THE ENGLISH LEGAL SYSTEM

In memoriam Gary Slapper 1958–2016

THE ENGLISH LEGAL SYSTEM

Eighteenth Edition

Gary Slapper, LLB (UCL), LLM (UCL),
PhD (LSE), PGCE (Law) (Manc)

Global Professor, New York University; Director, New York University,
London; Door Tenant, 36 Bedford Row; Visiting Professor of Law,
The Chinese University of Hong Kong, and The Open University, UK

David Kelly, BA, BA (Law), PhD

Previously Principal Lecturer in Law, Staffordshire University

Routledge
Taylor & Francis Group

LONDON AND NEW YORK

Eighteenth edition published 2017
by Routledge
2 Park Square, Milton Park, Abingdon, Oxon, OX14 4RN

and by Routledge
711 Third Avenue, New York, NY 10017

Routledge is an imprint of the Taylor & Francis Group, an informa business

First edition published by Cavendish 1994
Seventeenth edition published by Routledge 2016

British Library Cataloguing-in-Publication Data
A catalogue record for this book is available from the British Library

Library of Congress Cataloging-in-Publication Data
A catalog record has been requested for this book

ISBN: 978-1-138-28446-3 (hbk)
ISBN: 978-1-138-28447-0 (pbk)
ISBN: 978-1-315-26540-7 (ebk)

Typeset in Simoncini Garamond
by Apex CoVantage, LLC

MIX
Paper from
responsible sources
FSC™ C013985
www.fsc.org

Printed in the United Kingdom
by Henry Ling Limited

This edition is for Gary's family and particularly Suzanne, Hannah, Emily and Charlotte.

CONTENTS

1   LAW AND LEGAL STUDY   1

2   THE RULE OF LAW AND HUMAN RIGHTS   25

3   SOURCES OF LAW: LEGISLATION   81

17 THE FUNDING OF LEGAL SERVICES   689

PREFACE

In December 2016, as the preliminary text of this edition was being completed, the death of Gary Slapper was announced to the shock and grief of his many friends and colleagues, but most acutely to his family. Although I have had to edit bits subsequently, I thought it apt simply to reproduce, with minimum changes, the preface to the last edition which was written by Gary.

In a law lecture delivered on 25 October 1758, William Blackstone described law as 'this most useful and most rational branch of learning'. With the growth and pervasion of law in the succeeding two and a half centuries, the importance of legal study has risen accordingly.

Law permeates into every cell of social life. It governs everything from the embryo to exhumation. It governs the air we breathe, the food and drink that we consume, our travel, sexuality, family relationships, property, the world of sport, science, employment, business, education, health, everything from neighbour disputes to war. Taken together, the set of institutions, processes, laws and personnel that provide the apparatus through which law works, and the matrix of rules that control them, are known as the legal system.

This system has evolved over a long time. Today it contains elements that are very old, such as the coroners' courts, which have an 800-year history, and elements that are very new, such as electronic law reports and judges using laptops and tablets.

A good comprehension of the English legal system requires knowledge and skill in a number of disciplines. The system itself is the result of developments in law, economy and politics, sociological change and the theories which feed all these bodies of knowledge. This book aims to assist students of the English legal system in the achievement of a good understanding of the law, and of its institutions and processes. We aim to set the legal system in a social context, and to present a range of relevant critical views.

Being proficient in this subject also means being familiar with contemporary changes and proposed changes, and this new edition has been comprehensively revised and updated to take these into account.

Since the seventeenth edition of this book, the changes to the English legal system have been many and varied. We have included in the text a wide range of legislative, common law, constitutional and European developments that have occurred in the last year.

We are once again very grateful to all those who advanced suggestions for improvement of the book since the previous edition; many of those suggestions have been implemented in this edition.

David Kelly
22 January 25 March 2017

THE ENGLISH LEGAL SYSTEM – AN OVERVIEW

This book is about the English legal system. It is helpful to note, right at the very beginning, that the system was never designed in full at one point. It is over a thousand years old and it has evolved over that time.

Even some of the elements within the system which appear to run all the way through, such as the monarchy, have changed considerably over the centuries. Monarchs in the tenth century, for example, did not rule over the whole of what would be today seen as the UK, and their powers were not limited by conventions as they are in modern times.

It is also important to note that the system has not come to a stop today. It is still growing and developing and always will do. At one time in the long history of the legal system, there was no democratic parliament to make law, but now there is. At one time, law could be declared by the monarch, but now that is impossible.

For a long time before the twentieth century there was no organised system of appeals in criminal cases but today there is such a system. In its early stages of development, the legal system had no organised law reporting so, in law courts, previous cases were analysed only in an oral way with lawyers and judges giving accounts of previous cases from memory, whereas today we have libraries full of voluminous law reports and all major decisions published in full online. Indeed, communications technology is completely altering the way the system works by allowing for new relationships between lawyers and their clients to exist in an electronic sphere. Precedents (previous cases which are relevant to the one in dispute) from all around the world can be consulted instantly in court using a computer, and mobile telephony can be used to summon witnesses to legal cases.

The pen and parchment allowed law to work in one particular way; the printing press meant law could be developed to a higher level of sophistication; the prevalence of the typewriter and photocopying facilities changed things further; and the internet and mobile telephony take law into a different sphere. It is clear that the story has not stopped here and that law will continue to develop in relation to technology.

Law, though, is also affected by the politics and the economy that surround it. New laws affecting the way the legal system works can be passed by one parliament but subsequently repealed when a different group of politicians gain power and want to change the legal system in accordance with their political views. In this textbook we aim not only to explain the law and mechanisms of the legal system but to situate those changes in the context of such matters as *how the law came to be what it is* and *what social, economic and political issues arise from the legal system*.

In *Chapter 1* we examine the different approaches to legal study and the way that this book engages with such study. We also examine basic questions affecting the study of the legal system such as what is meant by law and how law can be classified according to different criteria.

In *Chapter 2* we examine the rule of law and human rights. These are very important ideas at the centre of the modern legal system. They are always in the thinking of lawyers, judges, legislators and civil servants and quite often they are ideas which are explicitly part of legal discussions. In its briefest form, the 'rule of law' is the idea that everyone is governed by the existing law, that no one is above it, and that random or capricious decisions in law courts are undesirable. The rule of law refers to an idea by which people are governed by rules, not by the whim of rulers.

The story of 'human rights' is a long one whose origins can be traced back many centuries, but such rights were systematically enshrined in documents by the United Nations and in Europe only from the middle of the last century. Since then they have become democratically implanted in many countries such as the UK. They cover basic unalterable rights, such as that no one should be tortured, and other rights such as the right to freedom of expression, which can only be taken away where there is a compelling need under such criteria that it is in the interests of a democracy.

In *Chapter 3* we examine various types of legislation as sources of law. In general language, people speak about 'the law' as if it were one single thing, but in fact there are various sorts of law, including law that we follow from being a member of the European Union, legislation direct from the UK Parliament, and the judicial decisions of the higher level courts in the UK. Legislation is a prodigious source of modern law. In recent times, Parliament has been making about 25 new Acts a year.

In *Chapter 4* we examine case decisions as a source of law. The higher courts – in particular the Court of Appeal and the Supreme Court – produce a large annual output of decisions that become part of English law.

In *Chapter 5*, we examine the third main source of law in the English legal system: law from both the European Union and the European Court of Human Rights. At this stage we have decided there is little purpose to be served by an in-depth analysis of the process leading to and the consequences of Brexit. Such analysis will be needed in the future but for the moment it is mainly a matter of speculation.

In *Chapters 6* and *7* we examine the civil courts and the civil process. In general terms 'civil law' means the law which governs the relationship *between* organisations like companies, and *between* individuals and organisations, and *between* individuals. This is different from the criminal process and courts, which we look at in *Chapters 9, 10,* and *11*, where one of the parties is the state and that party is prosecuting an individual or organisation for committing a crime.

In one sense, the civil courts and civil process are sub-compartments of the English legal system. It is, though, not quite as straightforward as that. It is not the case that the buildings and the people who work in the civil side of law are entirely separate from the people and buildings concerned with the criminal side of the system. Some judges and lawyers, and some of the court and governmental buildings, deal with both civil and criminal matters. The civil courts have their own system of procedures and rules and their own special set of court orders and remedies. Typically, for example, a litigant in the civil process wishes to have an award of damages to compensate them for some harm or loss, or an order (an injunction) to stop someone from doing something legally wrong.

In *Chapter 8* we examine the Family Courts and Process, a hugely important part of the system that deals with marriage, divorce, cohabitation, disputes between parents over the upbringing of their children, financial support for children upon separation or divorce, local authority powers to protect children and adoption.

In *Chapters 9, 10* and *11* we examine the Criminal Courts and criminal process. Prosecutions for crimes are brought by the state against individuals or groups of individuals or organisations such as companies. To be convicted of a crime is a serious matter and, where the crime is a serious one, conviction can result in a life-changing sentence for the convict. Of all prosecutions brought each year, of which there are over 1.5 million, 98 per cent are carried out in magistrates' courts, with the remainder being held as trials before a jury in Crown Courts.

The state is mighty and powerful and highly resourced, whereas the individual is comparatively weak and poorly resourced. So, over time, rules about what evidence can be heard in court have evolved to prevent the state getting a conviction where the evidence would not sustain a fair conviction. No one, for example, can be convicted on the basis of a confession alone – there must be other credible evidence against them. That rule is to prevent confessions being extracted from suspects by improper means. Today, there are debates about whether defendants in criminal trials have too many rights; we examine these issues in these chapters.

In *Chapter 12* we examine the judiciary. Much of modern law comes from democratically passed legislation but these laws will often be given clear meaning only once they are interpreted and applied by judges in law courts (we examine the rule of statutory interpretation in *Chapter 3*). So, as the judiciary plays such a critically important role in 'making law', it becomes very important to analyse and evaluate this body of people, this legal institution. In this chapter we examine the constitutional role of the judiciary and such issues as how judges are selected and trained, and how their conduct is regulated.

In *Chapter 13* we examine the role of judicial reasoning and politics. The scientific study of how judges arrive at the judgments in cases is of momentous importance because it is through that route that so much of English law is made real.

In *Chapter 14* we examine the jury. The system of the jury trial has ancient origins and has been an indispensable part of the English legal system ever since. It is now replicated in over 50 countries of the Commonwealth and is, according to one theory, the most important element in a legal system that guarantees against the tyranny of the state.

In *Chapter 15* we examine arbitration, tribunal adjudication and alternative dispute resolution. Going through the law courts to resolve a civil dispute or family law dispute is almost always a very long, expensive and confrontational event. There is considerable doubt about whether that approach is the best one in all cases. In this chapter we look at the alternative mechanisms to standard law court hearings. These began as adventurous innovations on the outskirts of the legal system, but their success in various ways has given them a progressively larger and more important role within the legal system. Arbitration, tribunal adjudication and alternative dispute resolution are now a central part of the legal system.

In *Chapter 16* we examine legal services. For most citizens the legal system's main manifestation is through its lawyers. This chapter examines and evaluates the systems through which legal advice and representation in court are provided. We examine the different types of lawyer, such as solicitors and barristers, and the changing structure of legal services. Recently we have moved into an era where lawyers can be involved in offering legal services in businesses which combine with other professionals such as accountants, and where commercial companies (even supermarkets) can own law firms.

In *Chapter 17* we examine the funding of legal services. Most citizens, of course, do not know any more about the law than they know about chemistry or medicine. It is therefore problematic if they have to try to defend themselves against a criminal or civil action without a lawyer. How should legal services be provided to people who could not otherwise afford to pay for a lawyer? In this chapter we examine the rules of the legal aid system and its changing features in the light of the economic and political environment. In 1950, 85 per cent of the English population was covered by the legal aid system, whereas by 2014 the proportion of people covered had fallen to 25 per cent. The significance and consequences of access to law are covered in this chapter.

ACKNOWLEDGEMENTS

I would like to thank Vicki Scoble for her help in editing Gary's text.

Guide to using the book

Chapter introductions

1.1 INTRODUCTION

Diagrams

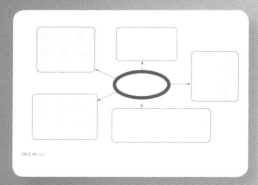

FIGURE 1.1

Chapter summaries

CHAPTER SUMMARY: LAW AND LEGA

THE STUDY OF LAW

FOOD FOR THOUGHT

1.

Food for thought

FURTHER READING

Further reading and useful
websites

COMPANION WEBSITE

-
-
-

-
-

Companion website

Guide to the companion website

www.routledge.com/cw/slapper

'One of the best sets of online resources I have ever seen.' *Richard Lee, Senior Lecturer, Manchester Metropolitan University*

For lecturers

Visit *The English Legal System's* companion website to discover a comprehensive range of resources designed to enhance the teaching and learning experience for both students and lecturers.

A free suite of exclusive resources developed to help you to teach the English legal system.

Testbank

Download a fully customisable bank of questions which test your students' understanding of the English legal system. These can be migrated to your university's Visual Learning Environment so that they can be customised and used to track student progress.

Diagrams

Use diagrams from the text in your own lecture presentations with our PowerPoint slides.

For students	Audio Introduction to The English Legal System.
	Listen to Gary Slapper describe the authors' aims and intentions in his audio introduction to *The English Legal System*
Legal skills guide	Improve your essential legal skills with our practical guides to Mooting, Negotiation, Finding Legal Information, Legal Writing and more.
Multiple choice questions	Test your understanding of the English legal system with more than 200 online questions, each including hints, commentary and links back to the textbook.
Glossary terms and flashcards	Search over 100 essential legal terms in our handy online Glossary or check your knowledge with our interactive flashcards.

LIST OF FIGURES

TABLE OF CASES

TABLE OF STATUTES

TABLE OF STATUTORY INSTRUMENTS

TABLE OF EUROPEAN LEGISLATION

LIST OF ABBREVIATIONS

ABH	actual bodily harm
ABS	alternative business structures
ACAS	Advisory, Conciliation and Arbitration Service
ACLEC	Advisory Committee on Legal Education and Conduct
ACSL	average custodial sentence length
ADR	alternative dispute resolution
AEO	attachment of earnings orders
AJF	Administrative Justice Forum
AJTC	Administrative Justice and Tribunals Council
ASBO	Anti-social Behaviour Order
ATE	After-The-Event
BCAT	Bar Course Aptitude Test
BME	black and minority ethnic
BPTC	Bar Practice Training Course
BSB	Bar Standards Board
CAB	Citizens Advice Bureau
Cafcass	Children and Family Court Advisory and Support Service
CBO	Criminal Behaviour Order
CC	Competition Commission
CCRC	Criminal Cases Review Commission
CCS	Consumer Complaints Service
CDS	Criminal Defence Service
CFAs	conditional fee arrangements
CILEx	Chartered Institute of Legal Executives
CJA	Criminal Justice Area
CJC	Civil Justice Council
CJEU	Court of Justice of the European Union
CJR	Civil Justice Review
CJSSS	*Criminal Justice: Simple, Speedy, Summary*
CLA	Civil Legal Aid
CLAD	Civil Legal Advice
CLS	Community Legal Service
CLSP	Community Legal Service Partnership
CMP	closed material procedure
CNR	cell nuclear replacement
COREPER	Committee of Permanent Representatives

CPD	continuing professional development
CPR	Civil Procedure Rules
CPS	Crown Prosecution Service
CRAR	Commercial Rent Arrears Recovery
CRASBO	Criminal Anti-social Behaviour Order
CSEW	Crime Survey for England and Wales
DCA	Department for Constitutional Affairs
DPA	Deferred Prosecution Agreement
DPP	Director of Public Prosecutions
EAT	Employment Appeal Tribunal
EC	European Community
ECF	Exceptional Cases Funding Scheme
ECHR	European Convention on Human Rights
ECJ	European Court of Justice
ECOFIN	economic and financial matters
ECtHR	European Court of Human Rights
EEC	European Economic Community
EMS	European Monetary System
EMU	European Monetary Union
EPA	Ending Power of Attorney
EVEL	English Votes for English Laws
FDAC	Family Drug and Alcohol Court
FGM	female genital mutilation
FSA	Financial Services Authority
FTA	failed to appear
GAD	Government Actuary's Department
GAR	guaranteed annuity rate
GCHQ	Government Communications Headquarters
GM	genetically modified
GRC	General Regulatory Chamber
GRO	General Register Office for England and Wales
HCA	Higher Court Advocates
HFEA	Human Fertilisation and Embryology Authority
HMCS	Her Majesty's Courts Service
HMCTS	Her Majesty's Courts and Tribunals Service
HMCPSI	**HM Crown Prosecution Service Inspectorate**
HMRC	Her Majesty's Revenue and Customs
ICAEW	Institute of Chartered Accountants in England and Wales
IPC	Investigatory Powers Commissioner
IPPs	Indeterminate Sentences for Public Protection
IPS	ILEX Professional Standards
IPSA	Independent Parliamentary Standards Authority
ISIL	Islamic State of Iraq and the Levant
JAC	Judicial Appointments Commission
JC	Judicial College

JCIO	Judicial Conduct Investigations Office
JO	Judicial Office
JP	Justice of the Peace
JSB	Judicial Studies Board
KPI	key performance indicators
LAA	Legal Aid Agency
LCD	Lord Chancellor's Department
LCF	Law Centres' Federation
LCS	Legal Complaints Service
LDP	Legal Disciplinary Practice
LETR	Legal Education and Training Review
LIP	litigant in person
LLP	limited liability partnership
LO	Legal Ombudsman
LPA	Lasting Power of Attorney
LPC	Legal Practice Course
LSB	Legal Services Board
LSC	Legal Services Commission
LSET	Legal services, education and training
LSO	Legal Services Ombudsman
MDP	multidisciplinary practices
MEP	Member of the European Parliament
MFR	minimum funding requirement
MIAM	Mediation Information and Assessment Meeting
MNP	multinational partnership
MoJ	Ministry of Justice
MRO	medical reporting organisation
NASS	National Asylum Support Service
NFIB	National Fraud Intelligence Bureau
NJPS	New Judicial Pension Scheme
NPO	Norwich Pharmacal order
NSPCC	National Society for the Prevention of Cruelty to Children
OFR	outcomes-focused regulation
OFT	Office of Fair Trading
OJC	Office for Judicial Complaints
OLC	Office for Legal Complaints
OOCD	out-of-court disposal of criminal offences
PAP	pre-action protocol
PC	practising certificate (solicitors)
PCA	Parliamentary Commissioner for Administration
PDS	Public Defender Service
PEP	profit per equity partner
PNC	Police National Computer
QBD	Queen's Bench Division
QC	Queen's Counsel

RTA	road traffic accidents
RUC	Royal Ulster Constabulary
SCPO	Serious Crime Prevention Order
SDT	Solicitors' Disciplinary Tribunal
SEC	Social Entitlement Chamber
SFO	Serious Fraud Office
SI	Statutory Instrument
SIAC	Special Immigration Appeals Commission
SRA	Solicitors Regulation Authority
SRL	self-represented litigants
STV	single transferable vote
TEU	Treaty on European Union
TFEU	Treaty on the Functioning of the European Union
TPIMs	terrorism prevention and investigation measures
TSI	Trading Standards Institute
UNCITRAL	United Nations Commission on International Trade Law
UT	Upper Tribunal
VHCC	very high cost cases
VOO	Violent Offender Order

1.1 INTRODUCTION

1.2   THE NATURE OF LAW

One of the most obvious and most central characteristics of all societies is that they must possess some degree of order to permit the members to interact over a sustained period of time. Different societies, however, have different forms of order. Some societies are highly regimented with strictly enforced social rules, whereas others continue to function in what outsiders might consider a very unstructured manner with apparently few strict rules being enforced (see Roberts 1979).

Order is therefore necessary, but the form through which order is maintained is certainly not universal, as many anthropological studies have shown (see Mansell 2015).

In our society, law plays an important part in the creation and maintenance of social order. We must be aware, however, that law as we know it is not the only means of creating order. Even in our society, order is not solely dependent on law, but also involves questions of a more general moral and political character. This book is not concerned with providing a general explanation of the form of order. It is concerned more particularly with describing and explaining the key institutional aspects of that particular form of order that is *legal* order.

The most obvious way in which law contributes to the maintenance of social order is the way in which it deals with disorder or conflict. This book, therefore, is particularly concerned with the institutions and procedures, both civil and criminal, through which law operates to ensure a particular form of social order by dealing with various conflicts when they arise.

Law is a *formal* mechanism of social control and, as such, it is essential that the student of law be fully aware of the nature of that formal structure. There are, however, other aspects to law that are less immediately apparent, but of no less importance, such as the inescapable political nature of law. Some textbooks focus more on this particular aspect of law than others, and these differences become evident in the particular approach adopted by the authors. The approach favoured by this book is to recognise that studying the English legal system is not just about learning legal rules, but is also about considering a social institution of fundamental importance.

1.2.1   LAW AND MORALITY

There is an ongoing debate about the relationship between law and morality and as to what exactly that relationship is or should be. Should all laws accord with a moral code, and, if so, which one? Can laws be detached from moral arguments? Many of the issues in this debate are implicit in much of what follows in the text, but the authors believe that, in spite of claims to the contrary, there is no simple causal relationship of dependency or determination, either way, between morality and law. We would rather approach both morality and law as ideological, in that they are manifestations of, and seek to explain and justify, particular social and economic relationships. This essentially materialist approach, to a degree, explains the tensions between the competing ideologies of law and morality and explains why they sometimes conflict and why they change, albeit asynchronously, as underlying social relations change.

Law and morality

At first sight it might appear that law and morality are inextricably linked. There at least appears to be a similarity of vocabulary in that both law and morality tend to see relationships in terms of rights and duties, and much of law's ideological justification comes from the claim that it is essentially moral. However, that is not necessarily the case and much modern law is of a highly technical nature (such as rules of evidence or procedure), dealing with issues that have very little, if any, impact on issues of morality as such. Opinions about the relationship between law and morality diverge between two schools of thought:

- One side adopts a 'natural law' approach which claims that law must be moral in order to be law, and that 'immoral law' is a contradiction in terms. Natural lawyers usually base their ideas of law on underlying religious beliefs and texts which are in the very literal sense sacrosanct, but this is not a necessity and opposition to specific law may be based on pure reason or political ideas.
- The other side can be characterised as 'legal positivists'. They argue that law has no necessary basis in morality and that it is simply impossible to assess law in terms of morality.

These issues feed into debates as to what is connoted by the rule of law, which will be considered in some detail in Chapter 2 of this text.

The legal enforcement of morality: the Hart v Devlin debate

This aspect of the law and morality debate may be reduced to the question: does the law have a responsibility to enforce a moral code, even where the alleged immorality takes place in private between consenting adults? Consider this example: in Britain there are over two million cohabiting gay couples. Homosexual sex was legalised in 1967 (for 21-year-olds, lowered to 18-year-olds in 1994), and consensual heterosexual anal intercourse was decriminalised by s 143 of the Criminal Justice and Public Order Act 1994. In British legal debate the moral issue was fought out in the 1960s by Lord Devlin and Professor HLA Hart. Devlin argued that 'the suppression of vice is as much the law's business as the suppression of subversive activities'. A shared morality, he argued, is the cement of society, without which there would be aggregates of individuals but no society. Hart argued that people should not be forced to adopt one morality for its own sake. He repudiated the claim that the loosening of moral bonds is the first stage of social disintegration, saying that there was no more evidence for that proposition than there was for Emperor Justinian's statement that homosexuality was the cause of earthquakes.

In any event it might be said that Hart 'won' the debate in the sense that it was his influence that led to the passing of the 1960s legislation liberalising the law on abortion, prostitution and homosexuality, and abolishing capital punishment. However, such issues can still arise – as was seen in the *Brown* case, considered later, and the ongoing issue of the 'rights' relating to assisted suicide as considered in *R (on the application of Purdy) v Director of Public Prosecutions* (2009).

The morality of the law maker

One particular aspect of the debate that will be repeatedly highlighted in what follows is the way in which certain individuals, particularly judges, have the power not just to make and mould law, but to make and mould law in line with their own ideologies, i.e. their individual values, attitudes and prejudices – in other words, their moralities.

> Morality *vis à vis* the law constitutes an external environment which interacts with the lawmaking process, not because law makers are blessed with divine insight into the 'general will', but rather because laws tend to be based on value – loaded information which percolates to the law-makers (*whose own individual values have a disproportionate influence upon the process*)
> (L Bloom-Cooper and G Drewry, *Law and Morality* (1976), p. xiv).

This issue is central to the Royal College of Nursing case considered in Chapter 3 and on the companion website at: www.routledge.com/cw/slapper.

1.3 CATEGORIES OF LAW

There are various ways of categorising law, which initially tend to confuse the non-lawyer and the new student of law. What follows will set out these categorisations in their usual dual form, while at the same time trying to overcome the confusion inherent in such duality. It is impossible to avoid the confusing repetition of the same terms to mean different things and, indeed, the purpose of this section is to make sure that students are aware of the fact that the same words can have different meanings, depending upon the context in which they are used.

1.3.1 COMMON LAW AND CIVIL LAW

In this particular juxtaposition, these terms are used to distinguish two distinct legal systems and approaches to law. The use of the term 'common law' in this context refers to all those legal systems that have adopted the historic English legal system. Foremost among these is, of course, the United States, but many other Commonwealth and former Commonwealth countries retain a common law system. The term 'civil law' refers to those other jurisdictions that have adopted the European continental system of law derived essentially from ancient Roman law, but owing much to the Germanic tradition.

The usual distinction to be made between the two systems is that the common law system tends to be case-centred and hence judge-centred, allowing scope for a discretionary, *ad hoc*, pragmatic approach to the particular problems that appear before the courts, whereas the civil law system tends to be a codified body of general abstract principles which control the exercise of judicial discretion. In reality, both of these views are

FIGURE 1.1 *Categorising Law.*

extremes, with the former overemphasising the extent to which the common law judge can impose their discretion and the latter underestimating the extent to which continental judges have the power to exercise judicial discretion. It is perhaps worth mentioning at this point that the Court of Justice of the European Union (CJEU), established, in theory, on civil law principles, is in practice increasingly recognising the benefits of establishing a body of case law.

It has to be recognised, and indeed the English courts do so, that, although the CJEU is not bound by the operation of the doctrine of *stare decisis* (see below, 4.2) it still does not decide individual cases on an *ad hoc* basis and, therefore, in the light of a perfectly clear decision of the CJEU, national courts will be reluctant to refer similar cases to its jurisdiction. Thus, after the ECJ, as it was then referred to, decided in *Grant v South West Trains Ltd* (1998) that Community law, now referred to as Union law, did not cover discrimination on grounds of sexual orientation, the High Court withdrew a similar reference in *R v Secretary of State for Defence ex p Perkins (No 2)* (1998) (see below, 5.3, for a detailed consideration of the CJEU).

1.3.2 COMMON LAW AND EQUITY

In this particular juxtaposition, the terms refer to a particular division within the English legal system.

The common law has been romantically and inaccurately described as the law of the common people of England. In fact, the common law emerged as the product of a particular struggle for political power. Prior to the Norman Conquest of England in 1066, there was no unitary, national legal system. The emergence of the common law represents the imposition of such a unitary system under the auspices and control of a centralised power in the form of a sovereign king; in that respect, it represented the assertion and affirmation of that central sovereign power.

Traditionally, much play is made about the circuit of judges travelling round the country establishing the 'King's peace' and, in so doing, selecting the best local customs and making them the basis of the law of England in a piecemeal but totally altruistic procedure. The reality of this process was that the judges were asserting the authority of the central state and its legal forms and institutions over the disparate and fragmented state and legal forms of the earlier feudal period. Thus, the common law was common *to* all in application, but certainly was not common *from* all. (The contemporary meaning and relevance and operation of the common law will be considered in more detail later in this chapter and in Chapter 3.)

By the end of the thirteenth century, the central authority had established its precedence at least partly through the establishment of the common law. Originally, courts had been no more than an adjunct of the King's Council, the *Curia Regis*, but gradually the common law courts began to take on a distinct institutional existence in the form of the Courts of Exchequer, Common Pleas and King's Bench. With this institutional autonomy, however, there developed an institutional sclerosis, typified by a reluctance to deal with matters that were not, or could not be, processed in the proper *form of action*. Such a refusal to deal with substantive injustices because they did not fall within the particular parameters of procedural and formal constraints, by necessity, led to injustice and the need to remedy the perceived weaknesses in the common law system. The response was the development of *equity*.

Plaintiffs unable to gain access to the three common law courts might directly appeal to the sovereign, and such pleas would be passed for consideration and decision to the Lord Chancellor, who acted as the king's conscience. As the common law courts became more formalistic and more inaccessible, pleas to the Chancellor correspondingly increased and eventually this resulted in the emergence of a specific court constituted to deliver 'equitable' or 'fair' decisions in cases that the common law courts declined to deal with. As had happened with the common law, the decisions of the Courts of Equity established principles that were used to decide later cases, so it should not be thought that the use of equity meant that judges had discretion to decide cases on the basis of their personal idea of what was just in each case.

The division between the common law courts and the Courts of Equity continued until they were eventually combined by the Judicature Acts (JdA) 1873–75. Prior to this legislation, it was essential for a party to raise an action in the appropriate court – for example, the courts of law would not implement equitable principles; the Acts, however, provided that every court had the power and the duty to decide cases in line with common law and equity, with the latter being paramount in the final analysis.

Some would say that, as equity was never anything other than a gloss on common law, it is perhaps appropriate, if not ironic, that now both systems have been effectively subsumed under the one term: common law.

Common law remedies are available as of right. Remedies in equity are discretionary: in other words, they are awarded at the will of the court and depend on the behaviour and situation of the party claiming such remedies. This means that, in effect, the court does not have to award an equitable remedy where it considers that the conduct of the party seeking such an award has been such that the party does not deserve it (*D & C Builders v Rees* (1965)).

This particular conjunction follows on from the immediately preceding section, in that the common law here refers to the substantive law and procedural rules that have been created by the judiciary through the decisions in the cases they have heard. Statute law, on the other hand, refers to law that has been created by Parliament in the form of legislation. Although there has been a significant increase in statute law in the twentieth and twenty-first centuries, the courts still have an important role to play in creating and operating law generally and in determining the operation of legislation in particular. The relationship of this pair of concepts is of central importance and is considered in more detail in Chapters 3 and 4.

1.3.4 PRIVATE LAW AND PUBLIC LAW

Private law deals with relations between individuals with which the state is not directly concerned or involved in. Public law, on the other hand, relates to the interrelationship of the state and the general population, in which the state itself is a participant. Somewhat confusingly, under the English legal system the state can enter into private law relationship with individuals, so the term public law is more accurately restricted to those aspects where the state is acting in a public capacity.

There are two different ways of understanding the division between private and public law. At one level, the division relates specifically to actions of the state and its functionaries vis-à-vis the individual citizen, and the legal manner in which, and form of law through which, such relationships are regulated: public law. In the nineteenth century, it was at least possible to claim, as AV Dicey did, that under the common law there was no such thing as public law in this distinct administrative sense and that the powers of the state with regard to individuals were governed by the ordinary law of the land, operating through the normal courts. Whether such a claim was accurate or not when it was made – and it is unlikely – there certainly can be no doubt now that public law constitutes a distinct and growing area of law in its own right. The growth of public law in this sense has mirrored the growth and increased activity of the contemporary state, and has seen its role as seeking to regulate such activity. The crucial role of judicial review in relation to public law will be considered in some detail in section 13.5, and the content and impact of the Human Rights Act 1998 will be considered in Chapter 2.

There is, however, a second aspect to the division between private and public law. One corollary of the divide is that matters located within the private sphere are seen as purely a matter for individuals themselves to regulate, without the interference of the state, whose role is limited to the provision of the forum for deciding contentious issues and mechanisms for the enforcement of such decisions. Matters within the public sphere, however, are seen as issues relating to the interest of the state and general public, and as such are to be protected and prosecuted by the state. It can be seen, therefore, that the category to which any dispute is allocated is of crucial importance to how it is dealt with. Contract may be thought of as the classic example of private law, but the extent to which this purely private legal area has been subjected to the regulation of public law, in such areas as consumer protection, should not be underestimated. Equally, the most obvious example of public law in this context would be criminal law. Feminists have argued, however, that the allocation of domestic matters to the sphere of private law has led to a denial of a general interest in the treatment and protection of women. By defining domestic matters as private, the state and its functionaries have denied women access to its power to protect themselves from abuse. In doing so, it is suggested that, in fact, such categorisation has reflected and maintained the social domination of men over women.

1.3.5   CIVIL LAW AND CRIMINAL LAW

Civil law is a form of private law and involves the relationships between individual citizens. It is the legal mechanism through which individuals can assert claims against others and have those rights adjudicated and enforced. The purpose of civil law is to settle disputes between individuals and to provide remedies; it is not concerned with punishment as such. The role of the state in relation to civil law is to establish the general framework of legal rules and to provide the legal institutions to operate those rights, but the activation of the civil law is strictly a matter for the individuals concerned. Contract, tort and property law are generally aspects of civil law.

Criminal law, on the other hand, is an aspect of public law and relates to conduct which the state considers with disapproval and which it seeks to control and/or eradicate. Criminal law involves the *enforcement* of particular forms of behaviour, and the state, as the representative of society, acts positively to ensure compliance. Thus, criminal cases are brought by the state in the name of the Crown and cases are reported in the form of *Regina v . . .* (*Regina* is simply Latin for 'queen' and case references are usually abbreviated to *R v . . .*) whereas civil cases are referred to by the names of the parties involved in the dispute, for example, *Smith v Jones*. In criminal law, a prosecutor prosecutes a defendant (or 'the accused'). In civil law, a claimant sues (or 'brings a claim against') a defendant.

In distinguishing between criminal and civil actions, it has to be remembered that the same event may give rise to both. For example, where the driver of a car injures someone through their reckless driving, they will be liable to be prosecuted under the Road Traffic legislation, but at the same time, they will also be responsible to the injured party in the civil law relating to the tort of negligence.

Standard of proof

A crucial distinction between criminal and civil law is the level of proof required in the different types of cases. In the criminal case, the prosecution is required to prove that the defendant is guilty beyond reasonable doubt, whereas in a civil case, the degree of proof is much lower and has only to be on the balance of probabilities. This difference in the level of proof raises the possibility of someone being able to succeed in a civil case, although there may not be sufficient evidence for a criminal prosecution. Indeed, this strategy has been used successfully in a number of cases against the police where the Crown Prosecution Service (CPS) has considered there to be insufficient evidence to support a criminal conviction for assault. A successful civil action may even put pressure on the CPS to reconsider its previous decision not to prosecute (see, further, below, 11.2, for an examination of the CPS). In June 2009, relatives of the victims of the Omagh bombing in Northern Ireland, which killed 29 people in 1998, won the right to take a civil case against members of the Real IRA, following the failure of a criminal prosecution to secure any convictions. In approving the action the judge in the case held that there was overwhelming evidence against four members of the terrorist group in relation to the atrocity. A subsequent criminal charge against one of the four was withdrawn in February 2016.

Burden of proof

It is essential not to confuse the standard of proof with the burden of proof. The latter refers to the need for the person making an allegation, be it the prosecution in a criminal case or the claimant in a civil case, to prove the facts of the case. In certain circumstances, once the prosecution/claimant has demonstrated certain facts, the burden of proof may shift to the defendant/respondent to provide evidence to prove their lack of culpability. The reverse burden of proof may be either *legal* or *evidential*, which in practice indicates the degree of evidence they have to provide in order to meet the burden they are under.

It should also be noted that the distinction between civil and criminal responsibility is further blurred in cases involving what may be described as hybrid offences. These are situations where a court awards a civil order against an individual, but with the attached sanction that any breach of the order will be subject to punishment as a criminal offence. As examples of this procedure may be cited the Protection from Harassment Act (PfHA) 1997 and the provision for the making of Anti-social behaviour orders available under s 1(1) of the Crime and Disorder Act 1998. Both of these provisions are of considerable interest and deserve some attention in their own right.

The Protection from Harassment Act was introduced as a measure to deal with 'stalking', the harassment of individuals by people continuously following them, and allowed the victim of harassment to get a court order to prevent the stalking. Stalking was made a fully-fledged criminal activity under s 111 of the Protection of Freedoms Act (PFA) 2012. Sub-section (1) inserted a new s 2A into the PfHA 1997 under which a person was guilty of the criminal offence of stalking if they pursued a course of conduct in breach of the prohibition on harassment in s 1(1) of the PHA 1997, and that course of conduct itself amounted to stalking.

Additionally, sub-section (2) inserted a new s 4A into the PfHA 1997 introducing the offence of stalking involving fear of violence or serious alarm or distress. A person will be guilty of that offence where they pursue a course of conduct amounting to stalking which causes another to fear, on at least two occasions, that violence will be used against them or it causes the victim serious alarm or distress that has a substantial adverse effect on their usual day-to-day activities.

Interestingly a new s 2A(3) provides a non-exhaustive list of examples of behaviour that are associated with stalking which includes such actions as 'following a person' and 'watching or spying on a person'.

Whereas stalking may have been the high-profile source of the Act, it is possible, however, that its most useful provision, if it is used appropriately, may actually lie in providing more protection for women who are subject to assault and harassment from their partners than is available under alternative criminal or civil law procedures.

Further, in March 2001, a black clerk in a City of London police station used the Act successfully against *The Sun* newspaper in an action. The newspaper had published three articles about the woman after she had reported four police officers in her station for making racist comments about a Somali asylum seeker and as a consequence had received hate mail. The paper admitted that the articles were 'strident, aggressive and inflammatory' and the judge held that they were also racist. In his view, the Protection from Harassment Act gave the claimant 'a right to protection from harassment by all the world including the press'. The Court of Appeal subsequently refused an application by the newspaper to strike out the action (*Thomas v News Group Newspapers* (2001)) and consequently it can be concluded that the Act potentially offers significant protection to the ordinary members of the public who have been the object of what many see as press harassment. Such protection is, of course, additional to any other protection provided under the Human Rights Act 1998.

While there certainly is potential for the Protection from Harassment Act to be used positively, many have claimed that in practice it has been used in a repressive way to prevent otherwise legitimate demonstrations. Perhaps significantly, the definition of harassment was extended by s 125 of the Serious Organised Crime and Police Act (SOCPA) 2005, to include 'a course of conduct . . . which involves harassment of two or more persons'. And as conduct is defined as including speech, this means that a person need only address someone once to be considered to be harassing them, as long as they have also addressed someone else in the same manner. Attention has to be drawn to the Anti-social Behaviour, Crime and Policing Act 2014 which conflates both standard and burden of proof in a very unsatisfactory way in relation to people who have suffered miscarriages of justice. The person claiming the miscarriage will still be freed if new evidence undermines the criminal standard of proof relied upon to convict them;

	Criminal law:	Civil law:
Courts:	Magistrates' and Crown Court	County Court and High Court
Aims:	Enforce standards of behaviour, protect, punish and rehabilitate	Resolve disputes between individuals
Outcomes:	Sentences include imprisonment and community service	To compensate for loss or harm caused
Terminology:	Prosecute, guilt, etc	Action, liability, etc
Standard of proof:	Beyond reasonable doubt	On the balance of probability
Procedure:	Arrest and charge by police, prosecution by CPS	Decision to bring an action made by claimant

FIGURE 1.2 *Differences Between Criminal and Civil Law.*

nonetheless s 175 provides that they will not be able to claim compensation for their imprisonment unless the evidence shows 'beyond reasonable doubt' that the person did not commit the original offence. Such a provision is tantamount to requiring the claimant to prove their innocence on the basis of the criminal standard of proof, thus not only reversing the normal burden of proof in criminal cases but also establishing a criminal law standard in relation to that test for a civil law action for compensation.

Anti-social behaviour orders

Anti-social behaviour orders (ASBOs) were introduced under the Crime and Disorder Act 1998 and were extended in the Police Reform Act (PRA) 2002 and the Anti-social Behaviour Act 2003. ASBOs are available to be used against individuals aged 10 or over. Their purpose was to control and minimise persistent problematic behaviour that seriously inconveniences other individuals or communities.

It is immediately apparent that the term 'anti-social behaviour' describes a very wide spectrum of behaviour, some of it criminal, but much of it not necessarily so. Nonetheless, what is consistent in such behaviour is the adverse impact it has on those who are subjected to it. While criminal law can be deployed where appropriate, it has been thought beneficial to introduce additional civil law measures to deal with anti-social behaviour, whether of a criminal nature or not. These civil measures allow the police and other agencies to deal with the cumulative harmful impact of an individual's behaviour, rather than focus on any one specific instance of criminal behaviour, with the aim of controlling and minimising persistent problematic behaviour that seriously inconveniences other individuals or communities.

The original anti-social behaviour orders (ASBOs) were introduced under the Crime and Disorder Act 1998 and the use of such orders was rapidly extended.

Initially the ASBO was a purely civil action distinct from, and an alternative to, criminal actions. However, the Police Reform Act 2002 introduced the possibility of such orders being made on conviction in criminal proceedings, in addition to, but separate from, any sentence imposed. The Serious Crime Act 2007 then introduced the possibility of courts awarding Serious Crime Prevention Orders (SCPO), and subsequently the Criminal Justice and Immigration Act 2008 introduced the concept of the violent offender orders (VOO).

R (on the application of McCann) v Manchester Crown Court

The exact legal categorisation of these orders and their consequences was considered by the House of Lords in two conjoined cases: *R (on the application of McCann) v Manchester Crown Court; Clingham v Kensington and Chelsea RLBC* (2002). The *McCann* case raised three issues. The primary issue related to the exact legal nature of the orders, whether they were emanations of civil or criminal law. The answers to two further questions depended upon the answer to that primary question. The first of these related to the difference in the way in which the rules of hearsay evidence operated in civil and criminal cases, with the former being less stringent than in criminal cases. The second, and perhaps the most important, related to the issue of what the appropriate standard of proof required to support the issuing of the order was: was it the civil law standard, on the balance of probabilities, or the criminal standard of beyond all reasonable doubt?

The House of Lords answered the questions as follows:

(1)   Proceedings for an anti-social behaviour order were civil under domestic law. In support of this conclusion the court relied on a number of factors. First, the Crown Prosecution Service was not involved in applications for the making of such an order as they were in criminal proceedings. Secondly, there was no need to show *mens rea*, or the guilty mind required to establish criminal liability. Thirdly, the issuing of the ASBO was not a penalty as such, as would be the outcome of a criminal case. As the House found no contrary cases in the European Court of Human Rights it concluded that ASBO procedures could not be seen to be criminal for the purposes of s 6 of the Human Rights Act 1998.

(2)   Following on from the first determination, that the proceedings were civil in nature, the Civil Evidence Act 1995 and the Magistrates' Courts (Hearsay Evidence in Civil Proceedings) Rules 1999 permitted the introduction of hearsay evidence. However, as regards the weight given to such evidence, that depended on the facts of each case, but its cumulative effect could be sufficient to support the issuing of the order.

(3)   As regards the issue of the standard of proof, however, the House held that *the criminal standard should be applied*. For the purposes of s 1(1)(a) of the Crime and Disorder Act, it would suffice for the magistrates '*to be sure*' that the defendant had acted in an anti-social manner. In the words of Lord Steyn:

> [the magistrates] must in all cases under section 1 apply the criminal standard . . . it will be sufficient for the magistrates, when applying section 1(1)(a) to be sure that the defendant has acted in an anti-social manner, that is to say in a manner which caused or was likely to cause harassment, alarm, or distress to one or more persons not of the same household as himself.

As with many of the previous government's initiatives, the ASBO and its related orders did not find favour with the coalition government and in July 2010 the Home Secretary, Theresa May, announced her wish to see ASBOs replaced by simpler sanctions that would be easier to obtain and to enforce and that, where possible, 'should be rehabilitating and restorative, rather than criminalising and coercive'. Subsequently in May 2012, the Home Office published a White Paper, *Putting victims first: more effective responses to anti-social behaviour*, which set out the government's proposals to replace the then 19 existing powers with six new ones, and giving victims a say in how agencies tackle anti-social behaviour. Those proposals were enacted in the Anti-social Behaviour, Crime and Policing Act 2014.

Anti-social behaviour, Crime and Policing Act (ABCP) 2014

In addition to reducing the 19 distinct anti-social behaviour orders to just six, the Act also introduced the concept of a 'community trigger' to ensure that the public had the power to demand that appropriate authorities take action in the event of a complaint about anti-social behaviour accompanied by a provision to allow for the implementation of 'community remedies'.

Section 2 of the Act defines anti-social behaviour as conduct:

(i) that has caused, or is likely to cause, harassment, alarm or distress to any person;

(ii) capable of causing nuisance or annoyance to a person in relation to that person's occupation of residential premises; or

(iii) capable of causing housing-related nuisance or annoyance to any person.

What actually amounts to anti-social behaviour is not defined in specific terms, but the sort of behaviour that is subject to this form of control includes, although it is not limited to:

- harassment of residents or passers-by;
- verbal abuse;
- vandalism;
- nuisance;
- smoking or drinking alcohol while under age;
- drug or alcohol abuse;
- begging;
- prostitution;
- kerb-crawling;
- and since October 2014, failing to control invasive plants such as Japanese knotweed.

An application for an ASBO is not made by individuals who are subjected to the antisocial behaviour, for the obvious reason that they might be subjected to further victimisation. It is the function of local authorities, police forces, including the British Transport Police, and registered social landlords to collect the evidence and put it to the courts.

Injunction to prevent anti-social behaviour (ss 1–21)

This action replaces a number of civil orders and injunctions including ASBOs and Anti-social Behaviour Injunctions. An injunction may be made against a person aged 10 or over if the court is satisfied, on the balance of probabilities (the civil standard of proof), that the person has engaged in, or is threatening to engage in, anti-social behaviour and that it is just and convenient to grant the injunction. There is no minimum or maximum term for an injunction for adults but in the case of under 18s, the maximum term is 12 months. The fact that the injunction can be issued on the civil rather than the criminal standard of proof, effectively obviates the decision of the House of Lords in the *McCann* case.

An injunction can be applied for by a number of authorities including the police, a local authority, and housing providers.

The injunction will name a person who will be responsible for supervising compliance with its terms and who will specifically be required to promote the respondent's compliance with the relevant requirements and to inform the person who applied for the injunction and the appropriate chief officer of police if the person subject to the injunction fails to comply with its requirements.

The injunction will require the person who is committing anti-social behaviour either to do a certain thing or prohibit them from doing a certain thing, with the aim of stopping the anti-social behaviour and also preventing the individual involved from getting into crime. The person subject to the injunction must keep in touch with the person supervising them and follow their instructions. The injunction is a purely civil order, and does not give the individual a criminal record. However, it may include a power of arrest in the event of any subsequent breach where the anti-social behaviour covered includes the use, or threatened use, of violence, or there is a significant risk of harm to others. Apart from the specific power to arrest in relation to violence, breach of an injunction will not be a criminal offence but rather will be dealt with by way of contempt of court for adults, potentially leading to imprisonment for up to two years or an unlimited fine. Breach of an injunction by someone aged under 18 could result in the youth court imposing a supervision order or a detention order. However, given the seriousness of the potential consequences, any subsequent breach of an injunction will need to be proved on the criminal standard of proof, beyond reasonable doubt.

Criminal Behaviour Order (CBO) (ss 22–33)

This is a civil order available on conviction for any criminal offence and replaced the previous ASBO-on-conviction (CRASBO). The criminal behaviour order is additional to the court's sentence for the offence, not a substitute for it, and may include positive action on the part of the recipient rather than simply negative restraints on their behaviour. However, in *Director of Public Prosecutions v Bulmer* (2015), the Divisional Court held that s 22 did not oblige a criminal behaviour order to contain a positive requirement which addressed the underlying cause of the offending behaviour; it simply enabled it to do so.

A court may make a criminal behaviour order only on the application of the prosecution and only on the basis of two conditions:

(i) that it is satisfied, beyond reasonable doubt, that the offender has engaged in behaviour that caused or was likely to cause harassment, alarm or distress to any person; and
(ii) that it considers that making the order will help in preventing the offender from engaging in such behaviour.

CBOs last for between one and three years for children (under 18) and in relation to adults must last a minimum of two years but, as with injunctions, they may be indefinite. If the offender is under 18, the prosecution must find out the views of the local youth offending team before applying for a criminal behaviour order. As with injunctions, a supervisor of the offender must be appointed under the CBO.

Breach of a CBO is a criminal offence with a maximum sentence of up to five years' imprisonment or a fine, or both for an adult. Breach proceedings for under 18s take place in the youth court, where the maximum custodial sentence that a young person can receive is a two-year detention and training order.

The anti-social behaviour covered by the CBO may be unrelated to the behaviour that leads to the criminal conviction and although the underlying criminal activity needs to be proved beyond reasonable doubt, once again, as with the injunction, the issuing of the CBO only needs to be proved on the civil standard of proof and as a result may be based on evidence that would not be admitted in a criminal case.

If the two orders considered above are the most significant powers included in the Act there are four other powers that require description. These are:

Dispersal powers (ss 34–42)

A constable in uniform may direct a person who is in a public place to leave the locality and not to return for a specified period up to a maximum 48 hours if:

(i)   the constable has reasonable grounds to suspect that the presence or behaviour of the person in the locality has contributed to or is likely to contribute to members of the public in the locality being harassed, alarmed or distressed, or the occurrence in the locality of crime of disorder; and

(ii) the constable considers that giving a direction to a person under this section is necessary for the purpose of removing or reducing the likelihood of the events mentioned in (i).

The constable may also require the surrender of an item being used to harass, alarm or distress members of the public.

The direction must be given in writing (unless not reasonably practicable), specifying the locality to which it relates and imposing requirements as to the time by which the person must leave and the manner in which they must do so (including the route). The constable should tell the person that failing without reasonable excuse to comply with the direction is an offence. If the constable reasonably believes that the offender is under 16, he or she may remove the person to a place where the person lives or a place of safety.

Community protection notice (ss 43–58)

An authorised person may issue a community protection notice to an individual aged 16 or over, or a body, if satisfied on reasonable grounds that:

(i)   the conduct of the individual or body is having a detrimental effect, of a persistent or continuing nature, on the quality of life of those in the locality; and

(ii) the conduct is unreasonable.

Such orders can only be issued if the offender has been given a written warning that the notice will be issued if their conduct doesn't change and that they have been given enough time to have reasonably made those changes, and yet have chosen not to do so.

It is a criminal offence not to comply with a community protection notice.

Public spaces protection order (ss 59–75)

A public spaces protection order is an order that identifies the public place and prohibits specified things being done in the restricted area and/or requires specified things to be done by persons carrying on specified activities in that area. The order may not last for more than three years and the local authority must consult with the chief police officer and the local policing body before issuing the order.

Failure to comply with a public spaces protection order is a criminal offence.

Closure of premises

A police officer of at least the rank of inspector, or a local authority, may issue a closure notice if satisfied on reasonable grounds that the use of particular premises has:

(i)   resulted, or is likely soon to result, in nuisance to members of the public; or

(ii)   there has been or is likely soon to be disorder near those premises associated with the use of those premises; and

(iii) the notice is necessary to prevent the nuisance or disorder from continuing, recurring or occurring.

A closure notice prohibits access to the premises for a period specified in the notice up to a maximum three months and may prohibit access by all persons except those specified, at all times and in all circumstances.

Whenever a closure notice is issued an application can be made to a magistrates' court for a closure order. This can be made by a constable or the local authority and must be heard by the magistrates' court not later than 48 hours after service of the closure notice.

The community trigger

The community trigger is intended as a means of recourse for those victims of antisocial behaviour who consider that there has not been an appropriate response to their complaints about such behaviour. The Act incorporates a mechanism for victims of persistent anti-social behaviour to request that relevant bodies, local authorities, the police, health providers and providers of social housing, undertake a case review involving a consideration of what action has previously been taken, and collectively deciding whether any further action could be taken in regard to the issue. An individual, community or business can make an application for a case review, and the relevant bodies are required to carry out a case review if the threshold is met. The Act provides that the threshold should be set no higher than three complaints, but agencies may choose to set a lower threshold.

The body which carries out a review must inform the applicant of the outcome of the review and any recommendations made. It must also publish annually how many triggers have been activated and how many case reviews have been carried out.

The community remedy document

A community remedy document contains a list of appropriate remedial actions to be carried out by a person who has been found liable for anti-social behaviour or has committed a minor criminal offence to be dealt with without court proceedings.

This provision looks to provide for the victim of low-level crime or anti-social behaviour to have a say in deciding the punishment imposed on, or actions required to be carried out by, offenders where they are dealt with without a formal court hearing. Among other things, such actions could include paying compensation to victims, repairing any damage caused or engaging in mediation to resolve ongoing disputes.

In order to ensure that the community remedy does not become the modern pillory or stocks, the local policing body is required to ensure that the actions in the community remedy document are reasonable and proportionate.

ASBO statistics

The most recent statistics available relate to the period 1 April 1999 to 31 December 2013, available at: www.gov.uk/government/statistics/anti-social-behaviour-order-statistics-england-and-wales-2013

In relation to ASBOs issued, the statistics reveal that:

- During the period covered, a total of 24,427 ASBOs were issued. The highest number of ASBOs issued in any calendar year was 4,122 in 2005, since when there was a year-on-year fall in the number issued. However, in 2013, 1,349 ASBOs were issued, a 2 per cent increase from the 1,329 ASBOs issued in 2012.
- Since 1 June 2000, 86 per cent of ASBOs have been issued to males, 20,836 as against 3,487 issued to females (Table 2).
- Since 2004, more ASBOs have been issued following conviction for a criminal offence rather than following a simple application. Thus in 2013, 65 per cent of ASBOs were issued following a conviction for a criminal offence (Table 3).

As regards breaches of ASBOs, the statistics show that:

- There have been a total of 70,770 separate breaches of ASBOs during the period covered. However, it should be noted that individual ASBOs tend to be breached on numerous occasions, on average five times (Table 10).
- The breach rate (by year of issue) shows that on average 29 per cent of ASBOs are breached within the year of issue.
- Immediate custodial sentences were given to 7,503 offenders for breaches of ASBOs with an average custodial sentence length of five months (Table 13).

Assessment of the ASBO regime

While the new procedure may seem initially to offer a welcome additional protection to the innocent individual, it has to be recognised that such advantage is achieved in effect by criminalising what was, and remains, in other circumstances non-criminal behaviour, and deciding its applicability on the basis of the lower civil law burden of proof.

In a joint letter to *The Observer* newspaper in October 2013, the children's commissioner Dr Maggie Atkinson and a number of others claimed that the new procedure will 'punish children over the age of 10 simply for being children' by widening the definition of anti-social behaviour and reducing the burden of proof so sharply that the effect could be to 'outlaw everyday activities' such as skateboarding or ball games. As they stated:

> We acknowledge that antisocial behaviour can blight the lives of individuals and communities, but this bill is not the answer. It promotes intolerance of youth, is a blow for civil liberties and will damage children's relationship with the police.

Anti-social behaviour orders have been subject to much criticism for the way they have been used in an attempt to define wider social problems as problems merely relating to social order. Of particular concern is the way that they and related orders are used to deal with political protestors, those suffering from mental health problems and young people generally.

As one commentator has put it:

> The reality is that ASBOs are being used far beyond their initial remit of dealing with vandals and nuisance neighbours. Behaviour that is overtly non-criminal is being criminalised and society's vulnerable groups are being targeted. Increasingly it is behaviour that is different rather than 'antisocial' that is being penalised. The form such punishment takes is perhaps of even greater concern because ASBOs effectively bypass criminal law and operate within their own shadow legal system. In effect, we no longer need to break the law to go to jail. In this sense they typify a growing abandonment of the rule of law (Max Rowlands, ECLN Essays no 9: 'The state of ASBO Britain – the rise of intolerance').

A further example of the relationship between criminal law and civil law may be seen in the courts' power to make an order for the confiscation of a person's property under the Proceeds of Crime Act 2002 (see below, 2.5.1.1).

Private prosecutions

It should not be forgotten that although prosecution of criminal offences is usually the prerogative of the state, it remains open to the private individual to initiate a private prosecution in relation to a criminal offence. It has to be remembered, however, that even in the private prosecution, the test of the burden of proof remains the criminal one requiring the facts to be proved beyond reasonable doubt. An example of the problems inherent in such private actions can be seen in the case of Stephen Lawrence, the young black man who was gratuitously stabbed to death by a gang of white racists while standing at a bus stop in London. Although there was strong suspicion, and indeed evidence, against particular individuals, the CPS declined to press charges against them on the basis of insufficiency of evidence. When the lawyers of the Lawrence family mounted a private prosecution against the suspects, the action failed for want of sufficient evidence to convict. As a consequence of the failure of the private prosecution, the rule against double jeopardy meant that the accused could not be retried for the same offence at any time in the future, even if the police subsequently acquired sufficient new evidence to support a conviction. The report of the Macpherson Inquiry into the manner in which the Metropolitan Police dealt with the Stephen Lawrence case gained much publicity for its finding of 'institutional racism' within the service, but it also made a clear recommendation that the removal of the rule against double jeopardy be considered. Subsequently, a Law Commission report recommended the removal of the double jeopardy rule and provision to remove it, under particular circumstances and subject to strict regulation, was contained in ss 75–79 of the Criminal Justice Act 2003.

In September 2010 two men, Gary Dobson and David Norris, were arrested for the murder of Stephen Lawrence. Dobson had been one of the people originally charged in the private prosecution, but the Court of Appeal held that there was sufficient new scientific evidence to justify a retrial under the Criminal Justice Act 2003. Following another review of the scientific evidence, and the discovery of new and substantial evidence, Dobson and Norris were prosecuted in 2011 and convicted of Stephen Lawrence's murder (3 January 2012).

In considering the relationship between civil law and criminal law, it is sometimes thought that criminal law is the more important in maintaining social order, but it is at least arguable that, in reality, the reverse is the case. For the most part, people come into contact with the criminal law infrequently, whereas everyone is continuously involved with civil law, even if it is only the use of contract law to make some purchase. The criminal law of theft, for example, may be seen as simply the cutting edge of the wider and more fundamental rights established by general property law. In any case, there remains the fact that civil and criminal law each has its own distinct legal system. The nature of these systems will be considered in detail in later chapters. The structure of the civil courts is considered in Chapter 6 and that of the criminal courts in Chapter 9.

1.4   APPROACHES TO LAW AND LEGAL STUDY

There are a number of possible approaches to the study of law, each of which has its own implications for how law is understood, located and studied.

The first is the traditional/formalistic approach. This 'black letter' approach to law, as it is commonly referred to, is posited on the existence of a discrete legal universe as the object of study. Such an approach is clearly manifested in the phrase 'the law is the law'. (In a lecture given more than 20 years ago I facetiously cited this statement as coming from the Fat Controller in the Thomas the Tank Engine books. It is with some amazement that I now find that there are posts on the internet making the same point.)

At their starkest, black letter law and legal formalism assume and claim to operate a form of mechanistic jurisprudence in which legal decisions are reached by means of marshalling and applying the appropriate legal rules. However, the nature and source of those rules appear as an unquestioned and unquestionable given, being derived from authoritative legal sources, again through the application of the correct rules of jurisprudential analysis and exegesis by those skilled in the arcane arts of legal hermeneutics. To simplify, the operation of legal formalism depends upon the application of legal rules by impartial experts to particular facts in order to derive inescapable and hence unquestionable outcomes, those outcomes being merely the result of the logical application of the rules.

This formalistic approach has a crucial impact on the way in which law is understood, taught and studied. As law is understood as being about purely legal rules, so legal study becomes seen as acquiring not just the knowledge of those rules but also the acquisition of the distinctly legal skills needed to derive and apply, not to say manipulate, those rules. Thus, the study of law is seen as establishing a knowledge of the specific legal rules that regulate social activity without reference to the social activity to which the legal rules are applied. However, as well as learning the law in the foregoing sense as simply a body of rules and principles and techniques to be mastered, it is important to learn something *about* law. The reason for this, and the justification for the approach adopted in this book, is that law cannot be examined merely in its own terms, for it amounts to considerably more than just the trade of lawyers.

The second approach to the study of law is the contextualist approach. This is by far the most common approach to law in modern academic institutions, and the intention behind it is to recognise that law is a *social* phenomenon and operates within a social context. Society requires particular tasks to be undertaken, be it the maintenance of order or the regulation of economic activity, and it is the function of law to perform those tasks.

The move from the black letter approach to the contextualist one involves an important shift in emphasis. No longer is law seen as simply a matter to be explained and justified in its own terms. It no longer constitutes its own discrete universe, but is analysed, and perhaps more importantly it can actually be assessed, within its socioeconomic context, and its performance can be evaluated in relation to the supposed purposes within that socio-economic context.

The contextualist approach may therefore be seen as an advance on the sterile legal-ism of the black letter approach to the extent that it takes cognisance of, and seeks to accommodate human behaviour within, the real world. I would suggest, however, that there is still one major shortcoming in its approach. True, it seeks to place law in its context, but what exactly is the context into which law is to be fitted? In our particular society the context is, and without any pejorative overtones, advanced capi-talism. The difficulty with the contextualist approach is that it tends to take that par-ticular context for granted: as a given, the assumed, unproblematic, and to that extent unquestioned, background in relation to which law has to operate. To that extent the concern of the contextualist is still the *legal* regulation of particular behaviour, with-out any great detailed consideration of the actual behaviour to which the legal rules are addressed.

It is only a third type of approach to the study of law that attempts to remedy that shortcoming in the contextualist approach; that third type of approach, and the one espoused by this particular text, is the critical/theoretical approach to law. From this perspective, not only is law in context an object of study, but equally, if not more essentially, the context within which law functions is itself an object of study. Neither law nor its social context is taken for granted, and the actual social relations and activity to which law is applied are examined in order to try to account for the existence of law in the first place.

In our society, as has been stated previously, law appears to, and does, play an important part in the creation and maintenance of social order, its centrality being typi-fied in the very phrase 'law and order', with its underlying suggestion that the two go together, with the latter, order, depending on the existence of the former, law. We must be aware, however, that law, as we know it, is not the only means of creating order. (Even in our society, order is not solely dependent on law, and we are not continuously having recourse to the courts in order to solve our problems.)

Critical legal study is concerned with seeking a general explanation of the form of order, but more particularly it is concerned with a search for the explanation of why our society has developed its particular form of *legal* order. In stressing the contribution that law makes to determining what we accept as order in our society, we are implicitly asserting the point that there can be no single universal idea of order, but rather that there are different versions of order. The version operating in our society, an order essen-tially shaped by law, is but one specific type of order; it is both culturally and historically specific to our present society.

Whichever approach one adopts to legal study – and each is valid within its own terms – will depend not just upon the individual student's approach and the ideological framework they operate within, but also the area of law that the student wishes to research. Some projects may be open to a merely expository analysis, while others, by the very nature of the subject, will demand a more critical analysis and explanation.

1.5 SKILLS

At the centre of any law student's course will be the law library, although, increasingly, paper-based resources are being supported by internet and other electronic sources. As well as general academic skills, law students need to develop particular skills relating to the finding and reading of legal texts. They are also required to develop the specific skills of writing legal essays and answering problem questions. The online Legal Skills Guide website that supports this text encourages the development of such skills; see http://routledgetextbooks.com/textbooks/_author/slapper.

CHAPTER SUMMARY: LAW AND LEGAL STUDY

THE STUDY OF LAW

The study of law is not just a matter of learning rules. It is a general misconception that learning the law is about learning a mass of legal rules. Critical, analytical thought should inform the work of the good student.

THE NATURE OF LAW

Legal systems are particular ways of establishing and maintaining social order. Law is a formal mechanism of social control. Studying the English legal system involves considering a fundamental institution in our society.

CATEGORIES OF LAW

Law may be categorised in a number of ways, although the various categories are not mutually exclusive.

Common law and civil law relate to distinct legal systems. The English legal system is a common law one, as opposed to Continental systems, which are based on civil law.

Common law and equity distinguish the two historical sources and systems of English law. Common law emerged in the process of establishing a single legal system throughout the country. Equity was developed later to soften the formal rigour of the common law. The two systems are now united, but in the final analysis, equity should prevail.

Common law and statute relate to the source of law. Common law is judge-made; statute law is produced by Parliament.

Private law and public law relate to whom the law is addressed. Private law relates to individual citizens, whereas public law relates to institutions of government.

Civil law and criminal law distinguish between law, the purpose of which is to facilitate the interaction of individuals, and law that is aimed at enforcing particular standards of behaviour.

APPROACHES TO LEGAL STUDY

Students of law can adopt a number of distinct approaches to legal study. Prominent among these are the traditional 'black letter' approach, the more evaluative 'contextualist' approach or the more radical 'critical legal studies' approach.

SKILLS

This textbook is supported by a Legal Skills Guide that can be found at www.routledge.com/cw/slapper. There you can improve the skills you'll need to be a successful law student, and ultimately a successful lawyer.

FOOD FOR THOUGHT

1   When asked to think of a law, most people immediately think of that archetypal public form of law, criminal law. However, although important, that is only one aspect of law and one that does not affect most people in the way that other elements of the law do. Most people can go through a day without the criminal law impinging on them, but it is almost certain that they will enter into contractual relationships, even if it is only riding on a bus or buying a sandwich. Equally the private law of property structures our society and is essential to its operation. Consider what other areas of law have an impact on how our society functions. If you are studying for a law degree, think of all the legal subjects you might possibly study.

2   Consider the relationship between law and morality. Is there any underpinning moral basis to law?

3   Consider the relationship of law and society and the following questions:

Does law exist independently of society?

Does law create society or does society create law?

Is law simply a matter of legal rules and legal reasoning?

What does law actually do?

4   Consider the roles of a law student, lawyer, judge:

What essential skills are required to perform these roles satisfactorily?

Do these skills differ, and if so, why?

FURTHER READING

Barnett, H, *Constitutional and Administrative Law*, 11th edn, 2015, Abingdon: Routledge

Bradney, A *et al*, *How to Study Law*, 7th edn, 2014, London: Sweet & Maxwell

Clinch, P, *Using a Law Library*, 2nd edn, 2001, London: Blackstone

Fitzpatrick, P (ed), *Dangerous Supplements*, 1991, London: Pluto

Mansfield, M, *Memoirs of a Radical Lawyer*, 2009, London: Bloomsbury

Slapper, G, and Kelly, D, *Questions and Answers on the English Legal System*, 2013 & 2014, Abingdon: Routledge

Susskind, R, *The End of Lawyers?*, 2009, Oxford: OUP

SOCIAL AND LEGAL ORDER

Mansell, W, *A Critical Introduction to Law*, 4th edn, 2015, London: Cavendish Publishing

Roberts, S, *Order and Dispute*, 1979, Harmondsworth: Penguin

LEGAL LANGUAGE

Friedman, L, 'On interpretation of laws' (1988) 11(3) Ratio Juris 252

Goodrich, P, *Reading the Law*, 1986, Oxford: Basil Blackwell

Jackson, B, *Making Sense in Law*, 1995, London: Deborah Charles

USEFUL WEBSITES

The constant impingement of legal issues on all aspects of social and individual life should be tracked and explored at:

www.bbc.co.uk
www.theguardian.com
www.independent.co.uk
www.ft.com
www.justice.gov.uk
The official website of the Ministry of Justice.

COMPANION WEBSITE

Now visit the companion website to:

- listen to Gary Slapper's audio introduction to the English legal system;
- test your understanding of the key terms using our Flashcard Glossary;
- revise and consolidate your understanding of 'Law and legal study' using our bank of multiple choice questions;
- view and follow all of the links to the Useful Websites above;
- keep up to date with the very latest developments in the law from the Student Law Review;
- access the supporting Legal Skills Guide, with guidance, exercises and activities across eight key skills from legal writing and research to understanding and using cases and statutes.

www.routledge.com/cw/slapper

2.1 INTRODUCTION

2.2 THE RULE OF LAW

implementation of its policies. The assumption and delegation of such power on the part of the state brought it into potential conflict with previous understandings of the rule of law, which had entailed a strictly limited ambit of state activity. The impact of this on the understanding and operation of the principle of the rule of law and its implications in relation to the judiciary are traced out below and will be returned to in Chapter 12.

Some might consider that it is not appropriate to have a section such as this in a textbook on the English legal system and that its proper place would be in a text on constitutional law or legal theory. However, it is essential to appreciate the central importance of the concept of the rule of law to the whole structure and operation of the English legal system. The fundamental nature of the concept of the rule of law is and always has been central, although perhaps implicit, in all the aspects of the legal system that are considered in this text. However, the Constitutional Reform Act (CRA) 2005 has for the first time recognised this centrality in the form of a statutory provision. As s 1 of the Act simply and clearly states, it does not adversely affect:

(a)   the existing constitutional principle of the rule of law; or

(b)   the Lord Chancellor's existing constitutional role in relation to that principle.

This very point was taken up by the former most senior judge in the House of Lords, the late Lord Bingham, whose speech on the issue will be considered in detail below.

As has been stated, although the idea of the rule of law is difficult to give a substantive definition of, that has not prevented a number of legal and social theorists from attempting to do just that. However, as will be seen and as has already been hinted at, the various explanations of what is, or should be, understood by the concept differ considerably and are different in accord with the socio-political approach adopted by the individual writers.

2.2.1   AV DICEY

According to AV Dicey in *An Introduction to the Study of the Law of the Constitution* (1885), the UK had no such thing as administrative law as distinct from the ordinary law of the land. Whether he was correct or not when he expressed this opinion – and there are substantial grounds for doubting the accuracy of his claim even at the time he made it – it can no longer be denied that there is now a large area of law that can be properly called administrative, that is, related to the pursuit and application of particular state policies, usually within a framework of statutory powers.

According to the notoriously chauvinistic Dicey, the rule of law was one of the key features that distinguished the English constitution from its Continental counterparts. Whereas foreigners were subject to the exercise of arbitrary power, the Englishman was secure within the protection of the rule of law. Dicey suggested the existence of three distinct elements, which together created the rule of law as he understood it:

An absence of arbitrary power on the part of the state: the extent of the state's power, and the way in which it exercises such power, is limited and controlled by law. Such control is aimed at preventing the state from acquiring and using wide discretionary powers, for, as Dicey correctly recognised, the problem with discretion is that it can be exercised in an arbitrary manner, and that above all else is to be feared, at least as Dicey would have us believe.

Equality before the law: the fact that no person is above the law, irrespective of rank or class. This was linked with the fact that functionaries of the state are subject to the same law and legal procedures as private citizens.

Supremacy of ordinary law: the fact that the English constitution was the outcome of the ordinary law of the land and was based on the provision of remedies by the courts rather than on the declaration of rights in the form of a written constitution.

It is essential to recognise that Dicey was writing at a particular historical period but, perhaps more importantly, he was writing from a particular political perspective that saw the maintenance of *individual* property and *individual* freedom to use that property as one chose as paramount. He was opposed to any increase in state activity in the pursuit of collective interests. In analysing Dicey's version of the rule of law, it can be seen that it venerated *formal* equality at the expense of *substantive* equality. In other words, he thought that the law and the state should be blind to the real concrete differences that exist between people, in terms of wealth or power or connection, and should treat them all the same, as possessors of *abstract* rights and duties.

There is an unaddressed, and certainly unresolved, tension in Dicey's work. The rule of law was only one of two fundamental elements of the English polity; the other was parliamentary sovereignty. Where, however, the government controls the legislative process, the sovereignty of parliament is reduced to the undisputed supremacy of central government. The tension arises from the fact that, whereas the rule of law was aimed at controlling arbitrary power, parliament could, within this constitutional structure, make provision for the granting of such arbitrary power by passing appropriate legislation.

This tension between the rule of law and parliamentary sovereignty is peculiar to the British version of liberal government. Where similar versions of government emerged on the Continent, and particularly in Germany, the power of the legislature was itself subject to the rule of law. This subordinate relationship of state to law is encapsulated in the concept of the *Rechtsstaat*.

This idea of the *Rechtsstaat* meant that the state itself was controlled by notions of law, which limited its sphere of legitimate activity. Broadly speaking, the state was required to institute general law and could not make laws aimed at particular people.

The fact that this strong *Rechtsstaat* version of the rule of law never existed in England reflects its particular history. The revolutionary struggles of the seventeenth century had delivered effective control of the English state machinery to the bourgeois class, who exercised that power through parliament. After the seventeenth century, the English bourgeoisie was never faced with a threatening state against which it had to protect itself; it effectively was the state. On the Continent, this was not the case and the emergent bourgeoisie had to assert its power against, and safeguard itself from, the power of a state machinery that it did not control. The development of *Rechtsstaat* theory as a means of limiting the power of the state can be seen as one of the ways in which the Continental bourgeoisie attempted to safeguard its position. In England, however, there was not the same need in the eighteenth and nineteenth centuries for the bourgeoisie to protect itself behind a *Rechtsstaat* version of the rule of law. In England, those who benefited from the enactment and implementation of general laws as required by *Rechtsstaat* theory – the middle classes – also effectively controlled parliament and could benefit just as well from its particular enactments. Thus, in terms of nineteenth-century England, as Franz Neumann stated, the doctrines of parliamentary sovereignty and the rule of law were not antagonistic, but complementary.

2.2.2   FA VON HAYEK

FA von Hayek followed Dicey in seeing the essential component of the rule of law as being the absence of arbitrary power in the hands of the state. As Hayek expressed it in his book *The Road to Serfdom* (1944):

> Stripped of all technicalities the Rule of Law means that government in all its actions is bound by rules fixed and announced beforehand.

Hayek, however, went further than Dicey in setting out the form and, at least in a negative way, the content that legal rules had to comply with in order for them to be considered as compatible with the rule of law. As Hayek expressed it:

> The Rule of Law implies limits on the scope of legislation, it restricts it to the kind of general rules known as formal law; and excludes legislation directly aimed at particular people.

This means that law should not be particular in content or application, but should be general in nature, applying to all and benefiting none in particular. Nor should law be aimed at achieving particular goals: its function is to set the boundaries of personal action, not to dictate the course of such action.

Hayek was a severe critic of the interventionist state in all its guises, from the fascist right wing to the authoritarian left wing and encompassing the contemporary welfare state in the middle. His criticism was founded on two bases:

Efficiency: from the microeconomic perspective – and Hayek was an economist – only the person concerned can fully know all the circumstances of their situation. The state cannot wholly understand any individual's situation and should, therefore, as a matter of efficiency leave it to the individuals concerned to make their own decisions about what they want or how they choose to achieve what they want, so long as it is achieved in a legal way.

Morality: from this perspective, to the extent that the state leaves the individual less room to make individual decisions, it reduces their freedom.

It is apparent, and not surprising considering his Austrian background, that Hayek adopted a *Rechtsstaat* view of the rule of law. He believed that the meaning of the rule of law, as it was currently understood in contemporary English jurisprudence, represented a narrowing from its original meaning, which he believed had more in common with *Rechtsstaat* than it presently did. As he pointed out, the ultimate conclusion of the current weaker version of the rule of law was that, so long as the actions of the state were duly authorised by legislation, any such act was lawful, and thus a claim to the preservation of the rule of law could be maintained. It should be noted that Hayek did not suggest at any time that rules enacted in other than a general form are not laws; they are legal, as long as they are enacted through the appropriate and proper mechanisms; they simply are not in accordance with the rule of law as he understood that principle.

Hayek disapproved of the change he claimed to have seen in the meaning of the rule of law. It is clear, however, that, as with Dicey, his views on law and the meaning of the rule of law were informed by a particular political perspective. It is equally clear that what he regretted most was the replacement of a free market economy by a planned economy, regulated by an interventionist state. The contemporary state no longer simply provided a legal framework for the conduct of economic activity, but was actively involved in the direct coordination and regulation of economic activity in the pursuit of the goals that it set. This had a profound effect on the form of law. Clearly stated and fixed general laws were replaced by open-textured discretionary legislation. Also, whereas the Diceyan version of the rule of law had operated in terms of abstract rights and duties, formal equality and formal justice, the new version addressed concrete issues and addressed questions of substantive equality and justice.

Hayek's views in relation to law and economics were extremely influential on conservative political thinking in the last quarter of the twentieth century and, in particular, on the Conservative government of Margaret Thatcher, which was elected in 1979 with the overt policy of reducing the impact and influence of the central state on economic activity and individuals. Thatcher was famous/infamous for, among other things, her declaration that there was no such thing as society, 'only individuals and families'.

2.2.3 EP THOMPSON

The rule of law is a mixture of implied promise and convenient vagueness. It is vagueness at the core of the concept that permits the general idea of the rule of law to be appropriated by people with apparently irreconcilable political agendas in support of their particular political positions. So far, consideration has been given to Dicey and Hayek, two theorists on the right of the political spectrum who saw themselves as proponents and defenders of the rule of law; however, a similar claim can be made from the left. The case in point is EP Thompson, a Marxist historian, who also saw the rule of law as a protection against, and under attack from, the encroaching power of the modern state.

Thompson shared Hayek's distrust of the encroachments of the modern state and he was equally critical of the extent to which the contemporary state intervened in the day-to-day lives of its citizens. From Thompson's perspective, however, the problem arose not so much from the fact that the state was undermining the operation of the market economy, but from the way in which the state used its control over the legislative process to undermine civil liberties in the pursuit of its own concept of public interest.

In *Whigs and Hunters* (1975), a study of the manipulation of law by the landed classes in the eighteenth century, Thompson concluded that the rule of law is not just a necessary means of limiting the potential abuse of power, but that:

> . . . the Rule of Law, itself, the imposing of effective inhibitions upon power and the defence of the citizen from power's all-intrusive claims, seems to me an unqualified human good.

In reaching such a conclusion, Thompson clearly concurs with Hayek's view that there is more to the rule of law than the requirement that law be processed through the appropriate legal institutions. He too argued that the core meaning of the rule of law involved more than mere procedural propriety and suggested that the other essential element is the way, and the extent to which, it places limits on the exercise of state power.

2.2.4   JOSEPH RAZ

Some legal philosophers have recognised the need for state intervention in contemporary society and have provided ways of understanding the rule of law as a means of controlling discretion without attempting to eradicate it completely. Joseph Raz ('The Rule of Law and its virtue' (1977) 93 LQR 195), for example, recognised the need for the government of men as well as laws, and that the pursuit of social goals may require the enactment of particular, as well as general, laws. Indeed, he suggested that it would be impossible in practical terms for law to consist solely of general rules. Raz even criticised Hayek for disguising a political argument as a legal one in order to attack policies of which he did not approve. Yet, at the same time, Raz also saw the rule of law as essentially a negative value, acting to minimise the danger that could follow the exercise of discretionary power in an arbitrary way. In that respect, of seeking to control the exercise of discretion, he shares common ground with Thompson, Hayek and Dicey.

Raz claimed that the basic requirement from which the wider idea of the rule of law emerged is the requirement that the law must be capable of guiding the individual's behaviour. He stated some of the most important principles that may be derived from this general idea:

> Laws should be prospective rather than retroactive. People cannot be guided by or expected to obey laws that have not as yet been introduced. Laws should also be open and clear to enable people to understand them and guide their actions in line with them.

Laws should be stable and should not be changed too frequently as this might lead to confusion as to what was actually covered by the law. There should be clear rules and procedures for making laws.

The independence of the judiciary has to be guaranteed to ensure that they are free to decide cases in line with the law and not in response to any external pressure.

The principles of natural justice should be observed, requiring an open and fair hearing to be given to all parties to proceedings.

The courts should have the power to review the way in which the other principles are implemented to ensure that they are being operated as demanded by the rule of law.

The courts should be easily accessible as they remain at the heart of the idea of making discretion subject to legal control.

The discretion of the crime preventing agencies should not be allowed to pervert the law.

It is evident that Raz saw the rule of law being complied with if the procedural rules of law-making were complied with, subject to a number of safeguards. It is of no little interest that Raz saw the courts as having an essential part to play in his version of the rule of law. This point will be considered further in section 13.5 in relation to judicial review.

2.2.5 ROBERTO UNGER

In *Law and Modern Society* (1976), the American critical legal theorist Roberto Unger set out a typology of social order, one category of which is essentially the rule of law system. Unger distinguished this form of social order from others on the basis of two particular and unique characteristics. The first of these is *autonomy:* the fact that law has its own sphere of authority and operates independently within that sphere without reference to any external controlling factor. Unger distinguished four distinct aspects of legal autonomy, which may be enumerated as follows:

substantive autonomy: this refers to the fact that law is not explicable in other, non-legal terms. To use the tautological cliché – the law is the law. In other words, law is self-referential, it is not about something else; it cannot be reduced to the level of a mere means to an end, it is an end in itself;

institutional autonomy: this refers to the fact that the legal institutions such as the courts are separate from other state institutions and are high-lighted in the fundamental principle of judicial independence;

methodological autonomy: this refers to the fact that law has, or at least lays claim to having, its own distinct form of reasoning and justifications for its decisions;

occupational autonomy: this refers to the fact that access to law is not immediate, but is gained through the legal professions, who act as gatekeepers and who exercise a large degree of independent control over the working of the legal system.

The second distinguishing feature of legal order, according to Unger, is its *generality:* the fact that it applies to all people without personal or class favouritism. Everyone is equal under the law and is treated in the same manner.

In putting forward this typology of social order, Unger recognised the advantages inherent in a rule of law system over a system that operates on the basis of arbitrary power, but he was ultimately sceptical as to the reality of the equality that such a system supports and questioned its future continuation. The point of major interest for this book, however, is the way in which each of the four distinct areas of supposed autonomy is increasingly being challenged and undermined, as will be considered at the end of the next section.

2.2.6   MAX WEBER

Unger saw the development of the rule of law as a product of Western capitalist society and, in highlighting the distinct nature of the form of law under that system, he may be seen as following the German sociologist Max Weber. Weber's general goal was to examine and explain the structure and development of Western capitalist society. In so doing, he was concerned with those unique aspects of that society which distinguished it from other social formations. One such distinguishing characteristic was the form of law that he characterised as a formally rational system, which prefigured Unger's notion of legal autonomy (see Weber, *Wirtschaft und Gesellschaft* (trans 1968)).

Weber's autonomous legal system was accompanied by a state that limited itself to establishing a clear framework of social order and left individuals to determine their own destinies in a free market system. In the course of the twentieth century, however, the move from a free market to a basically planned economy, with the state playing an active part in economic activity, brought about a major change in both the form and function of law.

2.2.7   THE RULE OF LAW AND THE CONTEMPORARY FORM OF LAW

While the state remained apart from civil society, its functions could be restricted within a limited sphere of activity circumscribed within the doctrine of the rule of law. However, as the state became increasingly involved in actually regulating economic activity, the form of law had by necessity to change. To deal with problems as and when they arose, the state had to assume discretionary powers rather than be governed by fixed pre-determined rules. Such discretion, however, is antithetical to the traditional idea of the rule of law, which was posited on the fact of limiting the state's discretion. Thus emerged the tension between the rule of law and the requirements of regulating social activity that FA von Hayek, for one, saw as a fundamental change for the worse in our society.

With specific regard to the effect of this change on law's previous autonomy, there is clear agreement among academic writers that there has been a fundamental alteration in the nature of law. Whereas legislation previously took the form of fixed and precisely stated rules, now legislation tends be open-textured and to grant wide discretionary powers to particular state functionaries, resulting in a corresponding reduction in the power of the courts to control such activity. The courts have resisted this process to a degree, through the expansion of the procedure for judicial review, but their role in the area relating to administration remains at best questionable. The growth of delegated legislation, in which parliament simply passes enabling Acts, empowering ministers of state to make regulations, as they consider necessary, is a prime example of this process (considered in detail in section 3.5). In addition, once made, such regulations tend not to be general but highly particular, even technocratic, in their detail.

The increased use of tribunals with the participation of non-legal experts rather than courts to decide disputes, with the underlying implication that the law is not capable of resolving the problem adequately, also represents a diminishment in law's previous power, as does the use of planning procedures as opposed to fixed rules of law in determining decisions. (Tribunals will be considered in Chapter 15.)

Legislation also increasingly pursues substantive justice rather than merely limiting itself to the provision of formal justice as required under the rule of law. As an example of this, consumer law may be cited: thus, in the Consumer Rights Act 2015, contract terms are to be evaluated on the basis of fairness and, under the Consumer Credit Act 1974, agreements may be rejected on the basis of their being extortionate or unconscionable. Such provisions actually override the market assumptions as to formal equality in an endeavour to provide a measure of substantive justice.

All the foregoing examples of a change can be characterised as involving a change from 'law as end in itself' to 'law as means to an end'. In Weberian terms, this change in law represents a change from *formal rationality*, in which law determined outcomes to problems stated in the form of legal terms through the application of abstract legal concepts and principles, to a system of *substantive rationality*, where law is simply a mechanism to achieve a goal set outside of law.

In other words, law is no longer seen as completely autonomous as it once was. Increasingly, it is seen as merely instrumental in the achievement of some wider purpose, which the state, acting as the embodiment of the general interest, sets. Paradoxically, as will be seen later, even when the law attempts to intervene in this process, as it does through judicial review, it does so in a way that undermines its autonomy and reveals it to be simply another aspect of political activity.

The return to a more Hayekian, free-market-based economy and polity since the election of the Thatcher Conservative government in 1979, and its continuation by all other governments, of whatever persuasion, since then has certainly changed the rhetoric and ideology about the relationship of the individual and the state. It can hardly be denied that the pursuit of essentially cost-cutting measures, by the previous coalition and present Conservative governments, in response to the economic imperatives of a perceived economic imbalance, has had a significant, not to say damaging, impact on the operation of the legal system. Indeed some have gone so far as to suggest that by treating the legal system in the same way as any other emanation of state provision it has undermined not only the independence of law and the legal system but also its own commitment to the rules of law as established in s 1 of the CRA 2005.

2.3   THE RULE OF LAW AND THE JUDICIARY

The commentators considered above came from a variety of academic backgrounds, but the essential practical importance of the concept of the rule of law was highlighted in a speech delivered by the former most senior Law Lord, the late Lord Bingham of Cornhill, in November 2006 under the deceptively simple title 'The Rule of Law' (the sixth *Sir David Williams Lecture* delivered at the Centre for Public Law at the University of Cambridge).

As has already been indicated, the Constitutional Reform Act (CRA) 2005 provides, in s 1, that the Act does not adversely affect 'the existing constitutional principle of the rule of law' or 'the Lord Chancellor's existing constitutional role in relation to that principle'. That provision is further reflected in the oath to be taken by Lord Chancellors under s 17(1) of the Act, to respect the rule of law and defend the independence of the judiciary. However, as Lord Bingham pointed out, the Act does not actually define what is meant by the rule of law, or indeed the Lord Chancellor's role in relation to it. He also recognised the difficulty in fixing a single meaning or in fact any substantive content to the principle, citing various different academic references to it, some of which have been considered above, but nonetheless he felt it appropriate to offer his own understanding of the rule of law.

In Lord Bingham's view, the authors of the 2005 Act apparently also recognised the difficulty of formulating a succinct and accurate definition suitable for inclusion in a statute, and consequently left the task of definition to the courts, if and when the occasion arose. The importance of such a task of definition cannot be underestimated, for it places an essential duty on, and considerable power in the hands of, the judiciary. If, as the CRA recognises, the rule of law is an existing constitutional principle, then the judges will be required to construe statutes in relation to that principle in such a way as to ensure that they do not infringe that constitutional principle. A further implication of the CRA is that the Lord Chancellor's conduct, in relation to role and duty to the rule of law, would be open to judicial review, were they to be challenged in that regard. As the rule of law already is an existing constitutional principle of the UK and one that may be more contentious in the future, it becomes imperative to attempt to define what it actually means. It is this task that Lord Bingham sets himself in the lecture under consideration and he suggests that at its core is the idea that 'all persons and authorities within the state, whether public or private, should be bound by and entitled to the benefit of laws publicly and prospectively promulgated and publicly administered in the courts'.

Bingham rests his basic understanding on John Locke's dictum that 'Wherever law ends, tyranny begins'. Yet, even in that regard, he demurs by admitting that in some proceedings justice can only be done if they are *not* dealt with in public.

However, the main importance is the detail that Lord Bingham introduces through his consideration of the eight implications, or sub-rules, that he holds are particular aspects of the general principle of the rule of law. These sub-rules are:

- The law must be accessible and so far as possible intelligible, clear and predictable.

The reasoning behind this requirement is that if everyone is bound by the law they must be able without undue difficulty to find out what it is, even if that means taking advice from their lawyers. Equally the response should be sufficiently clear that a course of action can be based on it. However, for this to be achieved, there has to be an end to what Lord Bingham refers to as the 'legislative hyperactivity which appears to have become a permanent feature of our governance'. This excessive legislation, exacerbated by baffling parliamentary draftsmanship, is particularly problematic in relation to the 'torrent of criminal legislation', not all of which is 'readily intelligible'.

However, Lord Bingham does not leave his fellow judges in doubt about their responsibilities in the creation of legal uncertainty and criticises 'the length, complexity and sometimes prolixity of modern common law judgments, particularly at the highest level'. However, on consideration he rejects the supposed benefit of single opinion decisions in the House of Lords, with only one judgment and four decisions in agreement with that, in favour of multiple judgments 'where the well-considered committee of five or more, can bring to bear a diversity of professional and jurisdictional experience which is valuable in shaping the law'.

As Lord Bingham saw it, the benefit of multiple decisions in shaping the law was, however, subject to the three caveats:

(i) Whatever the diversity of opinion the judges should recognise a duty, not always observed, to try *to ensure that there is a clear majority ratio*. Without that, no one can know what the law is until Parliament or a later case lays down a clear rule.

(ii) Excessive innovation and adventurism by judges had to be avoided. Without challenging the value or legitimacy of judicial development of the law, taken to extremes, such judicial creativity can itself destroy the rule of law.

(iii) All these points apply with redoubled force in the criminal field with the conclusion that judges should create new offences or widen existing offences so as to make punishable conduct that was not previously subject to punishment.

- Questions of legal right and liability should ordinarily be resolved by application of the law and not the exercise of discretion.

Lord Bingham does not share Dicey's complete antipathy to the exercise of discretion, and cites immigration law as an example where it has been advantageous. Nonetheless he does believe that the essential truth of Dicey's insight stands and that 'the broader and more loosely-textured a discretion is, *whether conferred on an official or a judge*, the greater the scope for subjectivity and hence for arbitrariness, which is the antithesis of the rule of law'. However, he is satisfied that the need for discretion to be narrowly defined, and its exercise to be capable of reasoned justification, are requirements which UK law almost always satisfies.

- The laws of the land should apply equally to all, save to the extent that objective differences justify differentiation.

However, if the law is to apply to all, then governments should also accept the converse, that the rule of law does not allow for any distinction between British nationals and others. Unfortunately, the second part of the reciprocal link did not appear to have been considered when Parliament passed Part 4 of the Anti-terrorism, Crime and Security Act 2001, which was held to be incompatible with the Human Rights Act in the *Belmarsh* cases (see 2.5.2).

- The law must afford adequate protection of fundamental human rights.

This sub-rule goes beyond the formalistic approaches of both Dicey and Raz to insist that the rule of law does in fact connote a substantive content, although Lord Bingham is less certain as to the particular detail of that content. In response to Raz he states:

> A state which savagely repressed or persecuted sections of its people could not in my view be regarded as observing the rule of law, even if the transport of the persecuted minority to the concentration camp or the compulsory exposure of female children on the mountainside were the subject of detailed laws duly enacted and scrupulously observed. So to hold would, I think, be to strip the existing constitutional principle affirmed by section 1 of the 2005 Act of much of its virtue and infringe the fundamental compact which, as I shall suggest at the end, underpins the rule of law.

But he also recognises that this is a difficult area and that there is not even a standard of human rights universally agreed among 'so-called' civilised nations. However, although he admits to this element of vagueness about the content of this sub-rule, he maintains that 'within a given state there will ordinarily be a measure of agreement on where the lines are to be drawn, and in the last resort (subject in this country to statute) the courts are there to draw them'.

Consequently, the rule of law must require the legal protection of such human rights as are recognised in that society.

- Means must be provided for resolving, without prohibitive cost or inordinate delay, bona fide civil disputes which the parties themselves are unable to resolve.

As a corollary of the principle that everyone is bound by and entitled to the benefit of the law is the requirement that people should be able, in the last resort, to go to court to have their rights and liabilities determined. In stating this sub-rule Lord Bingham makes it clear that he is not seeking to undermine arbitration, which he sees as supremely important, rather he is looking to support the provisions of a properly funded legal aid scheme, the demise of which he clearly regrets, as may be seen from the following:

> Whether conditional fees, various pro bono schemes and small claims procedures have filled the gap left by this curtailment I do not myself know. Perhaps they have, and advice and help are still available to those of modest means who deserve it. But I have a fear that tabloid tales of practitioners milking the criminal legal aid fund of millions, and more general distrust of lawyers and their rewards, may have enabled a valuable guarantee of social justice to wither unlamented.

Lord Bingham is equally concerned about the fact that successive governments have insisted that the civil courts, judicial salaries usually aside, should be self-financing: the cost of running the courts being covered by fees recovered from litigants. The danger with such an approach is that the cost of going to court in order to get redress may preclude some people from gaining access to the legal system.

- Ministers and public officers at all levels must exercise the powers conferred on them reasonably, in good faith, for the purpose for which the powers were conferred and without exceeding the limits of such powers.

As Lord Bingham saw it:

> The historic role of the courts has of course been to check excesses of executive power, a role greatly expanded in recent years due to the increased complexity of government and the greater willingness of the public to challenge governmental (in the broadest sense) decisions. Even under our constitution the separation of powers is crucial in guaranteeing the integrity of the courts' performance of this role.

This judicial role has of course been met through judicial review.

However, Lord Bingham is conscious, and unarguably so it would appear, of a shift away from the traditional relationship of the courts and the executive, under which the convention was that ministers, however critical of a judicial decision, and exercising their right to appeal against it or, in the last resort, legislate to reverse it retrospectively, did not engage in any public attack on the judiciary. In a muted, although nonetheless threatening, rejoinder to the present government Lord Bingham states his view that:

> This convention appears to have worn a little thin in recent times, as I think unfortunately, since if ministers make what are understood to be public attacks on judges, *the judges may be provoked to make similar criticisms of ministers*, and the rule of law is not, in my view, well served by public dispute between two arms of the state.

- Adjudicative procedures provided by the state should be fair.

The rule of law would seem to require no less. The general arguments in favour of open hearings are familiar, summed up on this side of the Atlantic by the dictum that justice must manifestly and undoubtedly be seen to be done and on the American side by the observation that 'Democracies die behind closed doors'.

While he sees application of this sub-rule to ordinary civil processes to be largely unproblematic, he does recognise that there is more scope for difficulty where a person faces adverse consequences as a result of what he is thought or said to have done or not done, whether in the context of a formal criminal charge or in other contexts such as deportation, precautionary detention, recall to prison or refusal of parole. The question in those circumstances is what does fairness ordinarily require? Lord Bingham's first response to the question is that, first and foremost, decisions must be taken by adjudicators who are:

> independent and impartial: independent in the sense that they are free to decide on the legal and factual merits of a case as they see it, free of any extraneous influence or pressure, and impartial in the sense that they are, so far as humanly possible, open-minded, unbiased by any personal interest or partisan allegiance of any kind.

But additionally a second element is involved, which relates to the presumption that any issue should not be finally decided against a person until they have had an adequate opportunity for their response to the allegation to be heard. In effect this means that:

> a person potentially subject to any liability or penalty should be adequately informed of what is said against him; that the accuser should make adequate disclosure of material helpful to the other party or damaging to itself; that where the interests of a party cannot be adequately protected without the

benefit of professional help which the party cannot afford, public assistance should so far as practicable be afforded; that a party accused should have an adequate opportunity to prepare his answer to what is said against him; and that the innocence of a defendant charged with criminal conduct should be presumed until guilt is proved.

In the context of criminal law this raises two pertinent issues:

(i)   *Disclosure*. This relates to material in the possession of the prosecutor, which they are for reasons of public interest unwilling to disclose to the defence. As the law stands at present, material need not be disclosed if in no way helpful to the defence; if helpful to the point where the defence would be significantly prejudiced by non-disclosure, the prosecutor must either disclose the material or abandon the prosecution.

(ii)   *Reverse burden of proof*. Some statutory offences place a reverse burden on the defendant; i.e. the defendant has to show that they did not commit the offence alleged. In Lord Bingham's opinion such reversals in the normal burden of proof are 'not in themselves objectionable, but may be so if the burden is one which a defendant, even if innocent, may in practice be unable to discharge'.

However, of much more concern to Lord Bingham in this regard was the increase in the instances, outside the strictly criminal sphere, in which Parliament has provided that the full case against a person, put before the adjudicator as a basis for decision, should not be disclosed to that person or indeed to their legal representative. One example of this procedure is of course the non-derogation control orders issued under the Prevention of Terrorism Act 2005. A further inroad in relation to this issue is to be found in the provisions of the Justice and Security Act 2013 (see p 73). In his Rule of Law lecture he expressed the view that:

> Any process which denies knowledge to a person effectively, if not actually, accused of what is relied on against him, and thus denies him a fair opportunity to rebut it, must arouse acute disquiet. But these categories reflect the undoubted danger of disclosing some kinds of highly sensitive information, and they have been clearly identified and regulated by Parliament, which has judged the departure to be necessary and attempted to limit its extent.

In *SSHD v E* (2007) he was required to provide a practical consideration of and decision in relation to the concerns raised above.

●   The existing principle of the rule of law requires compliance by the state with its obligations in international law.

This particular section of Lord Bingham's lecture is interesting for the indirect way in which he examines the involvement of the UK in the ongoing war in Iraq while, as he said, 'not for obvious reasons touch[ing] on the vexed question whether Britain's involvement in the 2003 war on Iraq was in breach of international law and thus, if this sub-rule is sound, of the rule of law'.

The way he achieved this was through a comparison between the procedures followed in 2003 and those followed at the time of the Suez invasion of 1956. While he concluded that the comparison suggests that over the period the rule of law has gained ground in the UK, it also allowed him to make some pointed comments in relation to the way the current war was initiated. In this regard he considered the different roles assumed by the law officers in both situations, and while he welcomed the involvement of the Attorney General in providing legal advice to the government, he raised doubts about to whom the Attorney General ultimately owed his duty – the government, as the then Attorney General had seen it, or the public at large, which Lord Bingham, personally, appears to support, as is evident from the following passage (the role of the Attorney General will be considered further in section 12.3.2):

> There seems to me to be room to question whether the ordinary rules of client privilege, appropriate enough in other circumstances, should apply to a law officer's opinion on the lawfulness of war: it is not unrealistic in my view to regard the public, those who are to fight and perhaps die, rather than the government, as the client . . . [a]nd the case for full, contemporaneous, disclosure seems to me even stronger when the Attorney General is a peer, not susceptible to direct questioning in the elected chamber.

In conclusion Lord Bingham correlated the rule of law with a democratic society based on:

> an unspoken but fundamental bargain between the individual and the state, the governed and the governor, by which both sacrifice a measure of the freedom and power which they would otherwise enjoy. The individual living in society implicitly accepts that he or she cannot exercise the unbridled freedom enjoyed by Adam in the Garden of Eden, before the creation of Eve, and accepts the constraints imposed by laws properly made because of the benefits which, on balance, they confer. The state for its part accepts that it may not do, at home or abroad, all that it has the power to do but only that which laws binding upon it authorise it to do. If correct, this conclusion is reassuring to all of us who, in any capacity, devote our professional lives to the service of the law. For it means that we are not, as we are sometimes seen, mere custodians of a body of arid prescriptive rules but are, with others, the guardians of an all but sacred flame which animates and enlightens the society in which we live

– a true Lockean view of the rule of law if there ever was one.

Inherent in Lord Bingham's speech is a tension between the judges and the other elements in the constitution – the executive/government and Parliament – with Lord Bingham seeing the role of the judges as protecting the society from unlawful inroads into its liberties and rights. This tension has been heightened by the enactment of the Human Rights Act 1998, to be considered in the following section; however, before that can be done it is necessary to examine the concept of the separation of powers and related concepts such as parliamentary sovereignty and judicial independence. Although the idea of the separation of powers can be traced back to ancient Greek philosophy, it was advocated in early modern times by the English philosopher Locke and the later French philosopher Montesquieu, and found its practical expression in the constitution of the United States. The idea of the separation of powers is posited on the existence of three distinct functions of government (the legislative, executive and judicial functions) and the conviction that these functions should be kept apart in order to prevent the centralisation of too much power. Establishing the appropriate relationship between the actions of the state and the legal control over those actions crucially involves a consideration of whether there is any absolute limit on the authority of the government of the day. Answering that question inevitably involves an examination of the general constitutional structure of the UK and, in particular, the interrelationship of two doctrines: parliamentary sovereignty and judicial independence. It also requires an understanding of the role of judicial review and the effect of the Human Rights Act 1998, and has caused no little friction between the judiciary and the executive, especially in the person of the Home Secretary.

There is, in any case, high judicial authority for claiming that the separation of powers is an essential element in the constitution of the UK (see *R v Hinds* (1979), p 212, in which Lord Diplock, while considering the nature of different Commonwealth constitutions in a Privy Council case, stated that 'It is taken for granted that the basic principle of the separation of powers will apply . . .'). In any case, the point of considering the doctrine at this juncture is simply to highlight the distinction and relationship between the executive and the judiciary and to indicate the possibility of conflict between the two elements of the constitution. This relationship assumes crucial importance if one accepts, as some have suggested, that it is no longer possible to distinguish the executive from the legislature as, through its control of its majority in the House of Commons, the executive (that is, the government) can legislate as it wishes and in so doing, can provide the most arbitrary of party political decisions with the form of legality. The question to be considered here is to what extent the judiciary can legitimately oppose the wishes of the government expressed in the form of legislation, or to what extent they can interfere with the pursuit of those wishes. As will be seen below, the power of the judiciary in relation to legislative provisions has been greatly enhanced by the passage of the Human Rights Act 1998.

The separation of powers and the Constitutional Reform Act 2005

The details of this major constitutional reform Act will be considered in detail in due course, but it cannot be denied that the force that drove the government to introduce the Act was an understanding of the imperatives of the separation of powers and the wish to regularise the constitution of the United Kingdom within that framework. Consequently, the anomalous position of the Lord Chancellor, who was a member of all three branches of the political structure, was to be resolved and the House of Lords, as the supreme court, was to be removed from its location within the legislative body.

2.3.2 PARLIAMENTARY SOVEREIGNTY

As a consequence of the victory of the parliamentary forces in the English revolutionary struggles of the seventeenth century, Parliament became the sovereign power in the land. The independence of the judiciary was secured, however, in the Act of Settlement 1701. The centrality of the independence of the judges and the legal system from direct control or interference from the state in the newly established constitution was emphasised in the writing of John Locke, who saw it as one of the essential reasons for, and justifications of, the social contract on which the social structure was assumed to be based. It is generally accepted that the inspiration for Montesquieu's *Spirit of Law (De L'Esprit des Lois)* was the English constitution, but if that is truly the case, then his doctrine of the separation of powers was based on a misunderstanding of that constitution, as it failed to take account of the express *superiority of parliament* in all matters, including its relationship with the judiciary and the legal system.

It is interesting that previous conservative thinkers have suggested that the whole concept of parliamentary sovereignty is itself a product of the self-denying ordinance of the common law. Consequently, they suggested that it was open to a subsequent, more robust, judiciary, confident in its own position and powers within the developing constitution, to reassert its equality with the other two elements of the polity. Just such an approach may be recognised as implicit in a number of the judgments of the augmented nine-person House of Lords in *Jackson v HM Attorney General* (2005). The case concerned the use of the Parliament Acts to pass legislation banning hunting with dogs, and in that respect it will be considered in detail in section 3.3, but in doing so it by necessity raised, without the requirement to deal definitively with, the essential constitutional question as to the relationship of the courts and parliament. While the majority of the judges, at the least, express reservations as to the power of the House of Commons under the Parliament Acts, the most overtly challenging statement can be seen in the judgment of Lord Steyn. His view of parliamentary sovereignty may be deduced from the following passage, in which he considers the argument of the Attorney General that the application of the Parliament Acts effectively is subject to no limitation:

> If the Attorney General is right the 1949 Act could also be used to introduce oppressive and wholly undemocratic legislation . . . The classic account given by Dicey of the doctrine of the supremacy of Parliament, pure and absolute as it was, can now be seen to be out of place in the modern United Kingdom. Nevertheless, the supremacy of Parliament is still the *general* principle of our constitution. It is a construct of the common law. The judges created this principle. If that is so, it is not unthinkable that circumstances could

arise where the courts may have to qualify a principle established on a different hypothesis of constitutionalism. In exceptional circumstances involving an attempt to abolish judicial review or the ordinary role of the courts, the Appellate Committee of the House of Lords or a new Supreme Court may have to consider whether this is a constitutional fundamental which even a sovereign Parliament acting at the behest of a complaisant House of Commons cannot abolish.

Lord Steyn's reasoning was subsequently questioned, and the traditional view of parliamentary sovereignty was reasserted by the former Master of the Rolls and current President of the Supreme Court, Lord Neuberger, in his Weedon Lecture in April 2011. As he put it:

Ultimately, it might be said that Lord Steyn's point that the courts had invented Parliamentary sovereignty and could therefore remove or qualify it involves an intellectual sleight of hand: Parliamentary sovereignty *was acknowledged* rather than *bestowed* by the courts. They acknowledged what had been clearly established by civil war, the Glorious Revolution of 1688, the Bill of Rights 1689 and the Act of Settlement 1701 (emphasis added).

Lord Neuberger went on:

[Parliament] can, if it chooses, and clearly and expressly states that it is so doing, enact legislation which is contrary to the rule of law . . . neither the Convention nor the Human Rights Act goes nowhere near to imposing a limit on Parliamentary legal sovereignty.

It is true that membership of the Convention imposes obligations on the state to ensure that judgments of the Strasbourg court are implemented, but those obligations are in international law, not domestic law. And, ultimately, the implementation of a Strasbourg, or indeed a domestic court judgment is a matter for Parliament. If it chose not to implement a Strasbourg judgment, it might place the United Kingdom in breach of its treaty obligations, but as a matter of domestic law there would be nothing objectionable in such a course. It would be a political decision, with which the courts could not interfere.

European Union Act 2011

In September 2011, Parliament passed the European Union Act 2011. The main purpose of the Act was to make provision for the application of the post-Lisbon treaties.

However, s 18 of the Act, for the first time, placed the common law principle of parliamentary sovereignty on a statutory footing in stating that all EU law takes effect in the UK only by virtue of the will of Parliament, as provided in the European Communities Act (ECA) 1972. The issue of parliamentary sovereignty in relation to the European Union and the UK's proposed exit therefrom will be considered in section 5.1.1.

R (Evans) v Attorney General (2015)

This case raises issues in relation to the interrelationship of the rule of law, the power of the judiciary and parliamentary sovereignty. Evans, a *Guardian* journalist, had made a request under the Freedom of Information Act (FOIA) 2000 for the release of correspondence between Prince Charles and various government ministers. As some of the letters related to environmental issues, a request was also made under the Environmental Information Regulations (EIR) 2004. Initially the request was refused, but was eventually approved after a six-day hearing before the Administrative Appeals Chamber of the Upper Tribunal. The government departments concerned did not appeal the UT decision, but on 16 October 2012 the Attorney General issued a certificate under s 53(2) of the FOIA 2000 and regulation 18(6) of the EIR 2004 stating that he had, on 'reasonable grounds', formed the opinion that the departments were entitled to refuse disclosure of the letters. Among his justifications for his action was 'the potential damage that disclosure would do to the principle of the Prince of Wales' political neutrality, which could seriously undermine the Prince's ability to fulfil his duties when he becomes King'. Evans's challenge to the issue of the certificate was ultimately decided by the Supreme Court, which decided by a majority of five to two that the certificate was unlawful under the 2000 Act (the court also decided by 6 to 1 that the certificate was contrary to EU law).

Lord Neuberger, with whom Lords Kerr and Reid agreed, concluded that 'reasonable grounds' could not mean that the Attorney General could issue a certificate merely because he would have reached a different conclusion to the Upper Tribunal.

> A statutory provision which entitles a member of the executive (whether a Government Minister or the Attorney General) to overrule a decision of the judiciary merely because he does not agree with it would not merely be unique in the laws of the United Kingdom. It would cut across two constitutional principles which are also fundamental components of the rule of law. First, . . . it is a basic principle that a decision of a court is binding as between the parties, and cannot be ignored or set aside by anyone including (indeed it may fairly be said, least of all) the executive. Secondly, it is also fundamental to the rule of law that decisions and actions of the executive are, . . . reviewable by the court at the suit of an interested citizen (paras 51–52).

These passages may be seen as Lord Neuberger's clarion call for the rights of the rule of law and the common law power of the judiciary in the face of executive and legislative power. However, his judgment actually rested on the unreasonable nature of the Attorney General's decision in the circumstances of the case. In so doing it may be said to recognise the pre-eminence of parliamentary sovereignty: for he recognises that properly constructed legislation can supersede either the final authority of judicial decisions or the requirement of judicial review, or indeed both.

Perhaps after all there is not so great a distance between Lord Neuberger's stance and the apparently contrary one expressed by Lord Hughes that:

> The rule of law is of the first importance. But it is an integral part of the rule of law that courts give effect to Parliamentary intention. The rule of law is not the same as a rule that courts must always prevail, no matter what the statute says (para 154).

R v (Miller) v Secretary of State for Exiting the European Union
[2017] UKSC 5

What is commonly referred to as the Brexit case related to the power of the government to give notice, under Article 50 of the Treaty on European Union, of the UK's intention to withdraw from the European Union. The consideration of the court and the reasoning supporting its conclusions involved the interplay of a number of issues considered here: the separation of powers, parliamentary sovereignty, and the use of the royal prerogative (the residual powers of the crown, now effectively exercised by the government, to take particular decisions and enter into binding agreements in areas such as international relations (see further at 3.5)).

In *Miller*, the Supreme Court was at pains to make it clear that it was not acting in a political way but purely on legal grounds in line with the separation of powers within the UK constitution. Nonetheless it held by a majority of 8 to 3 that, under the UK's constitutional arrangements, the government could not trigger Article 50 without the prior authorisation of an Act of Parliament. The fact that ministers were accountable to parliament for their actions was insufficient ground to legitimise the action of the government. Nor could the use of royal prerogative power sustain such action, as withdrawal from the EU would remove some substantive domestic rights of UK residents, an action well recognised as being beyond the scope of prerogative power.

2.3.3 JUDICIAL INDEPENDENCE

The exact meaning of 'judicial independence' became a matter of debate when some members and ex-members of the senior judiciary suggested that the former Conservative Lord Chancellor, Lord Mackay of Clashfern, had adopted a too-restrictive interpretation of the term, which had reduced it to the mere absence of interference by the executive in the trial of individual cases. They asserted the right of the legal system to operate independently, as an autonomous system apart from the general control of the state, with the judiciary controlling its operation, or at least being free from the dictates and strictures of central control.

According to Lord Mackay, in the first of his series of Hamlyn lectures entitled 'The Administration of Justice' (1994):

> The fact that the executive and judiciary meet in the person of the Lord Chancellor should symbolise what I believe is necessary for the administration of justice in a country like ours, namely, a realisation that both the judiciary and the executive are parts of the total government of the country with functions that are distinct but which must work together in a proper relationship if the country is to be properly governed . . . It seems more likely that the interests of the judiciary in matters within the concerns covered by the Treasury are more likely to be advanced if they can be pursued within government by a person with a lifetime of work in law and an understanding of the needs and concerns of the judiciary and who has responsibility as Head of the Judiciary, than if they were to be left within government as the responsibility of a minister with no such connection with the judiciary.

The tension inherent in the relationship between the courts and the executive government took on a more fundamental constitutional aspect with the passing of the Human Rights Act 1998. By means of that Act, the courts were given the right to subject the actions and operations of the executive and, indeed, all public authorities to the gaze and control of the law, in such a way as to prevent the executive from abusing its power. If the Human Rights Act represented a shift in constitutional power towards the judiciary, the Act was nonetheless sensitive to maintain the doctrine of parliamentary sovereignty. In the United States, with its written constitution, the judiciary in the form of the Supreme Court has the power to declare the Acts of the legislature unconstitutional and consequently invalid. No such power was extended to the UK courts under the Human Rights Act, although some commentators saw the Human Rights Act as eventually leading to a similar outcome in the UK. Such tension was further heightened when, in June 2003, the government announced its intention to radically alter the constitution, and the judges' role within it, at an apparent single stroke by the expedient of removing the role of Lord Chancellor.

Given the judiciary's suspicion of Lord Mackay as Lord Chancellor, it is not a little ironic that the government's announcement of its intention to abolish the position of Lord Chancellor was met by strong judicial reaction, in language very similar to that used by that former holder of the office. The judges, supported by many parliamentarians and commentators, made it absolutely clear that they thought that their independence would best be protected by a strong, legally qualified, champion within the cabinet. Such a role had been performed by the Lord Chancellor. Consequently, the judiciary generally regretted, not to say resisted, the abolition of the office as originally provided for in the Constitutional Reform Bill 2003. Although such resistance succeeded in retaining the office of the Lord Chancellor, its functions were greatly reduced and s 2 of the Constitutional Reform Act 2005 provides that the holder of the office should be 'qualified by experience', which need not include legal experience. Neither will the holder of the office necessarily sit in the House of Lords. However, in recognition of the sensitivities of the judiciary, s 3 of the Act, for the first time, places a legal duty on government ministers

> **The need for separation of legislative, executive and judicial powers:** acts as a 'check' on the potential for arbitrary government. This is known as 'the separation of powers'. It facilitates the 'rule of law'.

> Supported by **the 'rule of law'**:
> • requires that all people and organisations be subject to law, and no one is above the law.
> • enshrined in legislation for the first time by the ***Constitutional Reform Act 2005***

> **Examples of overlap between powers:**
> • **Prime Minister:** member of the executive (Cabinet) and of the legislature (Parliament)
> • **Lord Chancellor:** no longer head of the judiciary (since the ***Constitutional Reform Act 2005***) but still a member of the executive (Cabinet) and the legislature (Government)
> • **Monarch:** has a ***legislative*** function (provision of Royal Assent to bills), an ***executive*** function (appointing Government Ministers) and a ***judicial*** function (courts are the monarch's courts. judges are the monarch's judges and criminal prosecutions are brought in the name of the sovereign)

> **Examples of distinctions between powers:**
> • **Independence of the judiciary:** Now enshrined in legislation by means of the ***Constitutional Reform Act 2005 (CRA).*** In particular, ***s 3(1)*** provides that 'The Lord Chancellor, other Ministers of the Crown and all with responsibility for matters relating to the judiciary or otherwise to the administration of justice must uphold the continued independence of the judiciary'.
> • **Creation of a Supreme Court:** CRA established a new, independent, Supreme Court, separate from the House of Lords with its own independent appointments system, its own staff, budget and accommodation. Justices of the Supreme Court are no longer allowed to sit as members of the House of Lords.
> • **Judicial Review of the acts of the Executive by the judiciary:** While the courts enforce the will of Parliament by giving effect to its legislative acts, they retain the right to review activities of the Executive by means of Judicial Review.
> • **The Human Rights Act** has gone some way to ensure that basic rights cannot be removed by the state and are actionable in the courts.

FIGURE 2.1   *Constitutional Doctrines and the English Legal System.*

to uphold the independence of the judiciary and specifically bars them from trying to influence judicial decisions through any special access to judges.

When Gordon Brown replaced Tony Blair as Prime Minister in the summer of 2007, the resulting Cabinet reshuffle resulted in the abolition of the Department for Constitutional Affairs and its being replaced by a new Justice Ministry headed by Jack Straw, who also replaced Lord Falconer as Lord Chancellor, although remaining a member of the House of Commons. The new ministry, which is ultimately responsible for looking after the interests of the judiciary and courts, also assumed responsibility for the prison service, which caused the judges great concern as they feared that their allocation from the joint ministerial budget would be under pressure from the ever-expanding prison budget.

Following the General Election of 2010, the new coalition Justice Minister was the extremely experienced MP Kenneth Clarke QC, although his experience did not save him from being replaced in the Cabinet reshuffle in September 2012. The replacement was Chris Grayling, who became the first non-lawyer to hold the office of Lord Chancellor, and was subsequently replaced by another non-lawyer, Michael Gove. The current Justice Minister is Liz Truss, the first female Lord Chancellor, but another non-lawyer.

In an article published in the *London Review of Books* and *The Guardian* newspaper in May 1995, three years before the enactment of the Human Rights Act, the High Court judge, as he then was, Sir Stephen Sedley, made explicit the links and tensions between the doctrine of the rule of law and the relationship of the courts and the executive, and the implications for the use of judicial review as a means of controlling the exercise of executive power. In his view:

> Our agenda for the 21st century is not necessarily confined to choice between a 'rights instrument' interpreted by a judiciary with a long record of illiberal adjudication, and rejection of any rights instrument in favour of Parliamentary government. The better government becomes, the less scope there will be for judicial review of it.
>
> But, for the foreseeable future, we have a problem: how to ensure that as a society we are governed within a law which has internalised the notion of fundamental human rights. Although this means adopting the Rule of law, like democracy, as a higher-order principle, we do have the social consensus which alone can accord it that primacy. And, if in our own society the Rule of law is to mean much, *it must at least mean that it is the obligation of the courts to articulate and uphold the ground rules of ethical social existence which we dignify as fundamental human rights* . . . There is a potential tension between the principle of democratic government and the principle of equality before the law . . . The notion that the prime function of human rights and indeed the Rule of law is to protect the weak against the strong is not mere sentimentality. It is the child of an era of history in which equality of treatment and opportunity has become perceived . . . as an unqualified good, and of a significant recognition that you do not achieve equality merely by proclaiming it . . . fundamental human rights to be real, have to steer towards outcomes which invert those inequalities of power that mock the principle of equality before the law.

Such talk of fundamental human rights denies the absolute sovereignty of parliament in its recognition of areas that are beyond the legitimate exercise of state power. It also recognises, however, that notions of the rule of law cannot be satisfied by the provision of merely formal equality as Dicey and Hayek would have it and previous legal safeguards would have provided. For Sedley, the rule of law clearly imports, and is based on, ideas of substantive equality that market systems and legal formalism cannot provide and in fact undermine. His version of the rule of law clearly involves a reconsideration of the relationship of the executive and the judiciary, and involves the latter in a further reconsideration of their own previous beliefs and functions.

2.5   THE HUMAN RIGHTS ACT 1998

As is evident in the quotation from Sir Stephen Sedley above, some judges, at least, saw their role in maintaining the rule of law as providing protection for fundamental human rights. In attempting to achieve this end, they faced a particular problem in relation to the way in which the unwritten English constitution was understood, and was understood to operate. The freedom of individual action in English law was not based on ideas of positive human rights which could not be taken away, but on negative liberties: that is, individual subjects were entitled to do whatever was not forbidden by the law. This was particularly problematic when it was linked to the doctrine of the sovereignty of parliament, which, in effect, meant that parliament was free to restrict, or indeed remove, individual liberties at any time merely by passing the necessary legislation.

It is generally accepted that the courts developed the procedure of judicial review, as an aspect of the rule of law, in an attempt to protect individuals from the excesses of an over-powerful executive (see below, 13.5, for a detailed consideration). But, in so doing, they were limited in what they could achieve by the very nature of the procedure available to them. They could not directly question the laws produced by parliament on the basis of substance, as constitutional courts in other systems could, but were restricted essentially to questioning the formal or procedural proprieties of such legislation. There was, however, an alternative forum capable of challenging the substance of English law, and one that was based on the assumption of positive rights rather than negative liberties. That forum was the European Court of Human Rights (ECtHR).

It has to be established and emphasised from the outset that the substance of this section has absolutely nothing to do with the European Union as such; the Council of Europe is a completely distinct organisation and, although membership of the two organisations overlap, they are not the same. The Council of Europe is concerned not with economic matters, but with the protection of civil rights and freedoms (the nature of these institutions and the operation of the ECtHR will be considered in detail in Chapter 15).

The UK was one of the initial signatories to the European Convention on Human Rights and Fundamental Freedoms (hereafter the ECHR) in 1950, which was instituted in post-war Europe as a means of establishing and enforcing essential human rights. In 1966, the UK recognised the power of the European Commission on Human Rights to hear complaints from individual UK citizens and, at the same time, recognised the authority of the ECtHR to adjudicate in such matters. It did not, however, at that time incorporate the ECHR into UK law.

The consequence of non-incorporation was that the Convention could not be directly enforced in English courts. In *R v Secretary of State for the Home Department ex p Brind* (1991), the Court of Appeal decided that ministerial directives did not have to be construed in line with the ECHR, as that would be tantamount to introducing the ECHR into English law without the necessary legislation. UK citizens were therefore in the position of having to pursue rights, which the state endorsed, in an external forum rather than through their own court system and, in addition, having to exhaust the domestic judicial procedure before they could gain access to that external forum. Such a situation was extremely unsatisfactory, and not just for complainants under the ECHR. Many members of the judiciary, including the then Lord Chief Justice Lord Bingham, were in favour of incorporation, not merely on general moral grounds, but equally on the ground that they resented having to make decisions in line with UK law which they knew full well would be overturned on appeal to the European Court. Equally, there was some discontent that the decisions in the European Court were being taken, and its general jurisprudence was being developed, without the direct input of the UK legal system. The courts, however, were not completely bound to decide cases in presumed ignorance of the ECHR, and did what they could to make decisions in line with it. For example, where domestic statutes were enacted to fulfil ECHR obligations, the courts could, of course, construe the meaning of the statute in the light of the ECHR. It was also possible that, due to the relationship of the ECHR with European Community (as it then was) law, the courts could find themselves applying the former in considering the latter. More indirectly, however, where the common law was uncertain, unclear or incomplete, the courts ruled, wherever possible, in a manner which conformed with the ECHR or, where statute was found to be ambiguous, they presumed that parliament intended to legislate in conformity with the UK's international obligations under the ECHR. As the late Lord Bingham put it:

> In these ways, the Convention made a clandestine entry into British law by the back door, being forbidden to enter by the front (Earl Grey Memorial Lecture, 1998).

Even allowing for this degree of judicial manoeuvring, the situation still remained unsatisfactory. Pressure groups did agitate for the incorporation of the ECHR into the UK legal system, but when in 1995 a Private Member's Bill moving for incorporation was introduced in the House of Lords, the Home Office minister, Lady Blatch, expressed the then Conservative government's view that such incorporation was 'undesirable and unnecessary, both in principle and practice'. The Labour opposition, however, was committed to the incorporation of the ECHR into UK law and, when it gained office in 1997, it immediately set about the process of incorporation. This process resulted in the Human Rights Act (HRA) 1998.

Rights provided under the European Convention on Human Rights

The Articles incorporated into UK law, and listed in Sched 1 to the Act, cover the following matters:

- the right to life. Article 2 states that 'Everyone's right to life shall be protected by law';
- prohibition of torture. Article 3 actually provides that 'No one shall be subjected to torture or to inhuman or degrading treatment or punishment';
- prohibition of slavery and forced labour (Art 4);
- the right to liberty and security. After stating the general right, Art 5 is mainly concerned with the conditions under which individuals can lawfully be deprived of their liberty;
- the right to a fair trial. Article 6 provides that 'everyone is entitled to a fair and public hearing within a reasonable time by an independent and impartial tribunal established by law';

- the general prohibition of the enactment of retrospective criminal offences. Article 7 does, however, recognise the *post hoc* criminalisation of previous behaviour where it is 'criminal according to the general principles of law recognised by civilised nations';

- the right to respect for private and family life. Article 8 extends this right to cover a person's home and their correspondence;

- freedom of thought, conscience and religion (Art 9);

- freedom of expression. Article 10 extends the right to include 'freedom . . . to receive and impart information and ideas without interference by public authority and regardless of frontiers';

- freedom of assembly and association. Article 11 specifically includes the right to form and join trade unions;

- the right to marry (Art 12);

- prohibition of discrimination in relation to the enjoyment of the rights and freedoms set forth in the convention (Art 14);

- the right to peaceful enjoyment of possessions and protection of property (Art 1 of Protocol 1);

- the right to education (subject to a UK reservation (Art 2 of Protocol 1));

- the right to free elections (Art 3 of Protocol 1);

- the right not to be subjected to the death penalty (Arts 1 and 2 of Protocol 6).

The rights listed can be relied on by any person, non-governmental organisation or group of individuals. Importantly, they also apply, where appropriate, to companies that are incorporated entities and hence legal persons. However, they cannot be relied on by governmental organisations, such as local authorities.

The nature of rights under the Act, proportionality and derogation

The rights listed above are not all seen in the same way. Some are absolute and inalienable and cannot be interfered with by the state. Others are merely contingent and are subject to derogation, that is, signatory states can opt out of them in particular circumstances. The ECtHR also recognises the concept of 'a margin of appreciation', which allows for countries to deal with particular problems in the context of their own internal circumstances (see below, 5.4). The absolute rights are those provided for in Arts 2, 3, 4, 7 and 14. All the others are subject to potential limitations. In particular, the rights provided for under Arts 8, 9, 10 and 11 are subject to legal restrictions such as are:

. . . necessary in a democratic society in the interests of national security or public safety, for the prevention of crime, for the protection of health or morals or the protection of the rights and freedoms of others (Art 11(2)).

The UK entered such a derogation in relation to the extended detention of terrorist suspects without charge, under the Prevention of Terrorism (Temporary Provisions) Act 1989, subsequently replaced and extended by the Terrorism Act 2000. Those powers had been held to be contrary to Art 5 of the Convention by the ECtHR in *Brogan v UK* (1989). The UK also entered a derogation with regard to the Anti-terrorism, Crime and Security Act 2001, which was enacted in response to the attack on the World Trade Center building in New York on 11 September of that year. The Act allowed for the detention without trial of foreign citizens suspected of being involved in terrorist activity (see, further, below, 2.5.2).

In deciding the legality of any derogation, courts are required not just to be convinced that there is a need for the derogation, but they must also be sure that the state's action has been proportionate to that need. In other words, the state must not overreact to a perceived problem by removing more rights than is necessary to effect the solution.

In the Supreme Court decision *Bank Mellat (Appellant) v Her Majesty's Treasury (Respondent) (No. 2)* (2013) Lord Reed set out the determinant issues in relation to proportionality regarding any particular measure relating to the Human Rights Act. These were:

(1)   whether the objective of the measure is sufficiently important to justify the limitation of a protected right;

(2)   whether the measure is rationally connected to the objective;

(3)   whether a less intrusive measure could have been used without unacceptably compromising the achievement of the objective; and

(4)   whether, balancing the severity of the measure's effects on the rights of the persons to whom it applies against the importance of the objective, to the extent that the measure will contribute to its achievement, the former outweighs the latter . . . In essence, the question at step four is whether the impact of the rights infringement is disproportionate to the likely benefit of the impugned measure.

With further regard to the possibility of derogation, s 19 of the 1998 Act requires a minister, responsible for the passage of any Bill through parliament, either to make a written declaration that it is compatible with the Convention or, alternatively, to declare that although it may not be compatible, it is still the government's wish to proceed with it.

The structure of the Human Rights Act

The HRA has profound implications for the operation of the English legal system. However, to understand the structure of the HRA, it is essential to be aware of the nature of the changes introduced by the Act, especially in the apparent passing of fundamental powers to the judiciary. Under the doctrine of parliamentary sovereignty, the legislature could pass such laws as it saw fit, even to the extent of removing the rights of its citizens. The 1998 Act reflects a move towards the entrenchment of rights recognised under the Convention, but, given the sensitivity of the relationship between the elected parliament and the unelected judiciary, it has been thought expedient to minimise the change in the constitutional relationship of parliament and the judiciary.

Section 2 of the Act requires future courts to take into account any previous decision of the ECtHR. This provision impacts on the operation of the doctrine of precedent within the English legal system, as it effectively sanctions the overruling of any previous English authority that was in conflict with a decision of the ECtHR.

However, in *Price v Leeds City Council* (2006), the House of Lords held that where there were contradictory rulings from it and the European Court of Human Rights, English courts were required to follow the ruling of the House of Lords. The case is considered in detail at 4.4.

Section 3 requires all legislation to be read, so far as possible, to give effect to the rights provided under the Convention. As will be seen, this section provides the courts with new and extended powers of interpretation. It also has the potential to invalidate previously accepted interpretations of statutes that were made, by necessity, without recourse to the Convention (see *Mendoza v Ghaidan* (2002)).

Section 4 empowers the courts to issue a declaration of incompatibility where any piece of primary legislation is found to conflict with the rights provided under the ECHR. This has the effect that the courts cannot invalidate primary legislation, essentially Acts of Parliament but also Orders in Council, which are found to be incompatible; they can only make a declaration of such incompatibility, and leave it to the legislature to remedy the situation through new legislation. Section 10 provides for the provision of remedial legislation through a fast-track procedure, which gives a minister of the Crown the power to alter such primary legislation by way of statutory instrument.

Section 5 requires the Crown to be given notice where a court considers issuing a declaration of incompatibility and the appropriate government minister is entitled to be made a party to the case.

Section 6 declares it unlawful for any public authority to act in a way that is incompatible with the ECHR, and consequently the Human Rights Act does not *directly* impose duties on private individuals or companies unless they are performing public functions. Whether or not a private company is performing a public function can prove problematic; there are instances where they would clearly be considered as doing so: such as privatised utility companies providing essential services, or if a private company were to provide prison facilities then clearly it would be operating as a public authority. However, at the other end of an uncertain spectrum, it has been held that, where a local authority fulfils its statutory duty to arrange the provision of care and accommodation for an elderly person through the use of a private care home, the functions performed by the care home are not to be considered as of a public nature. At least that was the decision of the House of Lords by a majority of three to two in *YL v Birmingham City Council* (2007), a surprisingly conservative decision, and one that met with much dismay, given that there was the expectation that the public authority test would be applied generously.

Section 6(3), however, *indirectly* introduces the possibility of horizontal effect into private relationships. As s 6(3)(a) specifically states that courts and tribunals are public authorities they must therefore act in accordance with the Convention. The consequence of this is that although the HRA does not introduce new causes of action between private individuals, the courts, as public authorities, are required to recognise and give effect to their Convention rights in any action that can be raised.

In *R v (on the application of Al-Skeini) v Secretary of State for Defence* (2007), which related to the conduct of the armed forces in Iraq, the House of Lords held that s 6 applies to a public body even if it is acting outside the United Kingdom territory, as long as it is acting within the jurisdiction of the United Kingdom, and jurisdiction depends upon control of the relevant location.

Where a public authority is acting under the instructions of some primary legislation, which is itself incompatible with the ECHR, the public authority will not be liable under s 6.

Section 7 allows the 'victim of the unlawful act' to bring proceedings against the public authority in breach. However, this is interpreted in such a way as to permit relations of the actual victim to initiate proceedings.

Section 8 empowers the court to grant such relief or remedy against the public authority in breach of the Act as it considers just and appropriate.

Where a public authority is acting under the instructions of some primary legislation, which is itself incompatible with the ECHR, the public authority will not be liable under s 6.

Section 19 of the Act requires that the minister responsible for the passage of any Bill through parliament must make a written statement that the provisions of the Bill are compatible with ECHR rights. Alternatively, the minister may make a statement that the Bill does not comply with ECHR rights, but that the government nonetheless intends to proceed with it.

Reactions to the introduction of the HRA have been broadly welcoming, but some important criticisms have been raised. First, the ECHR is a rather old document and does not address some of the issues that contemporary citizens might consider as equally fundamental to those rights actually contained in the document. For example, it is silent on the rights to substantive equality relating to such issues as welfare and access to resources. Also, the actual provisions of the ECHR are uncertain in the extent of their application, or perhaps more crucially in the area where they can be derogated from, and at least to a degree they are contradictory. The most obvious difficulty arises from the need to reconcile Art 8's right to respect for private and family life with Art 10's freedom of expression. In *Weller v Associated Newspapers Ltd* (2015) the Court of Appeal upheld the judgment in the action by the musician Paul Weller against the proprietor of the *Mail Online* for publishing photographs of his young children. The court found that the children had a reasonable expectation of privacy and that their rights under Art 8 of the European Convention on Human Rights had outweighed the defendant's right under Art 10 of the Convention. Newspaper editors have expressed their concern in relation to this particular issue, and fear the development, at the hands of the court, of an overly limiting law of privacy that would prevent investigative journalism. This leads to a further difficulty – the potential politicisation, together with a significant enhancement in the power, of the judiciary. Consideration of this issue will be postponed until some cases involving the HRA have been examined.

Perhaps the most serious criticism of the HRA was the fact that the government did not see fit to establish a Human Rights Commission to publicise and facilitate the operation of its procedures. Many saw the setting up of such a body as a necessary step in raising human rights awareness and assisting individuals, who might otherwise be unable to use the Act, to enforce their rights.

2.5.1 JUDICIAL INTERPRETATION AND APPLICATION OF THE HUMAN RIGHTS ACT

Before and subsequent to the coming into effect in England of the HRA on 2 October 2000, the newspapers were full of dire warnings as to the damaging effect that the

Act would have on accepted legal principles and practices. However, an examination of some of the earliest cases to reach the higher courts may serve to dispel such a view.

Although the HRA was enacted in 1998, it did not come into force generally until October 2000. The reason for the substantial delay was the need to train all members of the judiciary, from the highest Law Lord to the humblest magistrate, in the consequences and implications of the new Act. However, the Act was in force before that date in Scotland as a consequence of the devolution legislation, the Scotland Act, which specifically applied the provisions of the HRA to the Scottish Parliament and executive. It is for that reason that the earliest cases under the Human Rights provisions were heard in the Scottish courts.

Road Traffic Act 1988

In *Brown v Stott* (2001), the claimant had been arrested at a supermarket on suspicion of the theft of a bottle of gin. When the police officers noticed that she smelled of alcohol, they asked her how she had travelled to the store. Brown replied that she had driven and pointed out her car in the supermarket car park. Later, at the police station, the police used their powers under s 172(2)(a) of the Road Traffic Act 1988 to require her to say who had been driving her car at about 2.30 pm, that is, at the time when she would have travelled in it to the supermarket. Brown admitted that she had been driving. After a positive breath test, Brown was charged with drink-driving, but appealed to the Scottish High Court of Justiciary for a declaration that the case could not go ahead on the grounds that her admission, as required under s 172, was contrary to the right to a fair trial under Art 6 of the ECHR.

In February 2000, the High Court of Justiciary supported her claim on the basis that the right to silence and the right not to incriminate oneself at trial would be worthless if an accused person did not enjoy a right of silence in the course of the criminal investigation leading to the court proceedings. If this were not the case, then the police could require an accused person to provide an incriminating answer which subsequently could be used in evidence against them at their trial. Consequently, the use of evidence obtained under s 172 of the Road Traffic Act 1988 infringed Brown's rights under Art 6(1).

Even before the HRA was in operation in England, the Scottish case was followed by a similar ruling in Birmingham Crown Court in July 2000.

The implication of these decisions was extremely serious, not just in relation to drink-driving offences, but also in relation to fines following the capture of speeding cars by traffic cameras. As can be appreciated, the film merely identifies the car; it is s 172 of the Road Traffic Act that actually requires the compulsory identification of the driver. If *Brown v Stott* stated the law accurately, then the control of speeding cars and drink-driving was in a parlous state.

However, on 5 December 2000, the Privy Council reversed the judgment of the Scottish appeal court in *Brown*. The Privy Council reached its decision on the grounds that the jurisprudence of the ECtHR, established through previous cases, had clearly established that while the overall fairness of a criminal trial could not be compromised, the constituent rights contained in Art 6 of the ECHR were not themselves absolute and could be restricted in certain limited conditions. Consequently, it was possible for individual states to introduce limited qualification of those rights, so long as they were aimed at 'a clear public objective' and were 'proportionate to the situation' under consideration. The ECHR had to be read as balancing community rights with individual rights. With specific regard to the Road Traffic Act, the objective to be attained was the prevention of injury and death from the misuse of cars, and s 172 was not a disproportionate response to that objective.

Subsequently, in a majority decision in *O'Halloran v UK* (2007), the European Court of Human Rights approved the use of s 172 in order to require owners to reveal who had been driving cars caught on speed cameras.

See also the related decision of the House of Lords in *Sheldrake v Director of Public Prosecutions* (2004), which concerned s 5(2) of the Road Traffic Act 1988 relating to the offence of being in charge of a vehicle after consuming excess alcohol. The court held that s 5(2) did not require the prosecution to prove that the defendant was likely to drive while intoxicated. Rather, the effect of s 5(2) was to allow the defendant to escape liability if they could prove, on a balance of probabilities, that there was no likelihood of their driving in their intoxicated condition. The House accepted that this interpretation of s 5(2) infringed the presumption of innocence and introduced a reverse burden of proof, but it considered that such a provision was neither arbitrary nor did it go beyond what was reasonably necessary, given the need to protect the public from the potentially lethal consequences of drink-driving. As Lord Bingham explained the matter:

> The defendant has a full opportunity to show that there was no likelihood of his driving, a matter so closely conditioned by his own knowledge and state of mind at the material time as to make it much more appropriate for him to prove on the balance of probabilities that he would not have been likely to drive than for the prosecutor to prove, beyond reasonable doubt, that he would. I do not think that imposition of a legal burden went beyond what was necessary.

Confiscation cases

Prior to the Proceeds of Crime Act 2002, a number of Acts of Parliament allowed for the property of individuals to be confiscated where it was assumed that such assets were the result of criminal activity. That legislation included the Criminal Justice Act 1988, as amended by the Proceeds of Crime Act 1995, the Drug Trafficking Act 1994 and the Terrorism Act 2000.

In allowing the court to make such an assumption, the Acts reversed the usual burden of proof to the extent that the person against whom the powers are used is required to demonstrate, on the balance of probabilities, that their assets are not the product of criminal activity. Section 1(1) of the Proceeds of Crime (Scotland) Act 1995 also allows for individuals' assets to be confiscated on the basis of similar assumptions.

In October 2000, in *McIntosh v AG for Scotland*, it was argued that the assumption made under s 3(2) of the 1995 Act displaced the presumption of innocence in Art

6(2) of the ECHR and hence was unlawful. McIntosh had been convicted for supplying heroin and the Crown had applied for a confiscation order under the 1995 Act. The Crown submitted that, since confiscation orders did not constitute a separate criminal offence, Art 6(2) of the Convention could not grant him the presumption of innocence in respect of such an action.

The High Court of Justiciary, Lord Kirkwood dissenting, approved McIntosh's submission and issued a declaration to that effect and, in so doing, threatened the efficacy of the whole confiscation policy.

In December 2000, the Court of Appeal in England, sitting with Lord Chief Justice Woolf on the panel, had the opportunity to consider the effect of the HRA on the assumptions relating to confiscation powers in the case of *R v Benjafield and Others* (2001). In the Court of Appeal's opinion, the express reversal of the burden of proof in confiscation proceedings amounted to a substantial interference with the normal presumption of innocence. However, it held that parliament had adequately balanced the defendant's interests against the public interest and cited the fact that the question of confiscation only arose after conviction and that the court should not make a confiscation order when there was a serious risk of injustice. It also considered that the court's role in the appeal procedure ensured that there was no unfairness to the individual concerned. As in the Privy Council's decision in *Brown*, the Court of Appeal held that where the discretion given to the court and prosecution was properly exercised, it was justifiable as a reasonable and proportionate response to a substantial public interest. In so doing, it declined to apply the High Court of Justiciary's decision in *McIntosh*, preferring the approach of the Privy Council in *Brown*.

When the further appeal in the *McIntosh* case came before the Privy Council in February 2001, the decision of the Scottish appeal court was unanimously overturned on two grounds:

- the confiscation order was not by way of a criminal action and therefore the assumptions were not in contravention of Art 6(2). An application for a confiscation order did not, of itself, lay a criminal charge against the convicted defendant. Although the court could assume that such a defendant had been involved in drug trafficking, there were no statutory assumptions as to a defendant's guilt for drug-trafficking offences;
- in addition, and more generally, Art 6(2) was not an absolute right and therefore, following *Brown*, could justifiably be encroached upon by the proportionate enactment of a democratically elected Parliament in the pursuit of its anti-crime policy.

In reaching this decision, the Privy Council expressly approved the Court of Appeal's decision in *R v Benjafield*.

Subsequently, in *Phillips v UK*, decided in July 2001, the ECtHR concurred with the decision of the Privy Council in *McIntosh* by holding, by a majority of five to two, that the confiscation procedure under the Drug Trafficking Act 1994 was not contrary to European Convention rights and, unanimously, that in any event the provisions of the Act represented a proportionate response to the problem under consideration.

Finally, when *R v Benjafield* came on appeal to the House of Lords, it felt comfortable in following the decisions and reasoning in both *McIntosh* and *Phillips*. At the same time, the House of Lords also applied that reasoning to confiscation procedure under the Criminal Justice Act 1988 in *R v Rezvi* (2002).

The courts' power to make confiscation orders was extended under the Proceeds of Crime Act (PCA) 2002, which came into full effect in March 2003.

Judicial interpretation of statutes under s 3 of the HRA

R v A (2001)

It has long been a matter of concern that in cases where rape has been alleged, the common defence strategy employed by lawyers has been to attempt to attack the credibility of the woman making the accusation. Judges had the discretion to allow questioning of the woman as to her sexual history where this was felt to be relevant, and in all too many cases this discretion was exercised in a way that allowed defence counsel to abuse and humiliate women accusers. Section 41 of the Youth Justice and Criminal Evidence Act (YJCEA) 1999 placed the court under a restriction that seriously limited evidence that could be raised in cross-examination of a sexual relationship between a complainant and an accused. Under s 41(3) of the 1999 Act, such evidence was limited to sexual behaviour 'at or about the same time' as the event giving rise to the charge that was 'so similar' in nature that it could not be explained as a coincidence.

In *R v A*, the defendant in a case of alleged rape claimed that the provisions of the YJCEA 1999 were contrary to Art 6 of the ECHR to the extent that they prevented him from putting forward a full and complete defence. In reaching its decision, the House of Lords emphasised the need to protect women from humiliating cross-examination and prejudicial but valueless evidence in respect of their previous sex lives; it nonetheless held that the restrictions in s 41 of the 1999 Act were *prima facie* capable of preventing an accused from putting forward relevant evidence that could be crucial to his defence.

However, rather than make a declaration of incompatibility, the House of Lords preferred to make use of s 3 of the HRA to allow s 41 of the YJCEA 1999 to be read as permitting the admission of evidence or questioning relating to a relevant issue in the case where it was considered necessary by the trial judge to make the trial fair. The test of admissibility of evidence of previous sexual relations between an accused and a complainant under s 41(3) of the 1999 Act was whether the evidence was so relevant to the issue of consent that to exclude it would be to endanger the fairness of the trial under Art 6 of the ECHR. Where the line is to be drawn is left to the judgment of trial judges. In reaching its decision, the House of Lords was well aware that its interpretation of s 41 did a violence to its actual meaning, but it nonetheless felt it within its power so to do. The words of Lord Steyn are illustrative of this process:

> In my view section 3 requires the court to subordinate the niceties of the language of section 41(3)(c), and in particular the touchstone of coincidence, to broader considerations of relevance judged by logical and common sense

criteria of time and circumstances. After all, it is realistic to proceed on the basis that the legislature would not, if alerted to the problem, have wished to deny the right to an accused to put forward a full and complete defence by advancing truly probative material. It is therefore possible under section 3 to read section 41, and in particular section 41(3)(c), as subject to the implied provision that evidence or questioning which is required to ensure a fair trial under Article 6 of the Convention should not be treated as inadmissible.

In this way, the House of Lords restored judicial discretion as to what can be raised in cross-examination in rape cases. It is to be hoped, sincerely but without much conviction on the basis of past history, that it is a discretion that will be exercised sparingly and sympathetically.

The acquittal of the footballer Ched Evans on a charge of rape brought the foregoing issues to prominence in October 2016. Evans had originally been found guilty of the offence and had served more than two years in prison, when he successfully applied to the Court of Appeal to have his case retried on the basis of the 'similar facts' defence, which allowed the alleged victim's sexual history to be questioned in the court.

Re S (2002)

In *Re S*, the Court of Appeal used s 3 of the HRA in such a way as to create new guidelines for the operation of the Children Act 1989, which increased the courts' powers to intervene in the interests of children taken into care under the Act. This extension of the courts' powers in the pursuit of the improved treatment of such children was achieved by reading the Act in such a way as to allow the courts increased discretion to make interim rather than final care orders, and to establish what were referred to as 'starred milestones' within a child's care plan. If such starred milestones were not achieved within a reasonable time, then the courts could be approached to deliver fresh directions. In effect, what the Court of Appeal was doing was setting up a new, and more active, regime of court supervision in care cases.

The House of Lords, however, although sympathetic to the aims of the Court of Appeal, felt that it had exceeded its powers of interpretation under s 3 of the HRA and, in its exercise of judicial creativity, it had usurped the function of parliament.

Lord Nicholls explained the operation of s 3:

> The Human Rights Act reserves the amendment of primary legislation to Parliament. By this means the Act seeks to preserve parliamentary sovereignty. The Act maintains the constitutional boundary. Interpretation of statutes is a matter for the courts; the enactment of statutes are matters for Parliament . . . [but that any interpretation which] departs substantially from a fundamental feature of an Act of Parliament is likely to have crossed the boundary between interpretation and amendment.

Unfortunately, the Court of Appeal had overstepped that boundary.

Mendoza v Ghaidan (2002)

In *Mendoza v Ghaidan* (2002), the Court of Appeal used s 3 to extend the rights of same-sex partners to inherit a statutory tenancy under the Rent Act 1977. In *Fitzpatrick v Sterling Housing Association Ltd* (1999), the House of Lords had extended the rights of such individuals to inherit the lesser assured tenancy by including them within the deceased person's family. It declined to allow them to inherit statutory tenancies, however, on the grounds that they could not be considered to be the wife or husband of the deceased as the Act required. In *Mendoza*, the Court of Appeal held that the Rent Act, as it had been construed by the House of Lords in *Fitzpatrick*, was incompatible with Art 14 of the ECHR on the grounds of its discriminatory treatment of surviving same-sex partners. The court, however, decided that the failing could be remedied by reading the words 'as his or her wife or husband' in the Act as meaning 'as if they were his or her wife or husband'. *Mendoza* is of particular interest in the fact that it shows how the HRA can permit lower courts to avoid previous and otherwise binding decisions of the House of Lords. It also clearly shows the extent to which s 3 increases the powers of the judiciary in relation to statutory interpretation.

In spite of this potential increased power, the House of Lords found itself unable to use s 3 in *Bellinger v Bellinger* (2003). The case related to the rights of transsexuals and the court found itself unable, or at least unwilling, to interpret s 11(c) of the Matrimonial Causes Act 1973 in such a way as to allow a male to female transsexual to be treated in law as a female. Nonetheless, the court did issue a declaration of incompatibility (see below for explanation).

Declarations of incompatibility under s 4 of the HRA

As has been stated previously, the courts are not able to declare primary legislation invalid, but, as an alternative, they may make a declaration that the legislation in question is not compatible with the rights provided by the ECHR.

The first declaration of incompatibility was actually issued in *R v (1) Mental Health Review Tribunal, North & East London Region (2) Secretary of State for Health ex p H* in March 2001. In that case, the Court of Appeal held that ss 72 and 73 of the Mental Health Act 1983 were incompatible with Art 5(1) and (4) of the ECHR inasmuch as they reversed the normal burden of proof, by requiring the detained person to show that they should not be detained rather than the authorities to show that they should be detained.

R v Secretary of State for the Environment, Transport and the Regions ex p Holding & Barnes plc and others (2001)

In this case, the House of Lords overturned an earlier decision of the Administrative Court that had called into question the operation of the planning system under the Town and Country Planning Act 1990. Under the Act, the ultimate arbiter in relation to planning decisions was the Secretary of State. The Administrative Court held that, as a member of the executive, determining policy, the Secretary of State should not be involved in the quasi-judicial task of deciding applications. It followed, therefore, that the operation of the planning system was contrary to the right to a fair hearing by an independent tribunal as provided for under Art 6 of the ECHR.

In overturning that decision, the House of Lords unanimously decided that the planning process was human rights compatible. In their Lordships' view, the possibility of judicial review was sufficient to ensure compliance with Art 6(1) of the ECHR, even though it could only remedy procedural rather than substantive deficiencies.

Indeed, their Lordships showed some displeasure at the manner in which Art 6 had been deployed in an attempt to undermine the democratically elected Secretary of State by seeking to pass the power to make policy decisions from him to the courts. Both Lords Slynn and Hoffmann quoted the words of the European Commission in *ISKCON v UK* (1994) with approval:

> It is not the role of Article 6 of the Convention to give access to a level of jurisdiction which can substitute its opinion for that of the administrative authorities on questions of expediency and where the courts do not refuse to examine any of the points raised . . .

Even more pointedly, Lord Hoffmann commented that:

> The Human Rights Act 1998 was no doubt intended to strengthen the rule of law but not to inaugurate the rule of lawyers.

2.5.1.4 The politics of the Human Rights Act

Historically, the Conservative Party argued against the enactment of the Human Rights Act (HRA) by the Labour government in 1998, on the grounds that it diminished the power of parliament and gave too much power to the unelected judiciary. In October 2009, in an article in the tabloid paper *The Sun*, the leader of the then opposition party, David Cameron, reaffirmed the Conservative Party's opposition to the HRA and promised that, if elected, he would replace it with a British Bill of Rights. However, subsequently, in 2010, on forming a coalition government with the Liberal Democrat Party, which was committed to the HRA, Cameron appeared to drop any proposals to repeal the Act

Nonetheless, rumblings of discontent continued to emanate from some parts of the Tory party. Thus in October 2011, at the Conservative Party annual conference, the then Home Secretary, Theresa May, reasserted her party's antagonism to the HRA, stating that it 'had to go'. In her notorious 'catgate' speech she justified the attack on the Act as follows:

> We all know the stories about the Human Rights Act. The violent drug dealer who cannot be sent home because his daughter – for whom he pays no maintenance – lives here. The robber who cannot be removed because he has a girlfriend. The illegal immigrant who cannot be deported because – *and I am not making this up* – he has a pet cat.

Regrettably for the Home Secretary and the truth, an examination of the transcripts of the case in point revealed that ownership of a cat was not actually the ground for refusing the deportation order and her claims were ridiculed as laughable by the then Justice Secretary Ken Clarke. Clarke subsequently had to apologise and was subsequently replaced by Chris Grayling, who, while in opposition – and like his leader David Cameron – famously announced that he was in favour of tearing up the HRA and replacing it with a British document.

At the Conservative Party annual conference in September 2013, Theresa May reasserted her attack on the Human Rights Act and even went as far as accusing the judiciary of using their powers under the Act 'to put the law on the side of foreign criminals instead of the public'. She further promised that her party's next manifesto would promise to scrap 'Labour's'[*sic*] Human Rights Act and that 'if leaving the European Convention is what it takes to fix our human rights laws, that is what we should do.'

Given what had been stated previously, and no doubt as a way of reasserting its right of centre credentials in the face of the challenge from UKIP, it was not unexpected that at the Conservative Party conference of 2014 various statements were made by May, Grayling and Cameron that they were prepared to withdraw from the European Convention on Human Rights (ECHR) after the upcoming election in 2015.

However, following the victory of the Conservative Party in that election, the previous statements and proposals were discounted as pre-election hyperbole when the subsequent Queen's speech on the opening of the new parliamentary session made only passing reference to the Human Rights Act. A subsequent plan to 'fast-track' a British Bill of Rights into UK law was not even attempted as the focus of political attention moved to the 'Brexit' referendum conducted in June 2016. The result of the referendum led to the appointment of a new Prime Minister, Theresa May and a new Justice Minister, Liz Truss. The latter confirmed the government's commitment to replacing the Human Rights Act with a British Bill of Rights which she maintained would 'protect our rights but in a better way'.

Few commentators shared the optimism of the new government as regards the likelihood of such a Bill securing an unobstructed passage through parliament, given the number of potential hazards in its way. Among these, in no particular order of danger, may be cited the government's slender 12 vote majority in the House of Commons and the stated opposition of some of its own members to the proposal, its overall lack of a majority in an antagonistic House of Lords, the stated opposition of the Scottish parliament with its now overwhelmingly strong representation at Westminster, and the fact that the Human Rights Act was an integral part to the intergovernmental Good Friday agreement which saw the establishment of the current settlement in Northern Ireland. All of these problems will be compounded by the ongoing Brexit negotiations when they are eventually triggered.

2.5.2 HUMAN RIGHTS AND ANTI-TERRORISM LEGISLATION

It is almost commonplace that the recognition of human rights is most sorely tested when those claiming the protection of those rights might not otherwise meet with sympathetic treatment. Thus it is the argument of those who would repeal the Human Rights Act that it is used as a block on the pursuit of substantive law and order by shyster lawyers who recognise its utility as a means of protecting the rights of criminals, prisoners, illegal immigrants and other supposedly blameworthy or morally dubious individuals at the expense of the rights of the good, and no doubt God-fearing (in a non-Islamic way), moral majority. However, it is precisely the universality and non-contingent nature of human rights, the fact that they are, or at least should be, an attribute of every person, irrespective of status, class, race, gender, religion or political belief, that provides the foundation for the very theory of human rights. It might also be said that the extent to which the universality of human rights is recognised and applied to even 'the undeserving' is the test of the very humanity of a society and its legal system.

What follows requires a consideration of perhaps the most essential tension between the courts, in their recognition and application of human rights, and the state in its desire to protect what it perceives as the public interest through controlling those it considers a threat to that public interest: a tension between judiciary and legislature, and perhaps one that prefigures future tension between the fairly recently established Supreme Court and parliament.

Anti-terrorism, Crime and Security Act 2001

Following the terrorist attack on the World Trade Center on 11 September 2001, the UK parliament introduced the Anti-terrorism, Crime and Security Act (ACSA) 2001. This Act allowed for the detention, without charge, of non-UK citizens suspected of terrorist activities, but who could not be repatriated to their own countries because of fear for their well-being.

Such a provision was clearly contrary to Art 5 of the ECHR. Consequently, the government was required to enter a derogation from the Convention by virtue of the Human Rights Act 1998 (Designated Derogation) Order 2001, the justification for the derogation being that the prospect of terrorism following 11 September 2001 threatened the life of the nation.

SIAC hearings and special advocates

The Special Immigration Appeals Commission (SIAC) was empowered under the ACSA 2001 to hear appeals in relation to decisions taken under it. The SIAC originally had been established by the Special Immigration Appeals Commission Act 1997 in response to a decision of the ECtHR in *Chahal v UK* (1997), in relation to the political deportations. Hearings before the SIAC are conducted on both an open basis and a closed basis. In the former, anyone can attend, but in the latter, which deal with matters of state security, not only the public but also the detained persons and their lawyers are excluded and therefore have no access to, let alone the possibility of challenging, the evidence used against them. In closed session, the detainees are represented by special advocates who are lawyers with clearance to access secret and security documents. These special advocates are neither appointed by the people they represent, nor are they at liberty to divulge any information to them. (See, further, Justice and Security Act 2013, p 73).

The Belmarsh cases

This title refers to a number of cases that focused on the issues of the compatibility of ACSA 2001 with the European Convention on Human Rights and the compliance with the convention of orders made under its auspices.

Protection of human rights in the UK:
- **The Human Rights Act 1998 (HRA)**: introduces into UK law rights contained in the **European Convention on Human Rights and Fundamental Freedoms (ECHR)**
- The **European Union Charter of Fundamental Rights** enshrines certain rights, many of which are also found in the ECHR, into EU and UK law (*see Chapter 5*)

The European Convention on Human Rights and Fundamental Freedoms (ECHR):
- International treaty, taking effect in 1953 to protect human rights and fundamental freedoms in Europe following World War II
- While the UK played a pivotal role in its creation, and is a signatory, the ECHR was not incorporated into UK law. In 1966 individuals were given the right to petition the **European Court of Human Rights (ECtHR)**
- **HRA 1998** entered into force in 2000, giving effect to the ECHR and allowing individuals to enforce ECHR rights in national courts

Enforcement of human rights in the UK

The Human Rights Act 1998:
- creates a domestic means of protecting rights by
  (i) requiring **public bodies** to comply with the **ECHR**, and
  (ii) obliging **national courts** to interpret national law in a manner compatible with the ECHR, in so far as it is possible to do so. Higher courts may also issue a *'Declaration of Incompatibility'* should UK statute conflict with the ECHR. However, Parliament cannot be compelled to amend the law
- When enacting a new statute, the minister responsible issues a **statement** as to whether the Bill is compatible or incompatible with the ECHR (the government may proceed with the Bill in either circumstance)

Interplay between national courts and the ECtHR:
- Statistics demonstrate that UK national courts and the ECtHR rarely disagree, with less than 2 per cent of cases finding a violation by a UK public body, which, it can be argued, is due to the high quality of UK court judgments
- While certain sections of the media may portray the ECtHR as unilaterally imposing its will on domestic courts, the two have demonstrated a willingness to engage in dialogue
- Where cases have been successfully brought before the ECtHR, many have resulted in significant milestones in protection of human rights

Enforcing rights under the ECHR:
- ECHR rights are only enforceable vertically (i.e. against a **public body** and not an individual)
- An individual who believes his rights have been breached may bring an action before a national court. (Remedy is usually a declaration of rights but can include compensation.)
- Where all national remedies have been exhausted, or there is no real prospect of achieving anything other than a declaration of incompatibility, it may be possible to bring a case before the **ECtHR** if that Court considers the case to be admissible. A final appeal may be available to the ECtHR's Grand Chamber
- As the ECHR has not been incorporated into UK law, UK courts are under a duty to do no more than 'take into account' (**s 2 HRA**) judgments of the ECtHR, while the government has discretion on how to remedy a breach, although its record on implementation has been described as 'exemplary'

FIGURE 2.2 *Enforcement of Human Rights in the UK.*

A v Secretary of State for the Home Department (SIAC and the Court of Appeal) *(2002)*

In July 2002, the SIAC held that the ACSA 2001 was not in compliance with the anti-discriminatory provisions of Art 14 of the Convention to the extent that it treated non-nationals differently from UK nationals.

The then Home Secretary, David Blunkett, attacked the SIAC decision and it was subsequently overturned by the Court of Appeal. According to the Court of Appeal, the case concerned an example of what is referred to as the 'area of due deference' within which the courts will 'defer on democratic grounds to the considered opinion of the elected body or person whose actual decision is said to be incompatible with the Convention'. As the Home Secretary was better qualified than the courts to decide what action had to be taken to safeguard national security, the courts should not intervene.

The approach of the Court of Appeal in this case was reminiscent of the quiescent attitude of previous courts when faced with the exercise of executive power. Perhaps the classic example of such subservience is to be found in *Liversidge v Anderson* (1942) in which a majority of the House of Lords approved the power of the Home Secretary to imprison a person without trial under wartime defence regulations. Lord Atkin, in the minority, famously railed against the granting of such uncontrolled power to the Home Secretary and accused his fellow members of the House of Lords of being '. . . more executive-minded than the executive'.

A v Secretary of State for the Home Department (House of Lords) *(2004)*

Somewhat surprisingly a further appeal to the House of Lords resulted in a crushing judgment against the Act and an undisguised and unmitigated rebuke to the government and its anti-terrorism policies. The strength of the decision was almost startling, especially in the light of the previously more accommodating decisions of the Court of Appeal in relation to state policy. The case was heard by a panel of nine Law Lords, Lord Steyn having stood down from the appeal because he had previously expressed the view that the derogation was unjustified, and it was decided by a majority of eight to one, only Lord Walker dissenting, that the ACSA was incompatible with the provisions of the ECHR.

Although the House of Lords recognised the deference due to the government and parliament and accepted that the government had been entitled to conclude that there was a public emergency, it nonetheless concluded that the response to the perceived threat had been disproportionate and incompatible with the rights under the ECHR.

The House pointed out the illogicality at the heart of the Act for, if the potential threat to the security of the UK *by UK nationals* suspected of being al-Qaida terrorists could be addressed without infringing their right to personal liberty, then why could not similar measures be used to deal with any threat presented by *foreign nationals*.

The House of Lords also held that ss 21 and 23 of the Act were disproportionate for the general reason that the provisions did not rationally address the threat to the security of the UK presented by al-Qaida terrorists.

As a result, the House of Lords decided that s 23 of the ACSA was incompatible with Art 5 and Art 14 of the ECHR and appropriately quashed the Derogation Order 2001, as it was secondary rather than primary legislation.

While the preceding report of *A v Secretary of State for the Home Department* provides an objective account of the House of Lords' decision, it does little to reflect the intensity of feeling expressed in the individual judgments of those involved in the case, which can only be appreciated through the words of the judges involved. While the leading judgment of Lord Bingham, the senior Law Lord, was delivered in measured, if critical, terms, it cannot but be recognised that some of the other members of the judicial panel expressed themselves in such florid language as to lay themselves open to the accusation of 'showboating' – an expression used to indicate a mixture of self- and over-indulgence.

The most patently (over-)rhetorical judgment was delivered by Lord Hoffmann, of which the following quotation is merely one example:

> 95. . . . Of course the government has a duty to protect the lives and property of its citizens. But that is a duty which it owes all the time and which it must discharge without destroying our constitutional freedoms. There may be some nations too fragile or fissiparous to withstand a serious act of violence. But that is not the case in the United Kingdom. When Milton urged the government of his day not to censor the press even in time of civil war, he said:
>
> > 'Lords and Commons of England, consider what nation it is whereof ye are, and whereof ye are the governors'
>
> 96. This is a nation which has been tested in adversity, which has survived physical destruction and catastrophic loss of life. I do not underestimate the ability of fanatical groups of terrorists to kill and destroy, but they do not threaten the life of the nation. Whether we would survive Hitler hung in the balance, but there is no doubt that we shall survive Al-Qa'ida.

However, perhaps the most overtly political speech was that of Lord Scott, which contained the following passages:

> 142. . . . The making of such a declaration [of incompatibility] will not, however, affect in the least the validity under domestic law of the impugned statutory provision. *The import of such a declaration is political not legal.*
>
> 154. . . . The Secretary of State is unfortunate in the timing of the judicial examination in these proceedings of the 'public emergency' that he postulates. It is certainly true that the judiciary must in general defer to the executive's assessment of what constitutes a threat to national security or to 'the life of the nation'. But judicial memories are no shorter than those of the public and the public have not forgotten the faulty intelligence assessments on the basis of which United Kingdom forces were sent to take part, and are still taking part, in the hostilities in Iraq.
>
> 155. . . . Indefinite imprisonment in consequence of a denunciation on grounds that are not disclosed and made by a person whose identity cannot be disclosed is the stuff of nightmares, associated whether accurately or inaccurately with France before and during the Revolution, with Soviet Russia in the Stalinist era and now associated, as a result of section 23 of the 2001 Act, with the United Kingdom (emphasis added).

It is significant to note that these speeches were delivered before the murderous bombings in London on 7 July 2005, or perhaps the rhetorical flourishes might have been more controlled. In any event, the House of Lords' decision, in what has become known as the *Belmarsh* case, represented a general exercise in judicial activism in relation to the executive power, but its declaration of incompatibility together with the quashing of the derogation order left the government with a particular problem: whether it would be able to renew the provisions of the ACSA in March 2005, as was required by the Act itself. When it became apparent that there was no such possibility, the government introduced new procedures for dealing with suspected terrorists under the Prevention of Terrorism Act 2005 (PTA 2005).

Prevention of Terrorism Act 2005 and control orders

The Act as eventually passed dealt with one of the shortcomings of the ACSA by widening the provisions of the previous legislation to control all terrorist-related activity, *irrespective of nationality* or indeed the particular cause the terrorists supported. But perhaps even more essentially, it did not attempt to continue the detention without trial regime under the ACSA, which was replaced with a new system of 'control orders'. These control orders were to be of two distinct types; derogating and non-derogating in relation to the ECHR.

Derogating control orders

As its title suggests, this type of control order required derogation from ECHR because it deprived the person affected of their liberty by requiring them to remain in a particular place at all times. It was equivalent to house arrest and consequently it clearly infringes the person's rights under Art 5 of the ECHR. In the event no derogation orders were ever sought.

Non-derogating control orders

This type of control order allowed the Home Secretary to impose a range of controls over people's activities from a ban on the use of mobile phones or the internet, to control of the movement of the individuals including the imposition of curfews and the use of tagging for the purposes of monitoring those curfews.

The 2005 Act retained the role of the *special advocate*, who was expected to support the interests of the suspect in regard to material that neither the accused nor his chosen legal representatives were allowed access to.

Any breach of a control order, without reasonable excuse, was a criminal offence punishable on indictment by imprisonment of up to five years.

The legal effect of non-derogation control orders issued under the PTA 2005 were considered by the House of Lords in a series of related appeals, the decisions in which were delivered in three judgments at the end of October 2007.

The maximum length of control orders

In the first, *Secretary of State for the Home Department v JJ and others* (2007), the issue was whether an order imposing an 18-hour curfew, coupled with other restrictions on the activities of those subject to the orders, amounted to deprivation of liberty and consequently were contrary to Art 5 of the ECHR. In deciding the question, the court recognised the distinction between the *unqualified* right to liberty and the *qualified* rights of freedom of movement, communication and association provided under the ECHR as previously expressed by the ECtHR.

The general effect of the particular control orders in question were summarised by the Court of Appeal in para 4 of its judgment as follows:

> The obligations imposed by the control orders are set out in annex I to Sullivan J's judgment. They are essentially identical. Each respondent is required to remain within his 'residence' at all times, save for a period of six hours between 10 am and 4 pm. In the case of GG the specified residence is a one-bedroom flat provided by the local authority in which he lived before his detention. In the case of the other five respondents the specified residences are one-bedroom flats provided by the National Asylum Support Service. During the curfew period the respondents are confined in their small flats and are not even allowed into the common parts of the buildings in which these flats are situated. Visitors must be authorised by the Home Office, to which name, address, date of birth and photographic identity must be supplied. The residences are subject to spot searches by the police. During the six hours when they are permitted to leave their residences, the respondents are confined to restricted urban areas, the largest of which is 72 square kilometres. These deliberately do not extend, save in the case of GG, to any area in which they lived before. Each area contains a mosque, a hospital, primary health care facilities, shops and entertainment and sporting facilities. The respondents are prohibited from meeting anyone by prearrangement who has not been given the same Home Office clearance as a visitor to the residence.

In addition, the controlled persons were required to wear an electronic tag and to report to a monitoring company on first leaving their flat after a curfew period and on returning to it before a curfew period. They were forbidden to use or possess any communications equipment of any kind except for one fixed telephone line in their flat maintained by the monitoring company. They were at liberty to attend a mosque of their choice if it was in their permitted area and approved in advance by the Home Office. A request by JJ to study English at a college outside his area was refused.

At first instance Sullivan J held that the cumulative effect of the obligations placed on the respondents went far beyond the mere restriction of liberty, recognised as potentially legitimate by the ECtHR, and was such as to deprive them of their liberty in breach of Art 5 of the Convention. As a result, Sullivan J held that the Secretary of State had had no power to make an order that was incompatible with Art 5 of the ECHR and any such purported order had to be treated as a nullity and totally ineffective.

Sullivan J's decision was subsequently approved by the Court of Appeal and, on further appeal to the House of Lords, it was decided by a majority of three to two that neither the judge at first instance nor the Court of Appeal had erred in their legal reasoning and the House of Lords expressly approved their rulings. In the view of the House, the effect of the 18-hour curfew, coupled with the effective exclusion of social visitors meant that the men subject to the control orders were practically in solitary confinement for an indefinite duration. Further, the House of Lords confirmed that as the control orders were a nullity, the defects in them could not be cured by the court simply amending the content of the provisions as was argued for by the Secretary of State.

Of the majority of the House of Lords who held that the control orders amounted to a deprivation of liberty, Lord Bingham and Baroness Hale were content simply to hold that the 18-hour curfew was contrary to Art 5 without considering the possibility of an alternative period that would count as merely a restriction on, rather than a deprivation of, liberty and hence be lawful. However, Lord Brown suggested that a 16-hour curfew period would be an acceptable limit.

The second of the linked cases, *Secretary of State for the Home Department v MB & AF* (2007) also concerned the issues considered in *JJ* and on this occasion the House of Lords unanimously held that a curfew of 14 hours with related restrictions did not amount to a deprivation of liberty. Consequently, if 14 hours did not count as a deprivation of liberty on the basis of *AF*, and 18 hours did amount to such a deprivation as in *JJ*, then Lord Brown's 16 hours appeared to be the appropriate time limit for curfews under PTA 2005 control orders.

However, in *Secretary of State for the Home Department v AP* (2010), which concerned someone subject to a control order confined to a flat for 16 hours a day in a Midlands town 150 miles away from his family in London, Lord Brown subsequently clarified/retracted his original suggestion.

In *AP* the Supreme Court unanimously decided that conditions that might be proportionate restrictions upon Art 8 rights to respect for private and family life can 'tip the balance' in relation to Art 5, which guarantees the right to liberty and security. In other words, the court should take account of the *effect* of any restrictions in deciding whether a control order amounts to a deprivation of liberty. However, in the leading judgment Lord Brown stated that:

> I nevertheless remain of the view that for a control order with a 16-hour curfew (*a fortiori* one with a 14-hour curfew) to be struck down as involving a deprivation of liberty, the other conditions imposed would have to be *unusually destructive* of the life the controlee might otherwise have been living (emphasis added).

The use of torture to extract evidence

After release from Guantanamo Bay, former detainees brought civil claims against UK ministers and intelligence agencies, alleging that the authorities had been complicit in their unlawful imprisonment and the abuse they received while in captivity. Initially, the

High Court allowed the possibility of the state raising a defence to the civil action based on evidence that could not be openly disclosed to the claimants. However, the Court of Appeal forcefully rejected such a possibility as being a fundamental breach of the common law.

A v Secretary of State for the Home Department *(2005)*

During the hearing relating to the appeals against their detention under the provisions of ACSA in October 2003, SIAC stated that the fact that evidence against the detainees had, or might have been, obtained through torture inflicted by foreign officials, but without the complicity of the British authorities, could be used in determining the outcome of the cases. SIAC held that *while the use of torture might affect the weight to be given to the evidence, its source did not render it legally inadmissible.*

    On appeal the Court of Appeal confirmed the approach previously taken by SIAC, holding by a majority that it would be contrary to the exercise of the statutory power and unrealistic to expect the Home Secretary to investigate each statement relied on, in order to determine whether it had been produced as a result of torture.

    Subsequently a seven-strong panel of the House of Lords heard a further appeal on two issues. The first related to the question as to whether evidence produced through torture could be used in any circumstances. The second related to the burden of proof in relation to showing whether or not torture had been used to produce the evidence in question.

    In relation to the first issue, the House was unanimous in its disapproval of the previous approaches of SIAC and the Court of Appeal. It was clear under the common law and under international law that no evidence obtained as a result of torture could be used, even if the torture was conducted by another state, without the complicity of the United Kingdom authorities. While parliament might have the power to approve the use of torture evidence, it had not done so through ACSA. This general view is encapsulated in the words of Lord Bingham at para 52:

> . . . it would of course be within the power of a sovereign Parliament (in breach of international law) to confer power on SIAC to receive third-party torture evidence. But the English common law has regarded torture and its fruits with abhorrence for over 500 years, and that abhorrence is now shared by over 140 countries which have acceded to the Torture Convention. I am startled, even a little dismayed, at the suggestion (and the acceptance by the Court of Appeal majority) that this deeply-rooted tradition and an international obligation solemnly and explicitly undertaken can be overridden by a statute and a procedural rule which make no mention of torture at all.

However, as to the second issue the House of Lords divided 4:3, with the majority holding that SIAC should only *not* admit evidence if it concluded, on a balance of probabilities that it was obtained by torture. If SIAC was in doubt as to whether the evidence was obtained by torture, then it should admit it, but it should bear its doubt in mind when evaluating the evidence.

On the other hand, a strongly argued minority opinion held that SIAC should refuse to admit evidence if it was unable to conclude that there was not a real risk that the evidence had been obtained by torture. *If it was in doubt whether the evidence had been procured by torture, then the commission should exclude the evidence.*

The majority did, however, state that the individual defendant would not be expected to shoulder the entire burden of demonstrating that a particular piece of evidence stated to justify their certification and detention was obtained by torture. According to Lord Hope, the defendant would only be required to raise the issue that the information used against them might have come from a country suspected of practising torture, after which the task of assessing the matter would be passed to SIAC itself.

Lord Rodger, rather naïvely, described how 'those in the relevant department who were preparing a case for a SIAC hearing would sift through the material, *on the lookout for anything that might suggest torture had been used*', and as he later pointed out (para 143, emphasis added):

> The Home Secretary accepted that he was under a duty to put any such material before the Commission. *With the aid of the relevant intelligence services, doubtless as much as possible will be done.* And SIAC itself will wish to take an active role in suggesting possible lines of inquiry.

Consequently defendants could rest assured, confident in the understanding that those who were seeking to have them detained would do everything in their power to ensure that the evidence against them was free from any taint of torture. Perhaps Lord Bingham deserves the final cutting comment on the flawed reasoning of the majority in the House of Lords:

> My noble and learned friend Lord Hope proposes, in paragraph 121 of his opinion, the following test: is it *established*, by means of such diligent enquiries into the sources that it is practicable to carry out and on a balance of probabilities, that the information relied on by the Secretary of State *was* obtained under torture? This is a test which, in the real world, can never be satisfied. The foreign torturer does not boast of his trade. The security services, as the Secretary of State has made clear, do not wish to imperil their relations with regimes where torture is practised. The special advocates have no means or resources to investigate. The detainee is in the dark. It is inconsistent with the most rudimentary notions of fairness to blindfold a man and then impose a standard which only the sighted could hope to meet. *The result will be that, despite the universal abhorrence expressed for torture and its fruits, evidence procured by torture will be laid before SIAC because its source will not have been 'established'* (at para 59, emphasis added).

The Terrorism Prevention and Investigation Measures Act 2011

In January 2011 the Home Secretary announced the government's intention with regard to the future of the control order regime, after some reportedly tense negotiations with her coalition partners in the Liberal Democrat party. The generally accepted assessment of the proposals was that they were a political compromise, which did little to live up to promises of the previous rhetorical claims as to a more liberal regime, with some commentators referring to the proposal as 'control order lite'.

The subsequent Terrorism Prevention and Investigation Measures Act 2011 included the following provisions:

- the new laws are permanent, doing away with the requirement for parliament to renew them on an annual basis;
- the replacement for the control order regime are to be known as Terrorism Prevention and Investigation Measures (TPIMs);
- there will be a two-year limitation on TPIMs, but they may be extended if new information emerges that leads the Home Secretary to believe that the person is still a danger;
- the Secretary of State must now have 'reasonable grounds to believe' rather than 'reasonable grounds to suspect' that a person may pose a terrorist threat;
- the Secretary of State is required to seek the court's permission before imposing the measures, except in the most urgent cases where the notice must be referred immediately to the court for confirmation;
- the previous curfew requirements were replaced by 'overnight residence' requirements;
- electronic tagging and restrictions on travel were retained;
- greater access to the internet, phones and personal meetings is allowed.

Nonetheless, the Terrorism Prevention and Investigation Measures Act 2011 retains the power to relocate individuals to another part of the country without consent under powers for the Secretary of State to impose enhanced TPIM notices. This, essentially emergency, power may only be used when Parliament is not in session, i.e. between the dissolution of a Parliament and the first Queen's Speech of the next Parliament.

Protection of Freedoms Act 2012

This Act relaxed a number of provisions introduced by the previous government. Among other measures (it has 121 sections and 10 schedules), the Act:

- introduced a new regime for police 'stop and searches' under the Terrorism Act 2000;
- reduced the maximum pre-charge detention period under the Terrorism Act from 28 to 14 days;

The Justice and Security Act 2013

The embarrassment suffered by the government as a result of the consideration of sensitive security-related material in open court in actions taken against it by former prisoners imprisoned by the United States at Guantanamo Bay fostered its determination to prevent such embarrassment in the future. The result was a Justice and Security Green Paper issued in October 2011, which allowed a relatively short time for consultation, closing in January 2012. Although the Green Paper was subject to much criticism, rather than issue a White Paper to allow further consideration, the government preferred to publish its Justice and Security Bill in May 2012 which subsequently became an Act in 2013. The Act has three purposes:

- the oversight of the Security Service, the Secret Intelligence Service, the Government Communications Headquarters and other activities relating to intelligence or security matters;
- the provision for closed material procedure in relation to certain civil proceedings;
- the prevention of making certain court orders for the disclosure of sensitive information; and for connected purposes.

Part 2 of the Act contains the most immediately controversial material, in that s 6 makes provision to enable the Secretary of State to apply to the court for a 'closed material procedure' (CMP) in certain civil proceedings in the courts. This is essentially an extension to other civil courts of the procedure previously considered in relation to SIAC under which the detained person and their legal representatives are prevented from hearing, and of course challenging, evidence presented to the court in their absence. Section 9 similarly allows for the appointment of special advocates to protect the interest of the detained person (see p 65). The minister triggers the process by deciding that a closed material procedure is needed, and applying to the judge, who decides whether to allow it or not. The judge *must* grant the application if one of the parties to the proceedings would be required to disclose material in the proceedings and the disclosure would be damaging to national security.

It has been suggested by supporters of the CMP that it will improve accountability and oversight on the ground that it will actually allow highly sensitive intelligence information to be heard in private as opposed to being completely excluded under a public interest immunity certificate, as is the case at present.

Section 17 relates to what are known as Norwich Pharmacal orders (NPOs). Such court orders apply in civil proceedings where one party seeks the disclosure of information from another party in order to identify the proper defendant, support their case or establish their defence to an action (*Norwich Pharmacal Co. & Others v Customs and Excise Commissioners* (1974)). The essential point, however, is that the involvement of the party required to provide the information may well be completely innocent, but nonetheless they are still required to supply the information, where it is deemed necessary in the interests of justice. It was on the basis of such a Norwich Pharmacal order that Binyam Mohamed, the leading Guantanamo Bay claimant, had gained access to the documents required to support his action against the UK security services.

Section 17 requires that a court may not order the disclosure of information sought if the information is sensitive information.

What is covered by the term 'sensitive information' is defined in sub-section 17(3) as information:

(a)   held by an intelligence service;

(b)   obtained from, or held on behalf of, an intelligence service;

(c)   derived in whole or part from information obtained from, or held on behalf of, an intelligence service;

(d)   relating to an intelligence service; or

(e)   specified or described in a certificate issued by the Secretary of State, in relation to the proceedings, as information which should not [be] ordered to disclose[d].

Such a provision goes a very long way to completely emasculating the operation of Norwich Pharmacal orders in matters relating to state security, much, one can only imagine, to the great delight of the government and the security services.

In considering the potential effect of what is now s 1[7], Fiona de Londras of University College Dublin School of Law commented:

> It is true that the certification is subject to review (s 1[8]), and it is quite possible that the courts would impose a demanding standard on the government to justify any decision ruling that certain information is sensitive, but that notwithstanding, section 1[7] is difficult to describe as anything but an affront. Its purpose is unquestioningly to ensure yet another avenue towards discovering the depth and breadth of the UK's involvement in what might charitably be called unsavoury activities is blocked.
>
> Even if the certification process – itself a stunning provision of quasi-judicial power to a government minister – were to disappear in the legislative process (and I don't believe it will), the remainder of section 1[4] is still a matter of extreme concern (www.guardian.co.uk/law/2012/may/29/justice-security-section-13).

The collapse of Syria, the emergence of ISIL and ongoing instability in Iraq led to the enactment of the Counter-terrorism and Security Act 2015. The Act contains provisions aimed at disrupting those intending to join the fighting by:

- providing the police with a temporary power to seize a passport at the border from individuals of concern;

- creating a Temporary Exclusion Order that will control the return to the UK of a British citizen suspected of involvement in terrorist activity abroad;

- enhancing border security by toughening transport security arrangements around passenger data, including 'no fly' lists and screening measures;

- enhancing existing TPIMs, including the introduction of stronger locational constraints and a power requiring individuals to attend meetings with the authorities as part of their ongoing management.

Various writers have different understandings of what the concept actually means, but see it essentially as involving a control of arbitrary power – Dicey, Hayek, Thompson, Raz, Unger and Weber.

The essential question is whether the UK is still governed under the rule of law, and of course the conclusion depends on the original understanding of the rule of law: Hayek and Thompson would have said not; Raz would say it was. Sir Stephen Sedley has a view as to the continued operation of the rule of law, which is based on substantive equality and challenges previous legal thought. Current judicial thought may be taken from the detailed consideration of the rule of law provided by the late Lord Bingham.

SEPARATION OF POWERS

The judges and the executive in the separation of powers have distinct but interrelated roles in the constitution. The question arises as to the extent to which the courts can act to control the activities of the executive through the operation of judicial review. The position of the Lord Chancellor as judge and member of the government has been questioned by many, including the current government.

THE HUMAN RIGHTS ACT 1998

The HRA incorporates the ECHR into domestic UK law. The Articles of the ECHR cover the following matters:

the right to life (Art 2);

prohibition of torture (Art 3);

prohibition of slavery and forced labour (Art 4);

the right to liberty and security (Art 5);

the right to a fair trial (Art 6);

the general prohibition of the enactment of retrospective criminal offences (Art 7);

the right to respect for private and family life (Art 8);

freedom of thought, conscience and religion (Art 9);

freedom of expression (Art 10);

freedom of assembly and association (Art 11);

the right to marry (Art 12);

prohibition of discrimination (Art 14).

1. Separation of Powers:
The principle that the primary functions of the state should not be carried out by the same body. Therefore Executive (administration of the law), Legislative (law-making) and Judicial (enforcement of the law) powers should be exercised by separate bodies

2. Parliamentary Sovereignty: Only Parliament may enact Acts of Parliament. Any such Acts are superior to all other sources of law and may not be challenged in the courts. Parliament may make any law that it wishes

CONSTITUTIONAL DOCTRINES AND THE ELS

3. Independence of the Judiciary: Part of the Doctrine of Separation of Powers, now upheld by s 3 of the Constitutional Reform Act 2005, which prevents the Executive from trying to influence judges

4. The Rule of Law: A widely argued principle that, at its most basic, provides that no one is above the law and that everyone must act within the law

FIGURE 2.3 *Constitutional Doctrines and the English Legal System.*

The incorporation of the ECHR into UK law means that UK courts must decide cases in line with the above Articles. This has the potential to create friction between the judiciary and the executive/legislature.

THE STRUCTURE OF THE HUMAN RIGHTS ACT 1998

Section 2 requires future courts to take into account any previous decision of the ECtHR.

Section 3 requires all legislation to be read so far as possible to give effect to the rights provided under the Convention.

Section 4 empowers the courts to issue a declaration of incompatibility where any piece of primary legislation is found to conflict with the rights provided under the Convention.

Section 6 declares it unlawful for any public authority to act in a way that is incompatible with the Convention.

Section 7 allows the 'victim of the unlawful act' to bring proceedings against the public authority in breach.

Section 8 empowers the court to grant such relief or remedy against the public authority in breach of the Act as it considers just and appropriate.

Section 10 provides for fast-track remedial legislation where an Act of Parliament has been declared incompatible with Convention rights.

Section 19 of the Act requires that the minister responsible for the passage of any Bill through Parliament must make a written statement as to whether its provisions are compatible with Convention rights.

CASES DECIDED UNDER THE HUMAN RIGHTS ACT 1998
Cases relating to s 3 powers:

R v A (2001);
Re S (2002);
Mendoza v Ghaidan (2003).

Cases relating to declarations of incompatibility:

R v (1) Mental Health Review Tribunal, North & East London Region (2001);
Wilson v Secretary of State for Trade and Industry (2003);
A v Secretary of State for the Home Department (2004).

Cases relating to sentencing:

R v Secretary of State for the Home Department ex p Anderson and Taylor (2002);
A v Secretary of State for the Home Department (2005).

Cases relating to anti-terrorism legislation:

A v Secretary of State for the Home Department (2002) & (2004);
Secretary of State for the Home Department v JJ and others (2007);
Secretary of State for the Home Department v AP (2010);
Secretary of State for the Home Department v MB & AF (2007);
Al Rawi & Ors v Security Service & Ors (2010);
A v Secretary of State for the Home Department (2005);
Mohamed, R (on the application of) v Secretary of State for Foreign & Commonwealth Affairs 1 & 2 (2010).

FOOD FOR THOUGHT

1   Consider what exactly is meant by the rule of law. Is it simply a matter of legal rules or does it connote something else? For example, Nazi Germany was notoriously legalistic, but were the legal rules it introduced and applied really the outcome of the rule of law?

2   Consider the distinction between the form and substance of the law. Is law 'right' simply because it has been introduced in the appropriate manner? If not, what grounds are there for criticising such law?

3   Consider the nature of human rights. What are they exactly and where do they come from? Would people have no human rights if there were no formal legal provisions, such as the Human Rights Act, recognising them?

4   Is it ever justifiable to torture suspects to acquire information? If not, why not? If it is, what limits can/should be placed on its use and who should regulate its use?

5   Some commentators and politicians complain that the Human Rights Act has increased the power of the judges. To what extent is this correct, and if it is correct, how has that been achieved, and is it a matter to be concerned about?

6   Human rights are currently politically controversial, with many members of the Conservative Party actively seeking the repeal and replacement of the Human Rights Act with a purely domestic Bill of Rights. To what extent is this proposal welcome, or feasible, in the current political/social context?

FURTHER READING

Anti-Social Behaviour Orders: Analysis of the First Six Years, 2004, London: National Association of Probation Officers

Bennion, F, 'A naked usurpation?' (1999) 149 NLJ 421

Bingham, T (Lord), 'The Way We Live Now: Human Rights in the New Millennium', Earl Grey Memorial Lecture [1998] 1 Web JCLI

Bingham, T (Lord), *The Rule of Law*, 2010, London: Allen Lane

Dicey, AV, *Introduction to the Law of the Constitution*, 1885, London: Macmillan

Feldman, D, 'The Human Rights Act and constitutional principles' (1999) 19(2) JLS, June

Fenwick, H, *Civil Liberties and Human Rights*, 4th edn, 2007, Abingdon: Routledge-Cavendish

Fenwick, H, Masterman, R and Phillipson, G (eds), *Judicial Reasoning under the UK Human Rights Act*, 2011, Cambridge: CUP

Fine, R, *Democracy and the Rule of Law*, 1984, London: Pluto

Hayek, FA von, *The Road to Serfdom*, 1944, London: Routledge

Hill, C, *Liberty Against the Law*, 1996, Harmondsworth: Penguin

Horowitz, MJ, 'The Rule of Law: an unqualified good?' (1977) 86 Yale LJ 561

Kairys, D (ed), *The Politics of Law: A Progressive Critique*, 1990, London: Pantheon

Kavanagh, A, 'Judging the judges under the Human Rights Act: deference, disillusionment and the "war on terror"' [2009] PL 287–304

Keating, D, 'Upholding the Rule of Law' (1999) 149 NLJ 533

Laws, J (Sir), 'Law and democracy' [1995] PL 72

Locke, J, *The Treatises of Government*, 1988, Cambridge: CUP

Raz, J, 'The Rule of Law and its virtue' (1977) 93 LQR 195

Rozenberg, J, 'Upholding the Rule of Law' (2009) 106(6) Law Soc Gazette 8

Sedley, S (Sir), *Freedom, Law and Justice*, 1998, Hamlyn Lectures, London: Sweet & Maxwell

Sedley, S (Sir), 'Human rights: a 21st century agenda' [1995] PL 386

Steiner, H and Alston, P, *International Human Rights in Context*, 3rd edn, 2007, Oxford: OUP

Steyn (Lord), 'Civil liberties in modern Britain' [2009] PL 228–36

Thompson, A, 'Taking the right seriously: the case of FA Hayek', in Fitzpatrick, P (ed), *Dangerous Supplements*, 1991, London: Pluto

Thompson, E, *Whigs and Hunters*, 1975, Harmondsworth: Penguin

Wadham, J, 'Rights and responsibilities' (2009) 106(39) Law Soc Gazette 8

Young A, 'R (Evans) v Attorney General – the Anisminic of the 21st Century?', UK Const L Blog (31 March 2015) (available at http://ukconstitutionallaw.org)

Young, J, 'The politics of the Human Rights Act' (1999) 26(1) JLS 27

Zander, M, 'The Prevention of Terrorism Act 2005' (2005) 155 NLJ 438

USEFUL WEBSITES

http://ukconstitutionallaw.org

The United Kingdom Constitutional Law Association (UKCLA) is the UK's national body of constitutional law scholars affiliated to the International Association of Constitutional Law. Its object is to 'encourage and promote the advancement of knowledge relating to United Kingdom constitutional law (broadly defined) and the study of constitutions generally'.

www.coe.int/en/

The Council of Europe site – it includes all the decisions of the Commission on Human Rights, the Court of Human Rights and the Committee of Ministers back to 1951.

www.equalityhumanrights.com

The official website for the Equality and Human Rights Commission.

www.lse.ac.uk/collections/LSEPublicLecturesAndEvents/pdf/20060222-Goldsmith.pdf

An online transcript of ' Government and the Rule of Law in the Modern Age ', a lecture given in 2006 by The Rt Hon Lord Goldsmith QC, Attorney General.

COMPANION WEBSITE

Now visit the companion website to:

- test your understanding of the key terms using our Flashcard Glossary;
- revise and consolidate your knowledge of 'The rule of law and human rights' using our Multiple Choice Question testbank;
- view all of the links to the Useful Websites above.

www.routledge.com/cw/slapper

3.1 INTRODUCTION

3.2 EUROPEAN UNION

3.3 PRIMARY LEGISLATION

legislation that is incompatible with the rights provided under the European Convention on Human Rights (ECHR). Whether this will remain the case in the future is, however, a moot point. Coupled with this wide power is the convention that no one parliament can bind its successors in such a way as to limit their absolute legislative powers.

This absolute power is a consequence of the historical struggle between parliament and the Stuart monarchy in the seventeenth century. In its conflict with the Crown, Parliament claimed the power of making law as its sole right. In so doing, Parliament curtailed the royal prerogative and limited the monarchy to a purely formal role in the legislative procedure. In this struggle for ultimate power, the courts sided with Parliament and, in return, Parliament recognised the independence of the courts from its control. Prerogative powers still exist and remain important, but are now mainly exercised by the government in the name of the Crown, rather than by the Crown itself. Some of the general prerogative powers are extremely important, such as the declaration of war and the power to issue, refuse or withdraw passport facilities, but others are less so, such as powers connected with prepaid postage stamps. It will not be lost on readers that perhaps the most important constitutional case in recent times, *Miller v Secretary of State for Exiting the European Union*, turned on the possibility of prerogative powers being used to initiate the UK's exit from the European Union.

Although we still refer to our legal system as a common law system, and although the courts still have an important role to play in the interpretation of statutes, it has to be recognised that legislation is the predominant method of law-making in contemporary times. It is necessary, therefore, to have some knowledge of the workings of the legislative process.

3.3.1 THE PRE-PARLIAMENTARY PROCESS

Any consideration of the legislative process must be placed in the context of the political nature of Parliament. Most statutes are the outcome of the policy decisions taken by government, and the actual policies pursued will of course depend upon the political persuasion and imperatives of the government of the day. Thus, a great deal of law creation and reform can be seen as the implementation of party political policies.

For example, previous Labour governments introduced considerable constitutional reform as proposed in its manifestos. Thus, the Scottish Parliament and the Welsh Assembly have been instituted and many hereditary peers have been removed from the House of Lords. As the election in May 2010 resulted in no one party having an overall majority of Members of Parliament, the government had to be formed by a coalition of the larger Conservative and smaller Liberal Democrat parties. As the basis for this coming together, the parties had to fashion a compromise programme, rather than insist on pursuing their individual manifesto promises. This generated some disquiet among some people who voted for a particular party on the basis of a specific manifesto promise, only to see that promise subsequently denied. This was particularly the case with some Liberal Democrat voters who expressed anger when their party subsequently supported an increase in university fees, in spite of its pre-election promise not to do so.

The establishment of the coalition government in 2010 clearly involved an increase in fissile tendencies, as the government faced not only the difficulty of controlling members of more than one party, but the much harder task of holding together two discrete memberships with sometimes incompatible political views. In response to this perceived potential difficulty one of the first decisions taken by the coalition was to introduce the constitutionally controversial Fixed-term Parliaments Act 2011. The stated purpose of this Act was to provide for five-year fixed-term parliaments. As a result, the date of the next General Election should have been 7 May 2020. The Act does allow the Prime Minister some leeway to alter the date by up to two months before or after that date. It also provides only two ways in which an election can be triggered before the end of the five-year term:

- if a motion of no confidence was passed and no alternative government was found;
- if a motion for an early General Election was agreed either by at least two-thirds of the House or without division.

The government took advantage of the second trigger in announcing the June 2017 election. As, by convention, the government is drawn from the party controlling a majority in the House of Commons, it can effectively decide what policies it wishes to implement and trust to its majority to ensure that its proposals become law. Accusations have been made that when governments have substantial majorities, they are able to operate without taking into account the consideration of their own party members, let alone the views of opposition members. It is claimed that their control over the day-to-day procedure of the House of Commons, backed with their majority voting power, effectively reduces the role of Parliament to that of merely rubber-stamping their proposals.

The government generates most of the legislation that finds its way into the statute book, but individual Members of Parliament may also propose legislation in the form of Private Member's Bills.

There are in fact three ways in which an individual Member of Parliament can propose legislation:

- through the ballot procedure, by means of which 20 backbench Members get the right to propose legislation on the 10 or so Fridays in each parliamentary Session specifically set aside to consider such proposals;
- under Standing Order 39, which permits any Member to present a Bill after the 20 balloted Bills have been presented;
- under Standing Rule 13, the 10-minute rule procedure, which allows a Member to make a speech of up to 10 minutes in length in favour of introducing a particular piece of legislation.

Of these procedures, only the first has any real chance of success and even then success will depend on securing a high place in the ballot and on the actual proposal not being too contentious. Examples of this include the Abortion Act 1967, which was introduced as a Private Member's Bill to liberalise the provision of abortion, and the various attempts that have subsequently been made by Private Member's Bills to restrict the original provision. The Mental Health (Discrimination) Act 2013 was another example of a successful use of the private member's procedure. In relation to particular reforms, external pressure groups or interested parties may very often be the original moving force behind them. When individual Members of Parliament are fortunate enough to find themselves at the top of the ballot for Private Member's Bills, they may well also find themselves the focus of attention from such pressure groups proffering pre-packaged law reform proposals in their own particular areas of interest.

The decision as to which government Bills are to be placed before Parliament in any Session is under the effective control of two Cabinet committees:

- the *Future Legislation Committee* determines which Bills will be presented to Parliament in the *following* parliamentary Session;
- the *Legislation Committee* is responsible for the legislative programme conducted in the *immediate* parliamentary Session. It is the responsibility of this Committee to draw up the legislative programme announced in the Queen's Speech, delivered at the opening of the parliamentary Session.

Green Papers are consultation documents issued by the government, which set out and invite comments from interested parties on particular proposals for legislation. After considering any response, the government may publish a second document in the form of a White Paper, in which it sets out its firm proposals for legislation.

The publication of draft Bills is a third way through which pre-legislative consultation and scrutiny can take place. In recent years it has become common for government departments to issue such draft Bills to allow for consultation and for more detailed scrutiny of the proposed text to take place before the Bill is formally introduced into the legislative process. Such draft Bills are made available on the UK Parliament website and are examined either by select committees in the House of Commons or in the House of Lords or by a joint committee of both Houses of Parliament.

3.3.2 THE LEGISLATIVE PROCESS

Parliament consists of three distinct elements: the House of Commons with 650 directly elected members; the House of Lords with 826 unelected members; and the monarch.

Before any legislative proposal, known at that stage as a Bill, can become an Act of Parliament, it must proceed through, and be approved by, both Houses of Parliament and must receive the Royal Assent. The ultimate location of power, however, is the House of Commons, which has the authority of being a democratically elected institution.

A Bill must be given three readings in both the House of Commons and the House of Lords before it can be presented for the Royal Assent. It is possible to commence the procedure in either House, although money Bills must be placed before the Commons in the first instance.

When a Bill is introduced in the Commons, it undergoes five distinct procedures:

- *First reading*. This is purely a formal procedure in which its title is read and a date set for its second reading.

- *Second reading.* At this stage, the general principles of the Bill are subject to extensive debate. The second reading is the critical point in the process of a Bill. At the end, a vote may be taken on its merits and, if it is approved, it is likely that it will eventually find a place in the statute book.
- *Committee stage.* After its second reading, the Bill is passed to a standing committee whose job it is to consider the provisions of the Bill in detail, clause by clause. The committee has the power to amend it in such a way as to ensure that it conforms with the general approval given by the House at its second reading. Very occasionally, a Bill may be passed to a special standing committee which considers the issues involved before going through the Bill in the usual way as a normal standing committee. Also, the whole House may consider certain Bills at committee stage. In general, these are Bills of constitutional importance, such as the House of Lords Bill, which proposed the reformation of the Upper House in 1999. Other Bills that need to be passed very quickly and certain financial measures, including at least part of each year's Finance Bill, are also considered by the committee of the whole House.
- *Report stage.* At this point, the standing committee reports the Bill back to the House for consideration of any amendments made during the committee stage.
- *Third reading.* Further debate may take place during this stage, but it is restricted to matters relating to the content of the Bill; questions relating to the general principles of the Bill cannot be raised.

When a Bill has completed all these stages, it is passed to the House of Lords for its consideration. After consideration by the Lords, the Bill is passed back to the Commons, which must then consider any amendments to the Bill that might have been introduced by the Lords. Where one House refuses to agree to the amendments made by the other, Bills can be repeatedly passed between them but, as Bills must usually complete their process within the life of a particular parliamentary Session, a failure to reach agreement within that period might lead to the total loss of the Bill. However, in 1998, the House of Commons Modernisation Committee agreed that, in defined circumstances and subject to certain safeguards, government Bills should be able to be carried over from one Session to the next, in the same way that Private and Hybrid Bills may be. The first Bill to be treated in this way was the Financial Services and Markets Bill 1998–99, which the House agreed to carry over into the 1999–2000 Session after a debate on 25 October 1999. The effect was to stay proceedings on the Bill in standing committee at the end of the 1998–99 Session and to carry it over into the next Session, when the committee resumed at the point in the Bill it had previously reached. In October 2004, a contested vote in the Commons made the carry-over process a permanent Standing Order of the House.

English Votes for English Laws (EVEL)

On 22 October 2015, a vote in the House of Commons agreed to alter its standing orders in order to introduce new legislative procedures for enacting Bills, or provisions in Bills, that apply only to England. Under the new procedure, English MPs, sitting as an English Grand Committee, will be able to block legislation deemed to solely affect England, although the Bill would ultimately be subject to a full vote of the House of Commons.

Introduction: *Most new legislation is introduced by the government as a result of policy decisions. However, legislation can be introduced by a Member of Parliament (MP) or peer (a member of the House of Lords). For the sake of simplicity, this flowchart concentrates on legislation introduced by the government, but a similar process will be followed for legislation introduced by others.*

Consultation stages: *Allow the opportunity for interested parties to provide their comments on legislative proposals. While the following stages are commonly employed, and provide an opportunity to influence future legislation, they are optional:*

(i) **White Paper:** *sets out proposals for change; interested parties are consulted. As a result:*
(ii) **Green Paper:** *a consultation paper may be issued.*

Draft Bill prepared: *undertaken by specialist lawyers. Allows for further scrutiny of proposals.*

Passage of a Bill: *The following stages are a requirement if a Bill is to become law:*

(i) **First Reading:** *comprises a formal introduction. Long title of Bill will be read out but no opportunity for debate is provided. Completion of this stage allows a Bill to be printed.*
(ii) **Second Reading:** *MPs discuss the main principles of a Bill. MPs may vote at the end of this stage, particularly if a Bill is controversial.*
(iii) **Committee stage:** *Bill is considered by a committee of MPs. Amendments may be proposed and voted on.*
(iv) **Report stage:** *Bill, with amendments or changes, is 'reported' to the House. All MPs can review the amended Bill. Those not involved at the previous stage may suggest further changes.*
(v) **Third reading:** *MPs debate and vote on the Bill in its final form.*

Transfer to the House of Lords: *If a Bill begins in the House of Commons – and is approved – it is then sent to the House of Lords, where it goes through the same stages. If the Lords make changes to a Bill, it returns to the Commons for MPs to consider any amendments. Both the Commons and Lords must agree on the final Bill before it can become law. If the Bill is a Finance Bill, the legislation can be passed after a year even if the House of Lords is opposed to it.*

Royal Assent: *Results in a 'Bill' becoming an 'Act':*

Once approval has been obtained from both the Commons and Lords, the Bill will require the approval of the monarch – called 'Royal Assent'. The monarch provides approval on the advice of ministers. Once assent has been provided, the Bill then becomes law (on a specified date) and is described as an **Act of Parliament.**

FIGURE 3.1 *The Legislative Process.*

The change was justified as a way of addressing the so-called 'West Lothian Question', the position where English MPs cannot vote on matters which have been devolved to other parts of the UK, but Scottish, Welsh and Northern Ireland MPs can vote on those same matters when the UK Parliament is legislating solely for England.

The policy paper supporting the proposed changes explained the procedure thus:

- When a Bill has been introduced in the Commons, the Speaker will certify whether the Bill, or parts of it, should be subject to the new process.

- Once the Speaker has certified a Bill, it continues to second reading and committee stage as normal.

- Any Bills that the Speaker has certified as England-only in their entirety will be considered by only English MPs at committee stage. The membership of this committee will reflect the numbers of MPs that parties have in England. After this the Bill continues to report stage as normal.

- For Bills containing English or English and Welsh provisions, there is then a process for gaining the consent of English or English and Welsh MPs. A legislative Grand Committee considers a consent motion for any clauses that the Speaker has certified as English or English and Welsh only. This is a new stage which will allow all English or English and Welsh MPs either to consent to or to veto those clauses.

- If clauses of the Bill are vetoed by the legislative Grand Committee, there is a reconsideration stage when further amendments can be made, to enable compromises to be reached. The whole House can participate in this stage, which is, in effect, a second report stage for disputed parts of the Bill. This is followed by a second legislative Grand Committee at which all English or English and Welsh MPs are asked to consent to the amendments made by the whole House. If no agreement is reached at this point, the disputed parts of the Bill fall.

- Following report stage and any consent motions, the Bill continues to third reading, in which now all MPs can participate. It then progresses to the House of Lords. If there are any consequential amendments to the rest of the Bill required as a result of disputed parts of the Bill falling, there will be an additional stage before third reading to allow this.

- The legislative process in the House of Lords is unchanged.

The alteration to the standing orders of the House was criticised for politicising the position of the Speaker, as that person would be in the position of having to adjudicate from which votes Scottish MPs should be excluded. However, the strongest opposition from both Labour and Scottish National opposition parties was on the grounds that the EVEL procedure undermined the equality of all Members of Parliament and that, in any event, it was no more than a device aimed primarily at securing future Conservative control over laws operating in England in the event of a Labour/SNP alliance majority in the UK.

The Parliament Acts

Given the need for legislation to be approved in both Houses of Parliament, it can be seen that the House of Lords has considerable power in the passage of legislation. However, the fact that it was never a democratically accountable institution, together with the fact that until 2005 it had an in-built Conservative Party majority reflecting its previous hereditary composition, meant that its legislative powers had to be curtailed. Until the early years of the twentieth century, the House of Lords retained its full power to prevent the passage of legislation. However, Lloyd-George's Liberal budget of 1909 brought the old system to breaking point when the House of Lords originally refused to pass it. Although the budget was eventually passed after a General Election in 1910, a second election was held on the issue of reform of the House of Lords. As a result of the Liberal victory the Parliament Act of 1911 was introduced, which removed the House of Lords' power to veto a Bill. As a matter of interest, the 1911 Act also reduced the maximum lifespan of a Parliament from seven years to its current five years and specifically retained the House of Lords' power to block any attempt to prolong the lifetime of a parliament. The Parliament Act of 1911 reduced the power of the Lords to delay a Bill by up to two years. In 1949 the Parliament Act of that year further reduced the Lords' delaying powers to one year, but it is significant that the 1949 Act was itself only introduced through the use of the previous Parliament Act of 1911.

Since 1949 the delaying powers of the House of Lords have been as follows:

- a 'Money Bill', that is, one containing only financial provisions, can be enacted without the approval of the House of Lords after a delay of one month;
- any other Bill can be delayed by one year.

Only four substantive Acts have been passed into law without the consent of the House of Lords:

- the War Crimes Act 1991;
- the European Parliamentary Elections Act 1999;
- the Sexual Offences (Amendment) Act 2000;
- the Hunting Act 2004.

The last piece of legislation, the Hunting Act, was introduced to prohibit the hunting of mammals with dogs and was particularly designed to outlaw the tradition of fox-hunting.

However, of essential importance in relation to this Act was that the use of the Parliament Act 1949 to pass it, in the face of the refusal of the House of Lords, gave rise to a consideration of the legality of the Act itself in *Jackson v HM Attorney General* (2005).

Jackson v HM Attorney General *(2005)*

The appellants argued that the 1949 Act was itself invalid on the basis that it did not receive the consent of the House of Lords, and the Parliament Act 1911 did not permit an Act such as the 1949 Act to be enacted without the consent of the House of Lords. Thus, although the Hunting Act gave rise to the case, the essential underlying issue related to the validity of the 1949 Act, which in turn depended on the effect of the 1911 Parliament Act. As Lord Bingham put it, 'The merits and demerits of the Hunting Act, on which opinion is sharply divided, have no bearing on the legal issue which the House, sitting judicially, must resolve.'

In its reading of the Parliament Acts, the Court of Appeal concluded that under the 1911 Act the House of Commons had the power to make a 'relatively modest and straightforward amendment'. The Court of Appeal went on to conclude that the Parliament Act of 1949 was within that ambit, as an example of a 'relatively modest' amendment, as was the Hunting Act. However, the Court of Appeal raised doubts as to the power of the House of Commons, acting without the agreement of the House of Lords, to make changes 'of a fundamentally different nature to the relationship between the House of Lords and the Commons from those which the 1911 Act had made'. Thus the Court of Appeal raised the fundamental constitutional question relating to the ultimate power of the House of Commons.

Once again an augmented nine-member panel of the House of Lords was required to deal with these fundamental constitutional issues. In doing so, the House of Lords unanimously held that the reasoning of the Court of Appeal could not be sustained. In reaching that conclusion the House of Lords rejected the argument that the Parliament Act of 1911 was an exercise in the *delegation* of powers from Parliament to the House of Commons, which could not later be used to extend those powers. Rather, as Lord Bingham stated:

> The overall object of the 1911 Act was not to delegate power: it was to restrict, subject to compliance with the specified statutory conditions, the power of the Lords to defeat measures supported by a majority of the Commons . . .

The House of Lords, however, did differ in their assessment of the extent of the power extended to the House of Commons under the Parliament Acts. It is clear that a majority of the House of Lords were of the view that the House of Commons could use the powers given to it under the Parliament Acts to force through such legislation as it wished, but a number of the judges were of the view that the Commons could not extend its own lifetime through such a procedure, as that would be in direct contradiction to the provisions of the Parliament Act 1911. Also, as has been pointed out at 2.3.2, although the decision in *Jackson* exemplifies the traditional deference of the courts to the supremacy of laws of Parliament, the possibility of future changes in the relationship between the two institutions was at least hinted at in the judgment of Lord Steyn.

The Royal Assent is required before any Bill can become law. There is no constitutional rule requiring the monarch to assent to any Act passed by Parliament. There is, however, a convention to that effect, and refusal to grant the Royal Assent to legislation passed by Parliament would place the constitutional position of the monarchy in jeopardy. The procedural nature of the Royal Assent was highlighted by the Royal Assent Act 1967, which reduced the process of acquiring Royal Assent to a formal reading out of the short title of any Act in both Houses of Parliament.

An Act of Parliament comes into effect on the date of the Royal Assent, unless there is any provision to the contrary in the Act itself. It is quite common either for the Act to contain a commencement date for some time in the future, or for it to give the appropriate Secretary of State the power to give effect to its provisions at some future time by issuing statutory instruments. The Secretary of State is not required to bring the provisions into effect and it is not uncommon for some parts of Acts to be repealed before they are ever in force.

An example of this is the massive, and hugely complex, Criminal Justice Act (CJA) 2003. As yet, not all of its provisions have come into effect, and full implementation will only take place over an extended timescale, if at all. One instance of this, which raises a number of issues that will be considered further in various sections of this book, relates to the provisions of s 43 of the CJA, which provides for the prosecution of certain serious and complex fraud cases to be conducted without a jury. Unusually, by virtue of s 330(5) of the CJA, any statutory instrument seeking to bring s 43 into force required an affirmative resolution of both Houses of Parliament. Following the failure of the Jubilee extension fraud cases the government announced its intention to implement s 43, and to that end a draft commencement order was produced. However, in July 2007 the House of Lords effectively killed off a Fraud (Trials without a Jury) Bill by postponing its consideration for six months and subsequently it never re-appeared. Eventually s 113 of the Protection of Freedoms Act 2012 repealed s 43 of the CJA.

Another example of this failure to implement legislative provisions may be seen in the Equality Act 2010, one of the last pieces of legislation passed by the previous Labour government. Although the coalition Home Secretary and Minister for Women and Equalities brought most of the provisions into effect through commencement orders, she let it be known that she would not do so with all its provisions and certainly not s 1 of the Act, which *imposed a duty on public bodies* to have due regard when making strategic decisions to reducing the inequalities of outcome that result from socio-economic disadvantage. In response, critics accused her of rendering the Act 'virtually toothless'.

Parliamentary reform

The 1997 Labour government was elected on the promise of the fundamental reform of the House of Lords, which it saw as undemocratic and unrepresentative. After establishing a Royal Commission, the government embarked on a two-stage process of reform. The first stage of reform was achieved through the House of Lords Act 1999, which removed the right of the majority of hereditary peers to sit in the House of Lords. The second stage of reform was set out, towards the end of 2001, in a White Paper entitled *Completing the Reform.*

The most controversial aspect of the White Paper was the relatively small proportion of directly elected members it proposed, especially when compared with the large proportion of members who would be nominated rather than elected. The government, faced with much criticism, even from its own MPs, set up a joint committee of both Houses of Parliament to consider the course of future reform. Somewhat surprisingly, that committee made no recommendation and merely listed seven possible options for determining the membership of a reformed House of Lords. The options were:

- a fully appointed house;
- a fully elected house;

- 80 per cent appointed, 20 per cent elected;
- 80 per cent elected, 20 per cent appointed;
- 60 per cent appointed, 40 per cent elected;
- 60 per cent elected, 40 per cent appointed;
- 50 per cent appointed, 50 per cent elected.

Even more surprisingly, in February 2003, the House of Commons voted against all of the options and thus failed to approve any of them. The closest vote, for an 80 per cent elected house, fell narrowly by 284 votes against to 281 in favour.

It should be noted that the House of Lords no longer has a majority of members taking the Conservative Party whip. It remains to be seen whether the difficulties suffered by the government in attempting to pass the Tax Credit Regulations 2015 (see below, 3.5.4.1) will result in any specific reform proposals, but it remains the case that the House of Lords, at least as presently constituted, appears to be untenable in the long term: the fact that it only has some 400 places to sit means that it can only function if most of its members do not attend.

On coming to power in 2010 the Conservative/Liberal Democrat coalition passed the Conservative-inspired Parliamentary Voting System and Constituencies Act (PVSCA) 2011, which provided for a future reduction in the number of MPs to 600 while equalising the numerical size of constituencies.

The proposed reduction in the number of MPs was included in the Conservative Party's pre-election manifesto in 2015, but Prime Minister Cameron was subsequently placed under pressure not to implement the policy by a number of his own MPs who feared for their positions in any such reduction. However, the new, Theresa May led, Conservative government has indicated its intention to pursue the reduction in the numbers of MPs.

3.3.3 THE DRAFTING OF LEGISLATION

In 1975, in response to criticisms of the language and style of legislation, the Renton Committee on the Preparation of Legislation (Cmnd 6053) examined the form in which legislation was presented. Representations were made to the Committee by a variety of people ranging from the judiciary to the lay public. The Committee divided complaints about statutes into four main headings relating to:

- obscurity of language used;
- over-elaboration of provisions;
- illogicality of structure;
- confusion arising from the amendment of existing provisions.

It was suggested that the drafters of legislation tended to adopt a stylised archaic legalism in their language and employed a grammatical structure that was too complex and convoluted to be clear, certainly to the layperson and even, on occasion, to legal experts. These criticisms, however, have to be considered in the context of the whole process of drafting legislation and weighed against the various other purposes to be achieved by statutes. The actual drafting of legislation is the work of parliamentary counsel to the Treasury, who specialise in this task. The first duty of the drafters must be to give effect to the intention of the department instructing them, and to do so in as clear and precise a manner as is possible. These aims, however, have to be achieved under pressure, and sometimes extreme pressure, of time. An insight into the various difficulties faced in drafting legislation was provided by a former parliamentary draftsman, Francis Bennion, in an article entitled 'Statute law obscurity and drafting parameters' ((1978) British JLS 235). He listed nine specific parameters which the drafter of legislation had to take into account. These parameters are as follows:

- *Legal effectiveness*. This is the need for the drafters to translate the political wishes of those instructing them into appropriate legal language and form.

- *Procedural legitimacy*. This refers to the fact that the legislation must conform with certain formal requirements if it is to be enacted. For example, it is a requirement that Acts be divided into clauses, and Bills not assuming this form would not be considered by Parliament.

- *Timeliness*. This refers to the requirement for legislation to be drawn up within particularly pressing time constraints. The effect of such pressure can be poorly drafted and defective provisions.

- *Certainty*. It is of the utmost importance that the law be clearly set down so that individuals can know its scope and effect and can guide their actions within its provisions. The very nature of language, however, tends to act against this desire for certainty. In pursuit of certainty, the temptation for the person drafting the legislation is to produce extremely long and complex sentences consisting of a series of limiting and refining sub-clauses. This process in turn, however, tends merely to increase the obscurity of meaning.

- *Comprehensibility*. Ideally, legislation should be comprehensible to the layperson, but given the complex nature of the situation that the legislature is dealing with, such an ideal is probably beyond attainment in practice. Nonetheless, legislative provisions certainly should be open to the comprehension of the Members of Parliament who are asked to vote on them, and they certainly should not be beyond the comprehension of the legal profession who have to construe them for their clients. Unfortunately, some legislation fails on both these counts.

- *Acceptability*. This refers to the fact that legislation is expected to be couched in uncontentious language and using a traditional prose style.

- *Brevity*. This refers to the fact that legislative provisions should be as short as is compatible with the attainment of the legislative purpose. The search for brevity in legislation can run counter to the wish for certainty in, and acceptability of, the language used.

- *Debatability*. This refers to the fact that legislation is supposed to be structured in such a way as to permit it, and the policies that lie behind it, to be debated in parliament.

- *Legal compatibility*. This refers to the need for any new provision to fit in with already existing provisions. Where the new provision alters or repeals existing provisions, it is expected that such effect should be clearly indicated.

A consideration of these various desired characteristics shows that they are not necessarily compatible; indeed, some of them, such as the desire for clarity and brevity, may well be contradictory. The point remains that those people charged with the responsibility for drafting legislation should always bear the above factors in mind when producing draft legislation, but if one principle is to be pursued above others, it is surely the need for clarity of expression and meaning.

3.3.4 TYPES OF LEGISLATION

Legislation can be categorised in a number of ways. For example, distinctions can be drawn between the following:

- *Public Acts*, which relate to matters affecting the general public. These can be further subdivided into either government Bills or Private Member's Bills.
- *Private Acts*, on the other hand, relate to the powers and interests of particular individuals or institutions, although the provision of statutory powers to particular institutions can have a major effect on the general public. For example, companies may be given the power to appropriate private property through compulsory purchase orders.
- *Enabling legislation* gives power to a particular person or body to oversee the production of the specific details required for the implementation of the general purposes stated in the parent Act. These specifics are achieved through the enactment of statutory instruments. (See below, 3.5, for a consideration of delegated legislation.)

Acts of Parliament can also be distinguished on the basis of the function they are designed to carry out. Some are *unprecedented* and cover new areas of activity previously not governed by legal rules, but other Acts are aimed at *rationalising* or *amending* existing legislative provisions.

- *Consolidating legislation* is designed to bring together provisions previously contained in a number of different Acts, without actually altering them. The Companies Act of 1985 was an example of a consolidating Act. It brought together provisions contained in numerous amending Acts that had been introduced since the previous consolidation Act of 1948. The new Companies Act 2006 also consolidated some previous legislation passed since the 1985 Act, but as it also contains previous common law provisions it may also be seen as an example of the next category.
- *Codifying legislation* seeks not just to bring existing statutory provisions under one Act, but also looks to give statutory expression to common law rules. The

classic examples of such legislation are the Partnership Act of 1890 and the Sale of Goods Act 1893 (now 1979).

- *Amending legislation* is designed to alter some existing legal provision. Amendment of an existing legislative provision can take two forms:

  (i)   a *textual amendment* is one where the new provision substitutes new words for existing ones in a legislative text or introduces completely new words into that text. Altering legislation by means of textual amendment has one major drawback, in that the new provisions make very little sense on their own, without the contextual reference of the original provision they are designed to alter;

  (ii)   *non-textual amendments* do not alter the actual wording of the existing text, but alter the operation or effect of those words. Non-textual amendments may have more immediate meaning than textual alterations, but they too suffer from the problem that, because they do not alter the original provisions, the two provisions have to be read together to establish the legislative intention.

Neither method of amendment is completely satisfactory, but the Renton Committee on the Preparation of Legislation favoured textual amendments over non-textual amendments.

3.4   STATUTORY INTERPRETATION

So far, attention has focused on the procedure through which the legislature makes law, but once it has come into being the law has to be applied and given effect, and ultimately that is the role of the judges. Parliament might have said what the law is; the task for the judges is to make sense of parliament's words.

3.4.1   PROBLEMS IN INTERPRETING LEGISLATION

The accepted view is that the constitutional role of the judiciary is simply to *apply* the law. The function of creating law is the prerogative of parliament. As will be seen, such a view is simplistic to the extent that it ignores the potential for judicial creativity in relation to the operation of the common law and the doctrine of judicial precedent. Equally, however, it ignores the extent to which the judiciary have a measure of discretion and creative power in the manner in which they interpret the legislation that comes before them.

Section 3.3.3 has already considered the general difficulties involved in drafting legislation from the point of view of the person carrying out the drafting; equally, however, it has to be recognised that determining the actual meaning of legislation presents judges with a practical difficulty. In order to *apply* legislation, judges must ascertain the meaning of the legislation, and in order to ascertain the meaning, they are faced with the difficulty of interpreting the legislation.

Before considering the way in which judges interpret legislation, it is pertinent to emphasise that, in spite of the best endeavours of those who draft legislation to be precise in communicating the meaning of what they produce, the process of interpretation is inescapable and arises from the nature of language itself. Legislation can be seen as a form of linguistic communication. It represents and passes on to the judiciary what parliament has determined the law should be in relation to a particular situation. Legislation, therefore, shares the general problem of uncertainty inherent in any mode of communication. One of the essential attributes of language is its fluidity: the fact that words can have more than one meaning and that the meaning of a word can change depending on its context. In such circumstances, it is immediately apparent that understanding is an active process. Faced with ambiguity, the recipient of information has to decide which of various meanings to assign to specific words, depending upon the context in which they are used.

Legislation gives rise to additional problems in terms of communication. One of the essential requirements of legislation is generality of application, the need for it to be written in such a way as to ensure that it can be effectively applied in various circumstances, without the need to detail those situations individually. This requirement, however, gives rise to particular problems of interpretation, for, as has been pointed out in 3.3.3, the need for generality can only really be achieved at the expense of clarity and precision of language. A further possibility that is not as uncommon as it should be is that the legislation under consideration is obscure, ambiguous, or indeed meaningless, or fails to achieve the end at which it is aimed, simply through being badly drafted. The task facing the judge in such circumstances is to provide the legislation with some effective meaning.

Legislation therefore involves an inescapable measure of uncertainty that can only be made certain through judicial interpretation. To the extent, however, that the interpretation of legislative provisions is an active process, it is equally a creative one, and inevitably it involves the judiciary in making law through determining the meaning and effect to be given to any particular piece of legislation. There is a further possibility that has to be considered: that judges might actually abuse their role as necessary interpreters of legislation in such a way as to insinuate their own particular personal views and prejudices into their interpretations, and in so doing misapply the legislation and subvert the wishes of the legislature.

3.4.2 APPROACHES TO STATUTORY INTERPRETATION

Having considered the problems of interpreting language generally and the difficulties in interpreting legislation in particular, it is appropriate to consider in detail the methods and mechanisms that judges bring to bear on legislation in order to determine its meaning. There are, essentially, two contrasting views as to how judges should go about determining the meaning of a statute – the restrictive, literal approach and the more permissive, purposive approach:

1   *The literal approach*

    The literal approach is dominant in the English legal system, although it is not without critics, and devices do exist for circumventing it when it is seen as too restrictive. This view of judicial interpretation holds that the judge should look primarily to the words of the legislation in order to construe its meaning and, except in the very limited circumstances considered below, should not look outside of, or behind, the legislation in an attempt to find its meaning.

2   *The purposive approach*

The purposive approach rejects the limitation of the judges' search for meaning to a literal construction of the words of legislation itself. It suggests that the interpretative role of the judge should include, where necessary, the power to look beyond the words of statute in pursuit of the reason for its enactment, and that meaning should be construed in the light of that purpose and so as to give it effect. This purposive approach is typical of civil law systems. In these jurisdictions, legislation tends to set out general principles and leaves the fine details to be filled in later by the judges who are expected to make decisions in the furtherance of those general principles.

European Union (EU) legislation tends to be drafted in the continental, civil law manner. Its detailed effect, therefore, can only be determined on the basis of a purposive approach to its interpretation. This requirement, however, runs counter to the literal approach that is the dominant approach in the English system. The need to interpret such legislation, however, has forced a change in that approach in relation to EU legislation and even with respect to domestic legislation designed to implement Community/ Union legislation. Thus, in *Pickstone v Freemans plc* (1988), the House of Lords held that it was permissible, and indeed necessary, for the court *to read words into* inadequate domestic legislation in order to give effect to EU law in relation to provisions relating to equal pay for work of equal value. (For a similar approach, see also the House of Lords' decision in *Litster v Forth Dry Dock* (1989) and the decision in *Three Rivers DC v Bank of England (No 2)* (1996), considered below at 3.4.4.2.)

In *Usdaw v Ethel Austin Limited (In Administration)* and *Usdaw v WW Realisation 1 Limited and Others* (2013), the Employment Appeal Tribunal (EAT) concluded that s 188(1) of the Trade Union and Labour Relations (Consolidation) Act (TULRA) 1992 did not properly implement the UK's obligations in Art 1(a) of the European Union Collective Redundancies Directive 98/59 EC of 20 July 1998. By virtue of s 188, employers are required to engage in collective consultation when proposing to make 20 or more employees redundant at one establishment within a period of 90 days or less. The ground of contention was whether 'one establishment' meant one specific location, i.e. one shop for example, or whether it referred to more than one of the employer's locations. At first instance the Employment Tribunals found that each shop was an 'establishment' and so only those employees who worked in shops with 20 or more employees were entitled to protective awards in breach of the consultancy provision. Consequently, those employees working in smaller stores (around 4,400 in total) were not entitled to the protection of the consultancy provision. On appeal, the EAT held that s 188 of TULRA did not give full effect to the original directive, which, in the tribunal's opinion, was to be operated by counting individual establishments together as a single entity. Accordingly, it held that, in order to give effect to the directive, s 188 must be *read without the words* 'at one establishment'. On further appeal, the Court of Appeal referred the case to the Court of Justice for the European Union for final determination under Art 267 of the Treaty on the Functioning of the European Union (see p 197).

In April 2015 the CJEU confirmed the earlier opinion of the Advocate General that employers were not required to aggregate dismissals in all establishments, merely those in individual establishments.

The purposive approach and updating construction

It has to be recognised that for some time there has been a move away from the over-reliance on the literal approach to statutory interpretation to a more purposive approach. As Lord Griffiths put it in *Pepper v Hart* [1993] 1 All ER 42 at 50:

> The days have long passed when the court adopted a strict constructionist view of interpretation which required them to adopt the literal meaning of the language. The courts now adopt a purposive approach which seeks to give effect to the true purpose of legislation and are prepared to look at much extraneous material that bears on the background against which the legislation was enacted.

Such a shift has been necessitated, to no little degree, by the need for the courts to consider matters that were not within the original contemplation of Parliament at the time when the legislation was passed, but which have since been brought into play by the effect of technological advances. As Lord Steyn in *R (Quintavalle) v Secretary of State for Health* [2003] 2 All ER 113 at 123 put it:

> The pendulum has swung towards purposive methods of construction. This change was not initiated by the teleological approach of European Community jurisprudence, and the influence of European legal culture generally, but it has been accelerated by European ideas . . .

That process may be traced through a number of controversial cases starting with *Royal College of Nursing of the United Kingdom v Department of Health and Social Security* (1981) (considered in detail at 3.4.3). In his minority judgment Lord Wilberforce, in that case, had expressed the view that ([1981] AC 800 at 822):

In interpreting an Act of Parliament it is proper, and indeed necessary, to have regard to the state of affairs existing, and known by Parliament to be existing, at the time. It is a fair presumption that Parliament's policy or intention is directed to that state of affairs. Leaving aside cases of omission by inadvertence . . . *when a new state of affairs, or a fresh set of facts bearing on policy, comes into existence, the courts have to consider whether they fall within the Parliamentary intention. They may be held to do so, if they fall within the same genus of facts as those to which the expressed policy has been formulated. They may also be held to do so if there can be detected a clear purpose in the legislation which can only be fulfilled if the extension is made.* How liberally these principles may be applied must depend upon the nature of the enactment, and the strictness or otherwise of the words in which it has been expressed . . . In any event there is one course which the courts cannot take, under the law of this country; they cannot fill gaps; they cannot by asking the question 'What would Parliament have done in this current case – not being one in contemplation – if the facts had been before it?' attempt themselves to supply the answer, if the answer is not to be found in the terms of the Act itself (emphasis added).

In other words, Lord Wilberforce thought that legislation *may not* be construed so as to cover new states of affairs, if the new construction required the court to fill gaps, or to ask what Parliament would have done in relation to situations that it could not have had any knowledge of, and hence were outside the ambit of the actual text of the legislation.

However, the court *could* use a purposive reading to extend the law to new situations where one of two things applied:

(i)   the genus of subject matter encompassed the new subject matter; or

(ii)   parliament's purpose was clear and an extended reading was necessary to give effect to it.

Given that Lord Wilberforce actually decided that the *Royal College of Nursing* case was not one in which the court should use the purposive approach, it is perhaps not a little ironic that his exposition of the appropriate circumstances under which the courts can adopt a purposive approach has been generally accepted, and, in many cases, used to extend the application of statutes in a way that he himself might very well not have agreed with.

In *R (Quintavalle) v Secretary of State for Health* (2003) the courts were asked to declare whether embryos created by cell nuclear replacement (CNR), a form of human cloning involving a human egg and a cell from a donor's body, were regulated under the Human Fertilisation and Embryology Act (HFE) 1990, which had been passed at a time when embryos were only ever created by fertilisation of an egg by a sperm. Section 1(1)(a) of the Act defines embryos as 'a live human embryo where fertilisation is complete'.

An organisation opposed to cloning and embryo experimentation, the Pro-Life Alliance, contested a statement from the government that therapeutic cloning research was permitted under the HFE Act 1990, subject to licensing by the regulatory authority, the Human Fertilisation and Embryology Authority (HFEA). The Alliance sought a declaration that the authority had no power to license such research on the grounds that an embryo created by cell nuclear replacement did not fall within the statutory definition of 'embryo'. The argument for the Alliance was that as cloned embryos created by CNR were never fertilised, as commonly understood, they could not be subject to the Act and, more importantly for them, the HFEA could not have any authority to license any such activity.

At first instance the declaration sought by the Alliance was granted 'with some reluctance', the judge saying that the government's argument to have the statute take account of new technology involved 'an impermissible rewriting and extension of the definition'. However, the Court of Appeal set aside the declaration, which decision the House of Lords subsequently confirmed, holding that the purposive interpretation argued for by the government did *not* require the court to assume the mantle of legislator. In so doing both Lord Bingham and Lord Steyn referred to the importance of a purposive approach in enabling the courts to give effect to the intention of Parliament in areas where legislative provisions need to be considered in the context of rapid scientific and technological change.

In deciding *Quintavalle*, the House of Lords based its decision on Lord Wilberforce's comments in the *Royal College of Nursing* case, which in the opinion of Lord Bingham 'may now be treated as authoritative'. In so doing the House of Lords held that embryos created by CNR, notwithstanding the fact that they were unfertilised, were within the same '*genus of facts*' as embryos created naturally or fertilised *in vitro*. In putting Lord Wilberforce's proposition into operation, the House of Lords held that CNR organisms were, in essence, sufficiently like other embryos to be considered as belonging to the same '*genus of facts*'. Parliament could not rationally have been assumed to have intended to exclude such embryos from the regulation; consequently, the fact of fertilisation was not to be treated as integral to the s 1 definition. As a result, they were subject to the control of the HFE Act 1990 and the HFEA could authorise research using such embryos.

In reaching his decision, Lord Bingham considered the purpose and procedure of statutory interpretation and concluded that ([2003] 2 All ER 113 at 118):

The basic task of the court is to ascertain and give effect to the true meaning of what Parliament has said in the enactment to be construed. But that is not to say that attention should be confined and a literal interpretation given to the particular provisions which give rise to difficulty. Such an approach not only encourages immense prolixity in drafting, since the draftsman will feel obliged to provide expressly for every contingency which may possibly arise. It may also (under the banner of loyalty to the will of Parliament) lead to the frustration of that will, because undue concentration on the minutiae of the enactment may lead the court to neglect the purpose which Parliament intended to achieve when it enacted the statute . . . The court's task, within the permissible bounds of interpretation, is to give effect to Parliament's purpose. So the controversial provisions should be read in the context of the statute as a whole, and the statute as a whole *should be read in the historical context of the situation which led to its enactment* (emphasis added).

With regard to the specific question of whether words in statutes should retain their original meaning, or whether they may be interpreted in the light of contemporary social factors, Lord Bingham concluded that legislation is akin to a living text, the meaning of which speaks differently as the social context in which it speaks changes. In his view (at 118):

> There is, I think, no inconsistency between the rule that statutory language retains the meaning it had when Parliament used it and the rule that a statute is always speaking . . . The meaning of 'cruel and unusual punishments' has not changed over the years since 1689, but many punishments which were not then thought to fall within that category would now be held to do so.

The impact of the preference for the purposive approach over the literal one may be seen in *R v Z and others* (2005) in which four men were charged with being members of a proscribed organisation contrary to s 11(1) of the Terrorism Act 2000. Schedule 2 of the Act listed the organisations proscribed under the Act. It referred to the IRA but did not specifically mention the 'Real IRA', which the men were allegedly members of. At first instance the judge found no case to answer, but following a reference by the Attorney General for Northern Ireland, the Northern Ireland Court of Appeal disagreed, concluding that it was the intention of the legislature to include the 'Real IRA' within the term 'the IRA' and that the legislation therefore had to be construed in such a way as to include that organisation.

In the House of Lords, counsel for the accused argued that the task of the court was 'to interpret the provision which parliament has enacted and not to give effect to an inferred intention of parliament not fairly to be derived from the language of the statute'. The House of Lords rejected that argument, holding that the historical context of the legislation was of fundamental importance. It decided that all the Westminster and Stormont statutes were directed towards the elimination of Irish-related terrorism and that the general approach in legislation had been to proscribe the IRA, using that title as a blanket description that 'embraced all emanations, manifestations and representations of the IRA, whatever their relationship to each other'.

The effect of *Pepper v Hart* (1993), permitting access to *Hansard*, will be considered at 3.4.4.2 below, but for the moment, it is still the case that the judges remain subject to the established rules of interpretation of which there are three primary rules of statutory interpretation, together with a variety of other secondary aids to construction.

In spite of the content of the preceding section, it is still necessary to consider the traditional and essentially literally based approaches to statutory interpretation. What follows in this and the following two sections should be read within the context of the Human Rights Act (HRA) 1998, which requires all legislation to be construed in such a way as, if at all possible, to bring it within the ambit of the European Convention on Human Rights (ECHR). The effect of this requirement is to provide the judiciary with powers of interpretation much wider than those afforded to them by the more traditional rules of interpretation, as can be seen from *R v A* (2001), considered above at 2.5.1.2. However, to quote Lord Steyn further in this particular context ([2001] 3 All ER 1 at 16):

> . . . the interpretative obligation under section 3 of the 1998 Act is a strong one. It applies even if there is no ambiguity in the language in the sense of the language being capable of two different meanings . . . [s]ection 3 places a duty on the court to strive to find a possible interpretation compatible with Convention rights. Under ordinary methods of interpretation a court may depart from the language of the statute to avoid absurd consequences: section 3 goes much further. Undoubtedly, a court must always look for a contextual and purposive interpretation: section 3 is more radical in its effect . . . In accordance with the will of Parliament as reflected in section 3 it will sometimes be necessary to adopt an interpretation which linguistically may appear strained.
>
> The techniques to be used will not only involve the reading down of express language in a statute but also the implication of provisions. A declaration of incompatibility is a measure of last resort. It must be avoided unless it is plainly impossible to do so.

Nonetheless, where the HRA is not involved, the courts still have to interpret legislative provisions. The three traditional rules of statutory interpretation are as follows:

1   *The literal rule*

  Under this rule, the judge is required to consider what the legislation actually says rather than considering what it might mean. In order to achieve this end, the judge should give words in legislation their literal meaning – that is, their plain, ordinary, everyday meaning – even if the effect of this is to produce what might be considered an otherwise unjust or undesirable outcome. The literal rule appears at first sight to be the least problematic method of interpreting legislation. Under this rule, the courts most obviously appear to be recognising their limitations by following the wishes of Parliament as expressed in the words of the legislation under consideration. When, however, the difficulties of assigning a fixed and unchallengeable meaning to any word is recalled, the use of the literal rule becomes less uncontroversial. A consideration of the cases reveals examples where the literal rule has been used as a justification for what otherwise might appear as partial judgments on the part of the court concerned in the case.

Inland Revenue Commissioners v Hinchy (1960) concerned s 25(3) of the Income Tax Act 1952, which stated that any taxpayer who did not complete their tax return was subject to a fixed penalty of £20 plus *treble the tax which he ought to be charged under the Act*. The question that had to be decided was whether the additional element of the penalty should be based on the total amount that should have been paid, or merely the unpaid portion of that total. The House of Lords adopted a literal interpretation of the statute and held that any taxpayer in default should have to pay triple their original tax bill.

In *R v Goodwin* (2005) the rider/driver of a jet-ski in the sea off Weymouth, crashed into another jet-ski, causing serious injuries to the rider/driver of the other machine.

The defendant was prosecuted under s 58 of the Merchant Shipping Act 1995, which makes it an offence for 'the master of . . . a United Kingdom ship' negligently to do any act which causes or is likely to cause serious injury to any person. Section 313 of the Act defines a ship as including every description of vessel 'used in navigation'. At first instance it was decided that a jet-ski was a ship for the purposes of the Merchant Shipping Act 1995 and as a result the defendant pleaded guilty.

On appeal, however, the Court of Appeal quashed his conviction, deciding that a jet-ski is not 'used in navigation' for the purpose of travel from one place to another and as s 58 only applies to sea-going ships and the jet-ski was used only within the port of Weymouth, it could not really be described as 'sea-going'.

A further problem with regard to the literal rule, relating to the difficulty judges face in determining the literal meaning of even the commonest of terms, can be seen in *R v Maginnis* (1987). The defendant had been charged under the Misuse of Drugs Act 1971, with having drugs in his possession and *with intent to supply them*. He claimed that, as he had intended to return the drugs to a friend who had left them in his car, he could not be guilty of *supplying* as charged. In this case, the judges, from first instance, through the Court of Appeal to the House of Lords, disagreed as to the literal meaning of the common word 'supply'. Even in the House of Lords, Lord Goff, in his dissenting judgment, was able to cite a dictionary definition to support his interpretation of the word. It is tempting to suggest that the majority of judges in the House of Lords operated in a totally disingenuous way by justifying their decision on the literal interpretation of the law while, at the same time, fixing on a non-literal meaning for the word under consideration. In actual fact, in *R v Maginnis*, each of the meanings for 'supply' proposed by the various judges could be supported by dictionary entries. That fact, however, only highlights the essential weakness of the literal rule, which is that it wrongly assumes that there is such a thing as a single, uncontentious, literal understanding of words. While *R v Maginnis* concerned the meaning of 'supply', *Attorney General's Reference (No 1 of 1988)* (1989) concerned the meaning of 'obtained' in s 1(3) of the Company Securities (Insider Dealing) Act 1985, since replaced by the Criminal Justice Act 1993, and led to similar disagreement as to the precise meaning of an everyday word. In another case relating to insider dealing, *Hannam v the Financial Conduct Authority* (2014) the Upper Tribunal held, on appeal, that 'precise' information must be such that it is possible to predict the direction of the movement in the share price which would or might occur if the information were made public.

However, subsequently, in March 2015 in *Jean-Bernard Lafonta v Autorité des Marchés Financiers* (Case C-628/13) the CJEU decided to the contrary that 'precise' does not require that a party be able 'to infer from that information, with a sufficient degree of probability, that, once it is made public, its potential effect on the prices of the financial instruments concerned will be in a particular direction'. All that is required is that the holder need know only that the information would affect the price of the shares, rather than knowing whether the share price would go up or down.

Bromley LBC v GLC (1983) may be cited as an instance where the courts arguably took a covert political decision under the guise of applying the literal meaning of a particular word in a piece of legislation.

In *Owens v Dudley Metropolitan Borough Council* (2011) the Court of Appeal confirmed that, where statute does not define a term, it should be given its ordinary meaning. In this case the claimant was employed as a special needs teacher and counsellor. Although her contract of employment described her as a teacher, her employer claimed that she was not in fact a teacher and consequently could not be a member of the Teachers' Pension Scheme. At first instance the High Court held that she was not a teacher as she merely provided services ancillary to teaching. The Court of Appeal held that, as there was no specific definition of 'teacher' in the Teachers' Pension Scheme, the dictionary definitions of the term should be referred to. As the dictionary definition was wide and went beyond people who stand in front of pupils in a classroom, the claimant was held to come within the definition.

2 *The golden rule*

This rule is generally considered to be an extension of the literal rule. In its general expression, it is used in circumstances where the application of the literal rule is likely to result in what appears to the court to be an obviously absurd result. The golden rule was first stated by Lord Wensleydale in *Grey v Pearson*

(1857), but its operation is better defined by the words of Lord Blackburn in *River Wear Commissioners v Adamson* (1877) as follows:

> [W]e are to take the whole statute and construe it all together, giving the words their ordinary signification, unless when so applied they produce an inconsistency, or an absurdity or inconvenience so great as to convince the Court that the intention could not have been to use them in their ordinary signification, and to justify the Court in putting them in some other signification, which, though less proper, is one which the Court thinks the words will bear.

It should be emphasised, however, that the court is not at liberty to use the golden rule to ignore, or replace, legislative provisions simply on the basis that it does not agree with them; it must find genuine difficulties before it declines to use the literal rule in favour of the golden one. How one determines or defines genuine difficulty is of course a matter of discretion and, therefore, dispute. As Lord Blackburn's definition makes clear, the use of the rule actually involves the judges in finding what they consider the statute should have said or provided, rather than what it actually did state or provide. As will be seen below, the justification for this judicial activity is based on that extremely wide, amorphous, not to say spurious, legal concept: public policy. However, such a justification immediately raises the questions of the judges' understanding of, and right to determine, public policy, which will be considered in the next section of this chapter.

It is sometimes stated that there are two versions of the golden rule:

(a) *The narrow meaning*. This is used where there are two apparently contradictory meanings to a particular word used in a legislative provision or the provision is simply ambiguous in its effect. In such a situation, the golden rule operates to ensure that preference is given to the meaning that does not result in the provision being an absurdity. An example of the application of the golden rule in this narrow sense is *Adler v George* (1964). The defendant had been charged, under the Official Secrets Act 1920, with obstruction in the vicinity of a prohibited area, whereas she had actually carried out the obstruction inside the area. The court preferred not to restrict itself to the literal wording of the Act and found the defendant guilty as charged.

(b) *The wider meaning*. This version of the golden rule is resorted to where, although there is only one possible meaning to a provision, the court is of the opinion that to adopt such a literal interpretation will result in Lord Blackburn's 'inconsistency, absurdity or inconvenience'. The classic example of this approach is to be found in *Re Sigsworth* (1935), in which the court introduced common law rules into legislative provisions, which were silent on the matter, to prevent the estate of a murderer from benefiting from the property of the party he had murdered. Just as it was contrary to public policy to allow a murderer to benefit directly from the proceeds of his offence, so it would equally be contrary to public policy to allow the estate of a murderer to benefit from his offence. However, the public policy issue becomes less certain when one realises that there was actually no question of the murderer benefiting directly in this case, as he had committed suicide. In that light, the decision can be seen as punishing those who would have benefited on his death for an offence that they had nothing to do with – effectively cutting them out from what had been a legitimate expectation before the murder. In October 2003, the Law Commission recommended a change in the rule in *Sigsworth* and proposed a change in the law to allow children to inherit from grandparents who have been murdered by the children's father or mother. As the report states, the law should penalise killers, not their children. Its provisional view was that the law should operate as though the killer had died, allowing the children to inherit the property.

Another example of this approach is found in *R v National Insurance Commissioner ex p Connor* (1981), in which the court held, in spite of silence in the actual legislation, that Connor was not entitled to a widow's pension on the grounds that she had been the actual cause of her widowed status by killing her husband. Once again, when taken at face value, the decision in *Connor* appears perfectly justifiable on the grounds of public policy as the court stated, but appears less so when it is pointed out that Connor was actually found guilty of manslaughter and sentenced merely to a two-year period of probation.

Subsequent to the *Connor* case, the Forfeiture Act 1982 was passed, giving courts the discretionary power to ignore the rule of public policy that precludes a person who has unlawfully killed another from acquiring a benefit as a consequence of the killing. The Act does not apply in relation to murder, but nonetheless it does give the courts discretion to mitigate the effects of the rule applied in *Connor* duct of the common law, so the courts have in any case felt free to distinguish and limit the strict application of the rule in *Connor* (see, for example *Re K (Deceased)* (1985)).

3   *The mischief rule*

At one level, the mischief rule is clearly the most flexible rule of interpretation, but in its traditional expression it is limited by being restricted to using previous common law rules in order to decide the operation of contemporary legislation. It is also, at least somewhat, paradoxical that this most venerable rule, originally set out in *Heydon's Case* (1584), is also the one which most obviously reveals the socio-political nature of judicial decisions.

In *Heydon's Case*, it was stated that in making use of the mischief rule, the court should consider the following four things:

(a)   What was the common law before the passing of the statute?

(b)   What was the mischief in the law which the common law did not adequately deal with?

(c)   What remedy for that mischief had Parliament intended to provide?

(d)   What was the reason for Parliament adopting that remedy?

It has to be remembered that, when *Heydon's Case* was decided, it was the practice to cite in the preamble of legislation the purpose for its enactment, including the mischief at which it was aimed. (An example where the preamble made more sense than the actual body of the legislation is the infamous Bubble Act of 1720.) Judges in this earlier time did not, therefore, have to go beyond the legislative provision itself to implement the mischief rule. With the disappearance of such explanatory preambles, the question arises as to the extent to which judges can make use of the rule in *Heydon's Case* to justify their examination of the policy issues that underlie particular legislative provisions. Contemporary practice is to go beyond the actual body of the legislation. This, however, raises the question as to what courts can legitimately consider in their endeavour to determine the purpose and meaning of legislation, which will be considered separately below.

The example usually cited of the use of the mischief rule is *Corkery v Carpenter* (1950), in which a man was found guilty of being drunk in charge of a 'carriage', although he was in fact only in charge of a bicycle. A much more controversial application of the rule is to be found in *Royal College of Nursing v DHSS* (1981), where the courts had to decide whether the medical induction of premature labour to effect abortion, under the supervision of nursing staff, was lawful. In this particularly sensitive area, whether one agrees with the ultimate majority decision of the House of Lords in favour of the legality of the procedure or not probably depends on one's view of abortion. This fact simply serves to highlight the socio-political nature of the question that was finally determined by the House of Lords under the guise of merely determining the legal meaning of a piece of legislation.

The relationship of the rules of interpretation

It is sometimes suggested that the rules of interpretation form a hierarchical order. On that basis, the first rule that should be applied is the literal rule, and that rule only cedes to the golden rule in particular circumstances where ambiguity arises from the application of the literal rule. The third rule, the mischief rule, it is suggested, is only brought into use where there is a perceived failure of the other two rules to deliver an appropriate result. On consideration, however, it becomes obvious that no such hierarchy exists. The literal rule is supposed to be used unless it leads to a manifest absurdity, in which case it will give way to the golden rule. The immediate question this supposition gives rise to is – what is to be considered as an absurdity in any particular case, other than the view of the judge deciding the case? The three rules are contradictory, at least to a degree, and there is no way in which the outsider can determine in advance which of them the courts will make use of to decide the meaning of a particular statute. Many may welcome the fact that the courts have moved towards a more explicitly purposive approach as outlined previously and as was recommended by the Law Commission report in 1969. It has to be recognised, however, that such a shift in approach provides the judiciary with additional power in relation to determining the meaning and effect of legislation. Cynics might say that such change merely makes overt the power that the judiciary always had, but previously exercised in a covert way.

3.4.4 AIDS TO CONSTRUCTION

In addition to the three main rules of interpretation, there are a number of secondary aids to construction. These can be categorised as either intrinsic or extrinsic in nature:

Intrinsic assistance

Intrinsic assistance is derived from the statute, which is the object of interpretation; the judge uses the full statute to understand the meaning of a particular part of it. The *title*, either long or short, of the Act under consideration may be referred to for guidance (*Royal College of Nursing v DHSS* (1981)). It should be noted, however, that a general intention derived from the title cannot overrule a clear statement to the contrary in the text of the Act.

It was a feature of older statutes that they contained a *preamble*, which was a statement, preceding the actual provisions of the Act, setting out its purposes in some detail and to which reference could be made for purposes of interpretation. Again, however, any general intention derived from the preamble could not stand in the face of express provision to the contrary within the Act.

Whereas preambles preceded the main body of an Act, schedules appear as additions at the end of the main body of the legislation. They are, however, an essential part of the Act and may be referred to in order to make sense of the main text.

Some statutes contain section headings and yet others contain marginal notes relating to particular sections. The extent to which either of these may be used is uncertain, although *DPP v Schildkamp* (1969) does provide authority for the use of the former as an aid to interpretation.

Finally, in regard to intrinsic aids to interpretation, it is now recognised that punctuation has an effect on the meaning of words and can be taken into account in determining the meaning of a provision.

Extrinsic assistance

Extrinsic assistance, that is, reference to sources outside of the Act itself, may on occasion be resorted to in determining the meaning of legislation – but which sources? Some external sources are unproblematic. For example, judges have always been entitled to refer to *dictionaries* in order to find the meaning of non-legal words. They also have been able to look into *textbooks* for guidance in relation to particular points of law, and in using the mischief rule, they have been able to refer to *earlier statutes* to determine the precise mischief at which the statute they are trying to construe is aimed. The Interpretation Act 1978 is also available for consultation with regard to particular difficulties. Unfortunately, its title is somewhat misleading, in that it does not give general instructions for interpreting legislation, but simply defines particular terms that are found in various statutes.

Other extrinsic sources, however, are more controversial. In 3.3, the various processes involved in the production of legislation were considered. As was seen, there are many distinct stages in the preparation of legislation. Statutes may arise as a result of reports submitted by a variety of commissions. In addition, the preparation of the precise structure of legislation is subject to consideration in working papers, known as *travaux préparatoires*. Nor should it be forgotten that in its progress through Parliament, a Bill is the object of discussion and debate, both on the floor of the Houses of Parliament and in committee. Verbatim accounts of debates are recorded and published in *Hansard*.

Each of these procedures provides a potential source from which a judge might discover the specific purpose of a piece of legislation or the real meaning of any provision within it. The question is, to which of these sources are the courts entitled to have access?

Historically, English courts have adopted a restrictive approach to what they are entitled to take into consideration. This restrictive approach has been gradually relaxed, however, to the extent that judges are allowed to use extrinsic sources to determine the mischief at which particular legislation is aimed. Thus, they have been entitled to look at Law Commission reports, Royal Commission reports and the reports of other official commissions. Until fairly recently, however, *Hansard* literally remained a closed book to the courts, but in the landmark decision in *Pepper v Hart* (1993), the House of Lords decided to overturn the previous rule. The issue in the case was the tax liability owed by teachers at Malvern College, a fee-paying school. Employees were entitled to have their sons educated at the school while paying only 20 per cent of the usual fees. The question was as to the precise level at which this benefit in kind was to be taxed. In a majority decision, it was held that where the precise meaning of legislation was uncertain or ambiguous or where the literal meaning of an Act would lead to a manifest absurdity, the courts could refer to *Hansard*'s reports of parliamentary debates and proceedings as an aid to construing the meaning of the legislation.

The operation of the principle in *Pepper v Hart* was extended in *Three Rivers DC v Bank of England (No 2)* (1996) to cover situations where the legislation under question was not in itself ambiguous but might be ineffective in its intention to give effect to some particular EC directive. Applying the wider purposive powers of interpretation open to it in such circumstances (see above, 3.4.2), the court held that it was permissible to refer to *Hansard* in order to determine the actual purpose of the statute. The *Pepper v Hart* principle only applies to statements made by ministers at the time of the passage of legislation, and the courts have declined to extend it to cover situations where ministers subsequently make some statement as to what they consider the effect of a particular Act to be (*Melluish (Inspector of Taxes) v BMI (No 3) Ltd* (1995)).

It is essential to bear in mind that *Pepper v Hart* was not intended to introduce a general purposive approach to the interpretation of non-European Community legislation. Recourse to *Hansard* is to be made only in the context of the mischief rule, as a further method of finding out the mischief at which the particular legislation is aimed.

The way in which *Pepper v Hart* should be used in relation to the HRA was considered by the House of Lords in *Wilson v Secretary of State for Trade and Industry* in 2003. This case was remarkable in that neither of the parties to the original issue took part in the House of Lords case. However, as it followed a previous declaration of incompatibility delivered by the Court of Appeal, it was pursued by the Attorney General on behalf of the Secretary of State. In addition, and for the first time ever, both the Speaker of the House of Commons and the Clerk of the Parliaments intervened in relation to the manner in which the Court of Appeal had scrutinised *Hansard* in order to determine the purpose of the legislation in question. The House of Lords proved much more sensitive than the Court of Appeal had been as to the tension between the courts and parliament in regard to the exercise of the powers of the courts in relation to compatibility issues under the HRA and equally restrictive in the use that could be made of *Hansard* in relation to the exercise of those powers. As Lord Nicholls put it:

> I expect the occasions when resort to Hansard is necessary as part of the statutory 'compatibility' exercise will seldom arise. The present case is not such an occasion. Should such an occasion arise the courts must be careful not to treat ministerial or other statements as indicative of the objective intention of Parliament. Nor should the courts give a ministerial statement, whether made inside or outside Parliament, determinative weight. It should not be supposed that members necessarily agreed with the minister's reasoning or his conclusions.

Consequently, it can be seen that the initial and primary role of the judge is to interpret the legislation as it stands and only, in limited circumstances, to have recourse to *Hansard* to look for enlightenment as to the meaning of the Act, and even then it must be done with circumspection.

3.4.5 PRESUMPTIONS

In addition to the rules of interpretation, the courts may also make use of certain presumptions. As with all presumptions, they are rebuttable. The presumptions operate:

* *Against the alteration of the common law*. Parliament is sovereign and can alter the common law whenever it decides to do so. In order to do this, however, Parliament must expressly enact legislation to that end. If there is no express intention to that effect, it is assumed that statute does not make any fundamental change to the common law. With regard to particular provisions, if there are

alternative interpretations, one of which will maintain the existing common law situation, then that interpretation will be preferred. In *R (Rottman) v Commissioner of Police* (2002), the claimant was arrested on a warrant issued under the Extradition Act 1989, and the police searched his house and seized various items that they believed to be evidence. The House of Lords affirmed the legality of this search and seizure. The common law power to search an arrested person's premises was not extinguished in relation to extradition offences by the Police and Criminal Evidence Act (PACE) 1984. According to Lord Hutton, while that Act clearly replaced the pre-existing common law in relation to domestic offences, it made no reference to extradition offences and so must be supposed to have left the common law intact in relation to them.

A more recent case in this area is *R v Hughes* (2013). A new s 3ZB of the Road Traffic Act 1988 was added by s 21(1) of the Road Safety Act 2006. It provides that a person is guilty of an offence if they *cause the death of* another person by driving while either disqualified, uninsured or without a licence. In October 2009, Hughes was driving a campervan without insurance when he was involved in a fatal crash with a man named Dickinson, who was described as driving erratically. Dickinson was said to be overtired, having worked a series of 12 hour nightshifts and driven long distances to and from his place of work. He was also found to have had a significant quantity of heroin in his system. While Hughes's driving was faultless and the blame for the crash was entirely with Dickinson, nonetheless Hughes was prosecuted under s 3ZB of the 1988 Act. Following a finding of liability in the Court of Appeal, the Supreme Court unanimously allowed the appeal.

In reaching its decision the Supreme Court stated that it would have been possible for Parliament to legislate in terms which left it beyond doubt that an uninsured driver would be guilty of causing death whenever a car which they were driving was involved in a fatal accident. However, it found that the legislation did not actually state that unambiguously. As a result of the section introducing the concept of causation, any action had to be judged in the light of the common law which required that Hughes should have contributed in some way to Dickinson's death rather than just be involved in it.

● *In favour of the assumption that a mental element is required for criminal offences.* It is a general requirement of the criminal law that, in order for a person to be convicted of a crime, he is proved not only to have committed the relevant act or conduct (or sometimes to have failed to do something), but also to have done this with a blameworthy state of mind. This state of mind is known by the Latin tag *mens rea* (the mental element).

The necessary mental element can include: (a) intention; (b) gross negligence; (c) recklessness; (d) inadvertence; or (e) simple knowledge of a state of affairs. Because the consequences of being convicted of a criminal offence are very serious and include a possible custodial sentence and a life-ruining conviction, there was always the assumption in the common law (judge-made law) that criminal law offences require some form of *mens rea* before a person can be convicted.

Today, more criminal law offences have been created through parliamentary legislation than those which existed by virtue of the common law. When interpreting statutes, the court will presume that Parliament intended that no criminal liability should arise without a requirement that *mens rea* be proven.

In some areas of social concern, however, like traffic accidents or underage drinking, Parliament has seen fit to pass what are known as 'strict liability' offences. These are criminal offences for which it is *not* necessary for the prosecution to prove that the defendant had a particular attitude towards the crime in question, for example, that he intended to commit it, but merely that the relevant conduct took place. The thinking behind such criminalisation of conduct is that because defendants will not be able to escape liability by pleading that they did not intend to produce a particular result or that they did not have relevant knowledge, everyone will be encouraged to be that much more vigilant that they do not offend that particular law.

Sometimes, someone comes before the criminal law courts accused of an offence created by statute, and the courts must decide whether the words of the statute imply that it is necessary for the prosecution to prove the defendant had a mental element. The general rule here is that Parliament will be presumed not to have wanted to create a strict liability criminal offence unless it has been explicit about wanting to do so. There are, though, a number of factors to be taken into account in answering this question, including the nature of the language used, the subject matter of the activity and the overall framework of the Act. In *Sweet v Parsley* (1970), the accused had a house just outside of Oxford, which she rented out and visited only occasionally. She was convicted of being concerned in the management of premises used for the purpose of smoking cannabis, contrary to s 5(b) of the Dangerous Drugs Act 1965; however, she had had no knowledge that the house was being used in this way. The House of Lords held that her conviction should be quashed, since it had to be proved that it was the accused's 'purpose' that the premises were used for smoking cannabis (that is, that she intended the premises to be so used). In the case, Lord Reid said that:

> . . . whenever a section is silent as to *mens rea* there is a presumption that . . . we must read in words appropriate to require *mens rea*.

In *R v Hussain* (1981), the Court of Appeal decided that possessing a firearm without a certificate is, under s 1 of the Firearms Act 1968, an offence of strict liability, so that the prosecution is not required to prove that the accused knew the article he had was a firearm. Similarly, the Court of Appeal decided in *R v Bradish* (1990) that, under s 5(1) of the Firearms Act 1968, the offence of being in possession of a prohibited weapon (a spray canister containing CS gas) is a crime of strict liability. It was therefore not a defence for the accused to argue that because the gas was concealed within the canister, he did not know, and could not reasonably have been expected to know, that the article in his possession was a prohibited weapon. The court's choice in these cases to impose strict liability is in furtherance of the general purpose of the firearms legislation, that is, to put everyone on their guard that so wrong is the possession of firearms that those who have them without the appropriate licence will effectively be deemed automatically to be guilty of an offence.

In another case, the Court of Appeal decided that the offence created by s 11 of the Company Directors (Disqualification) Act 1986 of acting as a director of a company while an undischarged bankrupt, except with the leave of the court, was one of strict liability. Thus, a mistaken but genuinely held belief that the bankruptcy had been discharged was no defence to the crime (*R v Brockley* (1994)). The court took the view that the mischief sought to be tackled by s 11 of the Act was of wide social concern and that, therefore, the creation of strict liability would promote the object of the Act by obliging bankrupts themselves to ensure that their bankruptcy was in fact discharged before they acted again as company directors.

In *R v K* (2001), the defendant was charged with indecently assaulting a 14-year-old girl, who had in fact consented and who had told him she was over 16. Section 14(1) of the Sexual Offences Act 1956 was silent as to *mens rea* so far as knowledge of the girl's age was concerned. On the other hand, s 14(4) expressly stated that genuine belief was to be a defence where an adult woman lacked the mental capacity to consent. Consequently, the Court of Appeal could legitimately infer that Parliament had *not* intended genuine belief to be a defence for s 14(1), otherwise it would have said so. The House of Lords reversed the finding of the Court of Appeal, holding that, as the 1956 Act was a consolidating Act, drawing together provisions from several previous Acts without making any substantive changes to them, the inference suggested by the Court of Appeal was not appropriate and the common law presumption against strict liability should prevail.

- *Against retrospective effect of new law.* The courts operate a presumption of interpretation that statutes will not operate retrospectively. It is one thing for Parliament to legislate that, for example, as from next year all fox-hunting is illegal. It would be quite another thing for Parliament to legislate that not only will fox-hunting be illegal if carried on in future, but that anyone who participated in such an event during the last five years is open to prosecution today. Such a presumption against retrospective effect is important in relation to crimes, but is relevant in other areas too, such as contractual arrangements and taxation. This principle operates not only to stop people whose conduct was innocent at the time from being convicted by a backward-looking Act, but also to stop people whose conduct was guilty at any given time from being free from blame just because an Act decriminalises certain conduct. So, if an Act abolishes an offence by repealing a statutory provision, then the repeal will not affect the punishment of someone who has been convicted of this crime at an earlier stage, nor the continuation of legal proceedings in respect of crimes that were committed before the law was changed. The presumption against retrospective effect was considered by the Court of Appeal in *Home Secretary v Wainwright* (2002). Two relatives visiting a prisoner were strip-searched as a condition of entry to the prison, and subsequently claimed a violation of their right to respect for private life. The court held that since the events in question had happened before the HRA 1998 came into force, s 3 of that Act could not be relied on. As Parliament had expressly made s 22(4) of the Act retroactive, its failure to do the same for s 3 must be taken to have been intentional. See also *R v Lambert* (2001) and *R v Kansal* (2001).

As Parliament is supreme, there being no body with higher constitutional powers, it can pass retrospective legislation if it wishes, but it must do so using express words to achieve this end. The War Damage Act 1965 was passed specifically to overrule the decision of the House of Lords in *Burmah Oil Co Ltd v The Lord Advocate* (1965), and to deprive Burmah Oil of the results of having won that case. The oil company's installations in Burma, which was then a British colony, had been destroyed by the British Forces in 1942 in order to prevent them being captured by Japanese forces. The company, which was registered in Scotland, sued the Crown for compensation. The Crown contended that no compensation was payable when property was destroyed under the royal prerogative. The House of Lords decided that compensation was payable. The Act of Parliament was then passed to override the House of Lords' decision and to prevent the burden of compensation having to be met by the taxpayer. An example of modern legislation which has been made expressly retrospective is the War Crimes Act 1991. This Act allows the Attorney General to authorise criminal proceedings for homicide committed in Germany or German-occupied territory during World War II. The prosecution can be against a person in the UK regardless of his nationality at the time of the alleged offence. The relaxation of the 'double jeopardy' rule by s 75 of the Criminal Justice Act 2003 has retrospective effect (s 75(6)).

Under the Jobseeker's Allowance (Employment, Skills and Enterprise Scheme) Regulations 2011 the unemployed could be required to engage in work or training or lose their benefits. Jamie Wilson, a qualified HGV driver, refused to undertake work for an organisation collecting, renovating and distributing unwanted furniture for six months for 30 hours a week. As a result, he was told that his benefits would be stopped for six months. Cait Reilly, a geology graduate who wanted to work in museums, was required to stop her voluntary work at a local museum and instead work for the retail business Poundland for two weeks. It was accepted that she was working rather than training, although she received no addition to her unemployment benefits.

In the subsequent challenge to how they were treated, *Wilson and Reilly v DWP* (2013), the Court of Appeal held that the Jobseeker's Allowance (Employment, Skills and Enterprise Scheme) Regulations 2011 were invalid because they failed to describe the schemes made under them in sufficient detail and that notices given under the regulations were inadequate. However, in order to save the estimated liability of up to £130 million, the government, in the form of the Secretary of State for Work and Pensions and former leader of the Conservative Party, Ian Duncan Smith, immediately introduced retroactive primary legislation, the Jobseekers (Back to Work Schemes) Act 2013, to counter the consequences of the Court of Appeal decision. The aim of the Act was simply to ensure that claimants who had had their benefits sanctioned unlawfully could not claim a refund on the basis of the Court of Appeal judgment, and that where benefit cuts had not yet been implemented for refusal to engage in the scheme, these could now be applied.

Subsequently, on appeal, the Supreme Court confirmed the reasoning of the Court of Appeal stating that:

> 'were it not for the 2013 Act and the 2013 Regulations, we would have affirmed the order of the Court of Appeal.'

However, the court had to recognise the efficacy of the new legislation in righting the previous procedural wrongs. Whether substantive wrongs were remedied is another question.

- *Against deprivation of liberty*. The law courts work on the assumption that Parliament does not intend to deprive a person of his liberty unless it is explicitly making provision for such a punishment. Thus, Lord Scarman has stated that:

> . . . if Parliament intends to exclude effective judicial review of the exercise of a power in restraint of liberty, it must make its meaning crystal clear (*R v Secretary of State for the Home Department ex p Khawaja* (1983)).

The House of Lords ruled that an immigration Act that it was examining did not have the effect of placing the burden of proof on an immigrant to show that the decision of the Home Office to detain him was unjustified. In other words, one could not read the Act in a way that allowed someone to be deprived of their liberty unless and until they proved that such imprisonment was unjustified.

- *Against application to the Crown*. Unless the legislation contains a clear statement to the contrary, it is presumed not to apply to the Crown.
- *Against breaking international law*. Where possible, legislation should be interpreted in such a way as to give effect to existing international legal obligations.
- *In favour of words taking their meaning from the context in which they are used*. This final presumption refers back to, and operates in conjunction with, the major rules for interpreting legislation considered previously. The general presumption appears as three distinct sub-rules, each of which carries a Latin tag.

The *noscitur a sociis* rule is applied where statutory provisions include a list of examples of what is covered by the legislation. It is presumed that the words used have a related meaning and are to be interpreted in relation to each other. (See *IRC v Frere* (1969), in which the House of Lords decided which of two possible meanings of the word 'interest' was to be preferred by reference to the word's location within a statute.) The *ejusdem generis* rule applies in situations where general words are appended to the end of a list of specific examples. The presumption is that the general words have to be interpreted in line with the prior restrictive examples. Thus, a provision which referred to a list that included 'horses, cattle, sheep and other animals' would be unlikely to apply to domestic animals such as cats and dogs. (See *Powell v Kempton Park Racecourse* (1899), in which it was held that, because a statute prohibited betting in a specified number of *indoor* places, it could not cover an *outdoor* location.) The *expressio unius exclusio alterius* rule simply means that where a statute seeks to establish a list of what is covered by its provisions, then anything not expressly included in that list is specifically excluded. (See *R v Inhabitants of Sedgley* (1831), where rates expressly stated to be payable on *coal* mines were held not to be payable in relation to *limestone* mines.)

For further examples and resources illustrating the way statutory interpretation is carried out, exercises and technical guidance, please go to: www.routledge.com/cw/slapper where you will find a guide to Using Legislation.

3.5 DELEGATED OR SUBORDINATE LEGISLATION

Delegated legislation is of particular importance. Generally speaking, delegated legislation is law made by some person or body to whom Parliament has delegated its general law-making power. A validly enacted piece of delegated legislation has the same legal force and effect as the Act of Parliament under which it is enacted but, equally, it only has effect to the extent that its enabling Act authorises it.

It should also be recalled that s 10 of the HRA 1998 gives ministers power to amend primary legislation by way of statutory instrument where a court has issued a declaration that the legislation in point is incompatible with the rights provided under the ECHR.

The output of delegated legislation in any year greatly exceeds the output of Acts of Parliament. For example, in the parliamentary year 2013 only 33 UK public general Acts were passed, as against 3,318 statutory instruments.

In statistical terms, therefore, it is at least arguable that delegated legislation is actually more significant than primary Acts of Parliament.

There are various types of delegated legislation:

● *Orders in Council.* Consideration of this type of legislation is confused by the interplay of related and overlapping concepts and the historical process that saw Parliament exercise control over the power of the Crown.

Historically, Orders in Council were the result of the exercise of the royal prerogative in consultation with the Privy Council, the monarch's close advisers. As has already been mentioned, some aspects of these prerogative powers remain and are exercised through the issuing of Orders in Council. Orders in Council made under prerogative powers are primary legislation. However, distinct from such exercise of prerogative powers are the statutory orders which arise from the fact that parliament, through statute, has given the Crown powers to make law through the issuing of Orders in Council. It is this latter type of Orders in Council that is correctly referred to as delegated legislation. The passing of statutory Orders in Council may also involve a parliamentary procedure, depending on the Act from which they stem. Consequently some Orders may need to be laid before Parliament in draft before being made, or after they have been made. Alternatively, the Act may require the Order to be approved by Parliament before it comes into force. The importance of this distinction lies in the fact that, as has already been explained, under the HRA 1998 the courts have greater power in relation to secondary legislation than they do in regard to primary legislation.

The Privy Council is nominally a non-party-political body of eminent parliamentarians, but in effect it is simply a means through which the government, in the form of a committee of ministers, can introduce legislation in the form of Orders in Council, without the need to go through the full parliamentary process. Although it is usual to cite situations of state emergency as exemplifying occasions when the government will resort to the use of Orders in Council, the use of this statutory form is far from uncommon. Perhaps the widest scope for Orders in Council is to be found in relation to EU law, for under s 2(2) of the European Communities Act 1972, ministers can give effect to provisions of Union law which do not have direct effect (see, further, below, 5.2.4).

Ministers may also be given statutory power to make orders to introduce or alter existing provisions, but such orders are not to be confused with Orders in Council. To add further potential confusion, since 1946, under s 1 of the Statutory Instruments Act (SIA) 1946, every power to make an Order in Council conferred by an Act of Parliament passed after 1 January 1948 must be in the form of a statutory instrument. Consequently, most Orders in Council are also statutory instruments, but there still exists the possibility of Orders in Council that are not to be issued as SIs, either being the result of the exercise of prerogative power or deriving from a pre-1948 statute.

- *Statutory instruments* are the means through which government ministers introduce particular regulations under powers delegated to them by parliament in enabling legislation.
- *Bylaws* are the means through which local authorities and other public bodies can make legally binding rules. Bylaws may be made by local authorities under such enabling legislation as the Local Government Act 1972.

- *Court Rule Committees* are empowered to make the rules which govern procedure in the particular courts over which they have delegated authority, under such Acts as the Senior Courts Act 1981 (originally passed as The Supreme Court Act 1981 but changed in name by the Constitutional Reform Act 2005, Sched 11), the County Courts Act 1984 and the Magistrates' Courts Act 1980.

- *Professional regulations* governing particular occupations may be given the force of law under provisions delegating legislative authority to certain professional bodies who are empowered to regulate the conduct of their members. An example is the power given to The Law Society, under the Solicitors' Act 1974, to control the conduct of practising solicitors.

3.5.1 ADVANTAGES IN THE USE OF DELEGATED LEGISLATION

The advantages of delegated legislation include the following:

- *Time saving*

  Delegated legislation can be introduced quickly, where necessary in particular cases, and can permit rules to be changed in response to emergencies or unforeseen problems.

  The use of delegated legislation, however, also saves parliamentary time generally. Given the pressure on debating time in Parliament and the highly detailed nature of typical delegated legislation, not to mention its sheer volume, Parliament would not have time to consider each individual piece of law that is enacted in the form of delegated legislation. It is considered of more benefit for Parliament to spend its time in a thorough consideration of the principles of the enabling Act, leaving the appropriate minister or body to establish the working detail under its authority.

- *Access to particular expertise*

  Related to the first advantage is the fact that the majority of Members of Parliament simply do not have sufficient expertise to consider such provisions effectively. Given the highly specialised and extremely technical nature of many of the regulations that are introduced through delegated legislation, it is necessary that those authorised to introduce the legislation should have access to the necessary external expertise required to formulate such regulations. With regard to bylaws, it practically goes without saying that local and specialist knowledge should give rise to more appropriate rules than reliance on the general enactments of parliament.

- *Flexibility*

  The use of delegated legislation permits ministers to respond on an *ad hoc* basis to particular problems, as and when they arise, and provides greater flexibility in the regulation of activity subject to the minister's overview.

The disadvantages in the use of delegated legislation include the following:

- *Accountability*

  A key issue involved in the use of delegated legislation concerns the question of accountability and erosion of the constitutional role of Parliament. Parliament is presumed to be the source of legislation, but with respect to delegated legislation, the individual members are not the source of the law. Certain people, notably government ministers and the civil servants who work under them to produce the detailed provisions of delegated legislation, are the real source of such regulations. Even allowing for the fact that they are, in effect, operating on powers delegated to them from parliament, it is not beyond questioning whether this procedure does not give them more power than might be thought appropriate, or indeed constitutionally correct, while at the same time disempowering and discrediting parliament as a body.

- *Scrutiny*

  The question of general accountability raises the need for effective scrutiny, but the very form of delegated legislation makes it extremely difficult for ordinary Members of Parliament to fully understand what is being enacted and to monitor it effectively. This difficulty arises in part from the tendency for such regulations to be highly specific, detailed and technical. This problem of comprehension and control is compounded by the fact that regulations appear outside the context of their enabling legislation, but only have any real meaning within that context.

- *Bulk*

  The problem faced by ordinary Members of Parliament in effectively keeping abreast of delegated legislation is further increased by the sheer mass of such legislation. If parliamentarians cannot keep up with the flow of delegated legislation, how can the general public be expected to do so?

In previous editions of this book the authors have, to a greater or lesser degree, focused on the increase in the power of Ministers of State to alter Acts of Parliament by means of statutory instruments in the pursuit of economic, business and regulatory efficiency.

The first of these (dis)empowering Acts of Parliament that brought this situation about was the Deregulation and Contracting Out Act (DCOA) 1994, introduced by the last Conservative government. It was a classic example of the wide-ranging power that enabling legislation can extend to ministers in the attack on such primary legislation as was seen to impose unnecessary burdens on any trade, business or profession. Although the DCOA 1994 imposed the requirement that ministers should consult with interested parties to any proposed alteration, it nonetheless gave them extremely wide powers to alter primary legislation without the necessity of having to follow the same procedure as was required to enact that legislation in the first place. For that reason, deregulation orders were subject to a far more rigorous procedure (sometimes referred to as 'super-affirmative') than ordinary statutory instruments. The powers were extended in its first term in office by the Labour government under the Regulatory Reform Act (RRA) 2001.

It was, however, only with the proposed Legislative and Regulatory Reform Bill 2006 that alarm bells started to ring generally. This critical reaction was based on the proposed power contained in the Act for ministers to create new criminal offences, punishable with less than two years' imprisonment, without the need for a debate in parliament.

The proposals under the Legislative and Regulatory Reform Bill 2006 were constitutionally dangerous to the extent that they gave to the executive powers that should be a function of the legislature.

As a result of opposition, the government amended the legislation to ensure that its powers could only be used in relation to business and regulatory efficiency.

Under s 1 of the Legislative and Regulatory Reform Act (LRRA) 2006, a minister of the Crown can make a legislative reform order for the purpose of removing or reducing any burden to which any person is subject as a result of any legislation. A burden is defined as:

- a financial cost;
- an administrative inconvenience;
- an obstacle to efficiency, productivity or profitability; or
- a sanction, criminal or otherwise, which affects the carrying on of any lawful activity.

However, it is at least somewhat reassuring that such powers cannot be used:

- to confer or transfer any function of legislation on anyone other than a minister;
- to impose, abolish or vary taxation;
- to amend or repeal any provision of the Human Rights Act 1998.

Nor can the Act be used to amend or repeal any provision of Part 1 of the LRRA, which includes the above prohibitions.

Similar fears were raised in relation to the Public Bodies Act 2011. Although not as wide-ranging as was originally proposed, the Act still gives government ministers wide powers to abolish non-government bodies and agencies, referred to as quangos.

3.5.4 CONTROL OF DELEGATED LEGISLATION

The foregoing difficulties and potential shortcomings in the use of delegated legislation are, at least to a degree, mitigated by the fact that specific controls have been established to oversee it:

Power to make delegated legislation is ultimately dependent upon the authority of Parliament and Parliament retains general control over the procedure for enacting such law. New regulations in the form of delegated legislation are required to be laid before Parliament. This procedure takes two forms depending on the provision of the enabling legislation. Some regulations require a positive resolution of one or both of the Houses of Parliament before they become law. Most Acts, however, simply require that regulations made under their auspices be placed before Parliament. They automatically become law after a period of 40 days unless a resolution to annul them is passed.

The problem with the negative resolution procedure is that it relies on Members of Parliament being sufficiently aware of the content, meaning and effect of the detailed provisions laid before them. Given the nature of such statutory legislation, such reliance is unlikely to prove secure.

Since 1973, there has been a *Joint Select Committee on Statutory Instruments* whose function it is to scrutinise all statutory instruments. The Joint Committee is empowered to draw the special attention of both Houses to an instrument on any one of a number of grounds specified in the Standing Orders (No 151 of the House of Commons and No 74 of the House of Lords) under which it operates, or on any other ground *which does not relate to the actual merits of the instrument or the policy it is pursuing*.

The House of Commons has its own *Select Committee on Statutory Instruments*, which is appointed to consider all statutory instruments laid *only* before the House of Commons. This committee is empowered to draw the special attention of the House to an instrument on any one of a number of grounds specified in Standing Order No 151; or on any other ground. However, as with the joint committee, it is not empowered to consider the merits of any statutory instrument or the policy behind it. As an example of its operation, after considering two statutory instruments, namely Personal Equity Plan (Amendment No 2) Regulations 2005 (SI 2005/3348) and Individual Savings Account (Amendment No 3) Regulations 2005 (SI 2005/3350), the Committee considered that they should be drawn to the attention of the House of Commons on the ground that there appeared to be a doubt whether they were *intra vires*.

EU legislation is overseen by a specific committee – as are local authority bylaws. In 2003 the House of Lords established a *Committee on the Merits of Statutory Instruments*, the task of which is to consider the policy implications of statutory instruments. It has wide-ranging remit and is specifically charged with the task of deciding whether the attention of the House should be drawn to a particular statutory instrument on any one of the following grounds:

- that it is politically or legally important or gives rise to issues of public policy likely to be of interest to the House;
- that it is inappropriate in view of the changed circumstances since the passage of the parent Act;
- that it inappropriately implements EU legislation;
- that it imperfectly achieves its policy objectives. (www.publications. parliament. uk/pa/ld/ldmerit.htm)

A case study on the passage of statutory instruments:
The Tax Credit Regulations 2015

As part of its continued austerity programme the Conservative government proposed that alterations be made to the regime of tax credits which were paid to people in work but previously thought not to be earning sufficient money to maintain themselves adequately. The treasury proposed significantly to limit people's eligibility for such tax credit payment, using a statutory instrument, the Tax Credits (Income Thresholds and Determination of Rates) (Amendment) Regulations 2015 under powers delegated to it under the Tax Credits Act 2002. The delegated powers required the approval of both Houses of Parliament and had been appropriately approved by the House of Commons. However, in its consideration in the House of Lords the members of that House voted in one motion for the cuts to be postponed pending an independent review of the proposals. On a second motion they also voted to provide transitional financial support for at least three years for those likely to be affected by the proposals.

The votes were not unexpected but nonetheless they did raise some anger and doubt about the constitutionality of the Lords' action.

As has been seen, the Parliament Acts certainly placed limitations on the Lords' powers in relation to ordinary Bills, but as delegated legislation was not a prominent feature of pre-1950 legislation, those Acts remained silent on the Lords' powers in relation to such secondary legislation. As a consequence, it would appear that the House of Lords had a formal veto over delegated legislation, but it was suggested, a suggestion supported by the government in the current issue, that a constitutional convention had emerged that the Lords should not vote on such matters. However, although it was certainly unusual for the Lords to vote on, and certainly vote against, secondary legislation, it has to be admitted that it was not unprecedented. Indeed, at the time when the majority of hereditary peers were removed from the Lords, the sometime Conservative Leader in the House Lord Strathclyde made a bold speech stating that 'I declare this convention dead', before using his voting power to vote down secondary legislation relating to the election of the mayor of London.

The government also questioned the right of the House of Lords to vote against the statutory instrument, as they maintained it was a financial matter and therefore subject to the normal rules under the Parliament Acts.

Where the Lords are concerned about the passage of a particular statutory instrument, they have the choice of two types of motion to vote on: the one most used is the 'non-fatal' motion, which merely expresses 'regret at the government's action', rather than looking to block it. One such motion was before the house in relation to the tax credits issue but was rejected. Also rejected was 'fatal' motion against the passage of the legislation, which would have completely curtailed the legislation in question. Instead the Lords chose the non-fatal options which resulted in the instrument being passed back to the Commons for it to be considered further.

Following the votes in the House of Lords, the government made known its extreme displeasure. Chancellor of the Exchequer, George Osborne, said he would heed the outcome of the vote, but said it raised constitutional issues of 'unelected Labour and Lib Dem lords defying the will of the elected House of Commons'. Somewhat ironically the government announced that Lord Strathclyde would be looking into the implications of the whole issue as it impacted on the future role of the House of Lords. Subsequently, in November 2016, the May government announced that it would not proceed with plans to take on the House of Lords. It is most likely that the decision was as a result of the realisation that they would struggle to pass the legislation, especially given the pressures of working within their self-imposed Brexit timetable. In its official response to the Strathclyde Review, subsequently published in December 2016, the government stated that while it agreed with the conclusion of the review as to the need to introduce legislation in the face of continued intransigence on the part House of Lords, nevertheless it would not introduce legislation in the current parliamentary session, with the warning that it would keep the situation under review.

Judicial control of delegated legislation

It is possible for delegated legislation to be challenged through the procedure of judicial review, on the basis that the person or body to whom Parliament has delegated its authority has acted in a way that exceeds the limited powers delegated to them. Any provision outside this authority is *ultra vires* and is void. Additionally, there is a presumption that any power delegated by Parliament is to be used in a reasonable manner, and the courts may on occasion hold particular delegated legislation to be void on the basis that it is unreasonable. The process of judicial review will be considered in more detail in Chapter 13. However, an interesting example of this procedure may illustrate the point. In January 1997, the Lord Chancellor raised court fees and, at the same time, restricted the circumstances in which a litigant could be exempted from paying such fees. In March, a Mr John Witham, who previously would have been exempted from paying court fees, successfully challenged the Lord Chancellor's action. In a judicial review, it was held that Lord Mackay had exceeded the statutory powers given to him by Parliament. One of the judges, Rose LJ, stated that there was nothing to suggest that Parliament ever intended 'a power for the Lord Chancellor to prescribe fees so as to preclude the poor from access to the courts'.

R (Public Law Project) v Secretary of State for Justice (2014) is a recent example of the courts finding the use of delegated legislation to alter primary legislation to be *ultra vires*. As its title indicates, the statutory instrument in questions, the Legal Aid, Sentencing and Punishment of Offenders Act 2012 (Amendment of Schedule 1) Order 2014, sought to amend Schedule 1 to the Legal Aid, Sentencing and Punishment of Offenders Act (LASPO) 2012 by introducing a residence test limiting the provision of legal aid to those who could show 'a meaningful connection' with the UK. The court held that the introduction of the residence test by way of secondary legislation exceeded the power to make delegated legislation conferred on the Secretary of State by the parent statute.

Lord Justice Moses (with whom Mr Justice Collins and Mr Justice Jay agreed) identified the objective of the primary legislation as being the provision of legal aid to those with the greatest need. As the proposed amendment actually had 'nothing to do with need or an order of priority of need . . . [but was], entirely, focused on reducing the cost of legal aid', it violated the principle that subsidiary legislation must serve and promote the object of the primary legislation under which it is made. Consequently it was held to be *ultra vires* and ineffective.

The power of the courts in relation to delegated legislation has been considerably increased by the enactment of the HRA 1998. As has been seen, the courts cannot directly declare primary legislation invalid, but can only issue a declaration of incompatibility. However, no such limitation applies in regard to subordinate legislation, which consequently may be declared invalid as being in conflict with the rights provided under the ECHR. This provision significantly extends the power of the courts in relation to the control of subordinate legislation, in that they are no longer merely restricted to questioning such legislation on the grounds of procedure, but can now assess it on the basis of content, as measured against the rights provided in the ECHR. It should be noted that some Orders in Council, as expressions of the exercise of the royal prerogative, are not open to challenge and control in the same way as other subordinate legislation.

A case study on ultra vires: HM Treasury v Mohammed Jabar Ahmed *(2010)*

In this, the first substantive case heard by the Supreme Court, it quashed fully the Terrorism (United Nations Measures) Order 2006 and quashed parts of the al-Qaida and Taliban (United Nations Measures) Order 2006 as being *ultra vires* the powers extended to the Treasury under the United Nations Act 1946.

Both Orders had been made by the Treasury under power conferred by s 1 of the United Nations Act (UNA) 1946, which was enacted to facilitate the taking of measures to implement decisions of the UN Security Council. In each case the Orders were made to give effect to resolutions of the United Nations Security Council, which were designed to suppress and prevent the financing and preparation of acts of terrorism.

The Orders specifically provided for the freezing of the funds, economic resources and financial services available to individuals who had been included on a United Nations list of associates of Osama Bin-Laden, or were involved in international terrorism, or were reasonably suspected of involvement with international terrorism.

In delivering the leading judgment, Lord Hope (with the agreement of Lord Walker and Lady Hale) emphasised the far-reaching and serious effect of the asset-freezing measures on not just the individuals concerned, but also their families. Using the scope afforded by the rule in *Pepper v Hart*, he concluded that the legislative history of the 1946 Act demonstrated that Parliament 'did not intend that the 1946 Act should be used to introduce coercive measures which interfere with UK citizens' fundamental rights'. The crucial question for the court to consider was whether s 1 of UNA conferred power on the executive, *without any parliamentary scrutiny*, to give effect in this country to decisions of the Security Council, which are targeted against individuals. And the answer to that question was a clear no.

In answering the question in that way, the Supreme Court was at pains to emphasise that it was in no way usurping the role of the legislature. Indeed as Lord Phillips put it:

> Nobody should form the impression that in quashing the TO and the operative provision of the AQO the Court displaces the will of Parliament. On the contrary, the Court's judgment vindicates the primacy of Parliament, as opposed to the Executive, in determining in what circumstances fundamental rights may legitimately be restricted.

3.6   LAW REFORM: THE ROLE OF THE LAW COMMISSION

At one level, law reform is either a product of parliamentary or judicial activity. Parliament tends, however, to be concerned with particularities of law reform, and the judiciary are constitutionally and practically disbarred from reforming the law in anything other than an opportunistic and piecemeal way. Therefore, there remains a need for the question of law reform to be considered generally and a requirement that such consideration be conducted in an informed but disinterested manner. Thereafter it is a matter for Parliament to introduce the necessary legislation to bring any proposed reform into effect.

Reference has already been made to the use of consultative Green Papers by the government as a mechanism for gauging the opinions of interested parties to particular reforms. More formal advice may be provided through various advisory standing committees. Among these is the *Law Reform Committee*. The function of this Committee is to consider the desirability of changes to the civil law which the Lord Chancellor may refer to it. The *Criminal Law Revision Committee* performs similar functions in relation to criminal law.

Royal Commissions may be constituted to consider the need for law reform in specific areas. The Commission on Criminal Procedure (1980) led to the enactment of the Police and Criminal Evidence Act 1984, and the recommendation of the 1993 Royal Commission on Criminal Justice (Runciman Commission) informed subsequent reform of the criminal law system.

Committees may be set up in order to review the operation of particular areas of law, the most significant of these being the Woolf review of the operation of the civil justice system. Similarly, Sir Robin Auld conducted a review of the whole criminal justice system and Sir Andrew Leggatt reviewed the tribunal system. Detailed analysis of the consequences flowing from the implementation of the recommendations of these reviews will be considered subsequently.

If a criticism is to be levelled at these Committees and Commissions, it is that they are all *ad hoc* bodies. Their remit is limited and they do not have the power either to widen the ambit of their investigation or to initiate reform proposals.

The *Law Commission* fulfils the need for some institution to concern itself more generally with the question of law reform. It was established under the Law Commissions Act 1965 and its general function is to keep the law as a whole under review and to make recommendations for its systematic reform to ensure that the law is as fair, modern, simple and cost-effective as possible. As part of its goal to make the law as simple as possible, the Commission has adopted three interrelated approaches: codification, consolidation and revision.

Codification

The Commission looks towards the codification of the law. Codification has already been mentioned in respect of Civil Law in Chapter 1 and the Commission has expressed its view that the law would be more accessible to the citizen, and easier for the courts to understand, if the English system also adopted a series of statutory codes. The

Commission has had a long-established aim of working towards a codification of criminal law; however, the tenth programme of law reform signalled a change in approach, reflecting a more realistic recognition of the difficulties involved in such a project and the need to reform the law before it can be successfully codified.

As the Commission stated in its 10th programme:

> The complexity of the common law in 2007 is no less than it was in 1965. Further, the increased pace of legislation, layers of legislation on a topic being placed one on another with bewildering speed, and the influence of European legislation, continue to make codification ever more difficult. The Commission continues to believe that codification is desirable, but considers that it needs to redefine its approach to make codification more achievable. Accordingly the Commission has decided that:
>
> (1)   It will continue to use the definition of codification used by Gerald Gardiner in Law Reform Now, that is, 'reducing to one statute, or a small collection of statutes, the whole of the law on any particular subject'.
> (2)   Consistently with Gardiner's concerns in 1964, the Commission's main priority is first to reform an area of the law sufficiently to enable it to return and codify the law at a subsequent stage. If it can codify at the same time as reforming, it will do so.
>
> The first direct effect of these decisions is that the Commission has removed from this programme, mention of a codification project in relation to criminal law. The duty in reforming the criminal law, as elsewhere, is to identify reform projects that will make the law accessible, remove uncertainties and bring it up to date with the aim that in the future we will return and codify the area if we cannot do so as part of the project. Rather than specifically referring to codification as the intended outcome, we have introduced a new item which seeks to undertake projects to simplify the criminal law. We see this work as the necessary precursor to any attempts to codify the criminal law.

One major codification project the Law Commission is currently working on involves the introduction of a single sentencing statute available and applicable to all sentencing tribunals. It is not intended that any such statute will interfere with mandatory minimum sentences or with sentencing tariffs in general, but will merely streamline the existing overly complicated procedure for determining sentences. The suggestion from the Commission is that the law currently lacks coherence and clarity, being spread across many statutes, and being frequently updated with a variety of transitional arrangements. As a result, the Commission rather worryingly concludes that '[t]his makes it difficult, if not impossible at times, for practitioners and the courts to understand what the present law of sentencing procedure actually is. This can lead to delays, costly appeals and unlawful sentences.' For an outline of the work done to date go to www.lawcom.gov.uk/project/sentencing-code/

Consolidation

This process brings together all existing statutory provisions, previously located in several different pieces of legislation, under one Act. As explained in Chapter 3 above, under this procedure the law itself remains unchanged, but those who use it are able to find it all in one place. An example, cited by the Commission, is the Powers of Criminal Courts (Sentencing) Act 2000, which brought together in a single piece of legislation sentencing powers which were previously to be found in more than a dozen Acts.

Statute law revision

The Commission continuously keeps under review the need to remove antiquated and/or anachronistic laws from the statute book, the continued existence of which make it subject to derision, even if they do not bring it into disrepute. As the Commission states, the purpose of its statute law repeals work is to modernise and simplify the statute book, reduce its size and save the time of lawyers and others who use it. Implementation of the repeal proposals is by means of special Statute Law (Repeals) Acts and 18 such Acts have been introduced since 1965, repealing more than 2,000 Acts either completely or partially.

It was as a result of this process, and following a 1995 Law Commission Report (No 230), that the Law Reform (Year and a Day Rule) Act was introduced in 1996. This Act removed the ancient rule which prevented killers being convicted of murder or manslaughter if their victim survived for a year and a day after the original offence. The Statute Law (Repeals) Act 2004 removed a Victorian Act which empowered the Metropolitan Police to license shoeblacks and commissionaires and, in so doing, removed the offence of fraudulently impersonating a shoeblack or commissionaire. The nineteenth, most recent, and biggest ever Statute Law (Repeals) Act (2013) repealed 817 whole Acts and part repealed 50 other Acts. The earliest repeal was from around 1322 (Statutes of the Exchequer) and the latest was part of the Taxation (International and Other Provisions) Act 2010. Repeals in the Act included:

- An 1856 Act passed to help imprisoned debtors secure their early release from prison.
- A 1710 Act to raise coal duty to pay for 50 new churches in London.
- A 1696 Act to fund the rebuilding of St Paul's Cathedral after the Great Fire 1666.
- An 1800 Act to hold a lottery to win the £30,000 Pigot Diamond.

The Commission is a purely advisory body and its scope is limited to those areas set out in its current programme of law reform, which has to be approved by the Lord Chancellor. It recommends reform after it has undertaken an extensive process of consultation with informed and/or interested parties. At the conclusion of a project a report is submitted to the Lord Chancellor and Parliament for their consideration and action.

Although the scope of the Commission is limited to those areas set out in its programme of law reform, its ambit is not unduly restricted, as may be seen from the range of matters covered in its twelfth programme set out in July 2014.

In addition to continuing work on 13 ongoing projects from the eleventh programme it lists nine new topic areas as follows:

- *Sentencing procedure:* a law reform project to recommend a single sentencing statute.
- *Mental capacity and detention:* a project to consider how deprivation of liberty should be authorised and supervised in settings other than hospitals and care homes. This follows sharp criticism of the present state of the law by Justices of the Supreme Court.
- *Land registration:* a project that will comprise a wide-ranging review of the Land Registration Act 2002 (itself a Law Commission Act).
- *Wills:* a law reform project to review the law of wills, focusing on mental capacity and will making, formalities that dictate how a will should be written and signed, and how mistakes in wills can be corrected.
- *Bills of sale:* a law reform review of the law relating to bills of sale loans, including logbook loans, which has become a recent area of concern in relation to non-controlled lending.

There are also two scoping exercises designed to see whether detailed proposals for law reform should be developed:

- *Firearms:* a scoping exercise to consider the enactment of a single statute containing modified and simplified versions of all firearms offence.
- *Protecting consumer prepayments on retailer insolvency:* a scoping review to assess the scale of the problem and consider whether to increase protection for consumers.

Finally, there are two wide-ranging topics specific to purposes of the Welsh Government:

- *The form and accessibility of the law applicable in Wales:* an Advice to Government, considering ways in which the existing legislation can be simplified and made more accessible, and how future legislation could reduce problems.
- *Planning and development control in Wales:* a law reform project to recommend a simplified and modernised planning system for Wales.

The Twelfth Programme of Law Reform is available on the Commission's website at: http://lawcommission.justice.gov.uk/areas/12th-programme.htm. Consultation on what should be included in the 13th programme closed at the end of October 2016.

In addition to these programme projects, ministers may refer matters of particular importance to the Commission for its consideration. As was noted in Chapter 1, it was just such a referral by the Home Secretary, after the Macpherson Inquiry into the *Stephen Lawrence* case, that gave rise to the Law Commission's recommendation that the rule against double jeopardy be removed in particular circumstances. An extended version of that recommendation was included in the Criminal Justice Act 2003.

Annual reports list all Commission publications. The Law Commission claims that, in the period since its establishment in 1965, over 100 of its law reports have been implemented. Examples of legislation following from Law Commission reports are: the Contracts (Rights of Third Parties) Act 1999, based on the recommendations of the Commission's Report No 180, *Privity of Contract*; and the Trustee Act 2000, based on the Commission's Report No 260. In February 2002 the Land Registration Act was passed, which has had a major impact on the land registration procedure. The Act implemented the draft Bill which was the outcome of the Commission's largest single project.

Current judicial review procedures are very much the consequence of a 1976 Law Commission report, and a review of their operation and proposals for reform were issued in October 1994.

In the area of criminal law, the preparatory work done by the Commission on several aspects of the criminal justice system (bail, double jeopardy and the revelation of an accused person's bad character) was incorporated into the Criminal Justice Act 2003.

In addition, ss 5 and 6 of the Domestic Violence, Crime and Victims Act 2004 reflect the recommendations of an earlier Commission report. The issue investigated related to situations where a child is non-accidentally killed or seriously injured, and it is apparent that one or more of a limited number of defendants must have committed the crime, but there is no evidence that allows the court to identify which of the defendants actually committed the offence. The Domestic Violence, Crime and Victims Act 2004 also contains provisions reflecting the Commission report relating to the prosecution of people charged with multiple offences.

In August 2004 the Commission published its Report on Partial Defences to Murder, recommending the reform of the defence of provocation, with particular reference to murders committed in the context of domestic violence. That report also included a recommendation that the Home Office undertake a wholesale review of the law of murder, including sentencing regimes, and subsequently in December 2005 the Commission published its proposals for reforming the law of murder, *Bringing the Law of Murder into the 21st Century*. Its initial conclusion was that the current law on murder 'is a mess' and in an attempt to remedy that situation it provisionally recommended that there should be three tiers of homicide:

- In the top tier would be cases where there is an intention to kill. This is the worst category and would retain the mandatory life sentence.

- In the second tier would be cases of killing through reckless indifference to causing death and intention to do serious harm but not to kill. This tier would also include revised versions of provocation, diminished responsibility and duress. The sentence would depend on the details of the case.

- In the third tier (manslaughter) would be cases of killing by gross negligence or intention to cause harm but not serious harm.

In November 2006 the Law Commission published its final report setting out recommendations for reform of the law of homicide proposing the adoption of the three-tier structure, comprising first-degree murder, second-degree murder and manslaughter. Although the recommendations on partial defences were implemented to a substantial extent in the Coroners and Justice Act 2009, in January 2011 the new government let it be known that it would not implement the remainder of the recommendations on the grounds that the time was not right to take forward such a substantial reform of the criminal law.

The Commission's recommendations in relation to the offence of corporate killing were incorporated in the Corporate Manslaughter and Corporate Homicide Act 2007, and its recommendations on inchoate liability for assisting and encouraging crime were enacted in the Serious Crime Act 2007. Finally, the Commission's report and draft Bill on bribery led to the passing of the Bribery Act 2010, which came into force in July 2011, and its 2013 report on juror misconduct and internet publication informed the provisions in Part 3 of the Criminal Justice and Courts Act 2015 (see 14.8).

Having emphasised the role of the Law Commission as a source of new law, it is a fact that many of its reports recommending reform remain to be implemented, even though a number of them have been accepted by the government (a table showing the current status of all Law Commission law reform reports can be accessed under the 'our work' tab on the Commission website).

In response to such failure of implementation, a former Law Lord, Lord Lloyd of Berwick, introduced the Law Commission Bill 2008–09 in the House of Lords. In support of the Bill, Lord Kingsland pointed out that: 'Over the years . . . [the Law Commission] has been tasked with many seemingly intractable problems, has grappled with them and produced a solution, only to find that solution spurned by the political classes.'

The resultant Act contains provisions to amend the Law Commissions Act 1965 so as to:

- require the Lord Chancellor to prepare an annual report, to be laid before Parliament, on the implementation of Law Commission proposals;

- require the Lord Chancellor to set out plans for dealing with any Law Commission proposals which have not been implemented and provide the reasoning behind decisions not to implement proposals;

- allow the Lord Chancellor and Law Commission to agree a protocol about the Law Commission's work. The protocol would be designed to provide a framework for the relationship between the UK government and the Law Commission, and the Lord Chancellor would have to lay the protocol before Parliament.

The fifth report on the implementation of Law Commission proposals was published in March 2015. It lists the reports that have been implemented or which are in the process of implementation. It also sets out the one report which the government has decided should not be legislated. As usual there is a long list of reports waiting for a government decision.

It should also be mentioned that in order to expedite the passage of such legislation, in 2008 the House of Lords Constitution Committee adopted a procedure to quicken the passage of non-controversial Law Commission Bills through the House of Lords and the procedure was adopted fully in 2010.

Mention should also be made of the relatively new Civil Justice Council (CJC), established under the Civil Procedure Act 1997. The remit of this Council, which is made up of a variety of judges, lawyers, academics and those representing the interests of consumers and others, under the chair of the Master of the Rolls, currently Lord Dyson, is to:

- keep the civil justice system under review;
- consider how to make the civil justice system more accessible, fair and efficient;
- advise the Lord Chancellor and the judiciary on the development of the civil justice system;
- refer proposals for change to the civil justice system to the Lord Chancellor and the Civil Procedure Rule Committee;
- make proposals for research.

Given the massive upheaval that resulted from the implementation of Lord Woolf's review of the civil justice system, it is to be hoped that the CJC will function effectively to bring about smaller alterations in the system as soon as they become necessary.

Access to Justice for Litigants in Person (or self-represented litigants)

In November 2011 the Civil Justice Council released a critical report entitled: *Access to Justice for Litigants in Person (or self-represented litigants)*. The report followed an examination of how litigants in person are likely to be affected by reductions to public funding for legal advice and representation, and ways in which public and voluntary bodies could best respond to the challenges arising as a result of this cutback in funding. The working party found that the numbers of litigants representing themselves will increase, giving rise to the fear that:

> Many of them will not know how to bring or defend legal proceedings in the absence of legal advice and representation and will either suffer a reduction in the quality of justice or they will entirely abandon their efforts to enforce or defend their rights or will try to take their cases to court but not do so properly.

The CJC report makes 10 recommendations for immediate action:

1. improving the accessibility, currency and content of existing online resources;
2. producing a 'nutshell' guide for self-represented litigants (SRLs);
3. improving judicial and court services for SRLs;
4. advice for judges on the availability of legal pro bono services;
5. guidance for court staff when dealing with SRLs;

6   guidance for legal professionals, and what SRLs can expect from lawyers;

7   notice of McKenzie Friends (these are people who volunteer to assist unrepresented parties);

8   introducing a code of conduct for McKenzie Friends;

9   freeing up in-house lawyers to provide pro bono services; and

10   a call for leadership from major advice and pro bono agencies across England and Wales to drive collaboration.

The report went on to make recommendations to be addressed in the medium term:

(a)   a systematic review should be undertaken of court leaflets, forms and information, involving consultation with experts in the field;

(b)   making a primary website available that pulls together and maintains the best independent guidance;

(c)   increasing the number of courts that offer Personal Support Units and information officers to assist SRLs;

(d)   producing a user-friendly guide to the Small Claims Court;

(e)   improving access to legal advice;

(f)   developing LawWorks' early electronic advice for SRLs and agencies;

(g)   finding new means of funding the administration of pro bono and other voluntary legal services;

(h)   offering surgeries and after-hours court information sessions for SRLs;

(i)   keeping records of numbers and circumstances of SRLs, and ensuring court user committees address their needs; and

(j)   reviewing the question of access to appeals after refusals by a judge on the 'paper' application.

The Council maintained its consideration for the self-represented litigant in its response to the proposed changes to judicial review. As it stated:

> The Council is particularly concerned that reforms do not have an adverse impact on the ability of self-representing litigants (SRLs) to seek effective access to justice through JR. Reforms could potentially have a disproportionate and adverse effect on SRLs due to the particular issues which they face in obtaining access to the courts. SRLs, specifically, face additional barriers to justice as:
>
> > They are generally unfamiliar with court procedure, how to go about obtaining necessary relevant evidence, how to structure their applications and how to comply with the relevant Pre-Action Protocols;

A disproportionate number of SRLs do not speak English as a first language, have a protected characteristic under the Equality Act or are vulnerable in some other way (such as for reasons of mental health). Any negative impact on effective access to justice can therefore be exacerbated in the case of such litigants.

Subsequent changes in the state funding of litigation have made the position of litigants in person, and the courts, even more problematic (see, further, 15.2.2).

CHAPTER SUMMARY: SOURCES OF LAW: LEGISLATION

LEGISLATION

Legislation is law produced through the parliamentary system. The government is responsible for most Acts, but individual Members of Parliament do have a chance to sponsor Private Member's Bills. The passage of a Bill through each House of Parliament involves five distinct stages: first reading; second reading; committee stage; report stage; and third reading. It is then given Royal Assent. The Supreme Court only has limited scope to delay legislation.

Among the problems of drafting Acts is the need to reconcile such contradictory demands as brevity and precision. Legislation can be split into different categories: public Acts affect the general public; private Acts relate to particular individuals; consolidation Acts bring various provisions together; codification Acts give statutory form to common law principles; amending Acts alter existing laws, and amendments may be textual, which alters the actual wording of a statute, or non-textual, in which case the operation rather than the wording of the existing law is changed.

STATUTORY INTERPRETATION

This refers to, and follows from, the previous consideration that law does not speak for itself and does not have meaning ascribed to it. That function belongs to the judiciary. However, in giving practical effect to legislation, judges may exercise creative power that rightly belongs to the legislature.

In deciding what meaning to ascribe to legislation, judges tend to adopt either a literal or a purposive approach. These two general approaches are traditionally divided into three supposedly distinct rules:

- the literal rule;
- the golden rule; and
- the mischief rule.

It should be recognised that such rules are not necessarily compatible.

In addition, judges make use of a number of presumptions in relation to the application of legislation.

DELEGATED LEGISLATION

Delegated legislation appears in the form of: Orders in Council; statutory instruments; bylaws; and professional regulations.

The main advantages of delegated legislation relate to: speed of implementation; the saving of parliamentary time; access to expertise; and flexibility.

The main disadvantages relate to: the lack of accountability of those making such law; the lack of scrutiny of proposals for such legislation; and the sheer amount of delegated legislation.

Controls over delegated legislation are: in parliament, the Joint Select Committee on Statutory Instruments; and, in the courts, *ultra vires* provisions may be challenged through judicial review.

LAW REFORM

Law reform in particular areas is considered by various standing committees particularly established for that purpose and Royal Commissions may also be established for such purposes. The Law Commission, however, exists to consider the need for the general and systematic reform of the law.

FOOD FOR THOUGHT

1. In relation to the concept of the separation of powers mentioned in Chapter 2, consider the extent to which Parliament as a whole decides on law. The ideal is of the legislature, the actual Members of Parliament, debating issues in order to produce the best possible legislation. However, is that really the case? Consider where most legislation comes from, who proposes it and who ensures that it is enacted. It has been suggested that the executive controls Parliament through its control of party politics. On that basis, the issue to consider is the extent to which the parliamentary process is just a rubber-stamping exercise for party political programmes.

2. Consider the current structure of the Houses of Parliament, an issue of some contemporary and long-standing debate. In particular, consider the function and membership of the House of Lords. What additional function does it perform over that of the House of Commons and how should its membership be decided?

3. Generally, law applies to everyone and ignorance of the law is no excuse for breaking it. Yet, to most new law students, let alone ordinary members of the public, certain pieces of legislation are almost totally incomprehensible. This raises certain issues for consideration as follows:

   Why can legislation not be written in ordinary language?

   Who is legislation actually written for?

Why do judges have to interpret legislation?

To what extent is interpretation creation?

4   There is a huge amount of law generated every year and lots of it comes in the form of delegated legislation. To what extent is this just a fact of contemporary political life, or is it a matter of concern?

FURTHER READING

Bates, T, 'The contemporary use of legislative history in the United Kingdom' (1995) 54(1) CLJ 127

Bell, J and Engle, G, *Cross: Statutory Interpretation*, 3rd edn, 1995, London: Butterworths

Bennion, F, 'Statute law: obscurity and drafting parameters' (1978) 5 British JLS 235

Bennion F, *Understanding Common Law Legislation: Drafting and Interpretation*, 2009, Oxford: OUP

Boulton, C (ed), *Erskine May's Treatise on the Law, Privileges, Proceedings and Usage of Parliament*, 1989, London: Butterworths

Committee on the Preparation of Legislation, *Renton Committee Report*, Cmnd 6053, 1975, London: HMSO

Cross, R, *Cross and Harris, Precedent in English Law*, 4th edn, 1991, Oxford: Clarendon

Editorial, 'Disability discrimination: tribunal interprets DDA to cover discrimination by association' (2008) 869 IDS Emp L Brief 3–5

Elliot, M and Perreau-Saussine, A, 'Pyrrhic public law: Bancoult and the sources, status and content of common law limitations on prerogative power' [2009] PL 697–722

Eskridge, W, *Dynamic Statutory Interpretation*, 1994, Cambridge, MA: Harvard UP

Friedman, L, 'On interpretation of laws' (1988) 11(3) Ratio Juris 252

Goodhart, A, 'The *ratio decidendi* of a case' (1959) 22 MLR 117

Holdsworth, W, 'Case law' (1934) 50 LQR 180

Jenkins, C, 'Helping the reader of Bills and Acts' (1999) 149 NLJ 798

Jones, O, *Bennion on Statutory Interpretation*, 6th edn, 2013, London: LexisNexis

MacCormick, N, *Legal Rules and Legal Reasoning*, 1978, Oxford: Clarendon

Manchester, C and Salter, D, *Exploring the Law: The Dynamics of Precedent and Statutory Interpretation*, 4th edn, 2011, London: Sweet & Maxwell

Masterman, R, 'Interpretations, declarations and dialogue: rights protection under the Human Rights Act and Victorian Charter of Human Rights and Responsibilities' [2009] PL 112–31

Mora, PD, 'The compatibility with art. 10 ECHR of the continued publication of a libel on the Internet: *Times Newspapers Ltd (Nos 1 and 2) v The United Kingdom*' (2009) 20(6) Ent LR 226–8

Simpson, A, 'The *ratio decidendi* of a case' (1957) 20 MLR 413; (1958) 21 MLR 155

Stone, J, 'The Ratio of the Ratio Decidendi' (1959) 22 MLR 597

Watson-Brown, A, 'In search of plain English – the Holy Grail or mythical Excalibur of legislative drafting' (2011) 33(1) Stat LR

USEFUL WEBSITES

www.uk-legislation.hmso.gov.uk/acts.htm
An extensive collection of Acts of Parliament.

www.lawcom.gov.uk
The official website of the Law Commission is a valuable resource because it carries scores of reports that provide very useful critical digests of whole areas of law.

www.legislation.gov.uk
The UK Statute Law database.

www.parliament.uk
The official website of Parliament.

www.hmcourts-service.gov.uk
The official website of Her Majesty's Courts Service.

www.supremecourt.uk
The official website of the Supreme Court.

COMPANION WEBSITE

Now visit the companion website to:

- test your understanding of the key terms using our Flashcard Glossary;
- revise and consolidate your knowledge of 'Sources of law: Legislation' using our Multiple Choice Question testbank;
- view all of the links to the Useful Websites above;
- read further about using cases and legislation in the Legal Skills Guide;
- view a sample exam question and answer on sources of law, taken from the authors' latest Questions & Answers book on The English Legal System.

www.routledge.com/cw/slapper

4.1 INTRODUCTION

4.2 PRECEDENT

4.3 LAW REPORTING

Consequently, they are expected to make themselves thoroughly aware of the current reports.

The Year Books

The earliest reports of particular cases appeared between 1275 and 1535 in what are known as *The Year Books*. These reports are really of historical interest as they were originally written in that peculiar language that was, and to a degree still is, the bane of law students and to the incomprehension of French students, Legal French. As with the common law generally, the focus was on procedural matters and forms of pleading. Those who are engaged in the study of legal history will find the most important cases translated and collected together in the Seldon Society series or the Rolls series but, for the main part, they represent a backwater little navigated by those whose concern is modern law.

Private reports (1535–1865)

These reports bear the name they do because they were produced by private individuals and cited by the name of the person who collected them. They were, however, published commercially for public reference. The ongoing problem with the private reports relates to their accuracy. At best it can be said that some were better, that is, more accurate than others. Of particular importance among the earlier reports were those of Plowden, Coke and Burrows, but there are many other reports that are of equal standing in their own right, with full and accurate reports of the cases submitted by counsel, together with the reason for the decisions in the particular case. A substantial number of the private reports have been collated and published as the *English Reports*. The series comprises 178 large volumes – 176 volumes being reports and the last two volumes providing an index of all the cases reported. In addition, the reports are accompanied by a useful wall chart to assist location of individual reports.

Modern reports (1865 to present)

As has been seen, the private reports were not without their problems. In addition to at least occasional inaccuracy, their publication could be both dilatory and expensive. This situation was at last remedied by the establishment of the Council for Law Reporting in 1865, subsequently registered as a corporate body in 1870 under the name of The Incorporated Council of Law Reporting for England and Wales. The Council was established under the auspices of the Inns of Court and The Law Society with the aim of producing quicker, cheaper and more accurate reports than had been available previously.

The Law Reports

These are the case reports produced by the Council. They have the distinct advantage of containing summaries of counsels' arguments and, perhaps even more importantly, they are subject to revision by the judges in the case before they are published. Not surprisingly, the Law Reports are seen as the most authoritative of reports, and it is usual for them to be cited in court cases in preference to any other report.

The current series of Law Reports from 1891 is issued annually in four parts:

- Appeal Cases (AC);
- Chancery Division (Ch);
- Family Division (Fam);
- King's/Queen's Bench (KB/QB).

Delays in reporting can obviously mean that cases decided in one year are not reported until the following year. Since the start of the current series, individual volumes of reports carry the year of publication in square brackets together with a volume number if there is a need for more than one. Cases are cited, therefore, in relation to the year and volume in which they are published, rather than the year they were decided.

Weekly Law Reports (citation WLR)

These have also been published by the Council since 1953 and, although they are not reports of cases decided in the current week as the name might suggest, they are produced much more quickly than the Law Reports. The need for speed means that these reports do not contain counsels' arguments, nor do they enjoy the benefit of judicial correction before printing. There are three volumes of reported cases, the last two containing the cases that will also appear in the Law Reports.

All England Law Reports (citation All ER)

These reports are produced by the legal publishers Butterworths, and, although they do enjoy judicial revision, they do not contain counsels' arguments. They are published weekly and are then collated annually in volumes.

Legal periodicals and newspapers

The *Solicitors Journal* (Sol Jo or SJ) has been reporting cases since 1851 and some cases are only to be found in its reports. In such circumstances, the reports may be cited in court. The same is also true for cases reported in other journals such as the *New Law Journal* or the other specialist legal journals.

The reports in the broadsheet newspapers *The Times* and *The Independent* may also be cited in such circumstances, as long as they have been produced by appropriately qualified individuals (the Courts and Legal Services Act 1990 extended the right to solicitors as well as barristers). It has to be recognised, however, that some of these reports are rather insubstantial in nature.

Specialist reports

There are a number of specialist reports. Indeed, there are more than can be mentioned here, but among the most important of these are:

- Industrial Relations Law Reports (IRLR);
- Knight's Local Government Reports (LGR);

- Lloyd's Law Reports (Lloyd's Rep);
- Report on Tax Cases (TC or Tax Cas);
- Criminal Appeal Reports (Cr App R).

European Community reports

Although European cases may appear in the reports considered above, there are two specialist reports relating to EC cases:

- *European Court Reports (ECR)*

  These are the official reports produced by the European Court of Justice (ECJ). As such, they are produced in all the official languages of the Community and consequently suffer from delay in reporting.

- *Common Market Law Reports (CMLR)*

  These are unofficial reports published weekly in English by the European Law Centre.

Reports of the European Court of Human Rights in Strasbourg are provided in the European Human Rights Reports (EHRR).

CD-ROMs and internet facilities

As in most other fields, the growth of information technology has revolutionised law reporting and law finding. Many of the law reports mentioned above are available both on CD-ROM and on the internet. See, for example, Justis, Lawtel, LexisNexis and Westlaw UK, among others. Indeed, members of the public can now access law reports directly from their sources in the courts, both domestically and in Europe. The first major electronic cases database was the Lexis system, which gave immediate access to a huge range of case authorities, some unreported elsewhere. The problem for the courts was that lawyers with access to the system could simply cite lists of cases from the database, without the courts having access to paper copies of the decisions. The courts soon expressed their displeasure at this indiscriminate citation of unreported cases trawled from the Lexis database (see *Stanley v International Harvester Co of Great Britain Ltd* (1983)).

The British and Irish Legal Information Institute (Bailii: www.bailii.org) is a charitable institution which provides online access to cases and legislation in the UK, Ireland and Europe.

Neutral citation

In line with the ongoing modernisation of the whole legal system, the way in which cases are to be cited has been changed. Thus, from January 2001, following *Practice Direction (Judgments: Form and Citation)* [2001] 1 WLR 194, a new neutral system was introduced and extended in the following year in a further Practice Direction in April 2002. Cases in the various courts are now cited as follows:

Supreme Court	[year]	UKSC case no
House of Lords	[year]	UKHL case no
Court of Appeal (Civil Division)	[year]	EWCA Civ case no
Court of Appeal (Criminal Division)	[year]	EWCA Crim case no

High Court

Queen's Bench Division	[year]	EWHC case no (QB)
Chancery Division	[year]	EWHC case no (Ch)
Patents Court	[year]	EWHC case no (Pat)
Administrative Court	[year]	EWHC case no (Admin)
Commercial Court	[year]	EWHC case no (Comm)
Admiralty Court	[year]	EWHC case no (Admlty)
Technology and Construction Court	[year]	EWHC case no (TCC)
Family Division	[year]	EWHC case no (Fam)

Tribunal decisions are now also reported using neutral citation. Thus a case decided by the Upper Tribunal (Administrative Appeals Chamber) would be reported in a similar format:

[year]   UKUT case no (AAC)

Those First-tier Tribunal decisions that are reported (e.g. a Health Education and Social Care case) would be cited:

[year]   UKFTT case no (HESC)

Within an individual case, the paragraphs of each judgment are numbered consecutively, and where there is more than one judgment, the numbering of the paragraphs carries on sequentially. Thus, for example, the neutral citation for the House of Lords' decision in *Jackson v HM Attorney General* considered above at 3.3.2 is [2005] UKHL 56 and the citation for the quotation from Lord Bingham in the case is at paragraph 25. The specific law report series within which the case is reported is cited after the neutral citation; thus, the decision may be found at [2005] 3 WLR 733 or [2005] 4 All ER 1253.

Citing authorities in court

In March 2012, Judge LCJ issued a Practice Direction to clarify the practice and procedure governing the citation of authorities in the Senior Courts of England and Wales. Consequently:

- where a judgment is reported in the Official Law Reports (AC, QB, Ch, Fam) published by the Incorporated Council of Law Reporting for England and Wales, that report must be cited. Other series of reports and official transcripts of judgment may only be used when a case is not reported in the Official Law Reports;

- if a judgment is not, or not yet, reported in the Official Law Reports but it is reported in the Weekly Law Reports (WLR) or the All England Law Reports (All ER), that report should be cited. If the case is reported in both the WLR and the All ER, either report may properly be cited;

- if a judgment is not reported in the Official Law Reports, the WLR or the All ER, but it is reported in any of the authoritative specialist series of reports which contain a headnote and are made by individuals holding a Senior Courts qualification, the specialist report should be cited;

- where a judgment is not reported in any of the reports referred to above, but is reported in other reports, they may be cited;

- where a judgment has not been reported, reference may be made to the official transcript if that is available. Handed-down text of the judgment should not be used, as that may have been subject to late revision after the text was handed down. In any event, an unreported case should not usually be cited unless it contains a relevant statement of legal principle not found in reported authority.

4.4 PRECEDENT WITHIN THE HIERARCHY OF THE COURTS

Supreme Court

Perhaps the most significant change to have taken place in the English legal system in recent times is the replacement of the judicial committee of the House of Lords by the Supreme Court. The Supreme Court began its work on 1 October 2009 and was officially opened by the Queen on 16 October 2009. The court will be considered in much more detail in later chapters, but as the replacement for the House of Lords it now clearly sits at the pinnacle of the English court hierarchy and, as such, its future decisions will have the same effect and binding power as those of its predecessor. Given the novelty of the Supreme Court, with the related lack of actual judgments, the decision has been taken that it would be wrong simply to delete references to the House of Lords and tedious to continually refer to the House of Lords as the House of Lords/Supreme Court. Consequently all future, and indeed previous, references to the House of Lords will be assumed to apply to the Supreme Court. However, it is inescapable that what follows will contain a mixture of the two titles as is considered appropriate. It should also be mentioned that the Supreme Court continues the previous alternative existence of the House of Lords as the distinct institution the Privy Council.

Supreme Court decisions

The decisions of the Supreme Court are binding on all other courts in the legal system, except the Supreme Court itself. The House of Lords was bound by its own previous decisions until it changed this practice in 1966. The old practice had been established in the nineteenth century and was reaffirmed in a famous case in 1898 – *London Tramways Co Ltd v London County Council*. The rationale for the old practice was that decisions of the highest court in the land should be final so that there would be certainty in the law and a finality in litigation.

The rule, however, did not appear to create certainty and had become very rigid by the end of the nineteenth century. The practice was eventually changed in July 1966 when Lord Gardiner, the Lord Chancellor, made a statement on behalf of himself and his fellow Law Lords. This *Practice Statement* [1966] 3 All ER 77 runs as follows:

> Their Lordships regard the use of precedent as an indispensable foundation upon which to decide what is the law and its application to individual cases. It provides at least some degree of certainty upon which individuals can rely in the conduct of their affairs as well as a basis for orderly development of legal rules.
>
> Their Lordships nevertheless recognise that too rigid adherence to precedent may lead to injustice in a particular case and also unduly restrict the proper development of the law. They propose, therefore, to modify their present practice and, while treating former decisions of this House as normally binding, to depart from a previous decision when it appears right to do so.
>
> In this connection they will bear in mind the danger of disturbing retrospectively the basis on which contracts, settlements of property, and fiscal arrangements have been entered into and also the special need for certainty as to the criminal law.
>
> This announcement is not intended to affect the use of precedent elsewhere than in this house.

The current practice enables the Supreme Court to adapt English law to meet changing social conditions and to pay attention to the decisions of superior courts in the Commonwealth. It was also regarded as important at the time that the House of Lords' practice be brought into line with that of superior courts in other countries, like the United States Supreme Court and state supreme courts elsewhere, which are not bound by their own previous decisions. It also has the effect of bringing the practice of the UK's highest domestic court into line with the practice of both the ECJ and the European Court of Human Rights (ECtHR), neither of which is bound by a rigid doctrine of precedent, although in practice they do not wilfully ignore previous decisions they have made. The possibility of the Supreme Court changing its previous decisions is a recognition that law, whether expressed in statutes or cases, is a living, and therefore changing, institution that must adapt to the circumstances in which and to which it applies if it is to retain practical relevance.

Any appellant who intends to ask the Supreme Court to depart from its own previous decision must draw special attention to this in the appeal documents (*Practice Direction (House of Lords: Preparation of Case)* [1971] 1 WLR 534). After 1966, the House used this power quite sparingly and no doubt the Supreme Court will continue this reluctance. It will not refuse to follow its earlier decision merely because that decision was wrong. A material change of circumstances will usually have to be shown.

In *Conway v Rimmer* (1968), the House of Lords unanimously overruled *Duncan v Cammell Laird and Co* (1942) on a question of the discovery of documents. *Duncan v Cammell Laird and Co* concerned the question of whether a plaintiff could get the defendant to disclose documents during wartime, which related to the design of a submarine. *Conway v Rimmer* concerned whether a probationary police officer could insist on getting disclosure of reports written about him by his superintendent. In the earlier case, the House of Lords held that an affidavit sworn by a government minister was sufficient to enable the Crown to claim privilege not to disclose documents in civil litigation, without those documents being inspected by the court. In the later case, their Lordships held that the minister's affidavit was not binding on the court. The second decision held that it is for the court to decide whether or not to order disclosure. This involves balancing the possible prejudice to the state if disclosure is ordered against any injustice that might affect the individual litigant if disclosure is withheld. Today, the minister's affidavit will be considered by the court, but it is no longer the sole determinant of the issue.

In *Herrington v British Railway Board* (1972), the House of Lords overruled *Addie and Sons v Dumbreck* (1929). In the earlier case, the House of Lords had decided that an occupier of premises was only liable to a trespassing child if that child was injured by the occupier intentionally or recklessly. In its later decision, the House of Lords changed the law in line with the changed social and physical conditions since 1929. Their Lordships felt that even a trespasser was entitled to some degree of care, which they propounded as a test of 'common humanity'.

In *R v United Railways of the Havana and Regla Warehouses Ltd* (1961), the House of Lords decided that damages awarded in an English civil case could only be awarded in sterling. The issue came up for reconsideration in 1976, by which time there had been significant changes in foreign exchange conditions, and the instability of sterling at the later date was of much greater concern than it had been in 1961. In the second case, *Miliangos v George Frank (Textiles) Ltd* (1976), the House of Lords overruled the earlier decision, stating that damages could be awarded in other currencies.

In *R v Secretary of State for the Home Department ex p Khawaja* (1983), the House of Lords departed from its own previous decision made two years earlier – *R v Secretary of State for the Home Department ex p Zamir* (1980). The earlier case had put the main burden of proof on an alleged illegal immigrant to show that his detention was not justified. In its decision two years later, the House of Lords expressed the view that the power of the courts to review the detention and summary removal of an alleged illegal immigrant had been too narrowly defined in the 1980 decision. It held that continued adherence to the precedent would involve the risk of injustice and would obstruct the proper development of law.

In *Murphy v Brentwood District Council* (1990), the House of Lords overruled its earlier decision in *Anns v Merton London Borough Council* (1978) on the law governing the liability of local authorities for the inspection of building foundations. In the earlier decision, the House of Lords held that a local authority was under a legal duty to take reasonable care to ensure that the foundations of a building complied with building regulations. The duty was owed to the owner and occupier of the building who had a legal action if the duty was broken. This created a very wide and extensive duty of care for local authorities, which was out of kilter with the development of this area of law (negligence) in relation to other property-like goods. There was considerable academic and judicial resistance to the decision in *Anns*. In overruling it, the House of Lords in *Murphy* cited the reluctance of English law to provide a remedy for pure economic loss, that is, loss that is not consequential upon bodily injury or physical damage.

If a person commits a murder or assists someone to do so under duress, that is, while under threat that unless they kill or help, they themselves will be murdered, should this afford them a legal defence? In *DPP for Northern Ireland v Lynch* (1975), the House of Lords decided that duress was available as a defence to a person who had participated in a murder as an aider and abettor. Twelve years later, the House of Lords overruled that decision. It held in *R v Howe* (1987) that the defence of duress is not available to a person charged with murder or as an aider and abettor to murder. Some people might regard it as unjust that a person who kills, or assists in a killing, while under duress should be so severely punished under the criminal law, but in taking away the defence of duress from murderers and those who assist them, the House of Lords founded its decision partly upon considerations of social policy (it made references to a rising tide of crimes of violence and terrorism that needed a strict response from the law) and a recognition that, where people killed others or assisted in such events while under duress, their conviction could be addressed by other mechanisms, such as the availability of parole and the royal prerogative of mercy.

Another significant example of the House of Lords recognising and accommodating changed circumstances can be seen in *Hall v Simons* (2000), in which it declined to follow the previous authority of *Rondel v Worsley* (1969), which had recognised the immunity of barristers against claims for negligence in their presentation of cases (see below, 16.5.1, for an extended analysis of this case).

In *R v G* (2003) the House of Lords disapproved of Lord Diplock's objective explanation of recklessness in relation to criminal law as stated previously in *R v Caldwell* (1982).

Whether or not the Supreme Court is inclined to be more active than the former House of Lords is a moot point, but it certainly is true that 2015 saw it changing precedents in two significant areas.

Thus *Montgomery v Lanarkshire Health Board (Scotland)* [2015] UKSC 11 saw a change in approach to medical negligence. In *Sidaway v Board of Governors of the Bethlem Royal Hospital* (1985) the House of Lords had no doubt reflected a historically more reverential/paternalistic approach to the medical profession in holding that it was generally a matter for doctors to decide how much patients should be told about their treatment and any dangers inherent in it. The principle was that, just as the standard of medical care was to be determined by medical evidence (the *Bolam* principle established in *Bolam v Friern Hospital Management Committee* [1957] 1 WLR 582), so the extent and quality of information provided to a patient about any such treatment was also for the medical experts to determine. Consequently, an uninformed patient, injured in the course of treatment, could not sue a doctor in negligence for failing to inform them of the inherent risk in the treatment, *if other reasonable doctors* would not have informed them of the risk.

In *Montgomery*, the Supreme Court rejected the majority decision in *Sidaway*, preferring the dissenting judgment of Lord Scarman which held that there was a duty for doctors to warn patients of any material risk inherent in their treatment.

In the course of their joint leading judgment, Lords Kerr and Reed not only made it clear that *Sidaway* was overruled, but that it had already been effectively sidelined before the present action of the Supreme Court:

> It follows that the analysis of the law by the majority in Sidaway is unsatisfactory . . . It is unsurprising that courts have found difficulty in the subsequent application of Sidaway and that the courts in England and Wales have in reality departed from it; a position which was effectively endorsed, particularly by Lord Steyn, in *Chester v Afshar* (para 86).

Also in 2015 the Supreme Court upheld the validity of two disputed penalty clauses in *Cavendish Square Holding BV (Appellant) v Talal El Makdessi (Respondent)* and *Parking-Eye Limited (Respondent) v Beavis (Appellant)* (2015). However, in doing so it altered the accepted the test for deciding whether or not such a clause was enforceable, as set out previously in *Dunlop Pneumatic Tyre Company Ltd v New Garage and Motor Company Ltd* (1915). In the latter case the House of Lords established the clear rule, and one that has featured in all contract textbooks since then, that the test was whether the clause in question was either:

(i)   a genuine pre-estimate of loss consequent upon breach of the contract, in which case it was enforceable; or

(ii)   a punitive deterrence designed to forestall the very possibility of breach, in which case it was not enforceable.

In the current cases, the Supreme Court rejected this approach as unhelpful and allowed itself to describe the old the rule as one that had '*not weathered well*'. However, the court also recognised that it was a well-established principle in the United Kingdom, Europe and other common law jurisdictions and consequently it was reluctant to, and did not, disapply it completely. Nonetheless it reformulated the test in such a way as to make *Dunlop* irrelevant. Now, the test for the enforceability of a damages clause in a contract is whether the innocent party can claim a legitimate interest in the enforcement of the clause:

> The true test is whether the impugned provision is a secondary obligation which imposes a detriment on the contract-breaker out of all proportion to any legitimate interest of the innocent party in the enforcement of the primary obligation (para 32).

As with the old test, the new one can be divided into two parts:

(i)   does the clause protect a legitimate business interest; and, if so,

(ii)   is the provision made in the clause extravagant, exorbitant or unconscionable?

The decisions in two cases delivered in February 2016 confirmed the Supreme Court's readiness to deal with awkward, not to say unfair, precedents set in previous House of Lords decisions.

R v Jogee and *Ruddock v R* (2016) related to conjoined appeals against murder convictions based on the doctrine of 'parasitic accessory liability' better known as the 'joint enterprise' doctrine, whereby someone who participated with another party in committing a specific crime, and *foresaw the possibility* that the other party might commit another crime in the course of the first criminal activity, then they could be tried as a joint principal in relation to that second criminal offence, even if they did not actually take part in it. The joint enterprise doctrine was first applied in the Privy Council case *Chan Wing-Siu v R* (1985) and was subsequently approved and adopted by the House of Lords in the cases of *R v Powell; R v English* (1997) and applied in many subsequent cases. The unanimous view of the Supreme Court was that:

> . . . we do not consider that the *Chan Wing-Siu* principle can be supported, except on the basis that it has been decided and followed at the highest level. In plain terms, our analysis leads us to the conclusion that the introduction of the principle was based on an incomplete, and in some respects erroneous, reading of the previous case law, coupled with generalised and questionable policy arguments. We recognise the significance of reversing a statement of principle which has been made and followed by the Privy Council and the House of Lords on a number of occasions. We consider that it is right to do so . . . (para. 79).
>
> We consider that the proper course for this court is to re-state, as nearly and clearly as we may, the principles which had been established over many years *before the law took a wrong turn*. The error was to equate foresight with intent to assist, as a matter of law; the correct approach is to treat it as evidence of intent (para 87, emphasis added).

In *Knauer v Ministry of Justice* (2016) a seven-strong panel of the Supreme Court over-turned two previous House of Lords judgments, *Cookson v Knowles* (1979) and *Graham v Dodds* (1983), in ruling that the multiplier in assessing damages for fatal accident claims should be calculated from the date of the trial, not the date of death. Delivering the judgment of the court, Lord Neuberger and Lady Hale stated the reason for the decision was that:

> Calculating damages for loss of dependency upon the deceased from the date of death, rather than from the date of trial, means that the claimant is suffering a discount for early receipt of the money when in fact that money will not be received until after trial (para 7).

This case is of particular interest in that the judge at first instance, in the High Court, was sympathetic to the claimant's case, which was supported by a Law Commission report on the issue, but recognised that he could not simply ignore the clear precedent set in the House of Lords decisions. He did, however, authorise an a 'leapfrog' appeal straight to the Supreme Court, which itself was very conscious of the issue of precedent, as its judgment made clear:

> . . . it is important not to undermine the role of precedent in the common law. Even though it appears clear that both the reasoning and conclusion on the point at issue in *Cookson v Knowles* and *Graham v Dodds* were flawed, at least in the light of current practice, it is important that litigants and their advisers know, as surely as possible, what the law is. Particularly at a time when the cost of litigating can be very substantial, certainty and consistency are very precious commodities in the law. If it is too easy for lower courts to depart from the reasoning of more senior courts, then certainty of outcome and consistency of treatment will be diminished, which would be detrimental to the rule of law.
>
> In our view, therefore, the issue is whether this is a case where this Court should apply the 1966 Practice Statement. In that connection, it is well established that this Court should not refuse to follow an earlier decision of this Court or the House of Lords merely because we would have decided it differently . . . More than that is required, not least because of the desirability of certainty in the law, as just discussed. However, as Lord Bingham said in the same passage, while 'former decisions of the House are normally binding . . . too rigid adherence to precedent may lead to injustice in a particular case and unduly restrict the development of the law'.
>
> This Court should be very circumspect before accepting an invitation to invoke the 1966 Practice Statement. However, we have no hesitation in concluding that we ought to do so in the present case (paras 21–23).

The jurisprudence of ex turpi causa non oritur actio

In *Jetivia SA v Bilta (UK) Ltd* [2015] UKSC 23 the Supreme Court considered the issue of '*ex turpi causa non oritur actio*', otherwise known as the 'illegality defence'. This term refers to the doctrine which holds that a party cannot pursue a legal remedy if it arises as a result of, or in connection with, their own illegal act. In this instance the Supreme Court had no doubt in holding that, where the directors of a company involve their company in a fraudulent transaction, the *ex turpi* doctrine cannot be used to prevent the company from taking action against those directors. In other words, the fraudulent directors cannot rely on their own wrongdoing to escape liability, as those dishonest acts are not attributable to the company.

The Court's decision in *Jetivia* was unanimous, but the same cannot be claimed for the underlying reasoning in the individual judgments as regards the jurisprudential underpinnings of the *ex turpi* doctrine. However, as the actual decision was on the basis of non-attribution, the detailed and differing considerations of the *ex turpi* doctrine were no more than *obiter dicta*. On the basis of the contradictory explanations of the operation of the doctrine, not only in this but also in previous Supreme Court cases (see *Hounga v Allen* [2014] 1 WLR 2889 and *Les Laboratoires Servier v Apotex Inc* [2015] AC 430), Lord Neuberger concluded in his judgment that the best course of action would be for an expanded Supreme Court panel to specifically address the doctrine of *ex turpi* as soon as possible. Such a hearing will of course depend on a suitable case arising and being argued as far as the Supreme Court.

The whole issue was considered in an interesting internet article by barrister Ryan S. Deane available at http://www.lexology.com/library/detail.aspx?g=68c8f065-b2b7-4883-a923-eecdae8028d6.

Deane's conclusion was:

> As things stand, the safe bet is that the law underpinning the illegality defence remains as stated in *Tinsley v Milligan.* The decision remains binding authority unless and until the Supreme Court expressly departs from its approach. With the prospect of a final battle involving every member of the Supreme Court, however, it is advisable to wait until the dust settles before a victor in this war about illegality can be declared.

It would be advisable to keep an eye open for future developments in this area.

A case study: the House of Lords, the Practice Statement and the Limitation Act 1980

Under s 2 of the Limitation Act 1980, the general rule is that the period of limitation for an action in tort is six years from the date on which the cause of action accrues. However, ss 11 to 14 establish a different regime for actions for damages for negligence, nuisance or breach of duty where the damages are in respect of personal injuries. In these latter cases, the limitation period is three years from either the date when the cause of action accrued or the 'date of knowledge' as defined in s 14, whichever is the later. In addition, s 33 gives the court discretion to extend the period within which a claim can be lodged when it appears that it would be equitable to do so. It can be seen that the latter regime is much more liberal than the strictly constrained s 2 procedure, and in recent cases the House of Lords has been required to consider the extent to which the more liberal s 11 regime should be applied. In doing so, however, it has had to consider the extent to which its own previous restrictive judgments should continue to apply or whether it should exercise its powers under the 1966 practice statement in order to overrule those previous authorities.

The first such decision, *Horton v Sadler* (2007), concerned the circumstances under which a court might exercise its discretion to allow an out-of-time claim under s 33 of the Act. In *Walkley v Precision Forgings Ltd* (1979) the House had previously decided that the exercise of such discretion was not possible where a writ had been issued before the limitation period expired, but the action had not been pursued to completion. The reasoning of the court appeared to be that, as the action had actually been started within the limitation period, it could not be argued that it was the limitation period as such that prevented its completion. However, in *Horton v Sadler* the House of Lords revealed the flaw in the earlier reasoning in *Horton*, which had focused on the first action to the exclusion of the later action. In the opinion of the House in *Horton* it was the circumstances of the later case, begun after the expiration of the limitation period, that had to be examined in deciding whether or not the s 33 discretion could be exercised. For that reason, the House of Lords overruled its previous ruling in *Walkley v Precision Forgings Ltd*.

The next issue relating to the operation of the Limitation Act 1980 arose in a series of unrelated cases in which six appellants, all of whom alleged that they had been victims of sexual abuse during their childhood, appealed against decisions of lower courts that their claims were statute-barred under s 2 of the Limitation Act 1980. The cases assumed a level of notoriety in the popular press due to the linked case of *A v Hoare* (2008) in which the defendant had been convicted in 1989 of an attempted rape of the claimant, involving a serious and traumatic sexual assault. He was sentenced to life imprisonment, but in 2004, while still serving his sentence, he won £7 million on the UK national lottery. Subsequently the claimant started proceedings for damages in December 2004.

In each of the cases, the respective judges had been constrained by judicial precedent to follow the previous House of Lords' judgment in *Stubbings v Webb* (1993), which had decided unanimously that s 11 of the Limitation Act 1980 did not apply in cases of deliberate assault, including indecent assault. The House clearly considered that an action for an intentional trespass to the person did not amount to an action for 'negligence, nuisance or breach of duty' within the meaning of s 11(1) of the Act. As a consequence of *Stubbings*, such claimants were subject to the three-year limitation period rather than the more generous provisions in ss 11–14 and s 33 which allowed for claims to be brought out of time if the court considered this was equitable.

In *A v Hoare* the House of Lords, again unanimously, held that *Stubbings v Webb* had been wrongly decided and concluded that ss 11 and 33 of the Limitation Act 1980 did extend to claims for damages in tort arising from trespass to the person, including sexual assault. As Baroness Hale pointed out, it is a common feature of claims for sexual abuse that they are instituted many years after the events complained of and thus very often after a limitation period of six years has passed. To subject such claims to the rigours of s 2 limitations effectively would be to deny access to justice to those who had suffered such abuse.

A's case was remitted to the Queen's Bench Division to decide whether the discretion under s 33 should be exercised in her favour and subsequently, and not very surprisingly, in June 2008 Mr Justice Coulson exercised the s 33 discretion in favour of A.

A subsequent appeal by Hoare to the ECtHR was rejected as inadmissible (*Hoare v UK* (2011)). In rejecting Hoare's argument that the House of Lords had effectively changed the law, retrospectively, the court stated that:

> however clearly drafted a legal provision may be, in any system of law, there is always an inevitable element of judicial interpretation. Equally, there will always be a need for elucidation of doubtful points and for adaptation to changing circumstances.

Perhaps the ultimate irony for Hoare lay in the fact that the ECtHR had previously refused to interfere in the original *Stubbings* case (*Stubbings v UK* (1993)).

Precedent, the Supreme Court and the European Court of Human Rights

The effect of the Human Rights Act on the operation of the doctrine of precedent, and in particular the impact of decisions of the ECtHR on the Supreme Court, has already been mentioned in Chapter 2. Reference may well be made to the stark expression of that relationship made by Lord Rodger in *Secretary of State for the Home Department v AF* (2009), one of the last cases to be heard by the House of Lords:

> Even though we are dealing with rights under a United Kingdom statute, in reality, we have no choice . . . Strasbourg has spoken, the case is closed.

However, a more considered, if no less resigned, expression of the relationship, with the ECtHR being clearly the superior court with its judgments overruling those of the domestic English court, may be found in Lord Hoffmann's pragmatic judgment in the same case. As he put it:

> I agree that the judgment of the European Court of Human Rights ('ECtHR') in *A v United Kingdom* (Application No 3455/05) requires these appeals to be allowed. I do so with very considerable regret, because I think that the

decision of the ECtHR was wrong and that it may well destroy the system of control orders which is a significant part of this country's defences against terrorism. Nevertheless, I think that your Lordships have no choice but to submit. It is true that section 2(1)(a) of the Human Rights Act 1998 requires us only to 'take into account' decisions of the ECtHR. As a matter of our domestic law, we could take the decision in *A v United Kingdom* into account but nevertheless prefer our own view. But the United Kingdom is bound by the Convention, as a matter of international law, to accept the decisions of the ECtHR on its interpretation. To reject such a decision would almost certainly put this country in breach of the international obligation which it accepted when it acceded to the Convention. I can see no advantage in your Lordships doing so.

On replacing the House of Lords, the Supreme Court adopted a more open and self-confident approach to the authority of the ECtHR. Thus in *R v Horncastle* (2009) ([2009] UKSC 14 for reference), one of the earliest cases heard by the newly constituted court, Lord Phillips explained the relationship as follows:

The requirement to 'take into account' the Strasbourg jurisprudence will normally result in the domestic court applying principles that are clearly established by the Strasbourg court. There will, however, be rare occasions where the domestic court has concerns as to whether a decision of the Strasbourg court sufficiently appreciates or accommodates particular aspects of our domestic process. In such circumstances it is open to the domestic court to decline to follow the Strasbourg decision, giving reasons for adopting this course. This is likely to give the Strasbourg court the opportunity to reconsider the particular aspect of the decision that is in issue, so that there takes place what may prove to be a valuable dialogue between the domestic court and the Strasbourg court.

Subsequently, in *Manchester City Council v Pinnock* (2011) ([2011] UKSC 6 for reference), before he became president of the Supreme Court, Lord Neuberger went further in stating that:

This Court is not bound to follow every decision of the ECtHR. Not only would it be impractical to do so: it would sometimes be inappropriate, as it would destroy the ability of the Court to engage in the constructive dialogue with the ECtHR which is of value to the development of Convention law (see e.g. *R v Horncastle* (2009)). Of course, we should usually follow a clear and constant line of decisions by the ECtHR: *R (Ullah) v Special Adjudicator* (2004). But we are not actually bound to do so or (in theory, at least) to follow a decision of the Grand Chamber. As Lord Mance pointed out in *Doherty v Birmingham* (2009), section 2 of the HRA requires our courts to 'take into account' EurCtHR decisions, not necessarily to follow them. Where, however, there is a clear and constant line of decisions whose effect is not inconsistent with some fundamental substantive or procedural aspect of our law, and whose reasoning does not appear to overlook or misunderstand some argument or point of principle, we consider that it would be wrong for this Court not to follow that line.

Then, as president of the Supreme Court, Lord Neuberger considered the role of judges in human rights jurisprudence in a speech delivered to a conference at the Supreme Court of Victoria, Melbourne, Australia. Perhaps rather disingenuously quoting his own passage in *Pinnock* above as the view of the court, he concluded, surely with an edge of irony, that:

> Save where we feel that Strasbourg has misunderstood or misappreciated our common law system, we UK judges have, I suspect, sometimes been too ready to assume that a decision, even a single decision of a section of that court, represents the law according to Strasbourg, and accordingly to follow it. That approach is attributable to our common law attitude to precedent . . . I think that we are beginning to see that the traditional common law approach may not be appropriate, at least to the extent that we should be more ready not to follow Strasbourg chamber decisions.

Such comments by Lord Neuberger not only pre-empted the Conservative Party's legislative proposals to remove the authority of the 'Strasbourg court'(see p 63), but revealed them as nugatory in practice and merely ideological in effect. Interestingly in a subsequent lecture at Bangor University in October 2014, Lord Neuberger also suggested the benefits of a written constitution, which also chimed in with Conservative Party proposals.

Mistakes by the Supreme Court

The following tautology may be applied in relation to the Supreme Court: as the ultimate authority on the law, it says what the law is; and as what it says is the law, it cannot be wrong. However, what happens if the Supreme Court subsequently believes that what it said the law was, was wrong? On rare occasions decisions of the House of Lords have almost immediately been recognised to have been wrong. Just such a situation arose in *Anderton v Ryan* (1985), when the House of Lords interpreted the Criminal Attempts Act 1981 in such a way as to virtually make the Act ineffective. Following much academic criticism, the House of Lords acknowledged its error and in *R v Shivpuri* (1986), after only one year, it overruled *Anderton v Ryan*. The leading judgment in *Shivpuri* was delivered by Lord Bridge, as was only fitting, as he had also been a member of the erroneous majority in *Anderton v Ryan*. As he stated:

> I have made clear my own conviction, which as a party to the decision . . . I am the readier to express, that the decision was wrong. What then is to be done? If the case is indistinguishable, the application of the strict doctrine of precedent would require that the present appeal be allowed. Is it permissible to depart from precedent under the Practice Statement (Judicial Precedent) [1966] 1 WLR 1234 notwithstanding the especial need for certainty in the criminal law? The following considerations lead me to answer that question affirmatively. First, I am undeterred by the consideration that the decision in *Anderton v Ryan* was so recent. *The Practice Statement is an effective abandonment of our pretension to infallibility. If a serious error embodied in a decision of this House has distorted the law, the sooner it is corrected the better* (emphasis added).

The foregoing was done in line with the operation of the doctrine of precedent within the English legal system, as a result of which only the House of Lords could overrule a previous decision of that court. However, it was fortunate that in *Shivpuri*, the House had an early opportunity to reconsider its previous exposition of the law. The question arises as to what would happen if an earlier legal determination by the House of Lords/Supreme Court were subsequently to be generally accepted as wrong. In strict terms, as all other courts are bound by the rules of precedent to follow the House of Lords/Supreme Court, no change could be considered until a similar case returned to the House of Lords/Supreme Court. Just such a situation arose in relation to the issue of provocation as a defence to a charge of murder. However, before considering the details of the situation it is necessary to explain the role of the Privy Council in regard to the doctrine of precedent.

The Judicial Committee of the Privy Council (see 6.11), although essentially made up of the Justices of the Supreme Court, is not actually a part of the English legal system. Consequently its decisions do not fit within the hierarchical structure of the English system and are not binding on any English court, although its decisions are of extremely strong persuasive authority. On the other hand, it has been previously accepted that decisions of the House of Lords are nonetheless to be followed by the Privy Council.

Thus in *Tai Hing Ltd v Liu Chong Hing Bank* (1986) the Committee (per Lord Scarman, p 14) stated that:

> Once it is accepted . . . that the applicable law is English, their Lordships of the Judicial Committee will follow a House of Lords' decision which covers the point in issue. The Judicial Committee is not the final judicial authority for the determination of English law. That is the responsibility of the House of Lords in its judicial capacity. Though the Judicial Committee enjoys a greater freedom from the binding effect of precedent than does the House of Lords, it is in no position on a question of English law to invoke the Practice Statement pursuant to which the House has assumed the power to depart in certain circumstances from a previous decision of the House.

Thus the traditional situation was that the House of Lords was supreme and in matters of English law it bound the Privy Council, which was never any more than of persuasive authority in relation to English law. However, this traditional view has been radically undermined by a series of cases relating to the interpretation of provocation as a defence under s 3 of the Homicide Act 1957.

Section 3 of the Homicide Act 1957 provides that a jury must decide two issues in assessing whether a defendant can make use of the defence of provocation:

(i)   whether the killer lost self-control in their reaction to words or acts; and

(ii)   whether a 'reasonable man' would have acted in that way.

Difference of opinion, not to say controversy, has arisen in relation to the second element of his test. In the House of Lords' decision in *R v Camplin* (1978), Lord Diplock stated that when considering whether the defendant's reaction to provocation had been that of a reasonable man, the jury should have regard to the fact that the reasonable man referred to:

> was a person having the power of self-control, to be expected of an ordinary person of the sex and age of the accused, but in other aspects *sharing such of the accused's characteristics* as they think would affect the gravity of the provocation to him (emphasis added).

However, the actual meaning of the words italicised in the above quotation has proved fertile ground for legal debate. Thus in *Luc Thiet Thuan v R* (1997), in the Privy Council the majority held that the standard of self-control to be applied was that of the ordinary person, not that of a brain-damaged person, as was involved in the case. In the minority, Lord Steyn suggested that the particular characteristics possessed by the defendant must be attributed to the reasonable man.

In two later decisions, the Court of Appeal declined to follow the majority in *Luc Thiet Thuan*, holding that, as the majority decision in that case was in conflict with decisions of the Court of Appeal, the doctrine of precedent required the Court of Appeal to follow its own decisions (see *R v Campbell* (1997) and *R v Parker* (1997)). However, in *R v Smith (Morgan)* (2001) a majority of the House of Lords held that *Luc Thiet Thuan* had been wrongly decided and by a majority of 3:2 held that juries could take account of the personal characteristics of defendants that made them particularly susceptible to losing self-control. As with *Anderton v Ryan*, this decision met with concentrated academic attack and it became generally, if certainly not universally, accepted that the House of Lords had got it wrong. The problem, however, was that no immediate opportunity presented itself for the House of Lords to reverse the decision in *Morgan Smith*. Instead, the Law Lords elected to make use of an appeal to the Privy Council in a case from Jersey, which has its own legal jurisdiction, but with a murder law based on English law. The case was *Attorney General for Jersey v Holley* (2005).

More in recognition of the potential consequences of their actions than the importance of the case *per se*, nine of the total of 12 Law Lords sat on the Privy Council hearing and ruled. As Lord Nicholls, in the majority, stated (para 1):

> The decision of the House in *Morgan Smith* is in direct conflict with the decision of their Lordships' board in *Luc Thiet Thuan v the Queen*. And the reasoning of the majority in the *Morgan Smith* case is not easy to reconcile with the reasoning of the House of Lords in *R v Camplin . . . This appeal, being heard by an enlarged board of nine members, is concerned to resolve this conflict and clarify definitively the present state of English law*, and hence Jersey law, on this important subject (emphasis added).

Such an intention was also accepted by the minority, who acknowledged the effect of the majority decision was to clarify the state of English law in relation to the partial defence of provocation. The conclusion, by a majority of six to three, was that the *Morgan Smith* case had been wrongly decided. Thus the Privy Council had made its decision; what remained was to consider the impact of that ruling in relation to the operation of the doctrine of precedent within the English court structure. The opportunity to do so came when the joined appeals in *R v James* and *R v Karimi* came before the Court of Appeal in January 2006.

The issue before the court was simple: was the Court of Appeal bound to follow the House of Lords' decision in *Morgan Smith*, or was the decision of the Privy Council in *Holley* to be preferred? Once again, a strengthened bench of the Court of Appeal, made up of five rather than the usual three members, indicated the importance of the case. In reaching its decision, the Court of Appeal was extremely sensitive to the manner in which *Holley* had been used as a device for subverting the traditional operation of the doctrine of precedent, but in an exercise of judicial realism it both raised, and dealt with, the central issues relating to precedent; thus per Lord Phillips, Chief Justice, paras 41–42:

> it is not this court, but the Lords of Appeal in Ordinary who have altered the established approach to precedent. There are possible constitutional issues in postulating that a Board of the Privy Council, however numerous or distinguished, is in a position on an appeal from Jersey to displace and replace a decision of the Appellate Committee on an issue of English law. Our principles in relation to precedent are, however, common law principles. Putting on one side the position of the European Court of Justice, the Lords of Appeal in Ordinary have never hitherto accepted that any other tribunal could overrule a decision of the Appellate Committee. Uniquely a majority of the Law Lords have on this occasion decided that they could do so and have done so in their capacity as members of the Judicial Committee of the Privy Council. We do not consider that it is for this court to rule that it was beyond their powers to alter the common law rules of precedent in this way.
>
> The rule that this court must always follow a decision of the House of Lords and, indeed, one of its own decisions rather than a decision of the Privy Council is one that was established at a time when no tribunal other than the House of Lords itself could rule that a previous decision of the House of Lords was no longer good law. *Once one postulates that there are circumstances in which a decision of the Judicial Committee of the Privy Council can take precedence over a decision of the House of Lords, it seems to us that this court must be bound in those circumstances to prefer the decision of the Privy Council to the prior decision of the House of Lords.* That, so it seems to us, is the position that has been reached in the case of these appeals (emphasis added).

As a consequence of the preceding cases it is now apparent that the Privy Council can in exceptional circumstances overrule precedents of the House of Lords. According to the Court of Appeal in *James*, those exceptional circumstances arose as a result of the following attributes in the case:

- All nine of the Lords of Appeal in Ordinary sitting in *Holley* agreed in the course of their judgments that the result reached by the majority clarified definitively English law on the issue in question.

- The majority in *Holley* constituted half the Appellate Committee of the House of Lords. We do not know whether there would have been agreement that the result was definitive had the members of the Board divided five/four.
- In the circumstances, the result of any appeal on the issue to the House of Lords is a foregone conclusion.

It might not be over-cynical to suggest that such 'exceptional' circumstances will occur as and when the Justices of the Supreme Court: (a) agree with advocates who in a case make such a suggestion, and (b) deem it desirable to change the law in such a case. It certainly cannot be denied that the decisions in *Holley* and *James* fundamentally alter the previous understanding of the way in which the doctrine of precedent operates within the English legal system and affords the Justices of the Supreme Court a second way of altering their previous decisions in addition to the Practice Statement of 1966.

The Court of Appeal

In civil cases, the Court of Appeal is generally bound by previous decisions of the House of Lords. Although the Court of Appeal, notably under the aegis of Lord Denning, attempted on a number of occasions to escape from the constraints of *stare decisis*, the House of Lords repeatedly reasserted the binding nature of its decisions on the Court of Appeal. The House of Lords emphasised the balance between the need for certainty in the law against the need to permit scope for the law to develop, and in so doing, it asserted its function, as the court of last resort at the head of the hierarchy, to undertake necessary reform. The relationship between and functions of the House of Lords and the Court of Appeal was clearly stated by Lord Diplock in *Davis v Johnson* [1978] 1 All ER 1132 at 1137–38:

> In an appellate court of last resort a balance must be struck between the need on the one side for legal certainty resulting from the binding effect of previous decisions and on the other side the avoidance of undue restriction on the proper development of law. In the case of an intermediate appellate court, however, the second desideratum can be taken care of by an appeal to a superior court, if reasonable means of access to it are available; while the risk to the first desideratum, legal certainty, if the court is not bound by its own previous decisions grows ever greater with increasing membership and the number of three-judge divisions in which it sits . . . So the balance does not lie in the same place as the court of last resort.

The decision to be taken by the Court of Appeal when faced with conflicting precedents from the Supreme Court and the Privy Council has been considered previously. The more general relationship between the Court of Appeal and the Privy

Council was clarified by Lord Neuberger MR in *Sinclair Investments (UK) Ltd v Versailles Trade Finance Ltd* (2011). In explaining the situation of the Court of Appeal he stated:

> We should not follow the Privy Council decision . . . in preference to decisions of this court, unless there are domestic authorities which show that the decisions of this court were *per incuriam*, or at least of doubtful reliability. Save where there are powerful reasons to the contrary, the Court of Appeal should follow its own previous decisions . . . It is true that there is a powerful subsequent decision of the Privy Council which goes the other way, but that of itself is not enough to justify departing from the earlier decisions of this court. . . . I do not suggest that it would always be wrong for this court to refuse to follow a decision of the Privy Council in preference to one of its own previous decisions, but the general rule is that we follow our previous decisions, leaving it to the Supreme Court to overrule those decisions if it is appropriate to do so. Two recent cases where this court preferred to follow a decision of the Privy Council rather than an earlier domestic decision which would normally be regarded as binding (in each case a decision of the House of Lords) are *R v James* and *Abou-Rahmah v Abacha*. In each case, the decision was justified, based as it was on the proposition that it was a foregone conclusion that, *if the case had gone to the House of Lords, they would have followed the Privy Council decision* (paras 72–74, emphasis added).

However, as has been seen in 2.5.1.2 above, the Court of Appeal in *Mendoza v Ghaidan* (2002) used s 4 of the HRA to extend the rights of same-sex partners to inherit a statutory tenancy under the Rent Act 1977. In so doing, it extended the earlier decision of the House of Lords in *Fitzpatrick v Sterling Housing Association Ltd* (1999), which had been decided before the HRA came into force. Thus, it can be seen that the HRA gives the Court of Appeal latitude to effectively overrule decisions of the House of Lords which were decided before the HRA came into effect and in conflict with the ECHR.

See also the reasoning of the Court of Appeal in *D v East Berkshire Community NHS Trust* (2004) in which the Court of Appeal held that the decision of the House of Lords in *X (Minors) v Bedfordshire County Council* (1995) could not be maintained after the introduction of the Human Rights Act 1998, as that Act had undermined the policy consideration that had largely dictated the House of Lords' decision. That approach was directly approved in *Kay v London Borough of Lambeth* (2005) (see below).

Similarly, decisions of the ECJ, which effectively overrule previous decisions of the House of Lords, will also be followed by the Court of Appeal.

The Court of Appeal generally is also bound by its own previous decisions in civil cases. There are, however, a number of exceptions to this general rule. Lord Greene MR listed these exceptions in *Young v Bristol Aeroplane Co Ltd* (1944):

• Where there is a conflict between two previous decisions of the Court of Appeal. In this situation, the later court must decide which decision to follow and, as a corollary, which to overrule. Such a situation arose in *Tiverton Estates Ltd v Wearwell Ltd* (1974). In that case, which dealt with the meaning of s 40 of the Law of Property Act 1925 (subsequently repealed), the court elected to follow older precedents rather than follow the inconsistent decision in *Law v Jones* (1974). The decision in *Tiverton Estates Ltd v Wearwell Ltd* can be justified as the mere working out of the rules of precedent. As *Law v Jones* must have been made in ignorance of, or based on a failure to properly understand, the earlier decisions (see *per incuriam*, below), it could have been ignored on that ground alone. However, this particular exception is wider than that, in that it allows the current Court of Appeal to choose between the previous conflicting authorities. Hence, the Court of Appeal could have decided to follow *Law v Jones* if it preferred.

• Where a previous decision of the Court of Appeal has been overruled, either expressly or impliedly, by the House of Lords. An express overruling would obviously occur where the House of Lords actually considered the Court of Appeal precedent, but it is equally possible that the *ratio* in a precedent from the Court of Appeal could be overruled without the actual case being cited and considered. In this situation, the Court of Appeal, in line with the normal rules of precedent, is required to follow the decision of the House of Lords. Thus, in *Family Housing Association v Jones* (1990), the Court of Appeal felt obliged to ignore its own precedents on the distinction between a licence and a tenancy in property law where, although they had not been expressly overruled, they were implicitly in conflict with later decisions of the House of Lords in *AG Securities Ltd v Vaughan* (1988) and *Street v Mountford* (1985).

• Where the previous decision was given *per incuriam* or, in other words, that previous decision was taken in ignorance of some authority, either statutory or case law, that would have led to a different conclusion. In this situation, the later court can ignore the previous decision in question. It is important to emphasise, however, that the missing authority must be such that it must have led to a different conclusion; the mere possibility is not enough. There are so many case authorities that it is simply not possible to cite all of them. However, the essential authorities, those that lead to a particular decision, must be considered. It is the absence of any such of these authorities that renders a decision *per incuriam*. As will be appreciated, the instances of decisions being ignored on the basis of a ruling of *per incuriam* are 'of the rarest occurrence' (*Morelle Ltd v Wakeling* (1955)). One example, however, may be seen in *Williams v Fawcett* (1985), in which the Court of Appeal did find such exceptional circumstances as would permit it to treat its previous decisions as having been made *per incuriam*. The facts of the case involved an appeal against a decision to commit a person to prison for contempt of court in breaching a non-molestation order. Previous decisions of the Court of Appeal had held that any such committal order had to be signed by the court officer who issued it. However, the present court found that the law as stated in the Criminal Court Rules did not allow for appeal simply on the grounds that the order was not signed by a proper officer as long as the seal of the court was applied. Of crucial importance among the circumstances that led to the finding of *per incuriam* in relation to the earlier decisions was the fact that, given the expense involved, the case would be unlikely to go to the House of Lords for its final determination of the legal situation. It should be noted that this justification can be seen to fit with the previous quotation from Lord Diplock in *Davis v Johnson*, to the extent that the Court of Appeal decided that, in this instance, there was no 'reasonable means of access to' the court of last resort. A similar justification for another finding of *per incuriam* can be found in *Rickards v Rickards* (1989), in which the Court of Appeal held that its previous decision in *Podberry v Peak* (1981) had misunderstood and wrongly applied the House of Lords' decision in *Laine v Eskdale* (1891). In overruling *Podberry*, the court held that it had the power to hear an appeal against a refusal to extend the time limit within which a person could appeal against the award of a lump sum in a clean-break divorce settlement. The court once again held that as the issue involved was so serious, and as it was unlikely to go to the House of Lords, then the Court of Appeal should itself remedy the earlier misunderstanding stated in its own previous decision. An interesting example of the principle can be found in *R (on the Application of W) v Lambeth LBC* (2002), in which the Court of Appeal overruled its earlier judgment of only six months previously in *R (A) v Lambeth LBC* (2001) as regards the interpretation and effect of s 17 of the Children Act 1989. The matter of interest is not so much that the later court held that the earlier one would have reached a different conclusion had the law been fully explained to it, but that one of the judges in the unanimous decision in *R (W) v Lambeth LBC* was Laws LJ, who had delivered a minority judgment to the same effect in *R (A) v Lambeth LBC*.

There used to be a further exception to the general rule that the Court of Appeal was bound by its own earlier decisions and that was in relation to an interlocutory or interim decision made by a panel of only two judges (*Boys v Chaplin* (1968)); even interim decisions by a full panel of three judges were still binding. However, as a consequence of the Woolf reforms and under the Civil Procedure Rules 1998, the distinction between interlocutory and final appeals was removed. Consequently, it was held in *Cave v Robinson, Jarvis and Rolf* (2002) that the decision in *Boys v Chaplin* was no longer sustainable, although the Court of Appeal stated that it might be possible to adjust the reasoning in *Boys v Chaplin* where the later court was satisfied that the earlier decision of the two-person court was 'manifestly wrong'.

Although on the basis *of R v Spencer* (1985) it would appear that there is no difference in principle between the operation of the doctrine of *stare decisis* between the criminal and civil divisions of the Court of Appeal, it is generally accepted that in practice, precedent is not followed as strictly in the former as it is in the latter. Courts in the Criminal Division are not bound to follow their own previous decisions that they subsequently consider to have been based on either a misunderstanding or a misapplication of the law. The reason for this is that the criminal courts deal with matters involving individual liberty and therefore require greater discretion to prevent injustice.

The European Courts and domestic precedent

The foregoing list deals with all the exceptions set out in *Young v Bristol Aeroplane Co Ltd*, but the following additional exceptions to the rule have become apparent since that decision:

- There is also the possibility/likelihood that, as a consequence of s 3 of the European Communities Act 1972, the Court of Appeal can ignore a previous decision of its own which is inconsistent with EC law or with a later decision of the ECJ. As s 3 requires courts either to refer cases dealing with Community law to the ECJ, or alternatively to decide the cases themselves in the light of the previous decision of the ECJ, it would appear that the section gives the Appeal Court grounds for ignoring any of its previous decisions which conflict with subsequent decisions of the ECJ. This effectively fits the ECJ into the traditional hierarchical structure of precedence as the court of last resort in relation to Community law matters.

- It has taken some time for the precise effect of the HRA 1998 to be seen, but as has been explained above at 2.5, s 2 of the Act requires all courts and tribunals to take into account any judgment, decision, declaration or advisory opinion of the ECtHR. As previously the decisions of the European Court of Human Rights were not directly binding on the UK courts, this means that the decisions and jurisprudence of the ECtHR will affect the way in which the UK courts reach decisions in cases involving the rights provided under the European Convention.

In *Director General of Fair Trading v Proprietary Association of Great Britain (No 2)* (2001) (see below, 12.2.3), the Court of Appeal felt able to refine the decision of the House of Lords in *R v Gough* (1993) to bring it into line with ECtHR jurisprudence, and it is almost without doubt that it will overrule its own decisions where those are in conflict with the provisions of the ECHR. The issue of the effect of s 2 of the HRA in relation to the domestic rules of precedent was considered extensively in *Lambeth London Borough Council v Kay; Price v Leeds City Council* (2006). These combined appeals, in essence, related to the effectiveness of orders to take possession of land owned by public authorities but occupied by the appellants, without right under domestic law. The argument that the appellants could rely on Art 8 of the ECHR was rejected by all the courts from the first instance to the House of Lords. In reaching its decision, the House of Lords, by a majority, held that it was not necessary for a local authority to prove that domestic law complied with Art 8. Courts could and should proceed on the assumption that domestic law was compatible with Art 8. The onus was on the occupier to show that there were highly exceptional circumstances to support their case. Much was made of the House of Lords' decision in these cases, especially as *Kay* related to the rights of travellers to occupy land. However, the cases also raised fundamental issues relating to the operation of precedent within the court hierarchy, with specific relevance to the authority of the ECtHR within the domestic structure.

In the *Kay* case, the Court of Appeal had held that it was bound by the decision of the House of Lords in *Harrow London Borough Council v Qazi* (2004), but it also expressed the opinion that the *Qazi* decision was incompatible with the later decision of the ECtHR in *Connors v United Kingdom* (2004). However, as neither the precise effect of s 2 of the Human Rights Act, nor the hierarchical authority of competing decisions of the ECtHR and the House of Lords, had previously received a definitive consideration in the English courts, the Court of Appeal granted leave to appeal to the House of Lords on the issue of precedent. On that issue Lord Bingham delivered the leading judgment, with which the other members of the court concurred. As Lord Bingham explained, there is a distinct difference in the consequences of decisions of the European Court of Justice and those of the European Court of Human Rights: the former are binding, the latter are not. As Lord Bingham put it (para 28):

> The mandatory duty imposed on domestic courts by section 2 of the 1998 Act is to take into account any judgment of the Strasbourg Court and any opinion of the Commission. Thus they are not strictly required to follow Strasbourg rulings, as they are bound by section 3(1) of the European Communities Act 1972 and as they are bound by the rulings of superior courts in the domestic curial hierarchy.

As regards the effect of decisions of the ECtHR within the English legal system of precedent, Lord Bingham addressed the fundamental issue of authority head-on (para 40):

> Reference has already been made to the duty imposed on United Kingdom courts to take Strasbourg judgments and opinions into account and to the unlawfulness of courts, as public authorities, acting incompatibly with Convention rights. The questions accordingly arise whether our domestic rules of precedent are, or should be, modified; whether a court which would ordinarily be bound to follow the decision of another court higher in the domestic curial hierarchy is, or should be, no longer bound to follow that decision if it appears to be inconsistent with a later ruling of the Court in Strasbourg.

His conclusion, with which the other members of the judicial panel concurred, was equally forthright in maintaining the integrity of the existing structure of binding precedent within the domestic hierarchical structure (para 43):

> . . . certainty is best achieved by adhering, even in the Convention context, to our rules of precedent. It will of course be the duty of judges to review Convention arguments addressed to them, and if they consider a binding precedent to be, or possibly to be, inconsistent with Strasbourg authority, they may express their views and give leave to appeal, as the Court of Appeal did here. Leap-frog appeals may be appropriate. In this way, in my opinion, they discharge their duty under the 1998 Act. But they should follow the binding precedent . . .

However, Lord Bingham did allow for one *exceptional* set of circumstances. As previously mentioned, he and the other members of the House of Lords specifically acknowledged that in such circumstances as occurred in *D v East Berkshire Community NHS Trust*, where the previous authority had been set without reference to the Human Rights Act, the Court of Appeal would be at liberty to avoid following the previous decision of the House of Lords.

Subsequently, in its judgment in *McCann v United Kingdom* (2008), the ECtHR disagreed with the majority of the House of Lords in *Kay* (2005), holding that *Connors* (2004) was not confined to cases involving the eviction of travellers, nor was it limited to cases where the applicant was seeking to challenge the law itself rather than its application or procedure in a particular case. However, in *Doherty v Birmingham City Council* the House of Lords decided that the basic rule in this area remained as laid down by the majority in *Qazi v Harrow* (2004) and reaffirmed by the majority in *Kay*. Although in *McCann* the European Court of Human Rights had endorsed the reasoning of the minority in *Kay*, the House of Lords in *Doherty* decided that the approach of the ECtHR could best be implemented by applying and developing the reasoning of the majority, rather than the minority, view expressly supported by the ECtHR.

In September 2010, when the *Kay* case reached the ECtHR, that court followed its own reasoning in *McCann* and reasserted its preference for the minority opinions in the House of Lords' judgments in *Kay*. The ECtHR judgment in *Kay* was handed down while the House of Lords was hearing another case relating to the same issue in *Manchester City Council v Pinnock*. The ECtHR's *Kay* decision was actually handed down after the oral hearing of the *Pinnock* case and the House of Lords asked for written submissions on its effect. The judgment of the House of Lords was delivered by Lord Neuberger, who was still sitting as a member of that court before taking up his position as Master of the Rolls and represents a falling in line, if ever so slightly hesitantly, with the jurisprudence of the ECtHR:

48. This Court is not bound to follow every decision of the ECtHR. Not only would it be impractical to do so: it would sometimes be inappropriate, as it would destroy the ability of the Court to engage in the constructive dialogue with the ECtHR which is of value to the development of Convention law. Of course, we should usually follow a clear and constant line of decisions by the ECtHR. But we are not actually bound to do so or (in theory, at least) to follow a decision of the Grand Chamber. As Lord Mance pointed out in *Doherty v Birmingham* [2009] 1 AC 367, para 126, section 2 of the HRA requires our courts to 'take into account' ECtHR decisions, not necessarily to follow them. Where, however, there is a clear and constant line of decisions whose effect is not inconsistent with some fundamental substantive or procedural aspect of our law, and whose reasoning does not appear to overlook or misunderstand some argument or point of principle, we consider that it would be wrong for this Court not to follow that line.

49. In the present case there is no question of the jurisprudence of the ECtHR failing to take into account some principle or cutting across our domestic substantive or procedural law in some fundamental way. That is clear from the minority opinions in *Harrow v Qazi* [2004] 1 AC 983 and *Kay v Lambeth* [2006] 2 AC 465, and also from the fact that our domestic law was already moving in the direction of the European jurisprudence in *Doherty v Birmingham* [2009] 1 AC 367. *Even before the decision in* Kay v UK *(App no 37341/06), we would, in any event, have been of the opinion that this Court should now accept and apply the minority view of the House of Lords in those cases. In the light of* Kay*, that is clearly the right conclusion.*

Therefore, if our law is to be compatible with Art 8, where a court is asked to make an order for possession of a person's home at the suit of a local authority, the court must have the power to assess the proportionality of making the order, and, in making that assessment, to resolve any relevant dispute of fact (emphasis added).

High Court Divisional Courts

The Divisional Courts, each located within the three divisions of the High Court, hear appeals from courts and tribunals below them in the hierarchy. They are bound by the doctrine of *stare decisis* in the normal way and must follow decisions of Supreme Court and the Court of Appeal. In turn, they bind the courts below them in the hierarchy, including those dealing with ordinary High Court cases. The Divisional Courts are also normally bound by their own previous decisions, although in civil cases, they may make use of the exceptions open to the Court of Appeal in *Young v Bristol Aeroplane Co Ltd* (1944) and, in criminal appeal cases and cases relating to judicial review, the Queen's Bench Divisional Court may refuse to follow its own earlier decisions where it feels the decision to have been made wrongly.

In *R v Greater Manchester Coroner ex p Tal* (1984), the Divisional Court held that it had supervisory jurisdiction in relation to coroners' courts, although this was contrary to its previous decision in *R v Surrey Coroner ex p Campbell* (1982). In so doing, the court stated that its power to depart from its previous decisions was conferred under the Senior Courts Act 1981, but it also held, on the basis of the House of Lords' decision in *O'Reilly v Mackman* (1982), that *Campbell* had wrongly applied *Anisminic v Foreign Compensation Commission* (1969). *Tal*, therefore, may also be seen as an example of the normal exceptions in *Young v Bristol Aeroplane Co Ltd*.

In *R v Stafford Justices ex p Commissioners of Customs and Excise* (1990), the Queen's Bench Divisional Court held that its previous decision in *R v Ealing Justices ex p Dixon* (1990) had been wrongly decided. Both cases related to the rights to undertake prosecutions where individuals had been charged, as required under s 37 of the Police and Criminal Evidence Act (PACE) 1984, by the police. Contrary to the *Ealing Justices* case, the Divisional Court in the *Stafford Justices* case held that merely being charged by the police did not require that the police should pursue the prosecution and that Customs and Excise could undertake the prosecution. In a similar case, although this time relating to the powers of the Inland Revenue to undertake prosecutions on indictment without the consent of the Attorney General, the Divisional Court approved the *Stafford Justices* decision and stated clearly that the *Ealing Justices* case should no longer be followed (*R v Criminal Cases Review Commission ex p Hunt* (2001)).

The House of Lords implicitly approved the Divisional Court's power to overrule its own previous decisions in *DPP v Butterworth* (1994). This case was the culmination of a number of cases relating to the refusal to provide a breath specimen contrary to s 7(6) of the Road Traffic Act 1988. In *DPP v Corcoran* (1993), a Divisional Court held that where a person was not informed for which of two potential offences he was being required to provide a specimen, any prosecution was undermined for duplicity. However, in *DPP v Shaw* (1993), a differently constituted Divisional Court subsequently held that *Corcoran* was wrongly decided and was an example of a *per incuriam* decision. *Shaw* rather than *Corcoran* was followed in the later Divisional Court decision in *DPP v Butterworth*. That decision was expressly approved by the House of Lords.

High Court

The High Court is also bound by the decisions of superior courts. Decisions by individual High Court judges are binding on courts inferior in the hierarchy, but such decisions are not binding on other High Court judges, although they are of strong persuasive authority and tend to be followed in practice. The simple reason for this is that different judgments would lead to confusion in relation to exactly how the particular law in question was to be understood. It is possible, however, for High Court judges to disagree and for them to reach different conclusions as to the law in a particular area. The question then becomes, how is a later High Court judge to select which precedent to follow? It is usually accepted, although it is not a rule of law, that where the later decision has actually considered the previous one and has provided cause for not following it, then that is the judgment which later High Court judges should follow (*Colchester Estates v Carlton Industries plc* (1984)).

Conflicting decisions at the level of the High Court can, of course, be authoritatively decided by reference upwards to the Court of Appeal and then, if necessary, to the Supreme Court, but when the cost of such appeals is borne in mind, it is apparent why, even on economic grounds alone, it is important for High Court judges not to treat their discretion as a licence to destabilise the law in a given area.

In relation to conflicting judgments at the level of the Court of Appeal, the High Court judge is required to follow the later decision.

Crown Courts cannot create precedent and their decisions can never amount to more than persuasive authority.

County Courts and magistrates' courts do not create precedents.

4.5 BINDING PRECEDENT

Not everything in a case report sets a precedent. The contents of a report can be divided into two categories:

• *Ratio decidendi*

   It is important to establish that it is not the actual decision in a case that sets the precedent; that is set by the rule of law on which the decision is founded. This rule, which is an abstraction from the facts of the case, is known as the *ratio decidendi* of the case. The *ratio decidendi* (Latin for 'reason for deciding') of a case may be understood as the statement of the law applied in deciding the legal problem raised by the concrete facts of the case.

• *Obiter dictum*

   This phrase is Latin for 'a statement by the way'. Any statement of law that is not an essential part of the *ratio decidendi* is, strictly speaking, superfluous, and any such statement is referred to as an *obiter dictum* (*obiter dicta* in the plural), that is, said 'by the way'. Although *obiter dicta* do not form part of the binding precedent, they are persuasive authority and can be taken into consideration in later cases if the judge in the later case considers it appropriate to do so.

The division of cases into these two distinct parts is a theoretical procedure. Unfortunately, judges do not actually separate their judgments into the two clearly defined categories, and it is for the person reading the case to determine what the *ratio* is. In some cases, this is no easy matter, and it may be made even more difficult in appellate cases where each of the judges may deliver their own lengthy judgments with no clear single *ratio*. (The potential implications of the way in which later courts effectively determine the *ratio* in any particular case will be considered below and in 13.4.2.) Students should always read cases fully; although it is tempting to rely on the headnote at the start of the case report, it should be remembered that this is a summary provided by the case reporter and merely reflects what that person thinks the *ratio* is. It is not unknown for headnotes to miss an essential point in a case.

4.6 ADVANTAGES OF CASE LAW

There are numerous perceived advantages of the doctrine of *stare decisis*, among which are the following:

- *Consistency*. This refers to the fact that like cases are decided on a like basis and are not apparently subject to the whim of the individual judge deciding the case in question. This aspect of formal justice is important in justifying the decisions taken in particular cases.

- *Certainty*. This follows from, and indeed is presupposed by, the previous item. Lawyers and their clients are able to predict what the outcome of a particular legal question is likely to be in the light of previous judicial decisions. Also, once the legal rule has been established in one case, individuals can orientate their behaviour with regard to that rule, relatively secure in the knowledge that it will not be changed by some later court.

- *Efficiency*. This refers to the fact that it saves the time of the judiciary, lawyers and their clients for the reason that cases do not have to be reargued. In respect of potential litigants, it saves them money in court expenses because they can apply to their solicitor/barrister for guidance as to how their particular case is likely to be decided in the light of previous cases on the same or similar points. (It should of course be recognised that the vast bulk of cases are argued and decided on their facts rather than on principles of law, but that does not detract from the relevance of this issue and is a point that will be taken up later in Chapter 13.)

- *Flexibility*. This refers to the fact that the various mechanisms by means of which the judges can manipulate the common law provide them with an opportunity to develop law in particular areas without waiting for Parliament to enact legislation. In practice, flexibility is achieved through the possibility of previous decisions being either overruled or distinguished, or the possibility of a later court extending or modifying the effective ambit of a precedent. (It should be re-emphasised that it is not the decision in any case which is binding, but the *ratio decidendi*. It is correspondingly and equally incorrect to refer to a decision being overruled.)

This apparently small measure of discretion, in relation to whether later judges are minded to accept the validity of *obiter* statements in precedent cases, opens up the possibility that judges in later cases have a much wider degree of discretion than is originally apparent in the traditional view of *stare decisis*. It is important in this respect to realise that it is the judges in the later cases who actually determine the *ratio decidendi* of previous cases.

Judges, as has been noted previously, in delivering judgments in cases do not separate and highlight the *ratio decidendi* from the rest of their judgment, which can lead to a lack of certainty in determining the *ratio decidendi*. This uncertainty is compounded by the fact that reports of decisions in cases may run to considerable length, and where there are a number of separate judgments, although the judges involved may agree on the decision of a case, they may not agree on the legal basis of the decision reached. This difficulty is further compounded where there are a number of dissenting judgments. In the final analysis, it is for the judge deciding the case in which a precedent has been cited to determine the *ratio* of the authority and thus to determine whether he or she is bound by the case or not. This factor provides later courts with a considerable degree of discretion in electing whether to be bound or not by a particular authority.

The main mechanisms through which judges alter or avoid precedents are as follows:

- *Overruling*

  This is the procedure whereby a court higher up in the hierarchy sets aside a legal ruling established in a previous case. It has generally been accepted that overruling acts retrospectively, that is to say that the law as stated in the higher court is held to have always been the law. Thus not only is the new precedent effective as to future situations, but it is deemed to have applied equally to situations in the past. This may be seen as an outcome of the declaratory theory of law, in which judges were seen as merely stating rather than making the law. Thus the judges in the court that overrules a precedent made by a lower court are understood to be merely removing a mistaken understanding of what the law was, rather than actually changing that law. Equally, when a higher court ruled that a previous interpretation of a statutory provision was wrong, there was no question of that court changing the law: it was merely correcting an error of interpretation (for a further consideration of this point see *R v R* below).

  However, the possibility of a change in this traditional approach to precedent was considered by the House of Lords in *National Westminster Bank plc v Spectrum Plus Ltd* (2005).

  Spectrum had opened an account with National Westminster Bank, and obtained an overdraft facility. As part of that procedure the company issued a debenture to secure its debt to the bank. As security, the debenture purported to provide a specific charge over the company's book debts and a floating charge over its property and undertaking. As regards the book debts, the company had to pay them into a special account with the bank, the use of which was limited. However, as long as the overdraft limit was not exceeded, the company was free to draw on the account for its business purposes. When the company went into voluntary liquidation the bank applied for a declaration that the debenture had created a fixed charge over the company's book debts, with the effect that it would receive payment from those funds before other preferred creditors, such as the company's former employees and, at that time, importantly the Commissioners of HM Revenue and Customs. However, were the security to be considered as merely a floating charge the bank would lose priority in relation to the preferred creditors, although it would still stand in front of ordinary unsecured creditors. At first instance the Vice Chancellor held that the charge granted to the bank was only a floating charge but the Court of Appeal allowed the bank's appeal.

In the House of Lords the main substantive issue related to the nature of the security provided by the book debts, whether a fixed or floating charge. The bank relied on the precedent set by the High Court in *Siebe Gorman and Co Ltd v Barclays Bank Ltd* (1979). In that case Slade J had decided that arrangements of the kind under consideration were of the nature of fixed charges. That precedent had been accepted and extended by the Court of Appeal in *Re New Bullas Trading Ltd* (1994) and was accepted and followed in the Court of Appeal in the present case. Nonetheless, the House of Lords unanimously held that the particular security given over Spectrum's book debts was not in the nature of fixed charges and in so doing overruled the precedent of *Siebe Gorman and Co Ltd v Barclays Bank Ltd* and consequentially the precedent in *Re New Bullas Trading Ltd*.

However, as a subsidiary issue in the case but a more essential one for the operation of the doctrine of precedent in the English legal system, the question as to whether the House of Lords had power to deliver prospective rulings, that is, decisions applicable only in the future, was considered. The argument put forward on behalf of the bank on this issue was that *Siebe Gorman* had stood unchallenged for many years and banks generally had followed it and organised their business relationships on the basis that it was an accurate statement of the law. Consequently it was argued that, even if *Siebe Gorman* was to be overruled, the effect of that decision should only be prospective, and should not provide grounds for invalidating the very many cases that had been settled in reliance upon *Siebe Gorman* precedent. The argument against prospective overruling was that it amounted to the judicial usurpation of the legislative function of Parliament, to the extent that the judiciary would be deciding how and when law was to have effect, and consequently it was outside the constitutional limits of judicial power.

The leading and wide-ranging decision in relation to the matter of prospective overruling was delivered by Lord Nichols, who concluded that (para 39):

> The objections in principle and difficulties in practice mentioned above have substance, particularly in respect of the traditional interpretation of statutes. These objections are compelling pointers to what should be the normal reach of the judicial process. But, even in respect of statute law, they do not lead to the conclusion that prospective overruling can

never be justified as a proper exercise of judicial power. *In this country the established practice of judicial precedent derives from the common law. Constitutionally the judges have power to modify this practice.*

Instances where this power has been in courts elsewhere suggest there could be circumstances in this country where prospective overruling would be necessary to serve the underlying objective of the courts of this country: to administer justice fairly and in accordance with the law. *There could be cases where a decision on an issue of law, whether common law or statute law, was unavoidable but the decision would have such gravely unfair and disruptive consequences for past transactions or happenings that this House would be compelled to depart from the normal principles relating to the retrospective and prospective effect of court decisions.*

If, altogether exceptionally, the House as the country's supreme court were to follow this course I would not regard it as trespassing outside the functions properly to be discharged by the judiciary under this country's constitution. Rigidity in the operation of a legal system is a sign of weakness, not strength. It deprives a legal system of necessary elasticity. Far from achieving a constitutionally exemplary result, it can produce a legal system unable to function effectively in changing times. *'Never say never' is a wise judicial precept, in the interest of all citizens of the country* (emphasis added).

Six of the other judges in the seven-strong panel of the House of Lords accepted Lord Nicholls' 'never say never' proposition; but of that number most adopted the more conservative approach of Lord Hope when he stated that (para 126):

I would respectfully agree with his comment about the wisdom of a 'never say never' approach but find myself unable to visualise circumstances in which it would be proper for a court, having reached a conclusion as to the correct meaning of a statute, to decline to apply to the case in hand the statute thus construed.

However, even though the House of Lords held open the possibility that in an exceptional case it could decide that its decision should only take effect for the future, in the instant case it decided that there was no good reason for postponing the effect of overruling *Siebe Gorman*. As a consequence of that decision it has been suggested that for those involved in previous cases, in which book debts were treated in accordance with what was then believed to be the law, apart from arguments of limitation, they may be able to seek further redress in the light of the restatement of the law. Alternatively, they may be able to rely on a defence that they have changed their position and therefore argue that their case should not now be reopened.

A similar decision about applying a decision to quash delegated legislation prospectively was taken in two related cases, *R (on the application of British Academy of Songwriters, Composers and Authors) v Secretary of State for Business, Innovation and Skills* (2015). The cases related to the introduction of a new s 28B into the Copyright, Designs and Patents Act 1988. This essentially provided for an exemption from copyright infringement so long as the copying was done for private use. The first of the two cases quashed the regulation on the basis of *ultra vires* for flaws in the consultation process; the second decided that the effect of the first decision should be prospective rather than retrospective as the claimants had requested.

It is somewhat anomalous that, within the system of *stare decisis*, precedents gain increased authority with the passage of time. As a consequence, courts tend to be reluctant to overrule long-standing authorities even though they may no longer accurately reflect contemporary practices or morals. In addition to the wish to maintain a high degree of certainty in the law, the main reason for judicial reluctance to overrule old decisions would appear to be the fact that overruling operates retrospectively, with the effect that the principle of law being overruled is held never to have been law. Overruling a precedent might, therefore, have the consequence of disturbing important financial arrangements made in line with what were thought to be settled rules of law. It might even, in certain circumstances, lead to the imposition of criminal liability on previously lawful behaviour. It has to be emphasised, however, that the courts will not shrink from overruling authorities where they see them as no longer representing an appropriate statement of law.

The decision in *R v R* (1992) to recognise the possibility of rape within marriage may be seen as an example of this, although, even here, the House of Lords felt constrained to state that it was not actually altering the law, but was merely removing a misconception as to the true meaning and effect of the law. As this demonstrates, the courts are rarely ready to challenge the legislative prerogative of Parliament in an overt way. For example, in *Curry v DPP* (1994), the Divisional Court attempted to remove the presumption that children between the ages of 10 and 14, who were charged with a criminal offence, did not know that what they did was seriously wrong and the prosecution had to provide evidence to rebut that presumption. Mann LJ justified reversing the presumption by claiming that although it had often been assumed to be the law, it had never actually been specifically considered by earlier courts. On such reasoning, he felt justified in departing from previous decisions of the Court of Appeal which otherwise would have bound him. The House of Lords subsequently restored the previous presumption. Although their Lordships recognised the problem, and indeed appeared to sympathise with Mann LJ's view, they nonetheless thought that such a significant change was a matter for parliamentary action rather than judicial intervention. The doctrine of *doli incapax* was finally removed by s 34 of the Crime and Disorder Act 1998. Of perhaps even greater concern is the fact that s 35 extended s 35 of the Criminal Justice and Public Order Act 1994 to cover all persons aged 10 or over. Thus, courts are now entitled to draw (adverse) inferences from the failure of such children to either give evidence or answer questions at their trial.

Bellinger v Bellinger (2003), considered at 2.5.1.2 above, provides a contemporary example of the courts' reluctance to overrule cases and change the law where Parliament is the appropriate forum for such change. In response to the House of Lords' decision in *Bellinger*, the complex issues relating to transsexual people were taken up in the Gender Recognition Bill, which had its first reading in November 2003 only seven months later. The subsequent Gender Recognition Act (GRA) 2004 came into full effect in April 2005 (see 3.5.6 *MB v Secretary of State for Work and Pensions* (2016) for a further consideration of the GRA 2004).

Overruling should not be confused with *reversing*, which is the procedure whereby a superior court in the hierarchy reverses the decision of a lower court in the same case. As 'overruling' refers to the *ratio* of a case and not its decision, it is quite possible for a higher court to overrule the *ratio* for a decision of a lower court yet still reach the same decision for a different reason. Equally, it is possible for the higher court to approve the *ratio* yet not agree with its application by the lower court and consequently reverse that court's decision.

● *Distinguishing*

In comparison to the mechanism of overruling which is rarely used, the main device for avoiding binding precedents is that of distinguishing. As was previously stated, the *ratio decidendi* of any case is an abstraction from, and is based upon, the material facts of the case. This opens up the possibility that a court may regard the facts of the case before it as significantly different from the facts of a cited precedent and thus, consequentially, it will not find itself bound to follow that precedent. Judges use the device of distinguishing where, for some reason, they are unwilling to follow a particular precedent and the law reports provide many examples of strained distinctions where a court has quite evidently not wanted to follow an authority that it would otherwise have been bound by.

4.7   DISADVANTAGES OF CASE LAW

It should be noted that the advantage of flexibility at least potentially contradicts the alternative advantage of certainty, but there are other disadvantages in the doctrine, which have to be considered. Among these are the following:

● *Uncertainty*

This refers to the fact that the degree of certainty provided by the doctrine of *stare decisis* is undermined by the absolute number of cases that have been reported and can be cited as authorities. This uncertainty is increased by the ability of the judiciary to select which authority to follow through use of the mechanism of distinguishing cases on their facts. A further element leading to uncertainty was highlighted by James Richardson, the editor of *Archbold* (1995), the leading practitioners' text on criminal law, who has claimed that the lack of practical experience of some judges in the Criminal Appeal Court is:

> . . . compounded by an apparent willingness, on occasion, to set aside principle in order to do what the court feels to be right (either way) in the individual case.

As Richardson suggests:

> In the long run, this can only undermine a system which claims to operate on the basis of a hierarchy of binding precedent.

- *Fixity*

  This refers to the possibility that the law in relation to any particular area may become ossified on the basis of an unjust precedent, with the consequence that previous injustices are perpetuated. An example of this is the possibility of rape within marriage, which has only relatively recently, given its long history, been recognised (*R v R* (1992)).

- *Unconstitutionality*

  This is a fundamental question that refers to the fact that the judiciary are overstepping their theoretical constitutional role by actually *making law* rather than restricting themselves to the role of simply applying it. This possibility requires a close examination of the role of the courts in the process of law-making.

  The traditional *declaratory theory of law* claims that judges do not make law, they simply state what it is. This view, however, gives rise to two particular conceptual difficulties:

  (a) *Innovation:* legal rules, as social institutions and creations, cannot be subject to infinite regression; they must have had a beginning at some time in the past when some person or group of people made or recognised them. Every common law rule must have had an origin. To put this in a simpler way, if a particular law was not created by statute, it must have been created by a judge; even if the level of creative activity was no more than recognising the legitimacy, or otherwise, of the practice in question, as was the role of the original circuit judges. Where an issue arises before a court for the first time, it follows, as a matter of course, that there can be no precedent for the court to follow and, given the rapid change in contemporary society, it can only be suggested that such innovations and potentially innovatory court cases are increasingly likely. In such novel circumstances, courts are faced with the choice of either refusing to decide a case, or stating what the law should be. In earlier times, judges did not shirk from this task and, even in modern times, courts are required on occasion to consider situations for the first time. Such cases are described as cases of first impression and inevitably involve judges in the creation of new law.

(b) *Reform:* the question arises as to how the law is to develop and change to cater for changed circumstances if cases are always to be decided according to precedent.

These considerations raise the question that if the law, as represented in either common law or statute law, is out of line with current social beliefs and practices, then should it not be incumbent upon the judiciary to decide cases in line with the currently prevailing standards, even if this means ignoring previous decisions and interpretations? Not to do so leaves the judges open to the charge of being out of touch with social reality. To overtly change the law, however, opens them up to the alternative charge of acting beyond their powers and of usurping the role and function of the legislature. Opinions on this matter range from those that would deny completely the right of judges to make or change the law, to those that would grant the judges the right to mould the law in line with their conception of justice. Others would recognise the fact that the common law was judge-made and restrict judicial creativity to the development of established common law principles. There is an important corollary to this latter position which links it with those who limit judicial creativity, for the implicit assertion is that judges have no place in reforming statutory provisions. They may signal the ineffectiveness of such provisions and call for their repeal or reform, but it would be a usurpation of the legislature's function and power for the courts to engage in such general reform.

In any case, this question unavoidably raises the issue of the actual extent of judicial creativity (compare and contrast *R v R* (1992) and *DPP v C* (1995) in this light). The previous consideration of distinguishing has demonstrated how the doctrine of *stare decisis* can be avoided by the judiciary. A further way in which judges have a creative impact on the law is in the way in which they adapt and extend precedent in instant cases. In addition, judicial reasoning, which will be considered in detail in Chapter 13, tends to be carried out on the basis of analogy, and judges have a large degree of discretion in selecting what are to be considered as analogous cases. They also have a tendency to extend, continuously, existing precedents to fit new situations, as the evolution of the tort of negligence will show.

It is now probably a commonplace of legal theory that judges do make law. Perhaps the more interesting question is not whether judges make law, but why they deny that they do so. In spite of the protestations of the judiciary, law and judicial decision-making is a political process to the extent that it is deciding which values are to be given priority within society. Through their choice of values, the judiciary sanction or prohibit particular forms of behaviour. Due to their position in the constitution, however, judges have to be circumspect in the way in which, and the extent to which, they use their powers to create law and impose values. To overtly assert or exercise the power would be to challenge the power of the legislature. For an unelected body to challenge a politically supreme parliament would be unwise to say the least. It is for that reason that the courts on occasion take refuge behind the cloak of a naïve declaratory theory of law.

The foregoing has set out the doctrine of binding precedent as it operates in theory to control and indeed limit the ambit of judicial discretion. It has to be recognised, however, that the doctrine does not operate as stringently as it appears at first sight and that there are particular shortcomings in the system that have to be addressed in weighing up the undoubted advantages with the equally undoubted disadvantages.

Nonetheless, the practical importance of the doctrine of precedent can be seen in the history of three conjoined cases, *Fairchild v Glenhaven Funeral Services Ltd and Others* (2002).

The cases related to claims for compensation for injury – mesothelioma, a terminal lung disease caused by the exposure of workers to asbestos fibre – during the course of their working lives with more than one employer. Both the High Court and the Court of Appeal held that the claimants' cases could not succeed, as they could not prove which exposure to asbestos fibre had actually caused the resultant disease. As they could not prove which employer was at fault, no employer could be held liable.

Only a matter of days before the House of Lords was due to hear the appeal, a consortium of insurance companies, which would have had to provide any recompense in the final analysis, offered to settle the present cases on a voluntary basis and set up a compensation scheme for the hundreds of other claimants who were waiting for the outcome of those cases. The point, however, was that the payments to be made would have been significantly less than would have been awarded if the claimants won their case in the House of Lords. The insurers decided that they would rather not risk an adverse decision in the House of Lords, and actually told the Lords' judicial office that the settlement had been reached, thus removing the need to hear the final appeal. In reality, no such settlement had been reached.

The representative of the claimants stated that the settlement scheme was a 'sordid attempt to manipulate the judicial process, the whole objective [being] to ensure that the Court of Appeal's decision remains intact'. The representative of the insurers stated that it was 'not cynical – it was practical'. Lord Bingham, the senior judge in the House of Lords, stated that the episode had been 'entirely regrettable'.

When the cases subsequently came before the House of Lords, the fears of the insurance companies were proved justified by that court overruling the decision of the Court of Appeal, thus laying the insurers open to significantly more liability than they would have had to meet under their voluntary scheme.

It has to be admitted, however, that this sort of manoeuvring also occurs in relation to trade union and other civil rights cases, where the specialist lawyers who deal with such issues attempt to ensure that potentially ground-breaking issues are argued in relation to relatively stronger cases rather than very weak ones. The practicality is that once a positive precedent, the legal rule, is established in the strong case, it can be extended into

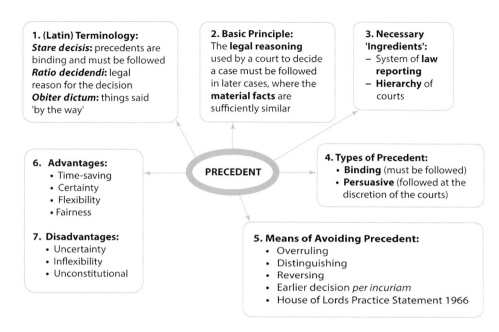

1. **(Latin) Terminology:**
Stare decisis: precedents are binding and must be followed
Ratio decidendi: legal reason for the decision
Obiter dictum: things said 'by the way'

2. **Basic Principle:**
The **legal reasoning** used by a court to decide a case must be followed in later cases, where the **material facts** are sufficiently similar

3. **Necessary 'Ingredients':**
– System of **law reporting**
– **Hierarchy** of courts

PRECEDENT

6. **Advantages:**
• Time-saving
• Certainty
• Flexibility
• Fairness

7. **Disadvantages:**
• Uncertainty
• Inflexibility
• Unconstitutional

4. **Types of Precedent:**
• **Binding** (must be followed)
• **Persuasive** (followed at the discretion of the courts)

5. **Means of Avoiding Precedent:**
• Overruling
• Distinguishing
• Reversing
• Earlier decision *per incuriam*
• House of Lords Practice Statement 1966

FIGURE 4.1 *Precedent: an aide-mémoire.*

a wider area. It would, however, be much more difficult to overturn a contrary precedent handed down in a weak case.

4.9   BOOKS OF AUTHORITY

When a court is unable to locate a precise or analogous precedent, it may refer to legal textbooks for guidance. Such books are subdivided, depending on when they were written. In strict terms, only certain works are actually treated as authoritative sources of law. Among the most important of these works are those by Glanvill from the twelfth century, Bracton from the thirteenth century, Coke from the seventeenth century and Blackstone from the eighteenth century. When cases such as *R v R* are borne in mind, it might be claimed, with justification, that the authority of such ancient texts may be respected more in the breach than in the performance. Given the societal change that has occurred in the intervening time, one can only say that such a refusal to fetishise ancient texts is a positive, and indeed necessary, recognition of the need for law to change in order to keep up with its contemporary sphere of operation. Legal works produced after Blackstone's *Commentaries* of 1765 are considered to be of recent origin, and they cannot be treated as authoritative sources. The courts, however, will look at the most eminent works by accepted experts in particular fields in order to help determine what the law is or should be. See, for example, the citation of Shetreet's *Judges on Trial*, and De Smith, Wolf and Jowell, *Judicial Review of Administrative Action*, in Lord Browne-Wilkinson's decision in *Re Pinochet* (1999), Bennion's *Statutory Interpretation* in *Wilson v Secretary of State for Trade and Industry* (2003), and Bruno Simma's *The Charter of the United Nations, A Commentary* in *HM Treasury v Mohammed Jabar Ahmed* (2010).

4.10   CUSTOM

There is some academic debate about the exact relationship of custom and law. Some claim that law is simply the extension of custom and that with the passage of time, customs develop into laws. From this point of view, law may be seen as the redefinition of custom for the purposes of clarity and enforcement by the legal institutions. The state institutions are seen as merely refining the existing customary behaviour of society. Others deny this evolutionary link and claim that law and custom are in fact contradictory, with law emerging in opposition to, and replacing, customary forms of behaviour. From this perspective, law is seen as being a new form of regulation handed down by the state rather than as emerging from society as a whole.

The traditional view of the development of the common law tends to adopt the first of these views. This overly romantic notion of the common law represents its emergence as no more than the crystallisation of common customs. This distillation is accomplished by the judiciary in the course of their historic travels around the land. This view, however, tends to play down the political process that gave rise to the procedure. The imposition of a common system of law represented the political victory of a state that had fought to establish and assert its central authority. Viewed in that light, the emergence of the common law can be seen actually to support the second of the two approaches suggested above.

Although some of the common law may have had its basis in general custom, a large proportion of these so-called customs were invented by the judges themselves and represented what they wanted the law to be, rather than what people generally thought it was.

One source of customary practice that undoubtedly did find expression in the form of law was business and commercial practice. These customs and practices originally were constituted in the distinct form of the law merchant, but gradually this became subsumed under the control of the common law courts and ceased to exist apart from the common law.

Notwithstanding the foregoing, it is still possible for specific local customs to operate as a source of law. In certain circumstances, parties may assert the existence of customary practices in order to support their case. Such local customs may run counter to the strict application of the common law and, where they are found to be legitimate, they will effectively replace the common law. Even in this respect, however, reliance on customary law as opposed to common law, although not impossible, is made unlikely by the stringent tests that have to be satisfied. The requirements that a local custom must satisfy in order to be recognised are that:

- it must have existed from 'time immemorial', that is, 1189;
- it must have been exercised continuously within that period;
- it must have been exercised peaceably without opposition;

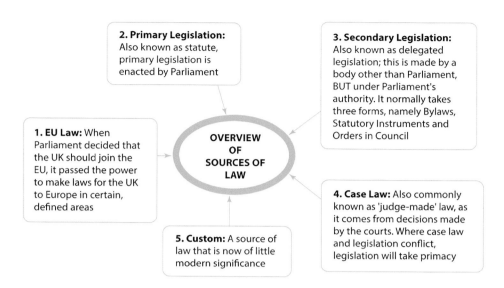

FIGURE 4.2 *Overview of Sources of Law.*

- it must also have been felt to be obligatory;
- it must be capable of precise definition;
- it must have been consistent with other customs;
- it must be reasonable.

Given this list of requirements, it can be seen why local custom is not an important source of law. However, the courts will have recourse to custom where they see it as appropriate, as may be seen in *Egerton v Harding* (1974), in which the courts upheld a customary duty to fence land against cattle straying from an area of common land.

CHAPTER SUMMARY: SOURCES OF LAW: CASE LAW

CASE LAW

Case law is that law created by judges in the course of deciding cases.

The doctrine of *stare decisis* or binding precedent refers to the fact that courts are bound by previous decisions of courts equal to or above them in the court hierarchy.

The Supreme Court can now overrule its own previous rules; the Court of Appeal cannot.

It is the reason for a decision, the *ratio decidendi*, that binds. Everything else is *obiter* and not bound to be followed.

Judges may avoid precedents through either overruling or distinguishing them. The advantages of the doctrine relate to:

- saving the time of all parties concerned;
- certainty;
- flexibility; and
- the meeting of the requirements of formal justice.

The disadvantages relate to:

- uncertainty;
- fixity; and
- unconstitutionality.

It should be recognised that supposed advantages and disadvantages conflict.

CUSTOM

Custom is of arguable historic importance as a source of law and is of very limited importance as a contemporary source.

FOOD FOR THOUGHT

1   The common law is the law made by judges, but under the separation of powers, judges are not supposed to make law. Judges are bound by precedent but can develop the law. How can both of these, apparently contradictory, sentences be reconciled?

2   The *ratio decidendi* in any case represents the binding precedent that has to be followed in later cases. However, who actually decides what the *ratio* is?

FURTHER READING

Goodhart, A, 'The *ratio decidendi* of a case' (1959) 22 MLR 117

Holdsworth, W, 'Case law' (1934) 50 LQR 180

Manchester, C, and Salter, D, *Exploring the Law: The Dynamics of Precedent and Statutory Interpretation*, 4th edn, 2011, London: Sweet and Maxwell

Simpson, A, 'The *ratio decidendi* of a case' (1957) 20 MLR 413; (1958) 21 MLR 155

Stone, J, 'The Ratio of the Ratio Decidendi' (1959) 22 MLR 597

USEFUL WEBSITES

www.justice.gov.uk/about/hmcts
The official website of Her Majesty's Courts and Tribunals Service.

www.supremecourt.uk
The official website of the Supreme Court.

COMPANION WEBSITE

Now visit the companion website to:

- test your understanding of the key terms using our Flashcard Glossary;
- revise and consolidate your understanding of 'Sources of law: Case law' using the multiple choice questions and the module on Using Cases in the online Legal Skills Guide;
- view all of the links to the Useful Websites above;
- view a sample exam question and answer on sources of law, taken from the authors' latest *Questions & Answers* book on The English Legal System.

www.routledge.com/cw/slapper

5.1   INTRODUCTION

It is also essential to distinguish between the two different courts that operate within the European context: the Court of Justice of the European Union (CJEU), formerly the European Court of Justice (ECJ), which is the court of the EU, sitting in Luxembourg; and the ECtHR, which deals with cases relating to the ECHR and sits in Strasbourg.

The development of the European Union

Following the accession of Croatia on 1 July 2013, the European Union is made up of 28 Member states and with a total population of 508 million inhabitants.

The initial impetus for European integration, eventually leading to the current structure and the, as yet still to be attained, establishment of an integrated EU, was a response to two factors: the disasters of World War II; and the emergence of the Soviet Bloc in Eastern Europe. The aim was to link the separate European countries, particularly France and Germany, together in such a manner as to prevent the outbreak of future armed hostilities. The first step in this process was the establishment of a European Coal and Steel Community. The next step towards integration was the formation of the European Economic Community (EEC) under the Treaty of Rome in 1957. The UK joined the EEC in 1973. The Treaty of Rome has subsequently been amended in the further pursuit of integration as the original Community has expanded. Thus, the Single European Act (SEA) 1986 established a single economic market within the EC and widened the use of majority voting in the Council of Ministers. The Maastricht Treaty further accelerated the move towards a federal European supranational state, in the extent to which it recognised Europe as a social and political – as well as an economic – community. Previous Conservative governments of the UK resisted the emergence of the EU as anything other than an economic market and objected to, and resiled from, various provisions aimed at social, as opposed to economic, affairs. Thus, the UK was able to opt out of the Social Chapter of the Treaty of Maastricht. The New Labour administration in the UK had no such reservations and, as a consequence, the Treaty of Amsterdam 1997 incorporated the European Social Charter into the EC Treaty which, of course, applies to the UK (see below).

As the establishment of the single market within the European Community (EC), as the EEC became, progressed, it was suggested that its operation would be greatly facilitated by the adoption of a common currency, or at least a more closely integrated monetary system. Thus, in 1979, the European Monetary System (EMS) was established, under which individual national currencies were valued against a nominal currency called the ECU and allocated a fixed rate within which they were allowed to fluctuate to a limited extent. Britain was a member of the EMS until 1992, when financial speculation against the pound forced its withdrawal. Nonetheless, other members of the EC continued to pursue the policy of monetary union, now entitled European Monetary Union (EMU), and January 1999 saw the installation of the new European currency, the Euro, which has now replaced national currencies within what is now known as the Eurozone. The UK did not join the EMU at its inception and there is little chance that membership will appear on the political agenda for the foreseeable future, especially given the financial crisis that is enveloping many of the EMU states, particularly those on the periphery of the EU. It remains to be seen whether the ongoing financial crisis results in the breakup of the EMU, or its strengthening, as the current members may be forced to seek more economic unity to address its consequences.

Treaty of Nice

In December 2000 the European Council met in Nice in the south of France. The Council consists of the heads of state or government of the member countries of the EU, and is the body charged with the power to make amendments to EU treaties (see below). The purpose of the meeting was to prepare the Union for expansion from its then 15 to 25 members by the year 2004, and so to its current 28 members. New members ranged from the tiny Malta with a population of 370,000 to Poland with its population of almost 39 million people. In order to accommodate this large expansion, it was recognised that significant changes had to be made in the institutions of the current Union, paramount among those being the weighting of the voting power of the Member states. Although parity was to be maintained between Germany, France, Italy and the UK at the new level of 29 votes, Germany and any two of the other largest countries gained a blocking power on further changes, as it was accepted that no changes, even on the basis of a qualified majority vote, could be introduced in the face of opposition from countries constituting 62 per cent of the total population of the Union. The recognition of such veto power was seen as a victory for national as against supranational interests within the Union and a significant defeat for the Commission. However, the number of matters subject to qualified majority voting was increased, although a number of countries, including the UK, refused to give up their veto with regard to the harmonisation of national and corporate tax rates. Nor would the UK, this time supported by Sweden, agree to give up the veto in relation to social security policy. Core immigration was another area in which the UK government retained its ultimate veto (see 5.3.1 for current voting power).

At the same time as these changes were introduced, the members of the Council of Europe also signed a new Charter of Fundamental Rights. Among the rights recognised by the charter are included:

* right to life;
* respect for private and family life;
* protection of family data;
* right to education;
* equality between men and women;
* fair and just working conditions;
* right to collective bargaining and industrial action;
* right not to be dismissed unjustifiably.

It is significant that the charter was not included within the specific Treaty issues at Nice, at the demand of the UK. The UK had also ensured that some of the references, particularly to employment matters, were subject to reference to domestic law.

Lisbon Treaty

Although the Treaty of Nice was difficult and time-consuming in its formation, it looked for some time as though its terms would be replaced before they had actually come into effect. This possibility came about as a result of the conclusions of the *Convention on the*

Future of Europe, which was constituted in February 2002 by the then members to consider the establishment of a European Constitution. The Convention, which sat under the presidency of the former President of France, Valéry Giscard d'Estaing, produced a draft constitution, which it was hoped would provide a more simple, streamlined and transparent procedure for internal decision-making within the Union and to enhance its profile on the world stage. Among the proposals for the new constitution were the following:

* the establishment of a new office of President of the European Union;
* the appointment of an EU foreign minister;
* the shift to a two-tier Commission;
* fewer national vetoes;
* increased power for the European Parliament;
* simplified voting power;
* the establishment of an EU defence force by 'core members';
* the establishment of a charter of fundamental rights.

In the months of May and June 2005 the move towards the European Constitution came to a juddering halt when first the French and then the Dutch electorates voted against its implementation. Such a signal failure meant that it was not necessary for the UK government to conduct a referendum on the proposed constitution as it had promised. However, as with most EU initiatives, the new constitution did not disappear and re-emerged as the Treaty of Lisbon, signed by all the members in December 2007. Once again the UK government, together with the Polish one, insisted that a protocol, number 7, be appended to the treaty ensuring that the charter of fundamental rights could not create new rights in the UK. The Lisbon Treaty gave rise to much ill-feeling in many states for the reason that it incorporated most of the proposals originally contained in the previously rejected constitutional proposal. In legal form, the Lisbon Treaty merely amended the existing treaties, rather than replacing them as the previous constitution had proposed. In practical terms, however, all the essential changes that would have been delivered by the constitution were contained in the treaty – a fact widely recognised by some EU leaders, although not the UK's. Thus Angela Merkel, Chancellor of Germany, was quoted in June 2007 in the *Daily Telegraph* as saying, 'The substance of the Constitution is preserved. That is a fact', and Valéry Giscard d'Estaing, Chairman of the Convention on the Future of Europe which drafted the Constitution was quoted, in a European Parliament press release on 17 July 2007, as saying, 'In terms of content, the proposals remain largely unchanged, they are simply presented in a different way . . . This text is, in fact, a rerun of a great part of the substance of the Constitutional Treaty.'

As a matter of interest and political significance, most member countries decided to ratify the new treaty through their legislatures rather than by hazarding it in a referendum, a decision that caused much discontent in many countries. In the UK, the government declined to have a referendum on the basis of the, not totally convincing, suggestion that the treaty was simply an amendment and a tidying-up measure and

1. The Council of Europe:	**2. The European Court of Human Rights:**	**3. The European Union (EU):**
– Set up in 1947 by European states following WWII, to protect human rights. It should be emphasised that this body is totally separate from the European Union – Enacted the **European Convention on Human Rights**, of which the UK is a signatory but which the UK has never fully incorporated into national law – **This body should not be confused with the European Council or the Council of the European Union**	– Established by the Council of Europe to enforce the rights contained in the European Convention on Human Rights – Following the enactment of the Human Rights Act in the UK, the decisions of this court now have to be considered by our national courts – **This court should not be confused with the Court of Justice of the European Union (CJEU)**	– Originally known as the European Economic Community (EEC) when established by the Treaty of Rome 1957, it was created in order to ensure peace in Europe through economic integration of its Member States – The EEC was subject to a change of name following the Treaty on European Union, 1992 (TEU or Maastricht Treaty) after which it became known as the European Community (EC) – The TEU also created the European Union (EU) of which the EC was a component part – Since the enactment of the Lisbon Treaty in 2009, the EC no longer exists and all references should now be to the EU – The UK became a member in 1973, after the enactment of the **European Communities Act 1972**

WHO'S WHO IN THE EUROPEAN CONTEXT

FIGURE 5.1 *Who's Who in the European Context.*

consequently did not need the confirmation of a referendum in the way necessary and promised for the constitution.

The necessary alterations to the fundamental treaties governing the EU, brought about by the Lisbon Treaty, were published at the end of March 2010 in the form of an updated *Treaty on European Union* (TEU), a newly named *Treaty on the Functioning of the European Union* (TFEU) (formerly the *Treaty Establishing the European Community*), together with *the Charter of Fundamental Rights of the European Union* (CFREU).

The Treaty on European Union (TEU)

The text of the treaty is divided into six parts as follows, with reference to some of the most important specific provisions:

1   *Common Provisions*

  •   Article 1 of this treaty makes it clear that 'The Union shall be founded on the present Treaty and on the Treaty on the Functioning of the European Union (hereinafter referred to as "the Treaties"). Those two Treaties shall have the same legal value. *The Union shall replace and succeed the European Community*.' This provision means that the previous confusion between when it was more appropriate to refer to EC rather than the EU has been removed and that it is now correct under all circumstances to refer to the EU. Article 47 provides further that the EU has legal personality, which means that the EU, as well as its constituent members, will be able to be a full member of the Council of Europe. As yet, the EU has not joined the Council, although an agreement to do so was established in July 2011.

- Article 2 establishes that the EU is 'founded on the values of respect for human dignity, freedom, democracy, equality, the rule of law and respect for human rights, including the rights of persons belonging to minorities'.

- Article 3 then states the aims of the EU in very general terms as follows:

  ○ the promotion of peace, its values and the well-being of its peoples; the assurance of freedom of movement of persons without internal frontiers but with controlled external borders;

  ○ the creation of an internal market . . . aiming at full employment and social progress, and a high level of protection and improvement of the quality of the environment;

  ○ the establishment of an economic and monetary union whose currency is the Euro; the promotion of its values, while contributing to the eradication of poverty and observing human rights and respecting the Charter of the United Nations;

  ○ the sixth aim requires that the EU pursue its objectives by 'appropriate means'.

- Article 6 binds the EU to the Charter of Fundamental Rights of the European Union and the European Convention on Human Rights.

2   *Provisions on democratic principles*

- Article 9 establishes the equality of EU citizens and that every national of a Member state shall be a citizen of the Union. It makes clear that citizenship of the Union is *additional to* and does *not replace* national citizenship.

3   *Provisions on the institutions*

- Article 13 establishes the institutions in the following order and under the following names (except for the ECB these will be considered in detail below):

  ○ the European Parliament;
  ○ the European Council;
  ○ the Council;
  ○ the European Commission;
  ○ the Court of Justice of the European Union;
  ○ the European Central Bank;
  ○ the Court of Auditors.

- Article 15 establishes the President of the European Council.
- Articles 15(2) and 18 establish the High Representative of the Union for Foreign Affairs and Security Policy to conduct the Union's common foreign and security policy.

4   *Provisions on enhanced co-operations*

- Article 20 allows a number of Member states to co-operate in furthering integration in a particular area where other members are blocking full integration.

5   *General provisions on the Union's external action and specific provisions on the Common Foreign and Security Policy*

- Articles 21–46 relate to the establishment and operation of a common EU foreign policy including:
  - compliance with the UN charter, promoting global trade, humanitarian support and global governance;
  - establishment of the European External Action Service, which will function as the EU's foreign ministry and diplomatic service;
  - the furtherance of military co-operation including mutual defence.

6   *Final provisions*

- Article 47 establishes the legal personality of the EU.
- Article 48 deals with the method of treaty amendment; either through the ordinary or the simplified revision procedures.
- Articles 49 and 50 deal with applications to join the EU and withdrawal from it.

The Treaty on the Functioning of the European Union (TFEU)

This document, going back through several iterations to the original Treaty of Rome, contains the detail of the structure and operation of the European Union.

Article 2 of this treaty provides that:

When the Treaties confer on the Union exclusive competence in a specific area, only the Union may legislate and adopt legally binding acts, the Member states being able to do so themselves only if so empowered by the Union or for the implementation of Union acts.

Article 3 specifies that the Union shall have exclusive competence in the following areas:

(a)   customs union;

(b)   the establishing of the competition rules necessary for the functioning of the internal market;

(c)   monetary policy for the Member states whose currency is the Euro;

(d)   the conservation of marine biological resources under the common fisheries policy;

(e)   common commercial policy.

Article 3 provides that the Union shall also have exclusive competence for the conclusion of an international agreement when its conclusion is provided for in a legislative act of the Union or is necessary to enable the Union to exercise its internal competence, or in so far as its conclusion may affect common rules or alter their scope.

The provision of specific articles will be considered below.

The Charter of Fundamental Rights of the European Union (CFREU)

The Charter contains 54 Articles divided into seven titles. The first six titles deal with substantive rights relating to:

- *dignity*, including the right to life and the prohibition of torture and inhuman or degrading treatment or punishment;
- *freedom*, including the right to liberty and security of person, the right to engage in work and the freedom to conduct a business;
- *equality*, including equality before the law, and the right not to be discriminated against;
- *solidarity*, which emphasises workers' rights to fair working conditions, protection against unjustified dismissal, information and consultation within the undertaking, together with the right to engage in collective bargaining and to engage in industrial action;
- *citizens' rights*, including the right to vote and to stand as a candidate at elections; and finally
- *justice*, which includes the rights to a fair trial, the presumption of innocence and the right of defence.

The last title, Arts 51–54, deals with the interpretation and application of the Charter.

Many Member states, including the UK, negotiated opt-outs of some of the provisions of the Charter.

5.1.1 PARLIAMENTARY SOVEREIGNTY, EUROPEAN UNION LAW AND THE COURTS

The doctrine of parliamentary sovereignty has already been considered with respect to the relationship between Parliament and the courts (see 2.3.2), and similar issues arise with regard to the relationship between EU law and domestic legislation. It has already been seen that the doctrine of parliamentary sovereignty is one of the cornerstones of the UK constitution. One aspect of the doctrine is that, as long as the appropriate procedures are followed, Parliament is free to make such law as it determines. The corollary of that is that no current Parliament can bind the discretion of a later Parliament to make law as it wishes. The role of the court, as also has been seen, is merely to interpret the law made by Parliament. Each of these constitutional principles is revealed as problematic in relation to the UK's membership of the EU and the relationship of domestic and EU law.

Before the UK joined the EU, its law was just as foreign as law made under any other jurisdiction. On joining the EU, however, the UK and its citizens accepted, and became subject to, EU law. This subjection to European law remains the case even where the parties to any transaction are themselves both UK subjects. In other words, in areas where it is applicable, European law supersedes any existing UK law to the contrary. The European Communities Act (ECA) 1972 gave legal effect to the UK's membership of the EEC, and its subjection to all existing and future Community/Union law was expressly stated in s 2(1), which provides:

> All such rights, powers, liabilities, obligations and restrictions from time to time created or arising by or under the Treaties, and all such remedies and procedures from time to time provided for by or under the Treaties, as in accordance with the Treaties *are without further enactment to be given legal effect or used in the UK* shall be recognised and available in law, and be enforced, allowed and followed accordingly (emphasis added).

Such statutory provision merely reflected the approach already adopted by the Court of Justice of the European Union (formerly the European Court of Justice):

> By contrast with ordinary international treaties, the EC Treaty has created its own legal system which . . . became an integral part of the legal systems of the Member states and which their courts are bound to apply (*Costa v ENEL* (1964)).

The impact of Community/Union law on, and its superiority to, domestic law was clearly stated by Lord Denning MR thus:

> If on close investigation it should appear that our legislation is deficient or is inconsistent with Community law by some oversight of our draftsmen then it is our bounden duty to give priority to Community law. Such is the result of s 2(1) and (4) of the European Communities Act 1972 (*Macarthys Ltd v Smith* (1979)).

Thoburn v Sunderland CC (2002) appeared a simple enough case, but it raised some fundamental constitutional issues. It concerned a Sunderland greengrocer who sold fruit only by imperial weight. He was given a conditional discharge after his conviction under an Order in Council implementing a European Directive. He appealed by way of case stated, arguing that the Weights and Measures Act 1985 took precedence over European law or Orders in Council. His appeal failed, but in deciding the issue, Laws LJ rejected the argument that the overriding force of European law in the UK depends on its own principles as enunciated by the European Court in *Costa v ENEL*. Laws LJ stated that EU law could not entrench itself, because when Parliament enacted the ECA in 1972, it could not and did not bind subsequent parliaments. The British Parliament, being sovereign, could not abandon its sovereignty, and there are no circumstances in which the jurisprudence of the Court of Justice could elevate Community law to a status within the corpus of English domestic law to which it could not aspire by any route of English law itself.

However, he went on, the traditional doctrine of parliamentary sovereignty has been modified by the common law, which has in recent years created classes of legislation that cannot be repealed by mere implication, that is, without express words to that effect. There now exists a clear hierarchy of Acts of Parliament – 'ordinary' statutes, which may be impliedly repealed, and 'constitutional' statutes, clearly including the ECA, which may not. The ECA is a constitutional statute and cannot be impliedly repealed, but that truth derives not from EU law but from the common law. In summary, the appropriate analysis of the relationship between EU and domestic law required regard to four propositions:

(i)   Each specific right and obligation provided under EC/EU law was, by virtue of the 1972 Act, incorporated into domestic law and took precedence. Anything within domestic law which was inconsistent with EC/EU law was either abrogated or had to be modified so as to avoid inconsistency.

(ii)   The common law recognised a category of constitutional statutes.

(iii)   The 1972 Act was a constitutional statute which could not be impliedly repealed.

(iv)   The fundamental legal basis of the UK's relationship with the EU rested with domestic rather than European legal powers.

Thus did Laws LJ maintain balance between the supremacy of EU law in matters of substantive law, and the supremacy of the UK Parliament in establishing the legal framework within which EU law operates. Clause 18 of the European Union Bill 2010/11 provides a statutory confirmation of Laws' reasoning.

An example of EU law invalidating the operation of UK legislation can be found in the *Factortame* cases. The Common Fisheries Policy established by the EEC had placed limits on the amount of fish that any member country's fishing fleet was permitted to catch. In order to gain access to British fish stocks and quotas, Spanish fishing boat owners formed British companies and reregistered their boats as British. In order to prevent what it saw as an abuse and an encroachment on the rights of indigenous fishermen, the British government introduced the Merchant Shipping Act 1988, which provided that any fishing company seeking to register as British would have to have its principal place of business in the UK and at least 75 per cent of its shareholders would have to be British nationals. This effectively debarred the Spanish boats from taking up any of the British fishing quota. Some 95 Spanish boat owners applied to the British courts for judicial review of the Merchant Shipping Act 1988 on the basis that it was contrary to Community law.

The High Court decided to refer the question of the legality of the legislation to the ECJ under Art 267 of the Treaty on the Functioning of the European Union (TFEU) (formerly Art 234 and Art 177 of previous versions of the treaty (see below, 5.3.6)), but in the meantime granted interim relief in the form of an injunction disapplying the operation of the legislation to the fishermen. On appeal, the Court of Appeal removed the injunction, a decision that was confirmed by the House of Lords. However, the House of Lords referred the question of the relationship of Community law and contrary domestic law to the ECJ. Effectively, they were asking whether the domestic courts should follow the domestic law or Community law. The ECJ ruled that the Treaty of Rome required domestic courts to give effect to the directly enforceable provisions of Community law and, in doing so, such courts are required to ignore any national law that runs counter to Community law. The House of Lords then renewed the interim injunction. The ECJ later ruled that in relation to the original referral from the High Court, the Merchant Shipping Act 1988 was contrary to Community law and therefore the Spanish fishing companies should be able to sue for compensation in the UK courts. The subsequent claims also went all the way to the House of Lords before it was finally settled in October 2000 that the UK was liable to pay compensation, which was estimated at between £50 million and £100 million.

The foregoing has demonstrated the way in which, and the extent to which, the fundamental constitutional principles of the UK are altered by its membership of the EU. Both the sovereign power of Parliament to legislate in any way it wishes and the role of the courts in interpreting and applying such legislation are now circumscribed by EU law. There remains one hypothetical question to consider and that relates to the power of Parliament to disapply legislation from the EU. While CJEU jurisprudence might not recognise such a power, it is certain that the UK Parliament retains such a power in UK law. If EU law receives its superiority as the expression of Parliament's will in the form of s 2 of the European Communities Act, as suggested by Lord Denning in *Macarthys*, it would remain open to a later Parliament to remove that recognition by passing new legislation. Such a point was actually made by the former Master of the Rolls in his judgment in that very case:

If the time should come when our Parliament deliberately passes an Act with the intention of repudiating the Treaty or any provision in it or intentionally of acting inconsistently with it and says so in express terms then I should have thought that it would be the duty of our courts to follow the statute of our Parliament.

Article 10 (formerly 5) requires:

> Member states to take all appropriate measures, whether general or particular, to ensure fulfilment of the obligations arising out of this Treaty or resulting from action taken by the institutions of the Community. They shall facilitate the achievement of the Community's tasks. They shall abstain from any measure which could jeopardise the attainment of the objectives of this Treaty.

This Article effectively means that UK courts are now EU law courts and must be bound by, and give effect to, that law where it is operative. The reasons for the national courts acting in this manner were considered by John Temple Lang, Director in the Competition Directorate General, in an article entitled 'Duties of national courts under Community constitutional law' [1997] EL Rev 22. As he wrote:

> National courts are needed to give companies and individuals remedies which are as prompt, as complete and as immediate as the combined legal system of the Community and of Member states can provide. Only national courts can give injunctions against private parties for breach of Community law rules on, for example, equal pay for men and women, or on restrictive practices. Private parties have no standing to claim injunctions in the Court of Justice against a Member state; they can do so only in a national court. In other words, only a national court could give remedies to individuals and companies for breach of Community law which are as effective as the remedies for breach of national law.

European Union Act 2011

In September 2011, Parliament passed the European Union Act 2011. The main purpose of the Act was to make provision for the application of the post-Lisbon treaties. However, the Act also amended the European Communities Act (ECA) 1972 to ensure that any proposed future EU treaty, or amendment to the treaties, which purports to transfer competences or areas of power from the UK to the EU will have to be subject to a domestic referendum. Section 18 of the Act, for the first time, places the common law principle of parliamentary sovereignty on a statutory footing and states that all EU law takes effect in the UK only by virtue of the will of Parliament, as provided in the ECA 1972. Such measures were taken in an endeavour to provide clear statutory authority for the superiority of domestic law over EU law and to circumscribe any suggestion that EU law constitutes a new higher autonomous legal order in its own right. It has been suggested that these measures were a sop to the Eurosceptic wing of the Conservative Party within the coalition government and their precise effect remains to be seen.

The UK's position in the EU

It cannot go unnoticed, and uncommented upon, that the UK's relationship with the EU and its constituent members is a matter that raises concerns among some politicians and some members of the public – a concern strengthened by the flow of refugees and asylum seekers towards Europe in the second half of 2015. Prior to the General Election in 2015 the Conservative Party declared that, if elected, it would seek to renegotiate the UK's terms of membership of the EU and put the results of such negotiation to the public in a referendum on the UK's continued membership of the union. Following his party's success in the election, Prime Minister Cameron initiated his campaign of renegotiation towards the end of 2015, with the intention of holding the in/out referendum in June 2016.

5.2 SOURCES OF EUROPEAN UNION LAW

European Union law, depending on its nature and source, may have a direct effect on the domestic laws of its various members; that is, it may be open to individuals to rely on it without the need for their particular state to have enacted the law within its own legal system (see *Factortame*).

There are two types of direct effect. Vertical direct effect means that the individual can rely on EU law in any action in relation to their government, but cannot use it against other individuals. Horizontal direct effect allows the individual to use the EU provision in an action against other individuals. Other EU provisions only take effect when they have been specifically enacted within the various legal systems within the Union.

The sources of EU law are fourfold:

- internal treaties and protocols;
- international agreements;
- secondary legislation;
- decisions of the CJEU.

5.2.1 INTERNAL TREATIES

Internal treaties govern the Member states of the EU, and anything contained therein supersedes domestic legal provisions. Upon the UK joining the then Community, the Treaty of Rome was incorporated into UK law by the ECA 1972. Since that date the UK has been subject to the various iterations of the ruling treaties. As was considered previously, the ruling treaties are now:

- Treaty on European Union (TEU);
- Treaty on the Functioning of the European Union (TFEU);
- Charter of Fundamental Rights of the European Union.

As long as treaties are of a mandatory nature and are stated with sufficient clarity and precision, then they have both vertical and horizontal effect (*Van Gend en Loos* (1963)).

5.2.2   INTERNATIONAL TREATIES

International treaties are negotiated with other nations by the European Commission on behalf of the EU as a whole and are binding on the individual members of the EU.

5.2.3   SECONDARY LEGISLATION

Secondary legislation is provided for under Art 249 (formerly 189) of the Treaty of Rome. It provides for three types of legislation to be introduced by the European Council and Commission:

- *Regulations* apply to, and within, Member states generally, without the need for those states to pass their own legislation. They are binding and enforceable from the time of their creation and individual states do not have to pass any legislation to give effect to regulations. Thus, in *Macarthys Ltd v Smith* (1979), on a referral from the Court of Appeal to the ECJ, it was held that Art 157 (formerly 141) entitled the plaintiff to assert rights that were not available to her under national legislation, the Equal Pay Act 1970, that had been enacted before the UK had joined the EEC. Whereas the national legislation clearly did not include a comparison between former and present employees, Art 157's reference to 'equal pay for equal work' did encompass such a situation. Smith was consequently entitled to receive a similar level of remuneration to that of the former male employee who had done her job previously. The horizontal direct effect of regulations was confirmed by the ECJ in *Munoz y Cia SA v Frumar Ltd* (2002), in which it was held that the claimant was entitled to bring a civil claim against the defendant for failure to comply with EU labelling regulations.

   Regulations must be published in the *Official Journal* of the EU. The decision as to whether or not a law should be enacted in the form of a regulation is usually left to the Commission, but there are areas where the Treaty of Rome requires that the regulation form must be used. These areas relate to: the rights of workers to remain in Member states of which they are not nationals; the provision of state aid to particular indigenous undertakings or industries; and the regulation of EU accounts and budgetary procedures.

- *Directives*, on the other hand, state general goals and leave the precise implementation in the appropriate form to the individual Member states. Directives, however, tend to state the means as well as the ends to which they are aimed and the CJEU will give direct effect to directives that are sufficiently clear and complete (see *Van Duyn v Home Office* (1974)). Directives usually provide Member states with a time limit within which they are required to implement the provision within their own national laws. If they fail to do so, or implement the directive incompletely, then individuals may be able to cite and rely on the directive in their dealings with the state in question. Further, *Francovich v Italy* (1991) has established that individuals who have suffered as a consequence of a Member state's failure to implement EU law may seek damages against that state.

● *Decisions* on the operation of European laws and policies are not intended to have general effect but are aimed at particular states or individuals. They have the force of law under Art 288 (formerly 249).

● Additionally, Art 17(1) TEU (formerly 211 TEC) provides scope for the Commission to issue *recommendations* and *opinions* in relation to the operation of EU law. These have no binding force, although they may be taken into account in trying to clarify any ambiguities in domestic law.

5.2.4   JUDGMENTS OF THE COURT OF JUSTICE OF THE EUROPEAN UNION

The CJEU is the judicial arm of the EU and, in the field of EU law, its judgments overrule those of national courts. Under Art 267 (formerly 234), national courts have the right to apply to the CJEU for a preliminary ruling on a point of EU law before deciding a case.

The mechanism through which EU law becomes immediately and directly effective in the UK is provided by s 2(1) of the ECA 1972. Section 2(2) gives power to designated ministers or departments to introduce Orders in Council to give effect to other non-directly effective EU law.

5.3   THE INSTITUTIONS OF THE EUROPEAN UNION

The major institutions of the EU are: the Council of Ministers; the European Parliament; the European Commission; and the CJEU.

5.3.1   THE EUROPEAN COUNCIL AND THE COUNCIL OF THE EUROPEAN UNION

Understanding this section is complicated by the multiple uses of the words council and European. First of all it should be remembered that the European Union and its internal organisation are completely different from the *Council of Europe*, which is a human rights organisation consisting of those 47 countries across wider Europe that have signed up to the European Convention on Human Rights.

Then, as regards the EU a distinction has to be clearly drawn between the *Council of the European Union* and the *European Council* which will be considered in turn below.

The European Council
This institution of the European Union is made up of the heads of government of the Member states. It has a designated permanent president, at the moment the former

MAIN SOURCES OF EUROPEAN UNION LAW

1. Primary Sources:
Primary Legislation of the EU: made up of the various **Treaties**, e.g. the Treaty of Rome 1957 and the Treaty on the Functioning of the European Union. All treaties are ratified by the Member states

2. Secondary Sources:
- **Secondary Legislation**, made up of **Regulations, Decisions & Directives,** enacted by the EU Institutions **(Art 288 TFEU)**
- **Judgments the Court of Justice of the European Union (CJEU),** binding on national courts

3. Other Sources
- **General Principles of Law,** e.g. equality and protection of fundamental rights
- **International Treaties** agreed with bodies outside the EU

Why are these Sources of Law so Important?
Not only does EU law have **supremacy** (also known as primacy) over UK law, but it also has **direct effect** (if it satisfies relevant criteria) which means that it gives rights and obligations to individuals as well as state authorities, which may be enforced before national courts (*Van Gend en Loos* **case**)

FIGURE 5.2 *Sources of EU Law.*

Polish Prime Minister, Donald Tusk, who is charged with organising the meeting of the council. The president of the Commission and the High Representative of the Union for Foreign Affairs and Security Policy also take part in its meetings.

Initially an informal body, the council was formalised as a distinct EU institution in 2009 under the Treaty of Lisbon. The European Council has no formal legislative power as such, rather it is the strategic body that provides the union with general political directions and priorities. Its meetings take place at least twice every six months and are chaired by its president. Decisions are made on a consensus basis, except where the Treaties provide otherwise.

The Council of the European Union (Council of Ministers)

This council is made up of ministerial representatives of each of the 28 Member states of the EU. The actual composition of the Council, in its 10 different configurations, varies depending on the nature of the matter to be considered. When considering economic and financial matters (ECOFIN), the various states will be represented by their finance ministers or, if the matter before the Council relates to agriculture, the various agricultural ministers will attend.

The organisation of the various specialist councils falls to the president of the council and that post is held for six-monthly periods in rotation by the individual Member states of the EU. The Presidency of the Council is significant to the extent that the country holding the position can, to a large extent, control the agenda of the Council and thus can focus EU attention on areas that it considers to be of particular importance. The Foreign Affairs Council, that is, the meeting of national foreign ministers, is chaired by the Union's High Representative for Foreign Affairs and Security Policy, who is currently the Italian politician, Federica Mogherini.

Historically, the Council of Ministers was the supreme decision-making body of the EU and, as such, it had the final say in deciding upon EU legislation. However, the current position is that, for the most part, both the Council and European Parliament pass legislation put before them by the EU Commission, through a process of 'co-decision'. Although it normally acts on recommendations and proposals made to it by the Commission, the Council does have the power to instruct the Commission to undertake particular investigations and to submit detailed proposals for its consideration. In addition, under the citizens' right of initiative introduced by the Treaty of Lisbon, a million citizens may sign a petition inviting the Commission to submit a proposal to the Commission.

Council decisions are taken on a mixture of voting procedures. Some measures only require a simple majority; in others, a procedure of qualified majority voting is used; and in yet others, unanimity is required. Qualified majority voting is the procedure in which the votes of the 28 member countries are weighted in proportion to their population from 29 down to three votes each. The distribution of votes is:

Germany, France, Italy, United Kingdom	29 votes
Spain, Poland	27 votes
Romania	14 votes
Netherlands	13 votes
Belgium, Czech Republic, Greece, Hungary, Portugal	12 votes
Austria, Sweden, Bulgaria	10 votes
Denmark, Croatia, Ireland, Lithuania, Slovakia, Finland	7 votes
Cyprus, Estonia, Latvia, Luxembourg, Slovenia	4 votes
Malta	3 votes

From 1 November 2014 a double majority voting system was adopted, meaning that the qualified majority is reached if a draft decision is supported by at least 55 per cent of the Member states (i.e. 15 Member states) representing at least 65 per cent of the EU population.

The use of qualified majority voting has been extended under various treaties, but unanimity is still required in what can be considered as the more politically sensitive areas, such as those relating to the harmonisation of indirect taxation or the free movement of individuals.

In addition to the need for unanimity in such sensitive areas, there is also the ultimate safeguard of what is known as the Luxembourg Compromise. This procedure, instituted at the behest of the French government in 1966, permits individual Member states to exercise a right of veto in relation to any proposals that they consider to be contrary to a 'very important interest' of theirs. It has been suggested that David Cameron considered using this procedure to prevent the appointment of Jean-Claude Junker to the presidency of the EU Commission in 2014, but in the event, that 'nuclear' option was not deployed.

As the format of particular councils fluctuates, much of its day-to-day work is delegated to a Committee of Permanent Representatives, which operates under the title of COREPER.

5.3.2   THE EUROPEAN PARLIAMENT

The European Parliament is the directly elected European institution and, to that extent, it can be seen as the body that exercises democratic control over the operation of the EU. As in national parliaments, members are elected to represent constituencies, the elections being held every five years.

The Treaty of Lisbon provides for a maximum number of 751 MEPs with a maximum possible allocation of 96 and a minimum allocation of six MEPs, depending on size of population. For the 2014–19 session, Germany will have 96 MEPs, France 74 and Italy and the United Kingdom 73 each. The smallest countries such as Malta and Luxembourg will have six MEPs. The European Parliament's general secretariat is based in Luxembourg, and although the Parliament sits in plenary session in Strasbourg for one week in each month, its detailed and preparatory work is carried out through 22 permanent committees, which usually meet in Brussels. These permanent committees consider proposals from the Commission and provide the full Parliament with reports of such proposals for discussion.

5.3.3   POWERS OF THE EUROPEAN PARLIAMENT

Originally the powers of the European Parliament were merely advisory and supervisory but its powers have significantly increased since the early days of the EEC until now; following the Lisbon Treaty, it shares the EU legislative function with the Council through the process of co-decision-making, now referred to as 'the ordinary legislative procedure'. In this way, the vast majority of European laws are adopted jointly and on an equal footing by the European Parliament and the Council. However, in the case of 'special legislative procedures', the Parliament still retains only a consultative role. Thus, in areas such as taxation, it can only provide an advisory opinion to the Council. If such consultation is obligatory the proposal cannot acquire the force of law unless the Parliament has delivered an opinion, but the Council is not required to accept the opinion proffered.

The powers of the European Parliament should not be confused, however, with those of national parliaments in terms of initiating legislation. While the Parliament can reject, amend, or at its weakest advise on proposals for legislation, it cannot, itself, make such a proposal, being dependent on the Commission putting proposals before it before anything can become law. However, it does now have a similar power to that of the Council to request the Commission to submit particular proposals to the Council.

The European Parliament is, together with the Council of Ministers, the budgetary authority of the EU. The budget is drawn up by the Commission and is presented to both the Council and the Parliament. As regards what is known as 'obligatory' expenditure, the Council has the final say, but in relation to 'non-obligatory' expenditure, the Parliament has the final decision whether to approve the budget or not. Such budgetary control places the Parliament in an extremely powerful position to influence EU policy, but perhaps the most draconian power the Parliament wields is the ability to pass a vote of censure against the Commission, requiring it to resign en masse.

The events of 1998/99 saw a significant shift in the relationship between the Parliament and the Commission. In December 1998, as a result of sustained accusations of mismanagement, fraud and cover-ups levelled against the Commission, the Parliament voted not to discharge the Commission's accounts for 1996. Such action was, in effect, a declaration that the Community's budget had not been properly handled and was tantamount to a vote of no confidence in the Commission. In January 1999, the Community's Court of Auditors delivered what can only be described as a devastating report on fraud, waste, mismanagement and maladministration on the part of the Commission. It was found that the Commission had understated its financial obligations by £3.3 billion, and was so lax in its control that it had not even noticed that its banks were not paying any interest on huge amounts of money they were holding. The report of the Court of Auditors led to a vote of no confidence in the Commission in early January 1999 and, although the Commission survived the vote by a majority of 293 to 232, it had to accept the setting-up of a 'committee of wise persons' to investigate and report on its operation. At the time, the appointment of this committee was thought to be a diplomatic fudge, allowing the Commission to carry on under warning as to its future conduct. However, when the committee submitted its report, it was so damning that it was immediately obvious that the Parliament would certainly use its power to remove the Commission. To forestall this event, the Commission resigned en masse.

However, by the first week of July 1999, a new Commission had been proposed and gained the approval of the European Parliament later that month.

5.3.4   ECONOMIC AND SOCIAL COMMITTEE

If the Parliament represents the directly elected arm of the EU, then the Economic and Social Committee represents a collection of unelected, but nonetheless influential, interest groups throughout the EU. This Committee is a consultative institution and its opinion must be sought prior to the adoption by the Council of any Commission proposal. The Economic and Social Committee represents the underlying 'corporatist' nature of the EU, to the extent that it seeks to locate and express a commonality of view and opinion on proposals from such divergent interest groups as employers, trade unions and consumers. It is perhaps symptomatic of the attitude of recent British governments to this underlying corporatist, essentially Christian Democratic, strand within the EU that it dispensed with its own similar internal grouping, the National Economic Development Council, in 1992.

5.3.5 THE EUROPEAN COMMISSION

The European Commission is the executive of the EU and, in that role, it is responsible for the administration of EU policies. As considered previously, it is also the prime initiator of EU legislation. There are 28 commissioners chosen from the Member states to serve for renewable terms of four years. Commissioners are appointed to head departments with specific responsibility for furthering particular areas of EU policy. Once appointed, commissioners are expected to act in the general interest of the EU as a whole rather than in the partial interest of their own home country.

As a result of the Treaty of Nice, the five largest countries gave up one of their appointees in order that each of the then 25 Member states would be able to nominate a commissioner. However, with further enlargement, it was intended that a system of rotation be implemented for the benefit of the smaller member countries, while preventing an increase in the number of commissioners to match the new membership. However, such a procedure had not yet been implemented when Croatia joined the European Union in 2013, so the Health and Consumer Protection portfolio was split to create a twenty-eighth portfolio.

In pursuit of EU policy, the Commission is responsible for ensuring that Treaty obligations between the Member states are met and that Union laws relating to individuals are enforced. In order to fulfil these functions, the Commission has been provided with extensive powers both in relation to the investigation of potential breaches of EU law and the subsequent punishment of offenders.

The classic area in which these powers can be seen in operation is competition law. Under Arts 101 and 102 (formerly Arts 81 and 82) of the TFEU, the Commission has substantial powers to investigate and control potential monopolies and anti-competitive behaviour, and it has used these powers to levy what, in the case of private individuals, would amount to huge fines where breaches of EU competition law have been discovered. In November 2001, the Commission imposed a record fine of £534 million on a cartel of 13 pharmaceutical companies that had operated a price-fixing scheme within the EU in relation to the market for vitamins. The highest individual fine was against the Swiss company Roche, which had to pay £288 million, while the German company BASF was fined £185 million. The lowest penalty levelled was against Aventis, which was only fined £3 million due to its agreement to provide the Commission with evidence as to the operation of the cartel. Otherwise its fine would have been £70 million. The Commission took two years to investigate the operation of what it classified as a highly organised cartel, holding regular meetings to collude on prices, exchange sales figures and co-ordinate price increases.

In the following month, December 2001, Roche was again fined a further £39 million for engaging in another cartel, this time in the citric acid market. The total fines imposed in this instance amounted to £140 million.

In 2012 the Commission imposed the biggest antitrust penalty in its history, fining six firms including Philips, LG Electronics and Panasonic a total of €1.47 billion (£132 billion) for running two cartels for nearly a decade.

The 2006 Fining Guidelines (http://ec.europa.eu/competition/antitrust/legislation/fines.html) give the Commission the power to increase fines by 100 per cent for repeat offending, even if the infringements took place long before the existence of the cartel in question. Saint-Gobain, the car glass manufacturer, had been the subject of previous Commission decisions relating to similar infringements in 1984 and 1988. In this instance, the Commission increased Saint-Gobain's fine by 60 per cent for the earlier violations, but in March 2014, the General court (see below, 5.3.6) announced its decision to reduce it, from €880 million to €715 million.

In 2004 the then EU Competition Commissioner, Mario Monti, levied an individual record fine of €497 million (£340 million) on Microsoft for abusing its dominant position in the PC operating systems market. In addition, the commissioner required Microsoft to disclose 'complete and accurate' interface documents to allow rival servers to operate with the Microsoft Windows system, or face penalties of €2 million (£1.4 million) for each day of non-compliance. In January 2006 Microsoft offered to make available part of its source code – the basic instructions for the Windows operating system. In an assertion of its complete compliance with Mario Monti's decision, Microsoft insisted it had actually gone beyond the Commission's remedy by opening up part of the source code behind Windows to rivals willing to pay a licence fee.

The offer, however, was dismissed by many as a public relations exercise. As a lawyer for Microsoft's rivals explained, 'Microsoft is offering to dump a huge load of source code on companies that have not asked for source code and cannot use it. Without a road map that says how to use the code, a software engineer will not be able to design inter-operable products.'

In February 2006 Microsoft repeated its claim that it had fully complied with the Commission's requirements. It also announced that it wanted an oral hearing on the allegations before national competition authorities and senior EU officials, a proposal that many saw as merely a delaying tactic postponing the imposition of the threatened penalties until the court of first instance has heard the company's appeal against the original allegation of abuse of its dominant position and, of course, the related €497 million fine. In July 2006, the Commission fined Microsoft an additional €280.5 million, €1.5 million per day from 16 December 2005 to 20 June 2006. On 17 September 2007, Microsoft lost their appeal and in October 2007, it announced that it would comply with the rulings.

However, in February 2008 Microsoft was fined an additional €899 million for failure to comply with the 2004 antitrust decision. In June 2012 Microsoft's appeal was rejected by the General Court of the EU (see below), although the total of the fine for non-compliance was reduced to €860. As a result, Microsoft was fined a total of €1.64 billion.

In May 2009 the Commission levied a new record individual fine against the American computer chip manufacturer Intel for abusing its dominance of the microchip market. Intel was accused of using discounts to squeeze its nearest rival, Advanced Micro Devices (AMD), out of the market. The amount of the fine was €1.06 billion

(£950 million, or $1.45 billion). Intel's subsequent appeal was rejected by the General Court in June 2014. The Court said that the fine amounted to 4.15 per cent of Intel's annual revenue, less than half of the maximum 10 per cent fine that the Commission had the power to levy.

The Commission also acts, under instructions from the Council, as the negotiator between the EU and external countries.

In addition to these executive functions, the Commission has a vital part to play in the EU's legislative process. The Council can only act on proposals put before it by the Commission. The Commission therefore has a duty to propose to the Council measures that will advance the achievement of the EU's general policies.

5.3.6 THE COURT OF JUSTICE OF THE EUROPEAN UNION

The CJEU is the judicial arm of the EU, and in the field of EU law its judgments overrule those of national courts. It consists of 28 judges, one from each Member state, assisted by eight Advocates General, and sits in Luxembourg. The Court may sit as a full court, in a Grand Chamber of 13 judges or in Chambers of three or five judges. The role of the Advocate General is to investigate the matter submitted to the Court and to produce a report, together with a recommendation, for the consideration of the Court. The actual Court is free to accept the report or not as it sees fit.

The SEA 1986 provided for a new Court of First Instance to be attached to the existing Court of Justice. Under the Treaty of Lisbon it was renamed the General Court. It has jurisdiction in first instance cases, with appeals going to the CJEU on points of law. The former jurisdiction of the Court of First Instance, in relation to internal claims by EU employees, was transferred to a newly created European Union Civil Service Tribunal in 2004. Together the three distinct courts constitute *the Court of Justice of the European Union*. The aim of introducing the two latter courts was to reduce the burden of work on the CJEU, but there is a right of appeal, on points of law only, to the full CJEU.

The Court of Justice performs two key functions:

(a) It decides whether any measures adopted, or rights denied, by the Commission, Council or any national government are compatible with Treaty obligations. Such actions may be raised by any EU institution, government or individual. In October 2000, the Court of Justice annulled EU Directive 98/43, which required Member states to impose a ban on advertising and sponsorship relating to tobacco products, because it had been adopted on the basis of the wrong provisions of the EC Treaty. The Directive had been adopted on the basis of the provisions of the Treaty relating to the elimination of obstacles to the completion of the internal market, but the Court decided that under the circumstances, it was difficult to see how a ban on tobacco advertising or sponsorship could facilitate the trade in tobacco products.

Although a partial prohibition on particular types of advertising or sponsorship might legitimately come within the internal market provisions of the

Treaty, the Directive was clearly aimed at protecting public health and it was therefore improper to base its adoption on the freedom to provide services (*Germany v European Parliament and EU Council* (Case C-376/98)).

A Member state may fail to comply with its Treaty obligations in a number of ways. It might fail or indeed refuse to comply with a provision of the Treaty or a regulation; alternatively, it might refuse to implement a directive within the allotted time provided for. Under such circumstances, the state in question will be brought before the CJEU, either by the Commission or another Member state, or indeed individuals within the state concerned.

In 1996, following the outbreak of 'mad cow disease' (BSE) in the UK, the European Commission imposed a ban on the export of UK beef. The ban was partially lifted in 1998 and, subject to conditions relating to the documentation of an animal's history prior to slaughter, from 1 August 1999, exports satisfying those conditions were authorised for despatch within the Community. When the French Food Standards Agency continued to raise concerns about the safety of British beef, the Commission issued a protocol agreement, which declared that all meat and meat products from the UK would be distinctively marked as such. However, France continued in its refusal to lift the ban.

Subsequently, the Commission applied to the CJEU for a declaration that France was in breach of Community law for failing to lift the prohibition on the sale of correctly labelled British beef in French territory. In December 2001, in *Commission of the European Communities v France*, the CJEU held that the French government had failed to put forward a ground of defence capable of justifying the failure to implement the relevant Decisions and was therefore in breach of Community law.

France was also fined in July 2005 for breaching EU fishing rules. On that occasion the CJEU imposed the first ever 'combination' penalty, under which a lump-sum fine was payable, but in addition France is liable to a periodic penalty for every six months until it had shown it was fully complying with EU fisheries laws. The CJEU set the lump-sum fine at €20 million and the periodic penalty at €57.8 million.

The Court held that it was possible and appropriate to impose both types of penalty at the same time, in circumstances where the breach of obligations has both continued for a long period and is inclined to persist.

(b) It provides authoritative rulings, at the request of national courts, under Art 267 (formerly 234) of the TFEU, on the interpretation of points of EU law. When an application is made under Art 267, the national proceedings are suspended until such time as the determination of the point in question is delivered by the CJEU. While the case is being decided by the CJEU, the national court is expected to provide appropriate interim relief, even if this involves going against a domestic legal provision, as in the *Factortame* case.

This procedure can take the form of a preliminary ruling where the request precedes the actual determination of a case by the national court.

Article 267 provides that:

The Court of Justice shall have jurisdiction to give preliminary rulings concerning:

(a)   the interpretation of treaties;
(b)   the validity and interpretation of acts of the institutions of the Union and of the European Central Bank;
(c)   the interpretation of the statutes of bodies established by an act of the Council, where those statutes so provide.

Where such a question is raised before any court or tribunal of a Member state, that court or tribunal may, if it considers that a decision on the question is necessary to enable it to give judgment, request the Court of Justice to give a ruling thereon.

Where any such question is raised in a case pending before a court or tribunal of a Member state against whose decision there is no judicial remedy under national law, that court or tribunal shall bring the matter before the Court of Justice.

The question as to the extent of the CJEU's authority arose in *Arsenal Football Club plc v Reed* (2003), which dealt with the sale of football souvenirs and memorabilia bearing the names of the football club and consequently infringing its registered trademarks. On first hearing, the Chancery Division of the High Court referred the question of the interpretation of the Trade Marks Directive (89/104) in relation to the issue of trademark infringement to the CJEU. After the CJEU had made its decision, the case came before Laddie J for application, who declined to follow that decision. The grounds for so doing were that the ambit of the CJEU's powers was clearly set out in Art 234. Consequently, where, as in this case, the CJEU makes a finding of fact that reverses the finding of a national court on those facts, it exceeds its jurisdiction and it follows that its decisions are not binding on the national court. The Court of Appeal later reversed Laddie J's decision on the ground that the CJEU had not disregarded the conclusions of fact made at the original trial and, therefore, he should have followed its ruling and decided the case in Arsenal's favour. Nonetheless, Laddie J's general point as to the CJEU's authority remains valid.

It is clear that it is for the national court and not the individual parties concerned to make the reference. Where the national court or tribunal is not the 'final' court or tribunal, the reference to the CJEU is discretionary. Where the national court or tribunal is the 'final' court, then reference is obligatory. However, there are circumstances under which a 'final' court need not make a reference under Art 267 (formerly 234). These are:

●   where the question of EU law is not truly relevant to the decision to be made by the national court;

- where there has been a previous interpretation of the provision in question by the CJEU so that its meaning has been clearly determined;
- where the interpretation of the provision is so obvious as to leave no scope for any reasonable doubt as to its meaning.

This last instance has to be used with caution given the nature of EU law; for example, the fact that it is expressed in several languages using legal terms that might have different connotations within different jurisdictions. However, it is apparent that where the meaning is clear, no reference need be made.

Mention has already been made to cases that have been referred under the Art 267 procedure. Thus, the first case to be referred to the CJEU from the High Court was *Van Duyn v Home Office* (1974), the first case to be referred from the Court of Appeal was *Macarthys Ltd v Smith* (1979), and the first from the House of Lords was *R v Henn* (1982).

MB v Secretary of State for Work and Pensions [2016] UKSC 53

Since the implementation of the Gender Recognition Act (GRA) 2004, it has been possible for transgender individuals to apply to a Gender Recognition Panel for a Gender Recognition Certificate confirming that for all legal purposes they are to be recognised and treated in line with their acquired gender. However, when the GRA 2004 was passed a legally valid marriage could only subsist in law between a man and a woman (a position altered subsequently by the Marriage (Same Sex Couples) Act 2013). For that reason, the GRA made specific provision for married applicants, whose change of legally recognised gender would have resulted in their being married to a person of the same gender as themselves. Thus as a result of this purely temporary legal incompatibility, although an unmarried person who satisfied the criteria for gender recognition was entitled to a full gender recognition certificate, a married person, even though they met the same criteria, would only be entitled to an interim gender recognition certificate, which did not give full legal recognition of their acquired gender status. The consequence of this concatenation of circumstances and laws was that, transgender people in opposite-sex marriages formed before 2013 could not be awarded a full gender recognition certificate unless they annulled their weddings, a provision specifically facilitated by the GRA. As a result, a number of transgender people who were unwilling to annul their marriages for a variety of reasons, be it friendship, love or religion, were effectively locked in to their birth gender with, for them, no acceptable way to obtain official recognition of their acquired gender and the rules that might apply as a consequence of that recognition. So much for English law, however Art 4 of Council Directive 79/7/EEC on the Progressive Implementation of the Principle of Equal Treatment for Men and Women in Matters of Social Security, including state benefits such old age and retirement pensions requires that there shall be 'no discrimination whatsoever on ground of sex either directly, or indirectly by reference in particular to marital or family status . . .'

In *MB* a married transgender woman appealed to the Supreme Court against a decision by the social security tribunal, that she would only be entitled to her state retirement pension at the age of 65, as if she were a man. Her case was that such a ruling was contrary to the directive and that is should take precedence over the UK law. The Supreme Court was divided on the question, and in the absence of Court of Justice authority directly in point, it considered itself unable to resolve the appeal without a reference to the Court of Justice. The stark question formulated by the Supreme Court was:

> whether Council Directive 79/7 EEC precludes the imposition in national law of a requirement that, in addition to satisfying the physical, social and psychological criteria for recognising a change of gender, a person who has changed gender must also be unmarried in order to qualify for a state retirement pension.

The immediate point of examining *MB* is to demonstrate the way in which under currently prevailing circumstances a decision in favour of *MB* would eventually require the government to change the existing rule preventing the full recognition of the rights of all transgender people. However, it is not really possible to predict what the political circumstances may be in the future, or indeed which aspects of EU law will still be applicable in the UK (or England for that matter), but what can be said is that the current unsatisfactory and unnecessary situation need not have arisen and should have been remedied when the Marriage (Same Sex Couples) Act 2013)) was implemented.

Mention has also been made in Chapter 4 of the methods of interpretation used by courts in relation to EU law. It will be recalled that, in undertaking such a task, a purposive and contextual approach is mainly adopted, as against the more restrictive methods of interpretation favoured in relation to UK domestic legislation. The clearest statement of this purposive, contextualist approach adopted by the CJEU is contained in its judgment in the *CILFIT* case:

> Every provision of EU law must be placed in its context and interpreted in the light of the provisions of EU law as a whole, regard being had to the objectives thereof and to its state of evolution at the date on which the provision in question is to be applied.

It can be appreciated that the reservations considered previously in regard to judicial creativity and intervention in policy matters in the UK courts apply *a fortiori* to the decisions of the CJEU.

Another major difference between the CJEU and the courts within the English legal system is that the former is not bound by the doctrine of precedent in the same way as the latter is. It is always open to the CJEU to depart from its previous decisions where it considers it appropriate to do so. Although it will endeavour to maintain consistency, it has, on occasion, ignored its own previous decisions, as in *European Parliament v Council* (1990), where it recognised the right of the Parliament to institute an action against the Council.

The manner in which EU law operates to control sex discrimination through the Equal Treatment Directive is of significant interest and, in *Marshall v Southampton and West Hampshire Area Health Authority* (1993), a number of the points that have been considered above were highlighted. Ms Marshall had originally been required to retire earlier than a man in her situation would have been required to do. She successfully argued before the CJEU that such a practice was discriminatory and contrary to Community Directive 76/207 on the equal treatment of men and women.

The action related to the level of compensation she was entitled to as a consequence of this breach. UK legislation, the Sex Discrimination Act 1975, had set limits on the level of compensation that could be recovered for acts of sex discrimination. Marshall argued that the imposition of such limits was contrary to the Equal Treatment Directive and that, in establishing such limits, the UK had failed to comply with the Directive.

The Court of Appeal referred the case to the ECJ, as it then was, under Art 267 (formerly 234) and the latter determined that the rights set out in relation to compensation under Art 5 of the Directive were directly effective, and that, as the purpose of the Directive was to give effect to the principle of equal treatment, that could only be achieved by either reinstatement or the awarding of adequate compensation. The decision of the ECJ therefore overruled the financial limitations placed on sex discrimination awards and effectively overruled the domestic legislation.

P v S and Cornwall CC (1996) extended the ambit of unlawful sex discrimination under the Directive to cover people who have undergone surgical gender reorientation (sex change). However, in *Grant v South West Trains Ltd* (1998), the ECJ declined to extend the Directive to cover discrimination on the grounds of sexual orientation (homosexuality), even though the Advocate General had initially supported the extension of the Directive to same-sex relationships. While *Grant* was in the process of being decided in the ECJ, a second case, *R v Secretary of State for Defence ex p Perkins (No 2)* (1998), had been brought before the English courts arguing a similar point, that discrimination on grounds of sexual orientation was covered by the Equal Treatment Directive. Initially, the High Court had referred the matter, under Art 267 (formerly 234), to the ECJ for decision, but on the decision in *Grant* being declared, the referral was withdrawn. In withdrawing the reference, Lightman J considered the proposition of counsel for Perkins to the effect that:

> . . . there have been a number of occasions where the ECJ has overruled its previous decisions; that the law is not static; and, accordingly, in a dynamic and developing field such as discrimination in employment there must be a prospect that a differently constituted ECJ may depart from the decision in *Grant* . . . But, to justify a reference, the possibility that the ECJ will depart from its previous decision must be more than theoretical: it must be a realistic possibility. The decision in *Grant* was of the full Court; it is only some four months old; there has been no development in case law or otherwise since the decision which can give cause for the ECJ reconsidering that decision . . . I can see no realistic prospect of any change of mind on the part of the ECJ.

It could be pointed out that there could be no change in case law if judges such as Lightman J refused to send similar cases to the CJEU, but there may well be sense, if not virtue, in his refusal to refer similar cases to the court within such a short timescale.

5.3.7   THE COURT OF AUDITORS

Given the part that the Court of Auditors played in the 1998/99 struggle between the Parliament and the Commission, the role of this body should not be underestimated.

As its name suggests, it is responsible for providing an external audit of the EU's finances. It examines the legality, regularity and soundness of the management of all the EU's revenue and expenditure.

5.4   THE EUROPEAN COURT OF HUMAN RIGHTS

The Convention for the Protection of Human Rights and Fundamental Freedoms, better known as the 'European Convention on Human Rights', was opened for signature in Rome on 4 November 1950; it entered into force on 3 September 1953. The European Court of Human Rights (ECtHR) was subsequently established to hear cases under the Convention in 1959.

It has to be established and emphasised from the outset that the substance of this section has absolutely nothing to do with the EU as such; the Council of Europe, of which the ECtHR is the adjudicatory institution, is a completely distinct organisation and, although membership of the two organisations overlaps, they are not the same. The Council of Europe has 47 countries as members with a combined population of more than 800 million people and is concerned not with economic matters but with the protection of civil rights and freedoms.

It is gratifying, at least to a degree, to recognise that the ECHR and its Court (the ECtHR) are no longer a matter of mysterious external control, the Human Rights Act (HRA) 1988 having incorporated the ECHR into UK law, making the ECtHR the supreme court in matters related to its jurisdiction. Much attention was paid to the ECHR and the HRA in Chapter 2 (see above, 2.5), so it only remains to consider the structure and operation of the ECtHR. Two points should be emphasised at this juncture. First, although the number of domestic cases relating to the ECHR will continue to increase and consequently domestic human rights jurisprudence will emerge and develop, it should be borne in mind that in relation to these cases, the ultimate court of appeal remains the ECtHR. Secondly, as has been considered at 2.5, s 2 of the HRA requires previous decisions of the ECtHR to be taken into consideration by domestic courts, and this means *all* decisions of the ECtHR, not just the cases that directly involve the UK. Consequently, it remains imperative that students of the UK legal system be aware of, and take into consideration, the decisions of that court.

The Convention originally established two institutions:

(a)   *The European Commission of Human Rights.* This body was charged with the task of examining, and if need be investigating the circumstances of, petitions submitted to it. If the Commission was unable to reach a negotiated solution between the parties concerned, it referred the matter to the Court of Human Rights.

(b)   *The ECtHR.* The ECHR provides that the judgment of the Court shall be final and that parties to it will abide by the decisions of the Court. This body, sitting in Strasbourg, was, and remains, responsible for all matters relating to the interpretation and application of the current Convention.

It is frequently stated, and with justification, that the ECHR and the ECtHR have been the victims of their own success, with the number of applications being made to them increasing year upon year. The ever-increasing pressure on the institutions was exacerbated by the break-up of the old Communist Eastern Bloc and the fact that the newly independent countries, in the full sense of the word, became signatories to the Convention. As the workload increased, so the incipient sclerosis of the original structure became apparent in the ever-increasing backlog of applications waiting to be dealt with. As a consequence of such pressure, it became necessary to streamline the procedure by amalgamating the two previous institutions into one Court. In pursuit of this aim, Protocol 11 to the Convention was introduced in 1994. A protocol to the Convention is a text which adds one or more rights to the original Convention or amends certain of its provisions. They are binding only on those states that have signed and ratified them.

The new ECtHR came into operation on 1 November 1998, although the Commission continued to deal with cases that had already been declared admissible for a further year. Nonetheless, it was still accepted that the court needed additional reform to allow it to function effectively under the ever-increasing burden of cases it has to deal with. The following are further suggestions and actions to achieve this necessary reform.

The Woolf Report

In 2005 the former Lord Chief Justice of England, Lord Woolf, led a panel to consider what steps could be taken to deal with the ECtHR's current and projected caseload.

As the review, issued in December 2005, repeated, the Court was a victim of its success. Nonetheless, it was faced with an enormous and ever-growing workload, thus it was quite clear that something had to be done, in the short term, if the Court was not to be overwhelmed by its workload.

Among the Review's main recommendations were the following:

(i)   *The Court should redefine what constitutes an application*

It should deal only with properly completed application forms that contain all the information required for the Court to process the application.

(ii)   *Satellite offices of the Registry should be established*

These would be located in key countries that produce high numbers of inadmissible applications. The satellite offices would provide applicants with information as to the Court's admissibility criteria, and the availability, locally, of ombudsmen and other alternative methods of resolving disputes. This could divert a significant number of cases away from the Court. Satellite offices would also be responsible for the initial processing of applications. They would then send applications, together with short summaries in either French or English, to the relevant division in Strasbourg. This would enable Strasbourg lawyers to prepare draft judgments more quickly.

(iii)   *Ombudsmen and other methods of alternative dispute resolution should be used more*

Not surprisingly, given his championing of alternative dispute resolution (ADR) in the English legal system, Lord Woolf's team recommended the encouragement of greater use of national Ombudsmen and other methods of ADR, thus diverting from the Court a large number of complaints that should never have come to it in the first place. As part of this approach the panel also recommended the establishment of a specialist '*Friendly Settlement Unit*' in the Court Registry, to initiate and pursue proactively a greater number of friendly settlements.

(iv)   *The Court should deliver a greater number of pilot judgments*

Pilot judgments refer to applications concerning similar issues, also known as 'systemic issues', that arise from the non-conformity of a particular country's domestic law with the convention. Following the Woolf recommendations, the Court has adopted the procedure of giving priority to examining one or more specific applications of that kind while adjourning similar cases. Once the pilot case is determined, the Court calls on the government concerned to bring the domestic legislation into line with the convention and indicates the general measures to be taken.

Priority rules

In June 2009 the Rules of Court were changed to alter the order in which cases may be dealt with. Until then, cases had been processed mainly on a chronological basis. As a consequence, however, some extremely serious allegations of human rights violations could take several years to be examined by the Court. This clearly unsatisfactory procedure was amended to allow for the prioritisation of certain applications.

Protocol 14

Protocol 14, although originally adopted in May 2004, was not fully ratified until 2010. The measure was designed to improve the efficiency of the Court through four provisions, which:

- extended the period of judicial service from six to nine years;
- allowed for a single judge, assisted by a non-judicial rapporteur, to reject cases where they are clearly inadmissible from the outset. This replaces the system where, previously, inadmissibility was decided by committees of three judges;
- allowed committees of three judges to give judgments in repetitive cases where the case law of the Court is already well established, where such cases were previously heard by chambers of seven judges;
- introduced a new admissibility criterion to the effect that the applicant must have suffered a 'significant disadvantage' as a result of the breach of their

rights. There is the safeguard that the case must have already been duly considered by a domestic tribunal, with the additional proviso that the case raises no general human rights concerns requiring the case to be examined on its merits.

Given the continued delay on the part of the Russian Federation in ratifying Protocol 14, the other members of the European Council decided in May 2009 that the protocol should be adopted by all those countries willing to agree to its immediate implementation. Subsequently, the Russian Federation ratified the protocol in January 2010, and given the fact that Russia remains the major source of applications coming before the ECtHR, this should have a considerable impact on the rate with which the court processes applications and cases.

Council of Europe conferences

Since 2010, three conferences have been convened to consider the future of the Court and to identify methods of guaranteeing long-term effectiveness.

In February 2010 the *Interlaken Declaration* stated that additional measures were urgently required in order to:

(i)   achieve a balance between the number of judgments and decisions delivered by the Court and the number of incoming applications;

(ii)   enable the Court to reduce the backlog of cases and to adjudicate new cases within a reasonable time, particularly those concerning serious violations of human rights;

(iii)   ensure the full and rapid execution of judgments of the Court and the effectiveness of its supervision by the Committee of Ministers.

While recognising and upholding the right of individuals to petition the Court it saw the need to:

* improve the filtering out of inadmissible claims;
* reduce the number of repetitive cases;
* facilitate the adoption of friendly settlements;
* encourage the use of pilot cases to decide general issues.

As for the Court, it was invited to:

* avoid reconsidering questions of fact or national law that have been considered and decided by national authorities;
* apply uniformly and rigorously the criteria concerning admissibility and jurisdiction;
* consider the possibility of applying the principle *de minimis non curat praetor* (to the effect that the court should not bother with petty cases).

Subsequently in April 2011 the *Izmir Declaration* invited Member states to 'ensure that effective domestic remedies exist . . . providing for a decision on an alleged violation of the convention and, where necessary, its redress', thus lessening the pressure on the ECtHR. It more specifically focused on the advisability of introducing 'a procedure allowing the highest national courts to request advisory opinions from the [Strasbourg] Court concerning the interpretation and application of the convention'.

Finally, in April 2012 the *Brighton Declaration* agreed the following measures designed to tackle perceived shortcomings in the operation of the court:

- amending the convention to specifically include the principles of subsidiarity and the margin of appreciation. The declaration emphasised the fundamental importance of the principle of subsidiarity and pointed out that the ECtHR acts as a safeguard for violations that *have not been remedied at a national level*;

- amending the convention to tighten the admissibility criteria in order that trivial cases can be passed over to allow the court to focus on more serious abuses. The declaration recognised the significant steps already undertaken to achieve this end within the framework of Protocol No 14;

- reducing the time limit for applications to the court from six to four months;

- improving the selection process for judges in recognition of their crucial role in deciding cases. It was emphasised that judgments of the court need to be clear and consistent in order to promote legal certainty. This was seen as helping national courts to apply the convention more precisely, and helping potential applicants decide whether they have grounds for making an application. However, it was also stressed that consistency in the application of the convention did not require the implementation of the convention uniformly through all 47 states, thus recognising the need to allow for a margin of appreciation;

- ensuring that state parties to the convention executed judgments of the court expeditiously by requiring the committee of ministers to take effective measures in respect of any state party that failed to comply with its obligations under Art 46 of the Convention;

- setting out a roadmap for further reform to anticipate future challenges and develop a vision for the future of the convention, so that future decisions can be taken in a timely and coherent manner.

The conference declarations above led to the adoption of Protocols 15 and 16 to the Convention. Protocol 15, adopted in 2013, inserted references to the principle of subsidiarity and the doctrine of the margin of appreciation into the Convention's preamble, as a means of reducing the number of cases that can be taken to the Court. It also reduces from six to four months the time within which an application must be lodged with the Court after a final national decision.

The same year, 2013, also saw the adoption of Protocol 16, which allows the highest domestic courts and tribunals to request the Court to give advisory opinions on questions of principle relating to the interpretation or application of the rights and freedoms defined in the convention. Not only would this reduce the need for cases to proceed to the Court but it was also designed to foster dialogue between courts and enhance the Court's 'constitutional' role. Any such requests would always be optional, could only be submitted by constitutional courts or courts of last instance, and the opinions given by the Court would not be binding.

Court statistics and further reform

In September 2014 in the course of a presentation to a joint meeting of various committees concerned with the reform of the Court, the Registrar of the Court, Erik Fribergh, presented statistics which he claimed showed the success of previous measures and undercut the need for further reform. As he stated, on 1 July 2014 the Court had 84,515 pending applications – half as many as in 2011. The Registrar presented the case for a temporary extraordinary budget of 30 million over eight years starting in 2015 to process the remaining backlog of cases and that thereafter the Court 'would deal with all incoming cases in a way which would roughly respect the Brighton criteria.'

Fribergh, rather sarcastically, concluded:

> The recent years have seen great success in terms of how the Court has got to grips with its case-load. The Court should be allowed to continue with this steady progress without the distraction of constant and sometimes confused calls for further reform. My view is that Member States should stop focusing on 'how to reform the Court' and rather focus on 'how can the Convention rights be better implemented in Member States' and how can we better implement the Court's judgments.

Whether those who still demand further reform of the Court and its operations, particularly those in the UK, will agree with Fribergh's conclusions remains to be seen.

Structure of the court

The ECtHR consists of 47 judges, representing the number of signatories to the ECHR, although they do not have to be chosen from each state and, in any case, sit as individuals rather than representatives of their state. Judges are elected, by the Parliamentary Assembly of the Council of Europe, generally for nine years, but arrangements have been put in place so that one-half of the membership of the judicial panel will be required to seek renewal every three years.

The Plenary Court elects its President, two Vice Presidents and two Presidents of Section for a period of three years. It is divided into four Sections, whose composition, fixed for three years, is geographically and gender balanced and takes account of the different legal systems of the contracting states. Each Section is presided over by a President, two of the Section Presidents being at the same time Vice Presidents of the Court. Committees of three judges within each Section deal with preliminary issues and, to that extent, they do the filtering formerly done by the Commission. Cases are actually heard by Chambers of seven members chosen on the basis of rotation. Additionally, there is a Grand Chamber of 17 judges made up of the President, Vice Presidents and Section Presidents and other judges by rotation. The Grand Chamber deals with the most important cases that require a reconsideration of the accepted interpretations of the ECHR. Again, the Grand Chamber is established with a view to geographical balance and different legal traditions. The Section President and the judge elected in respect of the state concerned sit in each case. Where the latter is not a member of the Section, he sits as an *ex officio* member of the Chamber.

Procedure before the Court

Any individual or contracting state may submit an application alleging a breach by a contracting state of one of the ECHR rights. Individuals can submit applications themselves, but legal representation is recommended and is required for hearings. Although a legal aid scheme has been set up by the Council of Europe for applicants who cannot fund their cases, recovery is usual from any award of monetary compensation.

Hearings are public, unless the Chamber decides otherwise on account of exceptional circumstances, and all documents filed with the Court's Registry are accessible to the public. It is, however, quite common for negotiations towards a friendly settlement to take place during proceedings, with the Registrar acting as intermediary, and such negotiations are confidential.

Admissibility procedure

Prior to Protocol 14 coming into full effect, each application was assigned to a Section whose President designated a rapporteur, who examined it and decided whether it should be dealt with by a three-member Committee or by a seven-member Chamber. Now the issue of admissibility is dealt with by a single judge under Protocol 14.

Procedure on the merits

The President of the Chamber may grant leave, or invite any contracting state that is not party to the proceedings or any person concerned who is not the applicant, to submit written comments and, in exceptional circumstances, to make representations at the hearing. A contracting state whose national is an applicant in the case is entitled to intervene as of right.

The Chamber hearing the case may at any time remit it to the Grand Chamber where it is concerned that it raises an important issue relating to the interpretation of the ECHR or a major extension of previous precedent.

In practice, only a minority of registered applications result in a judgment on the merits of the case. Other applications are completed at an earlier stage by being declared inadmissible, being otherwise struck out or following a friendly settlement. Examples of such friendly procedures are *Cornwell v UK* and *Leary v UK*, both reported in 2000. These cases both involved men whose wives died, leaving them solely responsible for their children. Had they been women in similar situations, they would have received benefits, namely a Widowed Mother's Allowance and a Widow's Payment, payable under the Social Security Contributions and Benefits Act 1992. The applicants complained that the lack of benefits for widowers under British social security legislation discriminated against them on grounds of sex, in breach of Art 14 (prohibition of discrimination) of the ECHR, taken in conjunction with both Art 8 (right to respect for private and family life) and Art 1 of Protocol No 1 (protection of property) of the ECHR. The cases were struck out following a friendly settlement in which Cornwell and Leary received back payment of monies due and further payments until the Welfare Reform and Pensions Act 1999 came into force, which equalised the position.

Judgments

Chambers decide by a majority vote and usually reports give a single decision. However, any judge in the case is entitled to append a separate opinion, either concurring or dissenting.

Within three months of delivery of the judgment of a Chamber, any party may request that a case be referred to the Grand Chamber if it raises a serious question of interpretation or application, or a serious issue of general importance. Consequently, the Chamber's judgment only becomes final at the expiry of a three-month period, or earlier if the parties state that they do not intend to request a referral. If the case is referred to the Grand Chamber, its decision, taken on a majority vote, is final. All final judgments of the Court are binding on the respondent states concerned. Responsibility for supervising the execution of judgments lies with the Committee of Ministers of the Council of Europe, which is required to verify that states have taken adequate remedial measures in respect of any violation of the ECHR.

In deciding cases, the ECtHR makes use of two related principles: the doctrine of the margin of appreciation; and the principle of proportionality.

Margin of appreciation

This refers to the fact that the ECtHR recognises that there may well be a range of responses to particular crises or social situations within individual states, which might well involve some legitimate limitation on the rights established under the ECHR. The Court recognises that in such areas, the response should be decided at the local level, rather than being imposed centrally. The most obvious, but by no means the only, situations that involve the recognition of the margin of appreciation are the fields of morality and state security. For example, *Wingrove v UK* (1997) concerned the refusal of the British Board of Film Classification to give a certificate of classification to the video film, *Visions of Ecstasy*, on the grounds that it was blasphemous, thus effectively banning it. The applicant, the director of the film, claimed that the refusal to grant a certificate of classification to the film amounted to a breach of his rights to free speech under Art 10 of the ECHR. The Court rejected his claim, holding that the offence of blasphemy, by its very nature, did not lend itself to precise legal definition. Consequently, national authorities 'must be afforded a degree of flexibility in assessing whether the facts of a particular case fall within the accepted definition of the offence'. In reaching its decision, the Court clearly set out how the doctrine was to operate and its justifications. It also explained the different ranges of the margin of appreciation that will be allowed in different areas. Thus:

> Whereas there is little scope under Article 10 para 2 of the Convention (Art 10(2)) for restrictions on political speech or on debate of questions of public interest, a wider margin of appreciation is generally available to the Contracting States when regulating freedom of expression in relation to matters liable to offend intimate personal convictions within the sphere of morals or, especially, religion. Moreover, as in the field of morals, and perhaps to an even greater degree, there is no uniform European conception of the requirements of 'the protection of the rights of others' in relation to attacks on their religious convictions. What is likely to cause substantial offence to persons of a particular religious persuasion will vary significantly from time to time and from place to place, especially in an era characterised by an ever growing array of faiths and denominations. By reason of their direct and continuous contact with the vital forces of their countries, State authorities are in principle in a better position than the international judge to give an opinion on the exact content of these requirements with regard to the rights of others as well as on the 'necessity' of a 'restriction' intended to protect from such material those whose deepest feelings and convictions would be seriously offended.

In *Civil Service Unions v UK* (1988), it was held that national security interests were of such paramount concern that they outweighed individual rights of freedom of association. Hence, the unions had no remedy under the ECHR for the removal of their members' rights to join and be in a trade union.

It should also be borne in mind that states can enter a derogation from particular provisions of the ECHR, or the way in which they operate in particular areas or circumstances. The UK entered such derogation in relation to the extended detention of terrorist suspects without charge under the Prevention of Terrorism (Temporary Provisions) Act 1989, subsequently replaced and extended by the Terrorism Act 2000. Those powers had been held to be contrary to Art 5 of the ECHR by the ECtHR in *Brogan v UK* (1989). The UK also entered a derogation in relation to the Anti-terrorism, Crime and Security Act 2001, which was enacted in response to the attack on the World Trade Center in New York on 11 September of that year. The Act allows for the detention without trial of foreign citizens suspected of being involved in terrorist activities (see above, *A v Secretary of State for the Home Department* (2002) at 2.5.2).

One point to note in relation to the operation of the margin of appreciation is that, by definition, it is a rule of international law, in that it recognises the different approaches of distinct states. Consequently, it is limited in operation to the supranational ECtHR and not to national courts. The latter may follow precedents based on the doctrine, but it is difficult to see how they could themselves apply it in a national context, although it would appear that the domestic courts' development of the doctrine of deference achieves similar ends to those allowed under the margin of appreciation.

Proportionality

Even where states avail themselves of the margin of appreciation, they are not at liberty to interfere with rights to any degree beyond what is required, as a minimum, to deal with the perceived problem within the context of a democratic society. In other words, there must be a relationship of necessity between the end desired and the means used to achieve it.

As the ECtHR stated in *Chorherr v Austria* (1994):

> The margin of appreciation extends in particular to the choice of the reasonable and appropriate means to be used by the authority to ensure that lawful manifestation can take place peacefully.

Proportionality as it might apply in the English legal system will be considered subsequently (see 13.5.3). However, in relation to the HRA, proportionality is central to the jurisprudence of the ECtHR and as such is now central to the jurisprudence of the UK courts in relation to human rights issues. It is suggested that it will not be restricted to this limited sphere for long and that it will expand into judicial review and other areas as the HRA becomes increasingly understood and used.

It also has to be recognised that the ECHR as a legal document is not a fixed text. As Luzius Wildhaber, the former president of the Court, stated:

> On the question of evolutive interpretation, it is precisely the genius of the Convention that it is indeed a dynamic and a living instrument, which has shown its capacity to evolve in the light of social and technological developments that its drafters, however far-sighted, could never have imagined. The Convention has shown that it is capable of growing with society; and in this respect its formulations have proved their worth over five decades. It has remained a live and modern instrument. The 'living instrument' doctrine is one of the best known principles of Strasbourg case law, the principle that the Convention is interpreted 'in the light of present-day conditions', that it evolves, through the interpretation of the Court.

The recognition of this approach may be seen in the Court's legal recognition of transsexuals' new sexual identity in *Goodwin v UK* (2002). Until that decision, the Court had found that there was no positive obligation for states to modify their civil status systems so as to have the register of births updated or annotated to record changed sexual identity. However, in *Goodwin*, the Court finally reached the conclusion that the fair balance now favoured the recognition of such rights, and ruled accordingly.

5.5 THE EUROPEAN CONVENTION AND THE EUROPEAN UNION

Having started this chapter by stressing the fundamental distinction between the CJEU and the ECtHR, it is necessary to end it by blurring it and pointing out the various ways in which the EC, and then European Union, have expressly recognised the rights provided in the ECHR and the decisions made by the ECtHR. Thus, in a joint declaration delivered in 1997, the European Parliament, the Council and the Commission emphasised the prime importance they attached to the protection of fundamental rights:

> . . . as derived particularly from the constitution of the Member states and the European Convention for the Protection of Human Rights and Fundamental Freedoms ((1977) OJ C103).

Also, as has already been pointed out, Art 6 of the TEU binds the EU, not just to the Charter of Fundamental Rights of the European Union, which is founded on the European Convention on Human Rights, but also the ECHR itself.

The CJEU, in the same way as English courts, has equally been guided by the Convention where EU law is silent. It still remains possible, however, for cases to be brought to either, or both, judicial forums. Issues relating to discrimination are a case in point, by being potentially both in breach of employment law regulated by the EU, and fundamental human rights regulated by the ECHR. It is also an unfortunate fact that it is possible for at least a degree of incompatibility between the decisions of the two courts in relation to very similar matters (for example, see *SPUC v Grogan* (1991) and *Open Door and Well Women v Ireland* (1992)).

It is to be hoped that the fact that the TEU now provides for the EU having its own legal personality, thus allowing it to be a signatory member to the Convention, will remove any such potential incompatibilities. On 5 May 2013 a draft accession agreement was concluded between the EU and the 47 members of the Council of Europe. However, in December 2014, the CJEU issued an opinion to the effect that the draft agreement lacked provisions to ensure that EU law was not open to being compromised by the fact of the EU joining the Council of Europe.

5.6 A CASE STUDY: THE GENESIS OF THE INVESTIGATORY POWERS ACT (IPA) 2016

What follows maps the interplay between European Convention and European Union provisions and their impact on one specific and increasingly important aspect of domestic law.

One particular area of UK law that has repeatedly drawn the attention of the ECtHR concerns the power of the security forces to collect incriminating information. In *Malone v UK* (1984), the ECtHR held that telephone tapping by the police, authorised by the UK government and condoned under common law powers by the High Court, was in breach of Art 8 of the ECHR, which guarantees the right to respect for private life. The Article provides:

> There shall be no interference by a public authority with the exercise of this right except such as is in accordance with the law and is necessary in a democratic society in the interests of national security . . .

The ECtHR held that the tapping was in breach of Art 8(2), because it was not 'in accordance with law', but was rather governed by an unregulated discretion. It could not be 'necessary in a democratic society', as there were no constitutional safeguards against misuse of the power. The government reacted by introducing legislation to control telephone tapping by the police. The Interception of Communications Act (IOCA) 1985 limits telephone tapping to cases where the Home Secretary has issued a warrant and, to safeguard against arbitrary use, the warrant can only be issued in three specified circumstances, one of which is the prevention of serious crime. Further safeguards are provided by a tribunal to investigate complaints about the use of these powers and by the establishment of a Commissioner to review annually how the Home Secretary has exercised their powers.

However, perhaps the most surprising aspect of *Malone* was the recognition in the UK courts that telephone tapping could not be unlawful in the UK, as there was no right of privacy at common law that could be breached. And of course, the right of respect for private life provided by the European Convention was not justiciable in the UK courts at that time (*Malone v Metropolitan Police Commissioner* (1979)).

At least somewhat surprisingly, the IOCA 1985 only applied to interceptions on public telecommunications systems and did not regulate private systems such as internal works' systems. As a consequence, the UK was also found in breach of Art 8 in *Halford v UK* (1997), where such a private system was abused to record conversations.

Even more surprising, not to say complacent, was the way in which the flaws inherent in the procedure relating to the interception of communication were not remedied in relation to the use of covert listening devices, commonly referred to as 'bugging'. Thus, a very similar situation, and corresponding decision, occurred in *Khan v UK* (2000). In *Khan*, the ECtHR held unanimously that there had been violations of Art 8 (right to respect for private and family life) and Art 13 (right to an effective remedy) of the ECHR, after the claimant had been convicted of drug dealing on the basis of evidence improperly obtained by a secret listening device installed by the police. As in *Malone*, the ECtHR held that, at the time in question, there was no statutory system to regulate the use of covert listening devices. As the Home Office Guidelines, which regulated such recordings, were neither legally binding nor publicly accessible, any such recording was consequently not 'in accordance with the law', as required by Art 8(2) of the ECHR. Khan had been arrested in 1993, but it was not until the enactment of the Police Act 1997 that a statutory basis for the authorisation of such surveillance operations was properly constituted.

As the last court in the UK, the approach of the House of Lords is of some interest and reveals the frustration that the court felt in relation to the case, which no doubt it was aware would eventually be decided in a contrary manner by the ECtHR. As it stated, in English law a breach of the provisions of Art 8 was not determinative of the outcome, and the judge's discretion to admit or exclude such evidence under s 78 of the Police and Criminal Evidence Act (PACE) 1984 was subject to common law rules that relevant evidence that was obtained improperly, or even unlawfully, remained admissible. As Lord Nolan expressed the situation:

> The sole cause of this case coming to your Lordships' House is the lack of a statutory system regulating the use of surveillance devices by the police. The absence of such a system seems astonishing, the more so in view of the statutory framework which has governed the use of such devices by the Security Service since 1989, and the interception of communications by the police as well as by other agencies since 1985. I would refrain from other comment because counsel for the respondent was able to inform us, on instructions that the government proposes to introduce legislation covering the matter in the next session of Parliament.

One can almost hear the additional words 'and not before time', but unfortunately it was too late in the *Khan* case, which had to make its way to the ECtHR.

The supposed remedial legislation, the Regulation of Investigatory Powers Act (RIPA) was enacted in July 2000 to ensure that the investigatory powers of state authorities are used in accordance with human rights, but in so doing, it significantly increased the state's power in relation to surveillance. Unfortunately, RIPA 2000 was introduced too late to prevent the UK being found to be in breach of Art 8 of the ECHR in *Allan v UK* in 2002, which arose from prior covert bugging actions taken by the police.

A critique of RIPA

The preceding text has been included in this book for approaching 15 years and it can be read as a very positive support of the Human Rights Act, the ECHR and the ECtHR, apart from the slight warning in the penultimate sentence. Given what has occurred subsequently it may no longer be right to leave this criticism implicit.

The introduction to the Act states its purpose as being:

> To *make provision* for and about the interception of communications, the acquisition and disclosure of data relating to communications, the carrying out of surveillance, the use of covert human intelligence sources and the acquisition of the means by which electronic data protected by encryption or passwords may be decrypted or accessed; to provide for commissioners and a tribunal with functions and jurisdiction in relation to those matters, to entries on and interferences with property or with wireless telegraphy and to the carrying out of their functions by the security service, the Secret Intelligence Service and the Government Communications Headquarters and for connected purposes.

The explanatory notes to the Act state that its purpose is 'to ensure that the relevant investigatory powers are used in accordance with human rights'. These powers are:

- the interception of communications;
- the acquisition of communications data (e.g. billing data);
- intrusive surveillance (on residential premises/in private vehicles);
- covert surveillance in the course of specific operations;
- the use of covert human intelligence sources (agents, informants, undercover officers);
- access to encrypted data.

Those are very wide-ranging and unspecific powers.

In an article in *The Guardian* newspaper, author John Lanchester wrote the following:

> The main law concerning [GCHQ's] activities is Ripa. If you read this 2000 Act (which, by the way, I don't recommend, since it's tortured and laborious even by the standards of statute-speak), it's clear that the main focus of its provisions is targeted surveillance. It's about what the spies and cops are allowed to do to catch specific bad guys. Ripa is pretty broad in its drafting, and it seems apparent that the intention was to let the authorities do anything they wanted with phones and email. And yet, it nowhere explicitly allows the mass interception of communications by people about whom the state has no reason for suspecting anything . . .

However, that is precisely the situation that the 2013 revelations of Edward Snowden made apparent: that the security agencies of both the UK and the US operated systems of mass rather than specific surveillance for collecting what they considered to be information sensitive to national security. Subsequently, in September 2014 it emerged that the police routinely used powers under RIPA to access the phone records of journalists in order to reveal their sources (although not conversations, it must be stressed), and even more concern was raised when in November of that year it was revealed that the security servicers MI5, MI6 and GCHQ had accessed legally privileged communications between lawyers and their clients without any regard to RIPA.

In 2006 the EU Data Retention Directive 2006/24/EC was issued, essentially requiring internet service providers to store and permit access to telecommunications data in order to facilitate the prevention and prosecution of crime. The Data Retention Directive was implemented in the United Kingdom with respect to fixed-network and mobile telephony by the Data Retention (EC Directive) Regulations 2007 (SI 2007/2199). These were superseded by the Data Retention (EC Directive) Regulations 2009 (SI 2009/859), which contained additional provisions relating to internet access, internet telephony and email.

In 2012, the then coalition government put forward a draft Communications Data Bill which would have required internet service providers and mobile phone companies to maintain records of each user's internet browsing activity (including social media), email voice calls, internet gaming, and mobile phone messaging services and store the records for 12 months. Although apparently in line with the EU directive, the proposed Bill, much maligned as a so-called snooper's charter, lost the support of the minority Liberal Democrat part of the then coalition government, which made it impossible for it to be enacted.

Subsequently, in April 2014, in *Digital Rights Ireland Ltd v Minister for Communications, Marine and Natural Resources and Others* (C-293/12) the CJEU held that the Data Retention Directive was in breach of Arts 7 and 8 of the EU Charter on Fundamental Rights (Art 7 enshrines the right to respect for private and family life as in the ECHR, but additionally Art 8 establishes a right to the protection and fair processing of personal data). The CJEU held that the directive did not include sufficient safeguards necessary for it to be compliant with individuals' rights under the Charter. The *Digital Rights Ireland* decision led to the UK government trying to ensure that its provision in this area remained watertight. To that end it unceremoniously rushed the Data Retention and Investigatory Powers Act (DRIPA) 2014 through parliament in 48 hours. The ill-fated outcome for that Act may be predestined in the hubris with which the government supported its passage:

> The ECJ struck down the European Data Retention Directive, not our own laws. The judgment upheld the principle that data could be retained at the request of government, but found that the Directive itself lacked proper safeguards. It did not consider the robust safeguards that already exist in the UK's communications data regime. We believe that our internationally respected retention and access regime already addresses most of the ECJ's criticisms. Th[is] Bill is compatible with the ECHR and will contain the normal statement to this effect from the Home Secretary.

The essential validity of DRIPA was challenged in a judicial review action brought by, among others, Conservative MP David Davis and Labour MP Tom Watson. For some inexplicable reason, the drafters of DRIPA had repeated the inadequacies of the EU directive and it was not surprising that the Court found that ss 1 and 2 of that Act were incompatible with the public's right to respect for private life and communications and to protection of personal data under Arts 7 and 8 of the EU Charter of Fundamental Rights. Ultimately DRIPA failed to provide clear and precise rules to ensure data was only accessed for the purpose of preventing and detecting serious offences, and consequently it failed to comply with the requirements of the EU charter. As a consequence of that failure, the UK legislation was quashed. However, the court suspended its disapplication until March 2016 specifically in order to give Parliament time to enact compliant legislation.

To that end and following pre-legislative scrutiny of a draft Bill, the then Home Secretary Theresa May introduced the Investigatory Powers Bill in March 2016. The Bill brought together all interception powers previously under RIPA and the Wireless

Telegraphy Act 2006. Internet and phone companies were to be required to maintain permanent capabilities to intercept and collect personal data passing over their networks. They were also to be placed under a wider duty to assist the security services and the police in the interests of national security. However, the proposed legislation did have the advantage of legalising what was previously unlawful and did include several new safeguards designed to overcome the faults in RIPA; among these are provisions:

- Replacing the existing system of three oversight commissioners with a single Investigatory Powers Commissioner (IPC) who will be a senior judge.

- Limiting the ability to seek interception warrants to the existing nine intercepting authorities and existing three statutory purposes subject to IPC oversight.

- Introducing a 'double-lock' on ministerial authorisation of intercept warrants with a panel of seven judicial commissioners given power of veto. Thus, judicial commissioners, as well as government ministers, will be required to approve warrants before they come into force. However, exemptions will apply in 'urgent cases'.

- Requiring that applications for targeted interception warrants will need to specify a particular person, premises or operation.

- Requiring the Prime Minister to be consulted in all cases involving interception of MPs' communications. It had previously been thought that the Wilson convention (named after the former Prime Minister) ensured that MPs' and peers' phones would not be tapped, and in 1997, the then Prime Minister, Tony Blair, said the doctrine extended to electronic communication, including emails. However, in October 2015 an Investigatory Powers Tribunal judgment confirmed that MPs' and peers' private communications were not protected from interception by the security services.

- Repealing the acquisition of communications under s 94 the Telecommunications Act 1984, under the very general powers of which successive governments had secretly allowed security services to access data from communications companies. As a replacement IPA provides for a new 'bulk acquisition' warrants for the security and intelligence agencies to obtain communications data.

- Making it a criminal offence to recklessly or knowingly obtain communications data without lawful authority.

CHAPTER SUMMARY: SOURCES OF LAW: THE EUROPEAN CONTEXT

THE EUROPEAN UNION

UK law is now subject to European Union law in particular areas.

In practice, this has led to the curtailment of parliamentary sovereignty in those areas.

SOURCES OF EUROPEAN UNION LAW

The sources of EU law are:

- internal treaties and protocols – the TEU, TFEU, and Charter of Fundamental Rights are examples;
- international agreements;
- secondary legislation; and
- decisions of the Court of Justice of the European Union.

Secondary legislation takes three forms:

- regulations that are directly applicable;
- directives that have to be given statutory form; and
- decisions that are directly applicable.

MAJOR INSTITUTIONS

The major institutions of the European Union (EU) are:

- the Council of Ministers;
- the European Parliament;
- the Commission; and
- the European Court of Justice.

THE EUROPEAN COURT OF HUMAN RIGHTS

Refer to Chapter 2 above for a consideration of the effect of the ECHR on United Kingdom law.

1. The UK Constitutional Principle of Parliamentary Sovereignty
– The UK Parliament is the highest legislative body in the UK
– It may enact any law which it sees fit, providing future Parliaments are not bound by that law
– No other body may overrule its laws

2. The Principle of Supremacy of EU Law
– Provides that where EU law and national law conflict, EU law will be supreme (*Costa v ENEL*)
– Acceptance of this principle in the UK is illustrated by Lord Bridge's *dicta* in *Factortame*

3. Maintenance of the UK Doctrine
In theory at least, the doctrine of parliamentary supremacy is maintained by the argument that the UK Parliament may repeal the European Communities Act at any time, thus removing the nee to comply with EU laws

THE PRINCIPLE OF UK PARLIAMENTARY SOVEREIGNTY AND EU LAW

FIGURE 5.3 *The Principle of UK Parliamentary Sovereignty and EU Law.*

1. Why Does the EU Need Institutions?
The EU Institutions (listed in Art 13 TEC) have a variety of functions as they act as the day-to-day 'government' of Europe, taking decisions relating to legislative, executive and judicial functions

2. The Council:
– A peripatetic body, representing the governments of the Member states. Its composition changes according to the subject matter under discussion
– It is an important decision-making body, with decisions normally taken by Qualified Majority Voting (QMV)
– The body is supported by a permanent body of staff known as COREPER

3. The European Parliament:
– A democratically elected body which represents the interests of EU citizens
– It has an important legislative role, which includes agreeing the EU budget
– It also has supervisory functions, primarily in relation to the Commission

THE INSTITUTIONS OF THE EC/EU

6. Other Bodies:
– **The European Council:** an institution composed primarily of the heads of government of the states
– It is responsible for directing EU policy
– **The Court of Auditors:** an institution which ensures EU money is spent in accordance with the EU's budget
– **The European Central Bank:** works to maintain a stable financial system

5. The Court of Justice of the EU (CJEU):
– The CJEU is the judicial arm of the EU and is charged with ensuring that the law of the EU is observed (Art 19 TE)
– It has the important function of interpreting EU law for the benefit of the Member states (Art 267 TFEU)
– It also hears actions relating to compliance with EU law by both the other Institutions (Art 263 TFEU) and the Member states (Art 258 TFEU)

4. The European Commission:
– The Commission represents the interests of the EU as a whole
– The Commission drafts EU legislation
– It also has a function in regard to the supervision of Member states, ensuring that they fulfil their EU obligations

FIGURE 5.4 *The Institutions of the EC/EU.*

The Council of Europe, the European Commission on Human Rights and the European Court of Human Rights are distinct institutions whose purpose is to regulate the potential abuse of human rights. They are not part of the EU structure.

Since the enactment of the Human Rights Act 1998, the European Convention on Human Rights has been incorporated into UK law. It remains to be seen what effect this has on domestic UK law, but it cannot but be significant.

FOOD FOR THOUGHT

1   Among the general public there is confusion between European institutions, their courts and their laws and it is quite common for even politicians to confuse decisions of the Court of Justice of the EU and the European Court of Human Rights. It is essential that the two are not confused, but how can this be achieved?

2   Within the European Union there exists a tension between those countries who would support a more integrationist approach towards a federal state of Europe and those who would prefer to see the Union in purely economic market terms.

3   In the context of national sovereignty, consider whether the United Kingdom could leave the EU, either in theory or in practice.

4   The European Court of Human Rights is threatened with sclerosis if it does not deal with more cases, or deals with those cases differently. What reform is necessary and how is it to be achieved, to ensure that the ECtHR continues to function adequately?

FURTHER READING

Benoetvea, J, *The Legal Reasoning of the European Court of Justice: Towards a European Jurisprudence*, 1993, Oxford: Clarendon

Borgsmit, K, 'The Advocate General at the European Court of Justice: a comparative study' (1988) 13 EL Rev 106

Craig, P and de Búrca, G, *EU Law: Text, Cases and Materials*, 5th edn, 2011, Oxford: OUP

Davies, K, *Understanding EU Law*, 5th edn, 2012, Abingdon: Routledge

Dickson, B, *Human Rights and the European Convention*, 1997, London: Sweet & Maxwell

Foster, N, *EU Treaties and Legislation*, 24th edn, 2013, Oxford: OUP

Gormsen, LL, 'The European Commission's priority guidelines on Article 82 EC' (2009) 14(3) Comms L 83

Kaczorowska, A, *EU Law*, 3rd edn, 2013, Abingdon: Routledge

Ward, I, *A Critical Introduction to European Law*, 3rd edn, 2009, London: Butterworths

USEFUL WEBSITES

http://eur-lex.europa.eu/en/index.htm
This site is the official database for all EU law. It includes the Official Journal, Treaties, recent case law, and legislation.

http://curia.europa.eu
The official website for the Court of Justice of the European Union.

www.echr.coe.int
The official website of the European Court of Human Rights (ECtHR).

COMPANION WEBSITE

Now visit the companion website to:

- test your understanding of the key terms using our Flashcard Glossary;
- revise and consolidate your knowledge of 'Sources of Law: The European context' using our multiple choice question testbank;
- view all of the links to the Useful Websites above.

www.routledge.com/cw/slapper

6.1 INTRODUCTION

person to pay the victim compensation, but this will be in addition to and separate from the sentence for the crime.

If a civil case is successful from the point of view of the person bringing the claim (the *claimant*), the outcome will be one of a number of civil remedies which are designed to benefit the *claimant* and in which the state, or wider community, has no direct interest. The exception to this is some judicial review claims that raise public interest points that will affect more people than just the individual claimant. Civil remedies include damages, court orders such as injunctions, orders of prohibition and specific performance. So, in civil proceedings, the *claimant* will sue the *defendant* and a successful claim will result in *judgment for* the *claimant*. In matrimonial cases, the party who brings an action is called the *petitioner* and the other party is known as the *respondent*.

Civil and criminal cases are processed differently by the English legal system. They use different procedures and vocabulary, and they are dealt with, on the whole, by different courts. It is very important not to confuse the vocabularies of the different systems and speak, for example, about a claimant 'prosecuting' a company for breach of contract. The law of contract is civil law, so the defendant would be 'sued' or 'litigated against' or have 'a claim taken against' him, her or it.

The following question then arises: 'What is the difference between a crime and a civil wrong; how am I to tell into which category a particular wrong falls?' The answer will be found simply by building up a general legal knowledge. There is nothing inherent in any particular conduct that makes it criminal. One cannot say, for example, that serious wrongs are crimes and that lesser transgressions will be civil wrongs: some crimes are comparatively trivial, like some parking offences, while some civil wrongs can have enormously harmful consequences, as where a company in breach of a contract causes financial harm to hundreds or thousands of people.

Sometimes a single event can be both a crime and a civil wrong. If you drive at 50 mph in a 30 mph zone and crash into another vehicle, killing a passenger, you may be prosecuted by the state for causing death by dangerous driving and, if convicted, imprisoned or fined. Additionally, you may be sued for negligence (a tortious civil wrong) by a dependant of the dead passenger and the driver.

6.2   HER MAJESTY'S COURTS AND TRIBUNALS SERVICE

The Courts Act 2003 provided for a new unified courts administration to be created, by combining the functions of the court service and the magistrates' courts committees. The new organisation, Her Majesty's Courts Service (HMCS), was established in April 2005. The aim of the agency was to deliver improved services to the community, taxpayer, victims, witnesses and all other users of the courts and to develop best practice with the most effective use of resources.

The proposal to set up a new system of courts administration in England and Wales derived from Sir Robin Auld's review of the criminal courts published in October 2001 (*A Review of the Criminal Courts of England and Wales*, The Right Honourable Lord Justice Auld, 2001). He recommended that a single centrally funded executive agency, as part of the Ministry of Justice, should be responsible for the administration of all courts, civil, criminal and family, replacing the court service and magistrates' courts committees.

The government accepted Sir Robin's proposals for a unified system of courts administration and the Courts Act 2003 was passed to implement the changes. Her Majesty's Courts Service was launched in 2005.

On 1 April 2011 Her Majesty's Courts Service and the Tribunals Service were amalgamated into one integrated agency, Her Majesty's Courts and Tribunals Service (HMCTS), providing support for the administration of justice in courts (up to and including the Court of Appeal) and most tribunals. HMCTS remains a separate agency of the Justice Ministry.

The courts are not in a good economic state. In 2008 the then Lord Chief Justice announced that the maintenance backlog in the courts had risen from £38 million in 2000 to £200 million, stating that it would remain at this level for three years. More recently the Lord Chief Justice has observed that 'Economic realities have led to budget cuts which have had direct effects on the administration of justice' (Lord Chief Justice's Report 2013).

The current economic situation poses significant challenges to the justice system; the coalition government took steps to cut £350 million from the legal aid budget alone and, following a consultation in 2010, 129 courts were closed. Such cuts cannot but have implications for access to justice. Lord Neuberger, President of the Supreme Court, said in June 2013: 'There are three principal problems: (i) legal services are expensive; (ii) court procedures are not always proportionate and (iii) money for legal aid is scarce.'

Grave concerns about the civil court system was raised by District Judge David Oldham, president of the Association of Her Majesty's District Judges (Woolf reforms and cost-cutting have led to acute shortages and a 'deficient' system, F Gibb, *The Times*, 16 April 2009). He argues that the civil courts were woefully under-resourced – a problem ever more acute in times of hardship. He has stated:

My mission is to persuade the Government to return to funding our civil courts to a realistic level and as the recession brings more and more individuals to the county courts, to ensure that all who need it have access to free and efficient expert advice and assistance from a duty solicitor or advice agency independent of the Courts Service.

Judge Oldham noted that the civil court system receives a smaller slice of public funds than criminal or family courts, and fees charged to court users had risen to 'draconian levels' under the policy of making civil courts pay for themselves.

The Commission of Inquiry into Legal Aid estimated that the legal aid cuts to the civil system are a false economy; according to figures supplied to the Inquiry by Citizens Advice, for every £1.00 of legal aid spent on benefits advice, the state saves up to £8.80, and for every £1.00 of legal aid spent on employment advice, the state saves up to £7.13 (see www.guardian.co.uk/law/2011/jun/14/legal-aid-cuts-false-economy).

Professor Dame Hazel Genn argued in her 2009 Hamlyn Lectures that the main thrust of civil justice reform in the last decade was not primarily about greater access, nor about greater justice, 'It is simply about diversion of disputants away from the courts' (F Gibb, *The Times*, 23 June 2009). She argued that:

> In England, we are witnessing the decline of civil justice, the degradation of court facilities and the diversion of civil cases to private dispute resolution – accompanied by an anti-court, anti-adjudication rhetoric that interprets these developments as socially positive.

She argued that a principal threat to civil justice was the 'unstoppable burgeoning of criminal justice' including the demands of human rights laws and costs of a growing prison population. The battle for resources was heightened at a time of economically imposed financial restraint. With a unified budget for all parts of the justice system now established under the Ministry of Justice, the importance of civil justice is, Genn has argued, obscured and under-rated. Arguably, evidence for this position can be seen in the enactment of the Legal Aid, Sentencing and Punishment of Offenders Act 2012 (LASPO), which made sweeping cuts to civil legal aid. Unlike any other common law system the civil courts in England are self-financing, paid for by litigants. However, Genn noted, any surplus generated from litigants' fees is not invested in the civil courts: instead it is 'redirected into the gaping maw of criminal justice'. Lady Hale, Justice of the Supreme Court, has contributed to this debate. In a speech in 2011 she observed that the coalition government's plans for cutting legal aid would 'of course have a dispropor-tionate effect on the poorest and most vulnerable in society. Indeed the government's own equality impact statement accepts that they will have a disproportionate impact on women, ethnic minorities and people with disabilities' ('Equal Access to Justice in the Big Society', speech by Lady Hale to The Law Society, 27 June 2011). The Judicial Executive Board expressed its concerns about the operation of the courts post-LASPO in written evidence to a parliamentary inquiry, available at http://www.parliament.uk/ business/committees/committees-a-z/commons-select/justice-committee/inquiries.

6.3 MAGISTRATES' COURTS

Magistrates' courts have a civil jurisdiction, but the main part of this, historically, was in relation to family law. This has been significantly changed by the Crime and Courts Act 2013 and the new system, which still involves magistrates, is summarised in Chap-ter 9. (A family proceedings court must normally be composed of not more than three justices, including, as far as is practicable, both a man and a woman. Justices who sit on such benches must be members of the 'family panel', which comprises people specially appointed to deal with family matters; see Chapter 8.) They have powers of recovery in relation to council tax and charges for water, gas and electricity. They also act as an appellate court from decisions of local authorities in licensing matters.

6.4   THE COUNTY COURT

The County Courts were introduced in 1846 to provide local, accessible fora for the adjudication of relatively small-scale litigation. There are 173 County Courts, now united under the single County Court. This was created by the Crime and Courts Act 2013, s 17, and removes jurisdictional and bureaucratic barriers to the way the County Court works. The court is served by circuit judges and district judges, the latter appointed by the Lord Chancellor from persons who have a seven-year qualification (s 71 of the Courts and Legal Services Act (CLSA) 1990). High Court judges may occasionally be deployed to sit in the County Court.

The Civil Procedure Rules (CPR), which we examine in Chapter 7, operate the same process irrespective of whether the case forum is the High Court or the County Court. Broadly speaking, the County Court will hear small claims and fast-track cases, while the more challenging multi-track cases will be heard in the High Court.

Certain types of actions set down for trial in the High Court are considered too important for transfer to a County Court. These are cases involving:

- professional negligence;
- fatal accidents;
- allegations of fraud or undue influence;
- defamation;
- malicious prosecution or false imprisonment;
- claims against the police.

The civil courts are under great pressure from the cutbacks being made as part of governmental budget strategy. Governmental plans announced in 2010 have seen the Ministry of Justice's budget cut from £9 billion to £7 billion, with £450 million coming out of administrative areas alone. The staffing of the law courts is already, by common judicial consent, quite inadequate but 14,250 of these demanding jobs have been cut, along with approximately 15,000 at the Ministry of Justice itself, leaving the residual workforce to toil in a hopeless Sisyphean challenge.

In 2007, Judge Paul Collins, London's most senior County Court judge, said that low pay and high turnover among staff meant that serious errors were commonplace and routinely led to incorrect judgments in court. He said that, with further cuts looming, 'we run the risk of bringing about a real collapse in the service we're able to give to the people using the courts'.

The main advantage to litigants using the small claims process is the fact that, if sued, they can defend themselves without the fear of incurring huge legal costs, since the costs that the winning party can claim are strictly limited. The average waiting period for trial was 31 weeks (as opposed to 56 weeks for fast- and multi-track cases). Although successful claimants are unable to recover costs of legal representation, the small claims procedure does not exclude litigants from seeking legal advice or engaging such legal representation. If a litigant is unrepresented, the district judge may assist him or her by putting questions to witnesses or to the other party, and by explaining any legal terms or expressions.

A litigant simply needs to complete a claim form, available from any County Court, and send it to the court with the issue fee appropriate to the amount claimed (ranging from £35 to £455, depending on the value of the claim). Claims may also be made online for a lower fee. If the case is defended, it will be dealt with at an informal hearing, sitting around a table in the district judge's office. This avoids the need for a trial in open court, which many litigants find daunting. There are further fees for hearings.

The working of the small claims system is looked at in greater detail in Chapter 7.

6.5   THE HIGH COURT OF JUSTICE

The High Court was created in 1873 as a part of the Supreme Court of Judicature. The Constitutional Reform Act 2005 established a new Supreme Court of the United Kingdom (which has been operational from 2009) to replace the House of Lords as the highest court of appeal. The new official collective name for the High Court, the Court of Appeal and the Crown Court (previously called 'The Supreme Court of Judicature') is the Senior Courts of England and Wales. The Supreme Court of Judicature of Northern Ireland was renamed the Court of Judicature of Northern Ireland.

The High Court has three administrative divisions: the Court of Chancery, the Queen's Bench Division (QBD) and the Family Division (Divorce and Admiralty and Exchequer and Common Pleas were merged with the QBD in 1880 and 1970). High Court judges sit mainly in the Royal Courts of Justice in the Strand, London, although it is possible for the High Court to sit anywhere in England or Wales.

The High Court judiciary comprises the Vice Chancellor; the Lord Chief Justice who presides over the QBD; the President, who presides over the Family Division; the Senior Presiding Judge (s 72 of the CLSA 1990); and 108 High Court judges or '*puisne judges*' (pronounced 'pewnee' and meaning 'lesser'). The number of High Court judges is fixed by statute.

To be qualified for appointment as a *puisne* judge, a person must have 10 years' qualification within the meaning of s 71 of the CLSA 1990 – essentially, someone who has had a general right of audience on all matters in that court for at least 10 years. The Constitutional Reform Act 2005 established the Judicial Appointments Commission. This body, with 14 members drawn from the judiciary, the lay magistracy, the legal professions and the public, was launched in 2006. It is responsible for selecting candidates to recommend for judicial appointment to the Secretary of State for Justice. This ensures that while merit will remain the sole criterion for appointment, the appointments system will be placed on a fully modern, open and transparent basis (see further at 12.4.3).

6.5.1   THE QUEEN'S BENCH DIVISION

The Queen's Bench Division – the main common law court – takes its name from the original judicial part of the general royal court, which used to sit on a bench in the Palace of Westminster. It is the division with the largest workload and has some criminal jurisdiction and appellate jurisdiction. The main civil work of this court is in contract and tort cases, as well as hearing more specialist cases such as applications for judicial review.

The Commercial Court is part of the QBD, being served by up to 15 judges with specialist experience in commercial law and presiding over cases concerning banking and insurance matters. The formal rules of evidence can be abandoned here, with the consent of the parties, to allow testimony and documentation that would normally be inadmissible. This informality can be of considerable benefit to the business keen to settle its dispute as quickly and easily as possible. Proceedings in the Commercial Court are governed by Part 58 of the Civil Procedure Rules. The QBD also includes an Admiralty Court to deal with the, often esoteric, issues of law relating to shipping. Commercial Court judges are sometimes appointed as arbitrators.

The Office of Fair Trading (OFT) was responsible for protecting consumer interests throughout the UK until 2014 when its responsibilities were passed to a number of different organisations. Consumer rights advice is available from Citizens Advice, and complaints about advertising can be made to the Advertising Standards Authority. The Competition and Markets Authority (CMA) deals with complaints regarding alleged anticompetitive practice (eg price fixing and bid rigging), and alleged unfair terms in a contract.

The Employment Appeal Tribunal is presided over by a High Court judge and either two or four laypersons, and hears appeals from employment tribunals. It is not part of the High Court, but is termed a superior court of record.

It is important to remember that most civil claims are settled out of court; only about 1 per cent of cases where claim forms are issued result in civil trials.

6.5.2 THE QUEEN'S BENCH DIVISIONAL COURT

The nomenclature can be puzzling here. This court, as distinct from the QBD, exercises appellate jurisdiction. Here, two or sometimes three judges sit to hear appeals in the following circumstances:

- appeals on a point of law by way of case stated from magistrates' courts, tribunals and the Crown Court;

- by exercising judicial review of the decisions made by governmental and public authorities, inferior courts and tribunals. However, leave to apply for judicial review is granted or refused by a single judge and some claims for judicial review can be heard by a single judge, sitting as the Administrative Court within the QBD. The majority of judicial review cases were immigration and asylum matters, which were transferred to the Tribunal system in November 2013 following a direction by the Lord Chief Justice on 21 August 2013 pursuant to his powers under Part 1, Schedule 2 of the Constitutional Reform Act 2005;

- applications for the writ of *habeas corpus* from persons who claim they are being unlawfully detained (there were 34 such cases in 2010 and no up-to-date figures have been published since).

6.5.3   THE CHANCERY DIVISION

The Chancery Division is the modern successor to the old Court of Chancery, the Lord Chancellor's court from which equity was developed. It has 18 judges. Its jurisdiction includes matters relating to:

- the sale or partition of land and the raising of charges on land;
- the redemption or foreclosure of mortgages;
- the execution or declaration of trusts;
- the administration of the estates of the dead;
- bankruptcy;
- contentious probate business, for example the validity and interpretation of wills;
- company law;
- partnerships;
- revenue law.

Like the QBD, the Chancery Division contains specialist courts; these are the Patents Court and the Companies Court. The Chancery Division hears its cases in London or in one of eight designated provincial High Court centres. The work is very specialised and there is a Chancery Bar for barristers who practise in this area. Chancery judges are normally appointed from this Bar.

6.5.4   THE CHANCERY DIVISIONAL COURT

Comprising one or two Chancery judges, this appellate court hears appeals from the Commissioners of Inland Revenue on income tax cases, and from the County Court on certain matters like bankruptcy.

6.5.5   THE FAMILY DIVISION

For details of the Family Division of the High Court, refer to Chapter 8.

6.5.6   THE COURT OF PROTECTION

The Court of Protection is a specialist court established by the Mental Capacity Act 2005. It is a supreme court of record with the same rights, privileges and authority as the High Court. The Court of Protection makes decisions, and appoints others (called deputies) to make decisions, on behalf of people who lack mental capacity under the Mental Capacity Act 2005. These decisions relate to incapacitous people's financial affairs, property, health and welfare. The Court sits at the Royal Courts of Justice in London as well

Supreme Court of the United Kingdom created by the **Constitutional Reform Act 2005**; replaced the House of Lords as the final UK court of appeal. Has jurisdiction to hear appeals from the Court of Appeal (Civil and Criminal Divisions) and, in limited circumstances, the High Court. Staffed by judges known as Justices of the Supreme Court.

Court of Appeal (Civil Division) one of the 'senior' Courts of England and Wales, hearing appeals from the High Court, County Courts and Employment Appeal Tribunals. The Court is largely staffed by senior judges known as Lord Justices of Appeal.

The Judicial Committee of the **Privy Council** is the final court of appeal for UK overseas territories, Crown Dependencies and some Commonwealth countries.

High Court one of the 'senior' courts of England and Wales. Hears more complex and higher value civil disputes (plus some limited criminal jurisdiction). Divided into three 'divisions' whose jurisdiction may overlap. Sometimes referred to as the '**Divisional Court**', which is not a separate court or division but relates to the number of judges sitting (it normally comprises a bench of two or, less often, three judges, rather than the more usual single judge). Exceptionally, the Court may include a jury (e.g. defamation). It has a supervisory function over subordinate courts and tribunals. It comprises:

Queen's Bench Division (QBD) hears actions in contract and tort and has three courts attached: Commercial, Admiralty and Technology and Construction. The OBD also hears actions relating to judicial review and writs of habeas corpus, while acting as an appellate court on criminal matters for the magistrates' and Crown courts.

Family Division has jurisdiction in family matters including matrimony, proceedings under the Children Act 1989 and non-contentious probate cases. Attached to it is the Family Divisional Court, which has appellate jurisdiction. See Chapter 8.

Chancery Division hears cases principally relating to business such as insolvency, mortgages, administration of estates, partnership disputes and intellectual property. The Companies and Patents Courts are attached to it. The Chancery Divisional Court has appellate jurisdiction in regard to tax and bankruptcy matters.

The County Courts have jurisdiction in claims which include contract tort, landlord and tenant disputes and uncontested divorce petitions. There are geographical and financial limitations on jurisdiction and more complex cases are heard by the High Court. The court is staffed by Circuit and District Judges.

Magistrates' courts, although largely criminal, jurisdiction includes civil matters such as granting licences (e.g. betting and alcohol) and 'family' matters (e.g. orders for protection against violence, maintenance orders and proceedings concerning the welfare of children, including adoption).

It should be remembered that many civil disputes never reach trial. Most are dealt with through statutory or voluntary complaints procedures, or through **mediation**, **negotiation** or **arbitration**. In addition, **Ombudsmen** have the power to determine complaints in the public sector and, on a voluntary basis, in some private-sector activities – e.g. banking. In addition, the relevance of tribunals to the machinery of justice in the UK should not be forgotten.

FIGURE 6.1 *Outline of the Civil Courts.*

as in a number of regional courts, including Newcastle, Bristol, Manchester and Cardiff. The Court is served by five High Court judges, 33 district judges and 40 circuit judges.

The Court of Protection has powers to:

- decide whether a person has the capacity to make a particular decision for themselves;
- make declarations, decisions or orders on financial or welfare matters affecting people who lack capacity to make these decisions;
- appoint a deputy to make ongoing decisions for people lacking capacity to make those decisions;
- decide whether a Lasting Power of Attorney (LPA) or Enduring Power of Attorney (EPA) is valid;
- remove deputies or attorneys who fail to carry out their duties; and
- hear cases concerning objections to the registration of an LPA or EPA.

In 2013, there were 25,000 applications made under the Mental Capacity Act 2005, roughly the same as the previous year. The majority of these (60 per cent) relate to applications for appointment of a property and affairs deputy.

6.6   APPEALS FROM THE HIGH COURT

Appeals from decisions made by a judge in one of the three High Court Divisions will go to the Court of Appeal (Civil Division). An exception to this rule allows an appeal to miss out or 'leapfrog' a visit to the Court of Appeal and go straight to the Supreme Court (ss 12–15 of the Administration of Justice Act 1969). In order for this to happen, the trial judge must grant a 'certificate of satisfaction' and the Supreme Court must give leave to appeal. Previously, in order for the judge to grant a certificate, he or she had to be satisfied that the case involved a point of law of general public importance, either concerned mainly with statutory interpretation or one where he or she was bound by a Court of Appeal or a Supreme Court decision. The Criminal Justice and Courts Act 2015 adds a further three conditions which now also entitle a judge to grant a certificate. These are that the proceedings entail a decision relating to a matter of national importance; that the result of the hearing is so significant that, in the opinion of the judge, a hearing by the Supreme Court is justified; and that the judge is satisfied that earlier consideration by the Supreme Court outweighs the benefits of consideration by the Court of Appeal. The 2015 Act also does away with the requirement that both parties must consent to the procedure.

6.7   THE COURT OF APPEAL (CIVIL DIVISION)

The Court of Appeal was established by the Judicature Act (JdA) 1873. Together with the High Court of Justice, the Court of Appeal formed part of the Supreme Court of Judicature. Why is it called 'Supreme' if the House of Lords was a superior court? The answer is that the JdA 1873 abolished the House of Lords in its appellate capacity, hence the Court of Appeal became part of the Supreme Court but, after a change of government, the House of Lords was reinstated as the final court of appeal by the Appellate Jurisdiction Act 1876.

The Court of Appeal is served by senior judges – currently 39 – termed Lord Justices of Appeal. Additionally, the President of the Family Division of the High Court, the Vice Chancellor of the Chancery Division and High Court judges can sit in the Court of Appeal. The court hears appeals from the three divisions of the High Court, the Divisional Courts, the County Court, the Employment Appeal Tribunal, the Immigration and Asylum Upper Tribunal, the Lands Tribunal, the Transport Tribunal and the Court of Protection. The most senior judge is the Master of the Rolls. Usually, three judges will sit to hear an appeal, although for very important cases five may sit. In the interests of business efficiency, some matters can be heard by two judges. These include:

- applications for leave to appeal;
- an appeal where all parties have consented to the matter being heard by just two judges;
- any appeal against an interim order or judgment (that is, one which is provisional).

Where such a court is evenly divided, three or five judges must rehear the case before it can be further appealed to the Supreme Court.

There may be four or five divisions of the court sitting on any given day. The court has a heavy workload. In the Court of Appeal Civil Division, a total of 4,291 applications were filed or set down in 2013, its highest level since 2005, and an increase of 12 per cent on 2012. In 2013 3,865 applications were disposed of, an increase of 4.5 per cent on 2012.

6.8 THE APPEAL PROCESS

6.8.1 THE ACCESS TO JUSTICE ACT 1999 (PART IV)

In relation to civil appeals, the Access to Justice Act (AJA) 1999 made several changes. It:

- provided for permission to appeal to be obtained at all levels in the system (s 54);
- provided that, in normal circumstances, there will be only one level of appeal to the courts (s 55);
- introduced an order-making power to enable the Lord Chancellor to vary appeal routes in secondary legislation, with a view to ensuring that appeals generally go to the lowest appropriate level of judge (s 56);
- ensured that cases which merit the consideration of the Court of Appeal reach that court (s 57);
- gave the Civil Division of the Court of Appeal flexibility to exercise its jurisdiction in courts of one, two or more judges (s 59).

Together, these measures are intended to ensure that appeals are heard at the right level, and dealt with in a way which is proportionate to their weight and complexity; that the appeals system can adapt quickly to other developments in the civil justice system; and that existing resources are used efficiently, enabling the Court of Appeal (Civil Division) to tackle its workload more expeditiously. The provisions relating to the High Court (ss 61–65) allow judicial review applications.

6.8.2 RIGHT TO APPEAL

The AJA 1999 provides for rights of appeal to be exercised only with the permission of the court, as prescribed by rules of court. Previously, permission was required for most cases going to the Civil Division of the Court of Appeal, but not elsewhere. Under the Act, with three exceptions, permission to appeal must be obtained in all appeals to the County Court, High Court or Civil Division of the Court of Appeal. The exceptions are appeals against committal to prison, appeals against a refusal to grant *habeas corpus*, and appeals against the making of secure accommodation orders under s 25 of the Children Act 1989 (a form of custodial 'sentence' for recalcitrant children). There is no appeal against a decision of the court to give or refuse permission, but this does not affect any right under rules of court to make a further application for permission to the same or another court.

The Act provides that, where the County Court or High Court has already reached a decision in a case brought on appeal, there is no further possibility of an appeal of that decision to the Court of Appeal, unless (s 55) the Court of Appeal considers that the appeal would raise an important point of principle or practice, or there is some other compelling reason for the court to hear it. This is known as the second appeals test.

6.8.3 DESTINATION OF APPEALS

Section 56 of the AJA 1999 enables the Lord Chancellor to vary, by order, the routes of appeal for appeals to and within the County Courts, the High Court and the Civil Division of the Court of Appeal. Before making an order, the Lord Chancellor will be required to consult the Heads of Division, and any order will be subject to the affirmative resolution procedure. The following appeal routes are specified by order:

- In fast-track cases heard by a district judge, appeals will be to a circuit judge.
- In fast-track cases heard by a circuit judge, appeals will be to a High Court judge.
- In multi-track cases, appeals of interim decisions made at first instance by a district judge will be to a circuit judge, by a master or circuit judge to a High Court judge, and by a High Court judge to the Court of Appeal.
- In multi-track cases, appeals of final orders, regardless of the court of first instance, will be to the Court of Appeal.

- The Heads of Division are the Lord Chief Justice, the Master of the Rolls, the President of the Family Division and the Vice Chancellor.
- A decision is interim where it does not determine the final outcome of the case.

The legislation provides for the Master of the Rolls or a lower court to direct that an appeal that would normally be heard by a lower court be heard instead by the Court of Appeal. This power would be used where the appeal raises an important point of principle or practice, or is a case that, for some other compelling reason, should be considered by the Court of Appeal.

6.8.4 CIVIL DIVISION OF COURT OF APPEAL

The 1999 Act makes flexible provision for the number of judges of which a court must be constituted in order for the Court of Appeal to be able to hear appeals. Section 54 of the Senior Courts Act 1981 provided that the Court of Appeal was constituted to exercise any of its jurisdiction if it consisted of an uneven number of judges not less than three. In limited circumstances, it provided that a court could be properly constituted with two judges. The 1999 Act allows the Master of the Rolls, with the concurrence of the Lord Chancellor, to give directions about the minimum number of judges of which a court must consist for given types of proceedings. Subject to any directions, the Act also allows the Master of the Rolls, or a Lord Justice of Appeal designated by him for the purpose, to determine the number of judges who will sit to hear any particular appeal.

6.8.5 JURISDICTION OF SINGLE JUDGE OF HIGH COURT

The 1999 Act allows certain applications to be routinely heard by a single judge of the High Court. It does this by removing an obstacle that existed in the earlier legislation by which the route of appeal for these cases was to the House of Lords, but the Administration of Justice Act 1960 provided that the Supreme Court would only hear appeals in these matters from a Divisional Court (that is, more than one judge) of the High Court. The 1999 Act amends the 1960 Act so that the Supreme Court can hear appeals from a single High Court judge.

6.8.6 THE CIVIL PROCEDURE RULES

Under Part 52 of the CPR, the general rule is that permission to appeal in virtually all cases is mandatory. It should be obtained immediately following the judgment from the lower court or appellate court. Permission will only be given where the court considers that the appellant shows a real prospect of success or there is some other compelling reason for the court to hear the appeal.

All appeals will now be limited to a review rather than a complete rehearing and the appeal will only be allowed if the decision of the lower court was wrong or unjust due to a serious procedural or other irregularity.

The rule now is that there should be only one appeal. Lord Justice Brooke emphasised in the leading case of *Tanfern v Cameron MacDonald and Another* (2000), 'the decision of the first appeal court is now to be given primacy'. An application for a second or subsequent appeal (from the High Court or County Court) must be made to the Court of Appeal, which will not accede unless the appeal raises an important point of principle or practice, or there is some other compelling reason to hear the appeal.

The general rule is that an appeal lies to the next level of judge in the court hierarchy, that is, district judge to Circuit judge to High Court judge. The main exception relates to an appeal against a final decision in a multi-track claim, which will go straight to the Court of Appeal.

Great emphasis is placed on ensuring that cases are dealt with promptly and efficiently, and on weeding out and deterring unjustified appeals. The result is that the opportunity to appeal a decision at first instance in a lower court is much more restricted. It is vital, therefore, that practitioners be properly prepared at the initial hearing.

6.9   THE SUPREME COURT

In October 2009, the UK Supreme Court assumed the jurisdiction of the Appellate Committee of the House of Lords and the devolution jurisdiction of the Judicial Committee of the Privy Council. It is an independent institution, presided over by 12 independently appointed judges known as Justices of the Supreme Court. The Court is housed in the refurbished Middlesex Guildhall on London's Parliament Square – opposite the Houses of Parliament and alongside Westminster Abbey and the Treasury – a fitting location for the apex of the justice system.

The official website of the Supreme Court (www.supremecourt.uk) notes that 'Courts are the final arbiter between the citizen and the state, and are therefore a fundamental pillar of the constitution'. The new court has been established to achieve a complete separation between the United Kingdom's senior judges and the Upper House of Parliament, emphasising the independence of the Law Lords and increasing the distance between Parliament and the courts. As with the previous decisions of the House of Lords, when it was the highest court in the land, the impact of Supreme Court decisions will extend far beyond the parties involved in any given case, shaping society and directly affecting our everyday lives. In their previous role as the Appellate Committee of the House of Lords the Justices gave many landmark rulings about such matters as marital rape, the defence of provocation, the detention without trial of alleged terrorists, the legality of the Hunting Act 2004 under European law, and whether or not a schoolgirl could be prevented from wearing traditional cultural dress.

The Supreme Court, as well as being the final court of appeal, plays an important role in the development of United Kingdom law. It has given a number of landmark rulings on subjects including police powers of stop and search, the territorial application of the Human Rights Act 1998, the legal status of prenuptial agreements and age discrimination in the workplace. As an appeal court, the Supreme Court cannot consider a case unless a relevant order has been made in a lower court.

The Supreme Court

- is the final court of appeal for all United Kingdom civil cases, and criminal cases from England, Wales and Northern Ireland;
- hears appeals on arguable points of law of general public importance;
- concentrates on cases of the greatest public and constitutional importance; and
- maintains and develops the role of the highest court in the United Kingdom as a leader in the common law world.

The Supreme Court hears appeals from the following courts in each jurisdiction:

England and Wales

- The Court of Appeal, Civil Division;
- The Court of Appeal, Criminal Division;
- (in some limited cases) the High Court.

This is extended by provisions in the Criminal Justice and Courts Act 2015, which allows the 'leapfrogging' procedure for decisions of the Employment Appeal Tribunal, Upper Tribunal and the Special Immigration Appeal Tribunal so that decisions from these bodies may, exceptionally, be appealed directly to the Supreme Court.

Scotland

- The Court of Session.

Northern Ireland

- The Court of Appeal in Northern Ireland;
- (in some limited cases) the High Court.

As the highest court of appeal in the United Kingdom, the Supreme Court acts as the final arbiter on cases. Occasionally, it will be called upon to interpret European law and the European Convention on Human Rights as they relate to UK domestic laws. Under European law, Member states' courts should always make their rulings according to principles laid down in relevant decisions by the Court of Justice of the European Union (CJEU). If the Supreme Court is considering a case where interpretation of a CJEU decision is unclear, the Justices must refer the question to the CJEU for clarification. They will then base their own decision on this answer.

In cases relating to the European Convention on Human Rights, it is accepted that no national court should 'without strong reason dilute or weaken the effect of the Strasbourg case law' (Lord Bingham of Cornhill in *R (Ullah) v Special Adjudicator* (2004)). If human rights principles appear to have been breached, it may be possible to make a claim to the European Court of Human Rights after all avenues of appeal in the United Kingdom have been exhausted, or if the Supreme Court has no jurisdiction in the particular case.

Lord Phillips of Worth Matravers, first president of the Supreme Court, said of its purpose:

> The object is to give formal effect to an important constitutional principle – the separation of powers, by transferring the function of the [highest] court from technically being a function carried out by Parliament to a function carried out by a court of judges.
>
> (*The Times*, 1 October 2009)

There have been changes to procedure from those adopted by the House of Lords. Lord Phillips favoured more sittings of bigger panels (seven or nine justices instead of five commonly collected for House of Lords' cases) and more single or majority judgments rather than each judge giving their own. The current president is Lord Neuberger and the appointment of Lady Hale as deputy president in 2013 represents the highest judicial office achieved by a woman in the UK.

Frances Gibb, legal editor of *The Times*, has noted that:

> Until now, the highest court in the land was a committee of the House of Lords known as the law lords. They were hidden from public view in an obscure corridor in the depths of the Palace of Westminster and the public scarcely knew they existed. So the idea of giving the 12 law lords their own building and distinct identity as Supreme Court justices quite separate from the legislature has constitutional logic.
>
> (*The Times*, 1 October 2009)

6.10   THE COURT OF JUSTICE OF THE EUROPEAN UNION AND THE EUROPEAN COURT OF HUMAN RIGHTS

These distinct courts, although outside of the English legal system as such, have an essential impact on English law. The precise nature of these courts and their impact on the English legal system was considered in detail in Chapter 5.

6.11   JUDICIAL COMMITTEE OF THE PRIVY COUNCIL

The Judicial Committee of the Privy Council was created by the Judicial Committee Act 1833. Under the Act, a special committee of the Privy Council was set up to hear appeals from the Dominions. The cases are heard by the judges (without wigs or robes) in the

Supreme Court in London. The Committee's decision is not a judgment but an 'advice' to the monarch, who is counselled that the appeal be allowed or dismissed.

The Committee is the final court of appeal for 23 Commonwealth territories and four independent Republics within the Commonwealth. The Committee comprises Privy Councillors who are Supreme Court Justices. In most cases, which come from places such as the Cayman Islands and Jamaica, the Committee comprises five Justices, sometimes assisted by a judge from the country concerned. The decisions of the Privy Council are very influential in English courts because they concern points of law that are applicable in this jurisdiction and they are pronounced upon by Supreme Court Justices (like their predecessor Lords of Appeal in Ordinary from the House of Lords) in a way which is thus tantamount to a Supreme Court ruling. These decisions, however, are technically of persuasive precedent only, although are likely to be followed in some circumstances by English courts; see, for example, *The Wagon Mound* (1963), a tort case in which the Privy Council ruled, on an appeal from Australia, that in negligence claims, a defendant is liable only for the reasonably foreseeable consequences of his tortious conduct. The Judicial Committee hears the following domestic appeals to Her Majesty in Council:

- from Jersey, Guernsey and the Isle of Man;
- from the Disciplinary Committee of the Royal College of Veterinary Surgeons;
- against certain schemes of the Church Commissioners under the Pastoral Measure 1983.

In 2016, 43 cases were dealt with. There were 49 petitions for special leave to appeal in 2016; of these only 7 were granted and 42 refused.

CHAPTER SUMMARY: THE CIVIL COURTS

THE DIFFERENCES BETWEEN CIVIL AND CRIMINAL LAW

There is no such thing as inherently criminal conduct. A crime is whatever the state has forbidden on pain of legal punishment. The conduct that attracts criminal sanctions changes over time and according to different social systems. The terminology and outcomes of the two systems are different. In criminal cases, the *prosecutor prosecutes the defendant* (or *accused*); in civil cases, the *claimant sues the defendant*.

HER MAJESTY'S COURTS AND TRIBUNALS SERVICE

Her Majesty's Courts and Tribunals Service was created in April 2011. It brings together Her Majesty's Courts Service and the Tribunals Service into one integrated agency providing support for the administration of justice in courts and tribunals.

Her Majesty's Courts and Tribunals Service is an agency of the Ministry of Justice. It uniquely operates as a partnership between the Lord Chancellor, the Lord Chief Justice and the Senior President of Tribunals.

The agency is responsible for the administration of the criminal, civil and family courts and tribunals in England and Wales and non-devolved tribunals in Scotland and Northern Ireland. Its aim is to provide for 'a fair, efficient and effective justice system delivered by an independent judiciary'.

MAGISTRATES' COURTS

Magistrates' courts have a civil jurisdiction. They hear some family proceedings and deal with non-payment of council tax.

COUNTY COURT

The County Court deals with various types of civil case, both small claims and fast-track cases. Over two million proceedings are started each year. The main advantage to litigants using the small claims process is the fact that, if sued, they can defend without fear of incurring huge legal costs, since the costs that the winning party can claim are strictly limited.

HIGH COURT

The High Court has three administrative divisions: the Court of Chancery, the Queen's Bench Division (QBD) and the Family Division. High Court judges sit mainly in the Courts of Justice in the Strand, London, although it is possible for the High Court to sit anywhere in England or Wales. Each branch also has a Divisional Court which is an appeal court, mainly for the magistrates' and County Court. The Court of Protection that deals exclusively with matters arising under the Mental Capacity Act 2005 has the same powers as the High Court.

THE COURT OF APPEAL (CIVIL DIVISION)

The court hears appeals from the three divisions of the High Court, the Divisional Courts, the County Court, the Employment Appeal Tribunal, the Asylum and Immigration Upper Tribunal, the Lands Tribunal, the Transport Tribunal and the Court of Protection. The most senior judge is the Master of the Rolls.

RIGHT TO APPEAL

Rights of appeal can be exercised only with the permission of the court, as prescribed by rules of court. There are three exceptions: appeals against committal to prison, appeals against a refusal to grant *habeas corpus* and appeals against the making of secure accommodation orders under s 25 of the Children Act 1989.

THE SUPREME COURT

In 2009 the Supreme Court assumed the jurisdiction of the Appellate Committee of the House of Lords and the devolution jurisdiction of the Judicial Committee of the Privy Council. It is an independent institution, presided over by 12 independently appointed judges, known as Justices of the Supreme Court.

FOOD FOR THOUGHT

1   In 2009, 36 per cent of the UK population were eligible for legal aid. Since 2004, civil legal aid expenditure has decreased by 15 per cent and following the

Legal Aid, Sentencing and Punishment of Offenders Act 2012, far fewer people are now eligible for legal aid in social welfare cases. What are the access to justice issues that arise when legal aid is cut? Are there other ways of improving access to justice in times of economic strife?

2   The civil justice system in the UK is adversarial. Should litigants be forced to use mediation before they go to court in order to reduce costs and alleviate the backlog in the court system?

FURTHER READING

Blackstone's Civil Practice, 2015, Oxford: OUP
Robins, J, 'Could do better' (2015) 165 NLJ 7648, p 8
Gold, S, 'Civil way' (2009) 159 NLJ 7378
Millett, T, 'A marked improvement' (2008) 158 NLJ 7321
Ministry of Justice, *Court Statistics Quarterly*, Jan–March 2014
New Law Journal, 'New charter for civil courts' [2007] 138
Parpworth, N, 'The hunt goes on' (2008) 158 NLJ 8118

USEFUL WEBSITES

www.justice.gov.uk/about/hmcts

www.gov.uk/government/organisations/hm-courts-and-tribunals-service
The official site of Her Majesty's Courts and Tribunals Service.

www.judiciary.gov.uk/about-the-judiciary/advisory-bodies/cjc
The site of the Civil Justice Council.

www.supremecourt.uk
The website of the Supreme Court.

COMPANION WEBSITE

Now visit the companion website to:

- test your understanding of the key terms using our Flashcard Glossary;
- revise and consolidate your knowledge of 'The civil courts' using our multiple choice question testbank;
- view all of the links to the Useful Websites above.

www.routledge.com/cw/slapper

7.1 INTRODUCTION

7.2   THE NEED FOR REFORM

According to the Civil Justice Review (CJR) 1988, delay in litigation 'causes continuing personal stress, anxiety and financial hardship to ordinary people and their families. It may induce economically weaker parties to accept unfair settlements. It also frustrates the efficient conduct of commerce and industry.' Despite some of the innovations in the five years following that CJR, the problems continued.

Historically, change has come very slowly and gradually to the legal system. The report of the CJR was largely ignored and, with the exception of a shift in the balance of work from the High Court to the County Court (under the Courts and Legal Services Act (CLSA) 1990), no major changes came from its recommendations. The whole process began again with the Woolf review of the civil justice system. In March 1994, the Lord Chancellor set up the Woolf Inquiry to look at ways of improving the speed and accessibility of civil proceedings, and of reducing their cost. Lord Woolf was invited by the government to review the work of the civil courts in England and Wales. He began from the proposition that the system was 'in a state of crisis . . . a crisis for the government, the judiciary and the profession'. The recommendations he formulated – after extensive consultation in the UK and in many other jurisdictions – form the basis of major changes to the system that came into effect in April 1999. David Gladwell, head of the Civil Justice Division of the Lord Chancellor's Department (LCD), stated (*Civil Litigation Reform*, 1999, LCD, p 1) that these changes represent 'the greatest change the civil courts have seen in over a century'.

The CJR 1988 recommended unification of the County Courts and the High Court. It accepted the need for different levels of judiciary, but argued that having different levels of courts was inefficient. This recommendation carried what Roger Smith, then director of the Legal Action Group, called an 'unspoken sting', namely, that a divided legal profession could hardly survive a unified court. The Bar rebelled and the judiciary were solidly opposed to such change. The recommendation was not legislated.

The CLSA 1990, following other recommendations in the CJR, legislated for large numbers of cases in the High Court being sent down to the County Courts to expedite their progress. No extra resources were given to the County Courts to cope with the influx of cases and so, not surprisingly, there has been a growing backlog of cases and a poorer quality of service in the County Courts. This problem may well have worsened rather than been helped by the introduction of the Civil Procedure Rules (CPR), as more cases are now heard in the County Courts.

7.3   THE CIVIL PROCESS

Following the Civil Procedure Act 1997, the changes have been effected through the Civil Procedure Rules (CPR) 1998, which came into force on 26 April 1999. These rules replaced the Rules of the Supreme Court 1965 and the County Court Rules 1981. The Rules are divided into parts and practice directions. There are also pre-action protocols. Each part deals with a particular aspect of procedure and within each part is a set of rules laying down the procedure relating to that aspect. Also, under most parts can be found practice directions that give guidance on how the rules are to be interpreted. In addition, the rules are kept under constant review and there are regular updates. By the end of 2014 the 77th update was issued; 2015 saw five further updates and on 3 October 2016 the 86th was introduced. Many of the updates are only minor, but some are substantive. Changes introduced in the 2015 updates included that for money claims where the defendant was an individual the case would be heard, if a hearing were necessary, in the defendant's local hearing centre, otherwise it would be the claimant's preference. The principal change in the eighty-sixth update relates to Part 52 appeals and supporting practice directions. Companies Acts proceedings are now commenced in the Central London County Court rather than the High Court. The pilot electronic working scheme set up in 2014 has been replaced for two years from 16 November 2015 with a new scheme. It has been extended to include the Chancery Division, Commercial Court, Companies Court, Mercantile Court, Probate, Technology and Construction, Arbitration, Intellectual Property, Estates, Trusts and Charities, Financial List, and the Admiralty Court, unless specifically excluded by the revised practice guides. It applies to existing proceedings and those started on or after 16 November 2015. Pre-action protocols are listed in 7.3.4.

A new not-for-profit company, MedCo Registration Solutions, was set up on 6 April 2015 to deal with soft tissue injuries arising from Road Traffic Accidents (RTA). All medico-legal experts and medical reporting organisations (MRO) will need to be registered with MedCo in order to provide medico-legal reports for RTA soft tissue injury claims. The qualifying criteria was updated 25 October 2016. Medco is awaiting the outcome of the Ministry of Justice consultation, which closes on 6 January 2017, on proposals to reduce the unacceptably high number of whiplash claims.

Of major importance has been the accessibility of the CPR, which can be found on the LCD website, including practice directions and updates. A further method of improving the civil process has been the introduction of pre-action protocols for certain types of case, which are designed to increase the opportunity for settling cases as early in the proceedings as possible by improving communication between the parties and their advisers. The rules are quoted as, for example, 'rule 4.1', which refers to Part 4, r 1 of the CPR.

The main features of the civil process are as follows.

The case control

The progress of cases is monitored by using a computerised diary monitoring system. Parties are encouraged to co-operate with each other in the conduct of the proceedings; which issues need full investigation and trial are decided promptly and others disposed of summarily.

Court allocation and tracking

The County Courts retain an almost unlimited jurisdiction for handling contract and tort claims. Where a matter involves a claim for damages or other remedy for libel or slander, or a claim where the title to any toll, fair, market or franchise is in question, then the proceedings cannot start in the County Court unless the parties agree otherwise. On 9 February 2012 the Ministry of Justice announced that non-personal injury claims under £100,000 cannot be heard in the High Court.

FIGURE 7.1 *The Reformed Civil Process.*

Issuing proceedings in the High Court is now limited to personal injury claims with a value of £50,000 or more; other claims with a value of more than £100,000 and equity claims where the property is worth at least £350,000; claims where an Act of Parliament requires a claim to start in the High Court; or specialist High Court claims. Cases are allocated to one of three tracks for a hearing, that is, small claims, fast track or multi-track, depending on the value and complexity of the claim.

The documentation and procedures

Most claims will be begun by a multipurpose form and the provision of a response pack, and the requirement that an allocation questionnaire is completed is intended to simplify and expedite matters.

7.3.1   THE CIVIL PROCEDURE RULES

The CPR are the same for the County Court and the High Court. The vocabulary is more user-friendly, so, for example, what used to be called a 'writ' is a 'claim form' and a *guardian ad litem* is a 'litigation friend'.

Although in some ways all the fuss about the CPR being so far-reaching creates the impression that the future will see a sharp rise in litigation, the truth may be different. The Queen's Bench Division of the High Court is the court that deals with all substantial claims in personal injury, breach of contract and negligence actions. According to official figures (*Judicial and Court Statistics 2011*, Ministry of Justice, 28 June 2012), 153,624 writs and originating summonses were issued by the court in 1995. By 2013, however, the number of annual actions issued was down to 13,035 (HM Government website of quarterly court statistics). The number of claims issued in the County Courts (which deal with less substantial civil disputes in the law of negligence) has also fallen. In 1998, the number of claims issued nationally was 2,245,324 but in 2014 it was 1,595,441 with 44,804 hearings or trials and in quarter 3 of 2016 claims were 494,148 with 12,675 hearings.

7.3.2   THE OVERRIDING OBJECTIVE (CPR PART 1)

The overriding objective of the CPR is to enable the court to deal justly with cases. It applies to all of the rules, and the parties to a case are required to assist the court in pursuing the overriding objective. Further, when the courts exercise any powers given to them under the CPR, or in interpreting any rules, they must consider and apply the overriding objective. The first rule reads:

> 1.1(1) These rules are a new procedural code with the overriding objective of enabling the court to deal with cases justly and at proportionate cost.

Costs are now fundamental to litigation and all parties, unless unrepresented, must file and exchange costs budgets in form H verified by a statement of truth. Under CPR 3.17, when making any case management decision, the court will have regard to any available budgets of the parties and will take into account the costs involved in each procedural step.

This objective includes ensuring that the parties are on an equal footing and saving expense. When exercising any discretion given by the CPR, the court must, according to r 1.2, have regard to the overriding objective and a checklist of factors, including the amount of money involved, the complexity of the issue, the parties' financial positions, and how the case can be dealt with expeditiously and fairly, and allot an appropriate share of the court's resources while taking into account the needs of others.

7.3.3   PRACTICE DIRECTIONS

Practice directions (official statements of interpretative guidance) play an important role in the civil process. In general, they supplement the CPR, giving the latter fine detail. They tell parties and their representatives what the court will expect of them in respect of documents to be filed in court for a particular purpose, and how they must co-operate with the other parties to their action. They also tell the parties what they can expect of the court; for example they explain what sort of sanction a court is likely to impose if a particular court order or request is not complied with. Almost every part of the rules has a corresponding practice direction. They supersede all previous practice directions in relation to the civil process.

7.3.4   PRE-ACTION PROTOCOLS

The pre-action protocols (PAPs) are an important feature of the reforms. They exist for cases of *clinical disputes* (formerly called medical/clinical negligence, but now extended to cover claims against dentists, radiologists and so on), personal injury, disease and illness, construction and engineering disputes, defamation, professional negligence, housing disrepair, housing possession following rent arrears, housing possession following mortgage arrears, low value personal injury claims in road traffic accidents, low value personal injury (employers' and public liability) claims, dilapidations at end of lease or tenancy of a commercial property and judicial review. Further protocols are likely to follow.

The protocols were drafted with the assistance of The Law Society, the Clinical Disputes Forum, the Association of Personal Injury Lawyers and the Forum of Insurance Lawyers. Most clients in personal injury and clinical dispute claims want their cases settled as quickly and as economically as possible. The spirit of co-operation fostered by the Woolf reforms should mean that fewer cases are pushed through the courts. The PAPs are intended to improve pre-action contact between the parties and to facilitate better exchange of information and fuller investigation of a claim at an earlier stage.

At the early stage of proceedings, when a case is being allocated to a track (that is, small claims, fast track or multi-track), after the defence has been filed, parties will be asked whether they have complied with the relevant protocol, and if not, why not. The court will then be able to take the answers into account when deciding whether, for example, an extension of time should be granted. The court will also be able to penalise poor conduct by one side through costs sanctions – an order that the party at fault pay the costs of the proceedings or part of them.

7.4   CASE CONTROL (CPR PART 3)

Case control by the judiciary, rather than leaving the conduct of the case to the parties, is a key element in the reforms resulting from the Woolf review. The court's case management powers are found in Part 3 of the CPR, although there is a variety of ways in which a judge may control the progress of the case. A judge may make a number of orders to give opportunities to the parties to take stock of their case-by-case management conferences, check they have all the information they need to proceed or settle by pre-trial reviews, or halt the proceedings to give the parties an opportunity to consider a settlement. When any application is made to the court, there is an obligation on the judge to deal with as many outstanding matters as possible. The court is also under an obligation to ensure that witness statements are limited to the evidence that is to be given if there is a hearing, and expert evidence is restricted to what is required to resolve the proceedings. Judges receive support from court staff in carrying out their case management role. The court monitors case progress by using a computerised diary monitoring system which:

- records certain requests, or orders made by the court;
- identifies the particular case or cases to which these orders/requests refer, and the dates by which a response should be made; and
- checks on the due date whether the request or order has been complied with.

Whether there has been compliance or not, the court staff will pass the relevant files to a procedural judge (a Master in the Royal Courts of Justice, or a district judge in the County Court), who will decide if either side should have a sanction imposed on them.

In the current system, the litigants have much less control over the pace of the case than in the past. They will not be able to draw out proceedings, or delay in the way that they once could have done, because the case is subject to a timetable. Once a defence is filed, the parties get a timetable order that includes the prospective trial date. The court now has a positive duty to manage cases. Rule 1.4(1) states that 'The court must further the overriding objective by actively managing cases'. The rule goes on to explain what this management involves:

1.4(2) Active case management includes –

(a)   encouraging the parties to co-operate with each other in the conduct of the proceedings;

(b)   identifying the issues at an early stage;

(c)   deciding promptly which issues need full investigation and trial and accordingly disposing summarily of the others;

(d)   deciding the order in which issues are to be resolved;

(e)   encouraging the parties to use an alternative dispute resolution procedure if the court considers that appropriate;

(f)   helping the parties to settle the whole or part of the case;

(g)   fixing timetables or otherwise controlling the progress of the case;

(h)   considering whether the likely benefits of taking a particular step justify the cost of taking it;

(i)   dealing with as many aspects of the case as it can on the same occasion;

(j)   dealing with the case without the parties needing to attend court;

(k)   making use of technology; and

(l)   giving directions to ensure that the trial of a case proceeds quickly and efficiently.

It is worth noting here that district judges and deputy district judges have had extensive training to promote a common approach. Training is being taken very seriously by the judiciary. District judges now occupy a pivotal position in the civil process.

Part 3 of the CPR gives the court a wide range of substantial powers. The court can, for instance, extend or shorten the time for compliance with any rule, practice direction or court order, even if an application for an extension is made after the time for compliance has expired. It can also hold a hearing and receive evidence by telephone or 'by using any other method of direct oral communication'.

This part of the CPR also gives the court powers to:

- strike out a statement of case;
- impose sanctions for non-payment of certain fees;
- impose sanctions for non-compliance with rules and practice directions;
- give relief from sanctions.

Part 3.9 of the CPR has been strengthened to make it more difficult to obtain relief from sanctions for failing to adhere to the strict timetables set by the courts. However, some judges have not applied the rule so strictly, as in the cases of *Wyche v Careforce Group plc* (2013) and *Raayan Al Iraq Co Ltd v Trans Victory Marine Inc* (2013).

There is, though, a certain flexibility built into the rules. A failure to comply with a rule or practice direction will not necessarily be fatal to a case. Rule 3.10 of the CPR states:

> Where there has been an error of procedure such as a failure to comply with a rule or practice direction:
>
> (a)   the error does not invalidate any step taken in the proceedings unless the court so orders; and
> (b)   the court may make an order to remedy the error.

The intention of imposing a sanction will always be to put the parties back into the position they would have been in if one of them had not failed to meet a deadline. For example, the court could order that a party carries out a task (like producing some sort of documentary evidence) within a very short time (for example, two days) in order that the existing trial dates can be met.

7.4.1   CASE MANAGEMENT CONFERENCES

Case management conferences may be regarded as an opportunity to 'take stock'. Many of these are now conducted by telephone. There is no limit to the number of case management conferences that may be held during the life of a case, although the cost of attendance at such hearings against the benefits obtained will always be a consideration in making the decision. They will be used, among other things, to consider:

- giving directions, including a specific date for the return of a listing questionnaire;
- whether the claim or defence is sufficiently clear for the other party to understand the claim they have to meet;
- whether any amendments should be made to statements of case;

- what documents, if any, each party needs to show the other;
- what factual evidence should be given;
- what expert evidence should be sought and how it should be sought and disclosed; and
- whether it would save costs to order a separate trial of one or more issues.

7.4.2   PRE-TRIAL REVIEWS

Pre-trial reviews will normally take place after the filing of listing questionnaires and before the start of the trial. Their main purpose is to decide a timetable for the trial itself, including the evidence to be allowed and whether this should be given orally; to determine instructions about the content of any trial bundles (bundles of documents including evidence, such as written statements, for the judge to read); and to confirm a realistic time estimate for the trial itself.

Rules require that, where a party is represented, a representative 'familiar with the case and with sufficient authority to deal with any issues likely to arise must attend every case management conference or pre-trial review'.

Both the Chancery Guide and the Queen's Bench Guide provide that where it is estimated that a case will last more than 10 days or where a case warrants it, the court may consider directing a pre-trial review.

7.4.3   STAYS FOR SETTLEMENT (CPR PART 26) AND SETTLEMENTS (CPR PART 36)

Under the CPR, there is a greater incentive for parties to settle their differences. Part 36 sets out the procedure for either party to make offers to settle. A Part 36 offer can be made before the start of proceedings and also in appeal proceedings. While there is no prohibition against a party to litigation making an offer to settle in any way they like, there can be advantages in making a formal offer to settle which complies with the rules of court (a 'Part 36 offer to settle'). Part 36 offers to settle in the prescribed form aim to encourage parties to try to settle a dispute. They set out the costs and other consequences that a party will face if it refuses a reasonable offer to settle. Making a Part 36 offer to settle should not be regarded as a sign of weakness but an appropriate way of putting pressure on an opponent to settle. What is a Part 36 offer to settle and when can one be made?

To be compliant with the rules of court, a Part 36 offer to settle must:

- be a genuine offer to settle;
- be made 'without prejudice except as to costs' (it cannot be referred to the judge having conduct of the proceedings until the conclusion of the matter);
- comply with the strict requirements of Part 36 of the rules of court.

Part 36 offers to settle can be made in the following instances:

- in both money (including claims for provisional damages) and non-money claims;
- in respect of the whole or part of the claim or in relation to an issue that arises;
- in respect of liability alone, thus leaving the issue of the amount of any damages to be dealt with later;
- in respect of counterclaims and any additional (Part 20) claim.

Part 36 offers to settle can be made by both a claimant and a defendant in a dispute, at any stage of a dispute before or after proceedings have commenced and in appeal proceedings. Part 36 offers to settle can be made prior to the commencement of court proceedings.

The party making the offer is called the 'offeror' and the party receiving it is called the 'offeree'. Under the revised Part 36 rule, where an offer relates to settlement of a money claim it is no longer possible to accompany the offer with the payment of funds into court. This provision applies irrespective of who the offeror is and whether that party has the means or assets to pay. When a Part 36 offer is accepted by the claimant the defendant must pay the sum offered within 14 days (unless the parties agree to extend the time period), failing which the claimant can enter judgment.

The court will take into account any pre-action offers to settle when making an order for costs. Thus, a side that has refused a reasonable offer to settle will be treated less generously in the issue of how far the court will order their costs to be paid by the other side. For this to happen, the offer must be one which is made to be open to the other side for at least 21 days after the date it was made (to stop any undue pressure being put on someone with the phrase 'take it or leave it, it is only open for one day then I shall withdraw the offer').

If an offer to settle is to be made in accordance with Part 36 it must be made in writing and state that it is intended to have the consequences of Part 36. Where the defendant makes the offer, it must specify a period of not less than 21 days within which the defendant will be liable for the claimant's costs if the offer is accepted. In addition, either party's offer must state whether it relates to the whole or part of the claim, or to an issue which arises in it and if so to which part or issue and whether any counterclaim is taken into account. The revised Part 36 rule allows the parties to withdraw any offer after the expiry of the 'relevant period' as defined in Rule 36.3.1.c without the court's permission. However, before the expiry of the 'relevant period' it is possible for a Part 36 offer to be withdrawn or its terms changed to be less advantageous to the 'offeree' only with the court's permission.

Several aspects of the rules encourage litigants to settle rather than take risks in order (as a claimant) to hold out for unreasonably large sums of compensation, or try to get away (as a defendant) with paying nothing rather than some compensation. The system of Part 36 payments or offers does not apply to a claim allocated to the small claims track but, for other cases, it seems bound to have a significant effect. Part 36 applies prior to a small claims track allocation and on reallocation from this track to the other two tracks.

Thus, if at the trial a claimant does not get more damages than a sum offered by the defendant, or obtain a judgment more favourable than a Part 36 offer, the court will, unless it considers it unjust to do so, order the claimant to pay any costs incurred by the defendant after the latest date for accepting the payment or offer without requiring the court's permission, together with interest on those costs.

Similarly, where, at trial, a defendant is held liable to the claimant for a sum at least equal to the proposals contained in a claimant's Part 36 offer (that is, where the claimant has made an offer to settle), the court may order the defendant to pay interest on the award at a rate not exceeding 10 per cent above the base rate for some or all of the period, starting with the date on which the defendant could have accepted the offer without requiring the court's permission. In addition, the court may order that the claimant be entitled to his costs on an indemnity basis together with interest on those costs at a rate not exceeding 10 per cent above base rate for the period from the latest date when the defendant could have accepted the offer without requiring the court's permission.

The court has a general and overreaching discretion to make a different order for costs than the normal order under Part 44.

District Judge Frenkel has given the following example:

> Claim, £150,000 – judgment, £51,000 – £50,000 paid into court. The without prejudice correspondence shows that the claimant would consider nothing short of £150,000. The claimant may be in trouble. The defendant will ask the judge to consider overriding principles of Part 1: 'Was it proportional to incur the further costs of trial to secure an additional £1,000?' Part 44.3 confirms the general rule that the loser pays but allows the court to make a different order to take into account offers to settle, payment into court, the parties' conduct including pre-action conduct and exaggeration of the claim ((1999) 149 NLJ 458).

Active case management imposes a duty on the courts to help parties settle their disputes. A 'stay' is a temporary halt in proceedings, and an opportunity for the court to order such a pause. Either party to a case can also make a written request for a stay when filing their completed allocation questionnaire. Where all the parties indicate that they have agreed on a stay to attempt to settle the case, provided the court agrees, they can have an initial period of one month to try to settle the case. If the court grants a stay, the claimant must inform the court if a settlement is reached, otherwise at the expiry of the stay it will effectively be deemed that a settlement has not been reached and the file will be referred to the judge for directions as considered appropriate.

The court will always give the final decision about whether to grant the parties more time to use a mediator or arbitrator or expert to settle, even if the parties are agreed they wish to have more time. A stay will never be granted for an indefinite period.

7.4.4   APPLICATIONS TO BE MADE WHEN CLAIMS COME BEFORE A JUDGE (CPR PART 1)

The overriding objective in Part 1 requires the court to deal with as many aspects of the case as possible on the same occasion. The filing of an allocation questionnaire, which is to enable the court to judge in which track the case should be heard, is one such occasion. Parties should, wherever possible, issue any application they may wish to make, such as an application for summary judgment (CPR Part 24), or to add a third party (CPR Part 20), at the same time as they file their questionnaire. Any hearing set to deal with the application will also serve as an allocation hearing if allocation remains appropriate.

7.4.5   WITNESS STATEMENTS (CPR PART 32)

In the *Final Report on Access to Justice*, Lord Woolf recognised the importance of witness statements in cases, but observed that they had become problematic because lawyers had made them excessively long and detailed in order to protect against leaving out something that later proved to be relevant. He said 'witness statements have ceased to be the authentic account of the lay witness; instead they have become an elaborate, costly branch of legal drafting' (para 55).

Witness statements must contain the evidence that the witness will give at trial. They should be drafted in lay language and should not discuss legal propositions. Witnesses will be allowed to amplify on the statement or deal with matters that have arisen since the report was served, although this is not an automatic right and a 'good reason' for the admission of new evidence will have to be established.

7.4.6   EXPERTS (CPR PART 35)

The rules place a clear duty on the court to ensure that 'expert evidence is restricted to that which is reasonably required to resolve the proceedings'. That is to say that expert evidence will only be allowed either by way of written report, or orally, where the court gives permission. Equally important is the rules' statement about experts' duties. Rule 35.3 states that it is the clear duty of experts to help the *court* on matters within their expertise, bearing in mind that this duty overrides any obligation to the person from whom they have received instructions or by whom they are paid.

There is greater emphasis on using the opinion of a single expert. Experts are only to be called to give oral evidence at a trial or hearing if the court gives permission. Experts' written reports must contain a statement that they understand and have complied with, and will continue to comply with, their duty to the court. Instructions to experts are no longer privileged and their substance, whether written or oral, must be set out in the expert's report. Thus, either side can insist, through the court, on seeing how the other side phrased its request to an expert.

7.5 COURT AND TRACK ALLOCATION (CPR PART 26)

Part 7 of the CPR sets out the rules for starting proceedings. A restriction is placed on which cases may be begun in the High Court. The County Courts retain an almost unlimited jurisdiction for handling contract and tort claims (that is, negligence cases, nuisance cases but excluding a claim for damages or other remedy for libel or slander unless the parties agree otherwise). Issuing proceedings in the High Court is now limited to:

- personal injury claims with a value of £50,000 or more; other claims with a value of more than £100,000;
- claims where an Act of Parliament requires proceedings to start in the High Court;
- specialist High Court claims which need to go to one of the specialist 'lists', like the Commercial List, the Technology and Construction List; or
- equity claims where the property is worth at least £350,000.

The civil system works on the basis that the court, upon receipt of the defence, requires the parties to complete 'allocation questionnaires' (giving all the relevant details of the claim, including how much it is for and an indication of its factual and legal complexity). Under Part 26 of the CPR, the case will then be allocated to one of three tracks for a hearing. These are: (a) small claims track; (b) fast track; and (c) multi-track. Each of the tracks offers a different degree of case management. The multi-track has, since 6 April 2009, a minimum limit of £25,000.01.

The small claims limit is £10,000, although personal injury (which in 2017 will increase to £5,000 for soft tissue injury and subject to consultation all injury claims) and housing disrepair claims for over £1,000, and illegal eviction and harassment claims are excluded from the small claims procedure. The limit for cases going into the fast-track system is £25,000. Applications to move cases 'up' a track on grounds of complexity will have to be made on the allocation questionnaire (see below). All small claims up to £5,000 will now be dealt with by mediation.

Directions (instructions about what to do to prepare the case for trial or hearing) will be proportionate to the value of the claim, its importance, its complexity and so on. Each track requires a different degree of case monitoring, that is, the more complex the claim, the more milestone events there are likely to be (i.e. important points in the process, like the date by which the allocation questionnaire should be returned). Time for carrying out directions, no matter which track, may be extended or shortened by agreement between parties, but must not, as a result, affect any of the milestones relevant to that track. The time for carrying out directions will be expressed as calendar dates rather than periods of days or weeks. Directions will include the court's directions concerning the use of expert evidence.

7.5.1 THE SMALL CLAIMS TRACK (CPR PART 27)

There is no longer any 'automatic reference' to the small claims track. Claims are allocated to this track in exactly the same way as to the fast track or multi-track. The concept of an '*arbitration*' therefore disappears and is replaced by a *small claims hearing*. Aspects of the old small claims procedure that are retained include their informality, the interventionist approach adopted by the judiciary, the limited costs regime and the limited grounds for appeal (misconduct of the district judge or an error of law made by the court).

Key features of the small claims track are:

- *Jurisdiction of claims limited to no more than £10,000* (with the exception of claims for personal injury where the damages claimed for pain and suffering and loss of amenity do not exceed £1,000 and the financial value of the whole claim does not exceed £10,000; and for housing disrepair where the claim for repairs and other work does not exceed £1,000 and the financial value of any other claim for damages is not more than £1,000).

  In George Osborne's autumn statement he proposed banning general damages for minor soft tissue (whiplash type) injuries and increasing the small claims procedure limit for all personal injury claims to £5,000. The proposed change is due to commence in 2017. The Treasury has confirmed the new limit, but that it would only apply to soft tissue injuries and other injury claims would be subject to consultation.

- *All small claims up to £5,000 to be dealt with by mediation* – the Ministry of Justice is encouraging all parties to financial disputes of up to £10,000 to use the Small Claims Mediation Service.

- *Hearings to be generally public hearings* – but subject to some exceptions (CPR Part 39).

- *Paper adjudication, if parties consent* – where a judge thinks that paper adjudication may be appropriate, parties will be asked to say whether or not they have any objections within a given time period. If a party does object, the matter will be given a hearing in the normal way.

- *Parties need not attend the final hearing* – a party not wishing to attend the final hearing will be able to give the court written notice before the hearing that they will not be attending. The notice must be filed with the court seven days before the start of the hearing. This will guarantee that the court will take into account any written evidence that the party has sent to the court. A consequence of this is that the judge must give reasons for the decision reached which will be included in the judgment.

- *Use of experts* – expert witnesses will only be allowed to give evidence with the permission of the court.

- *Costs* – these are not generally awarded, but a small award may be made to cover costs in issuing the claim, court fees, for legal advice and assistance relating to proceedings which included a claim for an injunction or an order for specific performance, the costs assessed by summary procedure in relation to an appeal and expenses incurred by the successful party, witnesses and experts. Under r 44.14 of the CPR, additional costs may be awarded against any party who has behaved unreasonably.

- *Preliminary hearings* – these may be called:

  (a)   where the judge considers that special directions are needed to ensure a fair hearing and where it appears necessary that a party should attend court so that it can be ensured that the party understands what he or she is required to do to comply with the special directions;

  (b)   to enable the judge to dispose of the claim where he or she is of the view that either of the parties has no real prospect of success at a full hearing;

  (c)   to enable the judge to strike out either the whole or part of a statement of case on the basis that it provides no reasonable grounds for bringing such a claim.

- *The introduction of tailored directions* – to be given for some of the most common small claims, for example, spoiled holidays or wedding videos, road traffic accidents, building disputes.

Parties can consent to use the small claims track even if the value of their claim exceeds the normal value for that track, but subject to the court's approval. The limited cost regime will not apply to these claims, but trial costs are at the discretion of the court and will be limited to the costs that might have been awarded if the claim had been dealt with in the fast track. Generally, the parties will be restricted to a maximum one-day hearing.

The milestone events for the small claims track are the date for the return of the allocation questionnaire and the date of the hearing.

7.5.2   THE FAST TRACK (CPR PART 28)

The fast track provides a streamlined procedure for the handling of cases not suitable for the small claims track and where the value of the claim does not exceed £25,000. It is appropriate where:

the trial is likely to last for no longer than one day; and oral expert evidence at trial will be limited to –

(i)   one expert per party in relation to any expert field; and
(ii)   expert evidence in two expert fields.

The procedures will ensure that the costs remain proportionate to the amount in dispute. The features of the procedure which aim to achieve this are:

- standard directions for trial preparation which avoid complex procedures and multiple experts, with minimum case management intervention by the court;

- a standard limited period between directions and the start of the trial: it will not be more than 30 weeks;

- a maximum of one day (five hours) for trial;

- trial period must not exceed three weeks and parties must be given 21 days' notice of the date fixed for trial unless in exceptional circumstances the court directs shorter notice;

- normally, no oral expert evidence is to be given at trial, but where allowed, will be limited to one expert per party in any expert field and expert evidence in two expert fields; and

- costs allowed for the trial are fixed depending on the level of advocacy.

Directions given to the parties by the judge will normally include a date by which parties must file a listing questionnaire. As with allocation questionnaires, the procedural judge may impose a sanction where a listing questionnaire is not returned by the due date. Listing questionnaires will include information about witnesses, and confirm the time needed for trial, parties' availability and the level of advocate for the trial.

The milestone events for the fast track are the date for the return of allocation and listing questionnaires and the date for the start of the trial or trial period.

7.5.3   THE MULTI-TRACK (CPR PART 29)

The multi-track is intended to provide a flexible regime for the handling of claims over £25,000, or lower, more complex claims if not appropriate for the fast track.

This track does not provide any standard procedure, such as those for small claims or claims in the fast track. Instead, it offers a range of case management tools – *standard directions*, *case management conferences* and *pre-trial reviews* – which can be used in a 'mix and match' way to suit the needs of individual cases. Whichever of these is used to manage the case, the principle of setting a date for trial, or a trial period at the earliest possible time, no matter that it is some way away, will remain paramount.

Where a trial period is given for a multi-track case, this will be one week. Parties will be told initially that their trial will begin on a day within the given week. The rules and practice direction do not set any time period for giving notice to the parties of the date fixed for trial.

7.6   DOCUMENTATION AND PROCEDURES

One of the main aims of the Woolf reforms is to simplify court forms. Under the old system, there were various forms that needed to be completed at the outset of a claim – different types including summonses, originating applications, writs and petitions. Under the current system, most claims will be begun by using a 'Part 7' claim form.

7.6.1   HOW TO START PROCEEDINGS – THE CLAIM FORM (CPR PART 7)

A Part 7 claim form has been designed for multipurpose use. It can be used if the claim is for a *specified* amount of money (the old term was *liquidated* damages) or an *unspecified* amount (replacing the term *unliquidated* damages). The form can also be used for non-monetary claims, for example, where the claimant just wants a court order, not money. The person issuing the claim form is called a claimant (plaintiff in old vocabulary) and the person at whom it is directed will continue to be known as a defendant.

Under the current rules, the court can grant any remedy to which the claimant is entitled, even if the claimant does not specify which one he wants. It is, though, as Gordon Exall has observed ((1999) SJ 162, 19 February), dangerous to start a claim without having a clear idea of the remedy you want. The defendant might be able to persuade the court not to allow the claimant a certain part of his costs if he (the defendant) finds himself having to consider a remedy that had not been mentioned prior to the trial.

There is now the facility to make a money claim online, which reduces the cost of commencing proceedings. A helpful free guide to starting and defending small claims produced by the Civil Justice Council is available at www.judiciary.gov.uk.

7.6.2 ALTERNATIVE PROCEDURE FOR CLAIMS (CPR PART 8)

Part 8 of the rules introduced the *alternative procedure for claims*. This procedure is commenced by the issue of a Part 8 claim form. It is intended to provide a speedy resolution of claims that are not likely to involve a substantial dispute of fact, for example applications for approval of infant settlements, or for orders enforcing a statutory right such as a right to have access to medical records (under the Access to Health Records Act 1990). The Part 8 procedure is also used where a rule or practice direction requires or permits its use.

The main differences between this and the Part 7 procedure are as follows:

- a hearing may be given on issue or at some later stage if required;
- only an acknowledgement of service is served with the claim form by way of a response document;
- a defendant must file an acknowledgement of service to be able to take part in any hearing;
- a defendant must serve a copy of the acknowledgement on the other parties, as well as filing it with the court;
- no defence is required;
- default judgment is not available to the claimant; the court must hear the case;
- there are automatic directions for the exchange of evidence (in this case, in the form of witness statements);
- Part 8 claims are not formally allocated to a track; they are automatically multitrack cases.

7.6.3 STATEMENT OF CASE – VALUE (CPR PART 16)

The 'value' of a claim is the amount a claimant reasonably expects to recover. Unless the amount being claimed is a specified amount, a claimant will be expected (Part 16) to state the value band into which the claim is likely to fall. The value bands reflect the values for the different tracks (for example, £1 to £10,000 for small claims). Value is calculated as the amount a claimant expects to recover, ignoring any interest, costs, contributory negligence or the fact that a defendant may make a counterclaim or include a set-off in the defence. If a claimant is not able to put a value on the claim, the reasons for this must be given.

Particulars of claim may be included in the claim form, attached to it, or may be served (that is, given or sent to a party by a method allowed by the rules) separately from it. Where they are served separately, they must be served within 14 days of the claim form being served. The time for a defendant to respond begins to run from the time the particulars of claim are served.

Part 16 is entitled *Statements of case* (replacing the term *pleadings*). Statements of case include documents from both sides: claim forms, particulars of claims, defences, counterclaims, replies to defences and counterclaims, Part 20 (third party) claims and any *further information* provided under CPR Part 18 (replacing the term *further and better particulars*). Part 16 also sets out what both particulars of claim and defences should contain.

Part 16 states:

(1)   The claim form must –

    (a)   contain a concise statement of the nature of the claim;
    (b)   specify the remedy which the claimant seeks;
    (c)   where the claimant is making a claim for money, contain a statement of value in accordance with rule 16.3;
    (cc)   where the claimant's only claim is for a specified sum, contain a statement of the interest accrued on that sum; and
    (d)   contain such other matters as may be set out in a practice direction.

The Woolf Report was against obliging the claimant to state the legal nature of the claim, as this would prejudice unrepresented defendants. If the nature of the claim is uncertain, then the court can take its own steps to clarify the matter.

Where a claimant is going to rely on the fact that the defendant has been convicted for a crime arising out of the same circumstances for which the claimant is now suing, then the particulars of claim must contain details of the conviction, the court which made it, and exactly how it is relevant to the claimant's arguments.

It is optional for the claimant also to mention any point of law on which the claim is based and the names of any witnesses which he proposes to call. All statements of case must also contain a statement of truth.

7.6.5 STATEMENTS OF TRUTH (CPR PART 22)

A statement of truth is a statement that a party believes that the facts or allegations set out in a document, which they put forward, are true. It is required in statements of case, witness statements and expert reports. Any document that contains a statement of truth may be used in evidence. This will avoid the previous need to swear affidavits in support of various statements made as part of the claim.

Any document with a signed statement of truth that contains false information given deliberately, that is, without an honest belief in its truth, will constitute a contempt of court (a punishable criminal offence) by the person who provided the information. Solicitors may sign statements of truth on behalf of clients, but on the understanding that it is done with the clients' authority, and with clients knowing that the consequences of any false statement will be personal to them.

7.6.6 RESPONSE TO PARTICULARS OF CLAIM (CPR PART 9)

When a claim form is served, it will be served with a response pack. The response pack will contain an acknowledgement of service, a form of admission and a form of defence and counterclaim. The response pack will be served with a claim form containing the particulars of claim, which are attached to it or, where particulars of claim are served after the claim form, with the particulars. A defendant must respond within 14 days of service of the particulars of claim. If a defendant ignores the claim, the claimant may obtain judgment for the defendant to pay the amount claimed. A defendant may:

- pay the claim;
- admit the claim, or partly admit it;
- file an acknowledgement of service; or
- file a defence.

Requirements have also been introduced regarding the content of a defence. A defence that is a simple denial is no longer acceptable and runs the risk of being struck out by the court (that is, deleted so that it may no longer be relied upon). A defendant must state in any defence:

- which of the allegations in the particulars of claim are denied, giving reasons for doing so, and must state their own version of the events if they intend to put forward a different version to that of the claimant;
- which allegations the defendant is not able to admit or deny but which the claimant is required to prove;
- which allegations are admitted; and
- if the defendant disputes the claimant's statement of value, the reasons for doing so and, if possible, stating an alternative value.

These rules mark a significant change of culture from the old civil procedure rules. Under the old rules, a defendant could, in their defence, raise a 'non-admission' or a 'denial'. The first meant that the defendant was putting the plaintiff (now claimant) to proof, that is, challenging them to prove their case on the balance of probabilities. The second meant that the defendant was raising a specific defence, for example, a 'development risks defence' under the Product Liability Act 1988. Defendants were allowed under the old rules to keep as many avenues of defence available for as long as possible. Under the rules, the defendant must respond according to the choices in the four options above. According to r 16.5(5), if the defendant does not deal specifically with an allegation, then it will be deemed to be admitted. However, where a defendant does not specifically deal with an allegation, but in any event sets out in their defence the nature of their case on that issue, it will be deemed that the matter be proved.

7.6.7   SERVICE (CPR PART 6)

Where the court is to serve any document (not just claim forms), it is for the court to decide the method of service. This will generally be by first-class post. The deemed date of service is two days after the day of posting for all defendants, including limited companies. Where a claim form originally served by post is returned by the Post Office, the court will send a notice of non-service to the claimant stating the method of service attempted. The notice will tell the claimant that the court will not make any further attempts at service. Service therefore becomes a matter for claimants. The court will return the copies of the claim form, response pack and so on, for claimants to amend as necessary and re-serve.

Claimants may serve claim forms, having told the court in writing that they wish to do so, either personally, by post, by fax, by document exchange (a private courier service operated between law firms) or by email or other electronic means. A claimant who serves the claim form must file a certificate of service within seven days of service with a copy of the document served attached.

7.6.8   ADMISSIONS AND PART ADMISSIONS (CPR PART 14)

The possibility of admitting liability for a claim for a specific amount and making an offer to pay by instalments, or at a later date, applies to both County Court and High Court cases. Where the claim is for a specific amount, the admission will be sent direct to the claimant. However, if a claimant objects to the rate of payment offered, there are changes that affect the determination process, that is, the process by which a member of a court's staff or a judge decides the rate of payment.

Cases involving a specific amount where the balance outstanding, including any costs, is less than £50,000, will be determined by a court officer. Those where the balance is £50,000 or more, or for an unspecified amount of any value, must be determined by a Master or district judge. The Master or judge has the option of dealing with the determination on the papers without a hearing or at a hearing.

A defendant in a claim for an unspecified amount of money (damages) will be able to make an offer of a specific sum of money in satisfaction of a claim, which does not have to be supported by a payment into court. A claimant can accept the admission and rate of payment offered as if the claim had originally been for a specific amount. The determination procedure described above will apply where a claimant accepts the amount offered, but not the rate of payment proposed.

If a claimant does not accept the amount offered, a request that judgment be entered for liability on the strength of the defendant's admission may be made to the court. This is referred to as *judgment for an amount and costs to be decided by the court* (replacing *interlocutory judgment for damages to be assessed*). Where judgment is entered in this way, the court will, at the same time, give case management directions for dealing with the case.

Where a request for such a judgment is received, the court file will be passed to a procedural judge. The judge may: allocate the case to the small claims track and give directions if it is of appropriate value; ask that the case be set down for a *disposal* hearing; or where the amount is likely to be heavily disputed, order a trial. Directions will be given as appropriate. A disposal hearing in these circumstances may either be a hearing at which the court gives directions, or at which the amount and costs are decided.

7.6.9 DEFENCE AND AUTOMATIC TRANSFER (CPR PART 26)

Claims for specified amounts will be transferred automatically to the defendant's 'home court' where the defendant is an individual who has filed a defence. The defendant's home court will be the court or district registry, including the Royal Courts of Justice, for the district in which the defendant's address for service as shown on the defence is situated. This means that, where a solicitor represents the defendant, this will be the defendant's solicitor's business address.

Where there is more than one defendant, it is the first defendant to file a defence who dictates whether or not automatic transfer will take place. For example, if there were two defendants to a claim, one an individual and one a limited company, there would be no automatic transfer if the limited company was the first defendant to file a defence.

7.6.10 ALLOCATION QUESTIONNAIRE (FORM N150)

The purpose of this document is to enable the judge to allocate in which track the case should be heard. When a defence is filed, the issuing court will send out a copy of the defence to all other parties to the claim, together with an allocation questionnaire, a notice setting out the date for returning it, and the name and address of the court (or district registry or the Royal Courts of Justice (that is, High Court), as appropriate) to which the completed allocation questionnaire must be returned. A notice of transfer will also be sent if the case is being automatically transferred.

The allocation questionnaire will not be served on the parties when a defendant files a defence if r 14.5 or r 15.10 applies or if the court decides to dispense with its service.

When all the parties have filed their allocation questionnaire, or at the end of the period for returning it, whichever is the sooner (providing the questionnaires have not been dispensed with or the case stayed under r 26.4), the court will allocate the claim to a track. If there is sufficient information, the judge will allocate the case to a track and a notice of allocation and directions will be sent out to each party. Where the judge has insufficient information, an order may be made for a party to provide further information. In particularly complex cases, for those allocated to the multi-track, the judge may first list the matter for a case management conference to formulate directions.

Where only one party has filed a questionnaire the judge may allocate the claim to a track, providing he or she has enough information, or will order that an allocation hearing be listed and that all parties must attend. Where none of the parties has filed a questionnaire, the file will be returned to the judge, who will usually decide to impose a sanction by ordering that the claim and any counterclaim be struck out unless a completed questionnaire is filed within three days from service of the order.

The questionnaire asks a number of questions, for example:

- Do you wish there to be a one-month stay to attempt to settle this case?
- Which track do you consider most suitable for your case (small claims, fast track or multi-track)? A party wishing a case to be dealt with on a track that is not the obviously suitable track must give reasons.
- At this stage, you are asked whether you have complied with any relevant protocols, and if not, why not and the extent of the non-compliance.
- You are asked for an estimate of costs to date and the overall costs up to trial.
- You are asked if you wish to use expert evidence at the trial, whether expert reports have been copied to the other side, who the expert is and, if the parties have not agreed upon a common expert, why not.

The purpose of this questionnaire is to make both sides have a clear overview of the case at an early stage, so it becomes very difficult for lawyers to bumble along buffeted by developments in a case. To reduce delays and therefore costs, it is desirable that a lawyer should be able to purposefully stride through a case along a planned route.

7.6.11 DEFAULT JUDGMENT (CPR PART 12)

If a defendant (to a Part 7 claim) files an acknowledgement stating an intention to defend the claim, this extends the period for filing a defence from 14 to 28 days from the date of service of the particulars. Failure to file an acknowledgement with the court or, later, failure to file a defence can result in 'default judgment'. That means the court will, without a trial, find in favour of the claimant, so the defendant will lose the case.

If the defendant does not reply to the claim, a claimant may apply for default judgment for the amount claimed if the amount claimed is a specified amount, or on liability if the amount claimed is unspecified, after the 14-day period from service has elapsed.

There are a number of cases in which it is not possible to obtain judgment in default, notably in claims for delivery of goods subject to an agreement controlled by the Consumer Credit Act 1974.

7.6.12   SUMMARY JUDGMENT (CPR PART 24)

Summary judgment is available to both claimants and defendants. Where either party feels that the other does not have a valid claim or defence, they can apply to the court for the claim or defence to be struck out and for judgment to be entered in their favour. The applicant, either claimant or defendant, must prove to the court's satisfaction that the other party has no real prospect of success and that there is no other compelling reason why the case or issue should be dealt with at trial.

Application for summary judgment cannot be made without the court's permission (replacing the term 'leave') or where a practice direction provides otherwise, before an acknowledgement of service or defence has been filed. Where the claimant makes an application before a defendant files a defence, the defendant against whom it is made need not file a defence. If a claimant's application is unsuccessful, the court will give directions for the filing of a defence.

7.7   PUBLIC AND PRIVATE HEARINGS (CPR PART 39)

Under the rules, the distinction between 'public' and 'private' hearings is not whether a claim or application is heard in a courtroom or the *judge's room* (formerly called *chambers*), but whether members of the public are allowed to sit in on the hearing wherever it takes place.

Courts are not required to make any special arrangements to accommodate members of the public, for example, if the judge's room is too small to accommodate more than those directly concerned with the claim. However, where a hearing is 'public', anyone may obtain a copy of the order made upon payment of the appropriate fee.

Rule 39.2 states that:

(1)   The general rule is that a hearing is to be in public.

(2)   The requirement for a hearing to be in public does not require the court to make special arrangements for accommodating members of the public.

(3)   A hearing, or any part of it, may be in private if –

    (a)   publicity would defeat the object of the hearing;

    (b)   it involves matters relating to national security;

    (c)   it involves confidential information (including information relating to personal financial matters) and publicity would damage that confidentiality;

    (d)   a private hearing is necessary to protect the interests of any child or protected party;

(e)   it is a hearing of an application made without notice and it would be unjust to any respondent for there to be a public hearing;

(f)   it involves uncontentious matters arising in the administration of trusts or in the administration of a deceased person's estate; or

(g)   the court considers this to be necessary, in the interests of justice.

7.8   APPEALS (CPR PART 52)

The appeal system is covered in Chapter 6.

There is generally no automatic right to appeal under the CPR, except as provided for in r 52.3 or statute. The exceptions include situations where the appeal is against:

(i)   a committal order;

(ii)   a refusal to grant *habeas corpus*; or

(iii)   a secure accommodation order.

Generally, parties need permission to appeal and this will be granted only where:

(a)   the court considers that the appeal would have a real prospect of success; or

(b)   where there is some other compelling reason why the appeal should be heard.

Permission to appeal will usually be made to the lower court at the hearing against which it is to be appealed. Alternatively, an appeal can be made to the appeal court in an appeal notice usually within 14 days after the date of the decision to be appealed unless directed otherwise by the lower court.

The important procedural points and the routes to appeal will vary depending on whether the matter involves a final decision.

Generally, an appeal will lie to the next court above. From a district judge of the County Court, appeal lies to a circuit judge; from a Master or district judge of the High Court, or a circuit judge, appeal lies to a High Court judge; and from a High Court judge, appeal lies to the Court of Appeal. In almost all cases, permission is needed in order to appeal.

Paragraph 2A.1 of the Practice Direction to Part 52 provides:

Where the decision to be appealed is a final decision –

1   in a Part 7 claim allocated to the multi-track; or
2   made in specialist proceedings (under the Companies Act 1985 or 1989 or to which sections I, II, or III of Part 57 or any of Parts 58 to 63 apply)

the appeal is to be made to the Court of Appeal (subject to obtaining any necessary permission).

A final decision 'is a decision of a court that would finally determine (subject to any possible appeal or detailed assessment of costs) the entire proceedings whichever way the court decides the issues before it'. A decision will not be deemed a final decision where an order is made on a summary or detailed assessment of costs or on an application to enforce a final decision. In these circumstances the appeal will follow the general appeal route.

If a decision of a circuit judge is in relation to fast-track claims, claims on the multi-track except for final decisions, and Part 8 claims including final decisions but excluding final decisions in specialist proceedings, appeal lies to the High Court. However, a Part 8 claim that is a final decision and is treated as allocated to the multi-track may be sent direct to the Court of Appeal if the court considers appropriate.

Under CPR 52.14 a lower court may order the appeal to be sent directly to the Court of Appeal, where it considers that the appeal would raise an important point of principle or practice or there is some other compelling reason for the Court of Appeal to hear it.

Generally an appeal will be limited to a review of the decision of the lower court unless a practice direction provides otherwise or the court considers that in the circumstances of the particular appeal it would be in the interests of justice to order a rehearing. The appeal court will not hear any oral evidence or new evidence unless it orders otherwise. An appeal will be allowed where the decision in the lower court was wrong, or unjust due to a serious procedural or other irregularity in the lower court's proceedings.

When the court deals with appeals it must have regard to the overriding objective in CPR 1.1. Consequently, the appeal court is only likely to deal with appeals where they are founded on an error of law, against a finding of fact, in respect of the exercise of a discretion, involving new evidence or a change of circumstances or where a serious procedural or other irregularity arises causing injustice.

Appeals from the Court of Appeal lie to the Supreme Court, but the appellant must be granted leave either by the Court of Appeal or by the Supreme Court. The application for leave must first be made to the Court of Appeal, and then if refused, by petition for leave to appeal, which will be heard by the Supreme Court sitting in public. Only cases involving points of public importance reach the Supreme Court and there are usually fewer than 50 civil appeals heard by the Supreme Court each year. It is possible, under the Administration of Justice Act 1969, for the Supreme Court to hear an appeal direct from the High Court, 'leapfrogging' the Court of Appeal. The agreement of both parties and the High Court judge is required. Such cases must concern a point of statutory interpretation (including the construction of a statutory instrument), which has been fully explored by the High Court judge, or concern a point that he or she was bound by precedent to follow.

7.9 REMEDIES

The preceding sections of this chapter have examined the institutional and procedural framework within which individuals pursue civil claims. What it has not addressed is the question why people pursue such claims. Taking a claim to court can be expensive, time-consuming and very stressful, but people accept these costs, both financial and personal, because they have a grievance that they require to be settled. In other words, they are seeking a remedy for some wrong they have suffered, or at least that they believe they have suffered. In practice, it is the actual remedy available that the litigant focuses on, rather than the finer points of law or procedure involved in attaining that remedy; those are matters for the legal professionals. It is appropriate, therefore, to offer a brief explanation of remedies, although students of the law will engage with the details of remedies in the substantive legal subjects, such as contract and tort. As will be seen, it is essential to distinguish between the common law remedy of damages, available as of right, and equitable remedies, which are awarded at the discretion of the court (see above, 1.3.2).

7.10 DAMAGES

As has been said, the whole point of damages is compensatory: to recompense someone for the wrong they have suffered. There are, however, different ways in which someone can be compensated. For example, in contract law, the object of awarding damages is to put the wronged person in the situation they would have been in had the contract been completed as agreed; that is, it places them in the position they would have been in after the event. In tort, however, the object is to compensate the wronged person, to the extent that a monetary award can do so, for injury sustained; that is, to return them to the situation they were in before the event.

7.10.1 TYPES OF DAMAGES

(a) *Compensatory damages:* these are the standard awards considered above, intended to achieve no more than to recompense the injured party to the extent of the injury suffered. Damages in contract can only be compensatory.

(b) *Aggravated damages:* these are compensatory in nature, but are additional to ordinary compensatory awards and are awarded in relation to damage suffered to the injured party's dignity and pride. They are, therefore, akin to damages being paid in relation to mental distress. In *Khodaparast v Shad* (2000), the claimant was awarded aggravated damages after the defendant had been found liable for the malicious falsehood of distributing fake pictures of her in a state of undress, which resulted in her losing her job.

(c) *Exemplary damages:* these are awarded in tort in addition to compensatory damages. They may be awarded where the person who committed the tort intended to make a profit from their tortious action. The most obvious area in which such awards might be made is in libel cases, where the publisher issues the libel to increase sales. Libel awards are considered in more detail at 14.6.1 below, but an example of exemplary awards can be seen in the award of £50,000 (originally

£275,000) to Elton John as a result of his action against *The Mirror* newspaper (*John v MGN Ltd* (1996)).

(d)   *Nominal damages:* these are awarded in the few cases which really do involve 'a matter of principle', but where no loss or injury to reputation is involved. There is no set figure in relation to nominal damages; it is merely a very small amount.

(e)   *Contemptuous damages:* these are extremely small awards made where the claimant wins their case, but has suffered no loss and has failed to impress the court with the standard of their own behaviour or character. In *Reynolds v Times Newspaper Ltd* (1999), the former Prime Minister of Ireland was awarded one penny in his libel action against *The Times* newspaper; this award was actually made by the judge after the jury had awarded Reynolds no damages at all. Such an award can be considered nothing if not contemptuous.

7.10.2   DAMAGES IN CONTRACT

The estimation of what damages are to be paid by a party in breach of contract can be divided into two parts: remoteness and measure.

Remoteness of damage

What kind of damage can the innocent party claim? This involves a consideration of causation, and the remoteness of cause from effect, in order to determine how far down a chain of events a defendant is liable. The rule in *Hadley v Baxendale* (1854) states that damages will only be awarded in respect of losses that arise naturally, that is, in the natural course of things, or which both parties may reasonably be supposed to have contemplated, when the contract was made, as a probable result of its breach.

The effect of the first part of the rule in *Hadley v Baxendale* is that the party in breach is deemed to expect the normal consequences of the breach, whether they actually expected them or not.

Under the second part of the rule, however, the party in breach can only be held liable for abnormal consequences where they have actual knowledge that the abnormal consequences might follow. In *Victoria Laundry Ltd v Newham Industries Ltd* (1949), the defendants contracted to deliver a new boiler to the plaintiffs, but delayed in delivery. The plaintiffs claimed for normal loss of profit during the period of delay, and also for the loss of abnormal profits from a highly lucrative contract, which they could have undertaken had the boiler been delivered on time. In this case, it was decided that damages could be recovered in regard to the normal profits, as that loss was a natural consequence of the delay. The second claim failed, however, on the grounds that the loss was not a normal one, but was a consequence of an especially lucrative contract, about which the defendant knew nothing.

As a result of the test for remoteness, a party may be liable for consequences which, although within the reasonable contemplation of the parties, are much more serious in effect than would be expected.

In *H Parsons (Livestock) Ltd v Uttley Ingham and Co* (1978), the plaintiffs, who were pig farmers, bought a large food hopper from the defendants. While erecting it, the defendants failed to unseal a ventilator on the top of the hopper. Because of lack of ventilation, the pig food stored in the hopper became mouldy. The pigs that ate the mouldy food contracted a rare intestinal disease and died. It was held that the defendants were liable for the loss of the pigs. The food affected by bad storage caused the illness as a natural consequence of the breach, and the death from such illness was not too remote.

Measure of damages

Damages in contract are intended to compensate an injured party for any financial loss sustained as a consequence of another party's breach. The object is not to punish the party in breach, so the amount of damages awarded can never be greater than the actual loss suffered. The aim is to put the injured party in the same position they would have been in had the contract been properly performed. Where the breach relates to a contract for the sale of goods, damages are usually assessed in line with the market rule. This means that, if goods are not delivered under a contract, the buyer is entitled to go into the market and buy similar goods, and pay the market price prevailing at the time. They can then claim the difference in price between what they paid and the original contract price as damages. Conversely, if a buyer refuses to accept goods under a contract, the seller can sell the goods in the market and accept the prevailing market price. Any difference between the price they receive and the contract price can be claimed in damages.

Non-pecuniary loss

At one time, damages could not be recovered where the loss sustained through breach of contract was of a non-financial nature. The modern position is that such non-pecuniary damages can be recovered. In *Jarvis v Swan Tours Ltd* (1973), the defendant's brochure stated that various facilities were available at a particular ski resort. The facilities available were in fact far inferior to those advertised. The plaintiff sued for breach of contract. The court decided that Jarvis was entitled to recover not just the financial loss he suffered, which was not substantial, but also for loss of entertainment and enjoyment. The Court of Appeal stated that damages could be recovered for mental distress in appropriate cases, and this was one of them.

7.10.3   DAMAGES IN TORT

Remoteness of damage

Even where causation is established, the defendant will not necessarily be liable for all of the damage resulting from the breach. The question to be asked in determining the extent of liability is whether the damage is of such a kind as the reasonable person should have foreseen, but this does not mean that the defendant should have foreseen precisely the sequence or nature of the events. The test for remoteness of damage in tort was set out in *The Wagon Mound (No 1)* (1961). The defendants negligently allowed furnace oil to spill from a ship into Sydney Harbour. The oil spread and came to lie beneath a wharf owned by the plaintiffs. The plaintiffs had been carrying out welding operations and, on seeing the oil, they stopped welding in order to find out whether it was safe to continue. They were assured that the oil would not catch fire and resumed welding. However, cotton waste that had fallen into the oil caught fire, which in turn ignited the oil, and the resultant fire spread to the plaintiff's wharf. It was held that the defendants were liable in tort, as they had breached their duty of care. However, they were only held liable for the damage caused to the wharf and slipway through the fouling of the oil. They were not liable for the damage caused by fire because that damage was unforeseeable due to the high ignition point of the oil.

Economic loss

There are two categories of economic loss that may form the basis of a claim in negligence. First, there is economic loss arising out of physical injury or damage to property and, second, there is what is known as 'pure economic loss', which is unconnected with physical damage. Following recent developments, only the former is recoverable unless the claimant can show that there was 'a special relationship' between them and the defendant (*Williams v Natural Life Health Foods Ltd* (1998)).

7.11 EQUITABLE REMEDIES

Equitable remedies are not available as of right and are awarded only at the discretion of the court. They will not be granted where the claimant has not acted properly. There are a number of maxims that relate to the awarding of equitable remedies. Thus, for example, it is frequently stated that '*He who comes to equity must come with clean hands*', which simply means that persons looking for the remedy must have behaved properly themselves (*D & C Builders v Rees* (1966)). The actual remedies are as follows.

Specific performance

It will sometimes suit a party to break their contractual obligations and pay damages; however, through an order for specific performance, the party in breach may be instructed to complete their part of the contract. An order of specific performance will only be granted in cases where the common law remedy of damages is inadequate, and providing the matter does not fall into a category where the courts will not order specific performance. It is not usually applied to contracts concerning the sale of goods where replacements are readily available. It is most commonly granted in cases involving the sale of land, where the subject matter of the contract is unique.

Generally, specific performance will not be available in respect of contracts of employment or personal service. However, in light of *C H Giles & Co Ltd v Morris and others* (1972), it would appear that the courts may be prepared to depart from this principle in certain circumstances.

Specific performance will not be granted if the court has to constantly supervise its enforcement. In *Ryan v Mutual Tontine Westminster Chambers Association* (1893), the landlords of a flat undertook to provide a porter, who was to be constantly in attendance to provide services such as cleaning the common passages and stairs, and delivering letters. The person appointed spent much of his time working as a chef at a nearby club. During his absence, his duties were performed by a cleaner or by various boys. The plaintiff sought to enforce the contractual undertaking. It was held that, although the landlords were in breach of their contract, the court would not award an order of specific performance.

The reason given was that to enforce the contract would require constant supervision by the court. In addition, it was held that damages were an adequate remedy and hence the only available course of action. By comparison, in *Posner and others v Scott-Lewis and others* (1986) an order for specific performance was granted. In this case, the landlord had covenanted (so far as it was in his power) with the tenants to employ a resident porter to carry out certain specified tasks. The court held that the covenant was specifically enforceable as they could order the landlord to employ a resident porter within a specified time, as this would not require constant supervision by the court. If the landlord failed to adhere to the order, the tenants could go back to the court and take appropriate action.

Injunction

This is the term used in relation to the courts' powers to order someone to either do something or, alternatively, to refrain from doing something. Injunctions are governed by s 37 of the Senior Courts Act 1981 and they may be granted on an interim or a permanent basis. Breach of an injunction is a contempt of court. Examples of specific injunctions are 'freezing orders', formerly known as Mareva injunctions, which are interim orders that prevent defendants from moving their assets out of the jurisdiction of the English courts before their case can be heard. Another well-known order is the search order, formerly known as an Anton Piller order, which prevents the concealment or disposal of documents that might be required in evidence at a later time. It can also authorise the searching of premises for such evidence.

In contrast, an injunction directs a person not to break their contract. It can have the effect of indirectly enforcing contracts for personal service. In *Warner Bros v Nelson* (1937), the defendant, the actress Bette Davis, had entered a contract that stipulated that she was to work exclusively for the plaintiffs for a period of one year. When she came to England, the plaintiffs applied for an injunction to prevent her from working for someone else. The court granted the order to Warner Bros. In doing so, the court rejected Nelson's argument that granting it would force her either to work for the plaintiffs or not to work at all. An injunction will only be granted to enforce negative covenants within the agreement, and cannot be used to enforce positive obligations (*Whitwood Chemical Co v Hardman* (1891)).

Rectification

This award allows for the alteration of contractual documents. It is generally assumed that written contractual documents accurately express the parties' terms, especially where the document has been signed. There are occasions, however, when the court will allow the written statement to be altered where it does not represent the true agreement (*Joscelyne v Nissen* (1970)).

Rescission

This action sets aside the terms of a contractual agreement and returns the parties to the situation they were in before the contract was entered into. The right to rescind a contract may be available as a result of fraud, misrepresentation of any type or the exercise of undue influence. The right can be lost, however, for a number of reasons, such as it being impossible to return the parties to their original position, affirmation, delay or the intervention of third party rights.

7.12 COSTS (CPR PARTS 44–48)

Fixed costs (CPR Part 45)

There are rates for the fixed costs allowed on issue of a claim and on entry of judgment where a party is represented by a solicitor.

The fee structure is designed so that fees become payable as the various stages of a claim are reached (a 'pay as you go' regime).

Courts are proactive in collecting fees, in particular those that are payable at allocation and listing stages, but *without interrupting* a case's progress. There are sanctions for non-payment of allocation and listing questionnaire fees, which could lead to a party's statement of case being struck out.

Assessment (CPR Part 47)

The terms *taxed* costs and *taxation* (which were previously used to denote that costs a lawyer was claiming had been approved by a senior officer of the court) are now redundant and have been replaced by *assessment*. Costs will either be assessed summarily, that is, there and then, or there will be a *detailed assessment* at some later stage where one party has been ordered to pay another's costs.

Summary assessment

Judges will normally summarily assess costs at the end of hearings, both interim and final, and particularly at the end of fast-track trials. Parties will be expected to bring any necessary documentation to the hearing for this purpose. In this way, the need for detailed assessment of costs is avoided so far as possible.

7.13 WHAT HAS THE REPLACEMENT SYSTEM ACHIEVED?

The CPR, the most fundamental changes in civil process for over 100 years, have radically altered the operation of civil justice. Since the current rules came into force (26 April 1999), they have been regularly reformed, the latest being the eighty-sixth update, which came into force in October 2016.

Part of the rationale of the new rules was to expedite the way cases were dealt with and to allow more cases to be settled early through negotiation between the parties or ADR. In this respect, there was some early evidence of success. During the May to August period in 1999, there was a 25 per cent reduction in the number of cases issued in the County Courts compared with the same period the previous year. By the end of January 2000, there was a further fall of 23 per cent. Mr Justice Burton of the QBD presented an interesting assessment of the new rules. Speaking at the City law firm, Kennedys, he outlined five benefits of the reforms, five problems and what he referred to as 'one big question mark' ((2000) Law Soc Gazette, 10 February).

The five problems with the reforms were: the courts' inflexibility in not allowing parties to agree extensions of time between themselves; the danger of the judiciary pushing time guillotines onto parties; the risk that lawyers and clients could exploit 'standard' disclosure to conceal important documents; single joint experts possibly usurping the role of judges; and summary assessments of costs leading to judges making assumptions replacing detailed costs analysis. The benefits were listed as: pre-action protocols; emphasis on encouraging settlement; judicial intervention; Part 24 strike-out provisions; and Part 36 offers to settle.

Mr Justice Burton said there had been three options for reforming appeals:

1   to extend the present system in order to discourage more than one appeal;

2   to refuse appeals without leave; or

3   to abolish the present system, giving no right to re-hearings, only appeals.

He said he regretted that all three had been adopted (in the Access to Justice Act 1999). The consequence will be pressure on judges 'to get it right first time' and higher costs for parties.

The issue of costs is a recurring theme that has been commented upon by many notable people in the legal world. Ted Greeno, a partner at Herbert Smith, believed that the Woolf reforms would result in higher costs for commercial cases. He was of the opinion that the rise in costs has nothing to do with the court's adversarial system but 'is a result of the introduction of pre-action protocols, case management and unnecessary bureaucracy, as well as unrealistic timetables and the unpredictable threat of costs sanctions which cause lawyers to practise "defensively"'.

Sir Anthony Clarke has commented that 'unless you are an extremely rich individual, a corporation or an organ of the state, no one can afford to litigate'. He believes that 'the most important issue that the civil justice system needs to worry about is control over costs' ((2006) Law Soc Gazette, 21 April).

Overall, it could be argued that the Woolf reforms can be seen as a triumphant step in the right direction as they have resulted in a wider proportion of society being able to achieve greater access to justice, especially where the problem is of a relatively small nature and can be dealt with quickly and cheaply in the lower courts. However, the reforms may not be so good where, for example, the problem involves complex commercial issues and/or where a matter goes to appeal, as costs rack up very quickly with the parties requiring the assistance of solicitors, barristers and experts and with the length of time it can take to resolve the more complex case. However, the Woolf reforms have been criticised by Dame Hazel Genn in her Hamlyn lectures (F. Gibb, 'Woolf v Genn: the decline of civil justice', *The Times*, 23 June 2009). Dame Hazel believed that the civil justice reforms were not about greater access or greater justice to society but rather a route to divert litigants away from the courts and instead direct them to mediation. Part of this rationale, she believed, was due to the self-financing of the civil court system and the government's lack of commitment to civil justice in favour of the criminal justice system. Dame Hazel believed that while society had strong views on civil justice, they were not picked up due to 'a lack of solid empirical evidence'. It was noted in this article that Lord Woolf has publicly commented upon Dame Hazel's views and expressed dissatisfaction with her argument that not enough empirical evidence was put forward. This is because Dame Hazel was one of Lord Woolf's review team when he was looking at proposed reforms to the civil justice system. In expressing criticism of Dame Hazel, Lord Woolf acknowledged that one commentator, Professor Michael Zander, was critical of his reforms but remained consistent with his views. Professor Zander did not consider that the government's intention was to utilise the reforms to reduce resources to the civil justice system and his proposed reforms required directly the opposite, namely proper resourcing. While Lord Woolf acknowledged that the civil justice system is not high profile as far as government is concerned compared to the criminal justice system, he emphasised that this has nothing to do with judges. Lord Woolf also believed that mediation is a 'proper functioning part of the justice system that does help in certain cases to achieve justice'.

7.14 ENFORCEMENT OF CIVIL REMEDIES

It is one thing to be awarded a remedy by the court against another party, but it is another thing to actually enforce that remedy. Consequently, an effective enforcement system is essential to providing access to justice.

In March 2003, the LCD issued the White Paper *Effective Enforcement*, in which it claimed to set out a strategy for reforming the current system by:

* improving methods of recovering civil debt; and
* establishing a more rigorous system of controls for enforcement agents, previously known as bailiffs.

On 12 June 2003 the Department for Constitutional Affairs (DCA) was created and took over the LCD's responsibilities for the court system and judiciary. In July 2006, the DCA published the draft Tribunals, Courts and Enforcement Bill and on 19 July 2007 the Tribunals, Courts and Enforcement Act 2007 received Royal Assent.

The 2007 Act provides for the abolition of the right of distress for rent. This is a common law right that allows landlords to recover unpaid rent from tenants without using the courts. Landlords can seize control of goods in the tenanted premises and sell them, utilising the money raised to offset against the rent arrears.

Part 3 of the 2007 Act came into force on 6 April 2014 and it created a statutory right for the landlord of tenanted commercial premises to recover unpaid rent. The new system is known as Commercial Rent Arrears Recovery (CRAR). As the name suggests, this procedure will not apply to residential premises, only leases of commercial premises. Furthermore it only covers rent, VAT and interest. It does not cover other costs reserved as rent, such as insurance and service charges.

Attachment of earnings orders

An attachment of earnings order (AEO) is a means of securing payment of certain debts by requiring an employer to make deductions direct from an employed debtor's earnings. Currently, the rate of deductions under an AEO made to secure payment of a judgment debt is calculated by a County Court using information provided by the debtor. The government identified weaknesses in the system and in particular the fact that information provided by debtors is often unreliable. The Act tackles this by making provision for a new method of calculation of deductions from earnings based on fixed rates, similar to the system used for council tax AEOs. Another weakness of the AEO system is that if a debtor changes job and does not inform the court of their new employer's details, the AEO lapses. The Act therefore enables the High Court, County Courts, magistrates' courts and fines officers to request the name and address of the debtor's new employer from Her Majesty's Revenue and Customs (HMRC) for the purpose of redirecting the AEO.

Charging orders

A charging order is a means of securing payment of a sum of money ordered to be paid under a judgment or order of the High Court or a County Court by placing a charge on the debtor's property (usually a house or land or securities such as shares). A charging order can be made absolute or subject to conditions. Once an order is in place, a creditor can subsequently apply to court seeking an order for sale of the charged property. Under the old law, the court could not make a charging order when payments due under an instalment order made to secure that same sum were not in arrears. In certain instances this could prejudice the creditor, allowing, for example, a debtor with large judgment debts, who is meeting his or her regular instalments, to benefit from the sale of a property without paying off the debt. The Tribunals, Courts and Enforcement Act 2007 removes this restriction and enables access to charging orders in circumstances where a debtor is not yet in arrears with an instalment order. As a safeguard, the Act allows the Lord Chancellor to set financial thresholds beneath which a court cannot make a charging order or order for sale, in order to ensure that charging orders are not used to secure payment of disproportionately small judgment debts.

CHAPTER SUMMARY: THE CIVIL PROCESS

THE NEED FOR REFORM

The Woolf Inquiry into the civil justice system was set up by the government in 1994 to examine why civil litigation was generally very costly, protracted, complicated and subject to long delays.

Starting Proceedings: Claimant commences proceedings by completing:
- *Claim form* to which may be attached the '*particulars of claim*' statement of case, which must include a '*statement of truth*'
- Court will serve documents on the defendant. who may provide a defence, counterclaim or fail to respond
- Once a defence is filed, an *allocation questionnaire* may be completed. The judge may then allocate the case to the appropriate 'track'. (Where the defendant has failed to respond, the court may issue a judgment in default)

Pre-trial Process: The judiciary now have an enhanced management role (case control), which involves encouraging greater co-operation between the parties, including the use of alternative dispute resolution (ADR) and giving directions in order that the case proceeds quickly and efficiently, involving:
- case management conferences
- pre-trial reviews
- consideration of pre-action offers to settle (known as Part 36 payments)

Courts have a duty to help parties settle their disputes, including the use of 'stays', which provide more time for the parties to settle

Court and Track Allocation:
- Where a case has been allocated to the '**small claims track**', parties are under no obligation to attend and 'paper adjudication' may be heard by agreement. As the procedure is intended to be quick and less formal, legal representation, use of expert witnesses and the awarding of costs are less common than under other tracks
- Where a case has been allocated to the '**fast track**', the period between directions and the start of the trial cannot be more than *30 weeks*, while the trial time is limited to *one day*. Advocacy costs will also be capped
- Where a case has been allocated to the '**multi-track**', a range of case management tools may be used in a 'mix and match' to suit the needs of the individual case

Remedies: Claimants initiate actions in order to seek a remedy for a wrong that they have suffered. The **common law** remedy available is damages
- **Equitable remedies** are only available at the discretion of the court and include specific performance and injunction

Costs: assessed by the judge at the end of a hearing
Court Fees: payable on a 'pay as you go' basis

FIGURE 7.2 *An Overview of the Civil Process.*

The Inquiry published its final report in 1996 and its proposals resulted in the Civil Procedure Act 1997 and the Civil Procedure Rules 1998. The Civil Procedure Rules (CPR) are the same for the County Court and the High Court.

THE CIVIL PROCESS
The changes were effected through the Civil Procedure Act 1997 and the CPR 1998. These have been supplemented by practice directions and pre-action protocols.

THE OVERRIDING OBJECTIVE (CPR PART 1)
The overriding objective of the CPR is to enable the court to deal justly with cases. The first rule reads:

1.1(1) These rules are a new procedural code with the overriding objective of enabling the court to deal with cases justly and at proportionate cost.

Practice directions (official statements of interpretative guidance) play an important role in the civil process. In general, they supplement the CPR, giving the latter fine detail. They tell parties and their representatives what the court will expect of them in respect of documents to be filed in court for a particular purpose, and how they must co-operate with the other parties to their action. They also tell the parties what they can expect of the court.

THE PRE-ACTION PROTOCOLS

The pre-action protocols (PAPs) are an important feature of the reforms.

They exist for cases of clinical disputes, personal injury, disease and illness, construction and engineering disputes, defamation, professional negligence, housing disrepair, housing possession following rent arrears, housing possession following mortgage arrears, low value personal injury claims in road traffic accidents, low value personal injury (employers' and public liability) claims, dilapidations at end of lease or tenancy of a commercial property and judicial review.

They are likely to be followed, over time, with similar protocols for cases involving other specialisms like debt.

CASE CONTROL (CPR PART 3)

Judges will receive support from court staff in carrying out their case management role. The court will monitor case progress by using a computerised diary monitoring system.

Active case management includes:

(a)   encouraging the parties to co-operate with each other in the conduct of the proceedings;

(b)   identifying the issues at an early stage;

(c)   deciding promptly which issues need full investigation and trial and, accordingly, disposing summarily of the others;

(d)   deciding the order in which issues are to be resolved.

Parties are required to adhere strictly to the timetable set by the courts, and r 3.9 has been strengthened to make it more difficult to obtain relief from sanctions. However, some recent cases have seen the courts not applying the rule so strictly.

CASE MANAGEMENT CONFERENCES

Case management conferences may be regarded as an opportunity to 'take stock'. There is no limit to the number of case management conferences that may be held during the life of a case, although the cost of attendance at such hearings measured against the benefits obtained will always be a consideration in making the decision.

PRE-TRIAL REVIEWS

Pre-trial reviews will normally take place after the filing of listing questionnaires and before the start of the trial. Their main purpose is to decide a timetable for the trial itself (including the evidence to be allowed and whether this should be given orally), to determine instructions about the content of any trial bundles (bundles of documents including evidence such as written statements, for the judge to read) and to confirm a realistic time estimate for the trial itself.

STAYS FOR SETTLEMENT (CPR PART 26) AND SETTLEMENTS (PART 36)

Under the CPR, there is a greater incentive for parties to settle their differences.

The court will take into account any pre-action offers to settle when making an order for costs. Thus, a side that has refused a reasonable offer to settle will be treated less generously in the issue of how far the court will order their costs to be paid by the other side. For this to happen, the offer, though, must be one that is made open to the other side for at least 21 days after the date it was made (to stop any undue pressure being put on someone with the phrase: 'take it or leave it; it is only open for one day, then I shall withdraw the offer').

WITNESS STATEMENTS (CPR PART 32)

Under the rules, witness statements must contain the evidence that the witness will give at trial, but they should be briefer than those drafted under the previous rules; they should be drafted in lay language and should not discuss legal propositions. Witnesses will be allowed to amplify on the statement or deal with matters that have arisen since the report was served, although this is not an automatic right and a 'good reason' for the admission of new evidence will have to be established.

EXPERTS (CPR PART 35)

These rules place a clear duty on the court to ensure that 'expert evidence is restricted to that which is reasonably required to resolve the proceedings'. That is to say, expert evidence will only be allowed either by way of written report or orally, where the court gives permission. Equally important is the rules' statement about experts' duties.

COURT AND TRACK ALLOCATION (CPR PART 26)

Part 7 of the CPR sets out the rules for starting proceedings. A restriction is placed on which cases may be begun in the High Court. County Courts retain an almost unlimited jurisdiction for handling contract and tort claims (that is, negligence cases, nuisance cases, but excluding a claim for damages or other remedy for libel or slander unless the parties agree otherwise). Issuing proceedings in the High Court is now limited to:

- personal injury claims with a value of £50,000 or more;
- other claims with a value of more than £100,000;
- equity claims where the property is worth at least £350,000;
- claims where an Act of Parliament requires an action to start in the High Court; or
- specialist High Court claims that need to go to one of the specialist 'lists', like the Commercial List, and the Technology and Construction List.

The civil system works on the basis of the court, upon receipt of the claim (accompanied by duly filled-in forms giving all the relevant details of the claim, including how much it is for and an indication of its factual and legal complexity), allocating the case to one of three tracks for a hearing. These are:

- small claims;
- fast track;
- multi-track.

The small claims limit is £10,000, although personal injury and housing disrepair claims for over £1,000 and illegal eviction and harassment claims will be excluded from the small claims court. Personal soft tissue injury claims will be increased to £5,000 in 2017 and other injury claims may follow after consultation. The limit for cases going into the fast-track system is £25,000, and only claims for over £100,000 can be issued in the High Court. Applications to move cases 'up' a track on grounds of complexity will have to be made on the new allocation questionnaire.

DOCUMENTATION AND PROCEDURES

HOW TO START PROCEEDINGS – THE CLAIM FORM (CPR PART 7)

Most claims will be begun by using a 'Part 7' claim form – a form which has been designed for multipurpose use. It can be used if the claim is for a *specified* amount of money (the old term was *liquidated* damages) or an *unspecified* amount (replacing the term *unliquidated* damages) and for non-monetary claims.

The court can grant any remedy to which the claimant is entitled, even if the claimant does not specify which one they want.

ALTERNATIVE PROCEDURE FOR CLAIMS (CPR PART 8)

Part 8 of the rules introduces the alternative procedure for claims. This procedure is commenced by the issue of a Part 8 claim form. It is intended to provide a speedy resolution of claims that are not likely to involve a substantial dispute of fact, for example, applications for approval of infant settlements, or for orders enforcing a statutory right such as a right to have access to medical records (under the Access to Health Records Act 1990). The Part 8 procedure is also used where a rule or practice direction requires or permits its use.

STATEMENT OF CASE – PARTICULARS OF CLAIM (CPR PART 16)

Particulars of claim may be included in the claim form, attached to it, or may be served (that is, given or sent to a party by a method allowed by the rules) separately from it. Where they are served separately, they must be served within 14 days of the claim form being served. The time for a defendant to respond begins to run from the time the particulars of claim are served.

Part 16 of the CPR is entitled 'statements of case' (replacing the word 'pleadings'). Statements of case include documents from both sides: claim forms, particulars of claims, defences, counterclaims, replies to defences and counterclaims, Part 20 (third party) claims and any further information provided under Part 18 of the CPR (replacing the term 'further and better particulars'). Part 16 of the rules also sets out what both particulars of claim and defences should contain.

STATEMENTS OF TRUTH (CPR PART 22)

A statement of truth is a statement that a party believes that the facts or allegations set out in a document, which they put forward, are true. It is required in statements of case, witness statements and expert reports. Any document that contains a statement of truth may be used in evidence. This will avoid the previous need to swear affidavits in support of various statements made as part of the claim.

DEFENCE AND AUTOMATIC TRANSFER (CPR PART 26)

Claims for specified amounts will be transferred automatically to the defendant's 'home court' where the defendant is an individual who has filed a defence. The defendant's home court will be the court or district registry, including the Royal Courts of Justice, for the district in which the defendant's address for service as shown on the defence is situated. This means that where a solicitor represents the defendant, this will be the defendant's solicitor's business address.

Where there is more than one defendant, it is the first defendant to file a defence who dictates whether or not automatic transfer will take place. For example, if there were two defendants to a claim, one an individual and one a limited company, there would be no automatic transfer if the limited company was the first defendant to file a defence.

ALLOCATION QUESTIONNAIRE (FORM N150)

The purpose of this document is to enable the judge to allocate in which track the case should be heard. When a defence is filed, the issuing court will send out a copy of the defence to all other parties to the claim together with an allocation questionnaire, a notice setting out the date for returning it and the name and address of the court (or district registry or the Royal Courts of Justice – that is, High Court – as appropriate) to which the completed allocation questionnaire must be returned. A notice of transfer will also be sent if the case is being automatically transferred.

The allocation questionnaire will not be served on the parties when a defendant files a defence if r 14.5 or r 15.10 applies or if the court decides to dispense with its service.

When all the parties have filed their allocation questionnaire, or at the end of the period for returning it, whichever is the sooner (providing the questionnaires have not been dispensed with or the case stayed under r 26.4), the court will allocate the claim to a track. If there is sufficient information, the judge will allocate the case to a track and a notice of allocation and directions will be sent out to each party. Where the judge has insufficient information, an order may be made for a party to provide further information.

Where only one party has filed a questionnaire, the judge may allocate the claim to a track providing he or she has enough information or will order that an allocation hearing be listed and that all parties must attend.

DEFAULT JUDGMENT (CPR PART 12)

If a defendant (to a Part 7 claim) files an acknowledgement stating an intention to defend the claim, this extends the period for filing a defence from 14 to 28 days from the date of service of the particulars. Failure to file an acknowledgement or, later, failure to file a defence can result in default judgment, that is, the court will find for the claimant, so the defendant will lose the case.

REMEDIES

It is essential to distinguish between the common law remedy of damages, available as of right, and equitable remedies, which are awarded at the discretion of the court.

DAMAGES

Damages are compensatory, to recompense someone for the wrong they have suffered. There are, however, different ways in which someone can be compensated.

In contract law, the object of awarding damages is to put the wronged person in the situation they would have been in had the contract been completed as agreed: that is, it places them in the position they would have been after the event. In tort, however, the object is to compensate the wronged person, to the extent that a monetary award can do so, for injury sustained: that is, to return them to the situation they were in before the event.

EQUITABLE REMEDIES

Specific performance

This remedy will only be granted in cases where the common law remedy of damages is inadequate. It is not usually applied to contracts concerning the sale of goods where replacements are readily available. It is most commonly granted in cases involving the sale of land, where the subject matter of the contract is unique.

Injunction

This is the term used in relation to the courts' powers to order someone either to do something or, alternatively, to refrain from doing something.

Rectification

This award allows for the alteration of contractual documents.

Rescission

This action sets aside the terms of a contractual agreement and returns the parties to the situation they were in before the contract was entered into.

COURT FEES

A new fee structure takes account of the different procedures, a movement towards a 'pay as you go' fees regime and the need for full cost recovery. 'Pay as you go' means that parties will be expected to contribute more in fees, the more court and judicial time they use, for example, if they do not settle and carry on to trial.

FOOD FOR THOUGHT

1   The English legal system has always been categorised as an adversarial system with the judge sitting as an umpire rather than a participant in cases. As a consequence the conduct of cases was to a large degree in the hands of the lawyers. Consider the consequences of such lack of judicial control for all the parties

concerned in the case. Then consider how the Woolf reforms were designed to overcome these problems by instituting a process of greater judicial control.

2   To what extent is it fair to claim that the reforms have been about saving time and money, both clients' and the state's? How exactly have these savings been pursued?

3   Although referred to as the 'new' civil process, the Woolf reforms have been in operation for more than 15 years. Is it not time to assess how successful they have been? How would such an assessment be made?

4   In relation to the small claims procedure, consider why there are different financial limits: £10,000 for the majority of claims but £1,000 for personal injury claims and housing disrepair actions. Why are the latter considered to need more judicial attention, and does this imply anything about possible shortcomings in the fast-track procedure?

5   It is accepted that 'justice delayed is justice denied', but can the same not be said in relation to a failure to provide adequate enforcement of remedies?

FURTHER READING

Blackstone's Civil Procedure (HH Judge William Rose (ed)), 2014, Oxford: OUP

Burns, R, 'A view from the ranks' (2000) 150 NLJ 1829

Genn, H, *Hamlyn Lectures 2008: Judging Civil Justice*, 2009, Cambridge: CUP

Genn, H, *Hard Bargaining: Out of Court Settlements in Personal Injury Claims*, 1987, Oxford: OUP

Gold, S, 'Civil Way' (2008) 158 NLJ 1370

Gold, S, 'Civil Way' (2008) 158 NLJ 1412

Harrison, R, 'Cry Woolf' (1999) 149 NLJ 1011

Kinley, A, 'Preparing the way' (2009) 153(40) SJ 8

Miller, F, 'The adversarial myth' (1995) 145 NLJ 743

New Law Journal, 'Increase in Civil Cases in High Court' [2007] 1628

Sime, S, *A Practical Approach to Civil Procedure*, 2014, Oxford: OUP

Solon, M, 'Selecting the best' (2008) 158 NLJ 1299

Squire, G, 'No more hired guns' (2009) 153(40) SJ 20

Thacker, R, 'The new Supreme Court' (2009) Legal Action 20

Zander, M, 'Are there any clothes for the emperor to wear?' (1995) 145 NLJ 154

Zuckerman, AAS, 'A reform of civil procedure – rationing procedure rather than access to justice' (1995) 22 JLS 156

USEFUL WEBSITES

www.justice.gov.uk/civil/procrules_fin/menus/rules.htm
This site, hosted by the Ministry of Justice, contains all the Civil Procedure Rules, and is regularly updated.

www.judiciary.gov.uk/about-the-judiciary/advisory-bodies/cjc
The official website of the Civil Justice Council.

COMPANION WEBSITE

Now visit the companion website to:

- test your understanding of the key terms using our Flashcard Glossary;
- revise and consolidate your knowledge of 'The civil process' using our multiple choice question testbank;
- view all of the links to the Useful Websites above.

www.routledge.com/cw/slapper

8.1 FAMILY COURTS

-
-
-
-
-
-
-

-

Although magistrates' courts and the new single County Court cannot hear family matters as of right, the Family Court can sit anywhere inside England and Wales and so it is able to sit inside county or magistrates' buildings.

Before family matters in England were given their own arena by way of dedicated family courts, governed by the state and secular in nature, the regulation of family matters was the domain of the Church, which tolerated a great deal of informality in its day-to-day administration of family matters. This often caused difficulties where, for example, two women claimed to be married to the same man (polygamy was, and still is, illegal in England), and it was scandals of this nature which ultimately led to the first series of law reforms in this area and which saw sustained legislation governing things like the dissolution of marriage and disputes over matrimonial finances, and a shift away from the church to the state.

The Births, Deaths and Marriages Registration Act 1836 formally created the General Register Office for England and Wales (GRO), which is today where births, deaths, adoptions, marriages and civil partnerships in England and Wales are registered. Prior to the 1836 Act, registration was left to the Church and carried out through local parishes, but with the progressive relaxation of the law in this area, and the growing number of marriages that were subsequently going unrecorded, the government felt they had no choice but to consider full-scale reform. The Marriage Act 1836, which was passed at the same time as the Births, Deaths and Marriages Registration Act, set out in law the formalities for getting married, with a view to preventing clandestine marriages and creating a streamlined system for the registration of marriages.

Non-compliance with the conditions set out in the Marriage Act 1836 was viewed as a felony, and rendered an attempted marriage null and void. However, precedent from this era shows that a clear presumption in favour of marriage existed, and parties who failed to comply with the conditions set down for the creation of a marriage would often be spared from an annulment. This may have been due in part to the Marriage Act 1836 itself and its subsequent interpretation by the judiciary of the time, which provided that marriages would be null and void if the parties knowingly and wilfully married in breach of various provisions in the Act. Ignorance of the law, therefore, provided the parties with a legitimate excuse, and the judges with a loophole, for upholding marriages in breach of the law.

With legislative reform came the need to look at the various forums in which matrimonial matters could be heard. Traditionally, Ecclesiastical courts presided over family matters, but with the passing of the Matrimonial Causes Act 1857 came the creation of a new court: the Court for Divorce and Matrimonial Causes, which effectively saw all family matters transferred to its jurisdiction. This court was then replaced in 1873 by the Probate Divorce and Admiralty Division, which was renamed the Family Division with the passing of the Administration of Justice Act 1970.

8.2   PRIVATE AND PUBLIC FAMILY LAW

Family courts are broadly divided into two areas: private and public family law. These areas are not mutually exclusive, as private family cases can often become public in nature, where, for example, a concern over a child's living arrangements may reveal more serious concerns about that child's day-to-day care. However, public family law cases must always start in the Family Proceedings Courts, though they can be transferred to County Courts to minimise delay, to consolidate proceedings or where the matter is exceptionally serious, complex or important.

Family court judges are charged with handling cases arising from these areas of law, which typically result in a series of directions, or orders, requiring a person to do or not to do something.

Private family law matters are brought by individuals, such as parents, spouses and next of kin, usually in connection with a divorce or parents' separation. Judges dealing with these matters can make various orders, including:

- parental responsibility: who holds the legal rights and responsibilities for a child (defined in s 3(1) of the Children Act 1989 as 'all the rights, duties, powers, responsibilities and authority which by law a parent of a child has in relation to the child and his property');

- family assistance orders, under s 16 of the Children Act 1989, which are designed to offer short-term support to families and children;

- special guardianship orders, which give a vetted guardian legal responsibility for a child without removing legal responsibility from the birth parents;

- Section 8 orders under the Children Act 1989, which can be used to determine where a child will live, time spent with each parent (contact), and other issues;

- prohibited steps orders, preventing a parent from doing something like changing a child's surname or removing them from the country (and effectively restricting that parent's parental responsibility);

- financial applications, for maintenance of a child or financial relief in divorce proceedings.

Public law cases are usually brought by local authorities (although the NSPCC, as an 'authorised person', currently also has powers to bring such cases), and can include issues such as:

- emergency protection orders, removing a child from harm by relocating them to a place of safety, or ensuring they are not removed from a safe environment;

- family assistance orders (s 16 of the Children Act 1989), as in private law proceedings;

- supervision orders, where children are placed under the supervision of their local authority;

- care orders, conferring parental responsibility of a child to the local authority that is applying for an order;

- adoption orders; a method of last resort, resulting in removing the rights, duties and obligations of the natural parents or guardian and transferring them to the adoptive parents. Once the adoption process is complete, an adopted child is viewed by the law as the child of his or her adoptive parents.

In August 2013, the Children and Family Court Advisory and Support Service (Cafcass), a non-departmental public body set up to safeguard and protect the welfare of children involved in family proceedings, received a total of 4,053 new private law cases (Cafcass Private Law Demand, August 2013 statistics, 9 September 2013). In July 2013, Cafcass received 870 care applications (Cafcass Care Applications, July 2013 statistics, 8 August 2013), a record month for care applications with the second highest number of care applications in a single month.

Adoption rates, too, have soared: the Department for Education reported in 2013 that 3,980 children were adopted between April 2012 and March 2013, up from 3,470 the previous year. This is higher than in any year since 1992, when comparable records began (Statistical First Release, Department for Education, 26 September 2013, SFR36/2013). It has been suggested that the increase in adoption rates is attributable to the government's efforts at finding loving homes for children in care ('Adoptions show "record" increase', *BBC News* online, 26 September 2013), though some argue that the increase is driven by a lucrative business which sees foster carers and the government profit from adoption agreements ('Big money to be made in the adoption trade', *The Telegraph* online, 19 June 2010). In recent times, however, there has been a significant reduction in adoptions. During July to September 2015, there were 1,463 adoption orders issued, down 17 per cent for the equivalent quarter in 2014. In 65 per cent of these, the adopters were a male/female couple, while in 18 per cent the adopter was a sole applicant (*Family Court Statistics Quarterly England and Wales*, July to September 2015, p 22, Ministry of Justice Statistics bulletin, December 2015).

8.3   THE CHILDREN ACT 1989 AND THE PARAMOUNTCY PRINCIPLE

The Children Act 1989 came into force on 14 October 1991 and was designed to:

> reform the law relating to children; to provide for local authority services for children in need and others; to amend the law with respect to children's homes, community homes, voluntary homes and voluntary organisations; to make provision with respect to fostering, child minding and day care for young children and adoption; and for connected purposes.
>
> (the Children Act 1989, introductory text, 18 November 1989)

It is the most important piece of child protection legislation in the United Kingdom. The Children Act 1989 is designed to make the welfare of every child the primary, or paramount, concern in cases involving children. This is often referred to as the 'paramountcy principle'.

The guiding principles found within the Children Act 1989, which apply to all proceedings concerning children brought under the Act, are:

- the welfare of the child will be the paramount consideration (the paramountcy principle) (s 1(1));
- delay to proceedings is likely to prejudice the welfare of the child and courts must be mindful of this when considering decisions relating to the upbringing of a child (s 1(2));
- the welfare checklist, which includes the consideration of the wishes and feelings of the child, their age, gender and other factors, must be considered by courts in relation to specific decisions (s 1(3));
- a court should not make an order under the Act unless the court considers that doing so would be better for the child than making no order at all (s 1(5)).

Covering a broad range of issues relating to children, and encompassing both private and public family law, the Children Act 1989 deals with:

- child welfare and parental responsibility issues (Part I);
- orders with respect to children in family proceedings (Part II);
- local authority support for children and families (Part III);
- care and supervision (Part IV);
- protection of children (Part V);
- community homes (Part VI);
- voluntary homes and voluntary organisations (Part VII);
- registered children's homes (Part VIII);
- private arrangements for fostering children (Part IX);
- child minding and day care for young children (Part X).

The Act's central principle focuses on the idea that responsibility in the first instance for a child's upbringing rests with that child's family, and that for the majority of children, their interests will be best served within their family unit. When that is no longer the case, the Act allows for government agencies to support the family where necessary, and to protect children where required. It also emphasises the need to ensure that all children and young people going through the family courts are consulted and are as fully informed as possible about decisions relating to them.

8.4 LEGAL AID AND THE FAMILY COURTS

Family legal aid covers both public and private law, and includes matters relating to the Children Act, domestic abuse, financial provision and mediation. As resources in the family justice system become scarce, largely due to ailing economic conditions, legal aid, which offers support through public funding, to families who are unable to pay for legal advice or proceedings, has been drastically reduced for civil cases by the newly enacted Legal Aid, Sentencing and Punishment of Offenders Act (LASPO) which came into effect in April 2013. As a result, only a very narrow set of family cases are now eligible for legal aid, including:

- cases where a victim of domestic violence is divorcing or separating from an abusive partner; and
- cases where a child is at risk of abuse from a partner.

Successful applications are now also dependent upon a further condition: evidence of abuse must be produced before legal aid may be granted.

Providing some relief to the very limited circumstances in which legal aid may now be considered for family matters is the Exceptional Cases Funding Scheme (ECF). The scheme allows cases to be considered if failure to grant legal aid would result in a breach of a client's rights under the European Convention on Human Rights (Lord Chancellor's Guidance on Exceptional Funding (Non-Inquests)).

Legal aid statistics produced for 2014 by the Ministry of Justice highlight a startling decrease in legal aid for family law matters, with a 60 per cent drop compared to figures for 2012. The largest drop was seen within private law Children's Act proceedings (there were 30,000 fewer certificates granted), and is attributed to the implementation of LASPO. Public family law cases were less affected, as they are driven by Local Authority applications to issue proceedings and are non-means and merits tested (Legal Aid Statistics in England and Wales, Legal Aid Agency, Ministry of Justice, 24 June 2014).

In 2015, the key issues of the family justice system include the increased number of litigants in person (21 per cent over one year); the lack of legal aid in family cases was cited as the most substantial problem of the system by 17 per cent of specialist lawyers responding to questions from the accountancy firm Grant Thornton, while the courts generally not being 'fit for purpose' was the main difficulty cited by 14 per cent (*Matrimonial Survey 2015*, Grant Thornton, 1 December 2015).

The National Audit Office has shown that across all family court cases starting there was a 30 per cent increase in those in which neither party had legal representation in 2013–14 compared with 2012–13 (*Implementing reforms to civil legal aid*, Report by the Comptroller and Auditor General Ministry of Justice and Legal Aid Agency, National Audit Office, HC 784 Session, 014–15 20 November, 2014) and in the first quarter of 2015, 76 per cent of private family law cases had at least one party who was not represented (Lord Falconer, *Five years in the death of the British justice system*, New Statesman, 8 September 2015).

The Justice Committee, which is appointed by the House of Commons to examine the expenditure, administration and policy of the Ministry of Justice and its associated public bodies, has also reported on this issue. It noted (Justice – Eighth Report, *Impact of changes to civil legal aid under Part 1 of the Legal Aid, Sentencing and Punishment of Offenders Act 2012*, 4 March 2015, para 92):

> The National Audit Office in its report, Implementing the civil legal aid reforms, found the number of cases in which neither party in a family law case had representation had increased by 18,519, around 30 per cent of all cases. In the first quarter of 2014, 80 per cent of all private family law cases had at least one party that was not represented. In contrast, the Minister told us, however, that the number of litigants in person in private family law cases had only risen by a 'small percentage' from 66 per cent of cases in which at least one party was not represented to 74 per cent. An additional complication is that the number of cases in the family courts has dropped since the introduction of the legal aid reforms by around 40 per cent. Whatever the true figure may be, evidence we have received strongly suggests not only a significant increase in parties without legal representation but also that litigants in person may be appearing in more complicated cases or be less able to represent themselves.

A steady decrease in public funding has led to an ever-widening gap in the system, leading to a rise in the number of court-goers representing themselves in family proceedings, as they are unable to afford legal representation but do not qualify for legal aid. Once referred to as self-represented litigants (SRLs), members of the public who process their own cases or represent themselves in court are now called Litigants in Person, or LIPs (Terminology for Litigants in Person, Practice guidance issued by the Master of the Rolls, Lord Dyson, 11 March 2013). As early as 2005, and based on an analysis of 1,334 family cases, a study found that 64 per cent of private adoption cases and 60 per cent of divorce cases featured at least one self-represented litigant (R Moorhead and M Sefton, 'Litigants in Person: unrepresented litigants in first instance proceedings', DCA Research Series 2/05, March 2005, Cardiff University (Department for Constitutional Affairs), p 97). In the first quarter of 2014, 74 per cent of private law children's cases featured at least one self-represented party (*Court Statistics Quarterly*, January to March 2014, Table 2.4, Litigants in Person in Private Family Law Cases, Ministry of Justice Analytical Series, 2014).

A Litigant in Person may choose to process their case solely on their own, or sporadically seek out legal assistance, rather than pay for long-term legal representation, which lowers costs and helps the LIP if they are not fully aware of the law surrounding their case. An increase in LIPs in the family courts has led to an increase in the use of lay advocates, known as McKenzie Friends. A McKenzie Friend is able to assist a self-represented litigant by:

- providing moral support;
- taking notes in court;
- helping with case papers;
- giving advice on any aspect of the conduct of the case.

(Practice Guidance, McKenzie Friends
(Civil and Family Courts), 12 July 2010).

McKenzie Friends vary in experience and competence, usually charge less for their assistance than solicitors and barristers, and often work for free. The name derives from a case in which the role was first recognised, *McKenzie v McKenzie* (1970). As the demand for McKenzie Friends has steadily increased inside the family justice system, a call to consider regulating their activity was made in April 2014 by the Legal Services Consumer Panel, with a view to protecting litigants in person from poor advice and unreasonable charges (Fee Charging McKenzie Friends, The Legal Services Consumer Panel, April 2014). However, there is a view that regulating the McKenzie sector at this time may deter lay advisers and reduce the level of support that litigants in person so desperately need as they try to navigate the system without conventional representation.

8.5   REFORMATION OF THE FAMILY JUSTICE SYSTEM

Reformation of a system can be viewed as a healthy response to environmental and societal changes, and an increased understanding of what needs to be improved upon. Yet it can also be the result of ongoing difficulties which are not properly addressed in the first instance. The family justice system is continuously trying to adapt to the ever-changing dynamics of society, but a lack of government funds and a slow turn-around time to implement much-needed changes on the ground means that the system continues to find itself subject to review and, ultimately, reform.

The latest series of recommendations for reform stem from the Family Justice Review, a report which focused on examining possible areas for reform with the family justice system, and which was published on 3 November 2011. The government's response to that review was laid before Parliament on 6 February 2012. A judge within the family courts, Mr Justice Ryder, was appointed by the then President of the Family Division, Sir Nicholas Wall, to make judicial proposals for what has been termed 'the modernisation of family justice'. The proposals were designed to make the family courts simpler and easier to use.

The proposals contained two key elements:

- a focus on strong judicial leadership and management; and
- robust case management of proceedings.

The key areas for reform included:

- a Single Family Court, to promote a significant culture change through strong judicial leadership, and focusing on evidence-based good practice;
- the provision of a network of Local Family Court Centres, under the umbrella of the Single Family Court, led by designated Family Judges where all levels of judges and magistrates will sit as judges of the Family Court;
- management of judicial resources to help reduce court delays;
- cultivating a good practice framework, to improve outcomes for children;
- robust case management of public family law cases;
- assisting Litigants in Person with the law and procedure;
- facilitating the voice of the child (the expression, by children where possible, of their wishes and feelings)

(Judicial Proposals for the Modernisation of Family Justice,
Mr Justice Ryder, July 2012).

Areas which remain untouched by the reforms include:

- the High Court, whose unique jurisdiction will be preserved;
- keeping England and Wales divided into geographical areas, judicially led and managed by the Designated Family Judge;
- the day-to-day management and administration of family cases.

Speaking at the national conference of Resolution, an organisation made up of family lawyers who practice a collaborative approach to handling family cases, Mr Justice Ryder said the aim of the reforms was to 'create a new court and better processes that work in the real world', which could only be achieved through a 'revolutionary culture of change' (Resolution National Conference, Stratford-upon-Avon, 12 April 2013). Many of the reforms have now been implemented, but it remains to be seen whether they are improving the quality of, and access to, justice.

8.6 MEDIA REPORTING IN THE FAMILY COURTS

Prior to 2009, only specific courts could be opened up to allow reporting of family matters, and members of the public and the media were often barred from attending family hearings.

However, on 27 April 2009, all levels of the family courts were opened, but only to accredited members of the media: qualified journalists working for authorised news outlets. Courts are still able to restrict access to hearings if they consider it to be in the best interests of any children involved, or to protect parties or witnesses in the case, who are also able to request such a restriction on their own behalf.

Courts also have the power to restrict what can be reported if they feel it would protect the welfare of any child or families involved in the proceedings. The court may also relax reporting restrictions in individual cases if they feel it would be appropriate or in the public interest to do so.

Further clarification on the position of media reporting by the President of the Family Division, Sir Nicholas Wall, consolidated and smoothed out some of the tensions between open justice, the need for justice to be seen to be done, and privacy and confidentiality concerns (A Wolanski and K Wilson, 'The Family Courts: Media Access and Reporting', Resources, Judicial College Office, Guidance, July 2011), but his successor, Sir James Munby, took reformation in this area a step further.

An outspoken advocate for greater transparency within the family courts, Sir James Munby released a draft Practice Guidance on media reporting, which was widely welcomed by the media, the general public and some members of the legal profession. The Practice Guidance, which has been issued for consultation and comment and is designed to be a guide for legal practitioners, recommends that decisions of family courts should always be published, unless there are compelling reasons against publication, and that some judgments should be published in anonymised form, where appropriate ('Transparency in the Family Courts and the Court of Protection, Publication of Judgments', Draft Practice Guidance, Sir James Munby, President of the Family Division, July 2013).

Section 12 of the Administration of Justice Act 1960 currently makes it a contempt of court to publish a judgment in a family court case involving children, unless the judgment has been delivered in public, or the judge has authorised publication. The July 2013 Practice Guidance effectively creates a presumption that all judgments should be published, unless compelling reasons exist to prevent publication and keep them private. The underlying notion of openness in family proceedings stems from a long-standing tenet in English law that any justice system should be transparent in its day-to-day workings, and allow itself to be examined by the very people who use the system.

The presumption of publication is wide and includes:

- cases brought by local authorities;
- cases involving the making or refusal of orders including emergency protection orders, orders involving a deprivation of liberty, or the withholding of significant medical treatment; and
- orders involving the restraint of publication on information relating to the proceedings.

In all other cases not specifically mentioned in the Practice Guidance, the Guidance suggests that a presumption of publication exists where:

- a party or member of the media applies for an order requesting publication of a judgment; and
- the judge is satisfied that, having taken into account any rights arising from relevant provisions within the European Convention on Human Rights (ECHR), the judgment may be published.

The Guidance suggests that reporting of cases and the extent to which a judgment is anonymised should be decided on a case-by-case basis, and places emphasis on ensuring anonymity does not extend beyond protecting the privacy of the families involved, unless there are good reasons to do so. The Draft Guidance also recommends that restrictions on reporting should be limited and that public authorities and expert witnesses should be named unless there are compelling reasons not to, a broad departure from previous reporting restrictions which shielded expert witnesses, for example, from being named in reported judgments. The number of judgments and family cases which explicitly reveal the names of expert witnesses has steadily increased over the last decade, allowing for debate over concerning issues inside the family courts (see for example 'The doctor who took my baby away', *The Telegraph* online, 1 April 2012).

The Practice Guidance is part of an incremental approach to increasing transparency in the family courts. Following a family case over which Mr Justice Munby presided, he said:

> We must have the humility to recognise – and to acknowledge – that public debate, and the jealous vigilance of an informed media, have an important role to play in exposing past miscarriages of justice and in preventing possible future miscarriages of justice . . . The remedy, even if it is probably doomed to only partial success, is . . . more transparency. Putting it bluntly, letting the glare of publicity into the family courts.
>
> (*Daily Telegraph*, 5 September 2013)

8.7   FAMILY LAW AND PHILOSOPHY

Family law affects every area of life and often incites policy-makers and governments to address some very difficult questions, questions which can be highly controversial in nature.

8.7.1   MARRIAGE, COHABITATION AND DIVORCE

The gradual decline in the twentieth century of people getting married, and an increased trend in divorce, has sparked an ongoing national debate about whether society is taking a step back or merely moving towards a way of life which is better suited to the human condition. And as more and more people choose cohabitation (living with a partner rather than being married or in a civil partnership with them, sometimes for many years) as a means of expressing their togetherness, family law has found it challenging to adapt to such choices.

In an attempt to reconcile the gaps in the law between married couples and cohabiting ones, Lord Lester proposed the Cohabitation Bill in 2009. The Bill sought to give cohabiting couples the right to make a claim for financial provision at the end of their relationship, either through separation or death – a right which is currently afforded to married couples. The Bill, although widely welcomed by family lawyers, was also opposed by some academics and peers in the House of Lords. Other dissenters took the view that people who chose to cohabit did so because they were making a conscious choice to opt out of formal legal commitments. At present, the Bill sits in limbo in Parliament and has not yet been ratified.

Official figures from the Office of National Statistics show that the number of people choosing to cohabit has doubled since 1996. This makes cohabitation the fastest growing family type in the United Kingdom (Short Report, 'Cohabitation in the UK', 1 November 2012).

Between 2011 and 2012, the number of divorces in England and Wales has increased from 117,558 to 118,140, a 0.5 per cent rise, with the highest number of divorces among men and women between the ages of 40 and 44 ('Divorces in England and Wales 2012', ONS, Statistical Bulletin, 6 February 2014). However, the number of marriages increased also, by an estimated 5.3 per cent to 262,240 from 249,133, in 2011 ('Marriages in England and Wales', (Provisional) ONS Statistical Bulletin, 11 June 2014).

8.7.2   DOMESTIC VIOLENCE

Domestic violence affects family units all over the country. The Home Office estimates that in 2011, 7 per cent of women aged 16 to 59 were victims of domestic violence; a further 5 per cent were men (British Crime Survey, 'Crime in England and Wales, 2010/11', July 2011).

The definition of domestic violence, which extends to include 16- and 17-year-old victims, is defined under the Legal Aid, Sentencing and Punishment of Offenders Act 2012 (as amended) as:

> any incident or pattern of incidents of controlling, coercive or threatening behaviour, violence or abuse between those aged 16 or over who are or have been intimate partners or family members regardless of gender or sexuality. This can encompass but is not limited to the following types of abuse:
>
> * psychological;
> * physical;
> * sexual;
> * financial;
> * emotional.

This definition came into force on 31 March 2013, and includes the remarkably misnamed 'honour' based violence, female genital mutilation (FGM), in which women and girls are forcibly mutilated in order solely to prevent them from experiencing sexual pleasure, as well as forced marriage.

Although domestic violence is viewed as a phenomenon which does not directly involve children in the family unit (emotional or physical harm experienced directly by children is usually addressed under the umbrella terms of abuse or neglect), it has been acknowledged that children who witness acts of domestic violence are in fact impacted and affected by it (*Re D (Contact: Reasons for Refusal)* [1997] 2 FLR 48). The NSPCC reported that in one study of 139 serious case reviews in England between 2009 and 2011, 63 per cent of cases were found to have domestic abuse as a risk factor (*New Learning From Serious Case Reviews: A Two Year Report*, 2009–2011, Department for Education, 2012).

Legal aid cutbacks have also had an impact on domestic violence cases, with leading charities warning that the new measures are putting children and women's lives at risk (M O'Hara, '"Women will die" as legal aid becomes more difficult for victims of legal abuse to get', *The Guardian*, 10 September 2014). In *R v (On the Application of Rights of Women) v The Lord Chancellor and Secretary of State for Justice* [2016] EWCA Civ 91, a case brought by the Public Law Project (PLP) on behalf of the charity Rights of Women, the Court of Appeal ruled that evidence requirements which had been operating to prevent survivors of domestic abuse from getting legal aid for family cases were unlawful. Although survivors of domestic violence were eligible for legal aid, applicants had to provide very specific evidence to prove their eligibility – evidence which was often difficult to get, particularly where applicants had suffered non-physical forms of abuse. In many cases it was also subject to a 24-month time limit, although evidence showed that perpetrators often remain a threat to survivors long after that period. The Court described a '. . . formidable catalogue of areas of domestic violence not reached by a statute whose purpose is to reach just such cases' [para. 44].

In February 2017 the government announced its intention to strengthen the law relating to domestic abuse, the Prime Minister Theresa May stating that she personally would take charge of preparations for a Domestic Violence and Abuse Act, with the aim to increase support for victims and ensure a common and comprehensive treatment across the UK in dealing with the issue.

8.7.3 CHILDREN

The culture surrounding children who are involved in family proceedings is fast becoming one of the most controversial areas of family law. With children increasingly either electing or being coerced by parties to become more involved in their own cases, the courts have found themselves under pressure to reform this area of family law, while maintaining appropriate levels of protection and privacy for children in these proceedings. This area of family law has come to be known as the Voice of the Child, and focuses exclusively on finding ways to include children who wish to be a part of the process, while balancing privacy and welfare needs of those children at the same time.

The first major step towards reform in this area occurred in 2010, when the Family Justice Council, a body set up to promote collaboration among professionals within the family justice system and to monitor the system, together with the Voice of the Child subcommittee, released guidelines for judges prepared to meet children going through proceedings ('Guidelines for Judges Meeting Children who are subject to Family Proceedings', April 2010). Although limited in its scope (the guidelines do not require judges to speak with children who wish to meet with them, and only allow a narrow range of subjects to be discussed, all linked to procedure rather than substantive issues in the case), it marked a significant shift away from a working culture which had traditionally kept children at arm's length.

In a further move to support and understand children better, the Voice of the Child sub-committee was asked to prepare another report, this time by the Children's Commissioner, in the form of a series of interviews with children as young as three who had experienced family proceedings. The report highlighted the need to look at the way proceedings might affect children, to make information more child-friendly and to give children the opportunity to produce a plan detailing how they would like to be supported and have their voice heard ('Do more than listen. Act' – Consultation response to the Family Justice Review undertaken for the Family Justice Council', 27 July 2011).

And in July 2014, at the newly established Voice of the Child Conference, Justice Minister Simon Hughes announced that children inside the family courts would be listened to and heard more effectively, with the government committing to allowing children as young as 10, and younger where appropriate, to have access to judges to make their views and feelings known ('Children will be seen and heard in family courts', government press release, 25 July 2014).

8.8   THE FUTURE OF THE FAMILY COURTS

The future of family law, while uncertain, and for all the controversy it courts, is a hopeful one. As society changes and our understanding of the human condition evolves, the family courts too must keep pace with and react to those changes. The modernisation of the family justice system in the twenty-first century is perhaps one of the most exciting periods in history for the family courts, and for its impact on future generations.

The enactment of the Marriage (Same Sex Couples) Act 2013 made provision, for the first time, for the marriage of same-sex couples in England and Wales. Maria Miller MP, who sponsored the Bill, told the media that the passing of the Bill was 'clear affirmation' that 'respect for each and every person is paramount, regardless of age, religion, gender, ethnicity or sexuality'. However, not everyone backed the Bill; the Conservative MP Sir Gerald Howarth viewed the Bill as having 'absolutely no mandate' (*BBC News* online, 17 July 2013). The first same-sex marriage ceremonies took place on 29 March 2014.

Other areas of family law, too, are wading into increasingly controversial waters. The Family Drug and Alcohol Court (FDAC), set up in 2008 by a pioneering family judge, District Judge Nicholas Crichton, has been accused of being a violation of judicial power, due to the extent of the interaction between judges in these courts and the families that come before them (BBC Radio 4, *Law In Action*, 15 March 2012). The judiciary did not agree though, and since its inception, FDAC, which uses a different approach from that adopted by mainstream family courts to help families with substance abuse, has won awards for its work and continues to lead the way in effective and humane care of families struggling with drug and alcohol addiction. Statistics for FDAC show that at the time of the final court order, 39 per cent of FDAC mothers were reunited with their children, compared to 21 per cent of mothers from a comparison group in ordinary care proceedings. There was also a marked reduction in costs for local authorities, as children stayed with their parents, care placements were shorter and there were fewer contested cases (Family Drug and Alcohol Court (FDAC), 'Evaluation Research Study', Brunel University, 2008–10).

CHAPTER SUMMARY: THE FAMILY COURTS AND PROCESS

FAMILY COURTS

Family courts are concerned with the law relating to the family unit. They deal with:

- marriage;
- divorce decrees;
- cohabitation;
- some types of domestic violence;
- disputes between parents over the upbringing of their children;
- financial support for children upon divorce or separation;
- local authority intervention where children may need to be protected from abuse or neglect; and
- adoption.

Jurisdiction to hear these matters is conferred to Family Proceedings Courts, which are specialist magistrates' courts, as well as County Courts and the Family Division of the High Court, through the umbrella of the Single Family Court, which may sit anywhere in England and Wales.

PRIVATE AND PUBLIC FAMILY LAW

Family courts are broadly divided into two areas: private and public family law. These areas are not mutually exclusive, as private family cases can often become public in nature, where for example a concern over a child's living arrangements may reveal more serious concerns about that child's day-to-day care. However, public family law cases must always start in the Family Proceedings Courts, though they can be transferred to

County Courts to minimise delay, consolidate proceedings or where the matter is exceptionally serious, complex or important.

Family court judges are charged with handling cases arising from these areas of law, which typically result in a series of directions, or orders, requiring a person to do or not to do something.

Private family law matters are brought by individuals, like parents, spouses and next of kin, usually in connection with a divorce or parents' separation. Judges dealing with these matters can make various orders, for example to control who holds the legal rights and responsibilities for a child.

Public law cases are usually brought by local authorities (although the NSPCC, as an 'authorised person', currently also has powers to bring such cases), and can include issues such as:

- emergency protection orders, removing a child from harm by relocating them to a place of safety, or ensuring they are not removed from a safe environment;
- family assistance orders (s 16 of the Children Act 1989), as in private law proceedings;
- supervision orders, where children are placed under the supervision of their local authority;
- care orders, conferring parental responsibility of a child to the local authority who are applying for an order.

THE CHILDREN ACT 1989 AND THE PARAMOUNTCY PRINCIPLE

The Children Act 1989 is designed to make the welfare of every child the primary, or paramount, concern in cases involving children. This is often referred to as the 'paramountcy principle'. This means the welfare of the child will be the paramount consideration for all decisions made under the Act.

LEGAL AID AND THE FAMILY COURTS

Legal aid has been drastically reduced for civil cases by the Legal Aid, Sentencing and Punishment of Offenders Act (LASPO) 2012. As a result, only a very narrow set of family cases are now eligible for legal aid, and include:

- cases where a victim of domestic violence is divorcing or separating from an abusive partner; and
- cases where a child is at risk of abuse from a partner.

REFORMATION OF THE FAMILY JUSTICE SYSTEM

The latest series of recommendations for reform stem from the Family Justice Review. A judge within the family courts, Mr Justice Ryder, was appointed to make judicial proposals for what has been termed 'the modernisation of family justice'. The proposals were designed to make the family courts simpler and easier to use.

The proposals contained two key elements:

- a focus on strong judicial leadership and management; and
- robust case management of proceedings.

Key areas which have been reformed:

- a single family court, to promote a significant culture change through strong judicial leadership, and focusing on evidence-based good practice;
- the provision of a network of Local Family Court Centres, under the umbrella of the Single Family Court, led by Designated Family Judges where all levels of judges and magistrates will sit as judges of the Family Court.

DOMESTIC VIOLENCE

The definition of domestic violence, which is not a legal formula, was recently extended to include 16- and 17-year-old victims, and is legally defined as:

> any incident or pattern of incidents of controlling, coercive or threatening behaviour, violence or abuse between those aged 16 or over who are or have been intimate partners or family members regardless of gender or sexuality. This can encompass but is not limited to the following types of abuse:
>
> - psychological;
> - physical;
> - sexual;
> - financial;
> - emotional.

This definition came into force on 31 March 2013, and includes female genital mutilation (FGM) in which women and girls are forcibly mutilated in order solely to prevent them from experiencing sexual pleasure, and forced marriage.

FOOD FOR THOUGHT

1 Scandals surrounding child sexual abuse and exploitation have become so acute that the government has now set up an Inquiry to find out the extent to which state and non-state institutions have failed to protect children from abuse. To date, there have been more than 67 inquiries in England alone looking at child protection issues – do you think another inquiry will make a difference? (Independent Panel Inquiry Into Child Sexual Abuse, https://childsexualabuseinquiry. independent.gov.uk)

2   The latest research on Litigants in Person suggests that engaging self-represented parties in the decision-making process would be beneficial to improving case outcomes. Do you agree? (Litigants in Person in Private Family Law Cases, Ministry of Justice Analytical Series 2014)

3   The administration and recording of marriage has steadily moved away from the church to the state. Should people now be able to marry privately without state intervention?

FURTHER READING

Cretney, S, *Family Law in the Twentieth Century: A History*, 2003, Oxford: OUP

Hewitt, L and Hughes, S, 'The changing Face(book) of family law' (2013) NLJ 7555

Ministry of Justice, *Family Court Statistics Quarterly, England and Wales*, July to September 2015, Ministry of Justice Statistics bulletin, December 2015

Moorhead, R and Sefton, M, 'Litigants in Person: unrepresented litigants in first instance proceedings', DCA Research Series 2/05, March 2005, Cardiff University (Department for Constitutional Affairs)

Munby, J, 'Sloppy practice in adoption', 20 September 2013, NLJ online

Wall, N, 'Changing the culture', 29 November 2011, Judiciary of England and Wales

Waller, P, 'Going the distance', 4 May 2012, NLJ online

Wolanski, A and Wilson, K, 'The Family Courts: Media Access and Reporting', Resources, Judicial College Office, Guidance, July 2011

USEFUL WEBSITES

http://unsafespaces.com/
The Not So Big Society Blog.

www.coram.org.uk/supporting-parents/family-drug-and-alcohol-court
The Family Drug and Alcohol Court.

https://www.publications.parliament.uk/pa/cm/cmallparty/170215/family-business.htm
All Party Parliamentary Group on Family Law and the Court of Protection.

http://researchingreform.net
Researching Reform.

COMPANION WEBSITE

Now visit the companion website to:

- test your understanding of the key terms using our Flashcard Glossary;
- revise and consolidate your knowledge of 'The family courts and process' using our multiple choice question testbank;
- view all of the links to the Useful Websites above.

www.routledge.com/cw/slapper

9.1 INTRODUCTION

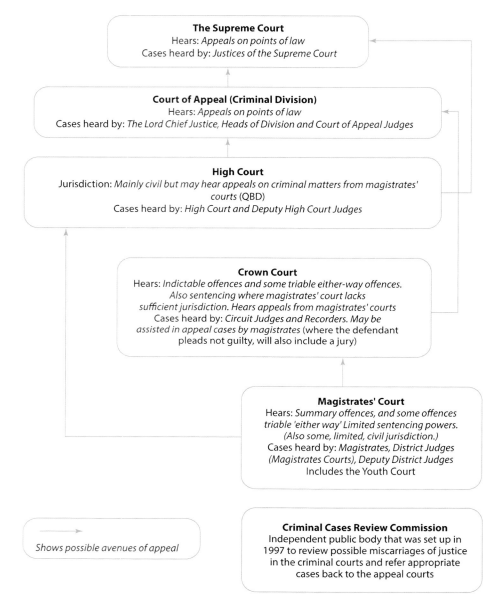

The Supreme Court
Hears: *Appeals on points of law*
Cases heard by: *Justices of the Supreme Court*

Court of Appeal (Criminal Division)
Hears: *Appeals on points of law*
Cases heard by: *The Lord Chief Justice, Heads of Division and Court of Appeal Judges*

High Court
Jurisdiction: *Mainly civil but may hear appeals on criminal matters from magistrates' courts* (QBD)
Cases heard by: *High Court and Deputy High Court Judges*

Crown Court
Hears: *Indictable offences and some triable either-way offences. Also sentencing where magistrates' court lacks sufficient jurisdiction. Hears appeals from magistrates' courts* Cases heard by: *Circuit Judges and Recorders. May be assisted in appeal cases by magistrates* (where the defendant pleads not guilty, will also include a jury)

Magistrates' Court
Hears: *Summary offences, and some offences triable 'either way' Limited sentencing powers. (Also some, limited, civil jurisdiction.)* Cases heard by: *Magistrates, District Judges (Magistrates Courts), Deputy District Judges* Includes the Youth Court

Shows possible avenues of appeal

Criminal Cases Review Commission
Independent public body that was set up in 1997 to review possible miscarriages of justice in the criminal courts and refer appropriate cases back to the appeal courts

FIGURE 9.1 *The Criminal Courts.*

26 November 2015). The aim is to move the courts from a Victorian paper-based system into the digital age. The IT reforms will enable more hearings to take place through video links with courts, and they reduce the costs of transporting prisoners to court, thus facilitating 90,000 cases a year to be heard in prison rather than court. Other pre-trial hearings will no longer be needed because judges and lawyers will agree the

management of cases via computer links. These changes, it must be kept in mind, are not driven by juridical preferences but rather by shortage of allocated resources. The Ministry of Justice budget will fall over the period 2015/16 to 2019/20 from £6.2 billion to £5.6 billion, a fall of 15 per cent.

9.2   MAGISTRATES' COURTS

In the 12 months ending March 2014, there were an estimated 1.4 million individuals proceeded against in criminal cases in magistrates' courts. This compares with 1.47 million individuals in the 12 months ending March 2013 (*Criminal Justice Statistics: March 2014*, Ministry of Justice, 2014).

The office of magistrate or Justice of the Peace (JP) dates from 1195, when Richard I first appointed 'keepers of the peace' to deal with those who were accused of breaking 'the King's peace'. The JPs originally acted as local administrators for the king in addition to their judicial responsibilities. Apart from the 21,704 lay justices who sit in some 330 courts, there are also 142 district judges (magistrates' courts) (formerly known as stipendiary magistrates) and 143 deputy district judges (magistrates' courts) who sit in cities and larger towns (*Court Statistics (quarterly) January – March 2014*, Ministry of Justice, June 2014). They are qualified, experienced lawyers who are salaried justices. A Practice Direction from the Lord Chief Justice sets out details concerning the classification and allocation of Crown Court business, and some of this is relevant to the magistrates' courts. For example, upon sending someone for trial at the Crown Court, the magistrates should, if the offence is a class I offence (for example murder, manslaughter or treason), specify the most convenient location of the Crown Court where a High Court judge or a circuit judge authorised to try such cases regularly sits (*Practice Direction (Criminal proceedings: Classification and allocation of business)*, 2005).

It became evident in 2009 that the workload of many magistrates' courts was being diverted away from the court system. Magistrates complained that increasing numbers of offenders were being dealt with by 'on-the-spot' fines and cautions – almost half of all offences are now dealt with in this way (*The Times*, 10 July 2009). John Thornhill, chairman of the Magistrates' Association, said: 'Magistrates are reporting to us cancelled sittings across the country, either because of no work, or disposing of the case out of court.' Costs were not saved in the long term, however, because nearly half of such fines went unpaid. Mr Thornhill observed that 'Many of these cases come back to the courts in the end, because the offender has failed to pay.' (See further at 12.9.3.)

9.2.1   SUMMARY TRIAL

Summary offences are created and defined by statute. There are thousands of different summary offences. They include traffic offences, common assault, taking a motor vehicle without consent and driving while disqualified: about 90 per cent of all cases are dealt with in the magistrates' court (*Court Statistics (quarterly) January – March 2014*, Ministry of Justice, June 2014).

Cases are heard in the court for the district in which the offence is alleged to have been committed. In most cases, the defendant will be in court, but it is possible for the accused in road traffic offences to plead guilty by post and not to attend court.

Two or three magistrates, whose powers of sentencing are limited by the Acts that govern the offences in question, will hear the cases. A district judge (magistrates' courts) may sit without lay magistrates. The maximum sentence that magistrates can impose on a private individual is an unlimited fine and/or a 12-month prison sentence for more than one either-way offence (see below), or six months for one offence. Businesses may be fined up to £20,000 for certain offences. The maximum sentences for many summary offences are much less than these limits. Where a defendant is convicted of two or more offences at the same hearing, the maximum custodial sentence for any one offence is 12 months (s 154 of the Criminal Justice Act 2003, to be brought into law at a date to be appointed). Several sentences to be served concurrently, including more than one 12-month sentence, will be permitted. Consecutive sentences amounting to more than 12 months are not permitted, but will be limited to 65 weeks once s 155 of the Criminal Justice Act 2003 is brought into force. A date for its coming into force has still not yet been appointed.

Many statutory offences are given particular 'levels' according to their seriousness. This means that if a government minister wishes to raise fines (say to be in line with inflation), he or she does not have to go through hundreds of different offences, altering the maximum fine in relation to each one separately; the maxima for each level are simply altered. The current figures are as follows: Level 5 unlimited; Level 4 up to £2,500; Level 3 up to £1,000; Level 2 up to £500; and Level 1 up to £200 (s 37 of the Criminal Justice Act 1982).

The Criminal Justice Act (CJA) 1991 (the framework statute for many of the sentencing powers of the courts until the enactment of a consolidating statute, the Powers of Criminal Courts (Sentencing) Act 2000) provided for a new system of fining in magistrates' courts: the 'unit fine' system. Under this system, fines were linked to the offender's income. The idea was that the rich should pay more than the poor for the same offence. Crimes were graded from 1 to 10 and the level of crime was then multiplied by the offender's weekly disposable income. The system's figures, however, resulted in many anomalies and it was eventually abolished. Nevertheless, in fixing the appropriate amount for a convicted defendant's fine, the magistrates must still take into account his income. Other sentences that the court may use include absolute discharge, conditional discharge, community orders (replacing the old probation orders, community service/ punishment orders and curfew orders, and including many new types of requirements which can be included in community orders) and compensation orders.

After a conviction, the magistrates will hear whether the defendant has a criminal record and, if so, for what offences. This is to enable them to pass an appropriate sentence. If, after hearing that record, they feel that their powers of sanction are insufficient to deal with the defendant, then the defendant may be sent to the Crown Court for sentencing.

A bench of lay magistrates is advised on issue of law by a justices' clerk, who is legally qualified and guides the justices on matters of law, sentencing and procedure. The justices' clerk may give advice even when not specifically invited to do so. It is an established principle of English law that 'justice should not only be done but manifestly and undoubtedly be seen to be done' (*R v Sussex Justices ex p McCarthy* (1924), per Lord Hewart CJ). This is not about the proceedings being visible from a public gallery! It means there must be nothing in the appearance of what happens in a trial that might create an impression that something improper happened. In the *Sussex Justices* case, Mr McCarthy had been convicted of dangerous driving. He found out that the clerk to the magistrates, the person giving them legal advice, was a solicitor who happened to be representing someone who was suing him as a result of the car accident. Even though the solicitor might have been perfectly professional, there was the appearance that he *could* have framed his advice to the magistrates (even subconsciously) to help secure a conviction because such an outcome would have assisted his client in the civil case. The clerk had retired with the magistrates when they went to consider their verdict. The conviction was quashed because of the possibility of bias.

The magistrates are independent of the clerks and thus the clerks should not *instruct* the magistrates as to what decision to make on any point, nor should they appear to be doing so. The clerk should not, therefore, normally retire with the justices when they go to consider their verdict in any case, although they may be called on by the magistrates to give legal advice on any point. The clerk should not give any judgment on matters of fact. The justices' clerk will employ legally qualified assistants to sit in court with magistrates – they are known as court legal advisers and carry out the advisory role described above. Court legal advisers have been given 'delegated powers' to deal with straightforward unopposed applications in the absence of the magistrates – for example, where both prosecution and defence agree an adjournment of a case or where a warrant for the arrest of the accused is to be issued in his/her absence. As these are formal matters the attendance of the magistrates in court is not required if the legal adviser is happy to deal with them in this way.

The court is required in certain cases to consider a compensation order and to give reasons if it decides not to make such an order. Compensation orders are governed by the provisions of ss 130–34 of the Powers of the Criminal Courts (Sentencing) Act (PCC(S)A) 2000. Section 130 states that a court before which a person is convicted, in addition to dealing with him or her in any other way, may make a compensation order. The order is to compensate personal injury, loss or damage resulting from the offence in question or any other offence 'taken into consideration' (that is, admitted by the defendant) by the court. The defendant can also be ordered to make payments for funeral expenses or bereavement in respect of a death resulting from an offence (other than a death due to a motor accident). The court, s 130(3) states, 'shall give reasons, on passing sentence, if it does not make such a compensation order in a case where this section empowers it to do so'. Unlike a fine, the compensation will go to the victim rather than to the state, so these orders save victims of crime from having to claim damages against defendants in the civil courts. They are not intended as an alternative to punishment, enabling the defendant to buy his way out of the penalties for the crime. Even so, s 130(12) gives priority to the issue of a compensation order over a fine. In 2010, the Crown Court and magistrates' courts issued 154,428 compensation orders. The total cost in 2010 was £44,620,426 (*Hansard*, 20 June 2011, col 86W).

Alongside any such compensation order, an offender may also be required to pay prosecution costs, on a scale currently starting at £85, and a so-called Victim Surcharge, currently priced from £15 to £120. This surcharge is statutorily imposed regardless of whether or not there was a victim or victims but goes to the Victims and Witness General Fund. In this way, it can be understood as a tax on the cost of a prosecution. It is also payable on conviction in the Crown Court. Section 54 of the Criminal Justice and Courts Act 2015 introduced the criminal courts charge, a mandatory charge payable on conviction (whether as a result of a plea or after trial) and refusal of an appeal in respect of all offences committed on or after 13 April 2015. The provisions are draconian, as judges and magistrates have no power to refuse to impose the charge or to determine the level of charge. Charges range from £150 for a conviction in the magistrates' court to £1,200 for a conviction after trial on indictment in the Crown Court. The charges raised concerns in a number of quarters about their effect on the poorest and most vulnerable defendants, and on 3 December 2015 the Lord Chancellor, Michael Gove, announced that as of 24 December 2015 they would no longer be imposed.

9.2.2 OFFENCES TRIABLE 'EITHER WAY'

Where the defendant is charged with an offence triable 'either way', the first matter to be established is whether he should be tried summarily (by magistrates) or on indictment (in the Crown Court by a judge and jury). The procedures by which this matter is resolved are known as plea before venue and allocation hearings. There were substantial changes made to this procedure in May 2013 when changes made by Sched 3 to the Criminal Justice Act 2003 to ss 17–21 of the Magistrates' Courts Act 1980 finally came into effect.

In a plea before venue hearing, that is, one where the accused is charged with an either-way offence, they are first asked if they wish to indicate a guilty plea. If they do, the magistrates will hear the facts of the case and see details of any previous convictions. The magistrates retain the power to commit them for sentence to the Crown Court if they feel that their powers of punishment are inadequate (this is dealt with later in more detail). If they feel that they have enough power to deal with the accused, then they proceed to sentence them.

If the defendant pleads not guilty or declines to indicate their plea, then an allocation hearing is held under s 19 Magistrates' Courts Act 1980. In this hearing the prosecution and defence make submissions about whether the case should be heard at the magistrates' or Crown Court. The magistrates then decide whether to agree to hear the case or decline to do so and commit it to the Crown Court. If they agree to hear the case, then the accused can still choose (elect) to have their case heard by a jury and – if they so choose – the case will be committed for Crown Court trial. If they decide in favour of the magistrates' court, then it will fix a date for a summary trial.

Secondly, if the determination is in favour of trial on indictment (by either method), the case will be sent to the Crown Court under s 51 Crime and Disorder Act (CDA) 1998. The old system of committal proceedings, where magistrates established whether there was a *prima facie* case to be heard before sending the case to the Crown Court, was abolished in May 2013.

Most defendants charged with 'either-way' offences are tried by magistrates: 36,167 cases were committed to the Crown Court in 2013 because the magistrates considered their sentencing powers to be inadequate and on average 4 per cent of cases go to the Crown Court because the defendants elect trial by jury (*Judicial and Court Statistics Quarterly, April – June 2014*, Ministry of Justice, 2014).

The defendant therefore can insist on trial on indictment, but cannot insist on being tried summarily if the magistrates decline jurisdiction. Similarly, the magistrates can decide that the defendant should be tried on indictment, but cannot insist that he or she be tried summarily. Prosecutions conducted by the Attorney General, the Solicitor General or the Director of Public Prosecutions must be tried on indictment if so requested by the prosecutor.

If a defendant charged with a number of related either-way offences pleads guilty to one of them at plea before venue and is sent to the Crown Court to be tried for the rest, the power in s 4 of the PCC(S)A 2000 – to send the offence to which he or she has pleaded guilty to the Crown Court for sentence – still exists.

9.2.3   SENTENCING IN THE MAGISTRATES' COURTS

Concern is often expressed at what sometimes appear to be quite notable discrepancies in sentencing practices employed by different benches of magistrates. It might be that these variations are unavoidable in circumstances where the rigidity of fixed penalties is unacceptable for most offences and regional differences in types of prevalent crime prompt justices to have certain attitudes to particular offences. Media reports from courtrooms are also unlikely to pick out the full detail and nuances of cases; there is clearly a difference between following a case in the press and watching it from the public gallery. There are several research surveys that demonstrate the discrepancies in magistrates' sentencing. Tarling, for example (*Sentencing and Practice in Magistrates' Courts*, 1979, Home Office Study 98), showed that in the 30 courts he surveyed, the use of probation (as it was then called) varied between 1 per cent and 12 per cent, suspended sentences between 4 per cent and 16 per cent, and fines between 46 per cent and 76 per cent. In one study, it was found that custody rates, average custodial sentence lengths (ACSL) and the use of life and Indeterminate Sentences for Public Protection (IPPs) vary significantly across the 42 Criminal Justice Areas (CJAs) in England and Wales. For example, of those CJAs with custody rates in the top five for 2006, three (Essex, Bedfordshire and London) were consistently in the top five for 2003, 2004 and 2005. Similarly, for those CJAs with custody rates in the bottom five for 2006, two (Dyfed – Powys and Lincolnshire) were consistently in the bottom five for 2003, 2004 and 2005 (T Mason, N de Silva, N Sharma, D Brown and G Harper, *Local Variation in Sentencing in England and Wales*, 2007, Ministry of Justice).

Committals for sentence

Currently, cases committed to the Crown Court for sentence must be heard in the Crown Court by a bench composed of a High Court judge, circuit judge or recorder sitting with between two and four JPs. The Powers of the Criminal Courts (Sentencing) Act 2000 ss 3–7 states that where, on a summary trial of an offence triable 'either way' a person aged 18 or over is convicted, the magistrates can commit the convicted person to the Crown Court for sentence if the magistrates are of the opinion that the offence was so serious that greater punishment should be inflicted for it than they have power to impose, or, in the case of a violent or sexual offence, that a custodial sentence for a period longer than the magistrates have power to impose is necessary to protect the public from serious harm, or, under s 4, the defendant is being sent to the Crown Court for a trial of related offences.

Warrant execution and fine default powers

The police used to be primarily responsible for arresting fine defaulters and those in breach of community sentences. Increasingly, however, some police forces have given this work a low priority. The Courts Act 2003 extended the use of the Department for Work and Pensions' long-standing Third Party Deduction Scheme, which allows deductions from benefits to enforce payment of fines. The level of deductions is contained in the Fines (Deductions from Income Support) (Amendment) Regulations 2004.

Deductions can be applied when the offender is first sentenced, subsequently applied if the offender defaults as part of a resetting of payment terms, or used as a further sanction by the fines officer. Other deductions can include council tax, rent arrears, fuel costs, housing costs and water charges.

9.2.4   YOUTH COURTS

The procedures previously discussed apply only to those aged at least 18. Defendants under 18 years of age will normally be tried by a youth court, no matter what the classification of the offence (summary, either way, indictable only). Section 51A of the Crime and Disorder Act 1998 provides for sending a defendant under 18 to the Crown Court for trial. If the charge is homicide or a firearms offence under either s 51A Firearms Act 1968 or s 29(3) Violent Crime Reduction Act 2006, it must be tried on indictment. Sending the young person to the Crown Court is also mandatory under s 51A(2) where:

- the charge is a specified offence under s 224 CJA 2003 and it appears to the court that the young person, if convicted, may be a 'dangerous' offender under s 226 CJA 2003; or
- the offence charged is a serious one (under s 91 Powers of Criminal Courts (Sentencing) Act 2000) and might attract a lengthy custodial sentence under the circumstances.

A young person may be tried on indictment where the offence in question is related to one which must be sent to the Crown Court under the provisions listed above. The court also has discretion where:

- the offence charged is a 'grave' crime punishable with at least 14 years' imprisonment, or a range of sexual and firearms offences;
- the defendant is jointly charged with an adult who is going to be tried on indictment and the court considers that it is in the interests of justice that both should be tried on indictment.

A defendant under 18 may be tried summarily in an adult magistrates' court where:

- he or she is to be tried jointly with an adult. This is subject to the power to commit both for trial on indictment, and also subject to a power to remit the defendant under 18 for trial to a youth court where the adult pleads guilty, or is discharged or committed for trial on indictment, but the defendant is not.

When defendants under 18 are tried by magistrates in the youth court, there will generally be three justices to hear the case, of whom one must be a man and one a woman. These justices will have had special training to deal with such cases. There are special provisions relating to punishment for this age group. Section 9 of the Criminal Justice and Immigration Act 2008 says a sentencing court must have regard to 'the principal aim of the youth justice system', which is to 'prevent offending (or re-offending) by persons aged under 18'. It identifies the purposes of sentencing as:

(a) the punishment of offenders;
(b) the reform and rehabilitation of offenders;
(c) the protection of the public; and
(d) the making of reparation by offenders to persons affected by their offences.

The current maximum fine for a child (under 14 years of age) is £250, and for a young person (under 18) £1,000. Members of both groups may be made the subject of a variety of orders, including the youth rehabilitation order, which is a generic community order which permits the imposition of a range of requirements for e.g. activity, supervision, a curfew, etc. A sentence of imprisonment may be imposed only on a defendant who is at least 21 years old. A sentence of detention in a young offenders' institution may be imposed only on a defendant who is at least 18 years old (the intention is to bring all those aged at least 18 within the imprisonment regime). For those under 18, the custodial sentence is a detention and training order, which may be imposed only where an adult could have been sentenced to imprisonment. Where the defendant is under 15, a detention and training order can be imposed only if he or she is a 'persistent' offender. In measures under Part III of the PCC(S)A 2000, the youth court will on some occasions be obliged, and on others will have the discretion, to refer the young offender to a youth offender panel, the members of which will agree with the young offender and his or her family a course of action designed to tackle the offending behaviour and its causes. This could involve actions such as making apologies, carrying out reparation, doing community work or taking part in family counselling.

Traditionally, the aim of the youth court system has been to take the young offender out of the normal criminal court environment, and this has involved strict rules about public access to the court. In general, members of the public have not been permitted to attend and reporting restrictions have been very tight. Parents can be required to attend, and must attend in the case of any person under the age of 16, unless such a requirement would be unreasonable in the circumstances. The name or photograph of any person under 18 appearing in a case must not be printed in any newspaper or broadcast without the authority of the court or the Home Secretary. Also the youth justice system has introduced a system of warnings and reprimands (formerly known as cautions) that are issued instead of court proceedings for many offenders in an attempt to divert them from the youth court system.

9.2.5   INDICTABLE OFFENCES – SENDING TO THE CROWN COURT

Under s 51 of the Crime and Disorder Act 1998, where an adult defendant is charged with an indictable-only offence – one which can be tried only by a Crown Court (for example, murder, manslaughter, rape or robbery), the court shall send them directly to the Crown Court for trial. They are 'sent forthwith'. Where they are also charged with an either-way offence or a summary offence, they may be sent directly to the Crown Court for that as well, provided the magistrates believe that it is related to the indictable offence and, in the case of a summary offence, it is punishable with imprisonment or involves obligatory or discretionary disqualification from driving. Under this procedure, the accused may apply to a Crown Court judge for the charge(s) to be dismissed, and the judge should so direct if it appears that the evidence would be insufficient to convict the accused (Sched 3 to the CDA 1998).

9.3   THE CROWN COURT

Until 1971, the main criminal courts were the Assizes and the Quarter Sessions. These courts did not sit continuously and were not held in locations that corresponded with centres of population, as had been the case when they developed. The system was very inefficient as circuit judges wasted much time simply travelling from one town on the circuit to the next, and many defendants spent long periods in gaol awaiting trial.

Change was made following the *Report of the Beeching Royal Commission on Assizes and Quarter Sessions* (1969). The Courts Act 1971 abolished the Assizes and Quarter Sessions. These were replaced by a single Crown Court, a part of the Supreme Court of Judicature. The Crown Court is not a local court like the magistrates' court, but a single court which sits in 77 centres. England and Wales are divided into six circuits, each with its own headquarters and staff. The centres are divided into three tiers. In first-tier centres, High Court judges hear civil and criminal cases, whereas circuit judges and recorders hear only criminal cases. Second-tier centres are served by the same types of judge, but hear criminal cases only. At third-tier centres, recorders and circuit judges hear just criminal cases.

Criminal offences are divided into three classes according to their gravity.

High Court judges are usually from the Queen's Bench Division (QBD). Circuit judges are full-time appointments made by the Queen on the advice of the Lord Chancellor. They are drawn from advocates with at least seven years' experience of Crown Court practice (s 71 of the CLSA 1990) or lawyers who have been recorders. Appointment is also possible for someone who has had three years' experience in a number of other judicial offices like that of the district judge (magistrates' courts). Circuit judges retire at the age of 72, or 75 if the Lord Chancellor thinks it in the public interest.

The Courts Act 2003, ss 65–67, introduced greater flexibility in the deployment of judicial resources, allowing district judges (magistrates' courts) to deal with and make orders in relation both to allocation and to other interim issues in cases reserved to the Crown Court. High Court judges, circuit judges and recorders are able to sit as magistrates when exercising their criminal and family jurisdiction.

A circuit judge may be removed from office by the Lord Chancellor on the grounds of incapacity or misbehaviour (s 17(4) of the Courts Act 1971). This right has not been exercised since 1983, when Judge Bruce Campbell, an Old Bailey judge, was removed from office a week after being convicted of two charges of smuggling.

To qualify for appointment as a recorder, a person must have seven years' experience of advocacy in the Crown Court or County Courts. JPs may also sit in the Crown Court, provided they are with one of the types of judge mentioned above. It is mandatory for between two and four JPs to sit when the Crown Court is hearing an appeal or dealing with persons committed for sentence by a magistrates' court.

The Crown Court hears all cases involving trial on indictment. It also hears appeals from those convicted summarily in the magistrates' courts. At the conclusion of an appeal hearing, it has the power to confirm, reverse or vary any part of the decision under appeal (s 48(2) of the Senior Courts Act 1981). If the appeal is decided against the accused, the Crown Court has the power to impose any sentence that the magistrates could have imposed, including one that is harsher than the one originally imposed on the defendant.

Defendants committed to the Crown Court to be tried might have to wait a long time. The *Judicial and Court Quarterly Statistics, January – March 2014* (Ministry of Justice, June 2014) reports that:

For cases completing at the Crown Court during Q1 2014, the number of days from offence to completion has remained unchanged at 304 days when compared with the same quarter in the previous year. However, changes can be seen when looking at the time spent in the magistrates' courts and the Crown Court. When comparing Q1 2014 with Q1 2013, the time spent at the magistrates' courts between first hearing and being sent to the Crown Court has fallen from 26 days to 8 days, whereas the time spent at the Crown Court has increased from 139 days to 155 days. This is mainly the result of the national abolition of committal hearings for triable either way cases.

Ever since the Streatfield Committee Report recommended in 1961 that the maximum time a defendant should have to wait after committal for trial should be eight weeks, there have been many schemes to help achieve this aim, but none has been particularly successful. Since 1985, for example, a person charged with an offence triable 'either way' can request the prosecution to furnish them with information (in the form of witness statements, a summary of the case, etc) of the case against them. This was aimed at increasing the number of guilty pleas by showing to the defendant at an early stage the strength of the prosecution's case.

When one remembers that the average time to try a case on a plea of 'not guilty' is about 14 hours, the burden of work on the Crown Court – dealing with over 90,000 trials and almost 120,000 defendants each year – is considerable. The consequent delay has very serious repercussions for the criminal justice system: justice delayed is justice denied. The accuracy of testimony becomes less reliable the longer the gap between the original reception of the data by a witness and his account of it in court. Also important is the stress and pain for those innocent defendants who have to wait so long before their case can be put to a jury.

9.4 MAGISTRATES' COURTS V CROWN COURTS

For offences triable 'either way', there has been much debate about the merits of each venue. The introduction of the 'plea before venue' procedure previously described has significantly reduced the number of cases committed for trial to the Crown Court and significantly increased the number committed for sentence. In 2013, 68 per cent of defendants pleaded guilty to all counts, 30 per cent pleaded not guilty to at least one count, and 2 per cent did not enter a plea. Since 2001, the guilty plea rate has steadily risen from 56 per cent to the current rate of 68 per cent. Initiatives in the Crown Court and other agencies, such as offering an early plea sentencing discount (a more lenient sentence if the defendant pleads guilty early) and providing early charging advice from the Crown Prosecution Service at police stations, have helped to increase the guilty plea rate.

One of the reasons defendants choose to have their cases tried at the Crown Court is that prosecution cases sometimes fall apart during the delay before a Crown Court hearing, allowing the defendant to go free. Another is that juries cannot be compelled to give reasons for convicting, unlike magistrates, who can be required to justify their reasons in writing for review in the High Court, which can overturn convictions or acquittals. Thus, there is a greater chance with jury convictions that an appeal court will regard a conviction (should there be one) as unsafe and unsatisfactory because the jury's reasons for having convicted will not be known. Thus, a defendant who suspects that they might be convicted can reasonably prefer to be convicted by a jury than by a magistrate because the former do not and cannot give reasons for their verdicts and are therefore perhaps easier to appeal. Jury verdicts are arguably more likely to be regarded as unsafe on appeal because it will not be known whether some improper factor (like a judge's misdirection) had entered their deliberation. The reports of the Court of Appeal (Criminal Division) contain many cases where the court states that a conviction should be quashed because a misleading statement from the judge might have influenced the jury. It might be said that a defendant should prefer the magistrates' court as the sentencing is generally lower, but when the defendant's antecedents are known (after a conviction), they can still be committed to the Crown Court for sentence, so the magistrates' courts are not really preferable to a defendant with a criminal record who fears another conviction is likely.

However, it is worth remembering that the Crown Court has more draconian powers of sentence compared to the magistrates' court – for example on a burglary it can sentence a defendant to 14 years' imprisonment whereas a magistrates' court's limit is six months.

9.5 CRIMINAL APPEALS

The process of appeal depends upon how a case was originally tried, whether summarily or on indictment.

9.5.1 APPEALS FROM MAGISTRATES' COURTS

Two routes of appeal are possible. The first route allows only a defendant to appeal. The appeal is to a judge and between two and four magistrates sitting in the Crown Court and can be: (a) against conviction (only if the defendant pleaded not guilty) on points of fact or law; or (b) against sentence. Such an appeal will take the form of a new hearing of the entire case (a trial *de novo*). In 2013, 44 per cent of appellants to the Crown Court had their appeals allowed or their sentences varied (*Court Statistics (Quarterly), January – March 2014*, Ministry of Justice, 2014).

Alternatively, the defendant can appeal 'by way of case stated' to the High Court (the Divisional Court of the QBD). This court consists of two or more judges (usually two), of whom one will be a Lord Justice of Appeal. Here, either the defence or the prosecution may appeal, but the grounds are limited to: (a) a point of law; or (b) that the magistrates acted beyond their jurisdiction. If the prosecution succeeds on appeal, the court can direct the magistrates to convict and pass the appropriate sentence. There is also an appeal by way of case stated from the Crown Court to the Divisional Court when the Crown Court has heard an appeal from the magistrates' court.

Appeal from the Divisional Court is to the Supreme Court. Either side may appeal, but only on a point of law and only if the Divisional Court certifies the point to be one of general public importance. Leave to appeal must also be granted either by the Divisional Court or the Supreme Court. Some magistrates' court decisions (not including conviction and sentence) can be appealed by way of a judicial review to the High Court if the magistrates were acting unlawfully, irrationally, in a way that was procedurally unfair, as a result of bias or in breach of the Human Rights Act 1998. Such decisions include a refusal to grant an adjournment, a decision to amend a charge or a decision to refuse bail.

Section 142(2) of the Magistrates' Courts Act 1980 gives the magistrates themselves power to re-open a case at the request of the defendant and to either set the conviction aside or vary or rescind an order made, if it is 'in the interests of justice to do so'. Rule (2009) suggests that this test has been too restrictively applied in *R v Croydon Youth Court ex parte DPP* (1997) and that the requirements of Art 6 ECHR must also be taken into account when construing s 142(2) (see: P Rule, *Criminal Law and Justice Weekly*, 3 April 2009).

9.5.2   APPEALS FROM THE CROWN COURT: DEFENCE

Appeals from the Crown Court in relation to trials on indictment lie to the Court of Appeal (Criminal Division), which hears appeals against conviction and sentence. Under s 28 of the Senior Courts Act 1981, the High Court has jurisdiction to hear cases stated by the Crown Court for an opinion of the High Court. The statute specifically excludes judgments and decisions relating to trials on indictment. Either party, prosecution or defence, can apply to the Crown Court to have a case stated on the ground that a decision is wrong in law or is in excess of jurisdiction. The procedure for such applications is set out in s 28A of the Senior Courts Act.

This court was established in 1966. The Division usually sits in at least two courts – one composed of the Lord Chief Justice sitting with two judges of the QBD and the other of a Lord Justice of Appeal and two Queen's Bench judges.

During 2013, a total of 6,851 applications for leave to appeal were received, a 10 per cent reduction on 2012. Of these, 1,554 were against conviction in the Crown Court and 4,997 against the sentence imposed. Of the 6,851 applications for leave to appeal, 4,863 (71 per cent) were considered by a single judge; and of these, 1,154 (17 per cent) were granted. During 2012, a total of 7,610 applications for leave to appeal were received, a 2 per cent increase on 2011 and a 10 per cent increase on 2006. Of these, 1,697 were against conviction in the Crown Court and 5,644 against the sentence imposed, the highest figures since 2006. Of the 7,610 applications for leave to appeal, 5,663 (74 per cent) were considered by a single judge; 1,541 (27 per cent) of these were granted.

All appeals against conviction and sentence must first have leave of the Court of Appeal or a certificate of fitness for appeal from the trial judge before the appeal can be taken. The Criminal Appeal Act (CAA) 1968 requires the Court of Appeal to allow an appeal against conviction under s 1 of the CAA 1968, an appeal against verdict under s 12 (insanity) or an appeal against a finding of disability (s 14) if it thinks that the conviction, verdict or finding is 'unsafe'. Before the passage of the Criminal Appeal Act (CAA) 1995, the law used the formula that the verdict was 'unsafe or *unsatisfactory*'.

During the parliamentary passage of the Act, there was much heated debate about whether the new provisions were designed to narrow the grounds of appeal. That would amount to a tilt in favour of the state in that it would make it harder for (wrongly) convicted people to appeal. Government ministers insisted that the effect of the new law was simply to restate or consolidate the practice of the Court of Appeal. One government spokesman said that:

> In dispensing with the word 'unsatisfactory', we agree with the Royal Commission on criminal justice that there is no real difference between 'unsafe' and 'unsatisfactory'; the Court of Appeal does not distinguish between the two.
>
> Retaining the word 'unsatisfactory' would imply that we thought there was a real difference and would only lead to confusion.

There were many attempts during the legislation's passage to insert the words 'or may be unsafe' after the word 'unsafe'. The Law Society, the Bar, Liberty and JUSTICE called on the government to make such a change. Also opposed to the use of the single word 'unsafe' was the eminent criminal law expert Professor JC Smith. The late Professor Smith argued cogently that there were many cases where a conviction was seen as 'unsatisfactory' rather than 'unsafe', so that there was a need for both words. Sometimes, the Court of Appeal might be convinced that the defendant is guilty (so the conviction is 'safe') but still wishes to allow the appeal because fair play, according to the rules, must be seen to be done. Accepting improperly extracted confessions (violating s 76 of the Police and Criminal Evidence Act (PACE) 1984) simply because it might seem obvious that the confessor is guilty will promote undesirable interrogation practices, because police officers will think that even if they break the rules, any resulting confession will nevertheless be allowed as evidence.

Professor Smith gave the example ((1995) 145 NLJ 534) of where there has been a serious breach of the rules of evidence. In *Algar* (1954), the former wife of the defendant testified against him about matters during the marriage. The Court of Appeal allowed his appeal against conviction, but Lord Goddard said: 'Do not think that we are doing this because we think that you are an innocent man. We do not. We think that you are a scoundrel' (*The Times*, 17 November 1953). The idea behind such remarks is that rules are rules, and the rules of evidence must be obeyed in order to ensure justice. Once you start to accept breaches of the rules as being justified by the outcome (ends justifying means), then the whole law of evidence could begin to collapse.

The proposal to include 'or might be unsafe' was rejected for the reason probably best summarised by Lord Taylor, the then Lord Chief Justice, who argued in the Lords that there was no merit in including the words 'or may be unsafe', as the implication of such doubt is already inherent in the word 'unsafe'.

Cases decided since the new formula was introduced have tended to indicate that the Court of Appeal has not adopted an entirely restrictive interpretation. Thus, a conviction was quashed as unsafe in *Smith (Patrick Joseph)* (1999) because of irregularities at trial, even though the accused had admitted his guilt during cross-examination. The Human Rights Act (HRA) 1998, incorporating the European Convention on Human Rights (ECHR), introduced a further significant element into the consideration of this issue. Article 6 ECHR, to which English courts must give effect unless incompatible with an Act of Parliament, gives the defendant a right to a fair trial. Irregularities in a trial, including misdirections by the judge, admission of improperly obtained evidence and so on, might cast doubt on the fairness of the trial without necessarily making the conviction unsafe on a narrow view of that word. In *Davis* (2001), the Court of Appeal suggested that since a conviction might be unsafe even where there was no doubt about guilt, but there were serious irregularities at the trial, English rules on appeals were compatible with Art 6. However, it went on to argue that a violation of Art 6 did not necessarily imply that the conviction must be quashed. Subsequently, Lord Woolf CJ argued in *Togher* (2000) that obligations under the ECHR meant that it was almost inevitable that if the accused had been denied a fair trial, his conviction would have to be regarded as unsafe. Confusingly the European Court of Human Rights itself does not always follow the restrictive approach, appearing to use consequentialist reasoning to justify using evidence obtained in violation of Art 3 ECHR (the prohibition against torture and inhuman and degrading treatment) in a criminal trial in the case of *Gäfgen v Germany* (2011).

The *Davis* decision was appealed to the House of Lords, where the reasoning and approach of the appellate court was confirmed as correct (2008). The *Davis* decision on the compatibility of anonymous witnesses with the demands of Art 6 ECHR should now be read in conjunction with the *Horncastle* decision of the UK Supreme Court ([2009] UKSC 14) and the affirmation of the Supreme Court's decision by the Grand Chamber of the European Court of Human Rights in *Al-Khawaja v United Kingdom* (2012). The upshot of these decisions is that Art 6 will not *automatically* be breached where hearsay statements amount to the 'sole and decisive' evidence in a criminal trial.

The Court is also vigilant about the operation of s 78 of the Police and Criminal Evidence Act (PACE) 1984, which allows a court to exclude unfair evidence or unfairly obtained evidence. Section 78 operates as a so-called exclusionary discretion rule.

The question may arise as to whether the Court of Appeal should receive fresh evidence. There is a discretion under s 23(1) of the CAA 1968 to receive fresh evidence if it is thought necessary or expedient in the interests of justice. Section 23(2) provides a set of criteria which the court must consider. They are:

- whether the evidence appears to the court to be capable of belief;
- whether it appears to the court that the evidence may afford any ground for allowing the appeal;
- whether the evidence would have been admissible at the trial on the issue under appeal; and
- whether there is a reasonable explanation for the failure to adduce the evidence at trial.

9.5.3 APPEALS FROM THE CROWN COURT: PROSECUTION APPEALS AND RELATED PROCEDURES

The prosecution has only limited rights of appeal, which may or may not affect the individual defendant in the case. There is no right of appeal as such against a defendant who has been acquitted, unless s 75 of the Criminal Justice Act 2003 applies (the abolition of the double jeopardy rule, discussed below). The options open to the prosecution if they are dissatisfied with the outcome of Crown Court proceedings are as follows.

The (limited) procedure for either party to apply to the Crown Court for a case to be stated to the High Court is discussed above at 9.5.2.

Attorney General's reference on a point of law

Under s 36 of the CJA 1972, the Attorney General can refer a case which has resulted in an acquittal to the Court of Appeal where he or she believes the decision to have been questionably lenient on a point of law. The Court of Appeal deals just with the point of law and the defendant's acquittal is not affected even if the court decides the point against the defendant. It merely clarifies the law for future cases.

Attorney General's reference on sentence

Sections 35–36 of the CJA 1988 allow the Attorney General to refer indictable-only cases to the Court of Appeal where the sentence at trial is regarded as unduly lenient. The Court can impose a harsher sentence.

Application to quash tainted acquittals

The High Court can quash tainted acquittals under s 54 of the Criminal Procedure and Investigations Act (CPIA) 1996. An acquittal is 'tainted' where someone has since been convicted of conspiring to pervert the course of justice in the case by interfering with the jury.

Prosecution appeals in respect of Crown Court rulings short of acquittal

Part 9 of the Criminal Justice Act (CJA) 2003 provides for prosecution appeals in respect of rulings in Crown Court trials which terminate the case. The right of appeal arises only in trials on indictment and lies to the Court of Appeal (s 57). Under s 57(2) the prosecution are prohibited from appealing rulings on discharge of the jury and those rulings that may be appealed by the prosecution under other legislation, for example, appeals from preparatory hearings against rulings on admissibility of evidence and other points of law.

Section 57(4) provides that the prosecution must obtain leave to appeal, either from the judge or the Court of Appeal.

Section 58 sets out the procedure that must be followed when the prosecution wishes to appeal against a terminating ruling, whether rulings that are formally terminating and those that are *de facto* terminating in the sense that they are so fatal to the prosecution case that, in the absence of a right of appeal, the prosecution would offer no or no further evidence. It applies to rulings made at any time before the start of the judge's summing up to the jury.

Where the prosecution fails to obtain leave to appeal or abandons the appeal, the prosecution must agree that an acquittal follow (s 58(8) and (9)).

Section 59 provides two alternative appeal routes: an expedited (fast) route and a non-expedited (slower) route. The judge must determine which route the appeal will follow (sub-s (1)). In the case of an expedited appeal, the trial may be adjourned (sub-s (2)). If the judge decides that the appeal should follow the non-expedited route, he or she may either adjourn the proceedings or discharge the jury, if one has been sworn (sub-s (3)). Sub-section (4) gives both the judge and the Court of Appeal power to reverse a decision to expedite an appeal, thus transferring the case to the slower non-expedited route. If a decision is reversed under this sub-section, the jury may be discharged.

Section 61 sets out the powers of the Court of Appeal when determining a prosecution appeal (and see s 67).

Section 61(1) authorises the Court of Appeal to confirm, reverse or vary a ruling that has been appealed against. After the Court of Appeal has ordered one or other of these disposals, it must then always make it clear what is to happen next in the case.

When the Court of Appeal confirms a ruling, it must then order the acquittal of the defendant(s) for the offence(s) which are the subject of the appeal (s 61(3) and (7)).

When the Court of Appeal reverses or varies a ruling, it must either order a resumption of the Crown Court proceedings or a fresh trial, or order the acquittal of the defendant(s) for the offence(s) under appeal (s 61(4) and (8)). The Court of Appeal will only order the resumption of the Crown Court proceedings or a fresh trial where it considers it necessary in the interests of justice to do so (s 61(5) and (8)).

Prosecution application for a retrial

The Criminal Justice Act also allows for the retrial of serious offences.

Section 75 sets out the cases that may be retried under the exception to the normal rule against *double jeopardy*. These cases all involve serious offences which in the main carry a maximum sentence of life imprisonment, and which are considered to have a particularly serious impact either on the victim or on society more generally. The offences to which the provisions apply are called 'qualifying offences' and are listed in Sched 5 to the Act. They include murder, manslaughter, rape and arson endangering life.

The cases that may be retried are those in which a person has been acquitted of one of the qualifying offences, either on indictment or following an appeal, or of a lesser qualifying offence of which he could have been convicted at that time. This takes into account cases of 'implied acquittals', in which, under the current law, an acquittal would have prevented a further prosecution being brought for a lower-level offence on the same facts. For example, an acquittal for murder may also imply an acquittal for the lower-level offence of manslaughter, but new evidence may then come to light, which would support a charge of manslaughter. A person may only be retried in respect of a qualifying offence.

In certain circumstances, cases may also be tried where an acquittal for an offence has taken place abroad, so long as the alleged offence also amounted to a qualifying offence and could have been charged as such in the UK. This would include, for example, offences such as war crimes, and murder committed outside the UK, for which the courts in England and Wales have jurisdiction over British citizens abroad. Such cases are likely to be rare. Sub-section (5) recognises that offences may not be described in exactly the same way in the legislation of other jurisdictions.

Prosecutor's application

Section 76 allows a prosecutor to apply to the Court of Appeal for an order that quashes the person's acquittal and orders him or her to be retried for the qualifying offence. A 'prosecutor' means a person or body responsible for bringing public prosecutions, such as the Crown Prosecution Service or HM Customs and Excise. Where a person has been acquitted outside the UK, the court will need to consider whether or not the acquittal would act as a bar to a further trial here and, if it does, the court can order that it must not be a bar.

Applications to the Court of Appeal require the personal written consent of the Director of Public Prosecutions (DPP). This provides a safeguard to ensure that only those cases in which there is sufficient evidence are referred to the Court of Appeal. The DPP will also consider whether it is in the public interest to proceed. This section also recognises any international obligations arising under the Treaty of the European Union, under which negotiations are taking place to support the mutual recognition of the decisions of the courts in other EU Member states.

Applications may also be brought by public prosecuting authorities if new evidence arises in cases that have previously been tried by means of a private prosecution.

Only one application for an acquittal to be quashed may be made in relation to any acquittal. In March 2006, a man accused of a 1989 murder became the first person to have his case referred to the Court of Appeal under this procedure. The body of Julie Hogg, 22, from Teesside, was found hidden behind her bath by her mother, Ann Ming. William Dunlop, 42, was acquitted of Ms Hogg's murder. In April 2005, police said they were to re-examine the case of Ms Hogg. William Dunlop previously faced two murder trials, but each time the jury failed to reach a verdict and he was formally acquitted in 1991. The then Director of Public Prosecutions, Ken Macdonald, said that after looking at submissions from the Chief Crown Prosecutor for Cleveland, Martin Goldman, he was satisfied the Crown Prosecution Service should apply to the Court of Appeal for a retrial. The Court of Appeal heard this application and ordered a retrial of Dunlop under s 75. In October 2006 he pleaded guilty to murdering Ms Hogg and was sentenced to life imprisonment. The Court of Appeal had applied s 75 when the CPS applied for a rehearing of Dunlop's case and felt that: (1) a jury could be selected which would not have any prior knowledge of Dunlop's earlier conviction; (2) any such recollection was outweighed by the fact that Dunlop had repeatedly confessed to Ms Hogg's murder since his acquittals in 1991 and that he had been convicted of perjury in relation to his denial of that offence; (3) the delay did not render a retrial unfair; (4) the new evidence under s 78 was both compelling and overwhelming (it consisted of Dunlop's repeated confessions) and he was in no position to rebut the new evidence; and (5) justice required that he face a retrial.

As the first example of this new procedure these comments by the Court of Appeal are clearly important. This provision was subsequently invoked by the Court of Appeal to quash the acquittal of Gary Dobson for the murder of the black teenager Stephen Lawrence in 1993 (*R v Dobson* (2011)) (see also 1.3.5). Following Dobson's second trial in 2011, he was convicted of murder.

Determination by the Court of Appeal

Section 77 sets out the decisions that the Court of Appeal may make in response to an application for an acquittal to be quashed. The court must make an order quashing an acquittal and ordering a retrial if it considers that the requirements set out in ss 78 and 79 of the Act are satisfied, namely that there is new and compelling evidence in the case, and that it is in the interests of justice for the order to be made. The court must dismiss an application where it is not satisfied as to these two factors.

New and compelling evidence

Section 78 sets out the requirement for there to be new and compelling evidence against the acquitted person in relation to the qualifying offence, and defines evidence which is 'new and compelling'. Evidence is 'new' if it was not adduced at the original trial of the acquitted person. Evidence is 'compelling' if the court considers it to be reliable and substantial and, when considered in the context of the outstanding issues, the evidence appears to be highly probative of the case against the acquitted person. The court is thus required to make a decision on the strength of the new evidence. So, for example, new evidence relating to identification would only be considered 'compelling' if the identity of the offender had been at issue in the original trial. It is not intended that relatively minor evidence, which might appear to strengthen an earlier case, should justify a retrial.

Interests of justice

Section 79 sets out the requirement that in all the circumstances it is in the interests of justice for the court to quash an acquittal and order a retrial. In determining whether it is in the interests of justice, the court will consider in particular: whether there are existing factors that make a fair trial unlikely (for example, the extent of adverse publicity about the case); the length of time since the alleged offence was committed; and whether the police and prosecution acted with due diligence and expedition in relation to both the original trial and any new evidence. The court may take into account any other issues it considers relevant in determining whether a retrial will be in the interests of justice.

The Criminal Justice and Immigration Act 2008 alters the test for ordering a retrial in England and Wales (or that the trial should resume) where the Court of Appeal allows a prosecution appeal against a terminating ruling. The original CJA 2003 provided that a court should not order a resumed or fresh trial unless it considered it necessary in the interests of justice to do so. Now, under s 44 of the 2008 Act, the court may not order that the defendant be acquitted unless it considers that he could not receive a fair trial/retrial.

9.6 CRIMINAL APPEALS TO THE SUPREME COURT

Following the determination of an appeal by the Court of Appeal or by the Divisional Court, either the prosecution or the defence may appeal to the Supreme Court. Leave from the court below or the Supreme Court must be obtained and two other conditions fulfilled according to s 33 of the CAA 1968:

(1)   the court below must certify that a point of law of general public importance is involved; and

(2)   either the court below or the Supreme Court must be satisfied that the point of law is one which ought to be considered by the Supreme Court.

Section 68(1) of the CJA 2003 amends s 33(1) of the Criminal Appeal Act 1968 to give both the prosecution and defence a right of appeal to the Supreme Court from a decision by the Court of Appeal on a prosecution appeal against a ruling made under Part 9 of the Act.

9.7 JUDICIAL COMMITTEE OF THE PRIVY COUNCIL

The Judicial Committee of the Privy Council was created by the Judicial Committee Act 1833. Under the Act, a special committee of the Privy Council was set up to hear appeals from the Dominions. The cases are heard by the judges (without wigs or robes) in a committee room in London. The Committee's decision is not a judgment but an 'advice' to the monarch, who is counselled that the appeal be allowed or dismissed.

The Committee is the final court of appeal for certain Commonwealth countries that have retained this option, and from some independent members and associate members of the Commonwealth. The Committee comprises Privy Councillors who are Justices of the Supreme Court.

Most of the appeals heard by the Committee are civil cases. In the rare criminal cases, it is only on matters involving legal questions that appeals are heard. The Committee does not hear appeals against criminal sentence.

The decisions of the Privy Council are very influential in English courts because they concern points of law that are applicable in this jurisdiction and they are pronounced upon by Supreme Court Justices in a way that is tantamount to a Supreme Court ruling. These decisions, however, are technically of persuasive precedent only, although English courts normally follow them; see, for example, the criminal appeal case

Abbot v R (1977). This was an appeal from Trinidad and Tobago. The Privy Council ruled that duress is no defence to the perpetrator of murder.

9.8   CRIMINAL CASES REVIEW COMMISSION

9.8.1   BACKGROUND

The Royal Commission on Criminal Justice was set up, under the chairmanship of Viscount Runciman, in March 1991, after the release of the Birmingham Six (an important case in a series of notorious miscarriages of justice in which people were found to have been wrongly convicted and sentenced for serious crimes). It reported in July 1993, with 352 recommendations largely designed to prevent wrongful conviction.

Research undertaken for the Royal Commission by Kate Malleson of the London School of Economics found that judges' mistakes are by far the most common ground for successful appeals against conviction. The research discovered that in about 80 per cent of cases where convictions were quashed, there had been an error at the trial and, in most instances, it was judicial error.

Of 300 appeals in 1990, just over one-third were successful. Of those appealing, almost two-thirds of defendants appealed against conviction on the ground that the trial judge had made a crucial mistake and, of those, 43 per cent succeeded in having their convictions quashed. Sixteen defendants were vindicated by the Court of Appeal in claims that the judge's summing up to the jury was biased or poor; a further 42 convictions were quashed because the judge was wrong about the law or evidence.

This research was critical of the way the Court of Appeal failed to consider cases where fresh evidence had emerged since the trial or where there was a 'lurking doubt' about the conviction. The Report urged that the court be given a new role allowing it to investigate the events leading up to a conviction.

The Commission recommended that the Home Secretary's power to refer cases to the Court of Appeal under s 17 of the CAA 1968 should be removed and a new body, independent of both the executive and the courts, should be set up to consider allegations that a miscarriage of justice might have occurred. This body should refer meritorious cases directly to the Court of Appeal. There should be neither a right of appeal nor a right to judicial review in relation to decisions reached by the Authority. The Authority should consist of both lawyers and lay people, should be supported by a staff of lawyers and should devise its own rules and procedures. It should be able to discuss cases directly with applicants and should have powers to direct its own investigations. These recommendations were largely met by the terms of the CAA 1995.

9.8.2   THE CRIMINAL CASES REVIEW COMMISSION: FUNCTION AND POWERS

The Criminal Cases Review Commission (CCRC) is an independent body set up under the CAA 1995. The CCRC came into being on 1 January 1997. It employs 90 staff members, including a core of 50 specialist caseworkers. It is responsible for investigating suspected miscarriages of criminal justice in England, Wales and Northern Ireland.

The CCRC cannot overturn convictions or sentences itself. Instead, it may refer to the Court of Appeal a conviction for an offence tried on indictment, or a finding of not guilty by reason of insanity, or a finding that a person was under a disability when they did the act or made the omission, and may also refer cases in respect of sentence where they were tried on indictment (s 9 of the CAA 1995). Additionally, the CCRC may refer to the Crown Court convictions and sentences imposed by magistrates' courts, though the Crown Court may not impose any punishment more severe than that of the court from which the decision is referred (s 11 of the CAA 1995). The Court of Appeal itself may direct the CCRC to carry out an investigation and it must report to the court when finished or as required to do so by the court. Once the reference has been made, it will be treated as an appeal for the purposes of the CAA 1968.

The Commission is given power by ss 17–21 of the CAA 1995 to obtain information and carry out investigations, including appointing investigating officers (who are likely to be police officers where there have been previous police investigations).

Any decision to refer a case to the relevant appellate court has to be taken by a committee of at least three members. The CCRC considers whether or not there is a real possibility that the conviction, finding, verdict or sentence would not be upheld were a reference to be made.

In order to establish that there is a real possibility of an appeal succeeding regarding a conviction, there has to be an argument or evidence which has not been raised during the trial or at appeal; or exceptional circumstances.

In order to establish that there is a real possibility of an appeal succeeding against a sentence, there has to be a legal argument or information about the individual or the offence which was not raised in court during the trial or at appeal.

Other than in exceptional circumstances, the Commission can only consider cases in which an appeal through the ordinary judicial appeal process has failed and, once a decision is taken to refer a case to the relevant court of appeal, the Commission has no other involvement.

The CCRC referred the notorious case of Derek William Bentley to the Court of Appeal. Mr Bentley was convicted at the Central Criminal Court on 11 December 1952 of the murder of PC Sidney Miles. Mr Bentley did not actually shoot the officer. His accomplice fired the gun in a failed burglary attempt, but Mr Bentley was convicted under the principles of 'joint enterprise', even though he was being held under arrest by a police officer, metres away from where his accomplice fired the pistol. An appeal against conviction was heard by the Court of Criminal Appeal on 13 January 1953 and dismissed. Mr Bentley was hanged on 28 January 1953.

Bentley's conviction and sentence were the subject of numerous representations to the Home Office. In July 1993, on the recommendation of the Home Secretary, Her Majesty The Queen, in the exercise of the Royal Prerogative of Mercy, granted to Mr Bentley a posthumous pardon limited to sentence.

Following submissions from the applicants' solicitors and the completion of its own inquiries, the CCRC concluded that the Court of Appeal should reconsider Mr Bentley's conviction. The trial was seen as unfair in a number of respects; for example the fact that, although aged 18, Bentley had a mental age of 11 was kept a secret from the jury, and the judge's summing up to the jury was astonishingly biased in favour of the police. In August 1998, on a momentous day in legal history, the Court of Appeal cleared Bentley of the murder for which he was hanged 46 years earlier. In giving judgment, the Lord Chief Justice, Lord Bingham, said: 'the summing up in this case was such as to deny the appellant that fair trial which is the birthright of every British citizen.'

The latest figures (CCRC *Case Statistics*, figures to 31 January 2017) show the following data:

Total applications:	21,831
Cases waiting:	306
Cases under review:	689
Completed:	20,831 (including ineligible), 629 referrals
Heard by Court of Appeal:	617 (190 quashed, 414 upheld)

Taking a global perspective on legal systems, it is unusual for any machinery of justice to provide as many opportunities for appeal and challenge as exist in the English system.

9.9   A MISCARRIAGE OF JUSTICE: SOME LESSONS FOR THE CRIMINAL JUSTICE SYSTEM

One of the English legal system's worst miscarriages of justice cases in recent history was exposed in the Court of Appeal in February 1998. In 1979, Vincent Hickey, Michael Hickey, Jimmy Robertson and Pat Molloy, who became known as the Bridgewater Four, were convicted of the murder of a 13-year-old boy, Carl Bridgewater. Although the men were not angelic characters (and two had serious criminal records), they strenuously protested that they were not guilty of the horrific child murder.

Eighteen years later, and after two earlier failed visits to the Court of Appeal and seven police investigations, three of the men were released on 21 February 1998 on unconditional bail in anticipation of an appeal hearing in April. The fourth defendant, Mr Molloy, died in jail in 1981. The appeal was eventually allowed.

The Crown had conceded that the case against the men was 'flawed' by evidence falsified and fabricated by police officers. There had also come to light significant fingerprint evidence, tending to exonerate the four, which was not disclosed to the defence by the prosecution. Mr Molloy was questioned for 10 days without access to a solicitor, and a fabricated statement from Vincent Hickey was used to persuade Mr Molloy to confess to the crime. Before he died, Mr Molloy claimed he had been beaten by police officers in the course of his interrogation. The former police officers alleged to have falsified the evidence were investigated but not prosecuted.

The case was given extensive coverage in the print and broadcast media in February 1997 and made a significant impact upon public consciousness. It did not reach the Court of Appeal through the Criminal Cases Review Commission, which had only been set up the year before. This major case raises many points germane to the operation of the criminal justice system. The following are of particular importance.

The case was originally investigated in 1978, before PACE 1984 had been passed. The requirements under PACE 1984 for suspects to be given access to legal advice (s 58, Code C) and for interviews to be recorded (s 60, Code E) may have reduced or eliminated the opportunity for police malpractice of the sort which occurred in the *Bridgewater* case.

Although the criminal justice system ultimately corrected an injustice, this result was achieved primarily through the indefatigable efforts of a few dedicated family members, campaigning journalists and Members of Parliament who would not let the issue disappear from the public forum. The case attracted attention because of the terrible nature of the crime – a child murder. It is quite possible that many other unjust convictions in cases with more mundane facts are never propelled into public discussion or overturned.

Miscarriages of justice cases involve two types of insult to notions of legal fairness: (a) the wrongly imprisoned endure years of incarceration; and (b) the real culprits (a child killer in the *Bridgewater* case) are never identified and could well go on to commit other offences.

The men were released due to the discovery of evidence that had been fabricated and falsified; yet the CPIA 1996 restricts defence access to prosecution evidence.

The CCRC was established to re-evaluate alleged cases of miscarriages of justice. One criticism of it has been that it does not have its own independent investigators, but must rely on police officers to re-examine cases.

The jury is only as good as the information and arguments put before it allows it to be. After the prosecution's case had been devastated by the discovery of new scientific evidence in 1993 (a forensic psychiatrist showed that Molloy's 'confession' used language the suspect would not have used), the foreman of the jury from the 1979 trial risked prosecution for contempt of court by issuing a statement to say that he thought that the men were not guilty. He, along with another juror, said they regretted that they had not been given all the evidence that was available at the time of the trial.

9.10 CORONERS' COURTS

The coroners' courts are one of the most ancient parts of the English legal system, dating back to at least 1194. They are not, in modern function, part of the criminal courts, but because of historical associations, it makes more sense to classify them with the courts in this chapter rather than that dealing with civil courts. The coroner was an appointment originally made as *custos placitorum coronae*, keeper of the pleas of the Crown. They had responsibility for criminal cases in which the Crown had an interest, particularly a financial interest.

Today, there are 110 coroners' jurisdictions. These are presided over by 32 full-time coroners. The rest are staffed on a part-time basis. The Chief Coroner is a new office, created by the Coroners and Justice Act 2009, intended to give national leadership to the coroner service across England and Wales. HHJ Peter Thornton QC has been appointed the first Chief Coroner. Coroners are usually lawyers (with at least a five-year qualification within s 71 of the Courts and Legal Services Act (CLSA) 1990), although about 25 per cent are medical doctors with an appropriate legal qualification. The main jurisdiction of the coroner today concerns unnatural and violent deaths (including those under Art 2 of the European Convention on Human Rights where the death in question may have been caused by state agents), although treasure trove is also something occasionally dealt with.

The classifying of types of death is clearly of critical importance, not just to the state, politicians and policy-makers, but also to the sort of campaign groups that exist in a constitutional democracy to monitor suicides, drug-related deaths, deaths in police custody and prison, accidental deaths, deaths in hospitals and deaths through industrial diseases.

In 2013, 227,984 deaths were reported to coroners. Anyone who is concerned about the cause of a death can inform a coroner about it, in the same way that members of the public are encouraged to report suspected crimes to the police. In practice, however, a death will be reported to the coroner by a doctor or the police.

The coroner will order a post-mortem and this may reveal a natural cause of death that can be duly registered. If not, or in certain other circumstances, such as where the death occurred in prison or police custody or if the cause is unknown, there will be an inquest.

Nearly all inquests concluded in 2013 (98 per cent), as in other years, were held without juries. Both the number and proportion of inquests held with juries have shown a downward trend in recent years but the trend appears now to have halted. The state, however, has historically been insistent that certain types of case must be heard by a jury in order to promote public faith in government. When, in 1926, legislation for the first time permitted inquests to be held without juries, certain types of death were deliberately marked off as still requiring jury scrutiny and these included deaths in police custody, deaths resulting from the actions of a police officer on duty and deaths in prison. This was seen as a very important way of fostering public trust in potentially oppressive aspects of the state. In 1971, the Brodrick Committee Report on the coronial system saw the coroner's jury as having a symbolic significance and thought that it was a useful way to legitimate the decision of the coroner.

Under s 7 of the Coroners and Justice Act 2009, and in order to comply with Art 2 of the European Convention on Human Rights, a jury must be summoned as follows:

(2)   An inquest into a death must be held with a jury if the senior coroner has reason to suspect –

    (a)   that the deceased died while in custody or otherwise in state detention, and that either –

        (i)   the death was a violent or unnatural one, or

        (ii)   the cause of death is unknown,

    (b)   that the death resulted from an act or omission of –

        (i)   a police officer, or

        (ii)   a member of a service police force, in the purported execution of the officer's or member's duty as such, or

(c)   that the death was caused by a notifiable accident, poisoning or disease.

(3)   An inquest into a death may be held with a jury if the senior coroner thinks that there is sufficient reason for doing so.

The coroner's court is unique in using an inquisitorial process. There are no 'sides' in an inquest. There may be representation for people such as the relatives of the deceased, insurance companies, prison officers, car drivers, companies (whose policies are possibly implicated in the death) and train drivers, etc, but all the witnesses are the coroner's witnesses. The coroner decides who shall be summoned as witnesses and in what order they shall be called.

Historically, an inquest jury could decide that a deceased had been unlawfully killed and then commit a suspect for trial at the local assizes. When this power was taken away in 1926, the main bridge over to the criminal justice system was removed. There then followed, in stages, an attempt to prevent inquest verdicts from impinging on the jurisdictions of the ordinary civil and criminal courts. Now, an inquest jury is exclusively concerned with determining who the deceased was and 'how, when and where he came by his death'. The court is forbidden to make any wider comment on the death and must not determine or appear to determine criminal liability 'on the part of a named person'.

Nevertheless, the jury may still now properly decide that a death was unlawful (that is, a crime). The verdict 'unlawful killing' is on a list of options (including 'suicide', 'accidental death' and 'open verdict') made under legislation and approved by the Home Office.

CHAPTER SUMMARY: THE CRIMINAL COURTS

THE MAIN COURTS

The trial courts are the magistrates' courts and Crown Courts. In serious offences, known as *indictable offences*, the defendant is tried by a jury in a Crown Court; for *summary offences*, he or she is tried by magistrates; and for 'either-way' offences, the defendant can be tried by magistrates if they agree, but he or she may elect jury trial in the Crown Court.

The main issues here concern the distribution of business between the magistrates' court and Crown Courts: what are the advantages of trial in the magistrates' court: (a) for the state; and (b) for the defendant? Conversely, what are the disadvantages?

APPEALS

Criminal appeals from the magistrates go to the Crown Court or to the QBD Divisional Court 'by way of case stated' on a point of law or that the JPs went beyond their proper powers, or by way of judicial review. If the prosecution succeeds on appeal, the court can direct the magistrates to convict and pass the appropriate sentence. There is also an appeal by way of case stated from the Crown Court to the Divisional Court when the Crown Court has heard an appeal from the magistrates' court. From the Crown Court, appeals against conviction and sentence lie to the Court of Appeal (Criminal Division). The High Court has jurisdiction to hear cases stated by the Crown Court for an opinion. The prosecution has some, limited, options to refer or appeal aspects of Crown Court decisions to the Court of Appeal.

The Judicial Committee of the Privy Council hears final appeals from some Commonwealth countries and its decisions are of persuasive precedent in English law.

REVIEW AFTER APPEAL

In an attempt to deal with possible miscarriages of justice, and following the recommendations of the Royal Commission on Criminal Justice in 1993 (the Runciman Commission), the Criminal Appeal Act 1995 established the Criminal Cases Review Commission (CCRC). The CCRC has power to investigate and to refer cases to the Court of Appeal (or, where appropriate, the Crown Court) where it considers that there is a real possibility of an appeal succeeding.

THE CORONERS' COURTS

These are not part of the criminal justice system. Their main function is to decide the cause of unnatural deaths. Verdicts such as unlawful killing might result in other legal processes like criminal prosecutions or human rights claims.

FOOD FOR THOUGHT

1   The age of criminal responsibility in the UK is 10. This is one of the lowest ages of criminal responsibility in the world. Where an adult defendant with the mental age of a 10-year-old could establish a defence of diminished responsibility or insanity, does it make sense for an actual 10-year-old to be tried as an adult?

2   Evidence obtained using oppressive techniques is not admissible in criminal proceedings. But what about the situation where the police believe that a child's life is in immediate danger and so threaten a suspect with physical violence if he does not tell them where the child is? If the suspect confesses and the child is found dead, should that confession be admissible evidence?

FURTHER READING

Bates, T, 'The contemporary use of legislative history in the United Kingdom' (1995) 54(1) CLJ 127

Bell, J and Engle, G (Sir), *Cross: Statutory Interpretation*, 3rd edn, 1995, London: Butterworths

Bennion, F, 'Statute law: obscurity and drafting parameters' (1978) 5 British JLS 235

Bennion, F, *Statutory Interpretation*, 2nd edn, 1992, London: Butterworths

Burrows, D, 'Enforcement matters: Part 1' (2009) 159 NLJ 334; Part II (2009) 159 NLJ 415

Carlen, P, *Magistrates' Justice*, 1976, Oxford: Martin Robertson

Committee on the Preparation of Legislation, *Renton Committee Report*, Cmnd 6053, 1975, London: HMSO

Dugg, A, Farmer, L, Marshall, S and Tadros, V (eds), *The Trial on Trial – Truth and Due Process*, 2004, Oxford: Hart Publishing

Eskridge, W, *Dynamic Statutory Interpretation*, 1994, Cambridge, MA: Harvard UP

Fitzpatrick, B, *Going to Court*, 2006, Oxford: OUP

Friedman, L, 'On interpretation of laws' (1988) 11(3) Ratio Juris 252

Gibb, F, 'The highest court in the land opens its doors to the public', *The Times*, 1 October 2009

Grove, T, *The Magistrates' Tale*, 2002, London: Bloomsbury

Hillman, M, 'For the public good?' (2008) 158 NLJ 661

Manchester, C, *Exploring the Law: The Dynamics of Precedent and Statutory Interpretation*, 2006, London: Sweet & Maxwell

Matthews, P and Foreman, J (eds), *Jervis: On the Office and Duties of Coroners*, 1993, London: Sweet & Maxwell

Moxon, D and Hedderman, C, 'Mode of trial decisions and sentencing differences between courts' (1994) 33(2) Howard J of Criminal Justice 97

New Law Journal, 'Increase in cases to CCRC' [2007] 1060

Richardson, PJ (ed), *Archbold: Criminal Pleading, Evidence and Practice*, 2016, London: Sweet & Maxwell

Stone, J, 'The Ratio of the Ratio Decidendi' (1959) 22 MLR 597

USEFUL WEBSITES

www.justice.gov.uk/about/hmcts/
The official website of Her Majesty's Courts and Tribunals Service.

www.magistrates-association.org.uk
The official website of the Magistrates' Association.

www.justice.gov.uk
The official website of the Criminal Justice System.

COMPANION WEBSITE

Now visit the companion website to:

- test your understanding of the key terms using our Flashcard Glossary;
- revise and consolidate your knowledge of 'The criminal courts' using our multiple choice question testbank;
- view all of the links to the Useful Websites above.

www.routledge.com/cw/slapper

10.1 INTRODUCTION

- Following an extension of the coverage of the survey, experimental statistics showed there were 3.6 million fraud and 2.0 million computer misuse offences for the first full year in which such questions have been included in the CSEW. The inclusion of these new offences yields a new headline estimate of 11.8 million incidents of crime covered by the survey, but it will be another year before a comparable time series is available.

- However, trend data on frauds referred to the police showed an annual rise of 3 per cent. Other industry data on financial fraud, the vast bulk of which is unreported to the police, showed there were 1.9 million cases of frauds on UK-issued cards (an increase of 39 per cent from the previous year).

- Across all crime types covered, the police recorded 4.7 million offences in the year ending September 2016, an annual rise of 8 per cent. Due to recording improvements affecting comparisons over time, this series is not currently a reliable measure of trends in crime.

- CSEW estimates showed no statistically significant change in levels of violence compared with the previous survey, with the underlying trend fairly flat in recent years. While the police recorded an annual rise of 22 per cent in Violence against the person offences, the volume increases were largely driven by changes in recording processes and the inclusion of additional harassment offences within the series. However, there appeared to be genuine smaller increases in some of the lower volume but higher harm categories of police recorded violence including homicide and knife crime.

The full report is available on National Statistics website at www.ons.gov.uk/peoplepopulationandcommunity/crimeandjustice

This chapter and the following one refer to the 'criminal justice system'. Governmental responsibilities overlap in this area, with the Home Office and the Ministry of Justice dealing with separate areas (for an overview see www.cps.gov.uk/about/cjs.html#a02). The Ministry of Justice describes its work as follows:

What we do

We work to protect the public and reduce reoffending, and to provide a more effective, transparent and responsive criminal justice system for victims and the public.

Responsibilities

We are responsible for these parts of the justice system:

- courts;
- prisons;

- probation services;
- attendance centres.

We also work in partnership with the other government departments and agencies to reform the criminal justice system, to serve the public and support the victims of crime. We are also responsible for making new laws, strengthening democracy, and safeguarding human rights. (www.gov.uk/government/organisations/ministry-of-justice/about#what-we-do)

A previous White Paper suggested that the idea of a 'system' might result in slowness, inefficiency and lack of transparency. Instead, a 'criminal justice service' might be more effective (*Swift and Sure Justice: The Government's Plans for Reform of the Criminal Justice System*, White Paper, July 2012).

10.2   MISTRUST OF THE SYSTEM

There exists mistrust of the criminal justice system from both those who believe innocent people have been convicted and those who think guilty people escape justice. The number of exposed miscarriages of justice involving malpractice and disastrous errors by agencies of the criminal justice system were discussed in Chapter 9, as was the Royal Commission on Criminal Justice and the establishment of the Criminal Cases Review Commission (CCRC) by the Criminal Appeal Act (CAA) 1995. In the course of this debate, great concern was expressed by pressure groups about the government's rejection of the Royal Commission's findings in relation to the so-called right to silence.

This right was effectively undermined by ss 34–37 of the Criminal Justice and Public Order Act (CJPOA) 1994, and this change arguably increased the chances of miscarriages occurring rather than reducing them. Confidence in the criminal justice system appeared at this period to be in decline. In a national survey for the 1962 Royal Commission on the Police (Cmnd 1728, 1962, HMSO), 83 per cent of respondents indicated that they had 'a great deal of respect' for the way the police operated. In a national poll in 1993, conducted by MORI for *The Sunday Times* and the Police Federation, under 50 per cent of respondents indicated that they had 'a great deal of respect' for the way the police operated. Ipsos MORI has asked the same question for over 30 years from 1983 to 2014: 'Do you generally trust the police to tell the truth?' Positive responses have ranged between 58 and 65 per cent (www.ipsos-mori.com/researchpublications/researcharchive/15/Trust-in-Professions.aspx).

10.2.1   A CONTRADICTION

There is a friction between the sorts of policies that these two concerns generate – that is, first, that people seem to want the police to have greater powers to combat crime; yet, contradictorily, the public want greater controls on the police and evidence so as to avoid more miscarriages of justice. The time of the troubles in Ireland, from the late 1960s to the Good Friday Agreement in 1998, was one of particular turbulence and impropriety with unjust convictions against the Winchester Three, the Guildford Four, the Birmingham Six, the Maguire Seven, the Tottenham Three, and the solitary Judith Ward. (When the jury system is considered subsequently and generally defended in Chapter 14 of this text, it should be always be borne in mind that such injustices as are cited above were all condoned by juries.)

Consequently, as the growing problem of crime, and the fear of crime, whether real or perceived, has become more politically important for governments, there are two lobbies arguing for change and these hold diametrically opposed views as to the nature, and consequences of 'so called' criminal behaviour.

In this text the criminal process is examined in the following three chapters. This chapter considers the law relating to important pre-trial matters up to and including the admissibility of confession evidence in court. Chapters 11 and 14 look at institutional and procedural aspects of prosecution and matters relating to bail, the classification of offences, trials, plea bargaining and the jury. In examining all these topics, it is important to keep in mind the various aims of the criminal justice system and the extent to which the existing law serves these aims. It could be argued that a criminal justice system should aim:

- to detect crime and convict those who have committed it;
- to have rules relating to arrest, search, questioning, interrogation and admissibility of evidence which do not expose suspects to unfair treatment likely to lead to unjust convictions;
- to have rules as above which do not unnecessarily impede the proper investigation of crime;
- to ensure that innocent persons are not convicted;
- to maintain public order;
- to maintain public confidence in the criminal justice system;
- to properly balance considerations of justice and fair procedure with those of efficiency and funding.

10.2.2 CONTEMPORARY ISSUES

The criminal justice system is showing signs of strain as it tries to cope with a society in the throes of major transitions. These include changes in the pattern of family life; changes in the nature of employment expectations; the economic downturn; and a revolution in information and communications technology.

In 1993, the prison population of England and Wales was 42,000 (this includes those incarcerated in young offender institutions). In December 2017 there were almost 86,000 people in prison.

Criminal justice has historically been regarded by government as a matter for the state. Recently, however, first under the Conservative government in the early 1990s, then under Labour, and then under the coalition government, various parts of the system have been privatised. Such moves have not generally been seen as runaway successes. Riots at one privately run prison are described at www.theguardian.com/business/2014/jan/06/prison-disorder-hmp-oakwood-g4s. After more than one fiasco, privatised prison escort services have come in for severe criticism. A provision of the CJPOA 1994 allowing for private sponsorship of police equipment was a boon for satirical cartoonists.

By contrast, there are several ways in which aspects of the criminal justice system, historically all independent from each other and detached from governmental control, have been drawn within the influence of central government. It has, for example, been a hallowed precept of the British constitution that police forces are local and not governmental agencies. Yet, under Conservative legislation, the Home Secretary became allowed to 'determine objectives for the policing of the areas of all police authorities'.

There is also reason for disquiet about the law contained in the Terrorism Act 2000, which makes the opinion of a police officer admissible evidence in court. Proof of membership of a proscribed organisation may be based in part upon the opinion of a senior police officer. Considerable evidence – from miscarriage of justice cases, especially those involving suspects of terrorism from Northern Ireland – showed that some police officers were apparently prepared to lie and falsify evidence to secure convictions. The new law has hence caused some people to become alarmed at the prospect that a person could be convicted of a serious offence on evidence taken mainly from the opinion of a police officer.

Proactive 'intelligence-led' policing has become increasingly commonplace in recent years, especially in relation to drugs, protestors and organised crime. Such techniques inevitably involve deception by police officers and their informers (see C Dunnighan and C Norris, 'A risky business: the recruitment and running of informers by English police officers' (1996) 19 Police Studies 1). This may involve testing whether a person is willing to commit an offence or infiltrating a protest group. Although English law has never recognised a defence of entrapment, entrapment may be a mitigating factor and a ground for excluding evidence (*R v Looseley; Attorney General's Reference (No 3 of 2000)* (2002); see A Ashworth, 'Re-drawing the boundaries of entrapment' [2002] Crim LR 161). Civil litigation is under way against the Metropolitan Police in respect of undercover police officers who allegedly had long-term sexual relationships with their targets under the direction of the Commissioner (*DIL v Commissioner of Police of the Metropolis* (2014)).

The long-running debate over how to deal with the policing and prevention of terrorism is also discussed in detail in Chapter 2 (at 2.5.2).

10.2.3   THE POLICE AND CRIMINAL EVIDENCE ACT 1984

The Police and Criminal Evidence Act 1984 (PACE) was designed to provide a comprehensive code for policing in response to some of the miscarriages of justice described above. It consists of the Act and accompanying Codes of Practice A – H, issued under s

66 of the Act, and updated at regular intervals. Current versions can be found at www. gov.uk/guidance/police-and-criminal-evidence-act-1984-pace-codes-of-practice. The Serious Organised Crime and Police Act 2005 (SOCPA) made major amendments to PACE by revising the framework of arrest and search powers.

10.3 STOP AND SEARCH

PACE 1984 gives the police power to search 'any person or vehicle' and to detain either for the purpose of such a search (s 1(2)). A constable may not conduct such a search 'unless he has reasonable grounds for suspecting that he will find stolen or prohibited articles' (s 1(3)). Any such item found during the search can be seized (s 1(6)). An article is 'prohibited' if it is either an offensive weapon or it is 'made or adapted for use in the course of or in connection with burglary, theft, taking a motor vehicle without authority or obtaining property by deception or is intended by the person having it with him for such use by him or by some other person' (s 1(7)).

Section 1 of PACE was amended by s 1 CJA to include articles made, adapted or intended for use in causing criminal damage, under s 1 of the Criminal Damage Act 1971. The effect is to give police officers power to stop and search where they have reasonable suspicion that a person is carrying, for example, a paint spray can, which they intend to use in producing graffiti.

An offensive weapon is defined as meaning 'any article made or adapted for use for causing injury to persons or intended by the person having it with him for such use by him or by some other person' (s 1(9)). This definition is taken from the Prevention of Crime Act 1953. It has two categories: things that are offensive weapons *per se* (that is, in themselves), like a baton with a nail through the end or knuckle-dusters, and things that are not offensive weapons, like a spanner, but which are intended to be used as such. If the item is in the first category, then the prosecution need prove only that the accused had it with them to put the onus onto the accused to show that they had a lawful excuse.

Stop and search powers can also be exercised under s 8A regarding items covered by s 139 of the CJA 1988. These items are any article that has a blade or is sharply pointed, except folding pocket knives with a blade of less than three inches. It is an offence to possess such items without good reason or lawful authority, the onus of proof being on the defendant. The courts will not accept the carrying of offensive weapons for generalised self-defence unless there is some immediate, identifiable threat.

Under s 2 of PACE 1984, a police officer who proposes to carry out a stop and search must state their name and police station, and the purpose of the search. A plain-clothes officer must also produce documentary evidence that they are a police officer. The officer must also give the grounds for the search. Such street searches must be limited to outer clothing; the searched person cannot be required to remove any article of clothing other than a jacket, outer clothes or gloves. The officer is required to make a record of the search immediately, or as soon as is reasonably practicable afterwards (s 3). The record of the search should include the object of the search, the grounds of the search and its result (s 3). A failure to give grounds as required by s 2(3)(c) will render the search unlawful (*R v Fennelley* (1989)).

Section 1 of the Crime and Security Act 2010 amends s 3 of PACE 1984 to reduce recording requirements where a search is conducted under s 2 (and see revised paras 4.1–4.10). There is no longer a requirement to record the person's name or description, whether anything was found or whether any injury or damage was caused as a result of the search. However, the police are obliged to record:

- ethnicity;
- objective of search;
- grounds for search;
- identity of the officer carrying out the stop and search;
- date;
- time;
- place.

It seems that failure to comply with these conditions will make the search unlawful. See *Fennelley* (1989), a case where the defendant was not told why he was stopped, searched and arrested in the street. Evidence from the search, some jewellery, was excluded at the trial. Evidence of drugs found on him at the police station was also excluded.

10.3.1 THE CODE OF PRACTICE FOR THE EXERCISE OF STATUTORY POWERS OF STOP AND SEARCH

As explained above, the Codes of Practice under PACE clarify how the police should exercise their powers. Code A details how searches under stop and search powers are to be conducted. The admissibility of evidence gained through the use of a dubious stop and search event may be in doubt if there are serious breaches of Code A. Someone charged with obstructing or assaulting a police officer in the exercise of duty may raise breaches of the Code in defence. Unlawful search or seizure may also provide a basis for an application for exclusion of evidence thus obtained under s 78 of PACE 1984.

The primary purpose of stop and search powers is to enable officers to allay or confirm suspicions about individuals without exercising their powers of arrest. The Code applies to powers of stop and search and states at para 2.1(a) that these are 'powers which require reasonable grounds for suspicion before they may be exercised; that articles unlawfully obtained or possessed are being carried'. The Code makes it clear beyond doubt that searches must not take place unless the necessary legal power exists. The importance of a non-discriminatory approach is stressed throughout.

If an officer asks a member of the public to account for their 'actions, behaviour, presence in the area or possession of anything', a record must be made. The person stopped will be entitled to a copy. The 2011 amendments to Code A removed the requirement for officers to record 'stops'. Police forces are now free to decide in consultation with their local communities whether to continue monitoring the stops on a local level.

In 2011 Code A was further amended to reflect the significant reduction in the quantity of information the police are required to record after a stop and search of a vehicle. While officers are still required to record the ethnicity of the occupant, they are no longer required to record their details, the registration number of the vehicle or even any injury or damage caused.

Reasonable suspicion can never be supported on the basis of personal factors alone. For example, a person's race, age, appearance, or the fact that the person is known to have a previous conviction cannot be used alone or in combination with each other as the reason for searching that person, and nor can generalisations or stereotypical images of certain groups or categories of people (para 2.2). Paragraph 2.6 states that:

> Where there is reliable information or intelligence that members of a group or gang habitually carry knives unlawfully or weapons or controlled drugs, and wear a distinctive item of clothing or other means of identification to indicate their membership of the group or gang, that distinctive item of clothing or other means of identification may provide reasonable grounds to stop and search.

Other means of identification might include jewellery, insignias, tattoos or other features that are known to identify members of the particular gang or group (Note 9).

Any search involving the removal of more than an outer coat, jacket, gloves, head-gear or footwear, or any other item concealing identity, may only be made by an officer of the same sex as the person searched and may not be made in the presence of anyone of the opposite sex unless the person being searched specifically requests it (para 3.6). All searches involving exposure of intimate parts of the body shall be conducted in accordance with para 11 of Annex A to Code C (para 3.7). All stops and searches must be carried out with courtesy, consideration and respect for the person concerned. Every reasonable effort must be made to reduce to the minimum the embarrassment that a person being searched may experience (para 3.1).

Paragraph 2.15 introduces powers to require removal of face coverings. (These powers were added by s 60A of the Criminal Justice and Public Order Act 1994; see below.) Paragraph 2.15 states:

> The officer exercising the power must reasonably believe that someone is wearing an item wholly or mainly for the purpose of concealing identity. There is also a power to seize such items where the officer believes that a person intends to wear them for this purpose. There is no power for stop and search for disguises. An officer may seize any such item which is discovered when exercising a power of search for something else, or which is being carried, and which the officer reasonably believes is intended to be used for concealing anyone's identity.

Section 60 of the CJPOA 1994 provides for a stop and search power in anticipation of violence, and was introduced to deal with violent conduct, especially by groups of young men. The section provides that, where authorisation for its use has been granted:

(4)   A constable in uniform may:

    (a)   stop any pedestrian and search him or anything carried by him for offensive weapons or dangerous instruments;

    (b)   stop any vehicle and search the vehicle, its driver and any passenger for offensive weapons or dangerous instruments.

(5)   A constable may, in the exercise of those powers, stop any person or vehicle and make any search he thinks fit whether or not he has any grounds for suspecting that the person or vehicle is carrying any weapons or articles of that kind.

(6)   If, in the course of such a search under this section, a constable discovers a dangerous instrument or an article which he has reasonable grounds for suspecting to be an offensive weapon, he may seize it.

The initial authorisation required by s 60 must be given by a police officer of, or above, the rank of inspector. The authorising officer must reasonably believe that:

(a)   incidents involving serious violence may take place in any locality in his area or that dangerous instruments or offensive weapons are being carried in that area; and

(b)   it is expedient to grant an authorisation to prevent their occurrence.

Such an authorisation, which must be in writing, will permit the exercise of stop and search powers within that locality for a period up to 24 hours. It may be extended to 48 hours by an officer of, or above, the rank of superintendent. The authorisation could conceivably be given in fear of a single incident, even though the CJPOA 1994 requires fear of 'incidents'. This is because s 6 of the Interpretation Act 1978 states that the plural includes the singular unless a contrary intention is shown.

    The word 'locality' is left undefined in the CJPOA 1994. It could be an area outside a particular club or pub, or it might extend to a large estate. The courts have the power to declare an authorisation invalid because of an overly expansive geographical area; they are unlikely to substitute their own view for that of the operational officer.

There is no power to detain especially conferred on officers by s 60 in order to carry out the search, but it does make failure to stop a summary offence. As it stands, there is nothing in s 60 that would permit an officer to use any force to conduct a non-consensual search. It is possible that the courts could imply such a power. Exercise of the s 60 power is subject to the safeguards in Code A.

The scope of s 60 and police powers to stop and search are being incrementally extended through various Acts of Parliament. For example, s 8 of the Knives Act 1997 amended s 60 to deal with anticipated violence in situations where gangs or persons may be 'tooled up' and travelling through various police areas en route to an intended scene of confrontation. Thus, the power may be invoked even where it is believed that the actual anticipated violence may occur in another police jurisdiction, for example, by football hooligans travelling to and from matches.

Further amendments to s 60 were made under the CDA 1998. This was mainly to deal with the problem of troublemakers deliberately wearing facial coverings to conceal their identities, especially when the police are using CCTV cameras. Section 25 of the CDA 1998 inserted a new s 4A under s 60, which conferred a power on any constable in uniform to demand the removal of, or seize, face coverings where authority had been given under s 60, if the officer reasonably believed that the face covering was being worn, or was intended to be used, to conceal a person's identity. The Anti-terrorism, Crime and Security Act 2001 replaced s 60(4A) with s 60AA. This is broader than the earlier sub-section and provides for the removal of 'disguises'. One case involved a protestor who wore a skeleton-type mask at a demonstration. A police officer asked her to remove it. When she failed to do so, he tried to remove it himself. The protestor responded by hitting him in the face. She was charged with assaulting a police officer in the course of his duty. The charge was dismissed by magistrates (partly because the policeman had failed to give his name, the location of his police station, or the reason why he wanted the mask to be removed). The Divisional Court took the view that an assault had been committed: *DPP v Avery* (2002).

Section 25 also extends s 60(8) and makes it a summary offence if a person fails to stop, or to stop a vehicle, or to remove an item worn by him or her, when required by the police in the exercise of their powers under s 60.

There are dangers that the powers under s 60 could be misused, as no reasonable suspicion is required and the requirements for authorisation are rather nebulous.

As the police have a common law power to take whatever action is necessary in order to prevent an imminent breach of the peace (*Moss v Mclachlan* (1985)), then, even if a challenge to the use of a s 60 power is technically successful, the police conduct in question may often be thus justified.

However, in *R (on the application of Roberts) v Commissioner of Police of the Metropolis* (2014), where the exercise of s 60 was challenged under the Human Rights Act 1998 as contrary to Arts 5, 8 and 14 ECHR, the Court of Appeal took a robust view of the s 60 powers. Maurice Kay LJ said that:

> In my judgment, the scheme of section 60 cannot be said to be arbitrary. It permits the use of stop and search powers only for a very limited period of time – up to 24 hours, extendable by a maximum of a further 24 hours. Its

temporal limitation is accompanied by a territorial limitation. The authorisation must relate to a 'locality' within a police area. Accordingly, there is no question of a 'rolling programme' across the whole area covered by a police authority. It is based on local intelligence of a specific kind, namely serious violence involving weapons.

He also noted that the individual officer 'is at all times controlled by Code A issued under the Police and Criminal Evidence Act 1984' and that Code A has specific provisions relating to the exercise of CJPOA powers (paras 2.12–2.18). In reaching his judgment, he rejected comparisons with *Gillan and Quinton v UK* (2010) (discussed below).

In a statement to Parliament in April 2014, the then Home Secretary, Theresa May, together with the College of Policing, announced a new code entitled *The Best Use of Stop and Search Scheme.* The stated principal aims of the Scheme were to achieve 'greater transparency, community involvement in the use of stop and search powers and to support a more intelligence-led approach, leading to better outcomes, for example, an increase in the stop and search to positive outcome ratio' and in so doing to improve public confidence and trust.

The specific features of the Scheme were:

- Data Recording – forces would be required to record the broader range of stop and search outcomes e.g. arrests, cautions, penalty notices for disorder and all other disposal types. Forces would be required to show the link, or indeed the lack of one, between the object of the search and its outcome.

- Lay observation policies – providing the opportunity for members of the local community to accompany police officers on patrol using stop and search.

- Stop and search complaints 'community trigger' – requiring the establishment of a local complaint policy requiring the police to explain to local community scrutiny groups how stop and search powers were being used where there was a large volume of complaints.

- Reducing 60 'no-suspicion' stop and searches by –

  (i) raising the level of authorisation to senior officer (above the rank of chief superintendent);

  (ii) ensuring that s 60 stop and search was only used where it is deemed necessary;

  (iii) making this clear to the public;

  (iv) in anticipation of serious violence, requiring the authorising officer to reasonably believe that an incident involving serious violence **would** take place rather than it might;

  (v) limiting the duration of initial authorisations to no more than 15 hours (down from 24); and

(vi)   communicating to local communities when there was to be a s 60 authorisation in advance (where practicable) and afterwards, so that the public is kept informed of the purpose and success of the operation.

Nonetheless, in November 2016 a special inspection by Her Majesty's Inspectorate of Constabulary found that forces in Greater Manchester, South Yorkshire, Northamptonshire and Derbyshire were not complying with the rules of the new code, although subsequently it was reported in February 2017 that Derbyshire remained the only one of 43 forces in England and Wales that did not comply with the code.

10.3.4   THE TERRORISM ACT 2000

The Terrorism Act 2000 gave exceptional powers of stop and search to uniformed police constables. A person of at least the rank of commander or assistant chief constable, who considered it expedient to do so for the prevention of acts of terrorism, could issue an authorisation specifying a particular area or place (to last for not more than 28 days). This gave a constable power to stop vehicles and pedestrians within that area or place and search the vehicle, driver, passengers, pedestrians (and anything with them) for articles of a kind that could be used in connection with terrorism. These powers could be exercised whether or not the constable had grounds for suspecting the presence of articles of that kind. The constable could seize and retain an article that they discovered in the course of such a search and that they reasonably suspected was intended to be used in connection with terrorism (ss 44 and 45). By s 47, it was an offence to fail to stop a vehicle when required to do so, fail to stop when required to do so, and wilfully to obstruct a constable in the exercise of these powers. The offences are punishable with six months' imprisonment and/or a fine of up to £5,000.

These provisions were not confined to terrorism in connection with Northern Ireland or international terrorism. 'Terrorism' means the use or threat of action involving serious violence against a person, serious damage to property, endangering the life of a person other than the 'terrorist'. This must be coupled with creating a serious risk to the health or safety of the public or a section of the public, or designing seriously to interfere with or seriously to disrupt an electronic system. The above action(s) must be designed to influence the government or to intimidate the public or a section of the public, and made for the purpose of advancing a political, religious or ideological cause. However, where the use or threat of action involves the use of firearms or explosives, it need not be designed to influence the government or to intimidate the public or a section of the public.

In *Gillan and Quinton v UK* (2010) the ECtHR held that the requirement on a person to submit to a stop and search under s 44 of the TA 2000 represented a clear interference with the right to respect for private life under Art 8 ECHR, finding that the provisions of the TA 2000 had been neither sufficiently circumscribed nor subject to adequate safeguards against abuse. The court was also influenced by the massive increase in the use of the power since it had been introduced and the fact that it was disproportionately used against ethnic minorities. As a result of the judgment, the coalition government made a remedial order under the Human Rights Act 1998 (the Terrorism Act 2000 (Remedial) Order 2011), which has the effect of repealing ss 44, 45, 46 and most of s 47. The new Protection of Freedoms Act 2012 now provides the police with more circumscribed powers to authorise stop and search of persons and vehicles without reasonable suspicion (s 47A) in exceptional circumstances. This places the powers provided by the Terrorism Act 2000 Remedial Order 2011 on a permanent footing. The Protection of Freedoms Act 2012 also changes stop and search powers in the Terrorism Act 2000 (ss 43 and 43A) which require reasonable suspicion to enable searches of vehicles or their occupants. Codes of practice supporting the new legislation were laid before Parliament in May 2012 in the form of the Terrorism Act 2000 (Codes of Practice for the Exercise of Stop and Search Powers) Order 2012. In addition PACE codes of practice C, G and H have been amended to introduce a new code of practice for the video-recording with sound of interviews carried out under s 41 of, and Sched 7 to, the Terrorism Act 2000 and post-charge questioning of terrorist suspects under the Counter-Terrorism Act 2008.

10.3.5   ENTRY AND SEARCH OF PREMISES

Section 18 of PACE provides powers to enter and search premises. These are further covered by Code B. Paragraph 1.3 states:

> The right to privacy and respect for personal property are key principles of the Human Rights Act 1998. Powers of entry, search and seizure should be fully and clearly justified before use because they may significantly interfere with the occupiers' privacy. Officers should consider if the necessary objectives can be met by less intrusive means.

Paragraph 7.7 states:

> The Criminal Justice and Police Act 2001, Part 2, gives officers limited powers to seize property from premises or persons so that they can sift or examine it elsewhere. Officers must be careful they only exercise these powers when it is essential and they do not remove any more material than necessary. The removal of large quantities of material, much of which may not ultimately be retainable, may have serious implications for the owners . . . Officers must carefully consider if removing copies or images of relevant material or data would be a satisfactory alternative to removing originals.

In 2011, amendments to Code B extended the conditions which must be met in order for a search under s 18 of PACE to be authorised. Under the previous version of the

Code, para 4.3 required that the authorising officer (of the rank of inspector or above) be satisfied that the necessary grounds under s 18 existed. This paragraph has now been extended to require the inspector to be satisfied, in addition to the grounds set out in s 18, 'that the premises are occupied or controlled by the arrested person'. This reflects the judgment in *Khan v Commissioner of Police of the Metropolis* (2008). A suspect had falsely provided Mr Khan's address as his own upon arrest. Entry and search of this address was duly authorised and undertaken under s 18. The Commissioner argued that s 18 should be interpreted so as to qualify the requirement of occupation and control by the suspect by reference to the belief of knowledge of the officer. The Court of Appeal rejected this submission and, dismissing the Commissioner's appeal, found that there was no justification for such a reading and that 'the requirement for occupation or control is central and fundamental to the operation of section 18'. The amended Code A was an attempt to achieve what the Metropolitan Police Commissioner failed to do in *Khan*: that is, to circumvent the clear wording of s 18 to protect the police from claims for damages in circumstances where the wrong address is searched in good faith.

10.4   ARREST

According to AV Dicey, 'individual rights are the basis not the result of the law of the constitution' (*Law of the Constitution*, 6th edn, p 203; cited by Judge LJ in *R v Central Criminal Court ex p The Guardian, The Observer and Bright* (2002)). Before considering the rights of the citizen and the law governing arrest and detention, what happens in the police station and what evidence is admissible in court, it is appropriate to look first at what the citizen can do if those rights are violated.

10.4.1   REMEDIES FOR UNLAWFUL ARREST

Like other areas of law where the liberty of the subject is at stake, the law relating to arrest is founded upon the principle of *justification*. If challenged, the person who has attempted to make an arrest must justify his actions and show that the arrest and subsequent detention was lawful. Failing this, the arrest will be regarded as unlawful. In *Roberts v Chief Constable of Cheshire Police* (1999), the Court of Appeal held that a failure to carry out a review of detention in accordance with s 40 of PACE 1984 rendered a subsequent period of detention unlawful. However, in *Lewis v Chief Constable of South Wales* (1991) it was held that informing an arrested person of reasons for their arrest made a previously unlawful arrest lawful from that moment onwards.

There are four possible remedies:

● The person, or someone on their behalf, can bring proceedings of *habeas corpus*. This ancient prerogative writ used to begin with the words 'habeas corpus', meaning 'you must have the body' and 'produce the body'. It is addressed to the detainer and asks them to bring the detainee in question before the court at a specified date and time. The remedy protects the freedom of those who have been unlawfully detained in prison, hospital, police station or private custody. The writ is applied for from a judge in chambers and can, in emergencies, be made over the telephone. It must be issued if there is *prima facie* evidence that the detention is unlawful. As every detention is unlawful, the burden of proof is on the detainer to justify their conduct. If issued, the writ frees the detainee and thus allows them to seek other remedies (below) against the detainer.

- To use the illegality of the detention to argue that any subsequent prosecution should fail. This type of argument is very rarely successful as illegally obtained evidence is not, *ipso facto*, *automatically rendered* inadmissible. The House of Lords ruled in *R v Sang* (1979) that no discretion existed to exclude evidence simply because it had been illegally or improperly obtained. A court could only exclude relevant evidence where its effect would be 'unduly prejudicial'. This is reflected in s 78(1) (and s 82(3)) of the Police and Criminal Evidence Act (PACE) 1984:

> 78(1) In any proceedings, the court may refuse to allow evidence on which the prosecution proposes to rely to be given if it appears to the court that, having regard to all the circumstances, including the circumstances in which the evidence was obtained, the admission of the evidence would have such an adverse effect on the fairness of the proceedings that the court ought not to admit it.

This perhaps surprising rule was supported by the Royal Commission on Criminal Justice (although the argument there was chiefly focused on the admissibility of confession evidence). Professor Zander, however, in a note of dissent, contested the idea that a conviction could be upheld despite serious misconduct by the prosecution if there is other evidence against the convicted person. He states: 'I cannot agree. The moral foundation of the criminal justice system requires that, if the prosecution has employed foul means, the defendant must go free if he is plainly guilty . . . the conviction should be quashed as an expression of the system's repugnance.' An extreme case might involve the admissibility of confession evidence obtained by torture by the authorities in another country (see for example *Gäfgen v Germany* (2011)). As well as interpretation of s 78(1) of PACE 1984, under the Human Rights Act 1998 any court must take Art 6 of the European Convention on Human Rights (ECHR) into account in appropriate circumstances.

- An action for damages for false imprisonment. In some cases, the damages for such an action would be likely to be nominal if the violation by the detainer does not have much impact on the detainee. Consider cases under this heading like *Christie v Leachinsky* (1947). Damages can, however, be considerable. In *Reynolds v Commissioner of Police for the Metropolis* (1982), a jury awarded £12,000 damages to the plaintiff. She had been arrested in the early hours in connection with charges of arson for gain, that is, that insured houses, which had been set alight deliberately, would be the subject of 'accidental fire' insurance claims. She was taken by car to a police station, a journey which took two-and-a-half hours. She was detained until about 8.00 pm, when she was told there was no evidence against her. She arrived home at about 11.00 pm. The judge, Caulfield J, ruled that the police had no reasonable grounds for suspecting the plaintiff of having committed an arrestable offence and he directed the jury in relation to damages. The jury awarded £12,000 and the defendant's appeal against this sum as excessive was dismissed.

- A judicial review of the detention. A judicial review of a decision to detain someone can be brought in the High Court on the ground that the detention is unlawful. The judicial review may include a claim under the Human Rights Act 1998 that the detention is in violation of Art 5 ECHR. If the High Court finds in favour of the detainee, it has the power to quash the decision to detain, order that the detainee be released and, in some limited circumstances, to award damages.

Apart from the question of civil remedies, it is important to remember that if the arrest is not lawful, there is the right to use reasonable force to resist it (*R v Waterfield* (1964); *Kenlin v Gardiner* (1967)). This is a remedy, however, of doubtful advisability, as the legality of the arrest will only be properly tested after the event in a law court. If a police officer was engaged in what the courts decide was a lawful arrest or conduct, then anyone who uses force against the officer might have been guilty of an offence of assaulting an officer in the execution of his duty, contrary to s 89(1) of the Police Act 1996.

10.4.2　GENERAL POWERS OF ARREST

In *Spicer v Holt* (1977), Lord Dilhorne stated:

> Whether or not a person has been arrested depends not upon the legality of the arrest, but on whether he has been deprived of his liberty to go where he pleases.

So, a person detained by the police against his will is arrested. Whether this arrest is lawful will depend on whether the conditions for a lawful arrest have been satisfied.

Lawful arrests are those: (1) under warrant; (2) without warrant at common law; or (3) without warrant under legislation.

10.4.3　ARREST UNDER WARRANT

The police lay a written information on oath before a magistrate that a person 'has, or is suspected of having, committed an offence' (s 1 of the Magistrates' Courts Act 1980).

The Criminal Justice Act (CJA) 1967 provides that warrants should not be issued unless the offence in question is indictable or is punishable with imprisonment.

Under the Extradition Act 2003, European arrest warrants may be obtained in the UK by other EU Member states. The traditional approach (found in extradition agreements) embodied the principle of 'dual criminality' – that is, a person would not be extradited from one state to another unless their alleged offence was an extraditable crime in both countries. This requirement has now been removed from a list of 32 offences. The inclusion of 'racism and xenophobia' has aroused some controversy. (See S Allegre, 'The myth and the reality of a modern European judicial space' (2002) 152 NLJ 986.)

10.4.4   COMMON LAW ARRESTS

The only power to arrest at common law is where a breach of the peace has been committed and there are reasonable grounds for believing that it will be continued or renewed, or where a breach of the peace is reasonably apprehended. Essentially, it requires *conduct* related to violence, real or threatened. A simple disturbance does not, in itself, amount to a breach of the peace unless it results from violence, real or threatened.

In 1981, two cases decided within months of each other offered definitions of a breach of the peace, in an attempt to bring some clarification to an area of law that previously was in doubt. In *R v Howell* (1981), the defendant was arrested after being involved in a disturbance at a street party in the early hours of the morning. Watkins LJ, who delivered the judgment of the court, observed that there was a power of arrest for anticipated breach of the peace, provided the arrestor had been witness to the earlier shouting and swearing of H. It followed that there must be reasonable grounds for belief, and the arrestor must believe at the time that the defendant's conduct, either alone or as part of a general disturbance, was likely to lead to the use of violence by the defendant or someone else in the officer's presence.

The court adopted the following definition of 'breach of the peace'. It occurs:

> Wherever harm is actually done, or is likely to be done to a person, or in his presence to his property, or a person is in fear of being so harmed through an assault, an affray, a riot, unlawful assembly or other disturbance.

In the second of the two cases, *R v Chief Constable of the Devon and Cornwall Constabulary ex p Central Electricity Generating Board (CEGB)* (1981), Lord Denning MR suggested that breach of the peace might be considerably wider than this. This case involved a group of protestors who had occupied private land in order to prevent CEGB employees from carrying out a survey to assess its suitability for a nuclear power station. The protest was intended to be peaceful and non-violent. Lord Denning MR suggested that:

> There is a breach of the peace whenever a person who is lawfully carrying out his work is unlawfully and physically prevented by another from doing it . . . If anyone unlawfully and physically obstructs the worker, by lying down or chaining himself to a rig or the like, he is guilty of a breach of the peace.

He appears to have been saying (Feldman, *Civil Liberties and Human Rights in England and Wales* (1993), pp 788–89) not that a breach of the peace is automatic in such circumstances. Instead, in the context of the *CEGB* case, any obstruction or unlawful *resistance* by the trespasser could give the police a reasonable apprehension of a breach of the peace, in the sense of violence.

However, in cases that have followed (such as *Parkin v Norman* (1982); *Percy v DPP* (1995); and *Foulkes v Chief Constable of Merseyside Police* (1998)), it is the definition in *R v Howell* that has been preferred. Despite earlier doubts, argues Parpworth ('Breach of the peace: breach of human rights?' (1998) 152 JP 6, 7 November), the decision of the European Court of Human Rights (ECtHR) in *Steel and Others v UK* (1998) brings clear and authoritative clarification to this area of law. This case represents 'a clear endorsement by a court largely unfamiliar with the common law concept of a breach of the peace that such a concept is in accordance with the terms of the European Convention on Human Rights'.

At common law, a constable may arrest a person for conduct that they genuinely suspect might be likely to cause a breach of the peace even on private premises where no member of the public is present (*McConnell v Chief Constable of Manchester* (1990)). Although mere shouting and swearing alone will not constitute a breach of the peace, it is an offence under s 28 of the Town Police Causes Act 1847. If it causes harassment, alarm or distress to a member of the public, it may constitute an offence under s 5 of the Public Order Act 1986. In either case, it could lead to arrest under the Police and Criminal Evidence Act 1984.

10.4.5   ARREST UNDER LEGISLATION

The right to arrest is generally governed by s 24 of PACE 1984 (as amended by SOCPA 2005 s 110) in respect of arrest by police officers and s 24A in respect of arrest by other people. PACE 1984 preserves an old common law distinction in respect of the powers of constables and private individuals when making such arrests (*Walters v WH Smith & Son Ltd* (1914)). Where an arrest is being made after an offence is thought to have been committed, then PACE 1984 confers narrower rights upon the private individual than on the police officer.

In particular, the changes made by SOCPA provide, in the case of a constable's power of arrest, for all offences to be 'arrestable' subject to a necessity test. This means that someone who has committed a relatively low-order criminal offence, like littering, could, in theory, be arrested if an officer deemed it necessary and was able to satisfy his or her desk sergeant at the police station that this was so. That might occur, for example, if the person being requested to pick up the litter refused to do so, and then refused to give his or her name to the officer.

24 Arrest without warrant: constables

(1)   A constable may arrest without a warrant –

    (a)   anyone who is about to commit an offence;

    (b)   anyone who is in the act of committing an offence;

    (c)   anyone whom he has reasonable grounds for suspecting to be about to commit an offence;

    (d)   anyone whom he has reasonable grounds for suspecting to be committing an offence.

(2)   If a constable has reasonable grounds for suspecting that an offence has been committed, he may arrest without a warrant anyone whom he has reasonable grounds to suspect of being guilty of it.

(3)   If an offence has been committed, a constable may arrest without a warrant –

    (a)   anyone who is guilty of the offence;

    (b)   anyone whom he has reasonable grounds for suspecting to be guilty of it.

(4)   But the power of summary arrest conferred by subsection (1), (2) or (3) is exercisable only if the constable has reasonable grounds for believing that for any of the reasons mentioned in subsection (5) it is necessary to arrest the person in question.

(5)   The reasons are –

    (a)   to enable the name of the person in question to be ascertained (in the case where the constable does not know, and cannot readily ascertain, the person's name, or has reasonable grounds for doubting whether a name given by the person as his name is his real name);

    (b)   correspondingly as regards the person's address;

    (c)   to prevent the person in question –

        (i)   causing physical injury to himself or any other person;

        (ii)   suffering physical injury;

        (iii)   causing loss of or damage to property;

        (iv)   committing an offence against public decency (subject to subsection (6)); or

        (v)   causing an unlawful obstruction of the highway;

(d)   to protect a child or other vulnerable person from the person in question;

(e)   to allow the prompt and effective investigation of the offence or of the conduct of the person in question;

(f)   to prevent any prosecution for the offence from being hindered by the disappearance of the person in question.

(6)   Subsection (5)(c)(iv) applies only where members of the public going about their normal business cannot reasonably be expected to avoid the person in question.

24A Arrest without warrant: other persons

(1)   A person other than a constable may arrest without a warrant –

(a)   anyone who is in the act of committing an indictable offence;

(b)   anyone whom he has reasonable grounds for suspecting to be committing an indictable offence.

(2)   Where an indictable offence has been committed, a person other than a constable may arrest without a warrant –

(a)   anyone who is guilty of the offence;

(b)   anyone whom he has reasonable grounds for suspecting to be guilty of it.

(3)   But the power of summary arrest conferred by subsection (1) or (2) is exercisable only if –

(a)   the person making the arrest has reasonable grounds for believing that for any of the reasons mentioned in subsection (4) it is necessary to arrest the person in question; and

(b)   it appears to the person making the arrest that it is not reasonably practicable for a constable to make it instead.

(4)   The reasons are to prevent the person in question –

(a)   causing physical injury to himself or any other person;

(b)   suffering physical injury;

(c)   causing loss of or damage to property; or

(d)   making off before a constable can assume responsibility for him.

SOCPA extended police powers in a highly controversial way. The case to extend powers for the police is built on the idea that those who have done nothing wrong will have nothing to fear from the exercise of the powers. The extension of police powers is also defended on the grounds that any arrest, to be lawful, must be 'necessary' (see s 24(5) of PACE as amended, above, by s 110 of the Serious Organised Crime and Police Act).

There are, however, clear reasons for concern at this development. A society in which the police have unlimited powers can be described as a 'police state', and such tyranny is almost universally disfavoured. That, of course, is very far from the position now in the UK, a country that has what are among the best-protected liberties in the world. However, the closer that law in the UK moves towards giving the police very wide powers to arrest, the greater the need for concern. A society in which people can be arrested for any offence, in which CCTV is ubiquitous (Surveillance UK, *The Independent*, 22 December 2005), and in which police 'success' is progressively measured by how many arrests and crimes are solved, might reduce certain sorts of offending (although many sorts of criminality are not reduced by such policies). But how comfortable a place would it be to live? The inhabitants of many countries in which there are dictatorial governments and no respect for civil liberties do not seem to rejoice in the crime-free streets. At all events, the most desirable balance between freedom not to be interfered with by police officers, and policing that improves society by effectively reducing crime, is ultimately a political question for the public, rather than the small section of the public comprising judges, lawyers and police officers.

10.4.6 WHAT IS THE MEANING OF 'REASONABLE GROUNDS FOR SUSPECTING'?

Many of the powers of the police in relation to arrest, search and seizure are founded upon the presence of reasonable 'suspicion', 'cause' or 'belief' in a state of affairs, usually that a suspect is involved actually or potentially in a crime.

In *Castorina v Chief Constable of Surrey* (1988), detectives reasonably concluded that the burglary of a company's premises was an 'inside job'. The managing director told them that she had recently dismissed someone (the plaintiff), although she did not think it would have been her, and that the documents taken would be useful to someone with a grudge. The detectives interviewed the plaintiff, having found out that she had no criminal record, and arrested her under s 2(4) of the Criminal Law Act (CLA) 1967 (which has now been replaced by s 24 PACE 1984). She was detained at the police station for almost four hours, interrogated and then released without charge. On a claim for damages for wrongful arrest and detention, a jury awarded her £4,500. The trial judge held that the officers had had a *prima facie* case for suspicion, but that the arrest was premature. He had defined 'reasonable cause' (which the officers would have needed to show they had when they arrested the plaintiff) as 'honest belief founded upon reasonable suspicion leading an ordinary cautious man to the conclusion that the person arrested was guilty of the offence'. He said an ordinary man would have sought more information from the suspect, including an explanation for any grudge on her part. In this, he relied on the *dicta* of Scott LJ in *Dumbell v Roberts* (1944) that the principle that every man was presumed innocent until proved guilty also applied to arrests. The Court of Appeal allowed an appeal by the chief constable.

The court held that the trial judge had used too severe a test in judging the officers' conduct.

Purchas LJ said that the test of 'reasonable cause' was objective and therefore the trial judge was wrong to have focused attention on whether the officers had 'an honest belief'. The question was whether the officers had had reasonable grounds to suspect the woman of the offence. There was sufficient evidence that the officers had had sufficient reason to suspect her.

Woolf LJ thought there were three things to consider in cases where an arrest is alleged to be unlawful:

- Did the arresting officer suspect that the person who was arrested had committed the offence? This was a matter of fact about the officer's state of mind.

- If the answer to the first question is yes, then was there reasonable proof of that suspicion? This is a simple objective matter to be determined by the judge.

- If the answers to the first two questions are both yes, then the officer did have a discretion to arrest, and the question then was whether they had exercised their discretion according to *Wednesbury* principles of reasonableness.

This case hinged on the second point and, on the facts, the chief constable should succeed on the appeal.

The *Wednesbury* principles come from *Associated Provincial Picture Houses Ltd v Wednesbury Corp* (1948). Lord Greene MR laid down principles to determine when the decision made by a public authority could be regarded as so perverse or unreasonable that the courts would be justified in overturning that decision. The case actually concerned whether a condition imposed by a local authority on cinemas operating on Sundays was reasonable. Lord Greene MR said:

> [A] person entrusted with a discretion must, so to speak, direct himself properly in law. He must call his own attention to matters which he is bound to consider. He must exclude from his consideration matters which are irrelevant to what he has to consider. If he does not obey those rules, he may be truly said, and often is said, to be acting 'unreasonably'.

Sir Frederick Lawton, the third judge in the Court of Appeal in *Castorina*, agreed. The facts on which 'reasonable cause' was said to have been founded did not have to be such as to lead an ordinary cautious man to conclude that the person arrested *was* guilty of the offence. It was enough if they could lead an ordinary person to *suspect* that he or she was guilty.

This creates quite some latitude for the police. Additionally, the House of Lords has decided in *Holgate-Mohammed v Duke* (1984) that, where a police officer reasonably suspects an individual of having committed an arrestable offence, they may arrest that person with a view to questioning them at the police station. The police officer's decision can only be challenged on *Wednesbury* principles if they acted improperly by taking something irrelevant into account. The police arrested a former lodger for theft of jewellery from the house where she had lived in order to question her at the police station. The trial judge awarded her £1,000 damages for false imprisonment. The Court of Appeal set aside the award and the decision was upheld by the House of Lords. The following passage from a judgment in the Court of Appeal in *Holgate-Mohammed* was approved in the House of Lords:

> As to the proposition that there were other things which [the police officer] might have done. No doubt there were other things which he might have done first. He might have obtained a statement from her otherwise than under arrest to see how far he could get. He might have obtained a specimen of her handwriting and sent that off for forensic examination against a specimen of the writing of the person who had obtained the money by selling the stolen jewellery, which happened to exist in the case. All those things he might have done. He might have carried out fingerprint investigations if he had first obtained a print from the plaintiff. But, the fact that there were other things which he might have done does not, in my judgment, make that which he did do into an unreasonable exercise of the power of arrest if what he did do, namely, to arrest, was within the range of reasonable choices open to him.

It has been forcefully contended, however, that, in some circumstances, a failure to make inquiries before making an arrest could show that there were insufficient grounds for the arrest. (See Clayton and Tomlinson, 'Arrest and reasonable grounds for suspicion' (1988) Law Soc Gazette, 7 September.)

Note, however, that the powers are *discretionary*. (See *Simpson v Chief Constable of South Yorkshire Police* (1991).)

10.4.7 DETENTION SHORT OF ARREST

For there to be an arrest, the arrestor must regard his action as an arrest. If they simply detain someone to question them without any thought of arrest, the action will be unlawful. It is often reported in criminal investigations that a person is 'helping police with their inquiries'. In *R v Lemsatef* (1977), Lawton LJ said:

> It must be clearly understood that neither customs officers nor police officers have any right to detain somebody for the purposes of getting them to help with their inquiries.

There is no police power to detain someone against his will in order to make inquiries about that person (see also *Franchiosy* (1979)). This is confirmed by s 29 of PACE 1984, which states that where someone attends a police station 'for the purpose of assisting with an investigation', they are entitled to leave at any time unless placed under arrest. They must be informed at once that they are under arrest 'if a decision is taken by a constable to prevent him from leaving at will'. There is, however, no legal duty on the police to inform anyone whom they invite to the station to help with their inquiries that they may go.

10.4.8 SUSPECTS STOPPED IN THE STREET

In *Kenlin v Gardiner* (1967), a police officer took hold of the arm of a boy he wanted to question about the latter's suspicious conduct. The boy did not believe the man was a policeman, despite having been shown a warrant card, and punched the officer in order to escape. The other boy behaved similarly, but their convictions for assaulting an officer in the execution of his duty were quashed by the Divisional Court. The court held that the boys were entitled to act as they did in self-defence as the officer's conduct in trying to physically apprehend them had not been legal. There is no legal power of detention short of arrest. As Lawton LJ observed in *R v Lemsatef* (see above), the police do not have any powers to detain somebody 'for the purposes of getting them to help with their inquiries'.

It is important, however, to examine the precise circumstances of the detaining officer's conduct. There are cases to suggest that if what the officer does amounts to only a *de minimis* interference with the citizen's liberty, then forceful 'self-defence' by the citizen will not be justified. In *Donnelly v Jackman* (1970), an officer approached a suspect to ask some questions. The suspect ignored the request and walked away from the officer. The officer followed and made further requests for the suspect to stop and talk. He tapped the suspect on the shoulder and the suspect reciprocated by tapping the officer on the shoulder and saying 'Now we are even, copper'. The officer tapped the suspect on the shoulder again, which was replied to with a forceful punch. Mr Donnelly's conviction was upheld and the decision in *Kenlin v Gardiner* was distinguished as, in the earlier case, the officer had actually taken hold of the boys and detained them. The court stated that 'it is not every trivial interference with a citizen's liberty that amounts to a course of conduct sufficient to take the officer out of the course of his duties'.

In *Bentley v Brudzinski* (1982), the facts were very close to those above. A constable stopped two men who had been running barefoot down a street in the early hours. He questioned them about a stolen vehicle as they fitted the description of suspects in an earlier incident. They waited for about 10 minutes while the officer checked their details over a radio and then they began to leave. Another constable, who had just arrived on the scene, then said, 'Just a minute', and put his hand on the defendant's shoulder. The defendant then punched that officer in the face. Unlike the decision in *Donnelly v Jackman*, the Divisional Court held that the officer's conduct was more than a trivial interference with the citizen's liberty and amounted to an unlawful attempt to stop and detain him. The respondent was thus not guilty of assaulting an officer in the execution of his duty.

Note, also, that a person may be arrested for being silent or misleading under s 25(5)(a) and (b) of PACE 1984, if the officer cannot ascertain or has reasonable doubts about the suspect's name and address.

The power to search after arrest somewhere other than at the police station is governed by s 32 of PACE 1984 (searches of detained persons are dealt with by s 54 and Code C, para 4.1). Section 32(1) allows the police to search someone arrested where there are grounds for believing that he may present a danger to himself or to others. Section 32(2) allows a search for anything that might be used to effect an escape or which might be evidence relating to any offence. Additionally, s 32(2)(b) gives the police power to enter and search the premises he or she was in when arrested, or immediately before he or she was arrested, for evidence relating to the offence for which he or she was arrested. Unlike the power to search under s 18, this is not limited to arrestable offences, nor do the searched premises need to be occupied or controlled by him or her. Such searches, however, are only lawful where there are reasonable grounds for believing that the search might find something for which a search is permitted under s 32(2)(b). Random or automatic searching is not lawful. Section 32(4) states that a person searched in public cannot be required to take off more than outer garments like coats, jackets and gloves. An officer may search the arrested person's mouth at the time of the arrest if he or she has reasonable grounds to believe that the arrested person is concealing therein evidence related to the offence (s 32(4)).

At common law (that is, before PACE 1984), it was necessary for the arrestor to make it clear to the arrestee that he was under compulsion either: (a) by physical means, such as taking him by the arm; or (b) by telling him, orally, that he was under compulsion. There was a danger, where words alone were used, that they might not be clear enough. Consider *Alderson v Booth* (1969). Following a positive breathalyser test, the officer said to the defendant: 'I shall have to ask you to come back to the station for further tests.' D did accompany the officer to the station. Lawful arrest was a condition precedent to anyone being convicted of driving with excess alcohol in their blood. At his trial, the defendant said he had not been arrested. He was acquitted and the prosecution appeal failed. Compulsion is a necessary element of arrest and the magistrates were not convinced that it was present in this case. The Divisional Court was not prepared to contradict the factual finding of the magistrates.

Additionally, where words alone were used, it was necessary for the arrestee to accede to the detention. There was no arrest where the arrestor said 'I arrest you' and the arrestee ran off before he could be touched (see *Sandon v Jervis* (1859)).

These principles remain good law after PACE 1984; see, for example, *Nichols v Bulman* (1985).

According to s 28(3) of PACE 1984, no arrest is lawful unless the arrestee is informed of the ground for the arrest at the time of, or as soon as reasonably practicable after, the arrest. Where a person is arrested by a constable, this applies (s 28(4)) regardless of whether or not the ground for the arrest is obvious.

The reasons for this rule were well put by Viscount Simon in *Christie v Leachinsky* (1947):

> [A] person is *prima facie* entitled to personal freedom [and] should know why for the time being his personal freedom is being interfered with . . . No one, I think, would approve of a situation in which when the person arrested asked for the reason, the policeman replied 'that has nothing to do with you: come along with me' . . . And there are practical considerations . . . If the charge . . . is then and there made known to him, he has the opportunity of giving an explanation of any misunderstanding or of calling attention to other persons for whom he may have been mistaken, with the result that further inquiries may save him from the consequences of false accusation.

An arrest, however, becomes lawful once the ground is given. In *Lewis v Chief Constable of the South Wales Constabulary* (1991), the officers had told the plaintiffs of the fact of arrest, but delayed telling them the grounds for 10 minutes in one case and 23 minutes in the other. The Court of Appeal said that arrest was not a legal concept but arose factually from the deprivation of a person's liberty. It was also a continuing act and therefore what had begun as an unlawful arrest could become a lawful arrest. The remedy for the plaintiffs was the damages they had been awarded for the 10 minutes and 23 minutes of illegality: £200 each.

In *Nicholas v Parsonage* (1987), N was seen riding a bicycle without holding the handlebars by two police officers. They told him twice to hold the bars and then he did so. When they drove off, N raised two fingers. They then stopped N and PC Parsonage asked him for his name, telling him it was required as he had been riding his bicycle in a dangerous manner. N refused. P then informed him of his powers under PACE 1984 and requested N's name and address. N again refused. P then arrested him for failing to give his name and address. N attempted to ride off and a struggle ensued. N was subsequently convicted of, *inter alia*, assaulting a police officer in the execution of his duty, contrary to s 51(1) of the Police Act 1964. His appeal was dismissed by the Divisional Court, which held that the arrest under s 25 of PACE 1984 (the law then in force) had been lawful as a constable exercising power under s 25(3) was not required to say why he wanted the suspect's name and address. N had been adequately informed of the ground of arrest under s 28(3) of PACE 1984. N was not arrested for failing to give his name and address; he was arrested because, having committed the minor offence of 'riding in a dangerous manner', it then became necessary to arrest him because the conditions in s 25(3)(a) and (c) were satisfied. These conditions were that an arrest for a minor offence is possible where the officer believes that the service of a summons is impracticable because he has not been given a proper name and address.

Is it necessary for an arrestor to indicate to the arrestee the grounds on which his 'reasonable suspicion' was based? In *Geldberg v Miller* (1961), the appellant parked his car outside a restaurant in London while he had a meal. He was asked by police officers to move the car. He refused, preferring to finish his meal first. On being told that the police would remove the car, he removed the rotor arm from the distributor mechanism. He also refused to give his name and address or show his driving licence and certificate of insurance. He was arrested by one of the officers for 'obstructing him in the execution of his duty by refusing to move his car and refusing his name and address'. There was no power to arrest for obstruction of the police as no actual or apprehended breach of the peace was involved. The court held, however, that the arrest was valid for 'obstructing the thoroughfare', an offence under s 56(6) of the Metropolitan Police Act 1839, an offence the officer had not mentioned. Lord Parker CJ said:

> In my judgment, what the appellant knew and what he was told was ample to fulfil the obligation as to what should be done at the time of an arrest without warrant.

An arrest will be unlawful, however, where the reasons given point to an offence for which there is no power of arrest (or for which there is only qualified power of arrest) and it is clear that no other reasons were present in the mind of the officer (*Edwards v DPP* (1993)). This principle was confirmed in *Mullady v DPP* (1997). A police officer arrested M for 'obstruction', an offence with the power of arrest only if the defendant's conduct amounted to a breach of the peace (for which there is a common law power of arrest) or if one of the general arrest conditions as set out in s 25 is satisfied. The police argued that the officer could have arrested M for a breach of the peace and merely gave the wrong reason. The Divisional Court held that the officer had acted unlawfully and that it would be wrong for the justices to go behind the reason given and infer that the reason for the arrest was another lawful reason.

In some circumstances, the court may infer a lawful reason for an arrest if the circumstantial evidence points clearly to a lawful reason (*Brookman v DPP* (1997)). However, if there is insufficient evidence to determine whether a lawful or unlawful reason was given for the arrest, then the police will fail to show that the arrest was lawful (*Clarke v DPP* (1998)).

10.4.11 THE USE OF FORCE TO EFFECT AN ARREST

The use of force by a member of the public when arresting someone is governed by s 3 of the CLA 1967. This states:

> (1) A person may use such force as is reasonable in the circumstances in the prevention of crime, or in effecting or assisting in the lawful arrest of offenders or suspected offenders or of persons unlawfully at large.

Reasonable force will generally mean the minimum necessary to effect an arrest. The use of force by police officers is governed by s 117 of PACE 1984. This states:

Where any provision of this Act:

(a) confers a power on a constable; and
(b) does not provide that the power may only be exercised with the consent of some person, other than a police officer, the officer may use reasonable force, if necessary, in the exercise of the power.

10.4.12 DUTIES AFTER ARREST

A person arrested by a constable, or handed over to one, must be taken to a police station as soon as is 'practicable', unless his or her presence elsewhere is 'necessary in order to carry out such investigations as it is reasonable to carry out immediately' (s 30(1), (10) of PACE 1984). Where a citizen makes an arrest, he 'must, as soon as he reasonably can, hand the man over to a constable or take him to the police station or take him before a magistrate', per Lord Denning in *Dallison v Caffery* (1965). There is no requirement, however, that this be carried out immediately (*John Lewis & Co v Tims* (1952)).

10.5 INTERROGATION, CONFESSION AND ADMISSIBILITY OF EVIDENCE

Before moving into the specific provisions of PACE 1984 and the Codes of Practice as they apply in the police station, it is important to be aware of the general issues at stake in this area of law. Are the rights of suspects being interrogated by the police sufficiently protected by law? Is there scope for abuse of power by the police? Are the police burdened by too many legal requirements when trying to induce a suspect to confess to a crime? What effects are likely to flow from the undermining of the right to silence (see ss 34–37 of the CJPOA 1994)?

Once again, it is also necessary to bear in mind the significance of the ECHR in this context. Unless impossible because of conflicting primary legislation, English courts must interpret rules of law so as to be compatible with obligations under the ECHR. Article 5 guarantees a right to liberty. To justify depriving a person of their liberty before conviction for an offence, for example, Art 5 requires that there be a lawful arrest or detention for the purpose of bringing the person before a competent authority on a reasonable suspicion of having committed an offence, or that arrest or detention is considered reasonably necessary to prevent them from committing an offence. Moreover, every person arrested shall be informed promptly in a language that they understand of the reasons for their arrest. The arrested person shall be informed of any charge against them, shall be brought promptly before a judge and shall be entitled to trial within a reasonable time or to release pending trial. Clearly, PACE requirements in relation to arrest and detention must be measured against Art 5. Equally, Art 6 requires a fair trial and declares a presumption of innocence, matters that bear on the conduct of the trial, the evidence presented, and the obligation to offer explanations or risk the consequences of adverse inferences being drawn from silence.

10.5.1 TIME LIMITS ON DETENTION WITHOUT CHARGE

Under s 40 of PACE 1984, the Custody Officer is obliged to review the detention of a suspect held at the police station as follows:

(a) the first review shall be not later than six hours after the detention was first authorised;

(b) the second review shall be not later than nine hours after the first;

(c) subsequent reviews shall be at intervals of not more than nine hours. The purpose of such reviews is to reduce the possibility that the suspect is being held for too long or unnecessarily while the investigation is ongoing. Both the suspect and/ or their solicitor are allowed to make representations about the termination or continuation of the detention.

Section 6 of the CJA 2003 introduced a new innovation – the use of telephones for review of police detention (s 40A PACE). This provision enables reviews of the continuing need for detention without charge carried out under s 40 of PACE 1984 to be conducted over the telephone rather than in person at the police station. Such reviews have to be carried out by an officer of at least inspector rank. PACE 1984 only allows telephone reviews where it is not reasonably practicable for the reviewing officer to be present at the police station.

Under s 41 of PACE 1984, a suspect can be held without being charged for 24 hours before any further authorisation needs to be given. At this point, the situation must be reviewed and further detention must be authorised by an officer of at least the rank of superintendent (s 42). This can only be done if an officer of sufficient rank is satisfied that detention is necessary to secure, preserve or obtain evidence, that the investigation is being conducted diligently and expeditiously, and that the relevant offence was an indictable offence. The period is measured from arrival at the police station. If they are arrested by another force, the time runs from their arrival at the station of the area where they are wanted. If further detention is authorised, this can continue for up to the 36-hour point. After 36 hours from the beginning of the detention, there must be a full hearing in a magistrates' court with the suspect and, if they wish, legal representation (s 43). The magistrates can grant a warrant of further detention for up to a further 60 hours – making a total of 96 hours (ss 43 and 44). However, the police could not be granted the 60-hour period as a whole because the maximum extension that a magistrates' court can grant at one time is 36 hours (ss 43(12) and 44).

The magistrates can only grant such extensions if the offence being investigated is an indictable offence and is being investigated diligently and expeditiously. Moreover, it must be shown that the further detention is necessary to secure or preserve evidence relating to an offence for which the suspect is under arrest or to obtain such evidence by questioning them (s 43(4)).

The capacity for extended detention without charge, which has been broadened since the original passage of PACE, assists the police in dealing effectively with a range of offences, for example robbery, where it will sometimes be extremely difficult or impossible to complete the necessary investigatory processes within 24 hours.

Section 38 states that, *after being charged*, the arrested person must be released with or without bail, unless:

- it is necessary to hold them so that their name and address can be obtained; or
- in the case of a person arrested for an imprisonable offence, the custody officer has reasonable grounds for believing that the detention of the person arrested is necessary to prevent them from committing an offence, if they have been arrested for an imprisonable offence; or
- the custody officer reasonably thinks that it is necessary to hold them for their own protection or to prevent them from causing physical injury to anyone or from causing loss of or damage to property; or
- the custody officer reasonably thinks that they need to be held because they would otherwise fail to answer bail or to prevent them from interfering with witnesses or otherwise obstructing the course of justice; or
- the custody officer believes that it is necessary for them to be detained in order that a sample under s 63B can be obtained; or
- they are a juvenile and ought to be held in their 'own interests'.

If the suspect is charged and not released, they will have to be brought before a magistrates' court 'as soon as practicable' – and not later than the first sitting after being charged (s 46(2)).

Custody officer

Under s 39 PACE, the custody officer has responsibility for ensuring that treatment at the police station complies with PACE and the codes of practice and has some decision-making powers in relation to detention, release and eventual charging (see Chapter 11).

The right to have someone informed

The right to have someone informed after arrest is given to all suspects after arrest (s 56 PACE). It can be delayed for up to 36 hours, however, if the case involves an indictable offence and it must be authorised by an inspector on certain grounds; for example, the arrested person would alert others involved in a crime.

Access to legal advice

Access to legal advice is provided for under s 58 and Code C. The notification must accord with details set out in Code C. Legal advice can be delayed if authorised by a superintendent on various grounds. In certain circumstances, questioning can begin before the detainee's legal adviser arrives.

Basic rights during detention

Code C, paras 8–9 and 12 cover basic rights to food, drink, sleep and an interpreter during detention, including interviews.

Searches at the police station

Searches of people detained at police stations are governed by s 54 PACE 1984 and Code C. Section 54 and Code C, para 4.1 require the custody officer (a particular officer with special responsibilities in police stations) to take charge of the process of searching detainees. He or she must ascertain what the suspect has with them unless they are to be detained for only a short time and not put in a cell. The person detained can be searched to enable this to happen, but the custody officer needs to believe it to be necessary; it is not an automatic right (s 54(6)). Anything the detainee has can be seized and retained, although clothes and personal effects can only be kept if the custody officer *believes* that the detained person *may* use them to escape, interfere with evidence, or cause damage or injury to themselves, to others or to property (s 54(4)). The police are not permitted, however, to retain anything protected by legal professional privilege, that is, private legal communications between the detainee and their legal adviser. The police can also seize things they *reasonably believe* to be evidence of an offence. A search must be carried out by a constable who is the same sex as the person to be searched. Strip searches can only be made where the custody officer thinks it necessary to get some item that the detainee would not be allowed to keep. The officer must make a record of the reason for the search and its result. Section 8 CJA removed the requirement of the custody officer to record or cause to be recorded everything a detained person has with him on entering custody. The custody officer is under a duty to ascertain what the person has with them, but the nature and detail of any recording is at the custody officer's discretion. They also have a discretion as to whether the record is kept as part of the custody record or as a separate record.

   Part V of PACE also includes a wide range of powers to take, for example, fingerprints, footwear impressions and both intimate and non-intimate samples, and details when this may be done without consent. The destruction, retention and use of those samples and DNA evidence derived from them has been very controversial given the massive scientific strides in this area. In *S and Marper v UK* (2009) the ECtHR held that, contrary to the House of Lords' earlier decision, holding DNA samples of people who were arrested but later acquitted or had the charges against them dropped was a violation of the right to privacy under Art 8 ECHR. The Protection of Freedoms Act 2012 introduced a new regime to govern this, which has been added to PACE as ss 63D – 63U. This is a complex regime. It is fully discussed and its compliance with Art 8 considered in Cape (2013) 'The Protection of Freedoms Act 2012: the retention and use of biometric data provisions' *Crim LR* 23.

The Policing and Crime Act 2017 extended the existing rules on retention of DNA and fingerprints of those with convictions in England and Wales to those with convictions elsewhere.

10.5.3 ANSWERING POLICE QUESTIONS AND THE RIGHT TO SILENCE

The police are free to ask anyone any questions. The only restriction is that all questioning is supposed to cease once a detainee has been charged. Code C, para 11.6 states that:

> The interview or further interview of a person about an offence with which that person has not been charged or for which they have not been informed they may be prosecuted must cease when the officer in charge of the investigation:
>
> (a) is satisfied all the questions they consider relevant to obtaining accurate and reliable information about the offence have been put to the suspect, this includes allowing the suspect an opportunity to give an innocent explanation and asking questions to test if the explanation is accurate and reliable, eg, to clear up ambiguities or clarify what the suspect said;
>
> (b) has taken account of any other available evidence; and
>
> (c) the officer in charge of the investigation, or in the case of a detained suspect, the custody officer, see *paragraph 16.1*, reasonably believes there is sufficient evidence to provide a realistic prospect of conviction for that offence if the person was prosecuted for it. See Note 11B.

This paragraph does not prevent officers in revenue cases or acting under the confiscation provisions of the Criminal Justice Act 1988 or the Drug Trafficking Act 1994 from inviting suspects to complete a formal question and answer record after the interview is concluded.

There is no *obligation* on a citizen to answer police questions. A person cannot be charged, for example, with obstructing the police in the execution of their duty simply by failing to answer questions. Although a judge or prosecutor cannot suggest to the jury that such silence is evidence of guilt, adverse inferences might be drawn in court from a defendant's earlier refusal to answer police questions if he or she has been given the police caution (see below – s 34 of the CJPOA 1994). 'Adverse inferences' can be drawn, the logic runs, on the basis that failure to answer questions suggests there is something to hide, or there is no explanatory, adequate answer. What is clear, however, is that a conviction cannot be founded on silence alone in the absence of any other evidence. Judges seem to have interpreted this section rather narrowly. Lord Bingham CJ, for example, said in *R v Bowden* (1999):

> Proper effect must of course be given to these provisions . . . But since they restrict rights recognised at common law as appropriate to protect defendants against the risk of injustice, they should not be construed more widely than the statutory language allows.

In *Rice v Connolly* (1966), the appellant was seen by officers in the early hours of the morning behaving suspiciously in an area where house-breaking had taken place on the same evening. On being questioned, he refused to say where he was going or where he had come from. He refused to give his full name and address, though he did give a name and the name of a road which were not untrue. He refused to accompany the officer to a police box for identification purposes, saying: 'If you want me, you'll have to arrest me.' He was arrested and charged with wilfully obstructing a police officer contrary to s 51(3) of the Police Act 1964.

His appeal against conviction succeeded. Lord Parker CJ noted that the police officer was acting within his duty in inquiring about the appellant and that what the appellant did was obstructive. The critical question, though, was whether the appellant's conduct was 'wilful' within the meaning of s 51. Lord Parker CJ, in the Divisional Court, took that word to mean 'intentional [and] without lawful excuse'. He continued:

> It seems to me quite clear that, though every citizen has a moral duty or, if you like, a social duty to assist the police, there is no legal duty to that effect, and, indeed, the whole basis of the common law is the right of the individual to refuse to answer questions put to him by persons in authority, and to refuse to accompany those in authority to any particular place; short, of course, of arrest.

The court was unanimous, although one judge, James J, cautioned that he would not go as far as to say that silence coupled with conduct could not amount to obstruction. It would depend on the particular facts of any given case.

There are certain circumstances where the citizen is under a duty to answer police questions. Where a constable has reasonable grounds for believing that a vehicle has been involved in an accident and he seeks the particulars of the driver, he or she may arrest that person if the information is not given. With the Home Secretary's consent, and on the authority of a chief constable, coercive questioning (that is, where a suspect's silence can be used in evidence against him) can be used in matters under s 11 (as amended) of the Official Secrets Act 1920. There are also wide powers under the Companies Acts to require officers and agents of companies to assist inspectors appointed to investigate the company.

Under s 2 of the CJA 1987, the Director of the Serious Fraud Office (SFO) (dealing with frauds worth over £5 million) can require anyone whom he or she has reason to think has relevant information to attend to answer questions and to provide information including documents and books. Such statements, however, cannot be used in evidence against the persons who make them unless they go into the witness box and give inconsistent testimony. Even this power, though, does not require the breach of legal professional privilege. Failure to comply with s 2 requests is a criminal offence and can result in an application for a magistrates' search warrant. These powers have been widely used. The SFO Annual Report for 2013–14 revealed that 18 defendants' cases had been prosecuted, amounting to eight trials, with an 85 per cent conviction rate at trial (*Serious Fraud Office Annual Report and Accounts 2013–14*, available at www.sfo.gov.uk). In *R v Director of the Serious Fraud Office ex p Smith* (1993), the House of Lords held that the SFO could compel a person to answer questions relating to an offence with which he or she had already been charged. It followed that in relation to such questions, the suspect did not have to be further cautioned.

Other powers to compel answers on pain of penalties for refusal exist under the Terrorism Act 2000, and refusal to answer certain allegations from the prosecutor can be treated as acceptance of them under the Drug Trafficking Act 1994.

The closest English law comes to creating a duty to give one's name and address is in s 24(5)(a) and (b) of PACE, where the need to ascertain the name and address of a suspect is one of the reasons why an arrest may be lawful.

There is no duty to offer information about crime to the police. However, s 19 of the Terrorism Act 2000 makes it an offence for a person who believes or suspects that another person has committed an offence under any of ss 15–18 (offences involving funding of terrorism), and bases their belief or suspicion on information that comes to their attention in the course of a trade, profession, business or employment to not disclose to an officer as soon as is reasonably practicable their belief or suspicion, and the information on which it is based. Additionally, s 5 of the CLA 1967 creates the offence of accepting money or other consideration for not disclosing information that would lead to the prosecution of a relevant offence.

There is an established common law rule that neither the prosecution nor the judge should make adverse comment on the defendant's silence in the face of questions. The dividing line, however, between proper and improper judicial comment has been a matter of great debate. In Scotland, a trial judge may not comment on a defendant's failure to answer questions. It is suggested that the position in England and Wales, whereby a judge may comment, not only undermines the right to silence but also provides fertile ground for judicial misdirections to the jury, in turn increasing the opportunities for appeal on points that arise simply in default of lack of judicial restraint. There are many reasons why a suspect might remain silent when questioned (for example fear, confusion, reluctance to incriminate another person) and the 'right to silence' enjoyed the status of a long-established general principle in English law. Thus, in *R v Davis* (1959), a judge was ruled on appeal to have misdirected the jury when he told them that 'a man is not obliged to say anything but you are entitled to use your common sense . . . [C]an you imagine an innocent man who had behaved like that not saying anything to the police . . . He said nothing.'

An exception, though, was that some degree of adverse suggestion was permitted where two people were speaking on equal terms and one refused to comment on the accusation made against them by the other. In *R v Parkes* (1974), the Privy Council ruled that a judge could invite the jury to consider the possibility of drawing adverse inferences from silence from a tenant who had been accused by a landlady of murdering her daughter. The landlady and tenant, for the purposes of this encounter, were regarded as having a parity of status, unlike a person faced with questions from the police. It was held in *R v Chandler* (1976) that the suspect was on equal terms with the police officer where the former was in the company of his solicitor. Chandler had refused to answer some of the questions he had been asked by the police officer before the caution. The judge told the jury that they should decide whether the defendant's silence was attributable to his wish to exercise his common law right or because he might incriminate himself. The Court of Appeal quashed Chandler's conviction since the judge had gone too far in suggesting that silence before a caution could be evidence of guilt.

It was proper for the judge to make some comment on a defendant's reticence before being cautioned, provided that the jury were directed that the issue had to be dealt with in two stages: (i) was the defendant's silence an acceptance of the officer's allegations?; and, if so, (ii) could guilt of the offence charged be reasonably inferred from what the defendant had implicitly accepted? The court said that it did not accept that a police officer always had an advantage over a suspect. Everything depended on the circumstances. In an inquiry into local government corruption, for example, a young officer might be at a distinct disadvantage when questioning a local dignitary. That type of interview was very different from a 'tearful housewife' being accused of shoplifting.

The Court of Appeal's decision in *Chandler* asserted that silence might only be taken as acquiescence to police allegations before a caution. The court excluded silence after the caution as being something from which anything adverse can be inferred, because a suspect could not be criticised for remaining silent having been specifically told of that right. This, however, seemed like an irrational dichotomy. If the suspect did, in fact, have a legal right to silence whether or not they had been cautioned, it was very odd that full enjoyment of the right could be effective only from the moment of it being announced by the police. Additionally, any questioning of a suspect at a police station prior to a caution being given was probably in contravention of Code C, para 10, which requires a caution to be given at the beginning of each session of questioning. Violation of the Code affords grounds for an appeal under s 78 of PACE 1984. Cautions need not be given according to para 10.1:

> . . . if questions are for other necessary purposes, eg:
>
> (a)   solely to establish their own identity or ownership of any vehicle;
> (b)   to obtain information in accordance with any relevant statutory requirement, see *paragraph 10.9*;
> (c)   in furtherance of the proper and effective control of a search, eg, to determine the need to search in the exercise of powers of stop and search or to seek co-operation while carrying out a search . . .

These cases must now all be read in the light of s 34 of the CJPOA 1994.

10.5.6   RIGHT TO SILENCE IN COURTS

Before the changes to the right to silence that were made by the CJPOA 1994, the value of maintaining the traditional approach was subjected to considerable scrutiny. From 1988, the right to silence was effectively abolished in Northern Ireland. It became possible for a court to draw adverse inferences from a defendant's silence when they were arrested. Adverse inferences could also be drawn from the defendant's failure to provide an explanation for any 'object, substance or mark' on their clothing, footwear or in their possession, which the arresting officer found suspicious and questioned the suspect about (Criminal Justice (Evidence etc.) (Northern Ireland) Order 1988).

Similar recommendations were made by the Home Office Working Group on the Right to Silence in 1989. The question was also considered by the Runciman Royal Commission on Criminal Justice. It had to decide whether to adopt a practice like the Northern Ireland system and the one recommended by the Home Office, or whether to retain the right to silence, as the Philips Royal Commission on Criminal Procedure had recommended in 1981. In evidence to the Runciman Royal Commission, the proposal to retain the right to silence was supported by The Law Society, the Bar Council and the Magistrates' Association. It was opposed by the police, the CPS, HM Council of Circuit Judges and several senior judges.

Professor Michael Zander's research on this issue suggested that the role of the right to silence in the real workings of the criminal justice system was in fact not as significant as often argued. In one of his studies, 'Investigation of crime' [1979] Crim LR 211, he looked at 150 cases randomly drawn from those heard at the Old Bailey. According to police statements, of the 286 defendants (in many cases there was more than one defendant), only 12 were said to have relied on their right to silence when confronted by police accusations. Of these, nine were convicted. Zander has also made the following points:

- Most defendants plead guilty, so the right to silence is unimportant in such a context.

- Common law rules permit the judge to *mention* the defendant's silence and, in some limited circumstances, to comment on it.

- In any event, the jury may draw adverse conclusions about the defendant's silence to police questions, that is, whether the judge is permitted to comment on this or not.

The Runciman Royal Commission eventually decided to recommend retaining the right to silence. Its Report (1993) states (para 82):

> The majority of us believe that adverse inferences should not be drawn from silence at the police station and recommend retaining the present caution and trial direction.

The Commission did, however, recommend (para 84) the retention of the current law regarding silence in investigations of serious and complex fraud under which adverse consequences can follow from silence. The Report notes that a large proportion of those who use the right to silence later plead guilty. The majority of the Commission felt that the possibility of an increase in convicting the guilty by abolishing the right would be outweighed by the considerable extra pressure on innocent suspects in police stations. The Commission did, however, meet the police and CPS concern about 'ambush defences', where a defence is entered late in a trial, thus leaving the prosecution no time to check and rebut the defence. The Commission recommended that if the defence introduces a late change or departs from the strategy it has disclosed in advance to the prosecution, then it should face adverse comment (para 136). Professor Zander, however, issued a note of dissent that the principle must remain that the burden of proof always lies with the prosecution. He stated:

> The fundamental issue at stake is that the burden of proof throughout lies with the prosecution. Defence disclosure is designed to be helpful to the prosecution and, more generally, to the system. But, it is not the job of the defendant to be helpful either to the prosecution or the system.

Since the abolition of the court of Star Chamber in 1641, no English court has had the power to use torture or force to exact confessions from suspects. The so-called right to silence really meant that a suspect could remain silent when questioned by police or in court without prosecution counsel or the judge being allowed to make adverse comment to the jury about such a silence. Traditionally, silence could not be used in court as evidence of guilt.

The government ignored the recommendations of the Runciman Commission and, in ss 34–37 of the CJPOA 1994, curtailed the right to silence. Everyone still has the right to remain silent in the same circumstances as they did before the CJPOA 1994, but what changed was the entitlement of a judge or prosecuting counsel to make adverse comment on such a silence.

Notwithstanding the 1994 Act, therefore, any person may refuse to answer questions put to him or her out of court. There are only a few exceptions to this (as with s 2 of the CJA 1987, which concerns the investigation of serious fraud, and requires certain questions to be answered under pain of punishment for refusal) and they existed before the Act. The CJPOA 1994 does not alter the position of the accused person as a witness – he or she remains a competent but not compellable witness in his or her own defence (s 35), although now the prosecution as well as the judge may comment upon such a failure to give evidence (s 168).

Except in so far as the new law makes changes, the old law still applies.

In enacting ss 34–37 of the CJPOA 1994, the government was adopting a particular policy. The general purpose of the Act was to assist in the fight against crime. The government took the view that the balance in the criminal justice system had become tilted too far in favour of the criminal and against the public in general, and victims in particular. The alleged advantage of the change in law was that it helped convict criminals who, under the old law, used to be acquitted because they took advantage of the right to keep quiet when questioned without the court or prosecution being able to comment adversely upon that silence. Introducing the legislation, the Home Secretary said that change in law was desirable because 'it is professional criminals, hardened criminals and terrorists who disproportionately take advantage of and abuse the present system'. There was also a feeling that defendants would wait until the last possible moment to formulate their defence, effectively 'ambushing' the prosecution.

Section 34 states that where anyone is questioned under caution by a police officer, or charged with an offence, then a failure to mention a fact at that time which he or she later relies on in his or her defence will allow a court to draw such inferences as appear proper about that failure. Inferences may only be drawn if, in the circumstances, a suspect could reasonably have been expected to mention the fact when he or she was questioned. The inferences that can be drawn can be used in determining whether the accused is guilty as charged. The section, however, permits adverse inferences to be drawn from silence in situations that do not amount to 'interviews' as defined by Code C of PACE 1984, and thus which are not subject to the safeguards of access to legal advice and of contemporaneous recording that exist where a suspect is interviewed at the police station. The caution to be administered by police officers is as follows (with appropriate variants for ss 36 and 37):

You do not have to say anything. But, it may harm your defence if you do not mention when questioned something which you later rely on in court. Anything you do say may be given in evidence.

Section 58 of the Youth Justice and Criminal Evidence Act (YJCEA) 1999 amended s 34 by adding a new s 34(2A). This restricted the drawing of inferences from silence in an interview at a police station (or similar venue) where the suspect was not allowed an opportunity to consult a solicitor prior to being questioned or charged (see Code D, Annex C). This amendment was intended to meet the ruling of the ECtHR in *Murray v UK* (1996) that delay in access to legal advice, even if lawful, could amount to a breach of Art 6, given the risk of adverse inferences being drawn.

An interesting illustration of the principle at work can be found in *R v Maguire (Glen)* (2008). The appellant offender (M) appealed against his conviction for two offences of wounding contrary to the Offences Against the Person Act 1861 s 20. M was accused, following an argument in a public house, first, of committing an unprovoked attack on a victim in a street with a rice flail, which he had allegedly taken from his pocket, and, second, of emerging from his house with a meat cleaver later the same evening, with which he struck a second victim on the arm. M gave two different accounts of the evening's events, one during a police interview and the other in evidence at the trial. Both versions raised the issue of self-defence. On the Crown's application, the trial judge gave a direction under the Criminal Justice and Public Order Act 1994 s 34 in conventional form, in which he identified two sets of facts on which M had relied at trial but which he had not mentioned in police interview, namely (i) that there had been no real gap between the incidents, that he had been confronted by a mob of people outside his house and that his need to act in self-defence arose at the same time in fending off what was a joint attack by the purported victims, and (ii) that, having emerged from his house, he was naked when obliged to confront the mob. M was convicted but appealed, saying his convictions were unsafe because the judge was wrong to give a direction under s 34 of the 1994 Act.

His appeal was dismissed. The Court of Appeal ruled that:

With or without such a direction, the Crown's case was plainly going to be that M's evidence had been shown to be untruthful, partly by other contradictory evidence in the case, and also by the way that his account had changed. The judge was virtually certain to refer to it, and he would no doubt have told the jury that it was up to them to say whether the explanation for the change in account might be an innocent one, or whether it was that M's evidence was untruthful. The s 34 direction was a formalised way of saying precisely the same. Section 34 did no more than seek to apply common sense.

Such a direction always raised the question whether the omission to refer to something in interview which appeared later in evidence was or was not an indication that the new material was untruthful. The object of the section and of the direction was to enable the jury to decide that question. In the instant case, the matters identified by the judge were capable of being facts within the meaning of s 34, but even if they were not, the judge's direction would have been substantially the same. The fact that the s 34 direction included the proposition that the jury were entitled to infer some additional support for the Crown from the change of evidence did not alter that. The jury had had the issues which arose in the case properly before them, and the convictions were safe.

The court also said that prosecutors should be cautious about too readily seeking to invite formalised directions under s 34. Anything that over-formalised common sense was to be discouraged.

Section 35 allows a court or jury to infer what appears proper from the refusal of an accused person to testify in his or her own defence, or from a refusal without good cause to answer any question at trial. In para 39.P. 2 of the *Criminal Practice Direction* (2013) ([2013] EWCA Crim 1631), the Lord Chief Justice indicates that where the accused is legally represented, the following should be said by the judge to the accused's lawyer at the end of the prosecution case if the accused is not to give evidence:

Have you advised your client that the stage has now been reached at which he may give evidence and, if he chooses not to do so or, having been sworn, without good cause refuses to answer any question, the jury may draw such inferences as appear proper from his failure to do so?

If the lawyer replies to the judge that the accused has been so advised, then the case will proceed. If the accused is not represented, and still chooses not to give evidence or answer a question, the judge must give him a similar warning, ending: '. . . the jury may draw such inferences as appear proper. That means they may hold it against you.'

Section 36 permits inferences to be drawn from the failure or refusal of a person under arrest to account for any object, substances or mark in their possession, on their person, in or on their clothing or footwear, or in any place at which they are at the time of arrest. Section 37 permits inferences to be drawn from the failure of an arrested person to account for their presence at a particular place where they are found.

Thus, as the late Lord Taylor, the then Lord Chief Justice, observed, the legal changes do not, strictly speaking, abolish the right to silence:

> If a defendant maintains his silence from first till last, and does not rely on any particular fact by way of defence, but simply puts the prosecution to proof, then [ss 34–37] would not bite at all.

The change was widely and strongly opposed by lawyers, judges and legal campaign groups. Liberty, for example, said that drawing adverse inferences from silence undermines the presumption of innocence. Silence is an important safeguard against oppressive questioning by the police, particularly for the weak and vulnerable.

John Alderson, former chief constable of Devon and Cornwall (1973–82) and a respected writer on constitutional aspects of policing, has written of the impending danger when police are able to 'exert legal and psychological pressure on individuals held in the loneliness of their cells'. He stated (*The Independent*, 1 February 1995) that:

> History tells us that, when an individual has to stand up against the entire apparatus of the modern State, he or she is very vulnerable. That is why, in criminal cases, the burden of proof has always rested on the State rather than on the accused. The Founding Fathers of America amended their constitution to that effect in 1791.

An example might be persons detained indefinitely at the Home Secretary's discretion at HMP Belmarsh and HMP Woodhill (see J Cooper, 'Guantanamo Bay, London' (2004) 154 NLJ 41).

Undermining the right to silence may constitute a significant constitutional change in the relationship between the individual and the state. It may be doubted whether the majority of suspects should be put under greater intimidation by the system because of the conduct of a few 'hardened criminals' – the justification for the legislation given by the then Home Secretary when he introduced it.

10.5.8   DIRECTIONS TO THE JURY ON SILENT DEFENDANTS

Following the enactment of the CJPOA 1994, there has been a steady stream of case law about the correct judicial practice when directing the jury about the drawing of adverse inferences under ss 34 and 35.

In *R v Cowan* (1995), the Court of Appeal considered what should be said in the summing up if the defendant decides not to testify. The jury must be directed that (as provided by s 38(3) of the CJPOA 1994) an inference from failure to give evidence could not on its own prove guilt. The jury had to be satisfied (on the basis of the evidence called by the prosecution) that the prosecution had established a case to answer before inferences could be drawn from the accused's silence. The jury could only draw an adverse inference from the accused's silence if that silence could only be sensibly attributed to the accused having no answer to the charge or none that could stand up to cross-examination.

The difficult issue as to correct judicial practice when the accused remains silent during interview on the advice of his or her solicitor was considered in three cases – *R v Beckles* (2004), *R v Hoare & Pierce* (2004) and *R v Howell* (2005). The Court of Appeal arrived at the following position:

- Where an accused gives evidence that they remained silent on the advice of their solicitor, the question for the jury/court is whether – in the situation existing at the time – it is reasonable to expect the accused to have mentioned the relevant fact(s).

- The fact that the court/jury accepts that the accused genuinely relied on legal advice when staying silent and not revealing facts that are subsequently relied on in court does not mean that the jury are obliged to conclude that it was reasonable for the accused not to mention those facts.

- A court might be more likely to conclude that reliance on legal advice not to put forward facts was reasonable if there was a sound foundation for it – examples being: little or no police disclosure; the case is too complex or too old to expect immediate answers from the accused; the accused has personal problems (for example, mental disability, shock, intoxication).

- A court might be less likely to conclude that reliance on legal advice not to put forward facts was reasonable if the advice was not based on a sound foundation – examples that The Law Society Guidance sets out are: a belief that the detention is unlawful; the victim has not made a written statement; a belief that the victim might withdraw the complaint; a belief that the police will charge anyway, whatever the accused says.

Where, however, a judge concludes that the requirements of s 34 have not been satisfied and therefore that it is not open to him or her to leave to the jury the possibility of drawing adverse inferences, he or she must direct the jury that it should not in any way hold against the accused the fact that they did not answer questions in interview (*R v McGarry* (1998)).

The provisions as to silence must also meet the requirements of Art 6 of the ECHR. The ECtHR held in *Murray v UK* (1996) that this right is not absolute and that a system under which inferences could be drawn from silence did not in itself constitute a breach of Art 6, though particular caution when drawing inferences was necessary. This was reaffirmed in *Condron v UK* (2001), where the Court asserted that though silence could not be the only, or even the main, basis for any conviction, it was right that it should be taken into account in circumstances which clearly called for an explanation from the accused (examples might be having to account for presence at the scene of the crime, or having to account for the presence of fibres on clothing). It should be noted that although the specimen direction issued by the Judicial Studies Board (JSB) and used by judges emphasises that silence cannot be the only basis for a conviction, it does not make any reference to whether it can be the *main basis* for conviction. Thus, there is a possible conflict between the approach under the ECHR and that currently adopted in English courts.

The ECtHR considers that legal advice is of great significance in this system. Thus, both *Murray v UK* and *Condron v UK* stressed the importance of access to legal advice at the time of any interview. As explained earlier, the finding in *Murray v UK* that denial of access to legal advice, in conjunction with the drawing of inferences, amounted to a breach of Art 6 led to the amendment to the CJPOA 1994 contained in s 34(2A). However, access in itself is not the end of the matter. The question which then arises is whether the drawing of inferences may be improper under the ECHR where silence results from legal advice, as discussed above. The ECtHR held in both *Condron v UK* and *Averill v UK* (2000) that legal advice may be a proper reason for declining to answer questions and that it may not be fair to draw adverse inferences in such cases. A solicitor representing a young or otherwise vulnerable person may recognise that the evidence against the client is very weak. Advising such a client to 'say nothing' will often make good sense (see A Keogh, 'The right to silence – revisited again' (2003) 153 NLJ 1352).

The jury should be informed that no adverse inference should be drawn where a defendant 'genuinely and reasonably' relies on a solicitor's advice to remain silent in interview (*R v Beckles* (2004)).

In *R v Robert Webber* (2004), the House of Lords decided that, for the purposes of working out whether a silent defendant in court was 'relying on a fact' used in their defence (and therefore something that could prompt the judge to allow the jury to draw adverse inferences about the defendant's silence), answers given by a witness for the prosecution who was being cross-questioned by the defendant's counsel were facts.

A positive suggestion put to a witness by or on behalf of a defendant could amount to a fact relied on in their defence for the purpose of s 34 of the CJPOA 1994, even if that suggestion was not accepted by a witness.

The defendant (W) appealed from a decision (summarised below) that the trial judge was correct to give a direction under s 34 of the CJPOA 1994. W and two codefendants had been charged with conspiracy to murder. The prosecution case against W was based on three incidents. When interviewed by police about each incident, W had either denied involvement in any conspiracy or said that he was not present. At trial, W's counsel put it to several prosecution witnesses that their evidence relating to the incidents was wrong. The witnesses rejected counsel's suggestions. The certified question for the House of Lords was whether a suggestion put to a witness by or on behalf of a defendant could amount to a 'fact relied on in his defence' for the purpose of s 34 of the Act, if that suggestion was not adopted by the witness. W submitted that s 34 was directed to evidence and that suggestions of counsel were not evidence unless or until accepted by a witness. The prosecution submitted that such suggestions were matters on which a defendant relied, whether or not they supported them by their own or other evidence, and whether or not prosecution witnesses accepted them.

The court held that a positive suggestion put to a witness by or on behalf of a defendant could amount to a fact relied on in his or her defence for the purpose of s 34 even if that suggestion was not accepted by a witness. The word 'fact' in s 34 covered any alleged fact that was in issue and was put forward as part of the defence case. If the defendant advanced at trial any pure fact or exculpatory explanation or account that, if true, he or she could reasonably have been expected to advance earlier, s 34 was potentially applicable. A defendant relied on a fact or matter in their defence not only when they gave or adduced evidence of it, but also when counsel, acting on their instructions, put a specific and positive case to prosecution witnesses, as opposed to asking questions intended to probe or test the prosecution case. That was so, whether or not the prosecution witness accepted the suggestion put. The appeal was dismissed.

10.5.9   TAPE-RECORDING OF INTERROGATIONS

The police were initially very hostile to the recommendation of the Philips Royal Commission on Criminal Procedure that there should be tape-recording of interviews with suspects. After a while, however, the police became more enthusiastic when it became apparent that the tape-recording of the interrogations increased the proportion of guilty pleas and reduced the challenges to prosecution evidence. Tape-recording of interviews is conducted in accordance with Code of Practice E. The tapes are time-coded so that they cannot be interfered with. It is compulsory for all police stations to record all interviews with suspects interrogated in connection with indictable offences and tape-recordings are used as a matter of course with all offences where an interview is held.

10.5.10   CONFESSIONS AND THE ADMISSIBILITY OF EVIDENCE

It was long established by the common law that a confession would not be admitted in evidence if it was 'involuntary', in the sense that it was obtained by threat or promise held out by a person in authority. This would include 'even the most gentle, if I may put it that way, threats or slight inducements', per Lord Parker CJ in *R v Smith* (1959). In that case, a sergeant major had put the whole company on parade and told them no one would be allowed to move until one of them gave details about which of them had been involved in a fight resulting in a stabbing. A confession resulting from this incident was ruled to have been something that should not have been admitted (although the conviction was not quashed as there was other evidence against the defendant).

In *R v Zavekas* (1970), a conviction was quashed where it had resulted from an improper promise. Z was told that the police were arranging an identification parade and that he would be free to go if he was not picked out. He asked whether he could be allowed to go at once if he made a statement. The officer agreed and then Z made a statement admitting guilt. The admission was given in evidence and Z was convicted. His conviction was quashed even though the inducement had not been proffered by the police. Similarly, the Court of Appeal regarded it as a 'fatal inducement' for a police officer to have agreed to a request by the defendant, in *R v Northam* (1968), for a second offence to be taken into account at a forthcoming trial rather than tried as a separate matter.

Apart from threats and promises, 'oppression' leading to a confession would render such a statement inadmissible. The Judges' Rules were a set of guidelines made by Divisional Court judges for excluding unreliable evidence, but they left it as discretionary whether violation of the rules should result in the exclusion of any resultant evidence.

The law is now contained in s 76 of PACE 1984, which renders inadmissible any confession (i) obtained as a result of oppression (s 76(2)(a)) or (ii) which was obtained in consequence of something 'likely in the circumstances to render unreliable any confession which might be made by the accused in consequence thereof' (s 76(2)(b)).

'Oppression' is defined by s 76(8) to include 'torture, inhuman or degrading treatment, and the use or threat of violence'.

10.5.11 OPPRESSION

The judge rules on whether evidence is admissible on these lines: if it is admitted, then the jury decides whether to believe it. There should be a 'trial within a trial' – without the jury – to determine whether the evidence is admissible (*R v Liverpool Juvenile Court ex p R* (1988)).

The courts have not found much evidence of 'oppression' in police questioning. In *Miller* (1986), a paranoid schizophrenic had confessed to killing his girlfriend. He had admitted the killing in an interview which contained both reliable and unreliable matter. He later retracted his confession. It was argued for him at trial that the confession should be excluded under s 76(2)(a) – that it had been obtained by 'oppression of the person who made it', as it had come as the result of protracted and oppressive interviews that had caused him to suffer an episode of 'schizophrenic terror'. Medical evidence was given that the style and length of questioning had produced a state of voluntary insanity in which his language reflected hallucinations and delusion. The judge would not exclude the evidence and the defendant was convicted of manslaughter. The Court of Appeal held that the mere fact that questions triggered off hallucinations in the defendant was not evidence of oppression.

In *R v Fulling* (1987), the Court of Appeal held that it was not oppression for the police to tell the defendant that her lover had been having an affair with another woman, which so affected her that she made a confession. The word 'oppression', the court held, should be given its ordinary dictionary meaning as stated in the *Oxford English Dictionary*:

> The exercise of authority or power in a burdensome, harsh or wrongful manner; unjust or cruel treatment of subjects, inferiors, etc; the imposition of unreasonable or unjust burdens.

In *R v Anthony Paris*, *R v Yusuf Abdullahi* and *R v Stephen Wayne Miller* (1993), it was held that it was perfectly legitimate for police officers to pursue their interrogation of a suspect with the intention of eliciting an account or gaining admissions, and they were not required to give up after the first denial or even a number of denials. However, it was undoubtedly oppressive within the meaning of s 76(2) of the Police and Criminal Evidence Act 1984 to shout at a suspect. That had occurred in the case of *Miller*, after he had denied involvement over 300 times. Thus the confessions obtained were unreliable, particularly in view of the fact that Miller was on the borderline of mental handicap. Accordingly, considering the tenor and length of the police interviews, those interviews ought not to have been admitted in evidence.

10.5.12   UNRELIABILITY

Evidence of a confession can be excluded if it was given:

> . . . in consequence of anything said or done which was likely in the circumstances existing at the time, to render unreliable any confession which might be made by him in consequence thereof . . . (s 76(2)(b)).

The phrase 'anything said or done' means by someone other than the suspect. In *R v Goldenberg* (1988), G, a heroin addict, was arrested on a charge of conspiracy to supply diamorphine. He requested an interview five days after his arrest and during this he gave information about a man who he said had supplied him with heroin. It was argued for G at trial that he had given the statement to get bail and thus to be able to feed his addiction. G contended that the words 'in consequence of anything said or done' included things said or done by the suspect and that the critical things here were the things G had said and done, namely, requested the interview and given any statement that would be likely to get him out of the station. G was convicted and his appeal was dismissed. Neill LJ stated:

> In our judgment, the words 'said or done' in s 76(2)(b) of the 1984 Act do not extend so as to include anything said or done by the person making the confession. It is clear from the wording of the section and the use of the words 'in consequence' that a causal link must be shown between what was said or done and the subsequent confession. In our view, it necessarily follows that 'anything said or done' is limited to something external to the person making the confession and to something which is likely to have some influence on him.

The reasoning in cases like *R v Zavekas* (see above) has now clearly been rejected. This view is confirmed by Code C; if a suspect asks an officer what action will be taken in the event of their answering questions, making a statement or refusing to do either, the officer may inform them what action he or she proposes to take in that event 'provided that the action is itself proper and warranted' (para 11.5).

'Confessions' made to fellow prisoners are particularly controversial. In 1996, Lin, Megan and Josie Russell were attacked while taking their dog for a walk. Lin and Megan were killed; Josie suffered serious injuries. Michael Stone was arrested and charged with the murders. He was then remanded into custody. At his trial in 1998, two fellow inmates, Damien Daley and Harry Thompson, were called as witnesses. Both alleged that Stone had 'confessed' to them. Stone was convicted. The next day,

Thompson contacted national newspapers. He said that he had lied in court because of police pressures. In 2001, Stone's convictions were quashed by the Court of Appeal. At his retrial, the prosecution used Daley's evidence and Stone was reconvicted. A strong argument could be made for excluding such dubious evidence under s 78 of PACE. The central problem has been described by Gwyn Morgan in 'Cell confessions' (2002) 152 NLJ 453:

> There may be a strong incentive for 'grasses' to come up with their incriminating stories. Deals may be done with the police as to the withdrawal of charges. Even where this is not the case, those on remand may well feel – even if they are wrong – that giving evidence for the prosecution will ease the way when their own cases come up. And where the grasses are already convicted, they may be anxious (again rightly or wrongly) to give a favourable impression to the prison authorities or the parole board. What's more, in contrast to most witnesses, coming to court does not adversely interfere with their lives; it's a day out.

See also 'Cell confessions – no stone left unturned' (2005) 155 NLJ 550.

10.5.13   CAN A SOLICITOR PROVIDE THE 'SOMETHING SAID OR DONE'?

In *R v Wahab* (2003) the accused was arrested on suspicion that he was involved in a conspiracy to supply drugs. He was interviewed in the presence of his solicitor. After the third interview he authorised his solicitor to approach the police to see whether his family, who were also in custody, might be released if he confessed his guilt. In accordance with those express instructions his solicitor approached the police, who made it clear that no promises could be made or guarantees given. The solicitor told W that if he made admissions, the police would look at the whole picture and that if the evidence against the family was 'borderline', they would be released. At a fourth interview W confessed to his involvement in the conspiracy, but only as a middleman.

The accused dismissed his solicitor and employed a different one for his trial, where he sought the exclusion of the fourth interview. The Court of Appeal held that advice properly given to a defendant by his solicitor did not normally provide a basis for excluding a subsequent confession under s 76(2) of the PACE 1984. The Court further held that one of the duties of a legal adviser, whether at a police station, or indeed at a pre-trial conference, or during the trial itself, is to give the client realistic advice. That emphatically did not mean that the advice had to be directed to 'getting the client off', or simply making life difficult for the prosecution; though it had to be sensibly robust considering the advantages that the client might derive from evidence of remorse and a realistic acceptance of guilt, or the corresponding disadvantages of participating in a no-comment interview.

At the beginning of the twenty-first century, we can see governmental recognition of the 'criminal justice system'.

REMEDIES

Remedies for unlawful arrest include: (1) an action for *habeas corpus* ; (2) that any subsequent prosecution arising from the arrest should fail – s 78 of the Police and Criminal Evidence Act (PACE) 1984; (3) a claim for damages for false imprisonment. If the arrest is not lawful, then reasonable force may be used to resist it; and (4) judicial review and human rights.

STOP AND SEARCH

Stop and search is governed by s 1 and Code A of PACE 1984. The judge can exclude evidence obtained in breach of the Codes (s 67(7) of PACE 1984). There are legal obligations on an officer conducting a search (ss 2 and 3 of PACE 1984). Note that the Code is quite specific about what indices can be grounds for reasonable suspicion and which, individually or combined, may not.

Section 60 of the Criminal Justice and Public Order Act (CJPOA) 1994 provides a stop and search power in anticipation of violence. Under it, with authorisation, an officer can stop any pedestrian and search them for offensive weapons or dangerous instruments, or even stop vehicles. The authorising officer must reasonably believe that incidents involving serious violence may take place in the area.

ARREST

Arrest can be: (1) under police warrant; (2) under common law for breach of the peace; or (3) under legislation, principally PACE 1984. The details in s 24 PACE 1984 are very important. Detention short of arrest does not exist. Note this confirmation by s 29 of PACE 1984.

SUSPECTS STOPPED IN THE STREET

Suspects stopped in the street are not legally obliged to help police with inquiries. Note the distinction between *Kenlin v Gardiner* (1967) and *Donnelly v Jackman* (1970). Note also that a person may be arrested for being silent or misleading under s 4(5)(a) and (b) if the officer has reasonable doubts about the suspect's name and address.

PROCEDURE ON ARREST

Procedure on arrest involves the arrestor having to inform the suspect of the grounds for arrest (s 28(3)). Note, though, that an arrest becomes lawful from when the information is given. The extent of the required information to the suspect is important (see *Geldberg v Miller* (1961); *R v Telfer* (1976)).

THE USE OF FORCE

The use of force to effect an arrest must be 'reasonable in all the circumstances' (s 3 of the Criminal Law Act 1967 (citizens); s 117 of PACE 1984 (police officers)).

SEARCH OF ARRESTED PERSONS

Search of arrested persons is governed by s 32 of PACE 1984. The person arrested cannot be required to take off more than outer garments. The place where they were arrested, or where they were immediately before, can also be searched under s 32. Note the differences between this power and those under s 18 regarding premises.

INTERROGATION, CONFESSION AND ADMISSIBILITY OF EVIDENCE

The main problem here is for the law to strike the proper balance between giving the police sufficient power to interrogate and protecting the interests of suspects. Too few rules governing how the police can conduct an interrogation and too few rules restricting the sort of evidence that can be put to a jury might easily lead to oppressive behaviour by the police interviewing suspects. Too many restrictive rules, conversely, will thwart the police in their endeavours to prosecute offenders successfully. The general rule in this area is that the courts have discretionary exclusionary powers under s 78 of the 1984 Act (the general overriding exclusionary provision) and s 76 (specifically pertaining to the admissibility of evidence derived from a purported confession by a defendant).

THE RIGHT TO HAVE SOMEONE INFORMED

The right to have someone informed after arrest is given to all suspects after arrest. It can be delayed under certain circumstances.

ACCESS TO LEGAL ADVICE

Access to legal advice is provided for under s 58 and Code C. The notification must accord with details set out in Code C.

TIME LIMITS

Note ss 42 and 38 of PACE 1984 for time limits operational before and after charges. Delayed access to legal advice is possible in cases of serious arrestable offences. A suspect can be held for up to 24 hours without being charged, up to 36 hours with authorisation from the superintendent and up to 96 hours with magistrates' permission.

SEARCH ON DETENTION

Search on detention is governed by s 54 of PACE 1984 and Code C, para 4.1, which require the custody officer to take charge of the process of searching the detained person. There is a complex statutory framework governing the taking, use, destruction and retention of biometric data, introduced into PACE by the Protection of Freedoms Act 2012.

THE RIGHT TO SILENCE

The right to silence means that a person cannot be charged with obstructing the police in the execution of their duty simply by failing to answer questions. Note the important difference between *Rice v Connolly* (1966) and *Ricketts v Cox* (1982). There are some circumstances where the suspect does have to answer on pain of penalty (s 2 of the Criminal Justice Act 1987).

Under ss 34–37 of the CJPOA 1994, certain adverse inferences may be drawn from a suspect's failure to answer police questions, or his failure to answer them in court.

CONFESSIONS

Confessions have proved problematic and may be excluded as evidence under s 76 PACE.

FOOD FOR THOUGHT

1   When a person is detained they have a right to legal advice. But what about the motorist who is pulled over and questioned by police at the side of the road? Or the protestor who is interrogated by the police while he or she is on a march? Should people have a right to legal advice even when their liberty has not been restricted?

2   Arrangements have recently been made for the appointment of directly elected politicians as police commissioners to oversee local police forces and hire and fire chief constables. Does this make the police force more accountable? Or does it compromise the independence of the police by making them serve a political agenda?

3   Do you think that the DNA profiles of individuals who have never been charged, prosecuted or convicted of any offence should be retained?

FURTHER READING

Ashworth, A and Redmayne, M, *The Criminal Process*, 2010, Oxford: OUP
Baldwin, J and McConville, M, *Jury Trials*, 1979, Oxford: Clarendon
Buckland, R, 'Update: police and criminal evidence' (2009) 153(9) SJ 20
Cape, E, 'Police station law and practice update', May (2009) Legal Action 10
Cape, E, 'The Protection of Freedoms Act 2012: the retention and use of biometric data provisions' (2013) Crim LR 23
Committee on Fraud Trials, *Roskill Report*, 1986, London: HMSO
Cragg, S, Murphy, T and Williams, H, 'Police misconduct and the law' (2013) (Oct) Legal Action 23
Crime Survey for England and Wales, Office for National Statistics, July 2014
Darbyshire, P, 'The lamp that shows that freedom lives – is it worth the candle?' (1991) Crim LR 740
Davies, M, Croall, H and Tyrer, J, *Criminal Justice: An Introduction to the Criminal Justice System in England and Wales*, 2010, Harlow: Longman
Devlin, P, *Trial by Jury*, 1956, London: Stevens
Findlay, M and Duff, P, *The Jury Under Attack*, 1988, London: Butterworths
Greer, S, 'The right to silence: defence disclosure and confession evidence' (1994) 21 JLS Office of National Statistics, *Crime in England and Wales 2010/2011*, July 2012

Owusu-Bempah, A, 'Silence in suspicious circumstances' (2014) Crim LR 126

Parpworth, N, 'Under control?' (2008) NLJ 1061

Royal Commission on Criminal Justice, *Runciman Report*, Cm 2263, 1995, London: HMSO

Sanders, A and Young, R, *Criminal Justice*, 2010, Oxford: OUP

Zander, M, 'Out of order' (2008) NLJ 1121

Zander, M, *The Police and Criminal Evidence Act 1984*, 6th edn, 2008, London: Sweet & Maxwell

USEFUL WEBSITES

www.cps.gov.uk/about/cjs.html
The official website of the Criminal Justice System – very useful across a range of subjects.

www.gov.uk/government/organisations/home-office
The website of the Home Office – very useful on matters of policing and crime.

COMPANION WEBSITE

Now visit the companion website to:

- test your understanding of the key terms using our Flashcard Glossary;
- revise and consolidate your knowledge of 'The criminal process: (1) The investigation of crime' using our multiple choice question testbank;
- view all of the links to the Useful Websites above.

www.routledge.com/cw/slapper

11.1 INTRODUCTION

Report and Accounts, 2015–16). The basis for charging is fully explained in the DPP's Guidance on Charging 2013.

Before 1986, there were five different forms of prosecution, those by:

- the police, who prosecuted most offences;

- the Attorney General/Solicitor General, whose permission was needed to prosecute for many serious crimes and who could enter a *nolle prosequi* to stop certain prosecutions or give a *fiat* to disallow them from the beginning;

- the Director of Public Prosecutions (DPP), who prosecuted in very serious cases and cases brought to him or her by the government;

- public bodies;

- private prosecutions, which involved having to persuade a magistrate of the propriety in issuing a summons. The Attorney General and the DPP both had the power to take over a private prosecution and then drop it for reasons of public policy. The right to bring private prosecutions was retained by s 6(1) of the POA 1985. Boyce and Gokani suggest that straitened economic times are leading to a substantial increase in private prosecutions from bodies such as Transport for London, the RSPCA (an increasingly active prosecutor) or Virgin or Sky prosecuting those using 'pirate' equipment (W Boyce and R Gokani, 'Private prosecutions' (2014) 111(31) LSG 22).

Today, the first three of the above list are conducted by the CPS. The CPS liaises where necessary with other public bodies which have the power to prosecute offenders: Attorney General's Office; Civil Aviation Authority; Department for Business, Energy and Industrial Strategy; Department for Work and Pensions; Environment Agency; Financial Conduct Authority; Food Standards Agency; Gambling Commission; Health and Safety Executive; Maritime and Coastguard Agency; Competition and Markets Authority; Office of Rail Regulation; Serious Fraud Office; and Service Prosecuting Authority.

11.2   THE CROWN PROSECUTION SERVICE

The move to establish a CPS was precipitated by a report from JUSTICE, the British section of the International Commission of Jurists, in its 1970 Report, *The Prosecution Process in England and Wales*. It argued that the police were not best suited to be prosecutors because they would often have a commitment to winning a case even where the evidence was weak, given the investment in a case that its investigation invariably represents. They were also not best placed to consider the public policy aspects of the discretion not to prosecute. The police were firmly opposed to such a change. They argued that statistics showed that the police were not given to pursuing cases in a way that led to a high rate of acquittal. They also showed that in cases involving miscarriages of justice, the decision to prosecute had been taken by a lawyer.

The question was referred to the Philips Royal Commission on Criminal Procedure, which judged the then existing system according to its fairness, openness and accountability. It proposed a new system based on several distinct features, including the following:

- that the initial decision to charge a suspect should rest with the police;
- that thereafter all decisions as to whether to proceed, alter or drop the charges should rest with another state prosecuting agency;
- this agency would provide advocates for all cases in the magistrates' courts apart from guilty pleas by post. It should also provide legal advice to the police and instruct counsel in all cases tried on indictment.

The POA 1985 established a national prosecution service under the general direction of the DPP. The 1985 Act gives to the DPP and the CPS as a whole the right to institute and conduct any criminal proceedings where the importance or difficulty of the case make that appropriate (s 3(2)(b)). This applies to cases that could also be started by the police or other bodies like local authorities. It can also, in appropriate circumstances, take over and then discontinue cases. The CPS relies on the police for the resources and machinery of investigation.

The CPS uses a mixture of employed staff and agents, that is, lawyers in private practice working for the CPS on a fee-for-case basis. At the end of March 2016, the CPS employed 5,915 people, with over 93 per cent being engaged in, or supporting, front-line prosecution activity. In 2015–16, 29.6 per cent of half-day sessions in magistrates' courts were covered by agents. Over that period the CPS prosecuted approximately 630,000 cases in the magistrates' courts and 99,000 in the Crown Courts. It secured 530,199 convictions, representing an overall success rate of 83.1 per cent, the magistrates' courts' rate was 83.8 per cent and the Crown Court 79.2 per cent.

According to its 2015–16 annual report, the Service has experienced a significant change in the profile of cases prosecuted. During the period 2009–16. Thus although the overall number of cases prosecuted in 2015–16 fell to 637,798 from 664,493 in 2014–15), there were increases in cases in the following areas:

- terrorism associated with Iraq and Syria;
- child sexual abuse, following the Savile Inquiry;
- other sexual and domestic violence offences; and
- fraud, involving digital technology.

11.2.1 THE DISCRETION TO PROSECUTE

The police have a very significant discretion as to what to do when a crime has possibly been committed. They could turn a blind eye, dispose of the case out of court or, in conjunction with the CPS, charge the suspect, in which case they must decide what is the most appropriate charge or charges commensurate with the facts and seriousness of the alleged conduct. Environmental health officers, the Health and Safety Executive and Environment Agency inspectors, as officers statutorily charged with investigative powers, are in a similar position.

As is very cogently argued by McConville, Sanders and Leng in *The Case for the Prosecution* (1991), prosecution cases are constructed from the evidence and testimony of many people including lay witnesses, victims, the police, CPS lawyers and expert witnesses. Each of these parties is fallible and prone to perceive events in line with their own sorts of experience. The net result of this is that the prosecution case is normally nothing more than an *approximation* of 'the truth'. In crude terms, we move further towards an explanatory account if we understand truth *as* proof. In their preface to *Reconstructing Reality in the Courtroom* (1981), Bennett and Feldman asserted that 'the use of stories to reconstruct the evidence in cases casts doubt on the common belief about justice as a mechanical and objective process'. Stories, their argument runs, serve as tools in the task of selecting from a glut of information what material will in fact be presented as evidence. Bennett and Feldman also contend that narrative devices like stories also serve to plug gaps. William Twining has, however, doubted this account of the somewhat subjective cherry-picking of stories in putting together a case. In particular, Twining argues, facts in issue, materiality, relevance, burdens of proof and presumptions, are peculiarly *lawyers*' concepts. Coupled with these, he continues, is the advocate's marshalling of 'the theory of the case' (see *Twining's Rethinking Evidence: Exploratory Essays*, Cambridge University Press (Law in Context series), 2nd edn, 2006).

The most influential role in what can neutrally be put as the narrative of a case is that of the police, as it is they who ultimately decide whether to charge anyone, and if so, whom and for what. Once these discretions have been exercised, there is a relatively narrow band of data on which the CPS can work.

In 1951, the Attorney General, Lord Shawcross, noted that:

> It has never been the rule in this country – I hope it never will be – that suspected criminal offences must automatically be the subject of prosecution (House of Commons Debates, vol 483, col 681, 29 January 1951).

This *dictum* has been almost universally accepted within the criminal justice system.

There is evidence, however, that the police do (for operational or social reasons) tend to focus their attention on particular types of conduct. Research, for example, by Andrew Sanders has shown a tendency for there to be a bias in favour of prosecuting working-class offenders as opposed to middle-class offenders. He compared the police response to offences with that of the Factory Inspectorate's response to violation of the health and safety laws, and found that the police were much more likely to initiate prosecutions against working-class suspects than were the factory inspectors against businesses and business executives. For the police, there was an institutional bias in favour of prosecution reflected in the principle 'let the court decide', whereas for the Factory Inspectorate, prosecution was a last resort pursued only after an attempt at negotiated compliance had failed. In 1980, there were 22,000 serious cases of tax evasion, but only one in 122 cases was prosecuted. By contrast, there were 107,000 social security frauds, of which one in four was prosecuted. Tax evasion resulted in a loss to the public purse 30 times larger than that caused by social security fraud, yet there was more state money spent on prosecuting people for social security fraud. (See Sanders, 'Class bias in prosecutions' (1985) 24 Howard J 176.) There is also evidence that the Environment Agency has a 'bottom-heavy' enforcement policy, that is, it is more concerned to prosecute minor offenders than large companies. Anglers who catch fish without licences are far more likely to appear in court than the directors of companies that pollute the environment. (See P de Prez, 'Biased enforcement or optimal regulation: Reflections on recent parliamentary scrutiny of the Environment Agency' (2001) 13(3) Environmental Law and Management 145.)

11.2.2 OUT-OF-COURT DISPOSALS

The Ministry of Justice guidance (July 2014) on out-of-court disposals identifies the following methods for diverting cases away from prosecution:

- community resolutions – adults (18+) and youths;
- cannabis (and khat) warnings – adults (18+);
- penalty notices for disorder – adults (18+);
- youth cautions – youths (10–17);
- simple cautions – adults (18+);
- conditional cautions – adults (18+) and youths (10–17);
- restorative justice – a technique which can be used out of court and in conjunction with an out-of-court disposal.

These disposals 'allow the police to deal quickly and proportionately with low-level, often first-time offending which could more appropriately be resolved without a prosecution at court' (www.justice.gov.uk).

Community resolutions

These are suitable for offenders who admit the offence and consent to a community resolution being administered. They encourage the offender to face up to the consequences of their behaviour and take responsibility for making good any harm caused. They may be used in conjunction with restorative justice. They do not form part of a criminal record but may have to be disclosed for an enhanced Disclosure and Barring Service check.

Cannabis (and khat) warnings

Police officers may administer an informal verbal warning to adults caught in possession of a small amount of these drugs consistent with personal use. The warnings, which may be administered on the street or at the police station, follow admission of the offence and consent to the warning and are suitable for first-time offences. A second offence leads to a penalty notice and a third to a charge.

Penalty notices for disorder

The Criminal Justice and Police Act 2001 established the penalty notice for disorder as an alternative method of disposing of cases such as low-level retail theft, being drunk and disorderly and causing fear, alarm or distress. An on-the-spot penalty of £60 is administered and this will rise to £90 if not paid within 21 days. The person concerned may opt to be tried for the offence instead. In some areas, schemes run whereby there is a short educational course as an alternative to paying the penalty (for example on the health implications of the behaviour concerned).

Youth cautions

Youth cautions are a statutory disposal governed by the Legal Aid, Sentencing and Punishment of Offenders Act 2012. They are available for any offence. Although principally designed for low-level offending, they may be used for any offence where it is not in the public interest to prosecute. While the young person must have admitted the offence (and not mentioned anything giving rise to a defence), consent is not required. Parents or other appropriate adults must have been given enough information about the options available and, in the case of sexual offences, the consequences of inclusion on the register of sex offenders must be explained to both the adult and the young person. The caution forms part of the young person's criminal record.

Simple cautions

These are non-statutory and available for any offence. Again, they are designed for low-level offending but may be used for any offence where it is not in the public interest to prosecute. The Crown Prosecution Service must be consulted if the offence is indictable only. The offender must admit the offence and consent and the caution will form part of the criminal record. As with young people, the offender may be placed on the sex offenders register if the offence is one covered by the Sexual Offences Act 2003.

Youth conditional cautions

These are youth cautions with conditions attached, and were introduced by the Crime and Disorder Act 1998. The police may offer these for summary and either-way offences, but a Crown Prosecutor must authorise conditional cautions for indictable-only offences.

The conditions may be rehabilitative, reparative or punitive but must be appropriate, proportionate and achievable. Punitive conditions may include unpaid work, but only in respect of youth conditional cautions.

These are adult cautions with conditions attached, and their main features are the same as youth conditional cautions (above). In addition, where the offender does not have permission to enter or remain in the UK, the conditions offered may be designed to ensure the offender leaves the UK and does not remain.

The problematic nature of such out- of-court disposals will be considered further at 12.9.3.

The Code for Crown Prosecutors (promulgated on behalf of the DPP) sets out the official criteria governing the discretion to prosecute. It is issued under s 10 of the POA 1985. The seventh edition of the Code was published in January 2013 and can be viewed in full at www.cps.gov.uk/publications/code_for_crown_prosecutors/. The CPS website also includes substantial legal guidance on every aspect of criminal law and procedure.

The Code sets out the basis on which prosecutions may be brought and the underlying principles. It provides two tests: the Threshold Test and the Full Code Test. Prosecution can only start or continue when the Full Code Test is satisfied. The Threshold Test is an exception to the Full Code Test. It may only be applied where the suspect presents a substantial bail risk and not all the evidence is available at the time when he or she must be released from custody unless charged.

The Full Code Test requires two tests to be satisfied before a prosecution is brought: there must be a 'realistic prospect of conviction' (the evidential test); and the prosecution must be 'in the public interest'.

The evidential test requires prosecutors to predict what a jury or bench, properly directed, would be likely to decide. The guidelines require prosecutors to assess the reliability of evidence, not just its admissibility. Glanville Williams ([1985] Crim LR 115) and Andrew Sanders ((1994) 144 NLJ 946) argued that earlier versions of this test, which dealt specifically with reliability in relation to personal characteristics, favoured people who are well respected in society – like police officers and businessmen – in whose favour juries and magistrates might be biased. It disfavoured the sort of victims who are unlikely to make good witnesses. Sanders proposed a better test: whether, on the evidence, a jury or bench ought (on the balance of probabilities) to convict. The Code now says that the test is whether the jury or bench 'is more likely than not to convict the defendant of the charge alleged' (para 4.5).

The public interest must be considered in each case where there is enough evidence to provide a realistic prospect of conviction. In cases of any seriousness, a prosecution will usually take place unless there are public interest factors tending against prosecution which clearly outweigh those tending in favour.

The Code lists some 'public interest factors in favour of prosecution' and some against (para 4.12). Crown Prosecutors and others must balance factors for and against prosecution, carefully and fairly.

In October 2013, a new Code of Practice for Victims of Crime was produced under s 33 of the Domestic Violence, Crime and Victims Act 2004. This Code, updated in October 2015, applies not just to the CPS, but to a wide variety of criminal justice organisations. The CPS is committed to 'championing justice and defending the rights of victims, fairly, firmly and effectively'. The public interest factors in the Full Test Code take into account the circumstances of the victim, for example the effect of a prosecution on the victim's health. If there is evidence that a prosecution is likely to have an adverse impact on the victim's health then it may make a prosecution less likely, taking into account the victim's views.

The Attorney General has commended the Code to prosecutors outside the CPS. This may help to correct inconsistent approaches between the police and CPS on the one hand and, on the other, prosecutors like HMRC and the Health and Safety Executive. As Sanders (see above) has observed, if you illegally gain a fortune or maim someone, you will probably be treated more leniently than ordinary disposals for such offences if the crimes are, technically, tax evasion and operating an unsafe place of work. Local authorities and the Environment Agency seem generally reluctant to prosecute environmental offenders. This can lead to a situation in which environmental crime, for example, makes good business sense. (See M Watson, 'Offences against the environment: the economics of crime and punishment' (2004) 16(4) Environmental Law and Management 2003–04. For the Health and Safety Executive, see G Slapper, *Blood in the Bank* (1999).)

11.2.4   CPS INDEPENDENCE FROM THE POLICE

The CPS is institutionally separate from the police. The police are no longer in a client – lawyer relationship with the prosecutor, able to give instructions about how to proceed. The CPS in practice exercises no supervisory role over the police investigation of cases; it simply acts on the file presented after the investigation by the police. It cannot instruct the police to investigate a particular incident.

The power of the CPS to discontinue prosecutions (under s 23 or s 23A of the POA 1985), or the continuing power to withdraw or offer no evidence, is an important feature of its independence.

However, the CPS itself identifies that the relationship between the CPS and the police is an important one. They recognise the importance of the role of the police in the prosecution process, not only the detection and investigation of criminal offences, but tasks such as warning witnesses to attend court, obtaining further witness statements as required and keeping victims informed as to the progress of the case.

Prosecutors are warned, however, that the CPS and the police have separate functions, and that they should not try to become an investigator or direct police operational procedures.

However, providing advice to the police in all matters relating to criminal offences is one of the core statutory functions of the CPS. Prosecutors should therefore be alert and open to all appropriate opportunities for giving such advice, where it may contribute to the effectiveness of an investigation and prosecution (www.cps.gov.uk/legal/a_to_c/ cps_relations_with_the_police/#a01).

11.2.5 JUDICIAL CONTROL OF PROSECUTION POLICY

There is a very limited way in which the courts could control the exercise of prosecutorial discretion by the police. Lord Denning MR gave the example in one 1968 case of a chief constable issuing a directive to his officers that no person should be prosecuted for stealing goods worth less than £100 (over £2,000 in modern prices), and said: 'I should have thought the court could countermand it. He would be failing in his duty to enforce the law.' More generally, the courts had no control, per Lord Denning MR, *R v Metropolitan Police Commissioner ex p Blackburn* [1968] 1 All ER 763 at 769:

> For instance, it is for the Commissioner of Police of the Metropolis, or the Chief Constable, as the case may be, to decide in any particular case whether inquiries should be pursued, or whether an arrest should be made or a prosecution brought. It must be for him to decide on the disposition of his force and the concentration of his resources on any particular crime or area. No court can or should give him directions on such a matter.

Apart from this, there is the doctrine of constabulary independence (see *Fisher v Oldham Corp* (1930)), which regards the constable as an independent office-holder under the Crown who cannot be instructed by organisational superiors or by governmental agencies about how to exercise his powers. The constable is accountable only to law. The judiciary has shown a marked reluctance to interfere with decisions made by police chiefs concerning, in particular, the allocation of resources and direction of police officers (see *Harris v Sheffield United Football Club Ltd* (1987); *R v Chief Constable of Sussex ex p International Trader's Ferry Ltd* (1997)).

An interesting instance of the courts being used to attack a use of police discretion is *R v Coxhead* (1986). The appellant was a police sergeant in charge of a police station. A young man was brought into the station to be breathalysed and the sergeant recognised him as the son of a police inspector at that station. The sergeant knew the inspector to be suffering from a bad heart condition. In order not to exacerbate this condition, the sergeant did not administer the test and allowed the motorist to go free. The sergeant was prosecuted and convicted for conduct tending and intended to pervert the course of justice. The sergeant's defence was that his decision came within the legitimate scope of discretion exercised by a police officer. The trial judge said the matter should be left for the jury to determine; they must decide the extent of any police discretion in accordance with the facts. The jury convicted the sergeant and his conviction was upheld by the Court of Appeal. In minor cases, the police had a very wide discretion whether to prosecute, but in major cases they had no discretion or virtually none. Thus, in a serious case like drink-driving, there was no discretion which the sergeant could have been exercising legitimately. It is odd, however, that this is left for the jury to decide after the event rather than being subject to clear rules to anticipate the proper exercise of police discretion.

It is possible to bring a judicial review of the decision to prosecute or not to prosecute. The courts are likely to direct the CPS to review its prosecutorial decisions where:

- it is apparent that the law has not been properly understood and applied (*R v DPP, ex p Jones (Timothy)* (2000));

- it can be demonstrated on an objective appraisal of the case that some serious evidence supporting a prosecution has not been carefully considered (*R (on the application of Joseph) v DPP* (2001); *R (on the application of Peter Dennis) v DPP* (2006));

- it can be demonstrated that in a significant area, a conclusion as to what the evidence is to support a prosecution is irrational (*R v DPP, ex p Jones (Timothy)* (2000));

- the decision is perverse, that is, one at which no reasonable prosecutor could have arrived (*R v DPP, ex p C* (1995));

- CPS policy, such as that set out in the Code for Crown Prosecutors, has not been properly applied and/or complied with (*R v DPP, ex p C* (1995); *R v DPP, ex p Manning* (2001); *R v Chief Constable of Kent, ex p L; R v DPP, ex p B* (1991));

- the decision has been arrived at because of an unlawful policy (*R v DPP, ex p C* (1995));

- it can be demonstrated that the decision was arrived at as a result of fraud, corruption or bad faith (*R v DPP, ex p Kebilene* (2000); *R v Panel on Takeovers and Mergers, ex p Fayed* (1992)).

11.2.6   STATE PROSECUTORS IN THE CROWN COURTS

Reference has already been made to the fact that Crown Prosecutors are now able to appear in the higher courts if they are suitably qualified. This has caused a great deal of concern in some quarters. The basis of the worry is that, as full-time salaried lawyers working for an organisation, CPS lawyers will sometimes be tempted to get convictions using dubious tactics or ethics because their own status as employees and prospects of promotion will depend on conviction success rates. Where, as now, barristers from the independent Bar are used by the CPS to prosecute, there is (it is argued) a greater likelihood of the courtroom lawyer dropping a morally unsustainable case.

Section 42 of the Access to Justice Act 1999 tries to overcome any possible difficulties with a provision (amending s 27 of the Courts and Legal Services Act (CLSA) 1990) that every advocate 'has a duty to the court to act with independence in the interests of justice', in other words, a duty that overrides any inconsistent duty that might lie, for example, to an employer. Professor Michael Zander QC has contended, however, that these are 'mere words'. He has said (letter to *The Times*, 29 December 1998) that they are unlikely to exercise much sway over CPS lawyer employees concerned with performance targets set by their line managers, and that:

> The CPS as an organisation is constantly under pressure in regard to the proportion of discontinuances, acquittal and conviction rates. These are factors in the day-to-day work of any CPS lawyer. It is disingenuous to imagine they will not have a powerful effect on decision making.

The Bar was also very wary of this change, an editorial in *Counsel* (the journal of the Bar of England and Wales) saying:

> [W]e are gravely concerned about the extent to which prosecutions will be done in-house by the CPS when the need for independent prosecutors is so well established in our democracy ((1999) *Counsel* 3, February).

It is important to set the arguments in a wider context. What are the social, economic or political debates surrounding this issue of how best to run a system of courtroom prosecutors? The change to having Crown Court prosecutions carried out by salaried CPS lawyers might well be expected to be more efficient, as the whole prosecution can be handled in-house, without engaging the external service of an independent barrister. This assumption has been discredited, however: CPS in-house cases are in fact more expensive to run than instructing chambers-based barristers (see Bar Council, 27 July 2009: 'Independent Study Heavily Criticises CPS Claims about In-House Advocates are Based on "Alice in Wonderland Accounting"'). Some will argue that justice is being sacrificed to the deity of cost-cutting. On the other hand, it could be argued that justice and efficiency are not mutually exclusive phenomena and – as has been shown above – the CPS has been actively recruiting Higher Court Advocates (HCAs) to prosecute in the Crown Court. Keir Starmer QC, the ex-Director of Public Prosecutions, committed himself to the view that 'in-house advocacy is here to stay for the CPS' (9 January 2009). However, the real-term costs of HCAs have been effectively queried, with recent Bar Council meetings discussing the relative expense of independent and in-house barristers. This has culminated in a turf war between in-house CPS advocates and independent practitioners at the Bar. (See the article by Frances Gibb, 'Bar Council says Crown Prosecution Service wasting millions with in-house prosecutions', *The Times*, 27 July 2009.)

It remains to be seen what effect the CPS Panel Advocate scheme, which is now up and running, will have on this debate.

11.2.7 HM CROWN PROSECUTION SERVICE INSPECTORATE

Her Majesty's Crown Prosecution Service Inspectorate (HMCPSI) oversees the work carried out by the Crown Prosecution Service (CPS) and other prosecuting agencies with the stated aim of enhancing the quality of justice and improving their efficiency effectiveness and fairness. It is independent from the prosecuting organisations it inspects and completely separately funded. In conducting such inspections HMCPSI employs:

- Legal inspectors, solicitors and barristers with backgrounds in prosecution, defence and private practice. These assess the quality of prosecution decisions and legal processes.
- Business management inspectors, experienced in areas such as management, business planning, audit, change management and governance. These assess the quality of management and planning in the organisations inspected.

HMCPSI may conduct an inspection in individual CPS areas to engage in thematic investigations across the whole service. It publishes the outcome of any such reports and in addition it submits an annual report to the Attorney General on the operation of the CPS generally which is laid before Parliament. HMCPSI has no regulatory powers in respect of the CPS or the SFO. Its role is merely 'to provide evidence-based findings on what is working well and where improvement is needed.' Then it is 'for those with responsibility for the CPS or the SFO, either within the organisation or through their powers of superintendence, to effect the necessary changes.'

11.3 BAIL

Bail is the release from custody, pending a criminal trial, of an accused. The relevant statute is the Bail Act (BA) 1976. Bail may be with or without conditions. Conditional bail may be granted, for example, on the promise that an accused will not contact witnesses or co-defendants in a case; that he or she will co-operate with probation or other state agencies; that he or she will report to a police station at specific times; or that he or she will observe a curfew (either a 'doorstop' curfew, where he or she is to present himself or herself to a police officer calling at the curfew address, or one which is electronically monitored via an ankle tag). Other conditions of remand on bail might include the promise that money will be paid to the court by a 'surety' (the person 'standing' the bail money) if he or she absconds, or the deposit of a security, where money is paid into court 'up-front' and is forfeit if the defendant absconds. All decisions on whether to grant bail therefore involve delicate questions of balancing interests, but the exercise begins with the presumption that an accused should be at liberty until proven guilty. The test to be applied is a threshold one. Where there are 'substantial grounds' for believing that the exceptions to bail in the Bail Act 1976 are met, a court may be satisfied that deprivation of the liberty of an accused can be justified.

A person is presumed innocent of a criminal charge unless he or she is proved guilty of it; this implies that no one should ever be detained unless he or she has been found guilty. It follows that there is a presumption of liberty, which the prosecution may oppose only by establishing 'substantial grounds' to overturn that presumption. For several reasons, however, it can be regarded as undesirable to allow some accused people to go back to society before the case against them is tried in a criminal court. Indeed, about 12 per cent of offenders who are bailed to appear in court fail to appear for their trials. In January 2005, the Attorney General called for a crack-down on defendants who skip bail. At the time in question, 60,000 'failed to appear' (FTA) warrants were outstanding. Lord Goldsmith said: 'They will see that they can't thumb their nose at the criminal justice system. Turning up at court is not optional. It is a serious obligation and we will enforce it' (C Dyer, 'Bail bandits blitz begins today', *The Guardian*, 14 January 2005).

In 2008, it was revealed that nearly one in seven people charged with murder and awaiting trial were released on bail. A survey by the Courts Service disclosed that at least 60 of the 455 people accused of murder were on the streets on 31 January 2008, while 35 out of 41 of those awaiting trial for manslaughter were bailed. (That survey has not been updated.) The disclosure came after Gary Weddell murdered Traute Maxfield, his mother-in-law, before killing himself. At the time, he was on bail charged with the murder of his wife (*The Times*, 25 February 2008). The Coroners and Justice Act 2009 has since reformed the law relating to the application and grant of bail. In particular, s 115 of that Act provides that a defendant who is charged with murder (and other offences) may not be granted bail except by a judge of the Crown Court. The power of magistrates to consider bail in murder cases – whether at the first hearing or after a breach of an existing bail condition – is thus removed. A bail decision in such cases must be made as soon as reasonably practicable. In any event, a decision must be made within 48 hours (excluding public holidays), beginning the day after the defendant's appearance in the magistrates' court.

To refuse bail to an accused might involve depriving someone of liberty who is subsequently found not guilty or convicted, but given a non-custodial sentence. Such a person will probably have been kept in a police cell or in a prison cell for 23 hours a day. Unlike the jurisdictions in the Netherlands, Germany and France, no compensation is payable in these circumstances. On the other hand, to allow liberty to the accused pending trial might be to allow him or her to abscond, commit further offences, interfere with witnesses and obstruct the course of justice. A suspected terrorist might commit further outrages (a controversial issue following the explosions in London on 7 July 2005).

The difficulties involved in finding the proper balance were highlighted by several cases of serious assault and rape being committed by persons who were on bail, and by the fleeing of Asil Nadir to Northern Cyprus in May 1993. Mr Nadir skipped his £3.5 million bail to travel to a jurisdiction that would not extradite him to England. He claimed that he would not be given a fair trial for the offences of theft and false accounting with which he was charged, and went on the public record as saying that his sureties would not suffer hardship as he would repay those who had put up bail for him. In 2010, Mr Nadir returned to the UK to clear his name. He was, however, convicted of fraud and the theft of £29 million from his former Polly Peck empire, and sentenced to 10 years' imprisonment.

The basic way in which the law currently seeks to find the right balance in such matters is by operating a general presumption in favour of bail, a presumption that can be overturned if one or more of a number of indices of suspicion exist in respect of a particular defendant. Even where bail is granted, it may be subject to certain conditions to promote public safety and the interests of justice. Bail may be granted by the police or by the court.

11.3.1   POLICE BAIL

In the criminal process, the first stage at which bail is usually raised as an issue is on arrest or at the police station. The police may grant bail using the same criteria as the courts but the governing law is the Police and Criminal Evidence Act 1984 (PACE).

Section 30A – D of PACE enables police officers to grant bail to persons following their arrest without the need to take them to a police station. It provides the police with additional flexibility following arrest and the scope to remain on patrol where there is no immediate need to deal with the person concerned at the station. It is intended to allow the police to plan their work more effectively by giving them new discretion to decide exactly when and where an arrested person should attend a police station for interview. (See A Hucklesby, 'Not necessarily a trip to the police station: the introduction of police bail' (2004) Crim LR 803.)

Section 30A(2) – (6) sets out the detail relating to this power to grant bail on arrest. The basic principle remains that a person arrested by a constable or taken into custody by a constable after being arrested by someone else must be taken by a constable to a police station as soon as is practicable. However, this is subject to the provisions dealing with release either on bail or without bail.

Sub-section (4) provides that a constable must release the person concerned without bail if, before reaching the police station, he or she is satisfied that there are no grounds for keeping them under arrest or releasing them on bail under the new provisions.

Sub-section (5) makes it clear that a constable may delay taking an arrested person to a police station or releasing them on bail if that person's presence elsewhere is necessary for immediate investigative purposes. The reason for such delay must be recorded either on arrival at the police station or when the person is released on bail.

Sub-section (7) provides police officers with the framework of powers to grant bail following arrest. Section 30A provides that a constable has power to release a person on bail at any time prior to arrival at a police station. It specifies that the person released on bail must be required to attend a police station and that any police station may be specified for that purpose. No other requirement may be imposed on the person as a condition of bail.

Section 30C(3) specifies that nothing in the BA 1976 applies in relation to bail under these new arrangements. The law that applies to this form of bail is set out in PACE 1984 as amended by the Criminal Justice Act 2003.

Section 30C(4) clarifies that a person who has been released under the new bail provisions may be re-arrested if new evidence justifying such a course of action has come to light since their release.

Under s 37(7) PACE, where it appears to the custody officer that there is sufficient evidence to charge a suspect, and either further enquiries are still in progress or a decision on charging needs to be made by the CPS, the custody officer may grant conditional or unconditional bail.

If a person is arrested on a warrant, this will indicate whether they are to be held in custody or released on bail. If the suspect is arrested without a warrant, then the police will have to decide whether to release the suspect after they have been charged. After a person has been charged, s 38(1)(a) of the PACE states that a person must be released unless: (a) their name and address are not known; or (b) the custody officer reasonably thinks that their detention is necessary for their own protection; or (c) to prevent them from injuring someone or damaging property, or because they might abscond, or interfere with the course of justice; or (d) the custody officer reasonably believes that the detention of that person is necessary to prevent them from committing any offence.

Sections 38 and 47 of PACE 1984 allow the police to grant conditional bail to persons charged. The conditions can be whatever is required to ensure that the person surrenders to custody, does not commit an offence while on bail, or does not interfere with witnesses or otherwise obstruct the course of justice. The powers of the custody officer, however, do not include a power to impose a requirement to reside in a bail hostel or to attend an interview with a legal adviser, or require the suspect to make him or herself available for inquiries and reports. The police have power to arrest without warrant a person who, having been granted conditional police bail, has failed to attend at a police station at the appointed time (s 46A PACE).

11.3.2   BAIL BY THE COURTS

The Bail Act 1976 created a statutory presumption of bail. It states (s 4) that, subject to Schedule 1, bail shall be granted to a person accused of an offence and brought before a magistrates' court or a Crown Court, and also to people convicted of an offence who are being remanded for reports to be made. The court must therefore grant bail (unless one of the exceptions applies), even if the defendant does not make an application. Schedule 1 provides that a court need not grant bail to a person charged with an offence punishable with imprisonment if it is satisfied that there are 'substantial grounds' (the relevant test) for believing that, if released on bail, the defendant would:

- fail to surrender to custody;
- commit an offence while on bail; or
- interfere with witnesses or otherwise obstruct the course of justice.

The court can also refuse bail if it believes that the defendant ought to stay in custody for his or her own protection, or if it has not been practicable, for want of time, to obtain sufficient information to enable the court to make its decision on bail, or he or she has previously failed to answer to bail (Sched 1, Part I, paras 2–6).

When the court is considering the grounds stated above, all relevant factors must be taken into account. These include: the nature and seriousness of the offence, the character, antecedents, associations and community ties of the defendant, and his or her record for satisfying his or her obligations under previous grants of bail.

Evidence accepted by the Home Office suggests that there is a link between drug addiction and offending. In addition, it is widely accepted that many abusers of drugs fund their misuse through acquisitive crime. There is thus a real concern that, if such offenders who have been charged with an imprisonable offence are placed on bail, they will merely re-offend in order to fund their drug use.

Under s 19 CJA 2003, an alleged offender aged 18 or over, who has been charged with an imprisonable offence, will not be granted bail (unless the court is satisfied that there is no significant risk of his committing an offence while on bail) where the three conditions below exist:

- there is drug test evidence that the person has a specified Class A drug in his or her body (by way of a lawful test obtained under s 63B of PACE or s 161 of this Act); and
- either the offence is a drugs offence associated with a specified Class A drug or the court is satisfied that there are substantial grounds for believing that the misuse of a specified Class A drug caused or contributed to that offence or provided its motivation; and
- the person does not agree to undergo an assessment as to his or her dependency upon or propensity to misuse specified Class A drugs, or has undergone such an assessment but does not agree to participate in any relevant follow-up action offered.

The assessment will be carried out by a suitably qualified person, who will have received training in the assessment of drug problems. If an assessment or follow-up is proposed and agreed to, it will be a condition of bail that it be undertaken. This provision can only apply in areas where appropriate assessment and treatment facilities are in place.

If the defendant is charged with an offence not punishable with imprisonment, Sched 1 provides that bail may be refused only if the court is satisfied that there are substantial grounds for believing that if released on bail (whether subject to conditions or not) he or she would fail to surrender to custody, commit an offence while on bail, or interfere with witnesses or otherwise obstruct the course of justice. Bail may also be refused for the defendant's own protection or there are substantial grounds for believing he or she may cause physical or mental injury (or fear of such) to an associated person.

Section 25 of the CJPOA 1994 provided that, in some circumstances, a person who had been charged with or convicted of murder, attempted murder, manslaughter, rape or attempted rape must not be granted bail. The circumstances were simply that the conviction must have been within the UK, and that, in the case of a manslaughter conviction, it must have been dealt with by way of a custodial sentence. The word 'conviction' is given a wide meaning and includes anyone found 'not guilty by way of insanity'.

There was debate about whether the changes wrought by s 25 were justifiable. A Home Office Minister, defending the section, stated that it would be worth the risk if it prevented just one murder or rape, even though there might be a few 'hard cases', that is, people eventually acquitted of crime, who were remanded in custody pending trial (David Maclean MP, Minister of State, Home Office, HC Committee, col 282, 1994). As Card and Ward remarked in a commentary on the CJPOA 1994, the government, when pushed, was unable to cite a single case where a person released on bail, in the circumstances covered by s 25, re-offended in a similar way. There is no time limit on the previous conviction and there is no requirement of any connection between the previous offence and the one in question. Card and Ward suggest that there is a world of difference between a person who was convicted of manslaughter 30 years ago on the grounds of complicity in a suicide pact and who is now charged with attempted rape (of which they must be presumed innocent), and the person who was convicted of rape eight years ago and now faces another rape charge. The first person is not an obvious risk to society and it is, they argue, regrettable that bail will be denied to him. There was also argument to be had with the contents of the s 25 list. Why should some clearly dangerous and prevalent crimes like robbery be omitted from it? In any case, it might have been better had the offences in the list raised a strong presumption against bail as opposed to an absolute ban, as the former could be rebutted in cases where there was, on the facts, no risk.

A further significant difficulty with this approach was that it appeared to be incompatible with the requirements of Art 5(3) of the European Convention on Human Rights (ECHR); decisions of the court which make it clear that the decision to remand a defendant in custody before trial must be a decision of the court based on the merits after a review of the facts. By precluding bail in the specified circumstances, s 25 denied the court the opportunity to take a decision based on the merits. Thus, in *CC v UK* (1999) (subsequently confirmed by the European Court of Human Rights in *Caballero v UK* (2000)), the European Court found that s 25 violated rights under Art 5(3) where the claimant had been denied bail on a rape charge in 1996 because of a conviction for manslaughter in 1987.

Anticipating this decision, s 25 was amended by the CDA 1998 to provide that bail should only be granted in homicide and rape cases if the court is 'satisfied that there are exceptional circumstances which justify it'. However, doubts have been expressed by the Law Commission and others about whether this change achieves compliance with obligations under the ECHR. The argument is that the presumption required by the ECHR is innocence and therefore that the defendant should be released, while the presumption under the amended s 25 is that the defendant should not be released. Nevertheless, what effectively operates as a presumption *against* bail in s 25 of the Criminal Justice and Public Order Act 1994 has been found by the courts as not incompatible with Art 5(3) (the liberty guarantee) of the ECHR, provided the overall burden is not on the defendant to prove that bail should be granted (see *R (O) v Harrow Crown Court* (2006)).

Bail can be granted as conditional or unconditional. Where it is unconditional, the accused must simply surrender to the court at the appointed date. Failure to appear without reasonable cause is an offence under the BA 1976 (s 6) and can result, if tried in a Crown Court, in a sentence of up to 12 months' imprisonment or a fine. Conditions can be attached to the granting of bail where the court thinks that it is necessary to ensure that the accused surrenders at the right time and does not interfere with witnesses or commit further offences. Bail conditions may also be imposed for a defendant's own protection or welfare, in the same circumstances that he or she might have been remanded in custody for that purpose. There is no statutory limit to the conditions the court may impose. The most common include requirements that the accused reports daily or weekly to a police station, resides at a particular address, surrenders his or her passport, or does not go to particular places or associate with particular people. The accused may also be required to attend interviews with a legal representative as a condition of bail.

Section 7 of the BA 1976 gives the police power to arrest anyone on conditional bail whom they reasonably suspect is likely to break the conditions or has already done so. Anyone arrested in these circumstances must be brought before a magistrate within 24 hours. The magistrate may then reconsider the question of bail.

Personal recognisances, by which the suspect agreed to pay a sum if he or she failed to surrender to the court, were abolished by the BA 1976 (s 3(2)), except in cases where it is believed that the defendant might try to flee abroad. The Act did retain the court's right to ask for sureties as a condition of bail. By putting sureties in a position where they can have large sums of money 'estreated' if the suspect does not surrender to the court, significant pressure (not using the resources of the criminal justice system) is put on the accused. The proportion of those who do not answer to bail is about 12 per cent of those given bail. Section 9 of the BA 1976 strengthens the surety principle by making it a criminal offence to agree to indemnify a surety. This sort of thing could happen, for example, if the accused agreed to reimburse the surety in the event that he or she skipped bail and the surety was requested to pay.

11.3.3   APPEALS AND REAPPLICATIONS

The rules that govern how someone who has been refused bail might reapply and appeal have also been framed with a view to balancing the interests of the accused with those of the public and justice. The original refusal should not be absolute and final but, on the other hand, it is seen as necessary that the refusals are not reversed too easily.

If the court decides not to grant the defendant bail, then Sched 1, Part IIA (inserted by s 154 of the Criminal Justice Act (CJA) 1988) provides that it is the court's duty to consider whether the defendant ought to be granted bail at each subsequent hearing. At the first hearing after the one at which bail was first refused, he or she may support an application for bail with any arguments, but at subsequent hearings, the court need not hear arguments as to fact or law which it has heard before. The CJA 1988 enables a court to remand an accused, in his or her absence, for up to three successive one-week remand hearings provided that he or she consents and is legally represented. Such repeated visits are costly to the State and can be unsettling for the accused, especially if he or she has to spend most of the day in a police cell, only to be told the case has been adjourned again without bail. If someone does not consent, they are prevented from applying for bail on each successive visit if the only supporting arguments are those that have been heard by the court before (*R v Nottingham JJ ex p Davies* (1980)).

To avoid unproductive hearings, that is, to promote courts being able to adjourn a case for a period within which reasonable progress can be made on it, s 155 of the CJA 1988 allows for adjournments for up to 28 days provided the court sets the date for when the next stage of the proceedings should take place.

The interests of the accused are also served by the variety of appeals he or she may make if bail has been refused. If bail has been refused by magistrates then, in limited circumstances, an application may be made to another bench of magistrates. Applications for reconsideration can also be made to a judge in chambers (through a legal representative) or to the Official Solicitor (in writing). Appeal can be made to a Crown Court in respect of bail for both pre-committal remands and where a defendant has been committed for trial or sentence at the Crown Court. There is also a right of appeal to the Crown Court against the imposition by magistrates of certain conditions of bail. The conditions that may be challenged in this way are requirements relating to residence, provision of a surety or giving a security, curfew, electronic monitoring or contact. This complements the removal by s 17 of the existing High Court power to entertain such appeals.

Section 3 of the BA 1976 allows for an application to vary the conditions of court bail to be made by the person bailed, the prosecutor or a police officer. Application may also be made for the imposition of conditions on unconditional court bail. Section 3 of the BA 1976 allows for the same thing in relation to police bail, although it does not allow the prosecutor to seek reconsideration of the decision to grant bail itself. Under the Bail (Amendment) Act 1993 (as amended), however, the prosecution does have a right to appeal against the grant of bail by a court in all cases of imprisonable offences. When this right of appeal is exercised, the defendant will remain in custody until the appeal is heard by a Crown Court judge, who will decide whether to grant bail or remand the defendant in custody within 48 hours of the magistrates' decision. Parliament was concerned that this power could be abused and has stated that it should be reserved 'for cases of greatest concern, when there is a serious risk of harm to the public' or where there are 'other significant public interest grounds' for an appeal.

Section 240 of the Criminal Justice Act 2003 states that time spent in custody pre-trial or pre-sentence can generally be deducted from the ultimate sentence. No compensation, however, is paid to people who have been remanded in custody but are subsequently found not guilty.

Section 240A of the Criminal Justice Act 2003, as inserted by s 21 of the Criminal Justice and Immigration Act 2008, provides for a deduction from the ultimate sentence if the offender has spent time on bail subject to a curfew of nine hours or more in any given day, coupled with an electronic monitoring condition. The defendant will generally be entitled to an order to the effect that half the number of days spent on bail subject to those conditions should count as time served by the prisoner as part of his or her sentence.

This area of law was subject to a comprehensive revision after a Home Office special working party reported in 1974, and has been legislatively debated and modified twice since the BA 1976. It is, however, still a matter of serious concern, both to those civil libertarians who consider the law too tilted against the accused, and to the police and commentators, who believe it too lenient in many respects. This criticism of the law from both sides of the debate might indicate a desirable state of balance reached by the current regulatory framework.

11.4   PLEA BARGAINING AND RELATED ISSUES

'Plea bargaining' has been defined as 'the practice whereby the accused enters a plea of guilty in return for which he will be given some consideration that results in a sentence concession' (Baldwin and McConville, *Negotiated Justice: Pressures on Defendants to Plead Guilty* (1977)). In practice, this can refer to:

- a situation either where there has been a plea arrangement for the accused to plead guilty to a lesser charge than the one with which he or she is charged (for example, charged with murder, agrees to plead guilty to manslaughter). This is sometimes called 'charge bargaining'; or

- where there is simply a sentencing discount available on a plea of guilty by the accused. This has been given statutory force by s 144 CJA 2003, which requires a court to award a reduced sentence for a timely guilty plea.

- A form of plea bargaining now also exists in respect of corporate bodies. Deferred Prosecution Agreements (DFAs) were introduced in Schedule 17 of the *Crime and Courts Act 2013*. Under a DPA a prosecutor charges a company with a criminal offence but proceedings are automatically suspended. The company agrees to a number of conditions, such as paying a financial penalty, paying compensation and co-operating with future prosecutions of individuals. If the company does not honour the conditions, the prosecution may resume.

11.4.1   ADVANCE INDICATION OF SENTENCE

Plea bargaining is widespread in some common law countries, for example the United States. It has always been considered impermissible in the English legal system. However, the related issue of whether a judge should give advance indications of sentence has been subject to change since the original leading case of *R v Turner* (1970) was decided. In *Turner* Lord Parker CJ said that the judge should never indicate the sentence which they are minded to impose, nor should they ever indicate that on a plea of guilty they would impose one sentence, but that on a conviction following a plea of not guilty they would impose a more severe sentence. The judge could say what sentence they would impose on a plea of guilty (where, for example, they have read the depositions and antecedents) but without mentioning what they would do if the accused were convicted after pleading not guilty. Even this would be wrong, however, as the accused might take the judge to be intimating that a more severe sentence would follow upon conviction after a guilty plea. The only exception to this rule is where a judge says that the sentence will take a particular form, following conviction, whether there has been a plea of guilty or not guilty.

This aspect of *R v Turner* was overruled in *R v Goodyear (Karl)* (2005), when Lord Woolf, giving the judgment of a specially convened five-judge Court of Appeal, said that a Crown Court judge could give an advance indication of sentence, if, but only if, the defendant requests one. He or she is not obliged to do so and the indication would normally be limited to the maximum sentence likely to be imposed if a plea of guilty were entered at that stage in proceedings (usually the plea and case management hearing). The Criminal Procedure Rules 2014, para 3.23, detail how this process works. In the *Attorney General's Reference (No. 34 of 2010) (R v Simon Roland Langridge)* (2010) the Court of Appeal stressed that it was essential that discussions take place in open court, unless circumstances were exceptionally sensitive.

11.4.2 ACCEPTANCE OF PLEAS BY THE PROSECUTOR

The role of the prosecutor in accepting guilty pleas is governed by the Attorney General's 'Guidelines on the acceptance of pleas and the prosecutor's role in the sentencing exercise (revised 2009)' and s 9 of the Code for Crown Prosecutors. The prosecutor can only accept the plea if the basis of the plea is accurate, so protecting the victim's interests and accuracy of sentencing. This also ensures fairness and transparency in the process. In relation to the advance indication of sentence, *Goodyear* makes it clear that the role of the prosecutor is reactive rather than proactive.

11.4.3 PLEA DISCUSSIONS IN SERIOUS FRAUD CASES

The complexity and expense of prosecuting serious fraud has led to specific provisions in relation to this. The 2009 *Attorney General's Guidelines on Plea Discussions in Cases of Serious or Complex Fraud* govern this.

The General Principles for prosecutors undertaking plea negotiations are as follows:

1. In conducting plea discussions and presenting a plea agreement to the court, the prosecutor must act openly, fairly and in the interests of justice.

2. Acting in the interests of justice means ensuring that the plea agreement reflects the seriousness and extent of the offending, gives the court adequate sentencing powers, and enables the court, the public and the victims to have confidence in the outcome. The prosecutor must consider carefully the impact of a proposed plea or basis of plea on the community and the victim, and on the prospects of successfully prosecuting any other person implicated in the offending. The prosecutor must not agree to a reduced basis of plea which is misleading, untrue or illogical.

3. Acting fairly means respecting the rights of the defendant and of any other person who is being or may be prosecuted in relation to the offending. The prosecutor must not put improper pressure on a defendant in the course of plea discussions, for example, by exaggerating the strength of the case in order to persuade the defendant to plead guilty, or to plead guilty on a particular basis.

4. Acting openly means being transparent with the defendant, the victim and the court. The prosecutor must:

    *   ensure that a full and accurate record of the plea discussions is prepared and retained;

- ensure that the defendant has sufficient information to enable him or her to play an informed part in the plea discussions;
- communicate with the victim before accepting a reduced basis of plea, wherever it is practicable to do so, so that the position can be explained; and
- ensure that the plea agreement placed before the court fully and fairly reflects the matters agreed. The prosecutor must not agree additional matters with the defendant which are not recorded in the plea agreement and made known to the court.

Section 45 and Sched 17 of the Courts and Crime Act 2013 introduced deferred prosecution agreements (DPAs). A DPA is an agreement between a prosecutor and an organisation (not an individual) facing prosecution for an alleged economic or financial crime in the Act. The organisation agrees to comply with a range of terms and conditions and the prosecutor agrees to institute but then defer criminal proceedings for the alleged offence. The aim is to protect organisations from the adverse effects of a criminal conviction while ensuring that they take appropriate action. Para 5(3) of Sched 17 provides that:

(3) The requirements that a DPA may impose on P [the organisation] include, but are not limited to, the following requirements –

(a)   to pay to the prosecutor a financial penalty;
(b)   to compensate victims of the alleged offence;
(c)   to donate money to a charity or other third party;
(d)   to disgorge any profits made by P from the alleged offence;
(e)   to implement a compliance programme or make changes to an existing compliance programme relating to P's policies or to the training of P's employees or both;
(f)   to co-operate in any investigation related to the alleged offence;
(g)   to pay any reasonable costs of the prosecutor in relation to the alleged offence or the DPA.

The DPA may impose time limits within which P must comply with the requirements imposed on P.

The Serious Fraud Office has issued a Code of Practice for DPAs: *Deferred Prosecution Agreements Code of Practice*, 2014.

The first DPA to be approved by the High Court involved the London-based ICBC Standard Bank admitting to wrongdoing and agreeing to penalties, compensation and costs totalling $32 million to avoid prosecution. The bank admitted failing to prevent bribery when its Tanzanian arm, Stanbic Bank Tanzania, raised $600 million (£400 million) for the government (*The Times*, 1 December 2015). The DPA was approved in a public hearing before Mr Justice Leveson, president of the High Court's Queen's Bench Division. The bank was given a penalty of $32.2 million, including a $16.8 million fine to be paid to the SFO. The penalty is one that includes a one-third reduction for self-disclosure and co-operation.

11.5   WHERE A PROSECUTION SUCCEEDS: SENTENCING AND THE HUMAN RIGHTS ACT

One area of criminal law that throws the relationship between the executive and the judiciary into particularly sharp focus is that of sentencing individuals who have been found guilty of particular offences. It is equally one that involves the interplay of judicial review, the European Convention on Human Rights (ECHR) and the Human Rights Act 1998 (HRA).

11.5.1   AUTOMATIC LIFE SENTENCE UNDER S 2 OF THE CRIME (SENTENCES) ACT 1997

In 1997, immediately prior to the election of that year, Parliament required the provision of automatic life sentences for those found guilty of a second serious offence. Thus, s 2 of the Crime (Sentences) Act 1997 required judges to pass indeterminate life sentences for those found guilty of a range of offences including attempted murder, rape, manslaughter, wounding, causing grievous bodily harm with intent and robbery with a real or imitation firearm, where the guilty person had been previously convicted of another offence on the list. Given their discontent with the provisions for mandatory sentencing in relation to convictions for murder, it can be appreciated that many of the judiciary, led by the late Lord Justice Taylor, saw the Act as a dangerous party-politicisation of the criminal justice system and an unwarranted interference by the legislature with the scope of judicial power and discretion, and were vociferous in their opposition to it.

However, even when the Act came into force, it still left some scope for judicial discretion whereby they could identify such 'exceptional circumstances' as could justify the non-application of the mandatory sentence. Until the implementation of the HRA, the question was as to what properly constituted such exceptional circumstances, and different courts tended to reach different conclusions of a more or less liberal nature. Thus, in *R v Stephens* (2000), the defendant, who already had a previous serious conviction, was found guilty of grievous bodily harm with intent and was consequently given an automatic life sentence. At his trial, the prosecution had offered, and Stephens had rejected, the opportunity to plead guilty to a lesser charge, which would not have led to the imposition of the automatic life sentence. When it emerged that his counsel had not advised him as to the possible consequences of his decision to defend the more serious charge, the Court of Appeal held that that fact amounted to sufficient exceptional circumstances to quash the life sentence. However, in *R v Turner* (2000), where the defendant was also found guilty of causing grievous bodily harm with intent, the court felt obliged to impose the automatic life sentence, even though a period of some 30 years had elapsed since his previous conviction for manslaughter at the age of 22. The court could find no exceptional circumstances.

This unsatisfactory situation was resolved by reference to the HRA in *R v Offen and Others* (2001), in which the Court of Appeal considered five related claims that the imposition of automatic life sentences was contrary to the ECHR. The facts of Offen's case provide a context for the decision.

Offen had robbed a building society using a toy gun. The cashiers thought the gun was real and placed £960 in his bag. During the robbery, he was nervous and shaking, and apologised to the staff as he left the building. A customer grabbed the bag with the money in it and gave it back to the building society. When he was arrested, Offen admitted the offence, but claimed he had not taken the medication he needed to deal with his schizophrenia. His previous conviction for robbery had been committed in similar circumstances. At his trial, he was subsequently sentenced automatically to life imprisonment.

In delivering its judgment, the Court of Appeal was extremely circumspect in considering its relationship with Parliament and its new powers under the HRA. It was equally firm, however, in its removal of the mandatory element from this aspect of the sentencing process.

As regards its relationship with Parliament, the court stressed that it was of the greatest importance to bear in mind Parliament's intention in establishing the automatic life sentences. In the present instance, it understood that intention as being to protect the public against a person who had committed two serious offences. The Court of Appeal went on, however, to draw the conclusion that, on the basis of that concentration on the importance of protecting the public, it could be assumed that the Act was not intended to apply to anyone who did not pose a future risk.

Focusing on the future danger posed by the offender to the public rather than on the mere fact of their having committed two offences would allow the court to decide each case on the basis of its own particular facts, and if the facts of any particular case showed that the statutory assumption was misplaced, then that would constitute exceptional circumstances for the purposes of s 2 of the 1997 Act. As examples, the committing of different offences, the age of the offender and the lapse of time between the offences could give rise to exceptional circumstances in the context of a particular case that could override the assumption as to the imposition of the mandatory life sentence.

The court's identification of Parliament's intention in passing the Act cannot be doubted. The supposed corollary of this intention is much less certain. However, its process of logic allowed the Court of Appeal to interpret the Act in such a way as to support its own preferred approach, which was effectively to remove the automatic element in the sentencing process and to reintroduce an element of judicial discretion. The foregoing interpretation of the Act was supported by the court's marshalling of the HRA. In their judgments, the three members of the Court of Appeal stated that s 2 of the 1997 Act did not contravene Arts 3 and 5 of the ECHR so long as, and only to the extent that, exceptional circumstances were construed in such a way that it did not result in offenders being sentenced to life imprisonment when they did not constitute a significant risk to the public: that is, as the Court of Appeal had already decided it should be construed. In reaching this conclusion, the Court of Appeal can be seen to be employing s 3 of the

HRA, in that it was interpreting the primary legislation of the Crime (Sentences) Act 1997 in such a way as to make it compatible with the ECHR rights. In so doing, the judiciary achieved its preferred end without having to issue a declaration of incompatibility and without having to rely on the government introducing an amendment to its own Powers of Criminal Courts (Sentencing) Act 2000, s 109 of which had re-enacted s 2 of the 1997 Act.

Indeterminate sentences for public protection

Section 109 of the Powers of Criminal Courts (Sentencing) Act 2000 was repealed by s 332 of the Criminal Justice Act 2003, and replaced by ss 224–236 of that Act. Those provisions introduced two new forms of custodial sentence under the heading of 'dangerous offenders':

(i)   imprisonment for public protection (IPP); and

(ii)   extended sentences for certain violent or sexual offences.

Imprisonment for public protection required the court to impose an indeterminate term in circumstances in which the offender satisfied the criteria of dangerousness therein defined.

In doing so, parliament replaced the relatively simple provision of two serious offences leading to an 'automatic' life sentence with an apparently more flexible concept of dangerousness. Thus under s 229 CJA 2003, courts were obliged to consider whether an offender has fallen into a category of dangerousness by virtue of being convicted of a 'specified offence' and such a determination required the judge to consider degrees of risks of serious harm from further offences by the offender. However, the apparent discretion given to the sentencing court by s 229 was undercut by the prescriptive language of the provision with the result that the courts were effectively bound by a similar test as had originally been required under s 109 of the Powers of Criminal Courts (Sentencing) Act 2000. As a result, individuals convicted of relatively trivial offences with comparatively short minimum periods to serve could receive indeterminate sentences under s 229. An attempt to remedy the clear inequity of such consequences was made in ss 13–18 of the Criminal Justice and Immigration Act 2008, to the effect that an *in*determinate sentence could only be imposed when the *determinate* term would have been at least four years' imprisonment. Subsequently the Legal Aid, Sentencing and Punishment of Offenders Act (LAPSO) 2012 abolished the penalty of an indeterminate sentence for public protection replacing it with the imposition of a life sentence on conviction for a second serious offence. LAPSO 2012 also amended the use of extended sentences. That being said, it must be recognised that the indeterminate sentence still exists as it still binds those who received it, and there are currently 3,998 prisoners serving such sentences.

In *James v UK* (2013) the ECtHR held that if a prisoner was beyond the expiry of the minimum term of their sentence of imprisonment for public protection without being able to access rehabilitative courses, this would violate the ECHR 1950 Art 5(1).

However, the Supreme Court did not apply this case in *R (on the application of Kaiyam) v Secretary of State for Justice* (2014), on the grounds that the availability of ancillary services could not affect the overall lawfulness of the detention. Subsequently, in November 2016, HM Inspector of Prisons, Peter Clarke, expressed the view that it was 'widely accepted that implementation of the sentence was flawed' and that 'decisive action' was needed for three main reasons:

- Fairness and justice.
- Cost to the public purse.
- The significant pressures that high numbers of IPP prisoners place on the system.

In the light of such criticism it came as no surprise that new rules came into force in November 2016 giving effect to a ministerial decision to allow the release of IPP prisoners without an oral hearing.

11.5.2   MANDATORY LIFE SENTENCES IN RELATION TO MURDER

When the death penalty for murder was removed in 1965, it was replaced by a mandatory life sentence, that is, if an individual is found guilty of murder, the court has no alternative but to sentence them to a period of life imprisonment. By definition, a 'life sentence' is for an indeterminate period, but the procedure is for a period to be specified, which the person must serve before they can be considered for release on parole. The problematic question of who sets this tariff is considered below. The judiciary have been consistently opposed to this fettering of their discretion; a number of leading judges, including the past Lord Chief Justices Bingham and Taylor, have spoken out against it, and in 1993 Lord Chief Justice Lane led a committee that recommended that the mandatory sentence be removed. In 1989, a Select Committee of the House of Lords, appointed to report on murder and life imprisonment, recommended the abolition of the mandatory life sentence. Lord Lane, formerly Lord Chief Justice, chaired a Committee on the Penalty for Homicide, which also produced a critical report in 1993:

> (1) The mandatory life sentence for murder is founded on the assumption that murder is a crime of such unique heinousness that the offender forfeits for the rest of his existence his right to be set free. (2) That assumption is a fallacy. It arises from the divergence between the legal definition of murder and that which the lay public believes to be murder. (3) The common law definition of murder embraces a wide range of offences, some of which are truly heinous, some of which are not. (4) The majority of murder cases, though not those which receive the most publicity, fall into the latter category. (5) It is logically and jurisprudentially wrong to require judges to sentence all categories of murderer in the same way, regardless of the particular

circumstances of the case before them. (6) It is logically and constitutionally wrong to require the distinction between the various types of murder to be decided (and decided behind the scenes) by the executive as is, generally speaking, the case at present . . .

As their Lordships correctly pointed out, there can be degrees of heinousness, even in regard to murder, and not all of those convicted deserve to be sentenced to life imprisonment. Mercy killers surely should not be treated in the same way as serial killers. This desire of the judges to remove the restriction in their sentencing power has, however, run up against the wish of politicians to be seen as tough on crime, or at least not soft on crime.

The uncomfortable relationship between criminal justice and party politics can be seen in the conviction for murder of Norfolk farmer Tony Martin in April 2000. Martin had used a shotgun to shoot two people who had broken into his farmhouse. One was injured and the other, 16-year-old Fred Barras, was killed. Martin was charged with murder and, at his trial, evidence was introduced to show that he had lain in wait for his victims, had set traps in his house and had used an illegal pump-action shotgun to shoot Barras in the back as he was attempting to run away. By a majority of 10:2 the jury found him guilty of murder and, as required, the judge sentenced him to life imprisonment. Much of the press considered the sentence to be outrageously severe on a man whom they portrayed as merely protecting his property against the depredations of lawless louts. (It has to be stated that Barras and his accomplice did have 114 previous convictions between them.) In focusing attention on the right of individuals to use force to protect their property – which, in any case, they already had so long as they did not use more than reasonable force – the press displaced attention from where it could best be focused. Had the court not been required to pass a mandatory sentence, then it would have been able to pass a more suitable sentence, if that had been appropriate in the circumstances. The press, however, would not countenance the granting of such discretionary sentencing power to the courts which, in other circumstances, they persistently characterise as being out of touch and dangerously soft on criminals.

The subsequent provision of s 76 of the Criminal Justice and Immigration Act 2008 did no more than provide a gloss on the existing law of self-defence. It maintained the existing common law test established in *Palmer v R* (1971), to the effect that the defence is available to someone only if they honestly believed it was necessary to use force and if the degree of force used was not disproportionate in the circumstances as they viewed them. Consequently a person who uses force is to be judged subjectively, on the basis of the circumstances as they saw them, and in the heat of the moment they will not be expected to have judged exactly what action was called for, and that a degree of latitude may be given to a person who only did what they honestly or instinctively thought was necessary.

In *R v Hussain* (2010) Munir Hussain had discovered three masked men in his house. The burglars tied up and threatened to kill him and his family. However, Hussain's son managed to escape and told his uncle what had happened. When help arrived, the intruders ran away, but Hussain and his brother chased and caught one of them. He was Walid Salem, a criminal with more than 50 previous convictions. The brothers then subjected Salem to what the judge described as a 'dreadful, violent attack'.

The revenge attack left Salem with a permanent brain injury after he was struck with a cricket bat so hard that it broke into three pieces. At their trial it was decided that the brothers' reaction was disproportionate and Munir Hussain was sentenced to 30 months' detention and his brother to 39 months' detention. The case caused a furore in the press and eventually, on appeal, Hussain and his brother were given suspended sentences on the ground that the assault on Salem was 'totally out of character'. Section 76 of the Criminal Justice and Immigration Act 2008 has now been amended by the Crime and Courts Act 2013 to allow homeowners to use disproportionate force against intruders, provided it is not 'grossly' disproportionate. Sub-section 5A now states:

> In a householder case, the degree of force used by D is not to be regarded as having been reasonable in the circumstances as D believed them to be if it was grossly disproportionate in those circumstances.

11.5.3   SENTENCE TARIFFS

In relation to mandatory life sentences, the Home Secretary formerly had the power to set what is known as the tariff, whereas in relation to other, non-mandatory life sentences, it was for the trial judge to set the tariff. The tariff was that part of the sentence that must be served before the person serving the prison sentence could be considered for release, on licence, by the Parole Board. Release after the tariff period was not automatic and depended on the decision of the Parole Board, which in turn depended on the behaviour of the individual while in prison and the extent to which they posed a threat to the public. The justification of the tariff was that it served to establish a minimum period of punishment and retribution. The question, however, was whether such a period should be determined by a member of the executive, by the Home Secretary or by the judiciary. As has been stated, the working out of this question involved an interplay of judicial review, the ECHR and the HRA, and demonstrated the way in which the HRA increased the powers of the courts in relation to the executive in a way that judicial review could never encompass.

There had been substantial criticism of the process of setting the tariff. In 1996, the Home Affairs Select Committee of the House of Commons took evidence and deliberated on the relevant issues. Their report (*Murder: The Mandatory Life Sentence*) recommended that the tariff and release decisions be removed from the Home Secretary and left with the trial judge and the Parole Board.

Before examining the situation in England, it should be noted that in Scotland, the Convention Rights (Compliance) (Scotland) Act 2001 now provides that in the case of mandatory life sentences, the trial judge fixes the 'punishment part' of the sentence, on the expiry of which the Parole Board decides on possible release on licence. The test applied to determine suitability for release is identical to that applied to discretionary life prisoners in England and Wales, namely, that the Parole Board is satisfied that the prisoner does not present a substantial risk of re-offending in a manner that is dangerous to life or limb, or of committing serious sexual offences.

The situation is similar in Northern Ireland: there, the Life Sentences (Northern Ireland) Order 2001 provides that the trial judge decides the tariff for a mandatory life prisoner and that release after serving the tariff is determined by Life Sentence Review Commissioners (with a status and functions very similar to those of the Parole Board operating in England and Wales). The test applied by the Commissioners is one of protection of the public from 'serious harm', this term meaning the risk of harm from violent or sexual offences.

There are in effect three distinct elements in a mandatory life sentence: the minimum term, the period after the minimum term has been served until the recommendation of the Parole Board to release the person on licence, and the overhanging possibility that the person might be recalled to prison if they breach the conditions of their release on licence at a later date. The first part – the minimum term – is punitive. The other elements are preventive and intended for public protection.

However, the question still arises as to what should happen where there is no need for any preventive element to a sentence. Precisely such situations arose in the related cases of *R v Lichniak* (2002) and *R v Pyrah* (2002). The two individuals concerned had been found guilty of murder, but in both cases the sentencing judges had clearly stated that neither of them represented a future danger to the community, nor was there any likelihood of their committing such offences in the future. Both were nonetheless subject to the mandatory life sentence for murder and appealed unsuccessfully to both the Court of Appeal and the House of Lords. Both courts held that the imposition of the mandatory life sentence did not violate Arts 3 or 5 of the ECHR and that such sentences were neither arbitrary nor disproportionate.

The decision of the House of Lords is, to say the least, somewhat surprising, especially when it is compared with the decision of the Privy Council in *Reyes v the Queen* (2002). In *Reyes*, it was held that a mandatory death sentence, operative in the jurisdiction of Belize, amounted to inhuman and degrading punishment. Among the grounds for that decision was the fact that the mandatory nature of the sentence precluded proper judicial consideration of the appropriate penalty. Although the Privy Council did expressly limit its reasoning to the Belize legal system in *Reyes*, and although the death penalty does stand alone as the harshest of penalties, it is nonetheless arguable that the mandatory life sentence in the United Kingdom achieves a similar, if less severe, consequence in limiting proper judicial consideration of the appropriate sentence to apply in different circumstances. It is apparent in both the *Lichniak* and *Pyrah* cases that the judges deciding the sentences did not really think that life sentences were appropriate, yet they had no choice but to pass such sentences. Can the imposition of an inappropriate sentence be anything other than arbitrary and disproportionate?

As will be considered below, perhaps Lichniak and Pyrah were unfortunate in the timing of their appeals. Those appeals followed a number of highly sensitive decisions in which the courts had used their powers under the HRA to remove the powers of the Home Secretary to set the punitive tariff in mandatory life sentences. Perhaps, given the highly charged, not to say antagonistic, nature of the relationship between the courts and past Home Secretaries, removing the mandatory sentence altogether was a step too far for the courts, or at least a step further than they thought it wise to take under political circumstances at that time.

Juveniles

Just as in the cases of adults sentenced to a mandatory life sentence, so the Home Secretary used to have the power to set the tariff for juveniles sentenced to detention at Her Majesty's pleasure, that is, for an indeterminate period. However, in 1999, the European Court of Human Rights held that the exercise of that power by the Home Secretary was in contravention of the ECHR. The Home Secretary subsequently relinquished the power. The path to such a resolution is traced below.

In 1993, Jon Venables and Robert Thompson, two 10-year-old boys, were found guilty of the murder of two-year-old James Bulger. As juveniles, they were both sentenced, as required under s 53(1) of the Children and Young Persons Act (CYPA) 1933, to be detained at Her Majesty's pleasure. The trial judge recommended a tariff of eight years as an appropriate period for retribution and deterrence, although, on review, Lord Chief Justice Taylor recommended that the tariff should be increased to 10 years. However, the ultimate decision as to the length of the tariff lay with the then Conservative Home Secretary, Michael Howard. Given the particularly brutal manner of the killing, there was very considerable public interest in the case and the sentencing of the two boys. *The Sun* newspaper organised a public petition to the effect that they should be 'locked up for life' or serve at least 25 years. Some 306,000 people signed and submitted petitions to that effect to the Home Secretary, who ultimately decided that the tariff should be set at 15 years. Doubts were raised as to whether, in ignoring the recommendations of the judges in reaching his decision, the Home Secretary had taken a (party) political rather than quasi-judicial decision to assuage the concerns of potential voters by demonstrating a willingness to be tough on crime and criminals.

R v Secretary of State for the Home Department ex p Venables and Thompson (1997)

Lawyers for Venables and Thompson successfully sought judicial review of the Home Secretary's decision. On final appeal to the House of Lords (*Secretary of State for the Home Department v V (A Minor) and T (A Minor)* (1997)), the Home Secretary having lost all the previous cases, it was held that in setting the tariff at 15 years, he had not taken into account the welfare of the children as required by s 44 of the CYPA 1933. Additionally, the House of Lords stated that although the Home Secretary was entitled to take into account considerations of a public character, he must distinguish between legitimate public concern and mere public clamour. The Home Secretary had therefore misdirected himself and his decision was unlawful and should be quashed. The mechanism of judicial review therefore allowed the court to insist that, even if statute permitted the executive, in the form of the Home Secretary, to take sentencing decisions, in reaching any such decision, he must act in a judicial rather than a political manner. As Lord Steyn expressed it ([1997] 3 All ER 97 at 147):

> In fixing a tariff the Home Secretary is carrying out, contrary to the constitutional principle of the separation of powers between the executive and the judiciary, a classic judicial function.

What judicial review could not achieve, however, was either the removal of the Home Secretary's general power or the substitution of the courts' decision for his particular decision. It would still have been for the Home Secretary to take the new decision as to the appropriate tariff, had the Strasbourg Court not intervened before such a decision could be taken.

T v UK; V v UK (1999)

Lawyers for Thompson and Venables had appealed to the ECtHR, claiming that many aspects of their clients' cases had been conducted in a manner that was contrary to the ECHR. In December 1999, the ECtHR delivered its judgment and found that although many of the grounds for appeal were unfounded, the applicants had been denied a fair trial in accordance with Art 6 of the ECHR, as they had not been able to participate effectively in the proceedings. The reason for this finding was that the conduct of the case in the Crown Court must have been at times incomprehensible and frightening to the two boys, and it was not sufficient that they were represented by skilled and experienced lawyers. The Court also held that there had been a violation of Art 6 on the grounds that they had been denied a fair hearing by 'an independent and impartial tribunal'. The fixing of the tariff was tantamount to a sentencing procedure and therefore should have been exercised by an impartial judge, rather than a member of the executive, as the Home Secretary clearly was.

Subsequent to, and consequent upon, this decision, the Home Secretary, by this time the Labour politician Jack Straw, announced in March 2000 that legislation would be introduced to provide that tariffs for juveniles should be set by trial judges, in open court, in the same way as they are for adults sentenced to discretionary life sentences. Until that legislation was passed by Parliament, the Home Secretary undertook that in using his statutory power, he would follow the recommendations of the Lord Chief Justice. In July 2000, Lord Chief Justice Woolf issued a practice statement setting out the criteria to be applied in establishing the tariff for juvenile offenders, and in October of that year, in line with those criteria, he set the tariff for both Thompson and Venables at eight years, which meant that they were immediately open to the operation of the normal parole system. Lord Woolf's decision did not go without challenge both in the media and in the courts, a subsequent application for judicial review being rejected, but perhaps the last words on the matter should remain with him ([2001] 1 All ER 737 at 741):

> The one overriding mitigating feature of the offence is the age of the two boys when the crime was committed. However grave their crime, the fact remains that if that crime had been committed a few months earlier, when they were under 10, the boys could not have been tried or punished by the courts. In addition, account has to be taken of the fact that the last seven years, the period of their adolescence, has been passed in custody.

In January 2001, Dame Elizabeth Butler-Sloss, President of the Family Division, granted a permanent injunction banning the media in England from revealing any information about the new identities that Thompson and Venables would live under when they were eventually released from custody. In the light of the many threats that had been made against Thompson and Venables, the order, the first of its kind, was made on the basis of the HRA and Art 2 of the ECHR, in that the court held that it was necessary in order to protect their right to life.

In June 2001, the new Home Secretary, David Blunkett, announced that the Parole Board had agreed to the release on life licence of Thompson and Venables. On 2 March 2010 it was confirmed by the Ministry of Justice that Jon Venables had been recalled to custody following a breach of his licence conditions (see www.publications.parliament.uk/pa/ld200910/ldhansrd/text/100308–0010.htm).

Adults

As has been pointed out above, the regime that once applied to juveniles sentenced to indeterminate sentences also applied to adults who were sentenced to mandatory, but indeterminate, life sentences. Not only did the courts accept the Home Secretary's general power to determine a tariff, but, more contentiously, it had been accepted that the Home Secretary could set an 'all life' tariff in appropriate circumstances, such as those in *R v Secretary of State for the Home Department ex p Myra Hindley* (2000). Hindley had been convicted of murder in 1966 and was sentenced as required by the Murder (Abolition of Death Penalty) Act 1965 to life imprisonment. As the House of Lords later stated, she was subject to a mandatory life sentence, itself subject to a discretionary executive power, vested in the Home Secretary to direct her release on licence at any time. The fact that the Home Secretary had such discretion to release on licence led to the conclusion that he equally had the discretion not to release her, as long as he complied with the duty to reconsider his decision at reasonable intervals.

Hindley's case was decided prior to the coming into effect of the HRA and, therefore, in deciding it, the courts considered themselves not at liberty to apply that Act. Subsequently, in an interview in the journal the *New Statesman*, Lord Chief Justice Woolf, who, as the then Master of the Rolls, had sat in the Court of Appeal in the *Hindley* case, expressed the view that, in reaching his decision in that case, he had been constrained by the law as it then was. He did concede, however, that the HRA had altered the situation. Consequently, it was likely that in the future domestic courts would follow the ECtHR in *T v UK* and *V v UK*, and hold that it would be in breach of Art 6 for the Home Secretary to continue to determine the tariff in murder cases, on the grounds that such a procedure would be a denial of the right to a fair hearing by 'an independent and impartial tribunal'. Lord Woolf's interview was widely reported in the news media, with the strong implication that the courts in the future might sanction the release of Myra Hindley.

Subsequent to his interview in the *New Statesman*, however, the Lord Chief Justice seemed to reconsider the wisdom of a direct challenge to the Home Secretary's power to set the tariff in mandatory life sentences.

R v Secretary of State for the Home Department ex p Anderson and Taylor (2001)

In November 2001, two convicted murderers complained that the Home Secretary had fixed their tariffs higher than had been recommended by the judges at their trial: 20 years instead of 15 years for the first, and 30 years instead of 16 years for the second. They argued that it was incompatible with Art 6(1) of the ECHR for a member of the executive to carry out what was in fact a sentencing exercise. The Court of Appeal, made up of Lord Woolf and Simon Brown and Buxton LJJ, rejected their arguments. In doing so, the Court of Appeal's disapproving views on mandatory life sentences in general were expressed by Simon Brown LJ, who stated that ([2001] EWCA Civ 1698 para 56):

> I accept of course that the mandatory life sentence is unique. But not all the offences for which it is imposed can be regarded as uniquely grave. Rather the spectrum is a wide one with multiple sadistic murders at one end and mercy killings at the other. Lifelong punitive detention will be appropriate only exceptionally.

Nonetheless, the Court of Appeal felt itself constrained by case law from the ECtHR and, in particular, the authority of *Wynne v UK* decided in 1994 and *T v UK* and *V v UK*. In *Wynne*, the ECtHR decided that no violation arose under Art 5(4) in relation to the continued detention after release, and recall to prison, of a mandatory life prisoner convicted of an intervening offence of manslaughter, the tariff element of which had expired. The ECtHR held that the sentence constituted a *punishment* for life. In *T v UK* and *V v UK*, while citing the *Wynne* judgment, the ECtHR reiterated that an adult mandatory life sentence constituted punishment for life. On the face of those authorities, the Court of Appeal in *Anderson and Taylor* declined to challenge the Home Secretary's power in relation to mandatory life sentences.

Perhaps the Court of Appeal's reluctance to challenge the executive's power head-on was based on the realisation that, as the court noted, a decision on the same point was expected within the following year in the ECtHR (*Stafford v UK* (2002)). It is perhaps not overly cynical to suggest that the Court of Appeal adopted its conservative approach in the realisation that, in the context of the prevailing tense relationship between the Home Secretary and the courts, it was perhaps politic to leave the final decision to remove the Home Secretary's power to the ECtHR, which decision their Lordships clearly expected.

Stafford v UK (2002)

Derek Stafford was convicted of murder in 1967 and released on licence in April 1979. His licence required him to remain in the United Kingdom, but he left to live in South Africa. In April 1989 he was arrested in the United Kingdom, having returned from South Africa on a false passport. Although the possession of a false passport only led to a fine, he remained in custody due to the revocation of his life licence. He was released in March 1991, once again on a life licence. In 1994 he was convicted of conspiracy to forge travellers' cheques and passports and sentenced to six years' imprisonment. In 1996 the Parole Board recommended his release on life licence, having reached the conclusion that he did not present a danger of violent re-offending. The Secretary of State rejected the Board's recommendation. But for the revocation of his life licence, the applicant would have been released from prison on the expiry of the sentence for fraud in July 1997, and in June 1997 he sought judicial review of the Secretary of State's decision to reject the Board's recommendation for immediate release. He was successful at first instance, but both the Court of Appeal and the House of Lords denied his claim and upheld the power of the Home Secretary to revoke his licence and thus effectively detain him under ss 39(1) and 35(2) of the Criminal Justice Act 1991 (the latter subsequently replaced by s 29 of the Crime (Sentences) Act 1997), even though there was no prospect of his committing any violent crime in the future. Both courts, however, expressed unease at their decisions. As Lord Bingham CJ stated in the Court of Appeal ([1998] 1 WLR 503 at 518):

> The imposition of what is in effect a substantial term of imprisonment by the exercise of executive discretion, without trial, lies uneasily with ordinary concepts of the Rule of Law. I hope that the Secretary of State may, even now, think it right to give further consideration to the case.

When the case came before the Grand Chamber of the ECtHR in May 2002, and as the Court of Appeal in *Anderson* had expected, it held that it was no longer in the interest of justice to follow its previous decision in *Wynne*. The ECtHR stated that although it was not formally bound to follow any of its previous judgments, it was 'in the interests of legal certainty, foreseeability and equality before the law that it should not depart, without cogent reason, from precedents laid down in previous cases'. However, it felt that the fixing of the tariff for mandatory life sentences was clearly a sentencing exercise, and that it was no longer possible to distinguish between mandatory life prisoners, discretionary life prisoners and juvenile murderers as regards the nature of that sentencing process. The ECtHR also held that the finding in *Wynne* that the mandatory life sentence constituted punishment for life could no longer be maintained. It was therefore open to the court to decide that the Secretary of State's role in fixing the tariff was a sentencing exercise and not merely a matter relating to the administrative implementation of the sentence. As a result, it concluded that the exercise of such power by the Home Secretary was contrary to Art 5(1) and (4) of the ECHR.

When the decision of the ECtHR in *Stafford* was delivered, the UK press immediately returned to the possibility of the imminent release of the child killer Myra Hindley. What they failed to indicate was that the ECtHR itself, in line with previous statements of the UK courts, had actually recognised the validity of 'whole life' tariffs in exceptional circumstances. Its decision was merely that it was for the courts rather than the executive to make such recommendations. In any event, Hindley died in prison in November 2002.

The first person actually to benefit from the *Stafford* decision was Satpal Ram, who was released from prison in June 2002 after having served more than 15 years for a murder he claimed was committed in self-defence in a racial attack. The previous Home Secretary had overturned a Parole Board recommendation to release Mr Ram in 2000. The succeeding Home Secretary preferred to release him rather than contest an action for judicial review of his predecessor's decision, recognising that *Stafford* made any argument to the contrary untenable.

R v Secretary of State for the Home Department ex p Anderson and Taylor (2002)

By November 2002, the appeals in the *Anderson* and *Taylor* cases had reached the House of Lords and were considered by a seven-member panel, indicating their importance. The essential issue under consideration was the effect that the *Stafford* decision in the ECtHR would have on English law, s 35(2) and (3) of the Criminal Justice Act 1991 having been replaced by similar provisions under s 29 of the Crime (Sentences) Act 1997. In the event, the House of Lords followed the decision of the ECtHR and held that the fixing of the tariff for a convicted murderer was legally indistinguishable from the imposition of sentence. Consequently, to ensure compatibility with Art 6(1), any such tariff should be set by an independent and impartial tribunal and not the Home Secretary, who was part of the executive. It was therefore incompatible with Art 6 for the Home Secretary to fix the tariff of a convicted murderer. However, the House of Lords went on to decide that it was not possible to interpret s 29 of the Crime (Sentences) Act 1997 in such a way as to make it compatible with the rights provided under the ECHR. As a result, the House of Lords issued a declaration of incompatibility to the effect that s 29 was contrary to the right under Art 6 to have a sentence imposed by an independent and impartial tribunal.

The above series of cases demonstrates how the implied wishes of the Court of Appeal in *Anderson* could be given express effect in the later House of Lords' decision, without the possibility of any direct accusation of political interference on the part of the judiciary.

The political sensitivity of the preceding cases, and the extent to which they challenge executive power, may go some way to explain the apparent conservatism of the decision of the House of Lords in the *Lichniak* and *Pyrah* cases, considered previously. A close reading of the cases certainly reveals grounds for the House of Lords to overturn those decisions and to remove mandatory life sentences altogether.

The foregoing analysis has used the term 'tariff' to refer to the period that a person sentenced to a life term must serve for the purposes of punishment. It should be noted, however, that, in a Practice Statement issued in May 2002, the Lord Chief Justice accepted the recommendation of the Sentencing Advisory Panel that it should be replaced by the clearer expression 'minimum term'.

The political tension around the issue of sentencing was further heightened when, in May 2003, Home Secretary Blunkett announced his intention to introduce proposals that would introduce a new statutory system in relation to sentencing in murder cases, together with a new Sentencing Guidelines Council to advise judges on appropriate sentencing. The Home Secretary made it clear that he considered that the judges had failed to provide clear and consistent sentencing. Indeed, the proposal can be seen as a direct attack on the Lord Chief Justice, Lord Woolf, whose directive on sentencing, issued in 2002, had indicated that the previous 14-year minimum 'starting point' should be replaced by 16 years for more serious cases and 12 years for lesser crimes such as mercy killings. The Home Secretary was quoted as saying: 'I share public concern that some very serious criminals seem to be serving a relatively short spell in prison . . . It will be Parliament that decides the structure. It will be judges that act within it.' Not surprisingly, the Bar Council described the proposal as 'constitutionally a leap in the dark' and said that the Home Secretary was trying to 'institutionalise the grip of the executive around the neck of the judiciary'.

The proposed scheme was subsequently attacked by Lord Woolf in a speech on the Bill in the House of Lords in June of that year and in the background notes for which he stated that:

> The indirect, knock-on effect of the proposed minimum period is highly undesirable . . . Sentencing, particularly in relation to murder, should be removed from the political arena. The present proposal will have the effect of increasing political involvement.

The Lord Chief Justice also took exception to the proposal to appoint a senior police officer to the Sentencing Council (formerly the Sentencing Guidelines Council) and more generally highlighted the logical contradiction in the Home Secretary's approach. As Lord Woolf stated:

> It is surely extraordinary to propose a council to make guidelines and at the same time include your own guidance in the legislation establishing the council.

Nonetheless, both the Council and the sentencing guidelines in relation to murder were implemented in the Criminal Justice Act 2003, and were the first of its major changes in the criminal justice system to be brought into effect in January 2004.

Section 269 of the Act applies to any murders for which sentence is passed on or after 18 December 2003. It introduces a three-tier system (detailed in Sched 21) and requires the courts to apply the following sentencing principles:

Level 1: whole life sentences will be the starting point for

- multiple murders, that is, two or more, that show a substantial degree of pre-meditation, involve abduction of the victim prior to the killing or are sexual or sadistic;
- murder of a child following abduction or involving sexual or sadistic conduct;
- murder carried out through acts of terrorism;
- murder where the offender has been previously convicted of murder.

Level 2: attracting a 30-year minimum sentence for

- murders of police and prison officers in the course of duty;
- murder involving the use of a firearm or explosive;
- killing done for gain (burglary, robbery, etc, including professional or contract killing);
- killing intended to defeat ends of justice (killing of a witness);
- race/religion/sexual orientation motivated murder;
- single sadistic or sexual murder of an adult;
- multiple murders (other than those above).

Level 3: attracting a 25 year sentence for

- murders where the offender took a knife or other weapon to the scene intending to commit any offence and then used that knife or other weapon in committing the murder.

Level 4: a 15-year minimum sentence will apply for

- other murders by adults and all murders by children under 17.

The whole life recommendation does not apply to offenders below the age of 21, but offenders aged 18 to 20 years of age will be subject to either the 15- or 30-year starting points. Those aged 17 years or under will be subject to a 12-year starting point (House of Commons Briefing Paper, Number 3626, 12 November 2015, *Mandatory life sentences for murder*, Sally Lipscombe and Jacqueline Beard, 2015, London: House of Commons Library).

It should be emphasised that the above recommendations state starting points in sentencing, and once trial judges have determined the starting point by applying the above principles, they may consider aggravating and mitigating factors (examples of which are set out in the Act) and may move up or down from the starting point to arrive at the appropriate minimum term.

Aggravating factors may include

- a significant degree of planning or premeditation;
- the fact that the victim was particularly vulnerable because of age or disability;
- mental or physical suffering inflicted on the victim before death;
- abuse of a position of trust;
- use of duress or threats against another person to facilitate commission of the offence;
- the fact that the victim was providing a public service or performing a public duty; or
- concealment, destruction or dismemberment of body.

Mitigating factors may include

- an intention to cause serious bodily harm rather than to kill;
- lack of premeditation;
- the fact that the offender was suffering a mental disorder or disability which lowered his degree of culpability (falling short of a defence of diminished responsibility);
- the fact that offender was provoked (for example by prolonged stress);
- the fact that the offender acted to any extent in self-defence or in fear of violence;
- a belief by the offender that the murder was an act of mercy; and
- the age of the offender.

In *R v Jones; R v Chandi, Multani, Khangura and Dosanjh; R v Ashman; R v Hobson* (2005), the Court of Appeal held that the guidance in the Criminal Justice Act 2003 was provided to help a court assess the appropriate sentence. Although a court was to have regard to this guidance, each case would depend crucially on its particular facts and a court, proposing to depart from the guidelines, would have to set out its reasoning.

In the light of previous experience in the courts, and in a clear endeavour to ensure compliance with the ECHR, s 269 provides that the scheme is not compulsory. However, s 270 requires any judge who departs from the recommended sentences to explain their reasons for so doing in open court. In any event, the Attorney General has the power to challenge unduly lenient sentences and will be able to challenge any minimum term that he or she considers to be unduly lenient under the Criminal Justice Act principles (for further consideration of the Criminal Justice Act 2003, see above, 11.5.1).

The Home Secretary has – therefore – since the *Anderson* case in 2002 played no role in the setting of the minimum term to be served by an offender sentenced to life imprisonment for murder. If an offender sentenced to life imprisonment for murder wishes to appeal against the minimum term fixed then he or she can do so to the Court of Appeal.

The Secretary of State has the power under s 30 of the Crime (Sentences) Act 1997 to order the release of a prisoner subject to a mandatory life sentence in 'exceptional circumstances', justifying release on compassionate grounds. The ECtHR criticised this provision taken in conjunction with s 269, CJA 2003 in *Vinter v United Kingdom* (2013) as incompatible with Art 3 ECHR. To be compatible there had to be the possibility of release or review. The Court of Appeal in *Attorney General's Reference (No. 69 of 2013) (R v Newell, R v McLoughlin)* (2013) declined to follow *Vinter*, arguing that the scheme was sufficiently certain and that the UK was acting within its margin of appreciation. The statute was not incompatible with Art 3 ECHR.

11.5.4   PRISONER VOTING

Hirst v UK (No 2)

Convicted prisoners are currently barred by s 3 of the Representation of the People Act 1983 from voting in parliamentary or local elections. In March 2004, the ECtHR ruled in *Hirst v UK (No 2)* that the UK government's blanket ban prohibiting sentenced prisoners from voting was unlawful. Despite rejection in 2005 of the appeal against this judgment, which was mounted by the UK government – two protracted public consultation exercises – the same exclusionary policy remains in place. In an open letter (dated 21 May 2010) addressed to the Committee of Ministers at the Council of Europe, Juliet Lyon CBE, Director of the Prison Reform Trust, stated that up to 73,000 prisoners had been unlawfully denied the right to vote in the UK general and local elections on 6 May 2010. Nineteen of the 47 countries in the Council of Europe – which include all 27 EU Member States – have no restrictions on prisoners voting. In France and Germany courts have the power to impose loss of voting rights as an additional punishment, while Sweden, Switzerland and Denmark are among countries with no ban at all on voting for prisoners. Ireland ended a voting ban in 2006, giving all prisoners a postal vote in the constituency where they would normally live. In July 2011, the ECtHR Grand Chamber accepted a referral in the case of *Scoppola v Italy* involving issues analogous to those which arose in *Hirst*. The UK government successfully applied to intervene in that case and the Court granted an extension of six months from the date of the final decision in the *Scoppola* judgment before the government had to comply with its obligations to change the current law as it applies to prisoners. During this time a further 2,500 applications from prisoners in the UK were submitted to the ECtHR.

   The Grand Chamber of the ECtHR handed down judgment in *Scoppola* in 2012. The judgment does not overrule *Hirst* but substantially increases the margin of appreciation afforded to governments to implement the decision. The ECtHR reaffirmed the principles set out in *Hirst*, in particular that disenfranchisement which affects a group of people generally, automatically and indiscriminately, based solely on the fact that they are serving a prison sentence, irrespective of the length of the sentence and irrespective of the nature or gravity of their offence and their individual circumstances, is not compatible with Art 3 of Protocol No 1. However, the ECtHR held that proportionality did not require that the decision to deprive a convicted prisoner of the vote be taken by a judge. The clock is now ticking again for the UK government to implement the decision of the ECtHR.

In November 2012, the government published the Voting Eligibility (Prisoners) Draft Bill for pre-legislative scrutiny by a joint committee of both houses. It set out three options: a ban for prisoners sentenced to four years or more, a ban for prisoners sentenced to more than six months and a restatement of the existing ban. The Committee published its report on 18 December 2013 and recommended that the government should introduce legislation to allow all prisoners serving sentences of 12 months or less to vote in all UK parliamentary, local and European elections. Apart from a brief response in February 2014, the government has not responded substantively and did not bring forward a Bill with the 2014 Queen's Speech.

In October 2013 the Supreme Court gave judgment in the case of *R (Chester) v Secretary of State for Justice*. Mr Chester, a prisoner serving a sentence for murder, sought a declaration of incompatibility, arguing that domestic law was in breach of the ECHR, as found by the ECtHR. The Supreme Court held that that while, under s 2(1) of the Human Rights Act 1998, the Courts were obliged only to 'take into account' judgments of the European Court of Human Rights, a decision of the Grand Chamber of that court would have to involve some truly fundamental principle of domestic law or some most egregious oversight or misunderstanding before it could be appropriate for the Supreme Court to contemplate an outright refusal to follow it; that the Grand Chamber had clearly and consistently concluded that a general ban on convicted prisoners voting, as contained in s 3(1) of the Representation of the People Act 1983 and s 8 of the European Parliamentary Elections Act 2002, was incompatible with Art 3 of the First Protocol to the ECHR and, therefore, there was no prospect of any further meaningful dialogue between the United Kingdom and the European Court of Human Rights on the issue. The court also stated that prisoner voting did not involve some fundamental aspect of domestic law such as would justify the court refusing to apply the ECtHR decisions, but that, in circumstances where a declaration of incompatibility had already been made in other domestic proceedings, the matter was under active consideration by Parliament and the European court would without doubt uphold a ban depriving murderers serving sentences of life imprisonment of the right to vote, it would not be appropriate for the court to grant a declaration of incompatibility.

A further decision by the Supreme Court in the summer of 2014, *Moohan v Lord Advocate* (2014), confirmed that a blanket ban on prisoner voting in respect of a referendum was not unlawful, whether in domestic law, under the ECHR or under EU law.

CHAPTER SUMMARY: THE CRIMINAL PROCESS: (2) THE PROSECUTION

THE CROWN PROSECUTION SERVICE

The Crown Prosecution Service (CPS) was introduced in 1986. It is important to understand the five types of prosecution that existed before this time and how the CPS was supposed to resolve the criticisms of the old system. What sort of biases can occur in the use of prosecutorial discretion and why? Why were the police regarded as unsuitable to exercise the prosecutorial discretion? What were the police defences to those criticisms? The police argued that conviction rates vindicated the way they exercised their discretion. The Code for Crown Prosecutors (2013) specifies factors that should weigh for and against a prosecution.

OUT-OF-COURT DISPOSALS

There are a range of out-of-court disposals available as an alternative to prosecution.

JUDICIAL CONTROL

Judicial control of prosecution policy is very limited and amounts to being able to correct only irrational, unlawful or fraudulent decisions or those contrary to CPS policy (see *R v Metropolitan Police Commissioner ex p Blackburn* (1968)).

BAIL

Bail is the release from custody (whether after arrest, police interview or remand in a prison), pending a criminal trial, of an accused. Bail may be granted with or without conditions. For example, conditional bail might include that a person connected with a defendant in some way stands *surety*, on the promise that money will be paid into the court if the defendant does not turn up for their trial or otherwise absconds. Other conditions that might be attached to the grant of bail include reporting at a police station at specified times or so-called doorstep conditions, whereby the police can turn up at any time to check that a defendant is in a place (their home or workplace, usually) at a time when they should be. Not contacting witnesses, living at a specified address and surrendering a passport or otherwise not applying for travel documents are all other possible bail conditions. The important issue raised here is how best the bail regulations should be framed so as to balance the conflicting interests of public safety and the liberty of the defendant, who enjoys the presumption of innocence until and in the event of their guilt being proven in a court of law. Public safety would perhaps be best served by keeping everyone accused of a crime in custody until their trial. This, though, would clearly be unnecessarily draconian. Conversely, civil liberty and the presumption of innocence might be best served by allowing every suspect to remain free, however heinous the crime of which they have been accused and whatever their past record.

PLEA BARGAINING AND RELATED MATTERS

Although English law does not recognise plea bargaining, the practice whereby judges give an advance indication of sentence on the basis of a guilty plea is now established. This must take place in open court. Prosecutors have a responsibility to scrutinise the basis of such guilty pleas and only to accept them if accurate.

THE SENTENCING PROCESS, THE SEPARATION OF POWERS AND THE HRA

Cases relating to s 3 powers:

- *R v A* (2001);
- *Re S* (2002);
- *Mendoza v Ghaidan* (2004).

Cases relating to declarations of incompatibility:

- *R v (1) Mental Health Review Tribunal, North & East London Region* (2001);
- *Wilson v Secretary of State for Trade and Industry* (2003);
- *A and others v Secretary of State for the Home Department* (2004);
- *R (Clift) v Secretary of State for the Home Department* (2006);
- *T v Chief Constable of Greater Manchester* (2013).

Cases relating to sentencing:

- *R v Offen and Others* (2001);
- *R v Secretary of State for the Home Department ex p Anderson and Taylor* (2002).

By s 229 of the Criminal Justice Act 2003, the courts are obliged to consider whether an offender has fallen into a category of dangerousness by virtue of being convicted of a 'specified offence' and it requires the courts to consider degrees of risks of serious harm from further offences by such an offender.

FOOD FOR THOUGHT

1   Currently one in 10 of the prison population are serving an imprisonment for public protection sentence (see the Prison Reform Trust report *Unjust Deserts: Imprisonment for Public Protection*, 2010). This imprisonment is based on an assessment of 'dangerousness'. In 2010 these indeterminate sentences cost the public purse in excess of £100 million. Are indeterminate sentences ethically and practically justifiable?

2   On 22 November 2013, the prison population in England and Wales was 85,363. When Ken Clarke was Home Secretary for the first time (from 1992 to 1993), the average prison population was 44,628. According to the government, the overall cost of the criminal justice system has risen from 2 per cent of GDP to 2.5 per cent over the last 10 years. That is a higher per capita level than the US or any EU country. Court-ordered community sentences were more effective (by seven percentage points) at reducing one-year proven re-offending rates than custodial sentences of less than 12 months for similar offenders. Prison has a poor record for reducing re-offending – 49 per cent of adults are reconvicted within one year of being released. For those serving sentences of less than 12 months, this increases to 59 per cent. For those who have served more than 10 previous custodial sentences the rate of re-offending rises to 77 per cent (see the *Bromley Briefing*, June 2011). Should short custodial sentences be abolished?

FURTHER READING

Ashworth, A, *Sentencing and Criminal Justice*, 2010, Cambridge: CUP

Ashworth, A and Redmayne, M, *The Criminal Process*, 2010, Oxford: OUP

Baldwin, J and McConville, M, *Negotiated Justice: Pressures on Defendants to Plead Guilty*, 1977, Oxford: Martin Robertson

Bindaman, D, 'Crown duals' (1999) Law Soc Gazette 22

Buxton, R, 'The private prosecutor as a minister of justice' [2009] 6 Crim LR 427

Carkeek, L, 'Assisted suicide guidance' (2009) 159 NLJ 1391

Cockburn, JS and Green, TA, *Twelve Good Men and True*, 1988, Princeton: Princeton UP

Devlin, P, *Trial by Jury*, 1956, London: Stevens

Findlay, M and Duff, P, *The Jury Under Attack*, 1988, London: Butterworth

Grieve, D, *The Case for the Prosecution: Independence and the Public Interest*, www.gov.uk/government/speeches/the-case-for-the-prosecution-independence-and-the-public-interest

Hastie, R, *Inside the Juror: The Psychology of Juror Decision Making*, 1993, Cambridge: CUP

Hucklesby, A and Wahidin, A (eds), *Criminal Justice*, 2013, Oxford: OUP

Lawrence, J, O'Kane, M, Rab, S and Nakhwal, J, 'Hardcore bargains: what could plea bargaining offer in UK criminal cartel cases?' (2008) 7(1) Comp LJ 17

Richardson, J (ed), *Archbold: Criminal Pleading, Evidence and Practice*, 2016, London: Sweet & Maxwell

Rose, D, *In the Name of the Law – The Collapse of Criminal Justice*, 1996, London: Jonathan Cape

Sanders, A, 'Class bias in prosecutions' (1985) 24 Howard J 176

Sanders, A and Young, R, *Criminal Justice*, 2010, Oxford: OUP

Spencer, J, ' "Fare-dodging" – strict liability for fraud?' (2014) Arch Rev 5 (on private prosecutions)

Thompson, EP, *Writing by Candlelight*, 1980, London: Merlin

Wurtzel, D, 'Spotlight on the CPS' (2009) *Counsel*, 1 October

USEFUL WEBSITE

www.cps.gov.uk
This is the website of the Crown Prosecution Service.

COMPANION WEBSITE

Now visit the companion website to:

- test your understanding of the key terms using our Flashcard Glossary;
- revise and consolidate your knowledge of 'The criminal process: (2) The prosecution' using our multiple choice question testbank;
- view the link to the Useful Website above.

www.routledge.com/cw/slapper

12.1   INTRODUCTION

12.2   THE CONSTITUTIONAL ROLE OF THE JUDICIARY

Not only did this mean that judges could be dismissed when the monarch so decided, but it highlighted the lack of independence of the law from the state in the form, and person, of the monarch. With the victory of Parliament and the establishment of a state based on popular sovereignty, and limited in its powers, the independence of the judiciary was confirmed in the Act of Settlement 1701. The centrality of the independence of the judges and the legal system from direct control or interference from the state in the newly established constitution was emphasised in the writing of the English philosopher, John Locke, who saw it as one of the essential reasons for, and justifications of, the social contract on which the social structure was assumed to be based.

In order to buttress the independence of the judiciary and remove them from the danger of being subjected to political pressure, it has been made particularly difficult to remove senior judges once they have been appointed. Their independence of thought and opinion is also protected by the doctrine of judicial immunity. Both of these principles will be considered in more detail below, as will the change in the procedure for appointing judges, which cannot but have had an impact on their perceived independence from politics and politicians.

12.2.1   THE CONSTITUTIONAL ROLE OF THE LORD CHANCELLOR

The following brief historical consideration of the constitutional position of the Lord Chancellor and the Appellate Committee of the House of Lords, as the highest court in England was correctly referred to, has to be placed within the immediate context of the changes made by the Constitutional Reform Act (CRA) 2005, which radically altered both institutions. The point of it is to highlight why those changes were, and arguably had to be, made.

The Lord Chancellor always held an anomalous position in respect of the separation of powers in the contemporary state, in that the holder of that position played a key role in each of the three elements of the state. The Lord Chancellor was the most senior judge in the English court structure, sitting as they did in the House of Lords. At the same time, however, the Lord Chancellorship was a party-political appointment, and the occupant of the office owed their preferment to the Prime Minister of the day. Not only was the incumbent a member of the executive, having a seat in the Cabinet, but they were also responsible for the operation of their own government department. In addition to these roles, it should not be overlooked that the Chancellor was also the Speaker of the House of Lords in its general role as a legislative forum.

The party-political role of the Lord Chancellor gave rise to a furore when, in February 2001, Lord Irvine, the then New Labour appointee, personally wrote to lawyers who were known sympathisers of the Labour Party, asking them to donate at least £200 to the party at a fundraising dinner he was to host. His political critics made much of the fact that, as the person ultimately responsible for appointing the judiciary, his soliciting of party funds from those who might apply for such positions in the future could be represented as improper. As such, the press immediately entitled it the 'cash for wigs' affair, echoing the previous 'cash for questions' scandal in the House of Commons and the subsequent 'cash for peerages' scandal. The Lord Chancellor, however, refused to apologise for his action. In a statement to the House of Lords, delivered in his political persona and therefore two paces apart from the woolsack on which he sat when acting as the Speaker of the House of Lords, he stated that:

> I do not believe I have done anything wrong nor do I believe that I have broken any current rules. If I did I would be the first to apologise.

According to Lord Irvine, it was misconceived to claim that the Lord Chancellor was not a party-political post, and that every minister from the Prime Minister down was involved in fundraising. The best that could be said for the Lord Chancellor was that, although he had done nothing unlawful, he had acted in an unwise, politically naïve and injudicious manner, and one that once again brought the anomalous constitutional role of his office to the political foreground and renewed calls for its reformation, if not removal.

In addition to difficulties arising directly from his responsibility for implementing political policies in relation to the legal system, the Lord Chancellor's judicial role also came into question. As a consequence of the fact that the appointment of the Lord Chancellor is a purely political one, there is no requirement that the incumbent should have held any prior judicial office. Indeed, in the case of Lord Irvine, he had never served in any judicial capacity, making his reputation as a highly successful barrister. Nonetheless, as Lord Chancellor, he was the most senior judge and was entitled to sit, as he thought appropriate (see below, 12.2.2, for further observations about the Lord Chancellor's residual powers).

There was, however, a much more fundamental issue relating to the manner in which the Lord Chancellor's former multifunctional role may be seen as having breached the doctrine of the separation of powers. There cannot but be doubts as to the impropriety of a member of the executive functioning as a member of the judiciary and Lord Irvine himself withdrew from sitting in a case in March 1999 in which he recognised the possibility of a conflict of interest. That case involved an action by the family of a man who had died in police custody. The suggestion was made that the Lord Chancellor's participation on the judicial panel raised doubts as to whether the case would be decided by an independent and impartial tribunal. Given his recent guidelines warning the judiciary about the need to be sensitive to issues of conflict of interest, the Lord Chancellor clearly felt himself required to stand down from hearing the case.

In *McGonnell v UK* (2000), the European Court of Human Rights (ECtHR) confirmed the previous decision of the Commission in relation to the judicial function of the Bailiff of the island of Guernsey. It was held that the fact that the Bailiff had acted as the judge in a case in which he had also played an administrative role was in breach of Art 6 of the European Convention on Human Rights (ECHR). In the words of the Commission decision:

> It is incompatible with the requisite appearance of independence and impartiality for a judge to have legislative and executive functions as substantial as those carried out by the Bailiff.

Although those words could apply equally to the Lord Chancellor, the actual court decision was limited to the situation of the Bailiff, and Lord Irvine made it clear that he considered its application to be limited to the particular facts of the Guernsey situation. In any event, the Lord Chancellor continued not to sit on cases where there might appear to be a conflict between his judicial and other roles. In February 2003, the Lord Chancellor's dual role as judge and member of the executive came under attack in the parliamentary assembly of the Council of Europe, which oversees the operation of the ECHR (see Chapter 5). A Dutch member, Erik Jurgens, a vice president of the assembly, tabled a motion that stated that:

> The assembly . . . has repeatedly stressed that judges should be a completely independent branch of government. It is undeniable that combining the function of judge with functions in other branches of government calls that independence seriously into question.

Mr Jurgens was quoted as saying that he was advising eastern European countries seeking entry to the Council of Europe that they would not be admitted unless their judges were totally independent, so it was an anomaly that one of the original members had a figure like the Lord Chancellor, and further that:

> Sooner or later a case is going to come to the European Court of Human Rights at Strasbourg, and I think they will certainly say that this is an unacceptable combination.

In April 2003, Lord Irvine defended the unique position of the Lord Chancellor in an appearance before the parliamentary select committee with oversight of the Lord Chancellor's Department. Questioned on the conflict inherent in his power to make law and still sit as a judge, he responded that he had 'difficulty seeing why this issue is so important', and argued against changing a legal system that had an enviable international reputation, simply for the sake of constitutional purity. As he put it:

> The basic point is that the higher judiciary accept this role – they believe profoundly that it is a superior system to any other.

The Constitutional Reform Act 2005

While Lord Irvine preferred to maintain his position rather than bow to constitutional purity, his views were apparently not shared by his colleagues in government and most importantly the Prime Minister, who sacked him in June 2003. As part of a Cabinet reshuffle, which appeared to involve a power struggle between the Home Secretary and the Lord Chancellor, which the former won, Lord Irvine was not only removed from office, but it was announced that his office itself was to disappear. A new ministry, the Department for Constitutional Affairs, was to replace the Lord Chancellor's Department and Lord Falconer was appointed Secretary of State for Constitutional Affairs to replace Lord Irvine as Lord Chancellor. It would appear that the announcement was made without anyone having thought through the constitutional implications, or indeed practicalities, of simply abolishing the position of the Lord Chancellor. Initially, Lord Falconer said he was not the Lord Chancellor and that he would not be assuming all of the functions of his predecessor. However, the realisation soon dawned that it was impossible to eradicate the role of the Lord Chancellor by simple diktat. Lord Falconer had to be Lord Chancellor even if by default, as someone had to perform the constitutional functions attached to the Lord Chancellor's office. So, on the first day in his new role, Lord Falconer was to be seen in wig and tights sitting on the woolsack in the House of Lords, for the simple reason that someone had to do it. As a consequence, Lord Falconer was, at least for the time being, both Secretary of State for Constitutional Affairs and Lord Chancellor, although in the former role he was charged with the duty of abolishing the latter role. It should be noted that from the outset Lord Falconer made it clear that he would not, and never did, sit as a judge. As regards his legislative role in chairing sessions of the House of Lords, the CRA subsequently provided for the election of an independent Lord Speaker and in July 2006 the House of Lords elected Baroness Hayman as the first office-holder.

The proposal of the original Constitutional Reform Bill for the complete abolition of the office of the Lord Chancellor was extremely controversial. Reference has already been made to the concerns of the judiciary as to the abolition of the role of the Lord Chancellor and those concerns were also shared by politicians and social commentators. Many of the latter argued against what they saw as the ditching of hundreds of years of history and practice for the sake of dressing up a Cabinet reshuffle as a matter of constitutional importance.

The government, nonetheless, insisted on pursuing its reforms, and justifying them on the basis of transparency and the recognition that it was no longer appropriate for one person to perform the disparate functions of the Lord Chancellor in clear contradiction of the doctrine of the separation of powers. However, as many correctly pointed out, the constitution of the UK never actually incorporated a strict separation of powers. Nonetheless, that recognition cannot be taken as justifying a situation that, as preceding analysis has shown, was clearly founded on fundamental conflicts of interest and was almost certainly contrary to the European Convention on Human Rights. In this regard, the changes introduced by the Constitutional Reform Act 2005 can be seen to be not only pertinent, but also timely, in their endeavour to address an issue before it became a problem. Nonetheless, as was explained above, the government did submit to the wish to retain the ancient office of Lord Chancellor, although the importance of the role was significantly reduced. Following a Cabinet reshuffle in 2007, which also involved the replacement of the Department of Constitutional Affairs by a new Justice Ministry, the Justice Minister, Jack Straw, became the first member of the House of Commons to assume the role and title of Lord Chancellor. Subsequently, in 2012, Chris Grayling, the Conservative MP, became the first Lord Chancellor to hold no legal qualifications.

As part of the reform of the office of Lord Chancellor, its former judicial functions transferred to the Lord Chief Justice in the role of President of the Courts of England and Wales, who took over responsibility for the training, guidance and deployment of judges. They are also responsible for representing the views of the judiciary of England and Wales to Parliament and ministers (see 12.3).

12.2.2   THE CONSTITUTION AND THE ROLE OF THE HOUSE OF LORDS AND THE SUPREME COURT

As has been mentioned previously, by virtue of the Constitutional Reform Act 2005, the Supreme Court replaced the House of Lords as the highest court in the United Kingdom in October 2009. The Judicial Committee of the Privy Council remains as a distinct entity, but follows the Supreme Court to its new location.

Consequently the Supreme Court is the final court of appeal for all United Kingdom civil cases, and criminal cases from England, Wales and Northern Ireland and hears appeals on arguable points of law of general public importance. However, once again, the explanation for this event requires a brief consideration of its historical and constitutional context. A number of issues came together to raise questions about the operation of the House of Lords as the final court of appeal in the English legal system and the role of the Privy Council. Among these were the devolution of parliamentary power to the Scottish Parliament and Welsh Assembly, the previous and proposed further reform of the House of Lords, the enactment of the Human Rights Act and the role of the House of Lords itself in the *Pinochet* case (see below). However, of far greater significance was the proposal in the Constitutional Reform Act 2005 to replace the currently constituted Appeal Committee of the House of Lords with a new Supreme Court.

The case for the reform of the Lord Chancellor's position and against the location of the most senior judges in the House of Lords was presented to the commission examining the reform of the House of Lords by JUSTICE, the civil rights organisation. Both aspects of the challenges were strongly rejected by the then Lord Chancellor Irvine in a speech to the Third Worldwide Common Law Judiciary Conference in Edinburgh, delivered in July 1999. Nonetheless, spring 2002 saw a spate of speeches and interviews highlighting disagreement, if not actual tension, between the Lord Chancellor and some of the most senior members of the judiciary. In March of that year Lord Steyn, then the second longest serving Law Lord, expressed the view that Lord Irvine's insistence on sitting as a judge in the House of Lords was a major obstacle to the creation of a Supreme Court to replace the House of Lords. In April, the Lord Chancellor's response was reported in the *Financial Times* newspaper. The article stated that 'Lord Irvine may have an impressive intellect, but his lack of diplomacy means he will seldom be short of enemies.' The point of that comment was supported by the Lord Chancellor's reaction to Lord Steyn's previous comments, dismissing them in a tone of effete arrogance as 'rather wearisome . . . he's not a political scientist, he knows nothing about the internal workings of government – or very little'. As reported, he reduced Lord Steyn's argument to a demand for 'a grand new architectural venture', stating that the argument that 'the Lord Chancellor, because of his desire to continue sitting, is preventing the judges from having a new building – that's just nonsense'.

Lord Irvine's views should, however, be contrasted with those of the former senior Law Lord, Lord Bingham, expressed in the Spring Lecture given at the Constitution Unit at University College London in May 2002. In a paper entitled 'A New Supreme Court for the UK', Lord Bingham directly addressed all of the issues raised above, except for the role of the Lord Chancellor, before stating his preference for:

> a supreme court severed from the legislature, established as a court in its own right, re-named and appropriately re-housed, properly equipped and resourced and affording facilities for litigants, judges and staff such as, in most countries of the world, are taken for granted.

As to the views and future role of the Lord Chancellor, the reduction of his direct judicial powers was implicit in the speech. As Lord Bingham concluded, 'inertia . . . is not an option'.

Once again, Lord Irvine's political antennae appear to have lacked acuity, in that not only was he replaced as Lord Chancellor by Lord Falconer, but as has been seen, his successor proposed the establishment of a Supreme Court much along the lines of that suggested by Lord Bingham. Thus Part 2 of the Constitutional Reform Act 2005 contained provisions for the following:

- The establishment of a new, independent Supreme Court, separate from the House of Lords with its own independent appointments system, its own staff and budget and its own building: Middlesex Guildhall. This new Supreme Court should not be confused with the old Supreme Court, which was the title previously given to the High Court and Court of Appeal. In future those courts will be known as the Senior Courts of England and Wales.

- The 12 judges of the Supreme Court will be known as Justices of the Supreme Court and will no longer be allowed to sit as members of the House of Lords. As a matter of fact, all of the present members are life peers and as a result will be able to sit in the House of Lords on their retirement from their judicial office, but this may not always be the case in the future.

- The current Law Lords will become the first 12 Justices of the Supreme Court, and the most senior will be appointed President of the Supreme Court. Lord Phillips, the former Lord Chief Justice, was appointed the first President of the new court and when it actually sat for the first time in October 2009 there were only 11 justices in office.

These measures can be considered in two parts: first, the creation of a Supreme Court, distinct from the House of Lords; and second, the removal of the right of the members of that new Supreme Court to sit as members of the Upper House. Neither of these proposals found favour with a majority of the members of the Law Lords; indeed, in their collective response to the Consultation Paper on constitutional reform, six of the 12 expressed their opposition to the creation of a Supreme Court and eight supported the retention of at least some judicial representation in the House of Lords. The minority supported the complete separation of judicial and legislative activity, as did Lord Falconer, who explained the need for reform thus:

> The present position is no longer sustainable. It is surely not right that those responsible for interpreting the law should be able to have a hand in drafting it. The time has come for the UK's highest court to move out from under the shadow of the legislature.

The relevance of Lord Falconer's argument was given added power by the decision of the Scottish Court of Sessions, the equivalent of the Court of Appeal, in *Davidson v Scottish Ministers (No 2)* (2002). The case involved a challenge to a previous court decision, on the grounds of Art 6 of the ECHR, for the reason that one of the judges in the earlier case, the former Lord Advocate Lord Hardie, had spoken on the issue before the court while a member of the Scottish Assembly. The Court of Sessions held that Lord Hardie should at least have declared his previous interest in the matter and that, in the light of his failure to do so, there was at least the real possibility of bias, and ordered the case to be retried.

In other constitutional systems, both civil, as in France, or common law, as in the United States of America, not only is there a clear separation of powers between the judiciary, the executive and the legislature, there is also a distinct Constitutional Court, with the power to strike down legislation on the grounds of its being unconstitutional. It has to be emphasised that the UK Supreme Court will not be in the nature of these other supreme courts, in that it will not be a constitutional court as such and it will not have the powers to strike down legislation. Consequently, although the proposed alterations clearly increase the appearance of the separation of powers, the doctrine of parliamentary sovereignty remains unchallenged. It was presumably the lack of such power that led Lord Woolf to comment that the new court would effectively replace a first-class appeal court (the House of Lords) with a second-class Supreme Court.

It remains to be seen, however, whether, under the changed circumstances of the contemporary constitution, the Supreme Court, as the highest court in the land, will simply assume the previously limited role of the House of Lords, or whether it will, with the passage of time, assume new functions and increased powers as are consonant with Supreme Courts in other jurisdictions. This issue arose in September 2009 when Lord Neuberger, the current President of the Supreme Court, spoke on a BBC radio programme and expressed the opinion that the advent of the Supreme Court was not unproblematic: as he put it, 'The danger is that you muck around with a constitution like the British constitution at your peril because you do not know what the consequences of any change will be', and he added that there was a real risk of 'judges arrogating to themselves greater power than they have at the moment'. Former Lord Chancellor, Lord

Falconer, also expressed the view that the Supreme Court 'will be bolder in vindicating both the freedoms of individuals and, coupled with that, being willing to take on the executive', but Lord Phillips, the first President of the Supreme Court, was more conciliatory towards the executive, expressing the view that, although he could not predict how the court would function in the future, he did not foresee it changing in the way suggested by Lord Neuberger.

It is a commonplace of politics that the devolution of power from the UK Parliament in London, particularly to the Scottish Parliament in Edinburgh, will give rise to disputes as to the relationship between the two bodies. Eventually, such issues will have to be resolved in the courts. Jurisdiction was originally with the Privy Council but has been subsequently transferred to the Supreme Court. During 2010 and 2011 there was considerable tension between the Supreme Court and the Scottish Executive in relation to the court's powers under the Human Rights Act, as a UK rather than a Scottish court, to determine criminal cases in relation to Scots law (see *Cadder v HM Advocate* (2010) and *Fraser v MH Advocate* (2011)). In *AXA General Insurance Limited v The Lord Advocate (Scotland)* (2011) the Supreme Court considered the constitutional position of the Scottish Parliament and concluded, in the words of Lord Hope:

> As a result of the Scotland Act, there are thus two institutions with the power to make laws for Scotland: the Scottish Parliament and, as is recognised in section 28(7), the Parliament of the United Kingdom. The Scottish Parliament is subordinate to the United Kingdom Parliament: its powers can be modified, extended or revoked by an Act of the United Kingdom Parliament. Since its powers are limited, it is also subject to the jurisdiction of the courts.

Lord Hope's judgment in *AXA* is also of general interest with respect to the constitutional relationship between Parliament and the courts.

Nor should it be forgotten that the Human Rights Act has, for the first time, given the courts clear power to declare the UK Parliament's legislative provision contrary to essential human rights (see above, 2.5). Even allowing for the fact that the HRA has been introduced in such a way as to maintain the theory of parliamentary sovereignty, in practice, the courts will inevitably become involved in political/constitutional issues. Once the courts are required to act in constitutional matters, it is surely a mere matter of time before they become Constitutional Courts, as distinct from ordinary courts, with specialist judges with particular expertise in such matters.

12.2.3 JUDICIAL IMPARTIALITY

Re Bow Street Metropolitan Stipendiary Magistrate ex p Pinochet Ugarte (1999)

No consideration of the operation of the judiciary generally, and the House of Lords in particular, can be complete without a detailed consideration of what can only be called the *Pinochet* case (the various cases are actually cited as *R v Bartle* and *R v Evans* (House of Lords' first hearing); *Re Pinochet* (House of Lords' appeal against Lord Hoffmann); *R v Bartle* and *R v Evans* (final House of Lords' decision)).

In September 1973, the democratically elected government of Chile was over-thrown in a violent army coup led by the then General Augusto Pinochet Ugarte; the President, Salvador Allende, and many others were killed in the fighting. Subsequently, in the words of Lord Browne-Wilkinson, in the final House of Lords' hearing ([1999] 2 All ER 97 at 100):

> There is no doubt that, during the period of the Senator Pinochet regime, appalling acts of barbarism were committed in Chile and elsewhere in the world: torture, murder and the unexplained disappearance of individuals on a large scale.

Although it was not suggested that Pinochet had committed these acts personally, it was claimed that he was fully aware of them and conspired to have them undertaken.

In 1998, General Pinochet, by now Senator for life and recipient of a Chilean amnesty for his actions (extracted as the price for his returning his country to democracy), came to England for medical treatment. Although he was initially welcomed, he was subsequently arrested on an extradition warrant issued in Spain for the crimes of torture, murder and conspiracy to murder allegedly orchestrated by him in Chile during the 1970s. Spain issued the international warrants, but Pinochet was actually arrested on warrants issued by the metropolitan stipendiary magistrate under s 8(1)(b) of the Extradition Act 1989. The legal question for the English courts was whether General Pinochet, as head of state at the time when the crimes were committed, enjoyed diplomatic immunity. In November 1998, the House of Lords rejected Pinochet's claim by a three-to-two majority, Lord Hoffmann voting with the majority but declining to submit a reasoned judgment.

Prior to the hearing in the House of Lords, Amnesty International, which campaigns against such things as state mass murder, torture and political imprisonment, and in favour of general civil and political liberties, had been granted leave to intervene in the proceedings, and had made representations through its counsel, Geoffrey Bindman QC. After the *Pinochet* decision, it was revealed, although it was hardly a secret, that Lord Hoffmann was an unpaid director of the Amnesty International Charitable Trust, and that his wife also worked for Amnesty. On that basis, Pinochet's lawyers initiated a very peculiar action: they petitioned the House of Lords about a House of Lords decision; for the first time, the highest court in the land was to be subject to review, but review of itself, only itself differently constituted. So, in January 1999, another panel of Law Lords set aside the decision of the earlier hearing on the basis that Lord Hoffmann's involvement had invalidated the previous hearing. The decision as to whether Pinochet had immunity or not would have to be heard by a new, and differently constituted, committee of Law Lords.

It has to be stated in favour of this decision that the English legal system is famously rigorous in controlling conflicts of interest, which might be seen to affect what should be a neutral decision-making process. The rule, which applies across the board to trustees, company directors and other fiduciaries as well as to judges, is so strict that the mere possibility of a conflict of interest is sufficient to invalidate any decision so made, even if in reality the individual concerned was completely unaffected by their own interest in coming to the decision. In the words of the famous *dictum* of Lord Hewart, it is of fundamental importance that 'justice must not only be done but should manifestly and undoubtedly be seen to be done' (*R v Sussex Justices ex p McCarthy* (1924)). With regard to the judicial process, it has been a long-established rule that no one may be a judge in his or her own cause, that is, they cannot judge a case in which they have an interest. This is sometimes known by the phrase *nemo judex in causa sua*. Thus, for example, judges who are shareholders in a company appearing before the court as a litigant must decline to hear the case (*Dimes v Grand Junction Canal* (1852)). It is therefore astonishing that Lord Hoffmann did not withdraw from the case, or at least declare his interest in Amnesty when it was joined to the proceedings. The only possible justification is that Lord Hoffmann assumed that all of those involved in the case, including the Pinochet team of lawyers, were aware of the connection. Alternatively, he might have thought that his support for a charitable body aimed at promoting civil and political liberties was so worthy in itself as to be unimpeachable: could not, and indeed should not, every English judge subscribe, for example, to cl 3(c) of the Amnesty International Charitable Trust memorandum, which provides that one of its objects is 'to procure the abolition of torture, extra-judicial execution and disappearance'?

In either case, Lord Hoffmann was wrong.

Once it was shown that Lord Hoffmann had a relevant interest in its subject matter, he was disqualified without any investigation into whether there was a likelihood or suspicion of bias. The mere fact of his interest was sufficient to disqualify him unless he had made sufficient disclosure. Hitherto, only pecuniary or proprietary interests had led to automatic disqualification. But, as Lord Browne-Wilkinson stated, Amnesty, and hence Lord Hoffmann, plainly had a non-pecuniary interest sufficient to give rise to an automatic disqualification for those involved with it.

The House of Lords therefore decided that Lord Hoffmann had been wrong, but it remained for the House of Lords to extricate itself, with whatever dignity it could manage, from the situation it had, through Lord Hoffmann, got itself into. This it endeavoured to do by reconstituting the original hearing with a specially extended committee of seven members. Political and legal speculation was rife before the decision of that court. It was suggested that the new committee could hardly go against the decision of the previous one without bringing the whole procedure into disrepute, yet the earlier court had actually contained the most liberal, and civil liberties minded, of the Lords. It was assumed that the new hearing would endorse the earlier decision, if with reluctance, but what was not expected was the way in which it would actually do so.

In reaching the decision that General Pinochet could be extradited, the House of Lords relied on, and established, Pinochet's potential responsibility for the alleged crimes from the date on which the UK incorporated the United Nations Convention on Torture into its domestic law through the Criminal Justice Act 1988–29 September 1988. Consequently, he could not be held responsible for any crimes committed before then, but was potentially liable for any offences after that date. Thus, although the later

House of Lords' committee provided the same decision as the first one, it did so on significantly different, and much more limited, grounds from those on which Lords Steyn and Nicholls, with the support of Lord Hoffmann, relied. Such a conclusion is neither satisfactory in law nor in political practice, and did nothing to deflect the unflattering glare of unwanted publicity that had been visited on the House of Lords.

It is important not to overstate what was decided in *Re Pinochet*. The facts of that case were exceptional and it is unlikely that it will lead to a mass withdrawal of judges from cases; however, there might well be other cases in which the judge would be well advised to disclose a possible interest. Finally, with regard to *Re Pinochet*, whatever one's views about the merits, sagacity or neutrality of the current judiciary, there is considerable evidence to support the proposition that, historically, judges have often been biased towards certain causes and social classes. For example, JAG Griffith's book, *The Politics of the Judiciary* (1997) (see 13.7.1), is brimming with concrete examples of judges who have shown distinctly conservative and illiberal opinions in cases involving workers, trade unions, civil liberties, Northern Ireland, police powers, religion and other matters. Lord Hoffmann was wrong, but it is nonetheless ironic that the first senior judge to have action taken against him for possible political bias was someone whose agenda was nothing more than being against torture and unjudicial killings.

Locabail (UK) Ltd v Bayfield Properties Ltd (1999)

Following a number of other cases in which lawyers sought to challenge a judgment on the grounds that through a social interest or remote financial connection the judge was potentially biased, the Court of Appeal delivered authoritative guidance on the matter in *Locabail (UK) Ltd v Bayfield Properties Ltd and Another* (1999).

The Court of Appeal ruled that all legal arbiters were bound to apply the law as they understood it to the facts of individual cases as they found them without fear or favour, affection or ill will: that is, without partiality or prejudice. Any judge, that term embracing every judicial decision-maker, whether judge, lay justice or juror, who allowed any judicial decision to be influenced by partiality or prejudice deprived the litigant of their important right and violated one of the most fundamental principles underlying the administration of justice. The law was settled in England and Wales by the House of Lords in *R v Gough* (1993), establishing that the relevant test was whether there was in relation to any given judge a real danger or possibility of bias. When applying the real danger test, it would often be appropriate to inquire whether the judge knew of the matter relied on as appearing to undermine their impartiality. If it were shown that they did not, the danger of its having influenced their judgment was eliminated and the appearance of possible bias dispelled. It was for the reviewing court, not the judge concerned, to assess the risk that some illegitimate extraneous consideration might have influenced his decision.

There was one situation where, on proof of the requisite facts, the existence of bias was effectively presumed, and in such cases it gave rise to automatic disqualification; namely, where the judge was shown to have an interest in the outcome of the case which they were to decide or had decided (see *Dimes v Proprietors of the Grand Junction*

Canal (1852), *R v Rand* (1866) and *R v Camborne Justices ex p Pearce* (1955)). However, it would be dangerous and futile to attempt to define or list factors which might, or alternatively might not, give rise to a real danger of bias, since everything would depend on the particular facts. Nonetheless, the court could not conceive of circumstances in which an objection could be soundly based on the religion, ethnic or national origin, gender, age, class, means or sexual orientation of the judge. Nor, at any rate ordinarily, could an objection be soundly based on his or her social, educational, service or employment background or history; nor that of any member of his or her family; nor previous political associations, membership of social, sporting or charitable bodies; nor Masonic associations; nor previous judicial decisions; nor extracurricular utterances, whether in textbooks, lectures, speeches, articles, interviews, reports or responses to consultation papers; nor previous receipt of instructions to act for or against any party, solicitor or advocate engaged in a case before him or her; nor membership of the same Inn, circuit, local Law Society or chambers.

By contrast, a real danger of bias might well be thought to arise if there existed personal friendship or animosity between the judge and any member of the public involved in the case; or if the judge were closely acquainted with any such member of the public, particularly if that individual's credibility could be significant in the decision of the case; or if in a case where the credibility of any individual were an issue to be decided by the judge, he or she had in a previous case rejected that person's evidence in such outspoken terms as to throw doubt on his or her ability to approach such a person's evidence with an open mind on any later occasion.

It might well be thought that the Court of Appeal was bound to come to this conclusion. Had it ruled that membership of certain societies, or a particular social background, or the previous political associations of a trial judge were grounds for appeal, two consequences would follow. First, there would be a rapid expansion of the use by law firms of special units that monitor and keep files on all aspects of judges' lives. Second, there would be a proliferation of appeals in all departments of the court structure at the very time when there is such a concerted effort to reduce the backlog of appeals. The decision in *Locabail* leaves a question of profound jurisprudential importance: how far can judges judge in an entirely neutral and socially detached manner?

Locabail was decided before the HRA 1998 came into force, but the Court of Appeal soon had the opportunity to assess the rules in *R v Gough* against the requirements of the European Court's approach to bias in relation to Art 6 of the ECHR. *Director General of Fair Trading v Proprietary Association of Great Britain (re Medicaments and Related Classes of Goods (No 2))* (2001) related to a case before the Restrictive Practices Court. Six weeks into the trial, one of the lay members of the panel hearing the case, an economist, disclosed that, since the start of the case, she had applied for a job with one of the main witnesses employed by one of the parties to the case. On learning this, the respondents argued that such behaviour must imply bias on her part and that consequently, the whole panel should stand down, or at least the member in question should stand down. The Restrictive Practices Court rejected the argument. On appeal, the Court of Appeal took the opportunity to refine the common law test as established in *R v Gough*. Previously, the court determining the issue had itself decided whether there had been a real danger of bias in the inferior tribunal. Now, in line with the jurisprudence of the ECtHR, the test was whether a fair-minded observer would conclude that there was a real possibility of bias. In other words, the test moved from being a subjective test on the part of the court to an objective test from the perspective of the fair-minded observer. In the case in question, the Court of Appeal held that there was sufficient evidence for a fair-minded observer to conclude bias on the part of one member of the panel and that consequently, at the stage the trial had reached, her discussions would have contaminated the other two members, who should also have been stood down. The approach adopted by the Court of Appeal in *re Medicaments and Related Classes of Goods (No 2)* was subsequently approved by the House of Lords in *Porter v Magill* (2001), and in the words of Lord Hope the test for bias is 'whether the fair-minded and informed observer, having considered the facts, would conclude that there was a real possibility that the tribunal was biased'.

Subsequently, in *Lawal v Northern Spirit Ltd* (2003), the House of Lords stated that 'public perception of the possibility of unconscious bias is the key' and while not finding it necessary to delve into the characteristics to be attributed to the fair-minded and informed observer, did suggest that such a person would adopt a balanced approach 'neither complacent nor unduly sensitive or suspicious'.

Finally, in *Meerabux v The Attorney General of Belize* (2005), Lord Hope in delivering the report of the Privy Council raised the possibility that had the House of Lords been able to apply the refined version of the test for apparent bias, rather than the test set out in *Gough*, then it is unlikely that it would have found it necessary to find a solution to the problem that it was presented with by applying the automatic disqualification rule. Not a little ironically, Lord Hoffmann himself was a member of this particular Privy Council panel.

12.3 JUDICIAL OFFICES

Although not required to know the names of present incumbents, students should at least be aware of the various titles of judges and equally know which courts they operate in. Much of what follows may be found on the judicial website: www.judiciary.gov.uk.

LORD CHANCELLOR

The history of this particular office has been considered previously and it only remains to state that in its contemporary, reduced state, the officeholder is the current Justice Minister Liz Truss MP.

LORD CHIEF JUSTICE

The holder of this position is now President of the Courts of England and Wales and the most senior member of the judiciary. As President of the Courts of England and Wales, the Lord Chief Justice is responsible for representing the views of the judiciary of England and Wales to Parliament, the Justice Minister and Ministers of the Crown generally. He or she is also to be responsible, within the resources made available by the Justice Minister, for maintaining appropriate arrangements for the welfare, training and guidance of the judiciary of England and Wales, and for maintaining appropriate arrangements for the deployment of the judiciary of England and Wales and allocating work within courts. The Lord Chief Justice is the President of the Criminal Division of the Court of Appeal and is formally the senior judge in the Queen's Bench Division of the High Court.

PRESIDENT OF THE SUPREME COURT AND DEPUTY PRESIDENT OF THE SUPREME COURT

These positions are currently held by Lord Neuberger and Lady Hale. They sit on the appointment commission for any new members of the Supreme Court.

MASTER OF THE ROLLS

The holder of this office is regarded as second in judicial importance to the Lord Chief Justice. He or she is President of the Civil Division of the Court of Appeal and is responsible for the allocation and organisation of the work of the judges of the Division, as well as presiding in one of its courts.

PRESIDENT OF THE FAMILY DIVISION OF THE HIGH COURT OF JUSTICE

This person is the senior judge in the Family Division and is responsible for organising the operation of the Court.

PRESIDENT OF THE QUEEN'S BENCH DIVISION AND JUDGE IN CHARGE OF THE ADMINISTRATIVE COURT

This post was instituted by the Constitutional Reform Act 2005 and the functions of the holder are apparent in the title.

CHANCELLOR OF THE HIGH COURT

This post was also created under the CRA 2005 and replaced the former office of Vice Chancellor of the Supreme Court. Although the Lord Chancellor is nominally the head of the Chancery Division of the High Court, the actual function of organising the Chancery Division falls to the Chancellor.

The Courts and Legal Services Act (CLSA) 1990 recognised the existing system and required that each of the six separate Crown Court circuits should operate under the administration of two presiding judges appointed from the High Court. In addition, a senior presiding judge is appointed from the Lords Justices of Appeal.

12.3.1   JUDICIAL HIERARCHY

The foregoing are specific judicial offices. In addition, the various judges who function at the various levels within the judicial hierarchy are referred to in the following terms:

Justices of the Supreme Court

When all appointed, these 12 judges now constitute the highest court in the United Kingdom and have been considered in some detail previously. The qualifications and procedure for appointment will be considered below.

Lords of Appeal in Ordinary

These were the people normally referred to as the Law Lords for the simple reason that they were ennobled when they were appointed to their positions and sat in the House of Lords. Historically, they constituted the highest court in the United Kingdom and have been replaced by the Supreme Court as considered above.

Lords Justices of Appeal

This category, of which there are currently 39 incumbents, constitutes the majority of the judges in the Court of Appeal, although the other specific office-holders considered previously may also sit in that court, as may High Court judges specifically requested to do so. They all used to be known as Lord Justice, even if they were female. The first female member of the Court of Appeal, Elizabeth Butler-Sloss, had to be referred to by the male title because the Senior Courts Act 1981 had not considered the possibility of a woman holding such high judicial office. The rules were changed subsequently to allow female judges in the Court of Appeal to be referred to as Lady Justices, and whereas their male counterparts receive knighthoods on their elevation, the women become Dames.

High Court judges

These are sometimes referred to as '*puisne*' (pronounced 'pew-nee') judges, in reference to their junior status in relation to those of superior status in the Supreme Court. There is a statutory maximum of 108 such judges appointed. Judges are appointed to particular divisions depending on the amount of work needing to be conducted by that division, although they may be required to hear cases in different divisions and may be transferred from one division to another by the Lord Chief Justice. Others, such as former High Court and Court of Appeal judges, or former circuit judges or recorders, may be requested to sit as judges in the High Court. High Court judges are referred to by their name followed by the initial 'J'.

The Lord Chancellor may also appoint deputy judges

of the High Court on a purely temporary basis, in order to speed up the hearing of cases and to reduce any backlog that may have built up. The Heilbron Report on the operation of the civil justice system was critical of the use of deputy judges and recommended that more permanent High Court judges should be appointed if necessary. The maximum numbers were subsequently increased to their present level, but the use of deputy judges has continued to provide grounds for criticism of the operation of the legal system, and has led to suggestions that the use of 'second-rate' judges might eventually debase the whole judicial currency.

Circuit judges

Although there is only one Crown Court, it is divided into six distinct circuits, which are serviced, in the main, by circuit judges who also sit as County Court judges to hear civil cases. There are currently some 626 circuit judges, each being addressed as 'Your Honour'.

Recorders

are part-time judges appointed to assist circuit judges in their functions in relation to criminal and civil law cases. There are currently over 1,035 recorders in post.

District judges

This category of judge, previously referred to as registrars, is appointed on a full-time and part-time basis to hear civil cases in the County Court. There are currently over 430 district judges.

All judicial statistics are available at www.gov.uk/government/collections/criminal-justice-statistics.

The situation of *magistrates* will be considered separately at 12.9 below and the situation of *chairmen of tribunals* and *tribunal judges* will be considered at 12.5.

12.3.2   LEGAL OFFICES

In addition to these judicial positions, there are three legal offices that should be noted:

- The *Attorney General*, like the Lord Chancellor, is a political appointee and a member of the executive, whose role is to act as the legal adviser to the government. For example, in March 2003, the former Attorney General, Lord Goldsmith, controversially advised the government that there was a legal basis for its use of military force against Iraq.

  The Attorney General alone has the authority to prosecute in certain circumstances and appears for the Crown in important cases. As may be recalled from 9.5 above the Attorney General also has powers to appeal against points of law in relation to acquittals under the Criminal Justice Act (CJA) 1972 and can also appeal against unduly lenient sentences under the CJA 1988. The crucially important decision of the House of Lords that DNA evidence, acquired in regard to another investigation and which should have been destroyed under s 64 of the Police and Criminal Evidence Act (PACE) 1984, could nonetheless be used, was taken as the result of a reference by the Attorney General (*Attorney General's Reference (No 3 of 1999)*). The current incumbent is Jeremy Wright MP.

- The *Solicitor General* is the Attorney General's deputy.

- The *Director of Public Prosecutions* (DPP) is the head of the national independent Crown Prosecution Service (CPS) established under the Prosecution of Offences Act 1985 to oversee the prosecution of criminal offences. The decision of the DPP whether to prosecute or not in any particular case is subject to judicial review in the courts. In *R v DPP ex p C* (1994), it was stated that such powers should be used sparingly and only on grounds of unlawful policy, failure to act in accordance with policy and perversity. Nonetheless, successful actions have been taken against the DPP in relation to decisions not to prosecute in *R v DPP ex p Jones* (2000) and in *R v DPP ex p Manning* (2000) (see 11.2 for an examination of the CPS). In November 2013, Alison Saunders was appointed DPP on the resignation of the previous incumbent, Keir Starmer.

12.4   APPOINTMENT OF THE JUDICIARY

The somewhat astonishing fact is that there are approximately 30,000 judicial officeholders in England and Wales if one includes judges, tribunal members and magistrates. This section of this book considers how such a number of people actually come to hold these judicial positions.

In the first of his Hamlyn Lectures of 1993, the then Lord Chancellor, Lord Mackay, stated that the pre-eminent qualities required by a judge are:

> good sound judgment based upon knowledge of the law, a willingness to study all sides of an argument with an acceptable degree of openness, and an ability to reach a firm conclusion and to articulate clearly the reasons for the conclusion.

Although the principal qualification for judicial office was experience of advocacy, Lord Mackay recognised that some people who have not practised advocacy may well have these necessary qualities to a great degree. This was reflected in the appointment of an academic and member of the Law Commission, Professor Brenda Hoggett, to the High Court in December 1993. Professor Hoggett, who sat as Mrs Justice Hale, was the first High Court judge not to have had a career as a practising barrister, although she qualified as a barrister in 1969 and was made a QC in 1989. As Dame Brenda Hale, she sat in the Court of Appeal; as Lady Hale of Richmond, she was the first female member of the Law Lords; and she is now Deputy President of the Supreme Court.

The Courts and Legal Services Act (CLSA) 1990 introduced major changes into the qualifications required for filling the positions of judges. Judicial appointment is still essentially dependent upon the rights of audience in the higher courts, but at the same time as the CLSA 1990 effectively demolished the monopoly of the Bar to rights of audience in such courts, it opened up the possibility of achieving judicial office to legal practitioners other than barristers.

The Tribunals, Courts and Enforcement Act 2007 extended the possibility of holding judicial office to Fellows of the Institute of Legal Executives. This provision came into effect in November 2010.

12.4.1 QUALIFICATIONS

The main qualifications for appointment are as follows (the CLSA 1990 is dealt with in detail at 16.6 below):

- *Lord of Appeal in Ordinary*
    - (a) the holding of high judicial office for two years; or
    - (b) possession of a 15-year Supreme Court qualification under the CLSA 1990.
- The Constitutional Reform Act retained the same qualifications for members of the new Justices of the Supreme Court. There is, however, a new statutory appointments procedure under the proposed legislation, which is considered below.
- *Lord Justice of Appeal*
    - (a) the holding of a post as a High Court judge; or
    - (b) possession of a 10-year High Court qualification under the CLSA 1990.
- *High Court judges*
    - (a) the holding of a post as a circuit judge for two years;
    - (b) possession of a 10-year High Court qualification under the CLSA 1990.
- *Deputy judges* must be qualified in the same way as permanent High Court judges.
- *Circuit judges*
    - (a) the holding of a post as a recorder;
    - (b) possession of either a 10-year Crown Court qualification or a 10-year County Court qualification under the CLSA 1990;

(c)   the holding of certain offices, such as district judge, Social Security Commissioner, chairman of an industrial tribunal, stipendiary magistrate for three years.

- *Recorders* must possess a 10-year Crown Court or County Court qualification under the CLSA 1990.

- *District judges* require a seven-year general qualification under the CLSA 1990.

12.4.2   SELECTION OF JUDGES

So far, attention has concentrated on the specific requirements for those wishing to fulfil the role of judge, but it remains to consider the more general question relating to the process whereby people are deemed suitable and selected for such office. Although the appointment procedure for judges has changed as a consequence of the Constitutional Reform Act 2005, with the establishment of the Judicial Appointments Commission, it is still necessary briefly to examine the former appointment procedure in order to explain the need for the reforms introduced by that Act.

Senior judicial positions

All judicial appointments remain, theoretically, at the hands of the Crown. Previously, however, the Crown was guided, if not actually dictated to, in regard to its appointment by the government of the day. Thus, as has been seen, the Lord Chancellor was a direct political appointment and the Prime Minister also advised the Crown on the appointment of other senior judicial office-holders such as the Law Lords and Appeal Court judges. Such apparent scope for patronage in the hands of the Prime Minister did not go without criticism.

Also under the previous system judges at the level of the High Court and Circuit Bench were appointed by the Crown on the advice of the Lord Chancellor, and the Lord Chancellor personally appointed district judges, lay magistrates and the members of some tribunals. This system did not go without challenge either, the question being raised as to how the Lord Chancellor actually reached his decision to recommend or appoint individuals to judicial offices.

High Court Bench

In the past, appointment to the High Court Bench was by way of invitation from the Lord Chancellor. However, in 1998, the Lord Chancellor's Department (LCD) issued an advertisement inviting applicants to apply for such positions. However, the Lord Chancellor retained their right to invite individuals to become High Court judges. As regards the system of invitation, the question immediately raised was as to exactly how the Lord Chancellor selected the recipients of their favour. There being no system as such, there could be no transparency and without transparency there had to be doubts as to the fairness of the process. Even where a candidate applied for the post of High Court judge, the procedure was different from applications at a lower level, for the reason that the candidate was not interviewed after the usual consultation process with the senior judiciary and the candidate's own referees. The Lord Chancellor simply decided whom to appoint on the basis of that consultation process. Thus doubts about the secretive nature of the consultancy procedure were compounded as regards applicants for the High Court Bench.

The previous procedure of appointment to the High Court was subject to some sharp criticism in a review conducted for the Bar Council under the chairmanship of the former Appeal Court judge Sir Iain Glidewell. The main review concluded that the system of appointment was not sufficiently transparent. More contentiously, however, it suggested that, given the increased role of the judiciary in matters relating to the review of administrative decisions, devolution issues and human rights, it was no longer constitutionally acceptable for judges to be appointed by the government of the day, of which the Lord Chancellor is a member.

Circuit judges and below

All appointments up to and including circuit judges were made on the basis of open competition but as part of the process comments were solicited from a wide range of judges and lawyers who were approached for assessments on the Lord Chancellor's behalf.

Relying on the recommendations and opinions of the existing judiciary as to the suitability of the potential candidates might appear sensible at first sight. However, it brought with it the allegation, if not the fact, that the system was over-secretive and led to a highly conservative appointment policy. Judges were suspected, perhaps not unnaturally, of favouring those candidates who have not been troublesome in their previous cases and who have shown themselves to share the views and approaches of the existing office-holders.

One of Lord Irvine's earliest actions as Lord Chancellor had been to declare the government's intention to inquire into the merits of establishing a Judicial Appointments Commission. However, rather than carry out that intention, he announced in 1999 that Sir Leonard Peach, the former Commissioner for Public Appointments, would be conducting an independent scrutiny of the way in which the current appointment processes for judges operated. In December of that year, Sir Leonard reported that he had been:

. . . impressed by the quality of work, the professionalism and the depth of experience of the civil servants involved.

Sir Leonard recommended that a Commission for Judicial Appointments be established, whose role would be to monitor the procedures and act as an Ombudsman for disappointed applicants. However, it was also recommended that the commission should not have any role in the actual appointments, but should merely maintain an independent oversight of the procedure.

Not surprisingly, Lord Irvine was most happy to accept such findings and Sir Leonard's proposals, and the system of appointing the judiciary remained essentially unchanged. The appointment of Sir Colin Campbell, Vice Chancellor of Nottingham University, as the first Commissioner was announced in March 2001. Nonetheless, the work of the Commission proved salutary in relation to the appointments process and its reports did not hold back on providing a constant flow of restrained if sometimes acerbic criticism of the process and indeed the continued role of the Lord Chancellor within that process.

Somewhat surprisingly, in April 2003 Lord Irvine announced – before the select committee with oversight of his department – that he intended to issue three separate consultation documents relating to:

- whether judges and lawyers should continue to wear wigs and gowns in court;
- whether the status of Queen's Counsel should be retained and the related appointment process; and
- the role of the Judicial Appointments Commission.

Once again, Lord Irvine's actions were forestalled by his dismissal from office and his replacement in June 2003 by Lord Falconer, who immediately issued a consultation paper on the establishment of a full-blown Judicial Appointments Commission, which subsequently formed the basis of the proposals in regard to judicial appointments contained in the Constitutional Reform Act 2005.

12.4.3   THE JUDICIAL APPOINTMENTS COMMISSION

Part 4 of the Constitutional Reform Act created a new independent Judicial Appointments Commission (JAC), which was in due course to assume responsibility for the process of selecting all judges for appointment in England and Wales from magistrates to members of the Supreme Court. However, following an agreement between the Lord Chancellor, the Judicial Appointments Commission (JAC), the Lord Chief Justice and the Magistrates' Association, it was decided that the JAC would not take responsibility for the recruitment and selection of magistrates. Consequently that function would remain with the Lord Chancellor's Advisory Committees on Justices of the Peace for the foreseeable future.

The Judicial Appointments Commission makes recommendations to the Lord Chancellor and no one may be appointed whom the Commission has not selected. The Lord Chancellor may reject a candidate, once, and ask the Commission to reconsider, once. However, if the Commission maintains its original recommendation, the Lord Chancellor must appoint or recommend for appointment whichever candidate is selected. The appointments of Lords Justices and above will continue to be made by the Queen formally, after the Commission has made a recommendation to the Lord

Chancellor. The Act makes special provision for the appointment of the Lord Chief Justice, Heads of Division and Lords Justices of Appeal. In these cases, the Commission will establish a selection panel of four members, consisting of two senior judges, normally including the Lord Chief Justice, and two lay members of the Commission.

Members of the Judicial Appointments Commission are appointed by the Queen, on the recommendation of the Lord Chancellor. Schedule 12 of the Act sets out the membership of the Judicial Appointments Commission, together with its powers and responsibilities. Of the total of 15 Commissioners:

- six must be lay members;
- five must be members of the judiciary (three judges of the Court of Appeal or High Court, including at least one Lord Justice of Appeal and at least one High Court judge, one circuit judge and one district judge);
- two must be members of the legal profession;
- one must be a tribunal member; and
- one must be a lay magistrate.

Significantly, the Chair of the Commission is one of the lay members. The Act requires that all candidates must be of good character and that selection shall be made strictly on merit. In addition, it gives the Lord Chancellor power to issue guidance to the Commission in regard to what considerations to take into account in assessing merit, which the Commission must have regard to. However, the Act does not prescribe detailed appointments procedures and makes it clear that any such procedures are a matter for the Commission to decide.

It can be seen that although the Lord Chancellor retains the ultimate power to decide whom to appoint, or to recommend to the Queen for appointment, and thus maintains Parliamentary accountability, their discretion has been tightly circumscribed by the provisions of the Act.

The Act also provides for the establishment of a Judicial Appointments and Conduct Ombudsman to whom unsuccessful or disgruntled applicants for judicial office can apply for a consideration of their case. As the full title suggests, the Ombudsman also will have a role to play in relation to matters of a disciplinary nature and s 110 allows complaints to be made to the Judicial Appointments and Conduct Ombudsman about judicial disciplinary cases.

The JAC has identified five core qualities and abilities that are required for any judicial office, although they may be adapted for different posts; thus for example a High Court judge would be expected to display a high level of legal knowledge, whereas a lay tribunal member would be expected to display expertise in their professional field.

1 *Intellectual capacity*
- high level of expertise in your chosen area or profession;
- ability quickly to absorb and analyse information;
- appropriate knowledge of the law and its underlying principles, or the ability to acquire this knowledge where necessary.

2   *Personal qualities*
- integrity and independence of mind;
- sound judgment;
- decisiveness;
- objectivity;
- ability and willingness to learn and develop professionally.

3   *An ability to understand and deal fairly*
- ability to treat everyone with respect and sensitivity whatever their background;
- willingness to listen with patience and courtesy.

4   *Authority and communication skills*
- ability to explain the procedure and any decisions reached clearly and succinctly to all those involved;
- ability to inspire respect and confidence;
- ability to maintain authority when challenged.

5   *Efficiency*
- ability to work at speed and under pressure;
- ability to organise time effectively and produce clear reasoned judgments expeditiously;
- ability to work constructively with others (including leadership and managerial skills where appropriate).

While the JAC is 'committed to widening the range of applicants for judicial appointment and to ensuring that the very best eligible candidates are drawn from a wider range of backgrounds', this goal is to be achieved by encouraging a wider range of applicants and through the provision of a fair and open selection process. That being said, all appointments will be made purely on merit. However, the first appointments of the Commission were subjected to criticism in the newspapers in early 2008 when it was discovered that the first 10 High Court judges appointed under the new system were all men and thus not very different from those appointed under the old system.

The JAC's role in the judicial appointments process begins when they receive a request from Her Majesty's Courts Service (HMCS), the Tribunals Service or on behalf of a tribunal outside the Tribunals Service. It then seeks out the best candidates, using the processes described below as measured against the qualities and abilities relevant to that post. The following sets out the procedures leading to the appointment of judicial office-holders (see also the JAC's website at http://jac.judiciary.gov.uk):

Stage 1: Application
Most positions are advertised widely in the national press, legal publications, the professional press and online. The application form is tailored for each individual selection exercise. Alongside the form, an information pack is available to applicants, which

includes details of the eligibility criteria and guidance on the application process. This too is tailored for each exercise. Both documents can be downloaded from the JAC website or are sent out to candidates on request. Once JAC has received a completed application form, it is required under s 63(3) of the Constitutional Reform Act to select people for appointment who are of 'good character' and has established guidance to help people to decide whether there is anything in their past conduct or present circumstances (for example business connections) which might affect their application for judicial appointment. The essential principles in determining good character are:

- the overriding need to maintain public confidence in the standards of the judiciary; and
- that public confidence will only be maintained if judicial office-holders and those who aspire to such office maintain the highest standards of behaviour in their professional, public and private lives.

Stage 2: Assessment

Candidates are asked on their application form to nominate up to three referees normally, or in some cases six. The Commission may also seek references from a list of Commission-nominated referees, which is published for each selection exercise. The time at which references are sought will depend on the assessment method used for shortlisting:

- If a qualifying test is used, references are taken up after the qualifying test and before interviews take place.
- If a paper sift is used, references are taken up before the sift and used to make the shortlisting decisions.

In all cases, references will form part of the information that JAC uses to make final selection recommendations to the Lord Chancellor.

Shortlisting

This may be done on the basis of qualifying tests or paper sift, using the application form and references. For senior appointments, where candidates will usually have an extensive track record, shortlisting will normally be done on information supplied by the candidate and from references.

Interviews and selection days

The next stage of the assessment will vary depending on the nature of the post to be filled. Candidates might be asked to attend a selection day, which may entail a combination of role-plays and an interview. For some specialist and the most senior appointments, there might be only a panel interview.

Panel members assess all the information about each candidate, prepare reports on their findings and agree which candidates best meet the required abilities.

As required under ss 88(3) and 94(3) of the CRA, the panel's reports on candidates likely to be considered by the Commission are sent to the Lord Chief Justice and another person who has held the post, or has relevant experience.

Stage 3: Selection and recommendation

The Commissioners consider all the information gathered on the candidates and select candidates to be recommended to the Lord Chancellor for appointment.

For existing judicial office-holders, checks are done with the Office for Judicial Complaints (OJC) that there are no complaints outstanding against them. For all other candidates recommended for appointment, a series of good character checks are done with the police, Her Majesty's Revenue and Customs and relevant professional bodies.

The Lord Chancellor may also require candidates to undergo a medical assessment before their appointment is confirmed. JAC recommends to the Lord Chancellor one candidate for each vacancy. The Lord Chancellor can reject that recommendation but they are required to provide their reasons to the Commission. They cannot select an alternative candidate.

As regards future appointments to the Supreme Court, s 25 of the Constitutional Reform Act (CRA) sets out three possible routes to qualification. These are:

1   having held high judicial office, for at least two years;
2   having satisfied the judicial-appointment eligibility condition on a 15-year basis;
3   having been a qualifying practitioner for at least 15 years.

Although appointment to office is by the Crown, ss 26, 27, 28, 29, 30 and 31 and Sched 8 CRA 2005 set out the procedure for appointing a member of the Supreme Court. The Lord Chancellor must convene an *ad hoc* selection commission if there is, or is likely to be, a vacancy. Subsequently, the Lord Chancellor will notify the Prime Minister of the identity of the person selected by that commission, and under s 26(4) the Prime Minister *must* recommend the appointment of that person to the Queen.

Schedule 8 contains the rules governing the composition and operation of the selection commission, which will consist of the President of the Supreme Court, who will chair the commission, the Deputy President of the Supreme Court and one member from each of the territorial judicial appointment commissions (see below), one of whom must be a person who is not legally qualified. The next most senior ordinary judge in the Supreme Court will take the unfilled position on the selection commission if either the President or Deputy President is unable to sit.

Section 27 sets out the process that must be followed in the selection of a justice of the Supreme Court. The commission decides the particular selection process to be applied, the criteria or competences against which candidates will be assessed, but in any event the requirement is that any selection must be made solely on merit. However, s 27(8) does require that the commission must take into account the need for the Court to have among its judges generally at least two Scottish judges and usually one from Northern Ireland. The Lord Chancellor, as provided for by s 27(9), may issue non-binding guidance to the commission about the vacancy that has arisen, for example on the jurisdictional requirements of the Court, which the commission must have regard to.

Under s 27(2) and s 27(3) the commission is required to consult:

(i) senior judges who are neither on the commission nor willing to be considered for selection;
(ii) the Lord Chancellor;
(iii) the First Minister in Scotland;
(iv) the Assembly First Secretary in Wales; and
(v) the Secretary of State for Northern Ireland.

Sub-section 28(1) provides that after a selection has been made the commission must submit a report nominating one candidate to the Lord Chancellor, who then must also consult the senior judges (or other judges) who were consulted by the commission, the First Minister in Scotland, the Assembly First Secretary in Wales and the Secretary of State for Northern Ireland.

Section 29 sets out the Lord Chancellor's options after they have received a name from the commission and carried out the further consultation under s 28. The procedure may be divided into three possible stages.

1 Stage 1, where a person has been selected and recommended by the appointments commission. At this stage the Lord Chancellor may:
(i) accept the nomination and notify the Prime Minister;
(ii) reject the selection;
(iii) require the commission to reconsider its selection.

2   Stage 2, where a person has been selected following a rejection or reconsideration at stage 1. In this event the Lord Chancellor can:

 (i)   accept the nomination and notify the Prime Minister;

 (ii)   reject the selection but only if it was made following a reconsideration at stage 1;

 (iii) require the commission to reconsider the selection, but only if it was made following a rejection at stage 1.

3   Stage 3, where a person has been selected following a rejection or reconsideration at stage 2. At this point, the Lord Chancellor *must* accept the nomination unless they prefer to accept a candidate who had previously been reconsidered but not subsequently recommended for a second time.

 In effect this means that the Lord Chancellor's options are as follows. They can:

 (i)   accept the recommendation of the commission;

 (ii)   ask the commission to reconsider; or

 (iii) reject the recommendation.

Where the Lord Chancellor requires the commission to *reconsider* its original selection, the commission can still put forward the same name with additional justifications for its selection. In such circumstances, the Lord Chancellor will either accept the recommendation or reject it. Alternatively, the commission can recommend another candidate, whom the Lord Chancellor can accept, reject or require reconsideration of.

However, if the Lord Chancellor *rejects* the original name provided by the selection commission, they must submit an alternative candidate giving reasons for their choice. At this point the Lord Chancellor can either:

(i)   accept the second candidate; or

(ii)   ask the selection commission to reconsider.

On reconsideration the commission can either resubmit the second candidate or propose an alternative candidate. At this point the Lord Chancellor must make a choice. They can either accept the alternative candidate or they can then choose the reconsidered candidate.

Under s 30(1), the Lord Chancellor's right of rejection is only exercisable where in their opinion the person selected is not suitable for the office concerned. The right to require reconsideration is exercisable under three conditions:

(i)   where they feel there is not enough evidence that the person is suitable for office;

(ii)   where they feel there is not enough evidence that that person is the best candidate on merit; or

(iii) where there is not enough evidence that the judges of the Court will between them have enough knowledge of, and experience in, the laws of each part of the United Kingdom, following the new appointment.

Should the Lord Chancellor exercise either of these options they must provide the commission with their reasons in writing (s 30(3)).

Details of the procedures involved in appointment may be found in the JAC pages of the judiciary website at http://jac.judiciary.gov.uk, together with an interesting collection of essays entitled *Judicial Appointments: Balancing Independence, Accountability and Legitimacy*.

The current membership of the Supreme Court

At the moment there are only 11 Supreme Court justices, Lord Toulson having retired in July 2016. As five other justices, including current president Lord Neuberger, are due to retire 2018 it has been decided to postpone the appointment of a replacement for Lord Toulson to allow the appointment process for all prospective retirees to be conducted collectively at a more appropriate time. Fortunately, s 39 of the Constitutional Reform Act 2005 provides for the appointment of a Supplementary Panel, upon which the Supreme Court can call when additional judges are needed to form a panel of the requisite number. The current panel consists of Lord Dyson, the former Supreme Court Justice and Master of the Rolls, the Scottish judges, Lords Gill and Hamilton, both former Lord Presidents of the Court of Session and Lord Toulson, whose effective retirement lasted only 72 days as he was a member of the panel that heard *AIG Europe Ltd v Woodman* in October 2016.

12.4.4 JUDICIAL DIVERSITY

Previous versions of this section have concentrated on an extensive, and admittedly rather dry, examination of available statistics and the pronouncements of various reports, committees and taskforces. While the importance of such evidence is not to be dismissed, perhaps they merely reflect underlying structural attitudes that have to be challenged before change can take place. To that end, and perhaps to better focus on such underlying issues, what follows will preface such consideration by placing it in the context of an apparent disagreement between two members of the current Supreme Court.

Lord Sumption

In an interview with the *Evening Standard* Lord Sumption was reported as offering his opinion on the gender structure of the judiciary. While many of his comments may well have been taken out of context to provide attention-seeking headlines, such as suggesting that rushing to achieve equal representation for women at the top of the legal profession could inflict 'appalling consequences' on the quality of British justice, nonetheless there are extensive, apparently verbatim, quotations from Lord Sumption that are no less worth comment, not to say concern. Thus he is quoted as expressing the view that it would take decades to have equal representation for women in the judiciary on the basis that:

> These things simply can't be transformed overnight, not without appalling consequence in other directions . . . One has to look at the totality of these problems and not simply at one of them. The lack of diversity is a significant problem, but it isn't the only one . . . It takes time. You've got to be patient. The change in the status and achievements of women in our society, not just in the law but generally, is an enormous cultural change that has happened over the last 50 years or so. It has to happen naturally. It will happen naturally. But in the history of a society like ours, 50 years is a very short time . . . We have got to be very careful not to do things at a speed which will make male candidates feel that the cards are stacked against them. If we do that we will find that male candidates don't apply in the right numbers. 85 per cent of newly appointed judges in France are women because the men stay away. 85 per cent women is just as bad as 85 per cent men . . . What we have in this country is a long cultural tradition which is genuinely based on public service, people feeling that at the end of a successful career at the Bar, that [becoming a judge] it is something that you ought to be willing to do. That's a terrific public asset . . . It's a tradition which you can destroy very easily and never recreate, not without waiting for a very long time. It would be very unfortunate . . . The Bar and the solicitors' profession are incredibly demanding in the hours of work and the working conditions are frankly appalling. There are more women than men who are not prepared to put up with that. As a lifestyle choice, it's very hard to quarrel with it, but you have to face the consequence which is that the top of the legal profession has fewer women in it than the profession overall does.

Lady Hale

In what may, or may not, have been a rejoinder to Sumption, Baroness Hale of Richmond, Deputy President of the Supreme Court, included the following in a speech delivered at the University of Birmingham:

> So how are we doing with appointments to our own Supreme Court? I was sworn in as a 'Lord of Appeal in Ordinary' on 12 January 2004. 15 people have been sworn in as Lords of Appeal in Ordinary or Justices of the Supreme Court of the United Kingdom since then. Even if we leave out the two who were sworn in the day after me, the Court has more than replaced itself since then. One might have hoped that the opportunity would have been taken to achieve a more diverse collegium. It has not happened.

All of those 13 appointments were men. All were white. All but two went to independent fee-paying schools. All but three went to boys' boarding schools. All but two went to Oxford or Cambridge. All were successful QCs in private practice, although one was a solicitor rather than a barrister. All but two had specialised in commercial, property or planning law. None had spent much, if any, time as an employee. I share with them the experience of being white and having been to Cambridge. In every other of those respects I am different: I went to a state day school, my profession was University teacher and then Law Commissioner, my specialism was family and social welfare law. How is it that, despite their very different characters and outlooks, they remain such a homogenous group? . . .

I believe that anyone who is appointing the Justices of the Supreme Court should be able to look at the body of Justices as a whole and ask how they can collectively best serve the needs of the UK justice system. Excellence is important (though I am embarrassed to claim it). But so is diversity of expertise. And so is diversity of background and experience. It really bothers me that there are women, who know or ought to know that they are as good as the men around them, but who won't apply for fear of being thought to be appointed just because they are a woman. We early women believed that we were as good as the men and would certainly not be put off in this way. I may well have been appointed because the powers that be realised the need for a woman. I am completely unembarrassed about that, because they were right, and I hope that I have justified their confidence in me. I don't think that all the talk about the best women being deterred is a plot to put them off, but I am sure that they should not be deterred by talk such as this. We owe it to our sex, but also to the future of the law and the legal system, to step up to the plate.

Judicial Diversity Taskforce final annual report, June 2014

This Judicial Diversity Taskforce was set up as the result of the recommendations of a previous Advisory Panel on Judicial Diversity which reported in 2010. It was given the task of overseeing an agreed action plan for change recommended by that panel. In June 2015 it published its final annual progress report, which outlined the progress of the recommendations of the Advisory Panel. The oversight function of the Taskforce will now be the responsibility of the Judicial Diversity Forum, which brings together most of the parties who were in the Taskforce. The Chairman of the JAC, Christopher Stephens, said of the report:

It is important that the JAC, government, the judiciary and the legal profession continue the work of the Taskforce, including through the Judicial Diversity Forum – it is only through our joint efforts that we will achieve a more diverse judiciary. Since the report was published the JAC has effectively completed all of its 15 allocated recommendations. The final two have been incorporated into our internal change programme, through which we are making improvements to our selection processes. Furthermore the quality of applications remains high and judicial diversity has continued to improve at all levels.

In the last four years (to 31 March 2014) the JAC has recommended 2,890 candidates for judicial office – 44% of them women, 11% Black, Asian and Minority Ethnic candidates and 6% with a self-declared disability. Women made up a third of recommendations for the 2013 High Court exercise and 40% of the previous Chancery Division exercise which has resulted in the highest ever number of women in the High Court. And there is good news for the future as women have shown that if they apply they are often very successful – and even outperform their male colleagues.

Additionally, we now collect and publish data on sexual orientation and religious belief, and are now turning our attention to whether we should monitor social mobility. We all acknowledge there is further work to be done, but the JAC is very encouraged by the results to date. (The report is available on the Ministry of Justice website.)

Judicial diversity statistics, July 2016 (introduction from the Lord Chief Justice Thomas)

Together with the Senior President of Tribunals I am pleased to announce the publication of the judicial diversity figures for 2016 and the first progress report of the Judicial Diversity Committee of the Judges' Council . . .

It is encouraging that the figures show that the overall percentage of female judges in courts has increased this year from 25% to 28% whilst remaining stable at the more impressive figure of 45% in the tribunals. The percentage of female judges in courts stood at 23% in 2012. Within these figures the numbers of female judges in the High Court and the Court of Appeal remain stable at their highest levels but have not increased this year. There has been marked improvement since 2015 in Upper Tribunals (up 8 percentage points), among District Judges (County Court) (up 5 percentage points), among Recorders (up 4 percentage points) and on the Circuit benches (up 3 percentage points)

The percentage of BAME judges under 50 years of age has increased from 12% to 16% which provides some encouragement for the future. However, we are disappointed that there has been no improvement in either courts or tribunals in the total percentage of judges from a Black Asian and Minority Ethnic background. This is an area of concern and one where the Committee will be considering what more needs to be done.

The judiciary must be truly open to everyone of the requisite ability and we are hopeful that the variety of initiatives being actively pursued – led by the Judicial Diversity Committee of the Judges' Council – will bring more diversity to the judiciary, more quickly.

The headline figures from the latest statistical report show:

- The number of woman Court of Appeal Judges remains the same as last year at eight out of 39 (21 per cent).

- Twenty two out of 106 High Court Judges are women (21 per cent). In April 2015 the number was 21 (20 per cent).

- In the courts the percentage of female judges has increased from April 2015 to April 2016 from 25 per cent to 28 per cent. In tribunals it remained stable at 45 per cent.

- The number of female Circuit Judges increased from 146 in April 2015 to 160 in April 2016 (from 23 per cent to 26 per cent).

- More than half (51 per cent) of the 85 courts judges under 40 years of age are women (53 per cent last year). In tribunals, 64 per cent of the 56 judges under 40 are women (56 per cent last year).

- The percentage of judges who identify as Black, Asian and Minority Ethnic is 5 per cent in courts (6 per cent last year), and in tribunals 9 per cent (stable since 2015). This is higher for judges under 40–8 per cent (6 per cent last year) for courts and 14 per cent (15 per cent last year) for tribunals.

- A third (34 per cent, compared with 36 per cent in 2015) of court judges and two thirds (65 per cent, compared with 67 per cent in 2015) of tribunal judges are from non-barrister backgrounds, This varies by jurisdiction for both courts and tribunals, with judges in lower courts more likely to come from a non-barrister background.

For further information see www.judiciary.gov.uk/about-the-judiciary/who-are-the-judiciary/diversity/judicial-diversity-statistics-2016/. The first progress report of the Judicial Diversity Committee of the Judges' Council emphasising the role of Diversity and Community Relations Judges can also be found on the judiciary website.

Case study: does the gender of the judge matter? Radmacher v Granatino

In *Radmacher (formerly Granatino) v Granatino* (the clue of the substance being in the full title of the case), for the first time the highest court in England was required to consider the issue of prenuptial agreements in which the parties, as a precursor to their marriage, establish a limit on subsequent claims on the event of the marriage breaking up. The question before the court was whether such 'freely entered into' contractual agreements are binding in law to the degree that they override the usual principles of fairness at the time of divorce in such a way as to limit the rights of the parties that the courts would otherwise apply.

There were two particular twists in the case:

- Whereas usually it is the husband looking to protect his interests upon divorce, in this instance it was the ex-wife who was trying to enforce the agreement.
- In recognition of the importance of the case the Supreme Court heard it as a panel of nine justices, including the first and, to date, only woman member of the UK's highest court, Baroness Hale.

In a judgment of 69 pages and 195 paragraphs, the court, by a majority of eight to one, determined that such prenuptial agreements were legal and enforceable. The one dissenting voice was Lady Hale. While seven of the justices produced a single majority judgment of 123 paragraphs, and Lord Mance delivered his own judgment, in essential agreement, in seven paragraphs, Hale delivered her minority judgment in 69 extensive paragraphs. However, the core of her difference may be found in paragraph 137:

> Above all, perhaps, the court hearing a particular case can all too easily lose sight of the fact that, unlike a separation agreement, the object of an ante-nuptial agreement is to deny the economically weaker spouse the provision to which she – it is usually although by no means invariably she – would otherwise be entitled . . . This is amply borne out by the precedents available in recent text-books . . . Would any self-respecting young woman sign up to an agreement which assumed that she would be the only one who might otherwise have a claim, thus placing no limit on the claims that might be made against her, and then limited her claim to a pre-determined sum for each year of marriage regardless of the circumstances, as if her wifely services were being bought by the year? Yet that is what these precedents do. *In short, there is a gender dimension to the issue which some may think ill-suited to decision by a court consisting of eight men and one woman* (emphasis added).

The questions that cannot be avoided in relation to this case are whether Baroness Hale's gender gave her an insight/awareness that was not shared with, or indeed open to, the other eight male judges and, if so, whether this awareness should have been allowed to influence her judgment (this last could of course be rewritten to question the privileging of the assumedly male perspective of the majority of the judges).

As a matter of coincidence, and no doubt one much appreciated by the authors, a book entitled *Feminist Judgments: From Theory to Practice* (Hunter, McGlynn and Rackley) had come out in September 2010 and had set itself the task of reconsidering and 're-judging' several notable cases from a feminist perspective, the application of which, they argued, would have led to very different decisions. Ironically, Baroness Hale's judgments were not found to be beyond criticism.

12.4.5   ALTERNATIVE APPROACHES TO APPOINTING JUDGES

A different approach, following the example of the United States, might be for the holders of the higher judicial offices to be subjected to confirmation hearings by, for example,
a select committee of the House of Commons. Lord Mackay dismissed any such possibility as follows:

> The tendency of prior examination . . . is to discover and analyse the previ-
> ous opinions of the individual in detail. *I question whether the standing of
> the judiciary in our country, or the public's confidence in it, would be enhanced
> by such an inquiry*, or whether any wider public interest would be served by
> it (emphasis added).

1. Who appoints the judiciary?
The Lord Chancellor is responsible for appointing judges based on candidates selected and recommended by the **Judicial Appointments Commission (JAC).**

2. On what basis are judges selected?
- All candidates for **judicial roles** are selected on merit through *'fair and open competition from the widest range of eligible candidates'* under procedures set out in the **Constitutional Reform Act 2005** (CRA, as amended), and selecting *'only people of good character and having "regard to the need to encourage diversity in the range of persons available for selection for appointments"'*.
- The main provisions relating to eligibility for judicial appointment are set out in the **Tribunals, Courts and Enforcement Act 2007** (TEC Act) which requires candidates to possess relevant qualifications and experience for a minimum period, dependent on the role sought.

The selection and appointment of judges

3. The process of selection up to and including High Court level:
- On notification of a vacancy by the Courts and Tribunals Service, JAC determine the requirements of the position, advertise the vacancy and set up a selection panel which will make its recommendation to the Lord Chancellor.
- Dependent on the post in question, eligibility rules (TCE Act) require that a relevant legal qualification be held for between five and seven years, and that the applicant has been engaged in law-related activity for the same minimum period. Since 2010, posts up to and including that of District Judge are open to ILEX Fellows, as well as to barristers and solicitors.
- **Becoming a magistrate**: no formal qualifications or legal training is required but applicants must be between the ages of 18 and 70, in good health and of good character.

4. The process of senior judicial appointment:
- When a vacancy arises for a senior judicial position (i.e. those above High Court level) the CRA requires that JAC advertise the vacancy and convene a selection panel of five members who consider nominations and make a recommendation to the Lord Chancellor.
- The Lord Chancellor may then accept the recommendation, reject or ask that the panel reconsider their recommendation. If the candidate recommended is not accepted by the Lord Chancellor, reasons must be provided. The Lord Chancellor does not have the authority to select an alternative candidate. (The composition of selection panels is set out by the CRA.)

FIGURE 12.1 *The Judiciary: selection and appointment.*

It is perhaps unfortunate that the italicised words in the above passage can be interpreted in a way that no doubt Lord Mackay did not intend but which, nonetheless, could suggest a cover-up of the dubious opinions of those appointed to judicial office.

The 2011 House of Lords Constitution Committee report also expressly rejected the possibility of parliamentarians being involved in pre- or post-appointment hearings of judicial candidates (see immediately above).

An even more radical alternative would be to open judicial office-holding to election as they also do in the United States, although in this case, one might well agree with Lord Mackay that:

> The British people would not feel that this was a very satisfactory method of appointing the professional judiciary.

Alternatively, and following Lord Mackay's emphasis on the professional nature of the judiciary, the UK could follow continental examples and provide the judiciary with a distinct professional career structure as an alternative to legal practice.

As has been seen, the changes made under the Constitutional Reform Act were subjected to many criticisms from the judges to the Commons Committee on Constitutional Affairs, with many social commentators and journalists joining in the attack. It is true that the reforms were an unlooked-for consequence of an ill-thought-out Cabinet reshuffle, and equally true that the proposed alterations provided the possibility of political interference with the independence and operation of the judiciary, especially with the future possibility of a weak Secretary of State for Justice and an overly strong Prime Minister or Home Secretary. Nonetheless, it was surely not appropriate, indeed it was inconsistent, for those concerned to resort to an uncritical pragmatic defence of the status quo on the basis that it had worked so far. The system may have worked, but did it do so in an open and transparent manner, and in whose interests did it operate? The opportunity for more radical reforms may not have been taken, but the measures that have been taken surely represent an improvement in the structure and operation of the judicial system.

12.5   TRAINING OF THE JUDICIARY

Following the Constitutional Reform Act 2005, two new judicial institutions were established: the Judicial Office and the Judicial College, both of which operate as independent judicial bodies within the Judicial Office for England and Wales and are funded directly by the Ministry of Justice.

JUDICIAL OFFICE (JO)

This was set up in 2006 to support the judiciary in discharging its responsibilities under the CRA 2005. It reports to the Lord Chief Justice and the Senior President of Tribunals. The Lord Chief Justice as head of the judiciary, has the responsibility for:

- representing the views of the judiciary of England and Wales to Parliament, the Lord Chancellor and ministers generally;
- maintaining arrangements for the welfare, training and guidance of the judiciary, within the resources made available by the Lord Chancellor;
- maintaining arrangements for the deployment of judges and the allocation of work within the courts.

The Senior President of Tribunals has parallel responsibilities for the First-tier and Upper Tribunals as well as the Employment Tribunals (for England and Wales; and Scotland) and the Employment Appeal tribunal.

    The creation of the JO brought together and replaced several units that had previously existed independently, including the Judicial Studies Board (JSB) and the Judicial Communications Office. In 2010 it assumed responsibility for providing secretariat support and sponsorship of the Family and Civil Justice Councils, both of which provide independent advice to government, and in 2011 it assumed responsibility for the work of the Office for Judicial Complaints. Also in 2011 the JO took over responsibility for the Tribunals Judicial Office and for provision of judicial training for the courts' and tribunals' judiciary through a new body, the Judicial College, which replaced the Judicial Studies Board.

    The JO provides a broad range of support to the judiciary, including:

- administrative support and advice for training and development for judicial office-holders;
- research, analysis, legal and secretarial support for the senior judiciary and its governance bodies on a wide range of jurisdictional, constitutional and other strategic matters;
- dealing with official complaints against judicial office-holders through the Office for Judicial Complaints;
- human resources and welfare support services;
- communication and media advice and information.

JUDICIAL COLLEGE

In April 2011, the newly established Judicial College brought together and replaced the Judicial Studies Board and the Tribunals Judicial Training Group and assumed responsibility for training judicial office-holders in the courts and in most tribunals. The Judicial College ensures that high-quality training is provided to enable judicial office-holders to carry out their duties effectively and in a way which preserves judicial independence and supports public confidence in the justice system.

The Judicial College aims to meet the highest professional standards in judicial learning and development.

The College is directly responsible for the development and delivery of training to judges in the Crown, county and higher courts in England and Wales and to tribunals, judges and members who come under the leadership of the Senior President of Tribunals. The Senior President's responsibilities extend to judges and members within reserved tribunals across the UK. The College also provides some direct training to those who exercise judicial functions in the magistrates' courts (in England and Wales), as well as training materials, advice and support to those providing training in the magistrates' courts. In April 2013, the training of all coroners and coroners' officers became part of the Judicial College's responsibilities.

Prior to the establishment of the JSB, now the JC, the training of judges in the UK was almost minimal, especially when considered in the light of the Continental practice where being a judge, rather than practising as an advocate, is a specific and early career choice, which leads to specialist and extensive training.

The Judicial College's activities fall under three main headings (what follows is taken from the publications of the JSB, but remains pertinent to the operation of the JC):

- initial training for new judicial office-holders and those who take on new responsibilities;
- continuing professional education to develop the skills and knowledge of existing judicial office-holders;
- delivering change and modernisation by identifying training needs and providing training programmes to support major changes to legislation and the administration of justice.

The Judicial College provides training and instruction to all part-time and full-time judges in judicial skills. As stated in its strategy document for 2015–17, judicial training has three elements:

- substantive law, evidence and procedure and, where appropriate, expertise in other subjects;
- the acquisition and improvement of judicial skills including, where appropriate, leadership and management skills;
- the social context within which judging occurs, this latter including diversity and equality.

An essential element of the philosophy of the College is that the training is provided by judges for judges.

The Board of the Judicial College is the governing body of the College. It sets the overall strategy for the College, agrees business plans and oversees the delivery of training within the budget allocated to the College.

The Board is supported by a series of committees responsible for the various detailed training programmes as follows:

- *The Tribunals Committee.* It considers the subject expertise required within tribunals as well as considering the overall training needs across the tribunals' judiciary;
- *The Courts' Committee.* It discusses plans and priorities for training across the entire courts' system;
- *The Diversity and Development Committee.* It functions across the entire College to identify issues common to all judiciary and areas of innovation and development for the Judicial College, the dissemination of best practice and ensure that issues of diversity and fair treatment are embedded in all areas of the College;
- *The Wales Training Committee.* It monitors issues that arise from the Welsh Assembly that impact on judicial training;
- *The International Committee.* It implements the College's international strategy to participate in international training projects that strengthen judicial independence, the rule of law and judicial skills.

Judicial training has probably never been of greater public concern or been executed with such rigour since the JSB was established in 1979. For example, the judiciary were subject to thorough retraining in the new civil procedure. This training included residential seminars for all full-time and part-time judges dealing with civil work, local training and conferences held at various national locations. In an interview in October 2009, Judge John Phillips, who was involved in devising the JSB's new programme, emphasised a change in judicial training, 'with less emphasis on the letter of the law and more on the acquisition of judicial skills'. As he added: 'There are, in any event, many ways for judges to keep pace with developments in the law – via JSB e-learning packages and e-letters, and other channels of communication such as professional legal publications, websites, law reports, judgments, textbooks and other sources.'

12.5.1   EQUAL TREATMENT TRAINING

Law is supposed to operate on the basis of formal equality: everyone is assumed to be equal before the law and to be treated equally, regardless of their personal attributes or situation (see Chapter 2). In the past, however, accusations have been levelled at the judiciary that allege that, at the very least, they themselves are insensitive to the sensitivities of others, particularly in matters of race, gender, sexual orientation and in relation to people with disabilities. Not only have they been accused of lacking understanding and sympathy towards others with different values or practices from their own, but it has also been claimed that many of them have been resistant to changing their attitudes.

However, such resistance runs the risk of alienating large sections of the population over which the judiciary exercises its power and, when law is reduced to the level of mere power rather than legitimate authority, its effectiveness is correspondingly reduced. In the light of the recognition that something had to be done to forestall such potential damage, the JSB instituted seminars for training part-time and circuit judges in racial awareness, for example, reminding them that, in a multicultural/multi-faith society, it is offensive to ask for people's 'Christian' names, as well as warning them as to the dangers of even more crassly offensive language and racial stereotyping that appears to be so much a part of the English use of metaphor.

In 1999, for the first time, JSB training included new guidance for all judges on equal treatment issues such as disability, gender and sexual orientation, and litigants in person. In announcing that equal treatment training was to be integral to all induction courses, Lord Justice Waller (the then chairman of the JSB) stated:

> There is absolutely no room for complacency in these areas. And I am not going to say just because someone has been on our course, they will be perfect, but I hope that, as a result, judges are better equipped to do their jobs (*The Times*, 13 July 1999).

A key component in the now Judicial College's strategy of overcoming the appearance of insensitivity and related perception of prejudice was the production of the *Equal Treatment Bench Book* (last updated in November 2013 specifically to take account of the Equality Act 2010), which it has to be said provides a truly comprehensive, first-class guide for the judiciary in ensuring awareness of the need to treat all those who come before them equally and with sensitivity and civility.

Ethnic minorities in the Criminal Justice System

An opportunity to assess the success of the then JSB's policy in assuring equality of treatment was provided in March 2003 by the publication of a research report entitled *Ethnic Minorities in the Criminal Court: Perceptions of Fairness and Equality of Treatment*.

The research project investigated the extent to which ethnic minority defendants and witnesses in Crown Courts and magistrates' courts perceived their treatment to have been unfair and whether those who did perceive unfairness attributed it to racial bias.

The conclusion of the research project was that there had been:

> a substantial change for the better in perceptions of ethnic minorities of racial impartiality in the criminal courts. Several judges mentioned that attitudes had altered markedly in recent years and magistrates reported a substantial decline in the frequency of racially inappropriate remarks. Many lawyers also reported that racial bias or inappropriate language was becoming 'a thing of the past'.

However, there was an undercurrent in the report which supported a more critical reading. While it was concerned with '*perceptions* of racial bias', dealing with such perceptions may not wholly correct the underlying reality. Eliminating inappropriate language may well be a good thing in itself, but if it merely provides camouflage for a system that remains fundamentally biased in terms of its outcomes, then doubts have to be raised about its fundamental worth. The difference in perception of the black lawyers and court staff as to the true nature of the system would seem to provide grounds to support such a possibility. Given that differential sentencing remains the major ground of complaint relating to allegations of racial bias, that surely remains the most pressing issue in relation to equality. As the report states:

> The findings of this study may go some way to dispelling the view that most minority ethnic defendants believe that their treatment by the courts has been racially biased. But *if it could be shown that the 'cultural change' which this study has identified has had a real impact on eliminating differential sentencing of white and ethnic minority defendants*, this would further encourage the confidence of ethnic minorities in the criminal courts (emphasis added).

Unfortunately, a remarkably unheralded report published by the Ministry of Justice in November 2013 appeared to confirm the continuation of the practice of differential sentencing. The report, *Statistics on Race and the Criminal Justice System 2012*, compared statistics relating to various criminal justice actions on both white and BME individuals during the period 2008–12. The conclusions would appear to indicate a disparity of treatment between the various groups over that period and, not unsurprisingly, the chair of the Society of Black Lawyers, Peter Herbert, was quoted as saying that the figures showed 'institutional racism', within the justice system that needed urgent attention. As he said, 'I am not sure what else you can call it. The effect is right across the criminal justice system. From stop and search, to arrest, to charge and to sentencing, every aspect of the process is stacked against defendants from ethnic minority backgrounds. It is not a pretty picture.'

The following are the report's most telling findings:

Victims

> The 2012/13 Crime Survey for England and Wales shows that adults from self-identified Mixed, Black and Asian ethnic groups were more at risk of being a victim of personal crime than adults from the White ethnic group.

Suspects

Stop and search

A person aged ten or older (the age of criminal responsibility), who self-identified as belonging to the black ethnic group was *six times more likely* than a white person to be stopped and searched under section 1 (s 1) of the Police and Criminal Evidence Act 1984 and other legislation in England and Wales; persons from the Asian or mixed ethnic group were just *over two times* more likely to be stopped and searched than a white person.

Arrest

For those aged 10 or older, a black person was nearly *three times more likely* to be arrested per 1,000 population than a white person, while a person from the mixed ethnic group was twice as likely to be arrested. There was no difference in the rate of arrests between Asian and white persons.

Defendants

Black persons were *less likely* to receive an out of court disposal for an indictable offence, and *more likely* to be proceeded against at magistrates' court, than all other ethnic groups. This remained consistent between 2009 and 2012 despite the overall decrease in the proportion of out of court disposals of those formally dealt with by the criminal justice system.

Between 2009 and 2012, for indictable offences, there was a decrease across all ethnic groups in the proportion receiving community sentences. In contrast there was *an increase* for most ethnic groups in the proportion receiving an immediate custodial sentence for an indictable offence. The most common sentence outcome for white and mixed ethnic group offenders was a community sentence, whilst for black, Asian and Chinese or other offenders the most common sentence outcome was immediate custody.

The average custodial sentence length for indictable offences was *higher* in all years between 2009 and 2012 for offenders from a BAME group compared with those from a white ethnic group. Different types of crime also show sentencing differences. A white person pleading guilty to burglary was sentenced to, on average, 25 months in prison compared with a black person who typically received a 28-month sentence. Of those pleading not guilty but convicted by the courts, the sentences were 40 months and 47 months respectively.

Similarly, 76 per cent of white people convicted of production or supply of a class A drug were sentenced to immediate custody compared with 84.8 per cent of black people.

The 2014 report, which continued to find that [i]n general, Black, Asian and Minority Ethnic (BAME) groups appear to be over-represented at most stages throughout the CJS, compared with the White ethnic group, together with an interesting 'info graphic' for those who are visual learners are available at www.gov.uk/government/statistics/race-and-the-criminal-justice-system-2014.

In January 2016, the former Prime Minister David Cameron, asked David Lammy MP to lead a review to investigate evidence of possible bias against black defendants and other ethnic minorities in the Criminal Justice System in England and Wales. Although the final findings were not due until 2017, the interim findings, released in November 2016 caused major concern. The core findings were:

- For every 100 white women handed custodial sentences at Crown Courts for drug offences, 227 black women were sentenced to custody. For black men, the figure is 141 for every 100 white men.

- Among all those found guilty at Crown Court in 2014, 112 black men were sentenced to custody for every 100 white men.

- Of those convicted at Magistrates' Court for sexual offences, 208 black men and 193 Asian men received custodial sentences for every 100 white men.

- BAME men were more than 16 per cent more likely than white men to be remanded in custody.

- In prisons, BAME males are almost five times more likely to be housed in high security for public order offences than white men.

- Mixed ethnic men and women were more likely than white men and women to have adjudications for breaching prison discipline brought against them – but less likely to have those adjudications proven when reviewed.

- 41 per cent of youth prisoners are from minorities backgrounds, compared with 25 per cent ten years ago, despite prisoner numbers falling by some 66 per cent in that time.

- The number of Muslim prisoners has almost doubled in the last decade.

- BAME defendants are more likely than their white counterparts to be tried at Crown Court. The interim report notes that 'black individuals account for about 3% of the total population of England and Wales yet make up about 9% of defendants prosecuted for indictable offences' at Crown Court.

- Court – with young black men around 56 per cent more likely than their white counterparts to be tried at the Crown Court rather than the Magistrates' Court.

- BAME men were 52 per cent more likely than white men to plead 'not guilty' at Crown Court.

- 51 per cent of the UK-born BAME population agree that 'the criminal justice system discriminates against particular groups', compared to 35 per cent of the UK-born white population.

12.6   RETIREMENT OF JUDGES

All judges are now required to retire at 70, although they may continue in office at the discretion of the Lord Chief Justice and with the approval of the Lord Chancellor. The

Judicial Pensions and Retirement Act 1993 reduced the retirement age from the previous 75 years for High Court judges and 72 years for other judges, although a judge already serving on the implementation of the Act (31 March 1995) retains the pre-existing retirement age. Part-time members of the judiciary were customarily required to retire at 65, but following an initial finding by an employment tribunal in February 2008 that such a policy was discriminatory, the Lord Chancellor announced that the retirement age for part-time judges would be increased to bring it into line with the general judicial retirement age of 70. The 2011 House of Lords Constitution Committee, previously considered, recommended that the retirement age for Court of Appeal judges and Supreme Court justices should be raised to 75.

The reduction of the retirement age may have been designed to reduce the average age of the judiciary, but of perhaps even more significance in this respect is the change that was introduced in judicial pensions at the same time. The new provision requires judges to have served for 20 years, rather than the previous 15, before they qualify for full pension rights. This effectively means that if judges are to benefit from full pension rights, they will have to take up their appointments by the time they are 50. Given that judges are predominantly appointed from the ranks of high-earning QCs, this will either reduce their potential earnings at the Bar or reduce their pay package as judges by approximately 7.5 per cent. This measure led to a great deal of resentment within both the Bar and the judiciary, Lord Chief Justice Taylor referring to its unfairness and meanness, and it was one of the issues that fuelled the antagonism between Lord Mackay and the other members of the judiciary.

With regard to compulsory retirement, many people thought it particularly regrettable that Lord Bingham's age meant that he could not assume the role of the first President of the new Supreme Court. That honour passed to Lord Phillips, who was a sprightly 71 when he assumed the office.

Following protracted litigation, including a hearing in the Supreme Court (*O'Brien v Ministry of Justice* [2013] UKSC 6), part-time fee-paid members of the judiciary were held liable to receive pension payments from the state, which increased the extent of the state's liability for judicial pension. However, under the Public Service Pensions Act 2013 future judicial pensions, alongside all other public sector provisions, were converted to a contributory basis with a significant reduction in value for future pensions. The New Judicial Pension Scheme (NJPS) 2015 which came into effect in April of that year, met with angry resistance from judges, many of whom suggested that they would resign rather than accept its terms, which they saw as reducing their remuneration packages to an unacceptable degree. In January 2017 a representative group of younger judges won an action in the employment tribunal on the basis that they had been subjected to discriminatory action on grounds of age, race and gender by being required to leave the existing judicial pension scheme in April 2015 while older judges were allowed to remain in it.

In the summer of 2005, Sir Hugh Laddie, a High Court Chancery Judge of some 10 years' standing, announced his intention to resign from his position and return to legal practice. He was the first judge to return to private practice for over 30 years and it is reported that his resignation upset the Lord Chancellor by breaking the 'unwritten rule that joining the judiciary is a one-way street'. Sir Hugh compounded the difficulties in the situation when, in February 2006, he delivered a lecture at the University of London, in which he told the audience that although he was an expert in intellectual property law, he was frequently asked to sit on tax and insolvency cases. As he admitted (*Law Society Gazette*, 23 February 2006):

> I knew nothing about tax, except that it came as a nasty shock at the end of the year. I had never studied it or did it at the bar, or insolvency . . . I had colleagues who said that it was marvellous to do cases outside their own field, that it was stimulating. When I resigned, I felt a certain sensitivity about deciding cases about which I had no knowledge. It would have been better to use a roulette wheel.

12.7 JUDICIAL CONDUCT AND DISCIPLINE

In March 2013 a revised *Guide to Judicial Conduct* was published by the Judges' Council after wide consultation with members of the judiciary. The guide:

- offers assistance to judges on issues rather than prescribing a detailed code; and
- sets up principles from which judges can make their own decisions and so maintain their judicial independence.

The guide accepts, as a basis for its more detailed consideration, what are referred to as the Bangalore principles, which were established following a United Nations initiative. The Bangalore principles may be understood as six underlying values with the stated intention of:

> establish[ing] standards for ethical conduct of judges. They are designed to provide guidance to judges and to afford the judiciary a framework for regulating judicial conduct. They are also intended to assist members of the Executive and Legislature, and lawyers and the public in general, to better understand and support the judiciary.

The essential principles are:

(i)   Judicial independence is a prerequisite to the rule of law and a fundamental guarantee of a fair trial. A judge shall therefore uphold and exemplify judicial independence in both its individual and institutional aspects.

(ii) Impartiality is essential to the proper discharge of the judicial office. It applies not only to the decision itself but also to the process by which the decision is made.

(iii)   Integrity is essential to the proper discharge of the judicial office.

(iv)   Propriety, and the appearance of propriety, are essential to the performance of all of the activities of the judge.

(v)   Ensuring equality of treatment to all before the courts is essential to the due performance of the judicial office.

(vi)   Competence and diligence are prerequisites to the due performance of judicial office.

The worked-out expression of those principles may be seen on the www.judiciary.gov.uk website.

In relation to matters of discipline, the Constitutional Reform Act 2005 gave powers to both the Lord Chancellor and the Lord Chief Justice. Consistent with previous provisions, the position of all senior judicial office-holders is protected, and removal from office of any judge in the High Court or above is only possible following resolutions in both the House of Commons and the House of Lords. Under s 108 CRA, the Lord Chief Justice was given new powers enabling them to:

- advise;
- warn; or
- formally reprimand judicial office-holders.

They may also suspend them in certain circumstances, mainly regarding allegations relating to criminal offences. Such powers are subject to the agreement of the Lord Chancellor. The Lord Chief Justice may, again with the agreement of the Lord Chancellor, make regulations and rules about the disciplinary process.

THE OFFICE FOR JUDICIAL COMPLAINTS/JUDICIAL CONDUCT INVESTIGATION OFFICE

The Constitutional Reform Act 2005 also established the Office for Judicial Complaints (OJC) and gave the Lord Chancellor and the Lord Chief Justice joint responsibility for a new system for dealing with complaints about the personal conduct of all judicial office-holders in England and Wales. The OJC was set up in April 2006 to handle these complaints and provide advice and assistance to the Lord Chancellor and Lord Chief Justice in the performance of their new joint role. In October 2013 the Judicial Conduct Investigations Office (JCIO) took over the functions of the OJC and from 18 August 2014 all complaints became subject to the Judicial Discipline (Prescribed Procedures) Regulations 2014 (http://judicialconduct.judiciary.gov.uk/rules-and-regulations.htm).

In its annual report for the year 2015/16 the JCIO revealed that, over the period, it had received 2,609 separate complaints against judicial office-holders, although 1,538 of these (59 per cent) related to judicial decisions, which are outside its remit. Unless there are elements of misconduct included in the complaint, issues can only be challenged through an appeal process.

The most common complaint, numbering 549 in total, related to inappropriate behaviour or comments. The next most frequent complaint, 43 in total, related to a failure to fulfil judicial duties and 14 alleged conflict of interest. In the period covered there were only 10 complaints referring to discrimination. Out of the 43 judicial office-holders subject to disciplinary action, 7 were from the mainstream judiciary, 5 were tribunals' judiciary and 30 were magistrates. This total represents less than 0.1 per cent of the 28,100 judicial office-holders in place during the period.

As a result of investigation:

- 16 judicial office-holders were removed from office;
- 9 received a reprimand; and
- 18 received formal advice/warning.

In June 2009, in rejecting an appeal by *The Guardian* newspaper under the Freedom of Information Act 2000, the Information Tribunal decided that the Ministry of Justice does not have to disclose the names of judges disciplined following complaints on the basis that 'Disclosure would risk undermining a judge's authority while carrying out his or her judicial function.'

In October 2013 the Judicial Conduct Investigations Office (JCIO) took over the functions of the Office for Judicial Complaints.

In March 2015 it was announced that three lower-level judges had been removed from office for viewing pornography via their official IT accounts. One other judge resigned before any action could be taken against him.

12.8 JUDICIAL IMMUNITY FROM SUIT

A fundamental measure to ensure the independence of the judiciary is the rule that they cannot be sued in relation to things said or acts done in their judicial capacity in good faith. The effect of this may be seen in *Sirros v Moore* (1975), in which a judge wrongly ordered someone's detention. It was subsequently held by the Court of Appeal that, although the detention had been unlawful, no action could be taken against the judge as he had acted in good faith in his judicial capacity. Although some judges on occasion may be accused of abusing this privilege, it is nonetheless essential if judges are to operate as independent representatives of the law, for it is unlikely that judges would be able to express their honest opinions of the law, and the situations in which it is being applied, if they were to be subject to suits from disgruntled participants.

Given the increased use of the doctrine of *ultra vires* to justify legal action by way of judicial review against members of the executive, it is satisfyingly ironic that at least one judge, Stephen Sedley, who now sits in the Court of Appeal, sees the possibility of a similar *ultra vires* action providing grounds for an action against judges in spite of their previously assumed legal immunity. As he expressed the point in the *London Review of Books* of April 1994:

> Judges have no authority to act maliciously or corruptly. It would be rational to hold that such acts take them outside their jurisdiction and so do not attract judicial immunity.

No doubt such a suggestion would be anathema to the great majority of the judiciary, but the point remains: why should judges be at liberty to abuse their position of authority in a way that no other public servant can?

Before 1991, magistrates could be liable for damages for actions done in excess of their actual authority, but the CLSA 1990 extended the existing immunity from the superior courts to cover the inferior courts, so magistrates now share the same protection as other judges.

It is worth stating at this point that this immunity during court proceedings also extends as far as advocates and witnesses, and of course jurors, although the controls of *perjury* and *contempt of court* are always available to cover what is said or done in the course of court proceedings.

Related to, although distinct from, the principle of immunity from suit is the convention that individual judges should not be subject to criticism in parliamentary debate, unless subject to an address for their removal: legal principles and the law in general can be criticised, but not judges.

12.9 MAGISTRATES

The foregoing has concentrated attention on the professional and legally qualified judges. It should not be forgotten, however, that there are some 17,500 unpaid part-time lay magistrates, 140 full-time professional magistrates (known as district judges (magistrates' courts)) and 125 deputy district judges (magistrates' courts) operating within some 300 or so magistrates' courts in England. These magistrates are empowered to hear and decide a wide variety of legal matters, and the amount and importance of the work they do should not be underestimated: as much as 90 per cent of all criminal cases are dealt with by the magistrates' courts.

Magistrates currently deal with around 500,000 traffic cases each year, which take up a great deal of their time and the time of those whose cases they hear. On average, traffic cases take nearly six months to reach completion, despite the fact that over 90 per cent of cases result in a guilty plea or are proved in the absence of the defendant. In an attempt to speed up the process, specialist traffic courts were established in nine pathfinder areas in England and the government subsequently announced that, from April 2014, there will be a specialist traffic court in each police area (see www.gov.uk/government/news/traffic-courts-in-every-area).

The operation of the magistrates' courts and the powers of magistrates have been considered in detail above at 6.3 and 9.2. Since April 2005, magistrates' courts in England and Wales have been administered by Her Majesty's Courts Service (HMCS, now the HMCTS). This amalgamation ended the previously long-standing separation between magistrates' courts, which were administered by a total of 42 independent local committees, and the government-run Court Service that ran the Court of Appeal, the High Court and all Crown and County Courts.

It remains, however, to examine the manner in which magistrates are appointed to their positions.

There is no requirement for lay magistrates to have any legal qualifications. On being accepted onto the bench, however, magistrates undertake a training process, under the auspices of the JC. Magistrates are required to attend training courses, with a special emphasis being placed on Equal Treatment Training. The way in which the training programme seeks to overcome conceptions as to the politically narrow nature of the magistracy is evident in the content of the extensive training materials produced for the magistrates. These include modules on raising awareness and challenging discrimination; discretion and decision-making; prejudice and stereotype; thus, the overall emphasis may be seen to be on equality of people, and equality of treatment. There is, however, a new emphasis on the practical skills involved in performing the duties placed on magistrates, and consequently much of the training will actually be based on sitting as magistrates with the input of specially trained mentors to give guidance and advice on how the new magistrates perform their tasks and fulfil their roles. About 12 to 18 months after appointment the new magistrate is appraised against a set of the competences covering each courtroom role from basic magistrates to chairmen in adult, youth and family courts. Competences include a checklist of observable behaviour and knowledge.

The training course is designed to give new magistrates an understanding of the functions and powers of the bench generally, and to locate that understanding within the context of national practice, particularly with regard to sentencing. On the topic of discretion and sentencing, Lord Irvine provided the magistrates with the following strong advice, not to say warning:

> You . . . must exercise your discretion in individual cases with great care within a system that needs to secure continuing public confidence. This is what makes the sentencing guidelines produced by the Magistrates' Association so important. They are guidelines – they do not curtail your independent discretion to impose sentences you think are right, case by case. But the guidelines exist to help you in that process, to give you more information in reaching your decision. And they help to assist the magistracy, to maintain an overall consistency of approach . . . I urge you to follow the guidelines, which are drawn up for your benefit and the magistracy as a whole (Speech to the Council of the Magistrates' Association, March 1999).

One aspect of sentencing that merits attention arises in relation to the increasingly important area of environmental crime. In response to this, and to make magistrates fully aware of its importance, the Magistrates' Association website made available an extremely useful guidance entitled 'Costing the Earth – guidance for sentencers'.

JUSTICES' CLERK

Although particular key legal issues may be considered in the course of the training, it is not the intention to provide the magistrate with a complete grasp of substantive law and legal practice. Indeed, to expect such would be to misunderstand both the role of the magistrates and the division of responsibility within the magistrates' court. Every bench of magistrates has a legally qualified justices' clerk, whose function it is to advise the bench on questions of law, practice and procedure, leaving matters of fact to magistrates to decide upon (see above, 9.2). This division of powers raises a further possible area of contention with regard to the operation of magistrates' courts, for in the case of some particularly acquiescent benches, the justices' clerks appear to run the court, and this leads to the suspicion that they actually direct the magistrates as to what decisions they should make. This perception is compounded by the fact that the bench is entitled to invite their clerk to accompany them when they retire to consider their verdicts. A *Practice Direction (Justices: Clerks to the Court)* (2000) set out the role and functions of the clerk to the court. Thus the clerk, or legal adviser who stands in for the clerk, is stated to be responsible for providing the justices with any advice they require to properly perform their functions, whether or not the justices have requested that advice, on the following matters:

- questions of law (including ECHR jurisprudence and those matters set out in s 2(1) of the HRA 1998);
- questions of mixed law and fact;
- matters of practice and procedure;
- the range of penalties available;
- any relevant decisions of the superior courts or other guidelines; other issues relevant to the matter before the court;
- the appropriate decision-making structure to be applied in any given case; and
- in addition to advising the justices, it shall be the legal adviser's responsibility to assist the court, where appropriate, as to the formulation of reasons and the recording of those reasons.

As regards when and where this advice should be given, the *Practice Direction* states that:

> At any time, justices are entitled to receive advice to assist them in discharging their responsibilities. If they are in any doubt as to the evidence which has been given, they should seek the aid of their legal adviser, referring to his/her notes as appropriate. This should ordinarily be done in open court. Where the justices request their adviser to join them in the retiring room, this request should be made in the presence of the parties in court. Any legal advice given to the justices other than in open court should be clearly stated to be provisional and the adviser should subsequently repeat the substance of the advice in open court and give the parties an opportunity to make any representations they wish on that provisional advice.

In October 2007 the senior presiding judge for England and Wales issued new guidelines for the conduct of justices' clerks and assistant justices' clerks. These emphasise the independence and impartiality of clerks.

12.9.1 APPOINTMENT

Under the Justices of the Peace Act 1997, magistrates are appointed to, and indeed removed from, office by the Lord Chancellor on behalf of the Queen, after consultation with local advisory committees. Following the Constitutional Reform Act 2005 it was the intention for the Judicial Appointments Commission eventually to deal with the appointment of magistrates. However, at least for the moment, the Ministry of Justice handles such appointments. In this interim period, recommendations on the appointment of magistrates continue to be made by local advisory committees. These are then passed to the Lord Chief Justice for approval, before being submitted to the Lord Chancellor to make the appointment.

Section 50 of the Employment Rights Act 1996 provides that employers are obliged to release their employees, for such time as is reasonable, to permit them to serve as magistrates. In the event of an employer refusing to sanction absence from work to perform magistrate's duties, the employee can take the matter before an employment tribunal. Understandably, there is no statutory requirement for the employer to pay their employees in their absence, but magistrates are entitled to claim expenses for loss of earnings in the exercise of their office.

Once candidates of a suitable quality have been identified, the local advisory committee is placed under the injunction to have regard to the need to ensure that the composition of the bench broadly reflects the community that it serves in terms of gender, ethnic origin, geographical spread, occupation and political affiliation. It may even be that individuals who are otherwise suitably qualified may not be appointed if their presence would exacerbate a perceived imbalance in the existing bench. Nonetheless, there remains a lingering doubt, at least in the minds of particular constituencies, that the magistracy still represents the values, both moral and political, of a limited section of society. A further significant step towards opening up the whole procedure of appointing magistrates was taken when local advisory committees were granted the power to advertise for people to put themselves forward for selection. As the chairman of the Mid-Staffordshire Magistrates' Bench stated in a local newspaper, although previously rank and social position were the main qualifications, nowadays:

> it is important a bench has a balance of sexes, professions and political allegiances.

In March 1999, the LCD launched a campaign to attract a wider section of candidates to apply to be magistrates. In announcing the campaign, Lord Irvine stated that:

> Magistrates come from a wide range of backgrounds and occupations. We have magistrates who are dinner ladies and scientists, bus drivers and

teachers, plumbers and housewives. They have different faiths and come from different ethnic backgrounds, some have disabilities. All are serving their communities, ensuring that local justice is dispensed by local people. The magistracy should reflect the diversity of the community it serves . . . Rest assured appointments are made on merit, regardless of educational background, social class or ethnic background.

The campaign was supported by adverts in some 36 newspapers and magazines, from broadsheets to tabloids, from TV listings to women's magazines. The campaign was particularly aimed at ethnic minorities, its adverts being carried in such publications as the *Caribbean Times*, the *Asian Times* and *Muslim News*. The 1999 campaign was followed in 2001 by a *Judiciary for All* scheme, which aimed to encourage more people from ethnic minority groups to apply to become magistrates. The next initiative to make the bench more reflective of the public was the 'National Strategy for the Recruitment of Lay Magistrates' announced by Lord Falconer in October 2003. As he stated:

> I consider it particularly important that the magistracy is seen to be representative of all sections of our society and that no one group of people should feel that they are under-represented on the magistrates' bench. My Department is already involved with a number of initiatives aimed at encouraging young people and minority ethnic groups to become involved in the judicial process and, although the ethnic make-up of the magistracy countrywide is close to the national average for cultural representation per head of population there are still regional variations, both in age and ethnicity, that need to be addressed.

The statistics demonstrate that the gender balance and ethnic mix of the magistracy does not appear to pose a major problem, but the same certainly cannot be said in terms of its class mix. In 1998, the Lord Chancellor's Department issued a consultation paper relating to the political balance in the lay magistracy, which suggested that political affiliation was no longer a major issue, and therefore did not have to be controlled in relation to the make-up of benches of magistrates. As support for its suggestion, the consultancy document made three points. First, that actually ensuring a political balance on the bench raises:

> the danger of creating a perception that politics do play a part in the administration of justice, notwithstanding that it is agreed on all sides that, in a mature democracy, politics have no place in the court room.

Secondly, that advisory committees:

> have increasingly found that many magistrates have declined to provide the information [relating to their political allegiance] or classed themselves as 'uncommitted'.

Thirdly, it claimed that in any case, 'geodemographic classification schemes', based on an analysis of particular personal attributes such as ethnicity, gender, marital status, occupation, home ownership and car-owning status, are much more sensitive indicators for achieving social balance on benches than stated political allegiance.

Such 'geodemographics' might well represent the emergence of the truly classless society. Alternatively, they might represent a worrying denial of the importance of political attitudes within law generally, and the magistrates' bench in particular.

In any case, in March 2001, Jane Kennedy MP, Parliamentary Secretary to the LCD, announced that, at least for the moment, the Lord Chancellor had reluctantly decided that political balance would have to remain an issue. This statement was made in response to the disclosure that the Magistrates' Advisory Committee in Stoke-on-Trent had sent out a letter to several local organisations, which stated that:

> whilst the overriding criterion for appointment is always the suitability of the candidate, the Advisory Committee is particularly keen to receive applications from members of ethnic minorities, shop floor workers, the unemployed and Labour Party supporters.

In answering charges that such a letter was politicising the magistracy, Ms Kennedy pointed out that:

> Public confidence in lay magistrates is vital. This is achieved, first and foremost, by individual magistrates discharging their duties effectively. It is also achieved when Benches reflect the diversity of the communities which they serve. In Stoke-on-Trent the Labour vote is significantly under-reflected on the magistrates' Bench. Of those who expressed political affiliation 40 per cent were Labour, compared to 60 per cent who voted Labour in the area at the last General Election. This compares to 47 per cent of the Bench being acknowledged Conservative voters, compared to 27 per cent in the area.

The Advisory Committee was simply and correctly trying to attract more Labour voters to apply to become magistrates, in order that the composition of the bench more broadly reflected the local voting pattern.

Magistrates are:
- Lay (unqualified), part-time and unpaid (expenses payable)
- Supported by a smaller number of professional judges, known as district judges

Appointment:
- Appointed on behalf of the monarch after consultation with the local advisory committee
- Bench is intended to reflect the local community
- Vacancies can now be advertised to encourage appropriate background, gender and ethnic mix

MAGISTRATES

Training:
- Magistrates are required to undertake training organised by the Judicial Studies Board
- Training is designed to give new magistrates an understanding of the functions and powers of the bench, including sentencing
- Magistrates are supported by a legally qualified clerk, who is responsible for providing the justices with advice on questions of law, practice and procedure

FIGURE 12.2 *Magistrates: an aide-mémoire.*

The age profile of magistrates

If the class make-up of the magistracy is possibly a problem, then a look at the current statistics will immediately show that the age profile and distribution of the current magistrates is certainly a matter for concern: 57 per cent of magistrates are aged 60 or above, 86 per cent of magistrates are at least 50 and only 0.19 per cent are below the age of 30. Given the strictures that are involved in being a magistrate, they have to commit to 13 full or 26 half-days sitting in court in addition to training days, it is obvious that the older members of society are more likely to have time to offer their services as magistrates, especially those who have retired. However, the inescapable question arises as to the representative nature of such a body, especially when the core clientele is likely to be a great deal younger than they are. It was an attempt to address this problem, at least of perception if not substance, that the age for service as a magistrate was reduced from 27 to 18 in 2003. Statistics on the magistracy are available at: www.judiciary.gov.uk.

12.9.2 THE FUTURE OF THE MAGISTRATES' COURTS

In December 2000, the results of a report, *The Judiciary in the Magistrates' Courts*, were published. The extensive report was jointly commissioned by the Home Office and the LCD and provided an extremely valuable comparison between the lay magistracy and stipendiaries, now known as District Judges (magistrates' courts). It found as follows.

As regards the lay magistracy

- they are drawn overwhelmingly from professional and managerial ranks;
- 40 per cent of them are retired from full-time employment;
- the cost of an appearance before lay magistrates was £52.10 per hour.

As regards the stipendiaries

- they are younger, but are mostly male and white;
- they hear cases more quickly;
- they are more likely to refuse bail and to make use of immediate custodial sentences;
- they are less likely to need legal advisers;
- the cost of an appearance before stipendiary magistrates was £61.78 per hour.

Those findings were essentially replicated in a later study conducted by Ipsos MORI for the Justice Ministry in 201. It was entitled The strengths and skills of the Judiciary in the Magistrates' Courts and is available at: www.justice.gov.uk.

In January, 2001, a report entitled *Community Justice* by Professor Andrew Sanders for the Institute for Public Policy Research called for the replacement of panels of lay justices by panels composed of district judges, the former stipendiary magistrates, assisted by two lay magistrates.

The Magistrates' Association saw the proposals as an attack on what was an extremely representative system of justice. According to its then Chair, Harry Mawdsley:

> Lay magistrates provide community justice: they are ordinary people who live and work in the local community and who have an intimate knowledge of that community.

Although praising the magistracy's gender and ethnic make-up, Mr Mawdsley nevertheless recognised the need to recruit more magistrates from working-class backgrounds.

Among many recommendations made by the House of Commons Justice Committee in its sixth report: *The role of the magistracy*, published in October 2016 it concluded that:

> The magistracy faces a range of unresolved issues relating to its role and its workload, together with serious problems with recruitment and training; we conclude that these now must be addressed as a matter of urgency. The wide range of recommendations that we have made indicate a need for

strategic leadership. It is unfortunate that the Government's evident goodwill towards the magistracy has not yet been translated into any meaningful strategy for supporting and developing it within a changing criminal justice system.

Magistrates' sentencing power

The Auld Report into the criminal court system, issued in 2001, suggested a compromise between these two positions: the retention of the magistrates' courts as one division in a unified criminal court, with the creation of a new District Division, made up of a district judge and two magistrates, to hear mid-range either-way offences (the third division, the Crown Division, retained the role of the current Crown Court). In the event, the government declined to adopt the Auld recommendations in this regard, but instead proposed to increase the sentencing powers of the magistrates to 12 months in detention in s 154 of the Criminal Justice Act 2003.

However, as yet, the increased sentencing power under s 154 of the Criminal Justice Act 2003 has not been implemented. Under the coalition government, the Justice Ministry had intended to remove this power to increase the sentencing powers of magistrates and included a section to that end in its Legal Aid, Sentencing and Punishment of Offenders Bill. However, following the riots that took place across England in the summer of 2011, the Attorney General, Dominic Grieve, put himself at odds with the then Justice Minister, Ken Clarke, by suggesting that increasing the sentencing powers of magistrates would make the court system more efficient. To the pleasure of the Magistrates' Association, Grieve would appear to have won any argument that took place as the proposal was omitted from the subsequent Legal Aid, Sentencing and Punishment of Offenders Act (LASPO) 2012.

LASPO 2012, however, did increase magistrates' powers in relation to the fines they could impose. Criminal offences are divided into five levels, on an ascending scale of seriousness. Before LASPO 2012, the general maximum fine for a level 5 offence was £5,000, but subsequently magistrates have the power to impose unlimited fines in the most serious cases.

The 2016 House of Commons Justice Committee report, *The role of the magistracy*, supported increasing magistrates' sentencing powers to 12 months' custody by commencing s 154 of the Criminal Justice Act 2003, and recommended that the Ministry of Justice provide a timetable for implementation. However, it also, and perhaps more worryingly, recommended that the Ministry of Justice publish any modelling of the potential impact on the prison population of extending magistrates' sentencing powers.

Criminal Justice and Courts Act 2015: trial by single justice on the papers

The Criminal Justice and Courts Act 2015 (ss 30, 31) introduced a new single-justice procedure under which proceedings against adults charged with summary-only, nonimprisonable offences can be considered by a single magistrate, on the papers. This means that the trial will take place without the attendance of either prosecutor or defendant, the defendant being able to engage with the court in writing. The stated purpose of this new procedure is to deal more proportionately with straightforward, uncontested cases, involving offences such as road traffic offences. Previously, many defendants either chose not to engage with the process or returned a written guilty plea. In such instances, hearings took place in an empty courtroom with only magistrates, prosecutors and court staff present. The new procedure allows such cases to be dealt with much more efficiently. Cases which prosecutors identify as being suitable for this process will be commenced by a written charge and a new type of document called a 'single justice procedure notice'. This notice will give a defendant a date to respond in writing to the allegation rather than a date to attend court; it will also be accompanied by all the evidence which the prosecutor would be relying on to prove the case. If a defendant pleads guilty and indicates they would like to have the matter dealt with in their absence, or doesn't respond to the notice, then a single magistrate will consider the case on the basis of the evidence submitted in writing by the prosecutor, and any written mitigation from the defendant. They can dismiss the charge, or convict and sentence as appropriate. However, if a defendant wishes to plead not guilty, or otherwise wants to have a hearing in a traditional courtroom, they can indicate their wishes and the current arrangements will apply.

In an article in *Criminal Law & Justice Weekly* in September 2010, entitled 'The future of the magistracy', Noel Cox used some recent changes in New Zealand practice to offer some suggestions as to the way that the role of the magistrates may evolve in England and Wales.

He sees two related processes emerging. First, the jurisdiction of magistrates has expanded in terms of number and complexity over the past few decades as a result of existing crimes being downgraded to summary or offences triable either way, with new offences tending to be categorised in that way from the outset. However, the increased use of fixed penalties for minor summary offences (see below) is a related, if apparently contradictory, development in that it reduces the number of less serious cases coming before the magistrates' courts. It should also be remembered that, to a very large extent, the role of the magistrates' courts as licensing bodies has been removed. Consequently there has been a radical shift of work to magistrates' courts and one that Cox sees as likely to continue. The threat for the lay magistracy is that the increase in the seriousness and complexity of the cases dealt with in their courts will lead, necessarily, to the further professionalisation of the magistracy in the form of increased use of district judges, and their role will be reduced to that of almost lay assessors or jury members, rather than judges.

Cox's conclusion, although not amounting to a death sentence, raised concerns among the magistracy. As he saw it:

In England and Wales the work of District Judges is currently expanding and their importance is likely to increase, as trial by jury is effectively restricted to the most serious cases. It is also possible that the powers of justices' clerks will continue to expand. They have acquired case management powers that were once reserved to magistrates and the Justices' Clerks Society have argued that its members should sit as chairmen of the bench. The days of the justice of the peace as an active lay magistrate may be drawing to a close. As a consequence, a long tradition of voluntary community service may be lost. But it would be premature to toll the death knell of the lay magistracy.

12.9.3   MAGISTRATES' COURTS AND OUT-OF-COURT DISPOSAL OF CRIMINAL OFFENCES (OOCDS)

In 2005 the government issued its *Supporting Magistrates' Courts to Provide Justice* initiative, which went out of its way to assure the magistracy of its support. However, in July 2006 a three-department initiative involving the then Constitutional Affairs Department, the Home Office and the Attorney General announced a new initiative: *Criminal Justice: simple, speedy, summary* or *CJSSS*.

- *Simple* – dealing with some specific cases transparently by way of warning, caution or some effective remedy to prevent re-offending without the court process;
- *Speedy* – those cases that need the court process will be dealt with fairly but as quickly as possible;
- *Summary* – a much more proportionate approach still involving due process – dealing with cases during the same week.

The intention was to improve the procedure within the lower courts so that those who pleaded guilty were dealt with as quickly as possible and those who elected to go for trial did not have to wait as long as previously for their hearing. The apparent success of *CJSSS* in four pilots led to its rollout to all magistrates' courts.

However, at the same time, the government was pursuing the increased use of non-court procedures for dealing with low-level criminal behaviour and disorder such as fixed penalty notices, penalty notices for disorder, and simple and conditional cautioning.

Fixed penalty notices

Similar to the already common road traffic fixed penalty notices, these generally deal with environmental offences such as litter, graffiti, fly posting and dog fouling. They can be issued to anyone over 10 years old by police, local authority officers and police community support officers.

Penalty notices for disorder

These procedures were introduced to address low-level anti-social behaviour, while also reducing police bureaucracy and paperwork. They can be issued to anyone over 16 years old. The Home Office suggests that such orders may be issued in relation to:

- intentionally harassing or scaring people;
- being drunk and disorderly in public;
- destroying or damaging property;
- petty shoplifting;
- selling alcohol to underage customers;
- selling alcohol to somebody who is obviously drunk;
- using fireworks after curfew.

Although not the same as criminal convictions, failure to pay the penalty may result in higher fines or imprisonment.

Simple cautions

These are used to deal quickly and simply with those who commit less serious crimes, without the need to take them through the court procedure. A caution is not a criminal conviction, but it will be recorded on the police database and may be used in court as evidence of bad character, or as part of an anti-social behaviour application (see above, 1.3.5). Cautions are issued where:

- there is evidence of criminal activity;
- the offender is 18 years of age or over (under the Crime and Disorder Act 1998 younger offenders are given 'reprimands' and 'final warnings' instead of simple cautions);
- the offender admits they committed the crime;
- the offender agrees to be given a caution; if they refuse they may be charged instead.

The use of cautions rather than court proceedings is at the discretion of senior police officers. However, the more serious crimes like robbery or assault must be referred to the Crown Prosecution Service.

Conditional cautions

These were introduced in the Criminal Justice Act 2003 and differ from simple cautions to the extent that the recipient must comply with certain conditions to receive the caution and to avoid prosecution for the offence allegedly committed.

The nature of the conditions that can be attached to a conditional caution must have one or more of the following objectives:

- rehabilitation – such conditions are aimed at helping to change the behaviour of the offender, in order to reduce the likelihood of their re-offending or help to reintegrate the offender into society. They may require attendance at drug or alcohol misuse programmes, or interventions tackling other addictions or personal problems, such as gambling or debt management courses;
- reparation – conditions that aim to repair, or compensate for, the damage done either directly or indirectly by the offender;
- retribution – conditional cautions can include punitive elements, which are designed to penalise the offender for their criminal activity. Such conditions, introduced in the Police and Justice Act 2006, may require the payment of a financial penalty, unpaid work for a period not exceeding 20 hours, or attendance at a specified place for a period not exceeding 20 hours.

The recipient of the caution must admit their guilt or they will be charged and face trial. As with the simple caution, a conditional caution is not a criminal conviction as such. However, it will be recorded on the police database and may be considered in court in the event of another offence. In addition the record will remain on the police database along with photographs, fingerprints and any other samples taken at the time. If the recipient breaches the condition, then they may be arrested and charged with the original offence.

It has been suggested that in the early enthusiasm for the *CJSSS* programme, the magistracy had not paid sufficient attention to the 'simple' aspect of *CJSSS* as set out above. However, it was not long until the magistrates and their association were complaining about the bypassing of the courts through the use of the non-court procedures.

The suspicion of the magistrates appears to be that the use of alternative mechanisms meant that incidents that should have been heard by them were being dealt with inappropriately and perhaps more leniently than they should have been in order to save police time and state money: it was estimated in October 2009 that only half the 1.4 million offenders dealt with by the justice system each year were actually prosecuted in the courts.

A report published in August 2008 by the Centre for Crime and Justice Studies at King's College London, entitled 'Summary Justice: fast – but fair?', written by Professor Rod Morgan, argued that the government policies aimed at diverting minor offences from court had actually resulted in an extensive widening of the criminal net, with individuals being brought within the ambit of the criminal justice system who would have previously been ignored or dealt with informally.

The report highlighted a rise in the numbers of convictions for violent offences, but much larger rises in the resort to cautions. Thus, convictions for serious indictable violent offences were 11 per cent higher in 2006 compared with 2001, but cautions increased by 92 per cent. The comparable figures for less serious indictable offences included a rise of 19 per cent for convictions but 195 per cent for cautions. Such findings would appear to suggest that cautions have been issued where previously no official sanction would have been applied. It also suggested that regional differences in the use of summary powers, and the fact that decision-making was made in private rather than in open court, resulted in an 'accountability deficit'.

In December 2011, the coalition Minister for Policing, Nick Herbert, addressed the National Council of the Magistrates' Association on the issue of summary justice in which he addressed some of their major concerns. He recognised the need to ask fundamental questions about the system of summary justice in order to reverse the proliferation of administrative disposals that had taken place over the previous few years. He also insisted that the magistracy should have an early role in overseeing how out-of-court sanctions are applied within their locality.

In January 2013, the then chairman of the Magistrates' Association wrote to the then Justice Secretary, Chris Grayling, calling for an inquiry into the police use of cautions, saying that the practice had 'got out of hand'. A subsequent review of simple cautions which were reported in November 2013 recommended that restrictions on their use be introduced and that a wider review of OOCDs be conducted. In response, in November 2014, the government published revised guidance on simple cautions and announced the introduction of a pilot scheme in three areas, to replace cautions with more stringent measures. It was revealed that in the 12 months to the end of March 2014, there had been 391,171 out-of-court disposals comprising 235,323 cautions, 77,933 cannabis warnings and 77,915 penalty notices for disorder.

Subsequently, in March 2015, the House of Commons Home Affairs select committee issued a report on use of out-of-court disposals and found that although the use of such measures had indeed declined from a high point in 2008, they were still being used inappropriately in up to 30 per cent of all cases. As the committee reported:

> Out-of-court disposals are not designed to deal with serious offences, nor with persistent offenders. It is alarming that they are used inappropriately in up to 30% of cases, although there might be certain circumstances where issuing an OOCD for a serious or repeat offence could be justified. One of the attractions of OOCDs is that they save the police time and administrative cost, allowing officers to spend more time on the front line, policing the community, but they must not be used by police merely as a time-saving tool when the circumstances of the offence suggest that prosecution is the right course of action. This is especially the case when there is a pattern of behaviour that needs to be addressed by the type of sentence that only a court can administer. The way in which OOCDs have originated, and how local police forces have used them, has created a postcode lottery. It is wrong that an offence committed in Cumbria should go to court, while the same offence, if it was committed in Gloucestershire, might be dealt with by a caution. The way in which OOCDs are recorded by the police does not help to instil public confidence in the system.

As the committee recognised, its conclusions were forestalled by provisions in the Criminal Justice and Courts Act 2015, s 17 of which placed restrictions on the circumstances in which cautions could be used. The restrictions are greater the more serious the offence. Thus:

- for indictable-only offences, a police officer will not be able to give a caution except in exceptional circumstances and with the consent of the Director of Public Prosecutions (DPP).
- for either-way offences, which have been specified in an order made by the Secretary of State, a police officer can only give a caution in exceptional circumstances but does not need the permission of the DPP.
- for repeat summary, or non-specified either-way offences, where a person has been convicted of, or cautioned for, a similar offence in the previous two years, a police officer may not give a caution except in exceptional circumstances.

Criminal Courts Charges

A more recent issue to cause perturbation among the magistracy was the compulsory requirement to charge people found guilty of criminal offences. By virtue of the Prosecution of Offences Act 1985 (Criminal Courts Charge) Regulations 2015, any person over the age of 18 who was convicted of a criminal offence was required to pay relevant court costs in addition to any other payments due such as fines or compensation orders.

The mandatory nature of the charge was objected to by a number of magistrates. While they are required to enquire into the means of the defendant before imposing compensation orders, there was no such discretionary element in relation to the court charges which had to be levied, irrespective of the defendant's wherewithal to pay the charge.

However, at the start of December 2015, the then Justice Minister Michael Gove announced that the criminal courts charge would no longer be imposed.

Magistrates and the public

In May 2012 the Magistrates' Association published the conclusions of what it described as 'a public engagement programme designed to gain an understanding of people's views on the future of summary justice and the role of magistrates'. The material gathered generated the following conclusions:

- Members of the public believe it is essential that those sitting in judgement on others should be people living or working in the communities they serve but, as judicial office-holders, should be totally independent, impartial, properly trained and competent.
- There is a lack of understanding about the extent of the role of the magistracy, although there does seem to be a belief that magistrates should be involved in all parts of the justice system including out-of-court disposals.

- The magistracy is not yet truly representative of the communities it serves especially in terms of class, age and diversity.

- For most people, and particularly victims, the processes of the justice system are still very difficult to comprehend and access.

- Punishment is expected to be part of a sentence but the priority for the public is for visible action such as community payback to stop re-offending and for magistrates to monitor and review sentences.

- The public wants to know more about the justice system from the practitioners themselves.

In the light of such conclusions, the association recognised the need to build the public's confidence in the magistracy and proposed that it should be the foundation of a community-focused justice system. However, in order to achieve such an objective, it also recognised and adopted the slogan that the magistracy must become more 'active, accessible and engaged' through strengthening and more clearly defining its roles and responsibilities.

CHAPTER SUMMARY: THE JUDICIARY

THE CONSTITUTIONAL ROLE OF THE JUDICIARY
Judges play a central role in the UK constitution. The doctrine of the separation of powers maintains that the judicial function be kept distinct from the legislative and executive functions of the state.

THE CONSTITUTIONAL ROLE OF THE LORD CHANCELLOR
The Lord Chancellor held an anomalous position in respect of the separation of powers within the UK constitution, in that they were at one and the same time: the most senior member of the judiciary and able to hear cases in the House of Lords as a court; a member of the legislature as Speaker of the House of Lords as a legislative assembly; and a member of the executive holding a position in the government. The Constitutional Reform Act 2005 dealt with the problem and subsequently the Lord Chancellor's Department has been replaced by a Ministry of Justice.

JUDICIAL OFFICES
The main judicial offices are the Lord Chancellor, the Lord Chief Justice, the Master of the Rolls, the President of the Family Division, the Vice Chancellor and the Senior Presiding Judge. Law Lords are referred to as Lords of Appeal in Ordinary. Court of Appeal judges are referred to as Lords Justices of Appeal.

APPOINTMENT OF THE JUDICIARY

The Constitutional Reform Act 2005 brought about a Judicial Appointment Commission, to replace the much-maligned previous system based on alleged secret soundings of the judiciary. However, the first appointments of the Commission have themselves been subjected to some criticisms for the conservative nature of the appointments made.

TRAINING OF THE JUDICIARY

Training of English judges is undertaken under the auspices of the Judicial College. Judges from the highest Law Lord to the lowest magistrate are subject to training. It is gratifying to note that anti-discriminatory training is a priority, although some have continued to express doubt about judicial attitudes in this regard. General training focuses on various aspects of discrimination, and special training was undertaken in relation to the Woolf reforms and the introduction of the Human Rights Act. This being said, it remains arguable that the training undergone by UK judges is not as rigorous as the training of judges on the Continent.

REMOVAL OF JUDGES

Senior judges hold office subject to good behaviour. They can be removed by an address by the two Houses of Parliament.

Judges below High Court status can be removed by the Lord Chancellor on grounds of misbehaviour or incapacity and they can remove magistrates without the need to show cause.

JUDICIAL IMMUNITY

To ensure judicial integrity, it is provided that judges cannot be sued for actions done or words said in the course of their judicial function.

This immunity extends to trial lawyers, witnesses and juries.

MAGISTRATES

Magistrates have powers in relation to both criminal and civil law.
District Judges (Magistrates' Courts) are professional and are legally qualified.
Lay magistrates are not paid and they are not legally qualified.
Magistrates are appointed by the Lord Chancellor.
Important issues relate to the representative nature of the magistracy.

THE CONSTITUTIONAL REFORM ACT

The essential features of the Act were designed to inspire transparency, openness and greater public confidence in Britain's constitution. Government ministers are now under a statutory duty to uphold the independence of the judiciary and are specifically barred from trying to influence judicial decisions through any special access to judges. The post of Lord Chancellor has been transformed with transfer of their judicial functions to the President of the Courts of England and Wales, the Lord Chief Justice. He will be responsible for the training, guidance and deployment of judges. He will also be responsible for representing the views of the judiciary of England and Wales to Parliament and ministers.

1. Selection and Appointment: Responding to criticism, the CLSA 1990 introduced major change to judicial appointment, opening up the judiciary to non-barristers, with senior judges appointed by the Crown on the advice of the Prime Minister, and High Court judges and below appointed on the advice of the Lord Chancellor. Transparency is encouraged, with vacancies for circuit judges and below being advertised. The CRA introduces a Judicial Appointments Commission who will report to the Lord Chancellor, who continues to make recommendations to the monarch

2. Training: Overseen and provided by the Judicial College Board, with emphasis on anti-discrimination training and application of the Human Rights Act. Still criticised for not being sufficiently rigorous in comparison to other European jurisdictions

4. Judicial Immunity: In order to ensure judicial integrity, judges cannot be sued for actions done or words said in the course of their judicial function

THE JUDICIARY

3. Retirement and Removal:
– Once appointed, it is unusual for a judge not to remain in post until retirement – which is normally 70
– Senior judges may only be removed (dismissed) by Parliament, while judges below High Court can be removed by the Lord Chancellor on grounds of misbehaviour or incapacity

5. Criticisms: Commonly criticised as being 'white, middle-class, middle-aged to elderly men', which it has been argued may lead to bias and lack of social awareness

FIGURE 12.3 *The Judiciary: an aide-mémoire.*

A new, independent Supreme Court, separate from the House of Lords, was established in 2009.

A new system of appointing judges, independent of the patronage of politicians, has been established. Appointments will be solely on the basis of merit and solely on the recommendation of the newly constituted Judicial Appointments Commission.

FOOD FOR THOUGHT

1   Much has been made of the creation of a new Supreme Court but the issue to consider is whether, as has been suggested, a first-class Appeal Court has been replaced by a second-class Supreme Court. In particular, what distinguishes the UK Supreme Court from, for example, the Supreme Court of the United States?

2   Consider whether judicial training should be for a profession in its own right, rather than as an adjunct to another profession, such as the Bar.

3   In the context of the magistrates' courts, consider whether there is a place for non-legally qualified judges and whether the age of most magistrates leads to particular problems.

4   Following the English riots of summer 2011, there was some accusation of heavy-handed sentencing policy in the magistrates' courts. This raises questions as to whether magistrates' current sentencing powers should be raised from six to 12 months. Consider the pros and cons of any such change.

FURTHER READING

Bell, J and Engle, G (Sir), *Cross on Statutory Interpretation*, 1995, London: Butterworths

Bennion, F, *Statutory Interpretation*, 1992, London: Butterworths

Bindman, G, 'Lessons of Pinochet' (1999) 149 NLJ 1050

Bindman, G, 'Lessons of history' (2009) 159 NLJ 1110

Blom-Cooper, L, 'Age of judicial responsibility' [2009] PL 429

Cox, N, 'The future of magistracy' (2010) CLJ Weekly, Sept 18

Denning (Lord), *Due Process of Law*, 1980, London: Butterworths

Denning (Lord), *The Discipline of Law*, 1979, London: Butterworths

Dowell, K, 'Neuberger gains political clout after attacking Supreme Court' (2009) 23(35) Lawyer 48

Hunter, R, McGlynn, C and Rackley, E, *Feminist Judgments: From Theory to Practice*, 2010, Oxford: Hart Publishing

Parker, C, 'Judicial decision making' (1999) 149 NLJ 1142

Pearl, D, 'Judging success' (2009) Counsel 13

Pickles, J, *Straight from the Bench*, 1987, London: Hodder and Stoughton

Rackley, E, *Women, Judging and the Judiciary: From Difference to Diversity*, 2014, London: Routledge

Reid (Lord), 'The judge as law maker' (1972) 12 JSPTL 22

Stevens, R, *English Judges: Their Role in the Changing Constitution*, 2005, Oxford: Hart

Weinreb, L, *Legal Reason: The Use of Analogy in Legal Argument*, 2004, Cambridge: CUP

USEFUL WEBSITES

http://webarchive.nationalarchives.gov.uk/+/www.dca.gov.uk/judges/diversity.htm
An archived webpage on information regarding the Lord Chancellor's commitment to ensuring 'a judiciary of the highest calibre, with candidates drawn from the widest possible range of available talent'.

www.judiciary.gov.uk
The official website for the Judiciary of England and Wales.

www.justice.gov.uk
Justice Ministry website.

www.supremecourt.uk
Official website of the Supreme Court.

www.gov.uk/government/uploads/system/uploads/attachment_data/file/217354/judicial-diversity-report-2010.pdf
Improving Judicial Diversity: Progress towards delivery of the 'Report of the Advisory Panel on Judicial Diversity 2010', May 2011.

COMPANION WEBSITE

Now visit the companion website to:

- test your understanding of the key terms using our Flashcard Glossary;
- revise and consolidate your knowledge of 'The judiciary' using our multiple choice question testbank;
- view all of the links to the Useful Websites above.

www.routledge.com/cw/slapper

13.1 INTRODUCTION

13.2 LAW AND LOGIC

ensure the best possible result, even if this means ignoring previously established legal rules.

At other times, however, the courts have appeared to base and justify their decisions on the working out of deterministic formal rules of law, categorised in such phrases as 'The Law is the Law' and 'The Law must run its course'. The suggestion behind such expressions of the *Declaratory Theory of Law* is that the judge is no more than the voice of an autonomous legal system that they, through their legal training, is able to gain access to but is in no way able to influence. If, as the declaratory theory of law maintains, judges do no more than give expression to already existing legal principles and rules, then the particular views, opinions or prejudices of the judiciary are of absolutely no consequence. If such a representation were accurate, then the logical conclusion would be that judges could be replaced by a computerised *expert system*, which could be programmed to make decisions on the basis of a strict application of general rules. It is doubtful, however, if anyone would actually accept such a suggestion. It cannot be denied that the bulk of cases are decided on the simple application of the legal rules to the particular facts of the case with little or no consideration of the legal principles. In other cases, however, the straightforward and automatic application of a legal rule might lead to the possibility of injustice.

Hard cases are decided on the basis of judicial reaction to the immediate facts of the case. Such a situation, however, is clearly antithetical to the declaratory theory of law.

These *hard cases* demand a consideration of the legal principles involved in order to achieve a just result. They may therefore be decided other than on the strict application of the law as it had been previously expressed. It should be pointed out that such cases are usually the province of the higher courts and of particularly active judges within those courts. The old maxim/cliché that ' *hard cases make bad law*' should also be borne in mind. (The career of Lord Denning might be cited as an example of this procedure and its shortcomings. Reference should be made to material covered previously in Chapters 3 and 4 of this book for a more detailed consideration of the problems inherent in judicial law-making and reform.)

13.3   REASONING IN GENERAL

In order to assess this apparent tension, if not divergence, of approach to the question whether legal reasoning is logical or not, it is necessary first of all to engage, at least minimally, in a consideration of what is to be understood by reasoning generally and logical reasoning in particular.

13.3.1   DEDUCTIVE REASONING

As regards reasoning in general, there is a division between deductive and inductive reasoning. *Deductive reasoning* may be categorised as reasoning from the whole to the part; from the general to the particular. Deductive reasoning finds its simplest and yet most powerful expression in the Aristotelian syllogism. The syllogism takes the following form:

> Major premise: A = B; for example, all men are mortal.
> Minor premise: B = C; for example, Socrates is a man.
> Conclusion: therefore A = C; that is, Socrates is mortal.

The power of the syllogism lies in its certainty. If the premises are true, then the conclusion cannot be false. The reason for this is that the conclusion is actually contained in the premises and amounts to no more than a restatement of those premises.

With regard to syllogisms, however, it is important to distinguish between *validity* of form and *truth* of content. It is quite possible for a syllogism to be logically valid but false. An example of this would be:

> Major premise: A = B; for example, all men are pigs.
> Minor premise: B = C; for example, Socrates is a man.
> Conclusion: therefore A = C; that is, Socrates is a pig.

The logical form of this argument, as represented in alphabetical terms, is valid, but the conclusion is not true. The reason for this is obviously that the major premise is false: the statement that all men are pigs is simply not true.

It is also possible for a syllogism to be both true and valid yet still be based on a false premise. An example of this would be:

> Major premise: A = B; for example, all men are Greek.
> Minor premise: B = C; for example, Socrates is a man.
> Conclusion: therefore A = C; that is, Socrates is Greek.

Once again, the logical form expressed in alphabetical terms is valid, and once again the major premise is false. On this occasion, however, the conclusion is true.

To reiterate the essential point, all that the syllogistic form of reasoning maintains is that *if the premises are true then the conclusion cannot be false* ; in itself, it states nothing as to the truth of those premises or the truth of the conclusion derived from them. As will be considered below, much legal argument is about the truth of particular premises rather than the validity of the logical form being operated.

Deductive reasoning can take another form as follows:

> If X then Y: If it rains, you will get wet.
> X: It is raining.
> Therefore, Y: You will get wet.

Again, the conclusion is contained in the premises, but equally again, if the premises are false, the conclusion may also be false.

The second classic form of reasoning, *inductive reasoning*, may be described as arguing from the part to the whole; from the particular to the general. Inductive reasoning differs from deductive reasoning in two major respects:

1   It reaches a conclusion that is *not* simply a restatement of what is already contained in the basic premises.

2   It is *less certain* in its conclusions than deductive logic.

An example of this type of reasoning would be:

> The sun has always risen in the east.
> Therefore, the sun will rise in the east tomorrow.

If the premise is true, then the conclusion is probably true, but not 100 per cent necessarily so because the conclusion is not contained in the premise, but is a projection from it. On the basis of past experience, we can reasonably expect the sun to rise in the east tomorrow, but there is the possibility, no matter how remote it might be, that something might happen to the sun, or indeed the earth, to prevent its appearance tomorrow. The point is that we cannot predict with 100 per cent accuracy what will happen in the future just because it happened in the past. Because the inductive argument goes beyond the content of its premises, it provides the power to predict events, but it gives predictive power at the expense of certainty in its conclusion.

An alternative example of this type of inductive reasoning would be:

> John is lying dead with a bullet in his head.
> Jane is standing over him with a smoking gun in her hand.
> Therefore, it can be concluded that Jane shot John.

Now, the conclusion may be reasonable under the circumstances, but there are other possible explanations for the scene. Jane may have simply picked up the gun after someone else had shot John. We cannot actually tell who killed John, but we may reasonably suspect Jane of the crime and she would be the first person to be questioned to confirm either her guilt or innocence. The investigation of this event would use a form of reasoning equivalent to scientific reasoning. From available data, a hypothesis would be formed; in this case, that Jane killed John. Investigations would then be undertaken to test the validity of the hypothesis. Depending on the outcome of the investigation, the original hypothesis would be either accepted, rejected or refined.

A third type of reasoning is *reasoning by example or analogy*. If deductive reasoning involves reasoning from the whole to the part, and inductive reasoning involves reasoning from the part to the whole, then reasoning by analogy involves reasoning from part to part.

An example of this type of reasoning would be:

Wood floats on water.

Plastic is like wood.

Therefore, plastic floats on water.

Or similarly:

Wood floats on water.

Stone is like wood.

Therefore, stone floats on water.

It can be seen that the truth of the conclusion depends completely on the accuracy of the analogy. The connection between the two objects that are being compared depends on weighing up and assessing their similarities and their differences. Only some characteristics are similar, and the question is whether those are more important than the differences between the two objects. If the analogy is valid, then the conclusion may very well be equally valid, although not necessarily correct, but, if it is not valid, then the conclusion will certainly be wrong, as the above examples demonstrate.

13.4 JUDICIAL REASONING

It is now appropriate to determine whether, or to what extent, judges use logical reasoning in reaching their decisions in particular cases and to determine which forms, if any, they make use of.

13.4.1 THE SYLLOGISM IN LAW

Some statutory provisions and also some common law rules can be expressed in the form of a syllogism. For example, the offence of theft may be reduced into such a formulation:

If A dishonestly appropriates B's property with the intention of permanently depriving B of it, then A is guilty of theft.

A has done this.

Therefore, A is guilty of theft.

This, however, represents an oversimplification of the structure of statute but, more importantly, the effect of concentrating on the logical form of the offence tends to marginalise the key issues in relation to its actual application. As has been stated previously, the great majority of cases are decided on the *truth* of the premises rather than the formal *validity* of the argument used. In other words, argument will concentrate primarily on whether A actually did the act or not and, second, on whether A appropriated the property either 'dishonestly' or 'with the intention of permanently depriving' B of it. Those are questions of fact, not logic.

13.4.2 THE LOGICAL FORM OF PRECEDENT

The operation of the rules of precedent appears, at first sight, to involve a similar operation of deductive logic to that applied in statute law: the judge merely applies the legal principle established in the precedent to the facts in hand to determine the outcome of the case. Thus:

> Precedent: in case X involving particular circumstances, legal principle Y was applied leading to conclusion Z.
>
> *Instant case:* in case W, similar circumstances to those in X have occurred.
>
> Therefore: principle Y must be applied to reach a conclusion similar to Z.

A closer consideration of the actual procedure involved in precedent, however, will reveal that it is not totally accurate to categorise precedent as a form of deductive reasoning.

In looking for a precedent on which to base a decision, judges are faced with a large number of cases from which to select. It is extremely unlikely that judges will find an authority that corresponds precisely to the facts of the case before them. What they have to do is to find an analogous case and use its reasoning to decide the case before them. This use of analogy to decide cases is prone to the same shortcomings as were revealed in the previous consideration of reasoning from analogy in general. The major difficulty is the need to ensure the validity of the analogy made, if the conclusion drawn is to be valid. There is, no doubt, considerable merit in the wish for similar cases to be treated similarly, but given the lack of precision that is inherent in the process of reasoning by analogy, it is not altogether certain that such a wish will be met.

A further reason why the operation of precedent cannot simply be considered as an example of deductive reasoning relates to the process through which the precedent is actually determined once an analogous case has been selected. The binding element in any precedent is the *ratio decidendi* of the decision. In delivering his decision, the judge does not separate the *ratio* of the case from other *obiter* comments. As has been considered previously, the *ratio* is a legal abstraction from the concrete facts of the case in which it appears, and in practice, it is for judges in subsequent cases to determine the *ratio* of any authority. The determination of the *ratio* and thus the precedent in a previous case may be seen as a process of *inductive reasoning*, in that the judge in the present case derives the *general* principle of the *ratio* from the *particular* facts of the previous case. This move from the particular to the general is by its nature inductive. The point to be remembered here is that, as was considered in relation to reasoning in general, the use of inductive reasoning cannot claim the certainty inherent in the use of deductive reasoning. The introduction of this increased element of uncertainty is inescapable and unconscious, but it is also appropriate to note that the determination of precedent by later courts gives the later judges scope to *consciously* manipulate precedents. This is achieved by the later judges formulating the *ratio* of a previous case in the light of their opinion as to what it *should* have been, rather than what it might actually have been. In other words, they have the scope to substitute their version of the *ratio*, even if it contradicts what the original judge thought the *ratio* was.

Thus, the apparent deductive certainty of the use of precedent is revealed to be based on the much less certain use of inductive reasoning and reasoning by analogy, with even the possibility of personal views of the judges playing some part in deciding cases. This latter factor introduces the possibility that judges do not in fact use any form of logical reasoning to decide their cases, but simply deliver decisions on the basis of an intuitive response to the facts of the case and the situation of the parties involved. The suggestion has been made that judges decide the outcome of the case first of all and only then seek some *post hoc* legal justification for their decision; and given the huge number of precedents from which they are able to choose, they have no great difficulty in finding such support as they require. The process of logical reasoning can be compared to the links in a chain, one following the other, but a more fitting metaphor for judicial reasoning would be to compare it with the legs of a chair: forced into place to support the weight of a conclusion reached *a priori*. Some critics have even gone so far as to deny the existence of legal reasoning altogether as a method of determining decisions, and have suggested that references to such are no more than a means of justifying the social and political decisions that judges are called upon to make.

In conclusion, however, it is not suggested that legal reasoning does not employ the use of logic, but neither can it be asserted that it is only a matter of logic. Perhaps the only conclusion that can be reached is that legal reasoning as exercised by the judiciary is an amalgam; part deductive, part inductive, part reasoning by analogy, with an added mixture of personal intuition, not to say personal prejudice.

13.4.3   LEGAL REASONING AND RHETORIC

Following on from the previous questioning of the logical nature of legal reasoning, it might be valuable to consider further the claim that legal decisions are not the outcome of a process of logical reasoning, but are in fact the products of a completely different form of communication. According to Peter Goodrich (*Reading the Law* (1986) at 171):

> the legal art is an art of interpretation; it is concerned not with a necessary or scientific logic, but with probable arguments, with evaluative reasoning and not with absolute certainty. Rhetoric is the discipline which most explicitly studies the techniques relevant to presenting and evaluating, affirming or refuting, such probable arguments . . . rhetoric, here, is defined as the reading of legal texts as acts of communication, as discourse designed to influence, to persuade and to induce action.

Goodrich analysed the use of rhetoric in law, from ancient Greece until the present time, in Chapter 6 of his book. In so doing, he revealed the specific rhetorical devices that judges bring to bear in their decisions in order to persuade their audience as to the objective validity of their decisions.

The question, however, is as to who constitutes the audience that the judiciary addresses. In the case of summings-up to juries, the answer is obvious, but there is still an audience being addressed when the judge delivers a judgment in any case. That audience, it is suggested, is the community at large, but with the community not as an active participant in the legal process, but as a passive body that merely has to be persuaded of the inherent and unquestionable validity of the judge's decision in any particular case.

As Goodrich points out (1986 at 188):

> The language of the legal decision strives for the appearance of objectivity and the exclusion of dialogue in favour of monologue. Its principal aim and function is that of achieving an image of incontestable authority and of correct legal meanings. Such a task is, essentially, a rhetorical one: the monologue is the language-usage of authority, it precludes dialogue or any questioning of the meanings given, and it closes legal discourse by privileging the voice of the judicial author as the supreme arbiter of meanings.

Rather than being presented as a particular individual's opinion, the legal text is typically expressed as in the language of objectivity. The use of such terms as 'thus', 'because', 'for the reason that' or 'in spite of' indicates the voice of necessity, not of choice. When this is combined with the use of terms such as 'therefore' or 'consequently', the outcome is to re-inforce the impression that the judge is merely engaged in a working out and presentation of the formal operation of the objective system that is law. In this fashion, the language of apparently objective, and logically determined, legal categories is revealed to be a mere rhetorical device marshalled by judges to provide their particular decisions with the justification of pseudo-objectivity. This process is complemented by the use of axioms, unquestioned and apparently unquestionable self-evident truths, to which the judiciary frequently have recourse in order to validate, without justifying, their own assumptions and presumptions. One should be on one's guard when one reads judges referring to principles that are 'so fundamental that they need not be debated', or where conclusions follow 'as a matter of course' on the basis of 'well-settled principle'. The question is whether such claims merely appeal to uncorroborated precedents and unsubstantiated prejudices.

One further aspect of the rhetorical nature of the judicial presentation directly relates to the inherently political nature of judicial decision-making. It is almost a commonplace in the most politically sensitive cases that the judges involved will ritually intone the mantra to the effect that 'it is fortunate that the court does not have to consider the political aspects of this case . . .', before going on to make what cannot but be a political decision. On the contrary, as this book maintains, all judicial decisions are political in that they reflect a disposition as to where power should be located in any particular situation.

Judgments, and judicial presentations to juries, therefore are not merely statements of law; they are equally, if not more fundamentally, exercises in rhetoric. To read a judgment in this way is to see it in a new revelatory light that shows the justificatory, if not manipulative, use of language and linguistic devices that are an essential element of the judgment. It has to be pointed out, however, that the nature and use of rhetoric has changed over time. The difference between the operation of rhetoric in the ancient world and its use by the judiciary today is that, whereas in the ancient world it was used as a means of *persuading* an audience to reach a particular decision, its contemporary role is that of justifying the decision that the judge has taken. The judge speaks; the audience listens and is persuaded: the role of the audience as a participant has been removed and it now merely exists as the passive receiver of the court's decision.

In *R (Smeaton) v Secretary of State for Health* ([2002] EWHC 610, paras 46 and 47), which considered the legality of the morning-after contraceptive pill, Munby J stated:

> I have said that this case raises moral and ethical questions of great importance. It would be idle to suggest otherwise. For those who view such matters in religious terms it raises religious and theological questions of great and, to some, transcending importance. But I must emphasise that, so far as the court is concerned, this case has nothing to do with either morality or religious belief. The issue which I have to decide is not whether the sale and use of the morning-after pill is morally or religiously right or wrong, nor whether it is socially desirable or undesirable. *What I have to determine is whether it may constitute an offence under the 1861 Act.*
>
> Cases such as this, and others in the field of medicine (one thinks of cases such as *Airedale NHS Trust v Bland* [1993] AC 789 and *Re A (Conjoined Twins: Medical Treatment)* [2001] Fam 147), raise moral, religious and ethical issues on which, as Lord Browne-Wilkinson pointed out in *Bland* at pp 879E, 880A, 'society is not all of one mind' and on which indeed 'society as a whole is substantially divided'. Our society, including the most thoughtful and concerned sections of our society, are deeply troubled by, and indeed deeply divided over, such issues. These are topics on which men and women of different faiths, or indeed of no faith at all, may and do hold, passionately and with the utmost sincerity, starkly differing views. *All of those views are entitled to the greatest respect but it is not for a judge to choose between them. The days are past when the business of the judges was the enforcement of morals or religious belief* (emphases added).

With the greatest of respect to Munby J, what he seeks to avoid is exactly what he is forced to do in making his 'legal' decision.

It is worth noting that in the most overtly political case to be heard in recent times, *Miller v Secretary of State for Exiting the European Union*, the judgment of the High Court felt it necessary to make the following statement at the outset:

> It is agreed on all sides that this is a justiciable question which it is for the courts to decide. *It deserves emphasis at the outset that the court in these proceedings is only dealing with a pure question of law.* Nothing we say has any bearing on the question of the merits or demerits of a withdrawal by the United Kingdom from the European Union; nor does it have any bearing on government policy, because government policy is not law (emphasis added). The Supreme Court subsequently emphasised the 'non- political' nature of its later decision.

13.5 JUDICIAL REVIEW

The effect of the Human Rights Act 1998 (HRA) on the interface between the judiciary and the executive has been considered previously at 2.5, but that Act merely heightened the potential for conflict in a relationship that was already subject to some tension as a consequence of the operation of judicial review. If the interface between judiciary and executive tends now to be most sharply defined in human rights actions, the previous and continued role of judicial review in that relationship should not be underestimated.

The growth in applications for judicial review prior to the HRA was truly startling, as individuals and the judiciary recognised its potential utility as a means of challenging administrative decisions. The records show that in 1980 there were only 525 applications for judicial review; in 1996, 4,586; in 1997, 4,636 such applications; and by 1998, applications had passed the 5,000 mark and were continuing to rise. Analysis of the statistics from 2004 to 2011 may be found on two websites: www.theguardian.com/news/datablog/2012/nov/19/judicial-review-statistics and http://fullfact.org/factchecks/judicial_reviews-28613.

As the analysis shows, the real push in the rise of judicial review cases is in the field of immigration and asylum: for example, in 2013, of the 15,000 applications for judicial review, 13,000 related to immigration and asylum matters. The year 2014, however, saw only 4,062 claims, reflecting the transfer of immigration cases to the Upper Tribunal for Immigration and Asylum Chamber in November 2013.

Thus at the outset, it should be noted that although this section focuses on those instances where the judiciary have decided against the exercise of executive power in a particular way, it has to be emphasised that the vast majority of judicial review cases are decided in favour of the executive. This may be significant when the views of Professor Griffith are examined at 13.7.1 below.

The remedies open to anyone challenging the decisions or actions of administrative institutions or public authorities can be divided into *private* or *public* law remedies.

There are three private law remedies:

Declaration

This is a definitive statement, by the High Court or County Court, of what the law is in a particular area. The procedure may be used by an individual or body to clarify a particularly contentious situation. It is a common remedy in private law, but it also has an important part to play in regard to individuals' relations with administrative institutions. This can be seen, for example, in *Congreve v Home Office* (1976), where the Court of Appeal stated that it would be unlawful for the Home Office to revoke annual television licences after only eight months because they had been bought in anticipation of an announced price rise but before the expiry of existing licences.

Declarations, however, cannot be enforced either directly or indirectly through the contempt of court procedure. Public authorities are, as a matter of course, expected to abide by them.

Injunctions

Usually, an injunction seeks to restrain a person from breaking the law; alternatively, however, a mandatory injunction may instruct someone to undo what they have previously done, or alternatively to stop doing what they are doing. Both types of injunction may be sought against a public authority. See *Attorney General v Fulham Corp* (1921), in which a local authority was ordered to stop running a laundry service where it only had the power to establish laundries for people to wash their own clothes.

Damages

Damages cannot be awarded on their own in relation to administrative misconduct, but may be claimed in addition where one of the other remedies considered above is sought, as, for example, in *Cooper v Wandsworth Board of Works* (1863). In this case, a builder had put up a building without informing the Board of Works as he was required to do. When the Board demolished the building, he nonetheless recovered damages against them on the basis that the Board had exceeded its powers by not allowing him to defend or explain his actions.

In order to seek one of these private law remedies, an individual merely had to issue a writ against a public authority in their own name. They did not require the approval of the court.

13.5.2   THE PREROGATIVE ORDERS

The prerogative orders are so called because they were originally the means whereby sovereigns controlled the operation of their officials. As a consequence, the prerogative orders cannot be used against the Crown, but they can be used against individual ministers of state and, since *R v Secretary of State for the Home Department ex p Fire Brigades Union* (1995), considered at 13.6.1 below, it is clear that ministers cannot avoid judicial review by hiding behind the cloak of prerogative powers. The prerogative orders are as follows.

A *quashing order*, formerly known as *certiorari*, is the mechanism by means of which decisions of inferior courts, tribunals and other authoritative bodies are brought before the High Court to have their validity examined. Where any such decision is found to be invalid, it may be set aside. An example of this can be seen in *Ridge v Baldwin* (1964). Here, the plaintiff had been dismissed from his position as Chief Constable without having had the opportunity to present any case for his defence. The House of Lords held that the committee that had taken the decision had acted in breach of the requirements of natural justice and granted a declaration that his dismissal was null and void.

A *prohibiting order*, formerly known as *prohibition*, is similar to *certiorari* in that it relates to invalid acts of public authorities, but it is different to the extent that it is pre-emptive and prescriptive in regard to any such activity and operates to prevent the authority from taking invalid decisions in the first place. An example of the use of the order arose in *R v Telford Justices ex p Badhan* (1991). In this case, an order was issued to stop committal proceedings in relation to an alleged rape that had not been reported until some 14 years after the alleged incident. The delay meant that the defendant would have been unable to prepare a proper defence against the charge.

A *mandatory order*, formerly known as *mandamus*, may be seen as the obverse of a prohibiting order, in that it is an order issued by the High Court instructing an inferior court or some other public authority to carry out a duty laid on them. Such an order is frequently issued in conjunction with an order of *certiorari*, to the effect that a public body is held to be using its powers improperly and is instructed to use them in a proper fashion. In *R v Poplar BC (Nos 1 and 2)* (1922), the court ordered the borough council to pay over money due to the county council and to levy a rate to raise the money if necessary. Failure to comply with the order led to the imprisonment of some of the borough councillors.

In *O'Reilly v Mackman* (1982), however, the House of Lords decided that issues relating to *public* rights could *only* be enforced by means of the judicial review procedure, and that it would be an abuse of process for an applicant to seek a declaration by writ in relation to an alleged breach of a public duty or responsibility by a public authority. In deciding the case in this way, the House of Lords did much to demarcate and emphasise the role of judicial review as the method of challenging public authorities in their performance of their powers and duties in public law.

13.5.3   GROUNDS FOR APPLICATION FOR JUDICIAL REVIEW

Judicial review allows people with a sufficient interest in a decision or action by a public body to ask a judge to review the lawfulness of:

(a)   an enactment; or

(b)   a decision, action or failure to act in relation to the exercise of a public function.

However, it is not an appeal on the merits of a decision. The grounds of application can be considered under two heads: *procedural ultra vires* and *substantive ultra vires*.

Procedural ultra vires, as its name suggests, relates to the failure of a person or body, provided with specific authority, to follow the procedure established for using that power. It also covers instances where a body exercising a judicial function fails to follow the requirements of natural justice by acting as prosecutor and judge in the same case or not permitting the accused person to make representations to the panel deciding the case.

Substantive ultra vires occurs where someone does something that is not actually authorised by the enabling legislation. In *Associated Provincial Picture House v Wednesbury Corp* (1947), Lord Greene MR established the possibility of challenging discretionary decisions on the basis of unreasonableness.

Lord Greene's approach was endorsed and refined by Lord Diplock in *Council of Civil Service Unions v Minister for the Civil Service* (1984), in which he set out the three recognised grounds for judicial review, namely:

- illegality;
- irrationality;
- procedural impropriety.

Lord Diplock, however, introduced the possibility of a much more wide-ranging reason for challenging administrative decisions: namely, the doctrine of *proportionality*. Behind this doctrine is the requirement that there should be a reasonable relation between a decision and its objectives. It requires the achievement of particular ends by means that are not more oppressive than they need be to attain those ends. The potentially innovative aspect of this doctrine is the extent to which it looks to the substance of the decisions rather than simply focusing on the way in which they are reached.

Lord Diplock's listing of proportionality within the grounds for judicial review was controversial, if not at the very least arguably mistaken. Proportionality, however, is a key principle within the jurisdiction of the ECtHR, and is used frequently to assess the validity of state action which interferes with individual rights protected under the Convention. Consequently, as the HRA has incorporated the European Convention into UK law, proportionality will be a part of UK jurisprudence and legal practice, at least in cases that fall within the scope of the HRA. Although HRA cases and judicial review are different and distinct procedures, nonetheless, it is surely a mere matter of time before the doctrine of proportionality is applied by the judges in judicial review cases unrelated to the Convention.

Indeed, such an approach was supported by Lord Slynn in *R v Secretary of State for the Environment, Transport and the Regions ex p Holding and Barnes* (2001), in which he stated ([2001] 2 All ER 929 at 975):

The European Court of Justice does of course apply the principle of proportionality when examining such acts and national judges must apply the same principle when dealing with Community law issues. There is a difference between that principle and the approach of the English courts in *Associated Provincial Picture Houses Ltd v Wednesbury Corporation* [1948] 1 KB 223. But the difference in practice is not as great as is sometimes supposed. The cautious approach of the European Court of Justice in applying the principle is shown *inter alia* by the margin of appreciation it accords to the institutions of the Community in making economic assessments. I consider that even without reference to the Human Rights Act the time has come to recognise that this principle is part of English administrative law, not only when judges are dealing with Community Acts but also when they are dealing with Acts subject to domestic law. Trying to keep the *Wednesbury* principle and proportionality in separate compartments seems to me to be unnecessary and confusing.

However, as Lord Reed pointed out in the Supreme Court case *R (on the application of Lumsdon) v Legal Services Board* [2015] UKSC 41, 'Although there is some common ground, the principle of proportionality in EU law is neither expressed nor applied in the same way as the principle of proportionality under the European Convention on Human Rights.'

In *Frank Cowl v Plymouth City Council* (2001), the Court of Appeal held that judicial review was not necessarily the proper action in the face of alternatives. The claimant had sought to use judicial review as a means of challenging the council's decision to close a residential care home for the elderly, even though the council had said it was willing to consider his situation as part of a statutory complaints procedure. According to Lord Woolf:

> The courts should not permit, except for good reason, proceedings for judicial review to proceed if a significant part of the issues between the parties could be resolved outside the litigation process. The disadvantages of doing so are limited. If subsequently it becomes apparent that there is a legal issue to be resolved, that can thereafter be examined by the courts which may be considerably assisted by the findings made by the complaints panel . . . This case will have served some purpose if it makes it clear that the lawyers acting on both sides of a dispute of this sort are under a heavy obligation to resort to litigation only if it is really unavoidable. If they cannot resolve the whole of the dispute by the use of the complaints procedure they should resolve the dispute so far as is practicable without involving litigation.

13.5.4   THE EXCLUSION OF JUDICIAL REVIEW

As will be considered in Chapter 15, one of the reasons for the setting up of extensive systems of administrative tribunals was precisely the wish to curb the power of the judges.

It was felt that judges, and indeed the common law itself, tended to be more supportive of *individual* rights and freedoms as opposed to *collective* notions of welfare pursued by post-war governments, and that they would not administer such policies sympathetically. The judges, however, asserted their ultimate control over such tribunals generally through the use of judicial review. There have been various attempts by parliamentary drafters to exclude the judiciary from certain areas by wording provisions in such a way as to deny the possibility of judicial review. These attempts, however, have mainly proved to be in vain and have been rendered ineffective by the refusal of the courts to recognise their declared effect. Examples are:

'Finality' or 'ouster' clauses

There is a variety of possible wordings for these clauses. For example, the legislation might provide that 'the minister's [or the tribunal's] decision shall be final', or alternatively it might attempt to emphasise the point by stating that the decision in question 'shall be final and conclusive', or it might even provide that 'it shall be final, conclusive and shall not be questioned in any legal proceedings whatsoever'. Unfortunately for the drafter of the legislation and the minister or tribunal in question, all three formulations are equally likely to be ineffective. The courts have tended to interpret such phrases in a narrow way, so as to recognise the exclusion of an appeal procedure but to introduce the possibility of judicial review, as distinct from appeal. The classic case on this point is *R v Medical Appeal Tribunal ex p Gilmore* (1957), in which Lord Denning stated that 'The word "final" . . . does not mean without recourse to *certiorari.*' This, however, raised the point of provisions which expressly sought to exclude *certiorari*.

In *South East Asia Fire Bricks Sdn Bhd v Non-Metallic Mineral Products Manufacturing Employees Union* (1980), the Privy Council decided that a Malaysian statute was sufficiently detailed in its wording to effectively exclude *certiorari for an error of law on the face of the record*. The Privy Council pointed out, however, that the exclusion could not be effective to prevent judicial review where the institution in question had acted *ultra vires* or in breach of natural justice.

The fury of the judiciary against the government's statutory proposals found its fullest expression in respect of the Asylum and Immigration (Treatment of Claimants etc) Bill. The Bill, which was designed to speed up asylum and immigration procedures by curtailing the appeal structure, introduced the most wide-ranging of ouster clauses to the effect that no court shall have any supervisory or other jurisdiction in relation to the Asylum and Immigration Tribunal. In particular, the original cl 11 of the Bill stated that the courts could not question the decisions of the tribunal even in the event of:

- lack of jurisdiction;
- irregularity;
- error of law;
- breach of natural justice; or
- any other matter.

As was stated at the time, such a proposal was the 'mother and father' of all ouster clauses. The judiciary were extremely vocal in their opposition to cl 11, which they saw, and publicly represented, as an attack on the rule of law in its refusal to allow access to the ordinary courts. When it became apparent that the Bill was not going to pass through the House of Lords, the government withdrew the original clause and the subsequent Asylum and Immigration (Treatment of Claimants etc) Act 2004 allowed appeals on a point of law.

Partial exclusion clauses

Where legislation has provided for a limited time period within which parties have to apply for judicial review, then applications outside of the period will not be successful. In *Smith v East Elloe Rural DC* (1956), the House of Lords, although only by a three-to-two majority, recognised the effectiveness of a six-week limitation clause in the Acquisition of Land (Authorisation Procedure) Act 1946. Although that case was subject to criticism in *Anisminic Ltd v Foreign Compensation Commission* (1969), it was explained and followed in *R v Secretary of State for the Environment ex p Ostler* (1976).

In response to the Franks Committee's recommendation that judicial review should not be subject to exclusion, s 14(1) of the Tribunals and Inquiries Act 1971 was enacted to that end. Unfortunately, it applies only to pre-1958 legislation.

The Criminal Justice & Courts Act 2015 and judicial review

In November 2012 the Prime Minister, David Cameron, announced that his government intended to 'get a grip' on people forcing unnecessary delays to government policy by 'cracking down' on the 'massive growth industry' of judicial review.

Following a consultation exercise in 2013, the Justice Ministry announced proposals to reduce the number of judicial review cases, including the following:

- reducing the time limits for bringing a judicial review relating to planning issues from the previous three months to six weeks;

- removing the right to an oral hearing where a judge refuses permission where there has been a prior judicial process, or where the claim was judged to be totally without merit. Consequently any right to appeal to the Court of Appeal would be on the papers;

- the introduction of a new fee for an oral renewal so that fees charged in Judicial Review proceedings better reflected the costs of providing the service. These were increased in line with all court fees under *The Civil Proceedings Fees (Amendment) Order 2014*;

- providing that immigration and asylum judicial review hearings be transferred to the specialist Upper Tier Tribunal rather than the High Court which had previously heard them.

In September 2013 the government's widely imputed antagonism towards judicial review was further evidenced when the Ministry of Justice issued a consultation document entitled *Judicial Review: Proposals For Further Reform*. The consultation exercise sought views on proposals in the following areas:

- a number of measures to rebalance the system of financial incentives so that those involved have a proportionate interest in the costs of the case, including amending payment of legal aid in judicial review cases (subsequently enacted in Part 4 of the Criminal Justice and Courts Act (CJ&CA) 2015 below).

- how the courts deal with minor procedural defects that would have made no difference to the final decision. (By virtue of s 84 of the CJ&CA 2015, where the court is of the view that it is 'highly likely' that the result would remain the same, irrespective of the error alleged, it is obliged to refuse the action for judicial review.)

- speeding up appeals to the Supreme Court in important cases. It is apparent from the outset that some cases are going to end up in the Supreme Court and the government wants to reduce the length of time and expense involved by cutting out the need for such cases to go through the Court of Appeal before their inevitable appearance there. (Sections 63–66 of the CJ&CA 2015 allows for this to take place in relation to cases which concern a point of law of general public importance. These provisions apply in all cases, not just those involving judicial review, so mark a considerable extension in relation to the rules relating to 'leapfrog appeals' (see above, 6.6). They also apply to decisions of the Upper Tribunal, the Employment Appeal Tribunal and the Special Immigration Appeals Commission.)

- a new specialist 'planning chamber' for challenges relating to major developments to be taken only by expert judges using streamlined processes. (This court was established in July 2014. In the previous November, immigration and asylum judicial review cases had been transferred from the High Court to the specialist Upper Tier Tribunal.)

- the potential to reform the test for standing, i.e. who is able to bring a judicial review. (This measure was not enacted.)

Such proposals met much opposition, including that of Lord Neuberger, President of the Supreme Court, who spoke out against the attack on judicial review in a speech, in October 2013, in which he expressed the view that:

> The courts have no more important function than that of protecting citizens from the abuses and excesses of the executive-central government, local government or other public bodies. We must look at any proposed changes with particular care . . . bearing in mind that the proposed changes come from the very body which is at the receiving end of judicial reviews.

In spite of such criticism, the government carried on with many substantive reforms. The most significant changes were contained in Part 3, Courts and tribunals, and Part 4, Judicial review, of the Criminal Justice and Courts Act 2015 as cited above.

Among the financial measures in Part 4 of the Act are the following:

- a requirement that applicants for judicial review reveal at the outset how their claim is to be funded and the resources available from others behind the scenes, including, in the case of companies with insufficient resources, their members;

- a requirement on the Court to consider making orders for costs against third parties who are providing financial support to claimants or who are likely to be able to do so;

- a rule that other parties may not be ordered to pay a third party intervener's costs other than in exceptional circumstances;

- a rule that third party interveners in judicial review claims be liable for their own costs and the costs of the other parties that arise from their intervention, other than in exceptional circumstances;

- restriction on the Court's ability to make protective costs orders limiting a claimant's exposure to liability to pay the other side's costs if unsuccessful.

In October 2015 the Bingham Centre, JUSTICE and the Public Law Project jointly published an extremely informative introduction to the judicial review reform provisions in Part 4 of the Criminal Justice and Courts Act 2015. The document was praised by no less an authority than Lord Woolf who, in a foreword to it, wrote: 'It deals with Part 4 of the Act in an exemplary manner. It sets out in clear terms what should be the approach. Its authors are to be congratulated for what they have achieved.' The full title of the document is *Judicial Review and the Rule of Law: An Introduction to the Criminal Justice and Courts Act 2015, Part 4*.

In the same month the Public Law Project also published a wider examination of judicial review under the title The Value and Effects of Judicial Review: The Nature of Claims, their Outcomes and Consequences, written by Varda Bondy, Lucinda Platt and Maurice Sunkin.

The authors preface their summary with the following cautionary comment:

> There are a number of widely held and influential assumptions about the costs and misuse of JR. First, that the past growth in the use of JR has been largely driven by claimants abusing the system, either deliberately or otherwise. Second, that the effect of JR on public administration is largely negative because JR makes it more difficult for public bodies to deliver public services efficiently. Third, that JR litigation tends to be an expensive and time consuming detour concerned with technical matters of procedure that rarely alters decisions of public bodies. These claims have been challenged for their lack of empirical basis and this study provides additional evidence which shows them to be at best misleading and at worst false.

The Administrative Court judicial review guide 2016

This comprehensive and excellent explanatory guide to the procedures and practice relating to judicial review process was published by HM Court and Tribunals service and is available on its website. The guide brings together all relevant statutory provisions, rules of procedure, practice directions, and case law on procedural aspects of judicial review. Much of the guide is aimed at helping litigants in person, but it is also designed to ensure consistency and efficiency in the Administrative Court by tackling bad practices, including late filing of bundles, authorities and skeleton arguments. The guidance states that sanctions may be applied to parties if they fail to comply. As is stated in its preface the guide:

> . . . is designed to make it easier for parties to conduct judicial reviews in the Administrative Court, by drawing together into one place the relevant statutory provisions, rules of procedure, practice directions, and case law on procedural aspects of judicial review. It provides general guidance as to how litigation in the Administrative Court should be conducted in order to achieve the overriding objective of dealing with cases justly and at proportionate cost.

13.6 POLITICS AND THE JUDICIARY

Law is an inherently and inescapably political process. Even assertions as to the substantive autonomy of law (see Chapters 1, 3 and 4) merely disguise the fact that, in making legal decisions, judges decide where the weight of public approval is to be placed and which forms of behaviour are to be sanctioned (see, for example *R v Brown* (1993), where the House of Lords criminalised the sexual activities of consenting sadomasochists, arguably without fully comprehending some aspects of what was going on).

There is, however, an increasingly apparent tendency for contemporary judges to become actively, directly and openly engaged in more overtly political activity. The 1955 Kilmuir rules, named after the Lord Chancellor who introduced them, were designed to control the instances when the judiciary could express opinion in the media. The rules were abrogated in 1987 by Lord Mackay and, since then, the judiciary have been more forthcoming in expressing their views, not just on matters strictly related to their judicial functions but also on wider political matters.

13.6.1 THE POLITICS OF JUDICIAL REVIEW AND THE HUMAN RIGHTS ACT

As has been stated, the HRA merely heightened the potential for conflict between the judges and the executive and Parliament, but the relationship was already subject to some tension as a consequence of the operation of judicial review, as can be seen in a number of cases.

In *M v Home Office* (1993), the House of Lords decided that the court has jurisdiction in judicial review proceedings to grant interim and final injunctions against officers of the Crown, and to make a finding of contempt of court against a government department or a minister of the Crown in either his personal *or his official capacity*.

M v Home Office is of signal importance in establishing the powers of the courts in relation to the executive. It is also interesting to note that in delivering the leading speech, Lord Woolf quoted extensively from, and clearly supported, Dicey's view of the rule of law as involving the subjection of all, including state officials, to the ordinary law of the land (see Chapter 2).

In November 1994, the government suffered two damaging blows from the judiciary. In *R v Secretary of State for Foreign Affairs ex p World Development Movement Ltd* (1995), the Queen's Bench Divisional Court held that the Secretary of State had acted beyond his powers in granting aid to the Malaysian government in relation to the Pergau Dam project. The financial assistance was given, not for the promotion of development *per se*, as authorised by s 1 of the Overseas Development and Co-operation Act 1980, but in order to facilitate certain arms sales.

In *R v Secretary of State for the Home Department ex p Fire Brigades Union* (1995), the Court of Appeal held that the Home Secretary had committed an abuse of power in implementing a scheme designed to cut the level of payments made to the subjects of criminal injuries. The court held that he was under an obligation, under the CJA 1988, to put the previous non-statutory scheme on a statutory basis. It was not open for the Secretary of State to use his prerogative powers to introduce a completely new tariff scheme contrary to the intention of Parliament as expressed in the CJA 1988. The decision of the Court of Appeal was confirmed by a three-to-two majority in the House of Lords in April 1995, the majority holding that the Secretary of State had exceeded or abused powers granted to him by Parliament. It is of interest to note that in his minority judgment Lord Keith warned that to dismiss the Home Secretary's appeal would be:

> an unwarrantable intrusion into the political field and a usurpation of the function of Parliament.

Even Lord Chancellors have not escaped the unwanted control of judicial review, and in March 1997 John Witham successfully argued that the Lord Chancellor had exceeded his statutory powers in removing exemptions from court fees for those in receipt of state income support (*R v Lord Chancellor ex p Witham* (1997)).

Given its centrality in the operation of the criminal justice system and immigration, it is hardly surprising that the Home Department is subject to more claims for judicial review than any other ministry, nor is it surprising that some of them go against it.

In *Alvi v Secretary of State for the Home Department* (2012), the Supreme Court ruled that the Home Secretary could not introduce substantive immigration requirements through policy decisions, guidance or instructions, rather than in the body of the immigration rules themselves. The list of skilled occupations used to assess immigration requests was held not to be part of the Immigration Rules, as the document in which that list was set out had not been laid before Parliament as was required under s 3(2) of the Immigration Act 1971.

R (on the application of Public Law Project) v Lord Chancellor [2016] UKSC 39

In April 2013, the Government announced it would introduce a residence test for civil legal aid funding under s 9(2)(b) of the Legal Aid, Sentencing and Punishment of Offenders Act, (LASPO) 2012. The intention was that individuals not lawfully resident in the UK would not be eligible for legal aid. The charitable organisation Public Law Project (PLP) successfully challenged the residence test on two grounds: (i) the secondary legislation was *ultra vires;* and, (ii) the test was unjustifiably discriminatory.

Ultimately, applying the ordinary principles of statutory interpretation, the Supreme Court held that the draft order was *ultra vires*. While s 9(2)(b) provides the power to vary or omit *services*, the relevant parts of the draft order did not look to vary or omit services; rather, they were intended to reduce *the class of individuals who were entitled to receive those services* by reference to a personal characteristics or circumstance unrelated to the services (i.e. length of residency).

R (on the application of ClientEarth) (appellant) v Secretary of State for the Environment, Food and Rural Affairs (respondent) [2015] UKSC 28

This case related to the UK government's obligations under the European Air Quality Directive (2008/50/EC), which required Member states to reduce the levels of nitrogen dioxide in outdoor air. The legal activist group ClientEarth raised an action against the state claiming that London and several other British cities had failed to meet EU standards on nitrogen dioxide (NO_2) levels since 2010. The Supreme Court held in favour of ClientEarth and granted a declaration that there has been a breach of Art 13 of the Air Quality Directive The fact that the breach has been conceded was not considered a sufficient reason to decline to grant the declaration. In addition, as Lord Carnwarth stated: 'The new government, whatever its political complexion, should be left in no doubt as to the need for immediate action to address this issue.'

Subsequently in December 2015, in purported compliance with the order of the Supreme Court and the provisions of the Directive, the Department for the Environment, Food and Rural Affairs (DEFRA) published the government's 2015 Air Quality Plan (AQP) which purportedly addressed the need to reduce nitrogen dioxide emissions. Once again ClientEarth challenged the government, this time on lawfulness of DEFRA's plan, seeking a declaration that the plan, like its predecessor, failed to comply with Art 23(1) of the Directive and Reg 26(2) of the Air Quality Standards Regulations 2010, and this time seeking for an order quashing the plan. In *ClientEarth (No.2) v Secretary of State for the Environment, Food and Rural Affairs* (2016) the High Court decided that it would be appropriate to make a declaration that the 2015 AQP failed to comply with Art 23(1) of the Directive and Reg 26(2) of the Air Quality Standards Regulations 2010, and an order quashing the plan.

In reaching that decision Mr Justice Garnham also held that:

- the proper construction of Art 23 meant that the Secretary of State must aim to achieve compliance by the soonest date possible and that she must choose a route to that objective which reduced exposure as quickly as possible, and that she must take steps which mean meeting the value limits is *not just possible, but likely*;

- the Secretary of State fell into error in fixing on a projected compliance date of 2020 (and 2025 for London);

- the Secretary of State fell into error by adopting too optimistic a model for future emissions.

Following the decision, the government said it would not appeal it and agreed to discuss with ClientEarth a new timetable for more realistic pollution modelling and the steps needed to bring pollution levels down to the legally required levels. At Prime Minister's questions, Theresa May said:

> We now recognise that DEFRA] has to look at the judgment made by the courts and we now have to look again at the proposals we will bring forward. *Nobody in this house doubts the importance of the issue of air quality.*
>
> (emphasis added).

Those outside parliament, such as ClientEarth, might have grounds to question that assertion.

Bedroom tax (also known as under occupancy charge or the spare room subsidy

In April 2013, when the Welfare Reform Act 2012 came into force, it cut the amount of housing benefit payment made to people renting social housing who were deemed to have 'spare bedrooms': the reduction applicable was 14 per cent for one bedroom and 25 per cent for those deemed to have two or more spare bedrooms. Actions against the new regime were raised and made their way through the legal system to the Supreme Court, which announced its decision as to the legality of the impositions on 9 November 2016. *R (on the application of Carmichael) v Secretary of State for Work and Pensions* [2016] UKSC 58 concerned a number of claimants, each of whom alleged that the bedroom tax amounted to unlawful discrimination, contrary to their Art 14 and Art 8 ECHR rights and the state's public sector duty not to discriminate against particular individuals on the basis of their disability.

In the *Carmichael* case, the claimant lived with her husband in a two bedroom flat. She was severely disabled and her husband was her full time carer. She needed a special bed with an electronic mattress and there was not enough space for her husband to have a separate bed in the same room, so he slept in the second bedroom. Their rent was reduced by 14 per cent under the 'under occupancy charge'. However, the Supreme Court held that Mrs Carmichael had suffered from disability discrimination in the reduction of their housing benefit payment.

A second successful linked case (*Rutherford*) related to two full-time carers of their disabled grandson. It was accepted that they needed a 'spare bedroom' to allow a further carer to stay overnight. However, a number of other linked cases were rejected including the case of a woman, *A*, who lived in a three-bedroom property which had been adapted by police to protect her from a violent and abusive ex-partner under what is known as the Sanctuary Scheme. The majority of the Supreme Court found that, while *A*, was entitled to receive protection she was not entitled to an exemption from the bedroom tax, even if the additional accommodation was provided under the Scheme. Lady Hale, with whom Lord Carnwath agreed, delivered a dissenting judgment, finding that the lack of exemption amounted to both unlawful discrimination and a breach of the public sector equality duty, the reason being that the government had not taken into account the disproportionate impact that the bedroom tax would have on survivors of domestic violence.

Coincidentally, the decisions of the Supreme Court were delivered only two days after the United Nations Committee on Rights of Persons with Disabilities issued a highly critical report on the way in which recent reforms had impacted on people with disabilities in the UK. The finding of the committee was that there was 'reliable evidence that the threshold of *grave or systematic violations of the rights of persons with disabilities* has been met in the State party.'

It can be seen from the foregoing that judicial review provided the judiciary with the means for addressing the potential for abuse that followed on from the growth of discretionary power in the hands of the modern state, particularly if it was operated on the basis of the doctrine of proportionality. Alongside the growth in the number of applications, there were also indications that at least some of the higher judiciary saw it as part of their function to exercise such control over the executive. For example, the former Master of the Rolls and former Lord Chief Justice, Lord Bingham, was quoted in *The Observer* newspaper of 9 May 1993 as saying that:

> Slowly, the constitutional balance is tilting towards the judiciary. The courts have reacted to the increase in powers claimed by the government by being more active themselves.

Judicial review is a delicate exercise and by necessity draws the judiciary into the political arena, using the word 'political' in its widest, non-party sense. That the judges were aware of this is evident from the words of Lord Woolf in the same article. As he recognised:

> Judicial review is all about balance: between the rights of the individual and his need to be treated fairly, and the rights of government at local and national level to do what it has been elected to do. There is a very sensitive and political decision to be made.

However, another former Law Lord, Lord Browne-Wilkinson, observed on a BBC radio programme, admittedly before his elevation to the House of Lords, that a great void was apparent in the political system, deriving from the fact that no government had a true popular majority and yet all governments were able to carry Parliament in support of anything they wanted. He went on to express the view that Parliament was not a place where it was easy to get accountability for abuse or misuse of powers. According to Lord Browne-Wilkinson, while judicial review could not overcome the will of Parliament, judges had a special role because *democracy was defective*. He then asked a rhetorical question as to who else but the judges could ensure that executive action is taken in accordance with law, *and not abused by increasingly polarised political stances*.

Such thinking is also evident in an article by Mr Justice Stephen Sedley (as he was then) in the May 1995 edition of the *London Review of Books*, in which he asserted that, after decades of passivity, there is a new 'culture of judicial assertiveness to compensate for, and in places repair, dysfunctions in the democratic process', and that the last three decades of the twentieth century may have seen the UK constitution being refashioned by judges 'with sufficient popular support to mute political opposition'.

The impact of the Human Rights Act 1998

As has been seen at 2.5 above, the introduction of the HRA greatly increased judicial power in relation to the other two branches of the constitution.

Initially the judges were reluctant to use their new powers, especially the Court of Appeal and the House of Lords, although the courts below them, and notably Collins J in the SIAC, adopted a much more robust approach.

This initial position was set by Lord Irvine in his inaugural Human Rights Lecture at the University of Durham:

> It is all about balance. The balance between intense judicial scrutiny and reasonable deference to elected decision-makers is a delicate one to strike. But the judiciary have struck it well: and I welcome that. Whilst scrutiny is undoubtedly an important aid to better governance, there are areas in which decisions are best taken by the decision-makers entrusted by Parliament to make them. This may be for reasons of democratic accountability, expertise or complexity.

The former Lord Chancellor may well have been of the view that the judges had got it right, but his views did not sound in harmony with those of his ex-colleague, the former Home Secretary, David Blunkett, who was a consistent source of attack on the judiciary. Perhaps his most severe attack came after Collins J's decision in *R (on the Application of Q) v Secretary of State for the Home Department* (2003), which declared unlawful his power under s 55 of the Nationality, Immigration and Asylum Act 2002 to refuse to provide assistance to those who had not immediately declared their intention to claim asylum when they arrived in the UK. In the press, the then Home Secretary was quoted as saying:

> Frankly, I am fed up with having to deal with a situation where Parliament debates issues and judges then overturn them. We were aware of the circumstances, we did mean what we said and, on behalf of the British people, we are going to implement it.

Of even more concern were the reports that the then Prime Minister was 'prepared for a showdown with the judiciary to stop the courts thwarting government's attempts to curb the record flow of asylum seekers into Britain', and that he was looking into the possibility of enacting legislation to limit the role of judges in the interpretation of international human rights obligations and reassert the primacy of Parliament. There were even reports that the Prime Minister was considering withdrawing completely from the ECHR, rather than merely issuing derogations where it was thought necessary.

Given such pressure, it is perhaps not surprising that when the Court of Appeal heard the *Q* case, while it supported Collins J's decision, it went out of its way to provide the Home Secretary with advice on how to make the Act, and the procedures under it, compatible with ECHR rights.

Critique of judicial activism

The fact that the judges increasingly see it as incumbent upon them to use judicial review and the HRA as the means of questioning and controlling what they see as the abuse of executive power does, at the very least, raise very serious questions in relation to their suitability for such a role. These doubts can be set out in terms of:

Competence

This refers to the question whether the judges are sufficiently competent to participate in deciding the substantive issues that they have been invited to consider under the guise of judicial review, and may be entitled to consider under the HRA. Judges are experts in law; they are not experts in the various and highly specialised areas of policy that by definition tend to be involved in judicial review cases. They may disagree with particular decisions, but it has to be at least doubted that they are qualified to take such policy decisions. A classic example of this difficulty was the 'fares' fair' cases (*Bromley London BC v GLC* (1983) and later, *R v London Transport Executive ex p GLC* (1983)), in which the courts got involved in deciding issues relating to transport policy for London on the pretext that they were judicially defining the meaning of particular words in a statute. The apparently technocratic, and hence neutral, application of rules of interpretation simply serves to disguise a political procedure and, in these cases, the policy issue concerned was certainly beyond the scope of the judges to determine. In *Bellinger v Bellinger* (2003), the House of Lords, although obviously sympathetic to the case, admitted their incompetence as regards deciding issues relating to the rights of transsexuals. For that reason, they issued a declaration of incompatibility under the HRA 1998 and thus passed the matter to Parliament for review and appropriate reform.

Constitutionality

This refers to the wider point that the separation of powers applies equally to the judiciary as it does to the executive. In interfering with substantive decisions and involving themselves in political matters, albeit on the pretence of merely deciding points of law, the judiciary may be seen to be exceeding their constitutional powers. It has to be remembered that judges are unelected and unaccountable.

Partiality

This refers to the possibility of individual, and indeed corporate, bias within the judiciary, as will be considered at 13.7.1 below.

The foregoing has indicated that the relationship between the state and the courts may, on occasion, involve a measure of tension, with the courts attempting to rein in the activities of the state. The relationship between the judiciary and the executive is well summed up in the words of Lord Justice Farquharson, again taken from an *Observer* article:

> We have to be very careful: the executive is elected. We have a role in the Constitution but, if we go too far, there will be a reaction. The Constitution only works if the different organs trust each other. If the judges start getting too frisky, there would be retaliation, renewed attempts to curb the judiciary.

Although no longer in force, the Kilmuir rules did have a valid point to make:

> the overriding consideration . . . is the importance of keeping the judiciary in this country isolated from the controversies of the day. So long as a judge keeps silent, his reputation for wisdom and impartiality remains unassailable; but every utterance which he makes in public . . . must necessarily bring him within the focus of criticism.

13.7 POLITICS OF THE JUDICIARY

When considering the role which the judiciary play in the process of applying the law, or indeed the process already adverted to in Chapter 4, whereby they actually make the law, criticism is usually levelled at the particular race, class and gender position of the majority of the judges. It is an objective and well-documented fact that the majority of judges are 'white, middle-class, middle-aged to elderly men', but the question that has to be considered is whether this *necessarily* leads to the conclusion that judges reach inherently biased decisions. It is always possible, indeed the newspapers make it relatively easy, to provide anecdotal evidence that apparently confirms either the bias or the lack of social awareness of the judiciary, but the fundamental question remains as to whether these cases are exceptional or whether they represent the norm.

Why should judges' class/race/gender placement make them less objective arbiters of the law? It is worth considering the fact that an *unsupported* general assertion as to the inherently partial approach of the judiciary is itself partial. Simon Lee, not totally fatuously, has highlighted the logical flaw in what he refers to as the 'Tony Benn thesis' (Benn, the former left-wing Labour Party Member of Parliament who created history by being the first hereditary peer to renounce his peerage in order to remain in the House of Commons). Just because judges are old, white, rich, upper middle class, educated at public school and Oxbridge does not mean that they all necessarily think the same way; after all, Benn was a product of the same social circumstances. There is, of course, the point that people from that particular background *generally* tend to be conservative in outlook, and the apparent validity of Lee's argument is clearly the product of logic-chopping that reverses the accepted relationship and uses the exception as the rule, rather than seeing the exception as proving/testing the rule. Nevertheless, Lee's point remains true: that proof of judicial bias is needed.

As previous sections of this book have pointed out, if law were completely beyond the scope of judges to manipulate to their own ends, then the race, class and gender placement of individual judges would be immaterial, as they would not be in any position to influence the operation of the law. As was demonstrated in Chapters 3 and 4, however, the way in which the doctrines that set the limits within which the judiciary operate are by no means as rigid and restrictive as they might at first appear. It was seen that, although judges are supposed merely to apply rather than create law, they possess a large measure of discretion in determining which laws to apply, what those laws mean, and how they should be applied. In the light of this potential capacity to create law, it is essential to ensure that the judiciary satisfactorily represent society at large in relation to which they have so much power, and to ensure further that they do not merely represent the views and attitudes of a self-perpetuating elite.

A Nuffield Foundation-funded report produced in November 1999 by Professor Hazel Genn in conjunction with the National Centre for Social Research, entitled *Paths to Justice*, revealed a truly remarkable lack of general confidence in the judiciary. The research surveyed a random selection of 4,125 people, from which total 1,248 people who had had experience of legal problems were selected for more detailed interview, with a smaller group of 48 being extensively interviewed. The results suggest that two out of three people think that judges are out of touch with ordinary people's lives, but, more worryingly, only 53 per cent thought that they would get a fair hearing if they ever went to court. Disappointingly, at the launch of the report, Lord Woolf claimed that this 'misconception' was due to 'irresponsible media reporting' and stated that:

> It behoves the media to learn from this and recognise the dangers posed to confidence in the judicial system.

Surely, it more behoves the judiciary and the Justice Ministry to do more to redress this negative perception than simply blame the media for focusing on silly judge stories of which, unfortunately, there are still too many.

One of the findings of the report was that judges could improve their image by getting rid of their wigs and gowns. Perish the thought: there are standards and distinctions to be maintained. Thus, in *Practice Direction (Court Dress) (No 3) (1998)*, the Lord High Chancellor, Lord Irvine of Lairg, provided:

> Queen's Counsel wear a short wig and silk (or stuff) gown over a court coat; junior counsel wear a short wig and stuff gown with bands; solicitors and other advocates authorised under the Courts and Legal Services Act 1990 wear a black stuff gown, *but no wig* (emphasis added).

The issue of wigs resurfaced in March 2006 when once again a proposal was put forward to consider getting rid of them. Somewhat surprisingly and counter-intuitively, some supported wigs as a means of benefiting the justice system by protecting the anonymity of counsel and providing suitable gravitas to the less experienced members of the barrister's profession.

In July 2008 the Lord Chief Justice issued a Practice Direction which introduced the wearing of a new civil robe in civil and family law cases together with the announcement that wigs will no longer be worn in such courts. The reforms, which took effect from 1 October 2008, do not apply in criminal cases. Justices of the Supreme Court do not wear wigs or gowns when hearing cases.

13.7.1 CRITICISMS

The treatment of some aspects of potential bias within the judiciary has already been dealt with at 12.2.3 above, but this section addresses a more amorphous form of prejudice, and therefore one that is correspondingly more difficult to recognise or deal with. Given the central position of judges in the operation of law and the legal system, particularly with regard to the growth in judicial review and their new role in relation to giving effect to the HRA, the question these reports raise is whether the social placement of the judiciary leads to any perceptible shortfall in the provision of justice. The pre-eminent critic of the way in which the judiciary permit their shared background, attitudes and prejudices to influence their understanding and statement of the law is Professor JAG Griffith. According to Griffith, bias can occur at two levels:

Personal bias

Personal bias occurs where individual judges permit their own personal prejudices to influence their judgment and thus the effective application of the law. It is relatively easy to cite cases where judges give expression to their own attitudes and in so doing exhibit their own prejudices. As examples of this process, two cases can be cited which consider the rule of natural justice, that a person should not be both the accuser and judge in the same case. In *Hannam v Bradford Corp* (1970), the court held that it was contrary to natural justice for three school governors to sit as members of a local authority education disciplinary committee, charged with deciding whether or not to uphold a previous decision of the governors to dismiss a teacher. This was so even though the three governors had not been present at the meeting where it was decided to dismiss the teacher. On the other hand, in *Ward v Bradford Corp* (1971), the Court of Appeal refused to interfere with a decision by governors of a teacher training college to confirm the expulsion of a student, although they had instituted the disciplinary proceedings and three members of the governors sat on the original disciplinary committee. What possible explanation can there be for this discrepancy? The only tenable explanation is to be found in the latter court's disapproval of the plaintiff's behaviour in that case. The truly reprehensible judgment of Lord Denning concludes that the student lost nothing, as she was not a fit person to teach children in any case. Can such a conclusion be justified on purely legal grounds or is it based on individual morality? Lord Denning did his best to buttress his judgment with spurious legal reasoning, but it could be suggested that, in so doing, he merely brought the process of legal reasoning into disrepute and revealed its fallaciousness.

Courts have also been notoriously unsympathetic to victims of rape and have been guilty of making the most obtuse of sexist comments in relation to such victims. Nor can it be claimed that depreciatory racist remarks have been totally lacking in court cases.

Such cases of bias are serious and reprehensible, but the very fact that the prejudice they demonstrate appears as no more than the outcome of particular judges, who are simply out of touch with current standards of morality or acceptable behaviour, suggests that it might be eradicated by the Lord Chancellor exercising stricter control over such mavericks and appointing more appropriate judges in the first place. Professor Griffith, however, suggests that there is a further type of bias that is actually beyond such relatively easy control.

Corporate bias

Corporate bias involves the assertion that the judges *as a body* decide certain types of cases in a biased way. This accusation of corporate bias is much more serious than that of personal bias, for the reason that it asserts that the problem of bias is *systematic* rather than merely limited to particular maverick judges. As a consequence, if such a claim is justified, it has to be concluded that the problem is not susceptible to treatment at the level of the individual judge, but requires a complete alteration of the whole judicial system. Griffith claims that, as a consequence of their shared educational experience, their shared training and practical experience at the Bar and their shared social situation as members of the Establishment, judges have developed a common outlook. He maintains that they share homogeneous values, attitudes and beliefs as to how the law should operate and be administered. He further suggests that this shared outlook is inherently conservative, if not Conservative in a party-political sense.

Griffith's argument is that the highest judges in the judicial hierarchy are frequently called upon to decide cases on the basis of a determination of what constitutes the public interest and that, in making that determination, they express their own corporate values, which are in turn a product of their position in society as part of the ruling Establishment. Griffith maintains that judges can be seen to operate in such a way as to maintain the status quo and resist challenges to the established authority. Underlying this argument is the implication that the celebrated independence of the judiciary is, in fact, a myth and that the courts will tend to decide cases in such a way as to buttress the position of the state, especially if it is under the control of a Conservative government.

In an attempt to substantiate his claims, Griffith examines cases relating to trade union law, personal rights, property rights and matters of national security, where he claims to find judges consistently acting to support the interests of the state over the rights of the individual. Some of the concrete examples he cites are the withdrawal of trade union rights from GCHQ at Cheltenham (*Council of Civil Service Unions v Minister for Civil Service* (1984)); the banning of publishing any extracts from the *Spycatcher* book (*AG v Guardian Newspapers Ltd* (1987)); and the treatment of suspected terrorists.

There certainly have been some overtly right-wing decisions taken by the courts, and the history of trade union cases is replete with them even at the highest level. The greater strength of Griffith's argument, however, would appear to be in the way that the courts have understood and expressed what is to be meant by 'public interest' in such a way as to reflect conservative, but not necessarily illiberal, values. It is surely only from that perspective that the higher judiciary's antagonistic response to some of the electorally driven policy decisions in relation to the legal system by *both* Conservative and New Labour administrations can be reconciled.

As would be expected, Griffith, and other academics associated with the left, have expressed their reservations about the extent to which the HRA will hand power to an unelected, unaccountable, inherently conservative and unreformed body, as they claim the judiciary is.

A notable, if somewhat complacent, response to Griffith's book was provided by Lord Devlin, who pointed out that, in most cases and on most issues, there tended to be plurality rather than unanimity of opinion and decision among judges. He also claimed that it would be just as possible for a more conservatively minded person than Griffith to go through the casebooks to provide a list of examples where the courts had operated in an over-liberal manner. Lord Devlin also adopted a different explanation of the judiciary's perceived reluctance to abandon the status quo. For him, any conservatism on the part of judges was to be seen as a product of age rather than class. In conclusion, he asserted that even if the judiciary were biased, their bias was well known and allowances could be made for it.

The issue of the way in which the criminal appeal procedure dealt with suspected terrorist cases is of particular relevance in the light of the Runciman Commission Report. General dissatisfaction with the trials and appeals involving suspected terrorists such as the Maguire Seven, the Birmingham Six, the Guildford Four, the Tottenham Three, Stefan Kiszko and Judith Ward helped to give rise to the widespread impression that the UK criminal justice system, and in particular the British appeal system, needed to be considered for reform.

In the light of the fact that the appeal system did not seem to be willing to consider the possibility of the accused's innocence once they had been convicted, the Runciman Commission's recommendation that a Criminal Case Review Authority be established, independent of the Home Office, was widely welcomed and resulted in the establishment of the CCRC in the Criminal Appeal Act 1995 (see above, 9.9). The question still remains, however, whether those earlier cases reflect an inherently and inescapably conservative judiciary, or were they simply unfortunate instances of more general errors of the system, which the implementation of the CCRC can overcome? And perhaps more importantly, will the Court of Appeal give a fair hearing to the cases referred to it by the CCRC?

It is apparent from the statistics produced by what was then the Department for Constitutional Affairs (DCA), cited previously, that senior judges were still being appointed from the same limited social and educational elite as they always have been. This gives rise to the suspicion, if not the reality, that the decisions that this elite make merely represent values and interests of a limited and privileged segment of society rather than society as a whole. Even if the accusations levelled by Professor Griffith are inaccurate, it is surely still necessary to remove even the possibility of those accusations.

It is not a little ironic that, in spite of the potential shortcomings that arise from the social composition of the current judicial body, there seems to be a distinct alteration in attitudes to the judiciary among those of a politically left-leaning persuasion. Following the introduction of the Human Rights Act and especially the decisions of the House of Lords in *A v Secretary of State for the Home Department* (2004) and *A v Secretary of State for the Home Department* (2005), many on the left now apparently see the courts as the bulwark of civilised society, against which beats the persistent tide of authoritarian legislation: the judges are now celebrated as the custodians of the rule of law, protecting the general populace from the depredations of the all-encompassing state. Thus, from previously being seen from this perspective, as reactionary, the courts are now seen as the appropriate defenders of generally accepted, and generally to be defended, liberal values. It is equally ironic that the same critics also hold the previously ineffable House of Lords in the same light as a safeguard of liberties of the ordinary person.

In support of this odd transition may be cited a series of BBC radio programmes delivered, at the end of the summer 2009, by the liberal barrister and Labour peer Helena Kennedy. In the second programme she examined the shifting history of attacks on judicial independence, admitting that in the 1970s and 1980s, it was she and a generation of liberal lawyers who attacked the judiciary for being too *right wing* and out of touch. Now, however, right-wing critics have taken up their language but with the twist that they now attack the judiciary for being too *liberal* and out of touch.

In the third programme she focused on the way in which restraining orders to protect the victims of domestic violence, once again championed by liberal lawyers like her, have in recent years been broadened in scope and application, in such a way as to operate as mechanisms for political control.

One would not have to be a confirmed cynic to recognise the dangers in such an approach. Those wishing to make radical changes in social order should not rely on the judges for support, nor place too much power in their hands. That is surely Griffith's underlying thesis?

13.7.2   THE POLITICS OF JUDICIAL INQUIRIES

During the summer of 2003, following the war in Iraq, the government established an inquiry to investigate the reasons why a British civil servant working for the Ministry of Defence (Dr David Kelly) apparently killed himself. The inquiry chairman was Lord Hutton, a Law Lord, and his task was set by the government as one to 'urgently conduct an investigation into the circumstances surrounding the death of Dr Kelly'. This prompts consideration of the judicial inquiry, and its place in the English legal system.

An inquiry is different from a tribunal, another quasi-judicial body with which it is sometimes compared. A tribunal is a permanent body whereas an inquiry is set up on an *ad hoc* basis to deal with one particular problematic issue. Tribunals are empowered to make decisions that affect the parties to the issue, whereas inquiries can only publish their 'findings' and make recommendations that might be implemented by the government.

A 'statutory inquiry' is one that is established because an Act permits or requires it to be set up in certain circumstances. For example, under s 78 of the Town and Country Planning 1990 Act, someone who seeks planning permission but is refused by their local planning authority has the right to appeal to the Secretary of State. In order to help decide the case, the Secretary can ask for a local public inquiry to be held.

A 'non-statutory inquiry' is one that has been set up by the government in order to examine matters of substantial public interest such as disasters or scandals. Senior members of the judiciary usually, but not necessarily, chair these.

There are, importantly, two sorts of judicial inquiry. First, there are those that are established under the Tribunals of Inquiry (Evidence) Act 1921. Such inquiries are similar in their formality and rules of procedure to court cases. The chair can summon witnesses under threat that they will commit an offence if they do not turn up to give evidence, and the chair can demand that documents be made available to the hearing. This type of inquiry can be established only upon a resolution of both houses of Parliament. The Bloody Sunday Inquiry into the killing of 13 Catholic civilians by British paratroopers in Derry in 1972 and chaired by Lord Saville of Newdigate was established under the 1921 Act. Similarly, the inquiry into the Dunblane shootings, in which many children at a primary school in Scotland were shot and killed in 1996, was also established under the 1921 Act.

Secondly, there are those judicial inquiries in which a judge is simply appointed by the government to chair the process but without the full powers of running it as a court case. For example Lord Denning investigated aspects of the Profumo affair, a scandal in 1963 involving the Secretary of State for War at the time. Lord Scarman conducted the inquiry into the Brixton riots of 1981; Lord Justice Taylor examined the safety of sports grounds following the Hillsborough stadium disaster in 1991; and Lord Justice Scott inquired into the arms-for-Iraq affair in 1994. Such investigations, however, are not necessarily conducted by a judge, as may be seen from the example of the Franks Report on the conduct of the Falklands War in 1983.

However, judges have often been selected to chair inquiries into matters of public importance because they are expert in conducting fair and methodical hearings, and are generally regarded as wise people who are well versed in using rules of evidence justly to evaluate competing arguments. The Hutton Inquiry into the death of Dr Kelly was of this second sort.

Lord Hutton conducted his inquiry in a scrupulously forensic manner and, while it was ongoing, the press was particularly effusive in its praise of him. It was only with the release of the final report, which totally exonerated all members of the New Labour government and its entourage, and castigated the BBC, that suggestions emerged that the Law Lord actually might not have been the best-equipped person to undertake such a politically sensitive inquiry, at least from the point of view of those who were opposed to the actions of the government. For example, an article in *The Guardian* newspaper of 29 January 2004 stated that:

> Lord Hutton's report caused little surprise yesterday among lawyers who know the newly retired Law Lord. Most describe him as an establishment man and not one to rock the boat. When he set out on his task, they predicted that he would keep his remit as narrow as possible. That prediction has been proved right.

Anthony Scrivener QC, a former chairman of the Bar, said:

> You get a conventional, conservative with a small 'c' judge. You ask whether the Prime Minister and other members of the government have been lying

through their teeth. As a conventional judge he applies the criminal standard of proof. You give him no right to get documents so he only sees the documents you give him. The result is entirely predictable.

One senior QC said: 'I think the report reflects his establishment background. He is a trusting man as far as officialdom is concerned.'

Another, who knows him personally and has appeared before him, said: 'There are judges in the House of Lords who are liberal and progressive and might possibly shake the establishment branches, but not Brian Hutton.'

Whether the Hutton Report provides evidence to support Professor Griffith's thesis as to the inherently establishment nature of the judiciary as a body is a moot point, but it certainly caused Lord Woolf to question the wisdom of using members of the senior judiciary in such situations. In a *New Statesman* journal interview in February 2004, the Lord Chief Justice was quoted as disapproving of the present system. He said, 'In America they are not keen on judges doing this sort of thing', and that inquiries conducted by non-judges 'might be a better way of doing it'.

It could, once again, only be the unwonted, not to say hostile, publicity that led the Lord Chief Justice to such a conclusion: a conclusion that might suggest that judges should not be seen to be meddling in the political arena, but might also carry the implication that what is wrong is not so much the interference in itself, as the being seen to be interfering.

The Inquiries Act 2005
This Act repealed the Tribunals of Inquiry (Evidence) Act 1921. Under the new Act:

- The inquiry and its terms of reference are to be decided by the executive in the form of the minister of state responsible for the issue under investigation. That minister may amend the terms of reference at any time if they consider that the public interest so requires. The terms of reference of the inquiry are defined as including:
  - (i)   the matters to which the inquiry relates;
  - (ii)   any particular matters as to which the inquiry panel is to determine the facts;
  - (iii) whether the inquiry panel is to make recommendations;
  - (iv)   any other matters relating to the scope of the inquiry that the minister may specify.
- In setting or amending the terms of reference, the minister must consult the chair, but is not obliged to consult any other person.

- The chair of the inquiry is appointed by the minister and the minister has the discretion to dismiss any member of the inquiry.

- The decision whether the inquiry, or any individual hearings, should be held in public or private is also at the discretion of the minister.

- The minister may terminate an inquiry at any time. If they do so before the inquiry has delivered its report, the minister must consult the chair, set out the reasons, and notify Parliament.

- Inquiries must deliver a report to the minister setting out the facts determined by the inquiry panel and their recommendations. There is no provision for dissenting reports, but if the panel is not unanimous the report must reasonably reflect any disagreements.

- The chair is responsible for publishing the report, unless the minister decides to take over that responsibility. Reports should be published in full but the person responsible for publishing a report may withhold material:

  (i)   as is required by any statutory provision, enforceable Community obligation or rule of law; or

  (ii)   as the person considers to be necessary in the public interest.

- Any decision to issue restrictive notices to block disclosure of evidence is also to be taken by the minister.

- Any judicial review of a decision made by a minister in relation to an inquiry or by the inquiry itself must be lodged within 14 days, which is shorter than the usual time limit of three months.

Critique of the Inquiries Act

In a trenchant assessment of the Inquiries Act 2005, the British and Irish Rights Watch, an independent human rights organisation, expressed the view that:

The Inquiries Act has brought about a fundamental shift in the manner in which the actions of government and public bodies can be subjected to scrutiny in the United Kingdom. The powers of independent chairs to control inquiries has been usurped and those powers have been placed in the hands of government Ministers. The Minister:

- decides whether there should be an inquiry;
- sets its terms of reference;
- can amend its terms of reference;

- appoints its members;
- can restrict public access to inquiries;
- can prevent the publication of evidence placed before an inquiry;
- can prevent the publication of the inquiry's report;
- can suspend or terminate an inquiry; and
- can withhold the costs of any part of an inquiry which strays beyond the terms of reference set by the Minister.

Parliament's role has been reduced to that of the passive recipient of information about inquiries, whereas under the 1921 Act reports of public inquiries were made to Parliament. Now, not only is there no guarantee that any inquiry will be public, but inquiry reports will go to the Minister.

The Minister's role is particularly troubling where the actions of that Minister or those of his or her department, or those of the government, are in question. In effect, the state will be investigating itself. In our view, the Inquiries Act is at odds with the United Nations' updated set of principles for the protection and promotion of human rights through action to combat impunity.

Where Article 2 of the European Convention on Human Rights (which protects the right to life) is engaged, the Inquiries Act is at variance with the United Nations' Principles on the Effective Prevention and Investigation of Extra-legal, Arbitrary and Summary Executions. Indeed, we doubt that the Inquiries Act can deliver an effective investigation in compliance with Article 2. The Minister's powers to interfere in every important aspect of an inquiry robs it of any independence. Even if a Minister were to refrain from exercising those powers that are discretionary, s/he still has absolute power over whether there should be an inquiry at all and over its terms of reference. There is no scope for victims to be involved in or even consulted about the process.

In support of their view, the organisation cited the views of Lord Saville, who chaired one of the most complex public inquiries in UK legal history, the Bloody Sunday Inquiry, who publicly expressed grave reservations about the Act. As they claimed, in a letter to Baroness Ashton at the Department of Constitutional Affairs, dated 26 January 2005, he stated his opinion that:

> I take the view that this provision makes a very serious inroad into the independence of any inquiry and is likely to damage or destroy public confidence in the inquiry and its findings, especially in cases where the conduct of the authorities may be in question.

He added that such ministerial interference with a judge's ability to act impartially and independently of government would be unjustifiable. He further stated that neither he nor his fellow judges on the Bloody Sunday Inquiry would be prepared to be appointed as a member of an inquiry that was subject to a provision of that kind.

The Inquiries Act came under critical attention in July 2008 when the United Nations Human Rights Committee issued its concluding observations on the UK's periodic report under the UN Covenant on Civil and Political Rights. As it stated:

> The Committee remains concerned that, a considerable time after murders (including of human rights defenders) in Northern Ireland have occurred, several inquiries into these murders have still not been established or concluded, and that those responsible for these deaths have not yet been prosecuted. Even where inquiries have been established, *the Committee is concerned that instead of being under the control of an independent judge, several of these inquiries are conducted under the Inquiries Act 2005 which allows the Government minister who is responsible for establishing an inquiry to control important aspects of that inquiry* (Art 6, emphasis added).

In March 2014, a House of Lords select committee published the results of its review of the law and practice relating to public inquiries, *The Inquiries Act 2005: post-legislative scrutiny*.

Its main recommendations were that:

* inquiries into matters of public concern should normally be held under the 2005 Act and ministers should give reasons for any decision to hold an inquiry otherwise than under the act;
* there should be stronger controls on the powers of ministers requiring them to seek the consent of, rather than merely consulting with, the chair of an inquiry before:
    (i) setting or amending terms of reference;
    (ii) adding another member to the inquiry panel or terminating the appointment of a panel member with the minister being required to lay reasons before parliament;
    (iii) except in matters of public security, only allowing the chair, not the minister, to withhold material from publication;
* interested parties, in particular, victims and victims' families, should have an opportunity to make representations about the final terms of reference;
* a central inquiries unit should be created to assist with the practical details of setting up an inquiry, including premises, infrastructure, IT, procurement and staffing;
* Parliament should do more to hold ministers to account following publication of the inquiry report, on responding to recommendations and implementation.

CHAPTER SUMMARY: JUDICIAL REASONING AND POLITICS

REASONING IN GENERAL

Deductive reasoning is reasoning from the whole to the part; from the general to the particular. The syllogism is a form of deductive reasoning. Inductive reasoning is reasoning from the part to the whole; from the particular to the general. Reasoning by analogy is reasoning from part to part.

JUDICIAL REASONING

Laws can be presented in the form of syllogisms but do not actually focus on questions of deductive reasoning. The doctrine of judicial precedent appears at first sight to involve deductive reasoning, but is in fact based on the much less certain use of inductive reasoning and reasoning by analogy.

JUDICIAL REVIEW

Under the constitution of the UK, and within the doctrine of the separation of powers, judges and the executive have distinct but interrelated roles.

Judicial review remedies are the prerogative remedies of *quashing orders, mandatory orders* and *prohibiting orders*, together with the private law remedies of declaration, injunction and damages. Private law remedies cannot be used in relation to public law complaints.

Increased judicial activity in relation to state programmes raises questions about the competence and authority of judges to act, as well as raising doubts as to their political views.

POLITICS OF THE JUDICIARY

Judges have a capacity to make law – the question is, do they exercise this power in a biased way?

Bias can take two forms: personal and corporate.

Accusations of corporate bias suggest that, as a group, judges represent the interest of the status quo and decide certain political cases in line with that interest. However, more recently there has been a reliance on the judiciary as the protectors of human rights.

FOOD FOR THOUGHT

1   Should the membership of the judiciary reflect the underlying social structure? In other words, do the class, race and gender of the judiciary matter, and if so, why?

2   Consider the extent to which the growth of judicial review and human rights actions are increasingly involving the judiciary in political decisions, and whether or not that is a good thing. In the words of the late Lord Denning, 'Someone

must be trusted. Let it be the judges.' Is such an assertion valid in the light of the unrepresentative nature of the judiciary? As Lord Justice Laws has recently asked with regard to the HRA:

Why should judges decide matters of social policy at all? The political rights, Articles 8–12, with the right set out in the first part and the derogation in the second, create a structure which means that a very large number of legal debates are about how the balance between private right and public interest should be struck. But what authority, expertise, do lawyers have to strike that balance, that is special to them?

FURTHER READING

Baldwin, J, 'The social composition of magistrates' (1976) 16 British J of Criminology 171

Blom-Cooper, L, 'Bias: malfunction in judicial decision-making' [2009] PL 199

Bondy, V, Platt, L and Sunkin, M, *The Value and Effects of Judicial Review: The Nature of Claims, their Outcomes and Consequences*, 2015, London: The Public Project

Browne-Wilkinson, N (Sir), 'The independence of the judiciary in the 1980s' [1988] PL 4

Clayton, R, 'Decision-making in the Supreme Court: new approaches and new opportunities' [2009] PL 682

Crawford, L, 'Race awareness training and the judges' (1994) Counsel 11

Griffith, JAG, *The Politics of the Judiciary*, 5th edn, 1997, London: Fontana

Hailsham (Lord), 'The office of Lord Chancellor and the separation of powers' (1989) 8 Civil Justice Quarterly 308 *Judicial Review and the Rule of Law: An Introduction to the Criminal Justice and Courts Act 2015, Part 4*,

Bingham Centre for the Rule of Law, JUSTICE and the Public Law Project, London, October 2015

Lee, S, *Judging Judges*, 1988, London: Faber & Faber

MacCormick, N, *Legal Rules and Legal Reasoning*, 1978, Oxford: Clarendon

Mackay (Lord), *The Administration of Justice*, 1994, London: Sweet & Maxwell

Malleson, K, *The New Judiciary: The Effect of Expansion and Activism*, 1999, Aldershot: Ashgate

McLachlin, B, 'The role of judges in modern Commonwealth society' [1994] LQR 260

Murdoch, S, 'Judges use discretion over discharges' (2009) 940 EG 131

Pannick, D, *Judges*, 1987, Oxford: OUP

Parker, H *et al*, *Unmasking the Magistrates*, 1989, Milton Keynes: OUP

Royal Commission on Criminal Justice, *Runciman Report*, Cm 2263, 1995, London: HMSO

Rutherford, A, 'Judicial training and autonomy' (1999) 149 NLJ 1120

Skordaki, E, *Judicial Appointments*, Law Society Research Study No 5, 1991, London: HMSO

Smith, R, 'Judging the judges' (2009) 159 NLJ 1154

Stevens, R, *The Independence of the Judiciary*, 1993, Oxford: OUP

Stevens, R, *The English Judge: Their Role in the Changing Constitution*, 2002, Oxford: Hart Publishing

Of general, as well as specific subject, interest, are the following books, written by two of the most erudite and literary of recent judges.

Bingham, T, *The Business of Judging: Selected Essays and Speeches: 1985–1999* and *Lives of the Law: Selected Essays and Speeches: 2000–2010*, 2011, Oxford: OUP

Sedley S, *Ashes and Sparks: Essays On Law and Justice*, 2011, Cambridge: CUP

USEFUL WEBSITE

www.bailii.org/databases.html
A list of the databases that BAILII holds.

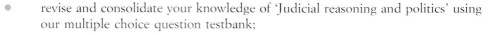

COMPANION WEBSITE

Now visit the companion website to:

- test your understanding of the key terms using our Flashcard Glossary;
- revise and consolidate your knowledge of 'Judicial reasoning and politics' using our multiple choice question testbank;
- view the link to the Useful Website above.

www.routledge.com/cw/slapper

14.1 INTRODUCTION

examples such as the *Clive Ponting* case with the series of miscarriages of justice relating to suspected terrorists in which juries were also involved.

Darbyshire is certainly correct in taking to task those who would simply endorse the jury system in an unthinking, purely emotional manner. With equal justification, she criticises those academic writers who focus attention on the mystery of the jury to the exclusion of the hard reality of the magistrates' court. It is arguable, however, that she goes to the other extreme. Underlying her analysis and conclusions is the idea that 'the jury trial is primarily ideological' and that 'its symbolic significance is magnified beyond its practical significance by the media, as well as academics, thus unwittingly misleading the public'. While one might not wish to contradict the suggestion that the jury system operates as a very powerful ideological symbol, supposedly grounding the criminal legal system within a framework of participative democracy and justifying it on that basis, it is simply inadequate to reject the practical operation of the procedure on that basis alone. Ideologies do not exist purely in the realm of ideas; they have real, concrete manifestations and effects – in relation to the jury system, those manifestations operate in such a way as to offer at least a vestige of protection to defendants. In regard to the comparison between juries and the summary procedure of the magistrates' courts, Darbyshire puts two related questions. First, she asks whether the jury system is more likely to do justice and get the verdict right than the magistrates' courts; then she goes on to ask why the majority of defendants are processed through the magistrates' courts. These questions are highly pertinent; it is doubtful, however, whether her response to them is equally pertinent. Her answers would likely be that the jury does not perform any better than the magistrates and, therefore, it is immaterial that the magistrates deal with the bulk of cases. Her whole approach would seem to be concentrated on denigrating the performance of the jury system. A not untypical passage from her article admits that, in relation to the suspect terrorist miscarriages of justice, juries 'were not to blame for these wrongful convictions'. However, she then goes on in the same sentence to accuse the juries of failing 'to remedy the lack of due process at the pre-trial stage', and thus blames them for not providing 'the brake on oppressive State activity claimed for the jury by its defenders'.

Although there is most certainly scope for a less romantic view of how the jury system actually operates in practice, Darbyshire's argument seems to be that the magistrates are not very good but then neither are the juries; and as they only operate in a small minority of cases anyway, the implication would seem to be that their loss would be no great disadvantage. Others, however, would maintain that the jury system does achieve concrete benefits in particular circumstances and would argue further that these benefits should not be readily given up. Among the latter is Michael Mansfield QC who, in an article in response to the Runciman Report, claimed that the jury 'is the most democratic element of our judicial system' and the one that 'poses the biggest threat to the authorities'. (These questions will be considered further in relation to future jury reform at 14.7.)

Having defended the institution of the jury generally, it has to be recognised that there are particular instances that tend to bring the jury system into disrepute. For example, in October 1994, the Court of Appeal ordered the retrial of a man convicted of double murder on the grounds that four of the jurors had attempted to contact the alleged victims using a Ouija board in what was described as a 'drunken experiment' (*R v Young* (1995)). A second convicted murderer appealed against his conviction on the grounds of irregularities in the manner in which the jury performed its functions. Among the allegations levelled at the jury was the claim that they clubbed together and spent £150 on drink when they were sent to a hotel after failing to reach a verdict. It was alleged that some of the jurors discussed the case, against the express instructions of the judge, and that on the following day the jury foreman had to be replaced because she was too hungover to act. One female juror was alleged to have ended up in bed with another hotel guest.

A truly remarkable case came to light in December 2000 when a trial, which had been going on for 10 weeks, was stopped on the grounds that a female juror was conducting what were referred to as 'improper relations' with a male member of the jury protection force who had been allocated to look after the jury during the trial. The relationship had become apparent after the other members of the jury had found out that they were using their mobile phones to send text messages to one another during breaks in the trial. That aborted trial was estimated to have cost £1.5 million, but it emerged that this was the second time the case had had to be stopped on account of inappropriate behaviour on the part of jury members. The first trial had been abandoned after some of the jury were found playing cards when they should have been deliberating on the case.

Another example of the possible criticisms to be levelled against the misuse of juries occurred in Stoke-on-Trent, where the son of a court usher and another six individuals were found to have served on a number of criminal trial juries. While one could praise the public-spirited nature of this dedication to the justice process, especially given the difficulty in getting members of jury panels, it might be more appropriate to condemn the possibility of the emergence of a professional juror system connected to court officials. Certainly, the Court of Appeal was less than happy with the situation, and overturned a conviction when the Stoke practice was revealed to it.

Over the past 15 years, the operation of the jury system has been subject to one Royal Commission (Runciman), one review (Auld) and several statutory attempts to alter it. An examination of these various endeavours will be postponed until the end of this chapter; for the moment, attention will be focused on the jury system as it currently functions.

14.2 THE ROLE OF THE JURY

It is generally accepted that the function of the jury is to decide on matters of fact, and that matters of law are the province of the judge. Such may be the ideal case, but most of the time the jury's decision is based on a consideration of a mixture of fact and law. The jurors determine whether a person is guilty on the basis of their understanding of the law as explained to them by the judge.

The oath taken by each juror states that they 'will faithfully try the defendant and give a true verdict according to the evidence', and it is contempt of court for a juror subsequent to being sworn in to refuse to come to a decision. In 1997, Judge Anura Cooray sentenced two women jurors to 30 days in prison for contempt of court for their failure to deliver a verdict. One of the women, who had been the jury foreman, claimed that the case, involving an allegation of fraud, had been too complicated to understand, and the other had claimed that she could not ethically judge anyone. Judge Cooray was quoted (*The Guardian*, 26 March 1997) as justifying his decision to imprison them on the grounds that:

> I had to order a re-trial at very great expense. Jurors must recognise that they have a responsibility to fulfil their duties in accordance with their oath.

The women spent only one night in jail before the uproar caused by Cooray's action led to their release and the subsequent overturning of his sentence on them.

It should be appreciated that serving on a jury can be an extremely harrowing experience. Jurors are the arbiters of fact, but the facts they have to contend with can be horrific. Criticisms have been levelled at the way in which the jury system can subject people to what in other contexts would be pornography, of either a sexual or violent kind, and yet offer them no counselling when their jury service comes to an end. Many jurors fear reprisals from defendants and their associates. In April 2003, two illegal immigrants, Baghdad Meziane and Brahim Benmerzouga, were convicted of various offences under the Terrorism Act 2000. It appears that they had raised hundreds of thousands of pounds for al-Qaida and other radical Islamic organisations. The trial at Leicester Crown Court became a 'drama unprecedented in legal history' (S Bird, 'Jurors too scared to take on case', *The Times*, 2 April 2003):

> The case began in February, amid extraordinary security arrangements. A jury was sworn in and retired overnight . . . The next morning one frightened female juror had worked herself up into such a state that she vomited in the jury room. Two others burst into tears . . . The jury was dismissed – as was a second after a male juror expressed fears for his family's safety.

The third jury was down to nine members when it was time to deliver a verdict, which it duly did: a verdict of guilty, the accused receiving sentences of 11 years.

The only recognition currently available is that the judge can exempt them from further jury service for a particular period. Many would argue that such limited recognition of the damage that jurors might sustain in performing their civic duty is simply inadequate. Jury service can make excessive (many would say unreasonable) demands on jurors. In May 2005 a fraud trial collapsed after jurors had spent almost two years at the Old Bailey in London (see, further, 14.6.2.2).

14.3   THE JURY'S FUNCTION IN TRIALS

Judges have the power to direct juries to acquit the accused where there is insufficient evidence to convict them, and this is the main safeguard against juries finding defendants guilty in spite of either the absence, or the insufficiency, of the evidence. There is, however, no corresponding judicial power to instruct juries to convict (*DPP v Stonehouse* (1978); *R v Wang* (2005)). That being said, there is nothing to prevent the judge summing up in such a way as to make it evident to the jury that there is only one decision that can reasonably be made, and that it would be perverse to reach any other verdict but guilty.

What judges must not do is overtly put pressure on juries to reach guilty verdicts. Finding of any such pressure will result in the overturning of any conviction so obtained. The classic example of such a case is *R v McKenna* (1960), in which the judge told the jurors, after they had spent all of two-and-a-quarter hours deliberating on the issue, that if they did not come up with a verdict in the following 10 minutes, they would be locked up for the night. Not surprisingly, the jury returned a verdict; unfortunately for the defendant, it was a guilty verdict; even more unfortunately for the judicial process, the conviction had to be quashed on appeal for clear interference with the jury.

In the words of Cassels J:

> It is a cardinal principle of our criminal law that in considering their verdict, concerning, as it does, the liberty of the subject, a jury shall deliberate in complete freedom, uninfluenced by any promise, unintimidated by any threat. They stand between the Crown and the subject, and they are still one of the main defences of personal liberty. To say to such a tribunal in the course of its deliberations that it must reach a conclusion . . . is a disservice to the cause of justice (*R v McKenna* [1960] 1 All ER 326 at 3290).

Judges do have the right, and indeed the duty, to advise the jury as to the proper understanding and application of the law that it is considering. Even when the jury is considering its verdict, it may seek the advice of the judge. The essential point, however, is that any such response on the part of the judge must be given in open court, so as to obviate any allegation of misconduct (*R v Townsend* (1982)).

In *R v Arshid Khan* (2008) Khan appealed against convictions on the ground that the judge at his trial had permitted new evidence to be put to the jury after it had retired to consider its verdict. The situation arose as a result of the jury returning to the court to ask for clarification of evidence relating to mobile phone calls. After the judge had answered the jury's questions, one of Khan's lawyers made further investigations which revealed that the evidence presented to the jury was inaccurate. The judge was informed of this fact and the jury was re-assembled within two hours of it having been given the information in answer to its questions.

The judge then informed the jury that some of the information may not have been correct. The jury were then told to go home and to return the following morning to resume their deliberations.

Further investigations revealed that the evidence presented to the jury was in fact inaccurate. On the following morning Khan's lawyers discussed the results of the investigation with him. And on the understanding that the new evidence might strengthen his case, he agreed that it should be put before the jury. Nonetheless, the jury returned guilty verdicts in relation to the charges against Khan, who subsequently appealed on the ground that the judge had erred in law in permitting the additional evidence to be put before the jury after it had retired.

In rejecting the appeal the Court of Appeal found that there was no reason in principle why the judge should not have agreed to allow the new evidence to be put before the jury. On the contrary, as they stated:

> [W]e can see every reason why he should have allowed this evidence to go before the jury. The defence invited the judge to do so on the basis that the evidence assisted the appellant's case. It was evidence which trial counsel believed was capable of supporting the appellant's case in an area which both counsel felt the appellant's evidence was weak and required some support. We have no doubt that the appellant agreed to this course of action.

On that basis the court rejected Khan's appeal.

The decision in *Khan* reflects the changed approach of the courts to such situations, as historically the authorities support the view that there was an absolute principle that no further evidence should be given after the judge's summing-up has been concluded and the jury has retired. Thus in *R v Owen* (1952), in which the trial judge allowed a doctor who had already given evidence in the case to be recalled to give evidence in answer to a question raised by the jury after their retirement, the subsequent conviction was quashed. The reason stated by Lord Goddard LCJ was that 'once the summing up is concluded, no further evidence ought to be given. The jury can be instructed in reply to any question they may put on any matter on which evidence has been given, but no further evidence should be allowed.'

Subsequently, in *R v Sanderson* (1953), the Court of Criminal Appeal, including Lord Goddard CJ, held that it was permissible for the evidence of a witness for the defence to be taken after the summing up had been completed, *but before the jury had retired*, and the 'very strict rule' that no evidence whatever must be introduced after the jury had retired was reiterated by Lord Parker CJ in *R v Gearing* (1968).

However, the introduction of the proviso under s 2(1) of the Criminal Appeal Act 1968 (see above, 9.5.2) led to a change in approach and in *R v Davis* (1976) the absolute nature of the rule was questioned and such an approach was approved of in *R v Karakaya* (2005).

More recently in *R v Hallam* (2007) the Court of Appeal actually held that a verdict was unsafe because a judge had refused to permit the jury to see a photograph which could potentially have assisted the appellant's defence, but which had come to light only after the summing-up. In that case the court defined the principle as follows:

> It used to be understood that there was a very firm rule that evidence cannot be admitted after the retirement of the jury, but more recent authorities confirm that there is no absolute rule to that effect. The question is what justice requires.

In criminal cases, even perversity of decision does not provide grounds for appeal against acquittal. There have been occasions where juries have been subjected to the invective of a judge when they have delivered a verdict with which he disagreed. Nonetheless, the fact is that juries collectively, and individual jurors, do not have to justify, explain or even give reasons for their decisions. Indeed, under s 8 of the Contempt of Court Act 1981, it would be a contempt of court to try to elicit such information from a jury member in either a criminal or a civil law case.

In *Attorney General v Associated Newspapers* (1994), the House of Lords held that it was contempt of court for a newspaper to publish disclosures by jurors of what took place in the jury room while they were considering their verdict, unless the publication amounted to no more than a re-publication of facts already known. It was decided that the word 'disclose' in s 8(1) applied not just to jurors, but to any others who published their revelations.

In an interview for *The Times* in January 2001, the Lord Chief Justice, Lord Woolf, expressed himself very strongly in favour of lifting the ban on jury research, though he emphasised that great care was needed in the conduct of any such research.

These factors place juries in a very strong position to take decisions that are 'unjustifiable' in accordance with the law, for the simple reason that they do not have to justify the decisions. Thus, juries have been able to deliver what can only be described as perverse decisions. In *R v Clive Ponting* (1985), the judge made clear beyond doubt that the defendant was guilty, under the Official Secrets Act 1911, of the offence with which he was charged: the jury still returned a not guilty verdict. Similarly, in the case of Pat Pottle and Michael Randall, who had openly admitted their part in the escape of the spy George Blake, the jury reached a not guilty verdict in open defiance of the law.

In *R v Kronlid* (1996), three protestors were charged with committing criminal damage, and another was charged with conspiracy to cause criminal damage, in relation to an attack on Hawk jet aeroplanes that were about to be sent to Indonesia. The damage to the planes allegedly amounted to £1.5 million and they did not deny their responsibility for it. They rested their defence on the fact that the planes were to be delivered to the Indonesian state, to be used in its allegedly genocidal campaign against the people of East Timor. On those grounds, they claimed that they were in fact acting to prevent the crime of genocide. The prosecution cited assurances, given by the Indonesian government, that the planes would not be used against the East Timorese, and pointed out that the UK government had granted an export licence for the planes. As the protestors did not deny what they had done, it was apparently a mere matter of course that they would be convicted as charged. The jury, however, decided that all four of the accused were innocent of the charges laid against them. A government Treasury minister, Michael Jack, subsequently expressed his disbelief at the verdict of the jury. As he stated:

> I, and I am sure many others, find this jury's decision difficult to understand. It would appear there is little question about who did this damage. For whatever reason that damage was done, it was just plain wrong (*The Independent*, 1 August 1996).

As stated above, jurors swear to return 'a true verdict according to the evidence'. Such verdicts may be politically inconvenient.

It is perhaps just such a lack of understanding, together with the desire to save money on the operation of the legal system, that has motivated the government's expressed wish to replace jury trials in relation to either-way offences (see below, 14.8). In any event, juries continue to reach perverse decisions where they are sympathetic to the causes pursued by the defendants. Thus, in September 2000, 28 Greenpeace volunteers, including its executive director Lord Melchett, were found not guilty of criminal damage after they had destroyed a field containing genetically modified (GM) maize. They had been found not guilty of theft in their original trial in April of that year. Judge David Mellor told the jury:

> It is not about whether GM crops are a good thing for the environment or a bad thing. It is for you to listen to the evidence and reach honest conclusions as to the facts.

However, the jury seemed to have adopted a different approach.

Fear of not achieving a successful conviction also appears to be the reason behind the CPS's belated decision, in February 2004, not to pursue the prosecution of Katherine Gun. Gun was the former GCHQ translator who revealed that the UK and the US were involved in spying on members of the United Nations before a crucial vote on whether the 2003 war on Iraq would be sanctioned by the UN. Although she admitted she was the source of the leak and was consequently, at least *prima facie*, in breach of the Official Secrets Act, her prosecution was dropped after she had put forward the defence of necessity. The decision was apparently taken on the guidance of the Attorney General, who was involved in the Iraq question from the beginning, being the source of the government's advice that the war was legal without the need for a specific resolution to that effect by the United Nations. In September 2008, six Greenpeace climate change activists were cleared of causing £30,000 of criminal damage at a coal-fired power station in Kent. They had admitted trying to shut down the station by occupying the smokestack and painting the word 'Gordon' down the chimney. However, the jury found them not guilty on the basis of their defence, which was that they were justified in their action as they were acting to prevent climate change causing greater damage to property around the world. In his summing-up at the end of an eight-day trial, the judge, David Caddick, said the case centred on whether or not the protestors had a lawful excuse for their actions, and the jury found that they did.

A non-political example of this type of case can be seen in the jury's refusal to find Stephen Owen guilty of any offence after he had discharged a shotgun at the driver of a lorry that had killed his child. And in September 2000, a jury in Carlisle found Lezley Gibson not guilty on a charge of possession of cannabis after she told the court that she needed it to relieve the symptoms of the multiple sclerosis from which she suffered. The tendency of the jury occasionally to ignore legal formality in favour of substantive justice is one of the major points in favour of its retention, according to its proponents.

14.3.1   APPEALS FROM DECISIONS OF THE JURY

In criminal law, it is an absolute rule that there can be no appeal against a jury's decision to acquit a person of the charges laid against him. Although there is no appeal as such against acquittal, there does exist the possibility of the Attorney General referring the case to the Court of Appeal, to seek its advice on points of law raised in criminal cases in which the defendant has been acquitted. This procedure was provided for under s 36 of the Criminal Justice Act (CJA) 1972, although it is not commonly resorted to. It must be stressed that there is no possibility of the actual case being reheard or the acquittal decision being reversed, but the procedure can highlight mistakes in law made in the course of Crown Court trial and permits the Court of Appeal to remedy the defect for the future. (See *Attorney General's Reference (No 1 of 1988)* (1988) for an example of this procedure, in the area of insider dealing in relation to shares on the Stock Exchange. This case is also interesting in relation to statutory interpretation. See also *Attorney General's Reference (No 3 of 1999)*, considered above at 12.3.2.)

In civil law cases, the possibility of the jury's verdict being overturned on appeal does exist, but only in circumstances where the original verdict was perverse; that is, no reasonable jury properly directed could have made such a decision (see *Grobbelaar v NGN Ltd* at 14.6.1).

14.3.2   MAJORITY VERDICTS

The possibility of a jury deciding a case on the basis of a majority decision was introduced by the CJA 1967. Prior to this, the requirement was that jury decisions had to be unanimous. Such decisions are acceptable where there are:

- no fewer than 11 jurors and 10 of them agree; or
- there are 10 jurors and nine of them agree.

Where a jury has reached a guilty verdict on the basis of a majority decision, s 17(3) of the Juries Act (JA) 1974 requires the foreman of the jury to state in open court the number of jurors who agreed and the number who disagreed with the verdict. See *R v Barry* (1975), where failure to declare the details of the voting split resulted in the conviction of the defendant being overturned. In *R v Pigg* (1983), the House of Lords held that it was unnecessary to state the number who voted against where the foreman stated the number in favour of the verdict, and thus the determination of the minority was a matter of simple arithmetic.

However, in *R v Mendy* (1992), when the clerk of the court asked the foreman of the jury how a guilty decision had been reached, he replied that it was 'by the majority of us all'. The ambiguity of the reply is obvious when it is taken out of context and this was relied on in a successful appeal. It was simply not clear whether it referred to a unanimous verdict, as the court at first instance had understood it, or whether it referred to a real majority vote, in which case it failed to comply with the requirement of s 17(3) as applied in *R v Barry*. The Court of Appeal held that in such a situation, the defendant had to be given the benefit of any doubt and he was discharged.

The Court of Appeal adopted a different approach in *R v Millward* (1999). The appellant had been convicted, at Stoke-on-Trent Crown Court, of causing grievous bodily harm. Although the jury actually had reached a majority decision, the foreman in response to the questioning of the clerk of the court mistakenly stated that it was the verdict of them all. The following day, the foreman informed the judge that the verdict had in fact been a majority verdict of 10 for guilty and two against.

The Court of Appeal met the subsequent challenge with the following exercise in sophisticated reasoning. The court at first instance had apparently accepted a unanimous verdict. Therefore, s 17 had not been brought into play at all. And, bearing in mind s 8 of the Contempt of Court Act 1981, discouraging the disclosure of votes cast by jurors in the course of their deliberations, the issue had to be viewed under the policy of the law. It would set a very dangerous precedent if an apparently unanimous verdict of a jury delivered in open court, and not then challenged by any juror, was reopened and subjected to scrutiny. It would be difficult to see how the court could properly investigate a disagreement as to whether jurors had dissented or not. In the instant case, there was a proper majority direction and proper questions asked of the jury and apparently proper and unambiguous answers given without challenge. Therefore, there should be no further inquiry.

There is no requirement for the details of the voting to be declared in a majority decision of not guilty.

14.3.3 DISCHARGE OF JURORS OR THE JURY

The trial judge may discharge the whole jury if certain irregularities occur. These would include the situation where the defendant's previous convictions are revealed inadvertently during the trial. Such a disclosure would be prejudicial to the defendant. In such a case, the trial would be ordered to commence again with a different jury. Individual jurors may be discharged by the judge if they are incapable of continuing to act through illness 'or for any other reason' (s 16(1) of the Juries Act (JA) 1974). Where this happens, the jury must not fall below nine members.

14.4 THE SELECTION OF THE JURY

In theory, jury service is a public duty that citizens should readily undertake. In practice, it is made compulsory, and failure to perform one's civic responsibility is subject to the sanction of a £1,000 fine.

14.4.1 LIABILITY TO SERVE

The JA 1974, as amended by the CJA 1988 and the CJA 2003, sets out the law relating to juries. Prior to the JA 1974, there was a property qualification in respect to jury service that skewed jury membership towards middle-class men. Now, the legislation provides that any person between the ages of 18 and 75, who is on the electoral register and who has lived in the UK for at least five years, is qualified to serve as a juror. The upper age limit was raised to 75 by the Criminal Justice and Courts Act 2015 s 68, although not brought into effect until December 2016.

The procedure for establishing a jury is a threefold process:

- An officer of the court summons a randomly selected number of qualified individuals from the electoral register.
- From that group, panels of potential jurors for various cases are drawn up.
- The actual jurors are then randomly selected by means of a ballot in open court.

As has been pointed out, however, even if the selection procedure were truly random, randomness does not equal representation. Random juries, by definition, could be all male, all female, all white, all black, all Conservative or all members of the Monster Raving Loony Party. Such is the nature of the random process; the question that arises from the process is whether such randomness is necessarily a good thing in itself, and whether the summoning officer should take steps to avoid the potential disadvantages that can result from random selection.

As regards the actual random nature of the selection process, a number of problems arise from the use of electoral registers to determine and locate jurors:

- Electoral registers tend to be inaccurate. Generally, they misreport the number of younger people who are in an area simply because younger people tend to move about more than older people and therefore tend not to appear on the electoral roll of the place in which they currently live.
- Electoral registers tend to under-report the number of members of ethnic minorities in a community. The problem is that some members of the ethnic communities, for a variety of reasons, simply do not notify the authorities of their existence.
- The problem of non-registration mentioned above was compounded by the disappearance of a great many people from electoral registers in order to try to avoid payment of the former poll tax. It has been suggested that the alteration of the registration procedure to an individual voluntary process from a compulsory household process will have an even greater impact on the register of voters.

14.4.2 INELIGIBILITY EXCEPTIONS, DISQUALIFICATION AND EXCUSAL

Prior to the CJA 2003, the general qualification for serving as a juror was subject to a number of exceptions.

A variety of people were deemed to be ineligible to serve on juries on the basis of their employment or vocation. Among this category were: judges; Justices of the Peace; members of the legal profession; police and probation officers; and members of the clergy or religious orders. Those suffering from a mental disorder were also deemed to be ineligible. Paragraph 2 of Sched 33 to the CJA 2003 removes the first three groups of persons ineligible – the judiciary, others concerned with the administration of justice, and the clergy – leaving only mentally disordered persons with that status.

This reform came into effect in April 2005. The extent to which 'ordinary' jurors will be influenced by contact with solicitors, barristers and judges remains to be seen (assuming that research into such matters is eventually permitted). In any event the provisions of the CJA 2003 as regards eligibility to serve were challenged, as being contrary to Art 6 of the ECHR, in *R v (1) Abdroikov (2) Green (3) Williamson* (2005), three otherwise unrelated cases. Each of the appellants appealed against their convictions on the grounds that the jury in their respective trials had contained members who were employed in the criminal justice system. The juries in the trials of the first and second appellants had contained serving police officers. The jury in the trial of the third appellant had contained a person employed as a prosecuting solicitor by the CPS. Their proposal was that, as prior to the CJA 2003 there would have been no doubt that the presence of such people on juries would have been unlawful, so their presence in the current cases ran contrary to the need for trials to be free from even the taint of apparent bias.

The Court of Appeal rejected such arguments as spurious, holding that the expectations placed on ordinary citizens in relation to jury service had to be extended to members of the criminal justice system.

However, by a majority of three to two the House of Lords held that the appeals of Green and Williamson should succeed, but that Abdroikov's appeal must fail. Lords Rodger and Carswell, in the minority, held that all the appeals should fail. In reaching its decision the majority looked at the reports of previous committees that had been tasked with examining the operation of juries. Thus they referred to the findings of the 1965 committee chaired by Lord Morris of Borth-y-Gest, which recommended that the police and those professionally concerned in the administration of the law should continue to be ineligible. Then in 2001, Auld LJ reviewed the issue and recommended that everyone should be eligible for jury service save for the mentally ill. He recognised that the risk of bias could not be totally eradicated and envisaged that any question about the risk of bias on the part of any juror could be resolved by the trial judge on the facts of the case. His recommendation was given effect by the Criminal Justice Act 2003 s 321. However, as the House of Lords made clear, Auld LJ's expectation that each doubtful case would be resolved by the trial judge could not be met if neither the judge nor counsel knew that the juror was a police officer or CPS solicitor. The House of Lords recognised that there were situations where police officers and CPS solicitors would meet the tests of impartiality; however, that did not mean they would always do so automatically.

However, according to Lords Rodger and Carswell in the minority, Parliament had endorsed the view that universal eligibility for jury service was to be regarded as appropriate. In reaching that conclusion Parliament had to be taken to have been aware of the test for apparent bias. It must, therefore, be taken to have considered that the risk of bias in the case of serving police officers or CPS solicitors was manageable within the system of jury trial. The consequence of the House of Lords majority decision was pointed out by Lord Rodger in the clearest of terms:

> I can see no reason why the fair-minded and informed observer should single out juries with police officers and CPS lawyers as being constitutionally incapable of following the judge's directions and reaching an impartial verdict. It must be assumed, for instance, that the observer considers that there is no real possibility that a jury containing a gay man trying a man accused of a homophobic attack will, for that reason alone, be incapable of reaching an unbiased verdict, even though the juror might readily identify with a fellow gay man. Despite this – if Mr Green's appeal is to be allowed – the observer must be supposed to consider that there is, inevitably, a real possibility that a jury will have been biased in a case involving a significant conflict of evidence between a police witness and the defendant, just because the witness and a police officer juror serve in the same borough or the juror serves in a force which commits its work to the trial court in question. Similarly, if Mr Williamson's appeal is allowed, the observer must be taken to consider that the same applies to any jury containing a CPS lawyer whenever the prosecution is brought by the CPS. In my view, an observer who singled out juries with these two types of members would be applying a different standard from the one that is usually applied. For no good reason, the observer would be virtually ignoring the other 11 jurors . . . your Lordships' decision to allow two of the appeals will drive a coach and horses through Parliament's legislation and will go far to reverse its reform of the law, *even though the statutory provisions themselves are not said to be incompatible with Convention rights*. Moreover, any requirement for police officers and CPS lawyers balloted to serve on a jury to identify themselves routinely to the judge would discriminate against them by introducing a process of vetting for them and them alone. Parliament cannot have considered that such a requirement was necessary since it did not impose it. The rational policy of the legislature is to decide who are eligible to serve as jurors and then to treat them all alike (emphasis added).

The issue of apparent juror bias on account of their occupation was considered further by the Court of Appeal in six conjoined cases in March 2008: *R v Khan* (2008). The occupations involved were those of serving police officers, employees of the CPS – although on this occasion in a prosecution brought by the Department of Trade and Industry – and prison officers. The judgment of the Court of Appeal was delivered by the then Lord Chief Justice, Lord Phillips, in the course of which he explained that, although the CJA 2003 had abolished automatic disqualification from jury service on account of an occupation associated with the administration of justice, it had not made those persons immune to claims of apparent bias and that 'the nature of some occupations is such that there is an obvious danger that the circumstances of a prosecution will give rise to an appearance of bias in relation to those who belong to them'. In its consideration of the issues, the Court of Appeal distinguished between apparent bias towards *a party* in the case and apparent bias towards *a witness* in the case. In the former instance, should it become apparent during a trial that a juror is partial then they should be discharged. If the bias only becomes apparent after the verdict, then the conviction must be quashed. However, the Court held that apparent bias towards *a witness* does not, automatically, have those consequences, and will do so only if it would appear to the fair-minded observer that the juror's apparent bias may affect, or have affected, the outcome of the trial. The fair-minded observer test was established in the House of Lords in *Porter v Magill* (2001).

As regards serving police officers, the Court of Appeal could find no clear principles for identifying apparent bias from the majority judgments in *R v Abdroikov*, but went on to hold that although such jurors may seem likely to favour the evidence of a fellow police officer, that would not automatically lead to the appearance that they favoured the prosecution. For example, if the police evidence was not challenged or was not an important part of the prosecution case, then there would be no reason to suspect bias on the part of the juror. It would only be appropriate to question a conviction for apparent bias if, and only if, the effect of the juror's partiality towards a fellow officer put in doubt the safety of the conviction and thus rendered the trial unfair.

More specifically, the court rejected the proposition that the mere fact that a police officer had taken part in operations involving the type of offence with which a defendant was charged gave rise, of itself, to an appearance of bias on the part of the police officer. As the court pointed out, police officers are likely to have had experience of most of the common types of criminal offence, not least drug dealing. Finally, as regards police jurors, the fact that the jury was told that a defendant had a previous conviction for assaulting a police officer would not of itself raise the issue of apparent bias.

As seen above, in *Abdroikov*, the majority of the House of Lords held that a juror who was a member of the Crown Prosecution Service had the appearance of bias where they acted as a juror in a case prosecuted by their employer. However, the Court of Appeal distinguished the situation under its consideration from that case in holding that there could be no objection to a member of the CPS sitting in a case prosecuted by some other authority, in this particular instance the Department of Trade and Industry.

With regard to the possibility of prison guards acting as jurors, the Court of Appeal made it clear that the mere suspicion that a juror might, by reason of employment in a prison where a defendant had been held, have acquired knowledge of that defendant's bad character could not, of itself, lead an objective observer to conclude that the juror had an appearance of bias. Where the juror had no knowledge of the defendant, there could be no objective basis for imputing bias towards the defendant. Indeed, even actual knowledge of a defendant's bad character would not automatically result in the juror ceasing to qualify as independent and impartial.

In concluding his judgment, Lord Phillips emphasised the court's concern with the need to regularise, and thus avoid appeals from, cases raising the issue of juror bias in relation to particular occupations. As he put it:

> It is undesirable that the apprehension of jury bias should lead to appeals such as those with which this court has been concerned. It is particularly

undesirable if such appeals lead to the quashing of convictions so that re-trials have to take place. In order to avoid this it is desirable that any risk of jury bias, or of unfairness as a result of partiality to witnesses, should be identified before the trial begins. If such a risk may arise, the juror should be stood down . . . It is essential that the trial judge should be aware at the stage of jury selection if any juror in waiting is, or has been, a police officer or a member of the prosecuting authority, or is a serving prison officer. Those called for jury service should be required to record on the appropriate form whether they fall into any of these categories, so that this information can be conveyed to the judge. We invite all of these authorities and Her Majesty's Court Service to consider the implications of this judgment and to issue such directions as they consider appropriate.

In an endeavour to maintain the unquestioned probity of the jury system, certain categories of persons are disqualified from serving as jurors. Among these are anyone who has been sentenced to a term of imprisonment, or youth custody, of five years or more. In addition, anyone who, in the past 10 years, has served a sentence, or has had a suspended sentence imposed on them, or has had a community punishment order made against them, is also disqualified. The CJA 2003 makes a number of amendments to reflect recent and forthcoming developments in sentencing legislation. Thus, juveniles sentenced under s 91 of the Powers of Criminal Courts (Sentencing) Act 2000 to detention for life, or for a term of five years or more, will be disqualified for life from jury service. People sentenced to imprisonment or detention for public protection, or to an extended sentence under ss 227 or 228 of the Act, are also to be disqualified for life from jury service. Anyone who has received a community order (as defined in s 177 of the Act) will be disqualified from jury service for 10 years. Those on bail in criminal proceedings are disqualified from serving as a juror in the Crown Court.

Certain people were excused as of right from serving as jurors on account of their jobs, age or religious views. Among these were members of the medical professions, Members of Parliament and members of the armed forces, together with anyone over 65 years of age. Paragraph 3 of Sched 33 to the CJA 2003 repeals s 9(1) of the JA 1974 and consequently no one will in future be entitled to excusal as of right from jury service.

It has always been the case that if a person who has been summoned to do jury service could show that there was a 'good reason' why their summons should be deferred or excused, s 9 of the JA 1974 provided discretion to defer or excuse service. With the abolition of most of the categories of ineligibility and of the availability of excusal as of right, it is expected that there will be a corresponding increase in applications for excusal or deferral under s 9 being submitted to the Jury Central Summoning Bureau (see below).

Grounds for such excusal or deferral are supposed to be made only on the basis of good reason, but there is at least a measure of doubt as to the rigour with which such rules are applied.

A Practice Note issued in 1988 (now *Practice Direction (Criminal: Consolidated)* [2002] 1 WLR 2870, para 42) stated that applications for excusal should be treated sympathetically and listed the following as good grounds for excusal:

(a)   personal involvement in the case;
(b)   close connection with a party or a witness in the case;
(c)   personal hardship;
(d)   conscientious objection to jury service.

However, a new s 9AA, introduced by the CJA 2003, placed a statutory duty on the Lord Chancellor, in whom current responsibility for jury summoning is vested, to publish and lay before Parliament guidelines relating to the exercise by the Jury Central Summoning Bureau of its functions in relation to discretionary deferral and excusal.

The guidelines were issued in 2004 and make clear that only in extreme circumstances should a person be excused from jury service. They require summoning officers to refuse requests in the absence of 'good reason'. Even where 'good reason' is shown why the person should not sit on the date they have been summoned, deferral should always be considered in the first instance. Excusal from jury service should be reserved only for those cases where the jury summoning officer is satisfied that it would be unreasonable to require the person to serve at any time within the following 12 months.

The previous, somewhat antiquated procedure for selecting potential jury members, with its accompanying disparity of treatment, was modernised by the introduction of a Central Summoning Bureau based at Blackfriars Crown Court Centre in London. The Bureau uses a computer system to select jurors at random from the electoral registers and issue the summonses, as well as dealing with jurors' questions and requests. The jury summoning system is linked to the national police records system to allow checks to be made against potentially disqualified individuals.

However, severe doubts have been expressed as to the accuracy of the Police National Computer (PNC), which might not only render the checks on juries inaccurate, but might actually contravene the Data Protection Act 1998. When the Metropolitan Police conducted an audit of the PNC in 1999, it was found to have 'wholly unacceptable' levels of inaccuracy, with an overall error rate of 86 per cent. In one case in 2000 at Highbury Corner magistrates' court in north London, a man charged with theft of £2,700 was granted bail on the grounds that the PNC showed that he had no previous convictions. In fact, he was a convicted murderer released from prison on licence.

It has to be stated that, as reported in a parliamentary answer in February 2007, the Secretary of State for the Home Department intimated that later audits carried out in August 2002 had indicated that the general position on data accuracy was far more favourable than had previously been suggested. According to his statement, the exercise found that in 94 per cent of cases, the key information was recorded entirely accurately, and that in the remaining 6 per cent some inaccuracies were found but, in the majority of instances, the inaccuracy was not critical.

TABLE 14.1 *Reproduced from Ministry of Justice Report*

Crown Court
Jury Central Summoning Bureau figures,[1] 2007–2012

	2007	2008	2009	2010	2011	2012
Total number of summons issued[2,3] (r)	388,362	395,503	373,871	373,650	343,949	349,606
Total number of jurors supplied to the court	182,661	183,506	176,351	181,281	170,421	168,914
Deferred to serve at a later date	66,174	66,806	61,892	62,051	57,982	61,252
Number refused deferral	122	103	87	78	54	33
Excused by right having served in past two years	4,518	4,244	3,470	3,881	3,331	3,280
Excused for other reasons[4]	103,064	104,290	96,563	93,782	76,008	76,578
All excused	**107,582**	**108,534**	**100,033**	**97,663**	**79,339**	**79,858**
Number refused excusal	1,641	1,515	1,342	1,485	1,303	1,141
Disqualified – residency, mental disorders, criminality	94,171	96,325	92,704	96,482	89,668	88,836
Disqualified – on selection	58,900	59,017	56,967	56,871	52,115	50,538
Disqualified – failed Police National Computer check	207	225	220	215	239	648
Failed to reply to summons	40,635	45,192	49,086	47,221	43,663	41,925
Summons undelivered	18,325	17,603	13,646	12,916	12,583	13,066
Postponed by Jury Central Summoning Bureau	7,274	9,621	7,439	6,569	4,937	5,427

Source: Jury Central Summoning Bureau
Notes:

[1] Numbers do not add up to the overall total within a given year, as the data reflect rolling 12-month periods with 'carry-over' rules applied to certain rows in the table. For example, the number of disqualifications reported for a given year may include disqualifications for summons that were issued in previous years.

[2] Previously published figures for 2007 to 2009 double-counted summons that were re-issued due to a change in court venue. In this publication, these figures have been revised to remove any double counting.

[3] This figure represents the number of summons that were issued in a year and not the number of people that actually served on a jury in that year. For example, a person summoned for jury service in 2011 may not actually serve until 2012.

[4] Including childcare, work commitments, medical issues, language difficulties, student status, moved from area, travel difficulties and financial hardship.

In 2015 there were 179,200 jurors supplied to the court by the Central summoning Bureau; a total of 361,300 juror summons being issued with around 27 per cent of all juror summons being excused.

It is to be hoped that the situation of people with disabilities has been altered for the better by the Criminal Justice and Public Order Act (CJPOA) 1994, which introduced a new s 9B into the JA 1974. Previously, it was all too common for judges to discharge jurors with disabilities, including deafness, on the assumption that they would not be capable of undertaking the duties of a juror.

Under this provision, where it appears doubtful that a person summoned for jury service is capable of serving on account of some physical disability, that person, as previously, may be brought before the judge. The new s 9B, however, introduces a presumption that people should serve and provides that the judge shall affirm the jury summons unless he is of the opinion that the person will not be able to act effectively.

It would appear, however, that the CJPOA 1994 does not improve the situation of profoundly deaf people who could only function as jurors with the aid of a sign language interpreter. That was the outcome of a case decided in November 1999 that profoundly deaf Jeff McWhinney, Chief Executive of the British Deaf Association, could not serve as a juror. For him to do so would have required that he had the assistance of an interpreter in the jury room and that could not be allowed as, at present, only jury members are allowed into the jury room.

Any person who has suffered from 'a disorder or disability of the mind' and, because of that condition, regularly visits a medical practitioner for treatment, is precluded from jury service. As campaigners have pointed out, many people are being excluded from jury service after being treated for conditions such as depression, schizophrenia and bipolar disorder, which are all perfectly manageable through medication. As they also point out, one in four Britons suffers from mental illness at some point in their lives, and one in 10 is prescribed antidepressants.

In 2012 Gavin Barwell MP successfully introduced a Private Member's Bill, which became the Mental Health (Discrimination) Act 2013. The Act outlaws discrimination against people who have experienced mental ill health, in relation to jury service and membership of the House of Commons.

That juries can be 'self-selecting' provides grounds for concern as to the random nature of the jury, but the traditional view of the jury is further and perhaps even more fundamentally undermined by the way in which both prosecution and defence seek to influence its constitution.

Under s 12(6) of the JA 1974, both prosecution and defence have a right to challenge the array where the summoning officer has acted improperly in bringing the whole panel together. Such challenges are rare, although an unsuccessful action was raised in *R v Danvers* (1982), where the defendant tried to challenge the racial composition of the group of potential jurors.

Challenge by the defence

Until the CJA 1988, there were two ways in which the defence could challenge potential jurors:

- *Peremptory challenge*

  The defence could object to any potential jury members, up to a maximum number of three, without having to show any reason or justification for the challenge. Defence counsel used this procedure in an attempt to shape the composition of the jury in a way they thought might best suit their client, although it has to be said that it was an extremely inexact process, and one that could upset or antagonise rejected jurors. In spite of arguments for its retention on a civil liberties basis, the majority of the Roskill Committee on Fraud Trials (January 1986, HMSO) recommended that the right be abolished, and abolition was provided for in the CJA 1988.

- *Challenge for cause*

  The defence retains the power to challenge any number of potential jurors for cause, that is to say that there is a substantial reason why a particular person should not serve on the jury to decide a particular defendant's case. A simple example would be where the potential juror has had previous dealings with the defendant or has been involved in the case in some way. There may be less obvious grounds for objection, however, which may be based on the particular juror's attitudes, or indeed political beliefs. The question arises whether such factors provide grounds for challenge. In what is known as *The Angry Brigade* case in 1972 (see *The Times*, 10–11 December 1971; *The Times*, 12–15 December 1972), a group of people were charged with carrying out a bombing campaign against prominent members of the Conservative government. In the process of empanelling a jury, the judge asked potential jurors to exclude themselves on a variety of socio-political grounds, including active membership of the Conservative Party. As a consequence of the procedure adopted in that case, the Lord Chief Justice issued a practice direction in which he made it clear that potential jurors were not to be excluded on account of race, religion, politics or occupation. Since that practice direction, it is clear that the challenge for cause can only be used within a restricted sphere, and this makes it less useful to the defence than it might otherwise be if it were to operate in a more general way.

It has been argued that the desire of civil libertarians to retain the right of the defence to select a jury that might be more sympathetic to its case is contradictory, because although in theory they usually rely on the random nature of the jury to ensure the appearance of justice, in practice they seek to influence its composition. When, however, the shortcomings in the establishment of panels for juries is recalled, it might be countered that the defence is attempting to do no more than counter the inbuilt bias that ensues from the use of unbalanced electoral registers.

If the defence attempts to ensure that any jury will not be prejudiced against its case, if not predisposed towards it, the same is true of the prosecution. However, the prosecution has a greater scope to achieve such an aim. While the prosecution has the same right as the defence to challenge for cause, it has the additional option of excluding potential jury members by simply asking them to stand by until a jury has been empanelled. The request for the potential juror to stand by is only a provisional challenge and, in theory, the person stood by can at a later time take their place on the jury if there are no other suitable candidates. In practice, of course, it is unlikely in the extreme for there not to be sufficient alternative candidates to whom the prosecution do not object and prefer to the person stood by.

When the Roskill Committee recommended the removal of the defence's right to pre-emptive challenge, it recognised that, in order to retain an equitable situation, the right of the Crown to ask potential jurors to stand by should also be withdrawn. Unfortunately, although the government of the day saw fit to follow the Committee's recommendation in relation to the curtailment of the defence rights, it did not feel under the same obligation to follow its corresponding recommendation to curtail the rights of the prosecution. Thus, the CJA 1988 made no reference to the procedure and, in failing to do so, established a distinct advantage in favour of the prosecution in regard to selecting what it considered to be suitable juries.

The manifest unreasonableness of this procedure led to the Attorney General issuing a practice note (1988) to the effect that the Crown should only exercise its power to stand by potential jurors in the following two circumstances:

- To prevent the empanelment of a 'manifestly unsuitable' juror, with the agreement of the defence. The example given of 'manifest unsuitability' is an illiterate person asked to sit in a highly complex case. It is reasonable to doubt the ability of such a person to follow the process of the case involving a number of documents, and on that basis they should be stood by.
- In circumstances where the Attorney General has approved the vetting of the potential jury members and that process has revealed that the particular juror in question might be a security risk. In this situation, the Attorney General is also required to approve the use of the 'stand by' procedure.

Jury vetting is the process by which the Crown checks the background of potential jurors to assess their suitability to decide particular cases. The procedure is clearly contrary to the ideal of the jury being based on a random selection of people, but it is justified on the basis that it is necessary to ensure that jury members are not likely to divulge any secrets made open to them in the course of a sensitive trial or, alternatively, on the ground that jurors with extreme political views should not be permitted the opportunity to express those views in a situation where they might influence the outcome of a case.

The practice of vetting potential jurors developed after the *Angry Brigade* trial in 1972, but it did not become public until 1978. In that year, as a result of an Official Secrets Act case, known by the initials of the three defendants as the ABC trial, it became apparent that the list of potential jurors had been checked to establish their 'soundness'. As a consequence of that case, the Attorney General published the current guidelines for vetting jury panels. Since that date, the guidelines have been updated and the most recent guidelines were published in 1988. These guidelines maintain the general propositions that jury members should normally be selected at random from the panel and should be disqualified only on the grounds set out in the JA 1974. The guidelines do, however, make reference to exceptional cases of public importance where potential jury members might properly be vetted. Such cases are broadly identified as those involving national security, where part of the evidence may be heard *in camera*, and terrorist cases.

Vetting is a twofold process. An initial check into police criminal records and police Special Branch records should be sufficient to reveal whether a further investigation by the security services is required. Any further investigation requires the prior approval of the Attorney General.

In addition to vetting properly so called, the Court of Appeal in *R v Mason* (1980) approved the checking of criminal records to establish whether potential jurors had been convicted of criminal offences in the past and therefore were not eligible to serve as jurors. The Runciman Commission recommended that this process of checking on those who should be disqualified on the basis of previous criminal conviction should be regularised when the collection and storage of criminal records is centralised. This was achieved when the Criminal Records Bureau was established as a result of Part V of the Police Act 1997.

The racial mix of the jury

In *R v Danvers* (1982), the defence had sought to challenge the array on the basis that a black defendant could not have complete confidence in the impartiality of an all-white jury. The question of the racial mix of a jury has exercised the courts on a number of occasions. In *R v Ford* (1989), the trial judge's refusal to accept the defendant's application for a racially mixed jury was supported by the Court of Appeal on the grounds that 'fairness is achieved by the principle of random selection' as regards the make-up of a jury, and that to insist on a racially balanced jury would be contrary to that principle, and would be to imply that particular jurors were incapable of impartiality. A similar point was made in *R v Tarrant* (1997), in which a person accused of drug-related offences was convicted by a jury that had been selected from outside the normal catchment area for the court. The aim of the judge had been to minimise potential jury intimidation, but nonetheless, the Court of Appeal overturned the conviction on the grounds that the judge had deprived the defendant of a randomly selected jury.

To deny people the right to have their cases heard by representatives of their own race, on the basis of a refusal to recognise the existence of racial discriminatory attitudes, cannot but give the appearance of a society where such racist attitudes are institutionalised. This has particular resonance given the findings of the Macpherson Inquiry that the police force was 'institutionally racist'. Without suggesting that juries as presently constituted are biased, it remains arguable that if, in order to achieve the undoubted appearance of fairness, jury selection has to be manipulated to ensure a racial mix, then it should at least be considered.

An interesting case study in this respect is the trial in 1994 of Lakhbir Deol, an Asian who was accused of the murder of a white youth in Stoke-on-Trent in 1993. Mr Deol's lawyers sought to have the case moved from Stafford to Birmingham Crown Court on the grounds that Stafford has an almost completely white population, whereas Birmingham has an approximately 25 per cent ethnic minority population. Mr Justice McKinnon repeatedly refused the request and the trial was heard in Stafford as scheduled. Mr Deol was acquitted, so his fears were proved groundless, but surely the worrying fact is that he had those fears in the first place.

In February 2010 the report on empirical research carried out by Professor Cheryl Thomas for the Ministry of Justice stated that:

> While these findings strongly suggest that racially balanced juries are *not needed* to ensure fair decision-making in jury trials with BME (black and minority ethnic) defendants, concerns about *the appearance of fairness* with all-white juries may still remain (emphasis added).

It is heartening to note that the Runciman Commission fully endorsed the views expressed above and recommended that either the prosecution or the defence should be able to insist that up to three jury members be from ethnic minorities, and that at least one of those should be from the same ethnic minority as the accused or the victim. Sir Robin Auld, in his review of the criminal courts, also recommended that provision should be made to enable ethnic minority representation on juries where race is likely to be relevant to an important issue in the case.

In *R v Smith* (2003), the Court of Appeal reaffirmed the traditional view in holding that it had not been unfair for Smith to be tried by a randomly selected all-white jury. In addition, however, the Court held that the selection process had not infringed Smith's rights under Art 6 of the ECHR.

Another case that raised a human rights issue was *R v Mushtaq* (2002), in which the defendant appealed against his conviction for conspiracy to defraud. He had admitted to police that he had played a minor part in the conspiracy, but later claimed that his confession had been obtained by oppression. The judge ruled during the trial that Mushtaq's confession had not been obtained by oppression and was therefore admissible, and in his summing-up to the jury, he emphasised that the confession was central and crucial to the case. Mushtaq claimed that the judge's direction to the jury was in breach of Art 6 of the ECHR and that the jury, *as a separate and distinct public authority*, had a duty to protect his rights. The Court of Appeal dismissed the appeal, holding that the separate functions allocated to the judge and the jury in relation to disputed confessions had significant advantages for ensuring that justice was done. The admissibility of a confession was a matter for the judge and if the prosecution failed to satisfy the judge that a confession was not obtained by oppression, the jury would not hear it. This division of function between judge and jury complied with the requirement to provide an adequate safeguard for a defendant's Art 6 rights, and it could not be said that the jury was a separate public authority having a distinct and separate duty from the judge to protect Mushtaq's rights. In a criminal trial, it was the court acting collectively that had the shared responsibility of ensuring a fair trial.

14.5   RACIAL BIAS IN JURIES

If the law does not allow for the artificial creation of ethnic balance in juries, then it must ensure that ethnically unbalanced juries do not become ethnically biased ones.

In May 2000, the ECtHR held by a majority of four to three that the right of a British Asian to be tried by an impartial tribunal had been violated on the basis of alleged racism within the jury that had convicted him. Kuldip Sander had been charged with conspiracy to commit fraud and was tried at Birmingham Crown Court in March 1995. During the trial, one of the jurors sent a note to the judge stating:

> I have decided I cannot remain silent any longer. For some time during the trial I have been concerned that fellow jurors are not taking their duties seriously. At least two have been making openly racist remarks and jokes and I fear are going to convict the defendants not on the evidence but because they are Asian. My concern is the defendants will not therefore receive a fair verdict. Please could you advise me what I can do in this situation.

The judge adjourned the case, but kept the juror who had written the letter apart from the other jurors while he listened to submission from counsel in open court. The defence asked the judge to dismiss the jury on the ground that there was a real danger of bias. The judge, however, decided to call the jury back into court, at which stage the juror who had written the complaint joined the others. The judge read out the complaint to them and told them the following:

> I am not able to conduct an inquiry into the validity of those contentions and I do not propose to do so. This case has cost an enormous amount of money and I am not anxious to halt it at the moment, but I shall have no compunction in doing so if the situation demands . . . I am going to ask you

all to search your conscience overnight and if you feel that you are not able to try this case solely on the evidence and find that you cannot put aside any prejudices you may have will you please indicate that fact by writing a personal note to that effect and giving it to the jury bailiff on your arrival at court tomorrow morning. I will then review the position.

The next morning, the judge received two letters from the jury. The first letter, which was signed by all the jurors including the juror who had sent the complaint, refuted any allegation of racial bias. The second letter was written by a juror who appeared to have thought himself to have been the one who had been making the jokes. The juror in question stated that he was sorry if he had given any offence, that he had many connections with people from ethnic minorities and that he was in no way racially biased.

The judge decided not to discharge the jury and it went on to find the applicant guilty, although it acquitted another Asian defendant. The applicant's appeal, partly on the grounds of bias on the part of the jury, was dismissed by the Court of Appeal.

The majority of the ECtHR, however, held that the trial was conducted contrary to Art 6(1) of the ECHR. The Court considered that the allegations contained in the note were capable of causing the applicant and any objective observer to have legitimate doubts as to the impartiality of the court, which neither the collective letter nor the redirection of the jury by the judge could have dispelled.

In reaching its decision, the Court distinguished the decision in the similar case of *Gregory v UK* (1998). In the *Gregory* judgment, there was no admission by a juror that he had made racist comments, in the form of a joke or otherwise; there was no indication as to who had made the complaint and the complaint was vague and imprecise. Moreover, in the present case, the applicant's counsel had insisted throughout the proceedings that dismissing the jury was the only viable course of action.

The Court accepted that, although discharging the jury might not always be the only means to achieve a fair trial, there were certain circumstances where this was required by Art 6(1) of the ECHR. As the Court stated:

> Given the importance attached by all Contracting States to the need to combat racism, the Court considers that the judge should have reacted in a more robust manner than merely seeking vague assurances that the jurors could set aside their prejudices and try the case solely on the evidence. By failing to do so, the judge did not provide sufficient guarantees to exclude any objectively justified or legitimate doubts as to the impartiality of the court. It follows that the court that condemned the applicant was not impartial from an objective point of view.

The Court, however, refused his claim for compensation of some £458,000, which suggests that it was not convinced that a substitute jury would not have convicted him as well.

It has already been seen that s 8 of the Contempt of Court Act 1981 prevents investigation into what occurs in the privacy of the jury room and such prohibition applies equally to judges. In *R v Qureshi* (2001), the defendant had been convicted of arson and of attempting to attain property by deception. Three days after the verdict, a juror in the trial informed the court that some members of the jury had been racially prejudiced against Qureshi and had decided he was guilty from the outset of the trial. Qureshi's application for permission to appeal against his conviction was rejected by the Court of Appeal on the grounds that the complaint did not arise during the trial, but only after an apparently regular verdict had been delivered. In order to pursue the allegation, the court would have had to investigate what had happened in the jury room and that was precluded by s 8 of the Contempt of Court Act 1981. In reaching this decision, the Court of Appeal distinguished *Sander*, where the complaint arose during the trial, and followed *R v Miah* (1997), where the complaint arose after the event. In the latter case, it was stated that the rule against breaching jury secrecy applied to 'anything said by one juror to another about the case from the moment the jury is empanelled, at least provided what is said is not overheard by anyone who is not a juror'. It has to be asked whether such a rule is acceptable, especially when it conceals possible injustice. For a detailed analysis of these cases, see P Robertshaw, 'Responding to bias amongst jurors' (2002) 66(1) Journal of Criminal Law 84.

In June 2007, the Department of Justice published an extremely illuminating report of the results of a series of four linked empirical studies into the operations of juries in the English and Welsh Crown Courts. The report, entitled 'Diversity and Fairness in the Jury System', was produced by academic Cheryl Thomas, with the assistance of Nigel Balmer.

The four studies had conducted:

- a survey of the socio-economic background of all jurors summoned in England and Wales in one week in 2003 and one week in 2005, involving a total of 15,846 jurors;

- a survey of the socio-economic background of all jurors in jury pools, on jury panels and juries at three Crown Courts over a four-week period, involving 640 jurors;

- a case simulation study with real jurors exploring whether ethnicity affects jury verdicts or juror votes, involving 28 juries with a total of 319 jurors (while this allowed the study to examine whether ethnicity affected jury decision-making, its use of simulation meant that it did not contravene s 8 of the Contempt of Court Act 1981);

- a study of the relationship between jury verdicts, the composition of juries and the ethnicity of defendants in actual cases at three Crown Courts, involving 186 verdicts.

The final report claimed to be the first study to compare the ethnic profile of jurors summoned and serving at each Crown Court in England and Wales with the ethnic population profiles for the areas in which each court operated.

Concern about ethnic minority under-representation on juries implicitly assumes that the ethnic composition of juries may affect jury verdicts, and this is the first research conducted in this country to examine whether the research used case simulation with real jurors, along with a study of jury verdicts in real cases.

Despite its scope and innovation, none of the research required exemption from the current restrictive rules, and illustrates just how much jury research can be conducted in this country within existing restrictions.

The studies set themselves the task of challenging various assumptions about the representative nature of jury service, which have influenced reviews of the jury system and policy development in that area. As the report stated, 'most of these assumptions paint a picture of widespread jury service avoidance and unrepresentative jurors'.

However, somewhat surprisingly, the report claimed to establish that most of those assumptions about jury service were based on myth, rather than reality, as substantiated by the following conclusions it reached, that:

- there was no significant under-representation of black and minority ethnic (BME) groups among those summoned for jury service at virtually all Crown Courts in England and Wales;

- ethnic minorities are summoned in proportion to their representation in the local population in virtually all Crown Courts in England and Wales. However, racially mixed juries are only likely to exist in courts where BME groups make up at least 10 per cent of the entire juror catchment area. The report explained that this was simply the consequence of BME population levels in these catchment areas and the process of random selection;

- while there was some evidence that BME jurors on jury panels appeared to be selected to serve on juries less often than white panel members, the report put this down to 'court clerks inadvertently avoiding reading out juror names that are difficult to pronounce';

- in addition, jury pools were found to closely reflect the local population in terms of gender and age, and the self-employed are represented among serving jurors in direct proportion to their representation in the population;

- the main factor affecting non-responses to summonses is high residential mobility, not ethnicity;

- there was no significant difference between BME and white respondents in their willingness to do jury service or indeed support for the jury system, which was strongly supported by both groups;

- the most significant factors predicting whether a summoned juror will serve or not were not ethnicity but income and employment status (those summoned for jury service who are economically inactive or in lower income brackets are far less likely to serve). Where ethnic minorities did not serve, this was primarily due to ineligibility or disqualification (residency or language);

- there is no mass avoidance of jury service by the British public (85 per cent of those summoned replied to their summonses and the vast majority served);

- the middle classes or 'the important and clever in society' do not avoid jury service. In fact the studies showed the contrary, that the highest rates of jury service are among middle- to high-income earners and higher-status professions. Again, perhaps surprisingly, the employed are over-represented among serving jurors, and the retired and unemployed are under-represented;

- the changes to juror eligibility under the Criminal Justice Act 2003 increased the proportion of those summoned who actually served, from 54 per cent to 64 per cent. Significantly, the proportion of serving jurors between 65 and 69 years of age doubled from 3 per cent in 2003 to 6 per cent in 2005, after their right of excusal was removed.

Perhaps the most controversial study informing the report was the research into the relationship of race and jury decision-making.

As the report recognised, the unstated but underlying assumption for those arguing possible under-representation of ethnic minorities on juries assumes that the ethnic composition of juries can affect jury outcomes.

- The research used case simulation with real jurors, supplemented by a study of jury verdicts in actual cases.

- The simulations were based on a real case, filmed in a real courtroom, with a real judge, barristers, court staff, police and witnesses. Real jurors were the study participants, jury panels were selected by the Court Service random selection programme, all juries included enough jurors to constitute a valid jury (10 to 12 jurors) and they deliberated in a real deliberating room.

All juries saw a film of an identical case where the defendant was charged with causing actual bodily harm (ABH), but where specific case elements were altered for different juries (race of defendant, victim and charges).

In examining the conclusions of the report it is important to distinguish between the decisions of individual jurors and the decision of the jury that they were a member of.

The main finding in relation to juries was that the verdicts of racially mixed *juries* did not discriminate against defendants based on the defendant's race. In the 28 separate jury verdicts, outcomes for the white, black and Asian defendants were remarkably similar.

However, as regards the voting of individual jurors on racially mixed juries, even though the defendant's ethnicity did not have an impact on jury verdicts, the research found that in certain cases ethnicity did have a significant impact on the individual decisions of some jurors. Indeed, the report claimed that 'in certain cases BME jurors were significantly less likely to vote to convict a BME defendant than a white defendant'.

However, any 'same race leniency' among BME jurors was only found when race was not an explicit element of the case, and where the prosecution was racially aggravated actual bodily harm (ABH), BME jurors and white jurors had similar conviction rates for both the white and BME defendants. The report suggested that such leniency among BME jurors reflected their belief that the courts treat ethnic minority defendants more harshly than white defendants. Somewhat disconcertingly, while both black and Asian jurors showed leniency for the black defendant, there was apparently no leniency for the Asian defendant by either Asian or black jurors.

The report also claimed to find evidence of race leniency among white jurors, but again only in cases where race was not an issue in the case. As the report stated: 'In non-race salient cases, white jurors had very low conviction rates for the white defendant, despite consistently stating that they did not believe his evidence and felt he was dishonest.'

Nonetheless, even in the face of these findings the report was confident that any same-race leniency did not have an impact on the verdicts of the juries of which they were members on the basis that '12 jurors must jointly try to reach a decision and that majority verdicts are possible meant that more verdicts were achieved and individual biases did not dictate the decision-making of these racially mixed juries'. However, it was careful to warn that: 'If juries were smaller or if unanimous verdicts were required, then individual juror bias might potentially have a greater impact on jury verdicts.'

In February 2010 a second report for the Ministry of Justice by Professor Thomas entitled 'Are juries fair?' concluded that, in essence, they were, that there was 'little evidence that juries are not fair' and that 'juries overall appear efficient and effective'.

The specific findings concluded that:

- there were no courts with a higher jury acquittal than conviction rate, and this dispels the myth that there are courts where juries rarely convict;
- all-white juries did not discriminate against BME defendants;
- differences in jury conviction rates for different specific offences suggest that juries try defendants on the evidence and the law;
- contrary to popular belief and previous government reports, juries actually convict more often than they acquit in rape cases (55 per cent jury conviction rate);
- while over half of the jurors perceived the judge's directions as easy to understand, only a minority (31 per cent) actually understood the directions fully in the legal terms used by the judge;
- younger jurors were better able than older jurors to comprehend the legal instructions, with comprehension of directions on the law declining as the age of the juror increased.

14.6   THE DECLINE OF THE JURY TRIAL

Many direct attempts have been made in the recent past to reduce the operation of the jury system within the English legal system. These particular endeavours, however, have to be understood in the context of the general historical decline in the use of the jury as the mechanism for determining issues in court cases. Perhaps the heat engendered in the current debate is a consequence of the fact that the continued existence of the jury as it is presently constituted is a matter of political contention.

There can be no doubt as to the antiquity of the institution of trial by jury, nor can there be much doubt as to its supposed democratising effect on the operation of the legal system. Neither, unfortunately, can there be any grounds for denying the diminishment that has occurred in the fairly recent past in the role of the jury as the means of determining the outcome of trials, nor can the continued existence of the jury as it is presently constituted be taken for granted.

In respect of civil law, the use of juries has diminished considerably and automatic recourse to trial by jury is restricted to a small number of areas and, even in those areas, the continued use of the jury is threatened. Prior to 1854, all cases that came before the common law courts were decided by a judge and jury. The Common Law Procedure Act of that year provided that cases could be settled without a jury where the parties agreed, and since then, the role of the jury has been gradually curtailed until, at present, under s 69 of the Senior Courts Act 1981, the right to a jury trial is limited to only four specific areas: fraud, defamation (i.e. libel and slander), malicious prosecution and false imprisonment. (Similar provisions are contained in the County Courts Act 1984.) Section 11 of the Defamation Act 2013 removes libel and slander from that list, unless the court decides otherwise. Even in these areas, the right is not absolute and can be denied by a judge under s 69(1) where the case involves 'any prolonged examination of documents or accounts or any scientific or local investigation which cannot conveniently be made with a jury'. (See *Beta Construction Ltd v Channel Four TV Co Ltd* (1990) for an indication of the factors that the judge will take into consideration in deciding whether a case should be decided by a jury or not.)

The question of whether or not juries should be used in libel cases gained wider consideration in the case involving McDonald's, the fast-food empire, and two environmentalists, Dave Morris and Helen Steel. McDonald's claimed that their reputation was damaged by an allegedly libellous leaflet issued by members of an organisation called London Greenpeace including Morris and Steel, which linked McDonald's' products to heart disease and cancer as well as the despoliation of the environment and the exploitation of the Third World. In a preliminary hearing, later confirmed by the Court of Appeal, it was decided that the evidence to be presented would be of such scientific complexity that it would be beyond the understanding of a jury (see *The Times*, 10 June 1997).

The right to jury trial in defamation cases has been the object of particular criticism. In 1975, the Faulks Committee on the Law of Defamation recommended that the availability of jury trial in that area should be subject to the same judicial discretion as all other civil cases. In its conclusions, the Faulks Report shared the uncertainty of the Court of Appeal in *Ward v James* (1965) as to the suitability of juries to determine the level of damages that should be awarded. Support for these views has been provided by a number of defamation cases decided since then, such as *Sutcliffe v Pressdram Ltd* (1990), in which the wife of a convicted serial killer was awarded damages of £600,000. She eventually settled for £60,000 after the Court of Appeal stated that it would reassess the award.

In *Aldington v Watts and Tolstoy* (1990), damages of £1.5 million were awarded. This huge award was subsequently held by the ECtHR to be so disproportionate as to amount to a violation of Tolstoy's right to freedom of expression under Art 10 of the ECHR (*Tolstoy Miloslavsky v UK* (1995)). Domestic law has also sought to deal with what could only be seen as excessive awards of damages in defamation cases, even prior to the Human Rights Act (HRA) 1998, which makes the ECtHR *Tolstoy* decision and Art 10 of the ECHR binding in UK law.

Section 8 of the Courts and Legal Services Act (CLSA) 1990 gave appeal courts the power to alter damages awards made by juries to a level that they felt to be 'proper'. Nonetheless, the question of what actually constitutes a proper level of damages continued to present problems for juries, which continued to award very large sums. The problem arose from the limited guidance that judges could give juries in making their awards. In *Rantzen v Mirror Group Newspapers* (1993), the Court of Appeal stated that judges should advise juries, in making their awards, to consider the purchasing power of the award and its proportionality to the damage suffered to the reputation of the plaintiff, and should refer to awards made by the courts under s 8 of the CLSA (Rantzen's original award of £250,000 was reduced to £110,000). Still, extremely large awards continued to be made, and in *John v MGN Ltd* (1996), the Court of Appeal stated that past practice should be altered to allow juries to refer to personal injury cases to decide the level of award, and that the judge could indicate what sort of level would be appropriate (John's awards of £350,000 for the libel and £275,000 in exemplary damages were reduced to £75,000 and £50,000, respectively).

In 1996, statute law intervened in the form of the Defamation Act, which was designed to simplify the procedure of defamation cases. The main provisions of the Act are:

(a)   a one-year limitation period for defamation claims;

(b)   a statutory defence based on responsibility for publication. This replaces the common law defence of innocent dissemination;

(c)   an updating of defences in relation to privilege, that is, reporting on the proceedings and publications of, for example, the courts and government;

(d)   a streamlined procedure for dealing with a defendant who has offered to make amends. This would involve paying compensation, assessed by a judge, and publishing an appropriate correction and apology;

(e)   powers for judges to deal with cases without a jury. Under this provision, the judge can dismiss a claim if he considers it has no realistic prospect of success. Alternatively, if he considers there to be no realistic defence to the claim, he can award summary relief. Such relief can take the form of a declaration of the falsity of the statement; an order to print an apology; an order to refrain from repeating the statement; and damages of up to £10,000.

The most significant elements of the Defamation Act came into effect at the end of February 2000, but in January 2001 the Court of Appeal used its common law powers to completely overturn the award of damages in the case of *Grobbelaar v News Group Newspapers Ltd* (2001). Grobbelaar, an ex-football player, had been accused of accepting money to fix football matches. He had been found not guilty in a criminal case and had been awarded £85,000 damages for defamation in a related civil case against *The Sun* newspaper. On appeal, the Court of Appeal held that the newspaper could not rely on the defence of limited qualified privilege, as recently recognised in *Reynolds v Times Newspapers Ltd and Others* (1999), and could be held to account for such defamatory statements as could not be proved true. However, although the Court stated that it would be most reluctant to find perversity in a jury's verdict, it had such jurisdiction and, therefore, duty to consider that ground of appeal. The Court then went on to conclude that no reasonable jury could have failed to be satisfied on the balance of probabilities, and to a relatively high degree of probability, that Grobbelaar had been party to corrupt conspiracies. The court considered that the evidence led inexorably to the view that Grobbelaar's story was 'quite simply incredible. All logic, common sense and reason compelled one to that conclusion'.

As regards overturning the decision of the jury, in the words of Thorpe LJ:

> I recognise and respect the unique function of a jury that heard all of the evidence over some 16 days of trial, nevertheless it would be an injustice to the defendants to allow the outcome to stand.

On further appeal, the House of Lords held that the Court of Appeal was correct in holding that the jury's decision was open to review on the grounds of perversity. However, it found that the Court of Appeal had been wrong to overturn the jury's verdict on the grounds of perversity in this instance, as the verdict could have been explained in such a way that did not necessarily require the imputation of perversity. Grobbelaar's victory, however, was pyrrhic in the extreme; due to his breach of his legal and moral obligations, the damages awarded by the jury were quashed and substituted by the award of nominal damages of £1, with no costs awarded.

The extent of damages and, in particular, exemplary damages awarded against the police in a number of civil actions have also been problematic (see 7.10 for a consideration of types of damages). These actions have arisen from wrongful arrest, false imprisonment, assault and malicious prosecution and usually have involved connotations of racist behaviour on the part of the police. In setting the level of damages, juries have wished signally to demonstrate their disapproval of such police behaviour, but as the courts have correctly pointed out, any payments made come from the public purse, not from the individuals involved. The issue came to a head in *Thompson and Another v Commissioner of Police for the Metropolis* (1997), in which the Court of Appeal considered awards made to two plaintiffs. The first had been assaulted in custody and false evidence was used against her in a criminal trial during which she was held in prison. In a civil action, she was awarded £51,500 damages, of which £50,000 was exemplary damages. The second plaintiff was physically and racially abused by police when they broke into his house and arrested him. In a consequential civil action, he was awarded £220,000 for wrongful arrest, false imprisonment and assault, of which £200,000 was exemplary damages. On appeal, the Court of Appeal stated that in such cases, the judge should direct the jury that:

(i)   damages, save in exceptional circumstances, should be awarded only as com-
        pensation and in line with a scale which keeps the damages proportionate with
        those payable in personal injury cases;
(ii)   where aggravated damages are appropriate, they are unlikely to be less than
        £1,000, or to be more than twice the basic damages except where those basic
        damages are modest;
(iii)   in relation to the award of exemplary damages the jury should be told of the
        exceptional nature of the remedy, and told that the basic and aggravated dam-
        ages together must be insufficient to punish the defendant before any exemplary
        damages can be considered. Where exemplary damages are appropriate they are
        unlikely to be less than £5,000. Conduct must be particularly deserving of con-
        demnation to warrant an award of £25,000 and the absolute maximum should
        be £50,000. It would be unusual for such damages to be more than three times
        the basic damages being awarded unless those basic damages are modest.

In the two cases in question, the first exemplary award was reduced from £50,000 to £25,000; and in the second, the exemplary component was reduced from £200,000 to £15,000.

The reasoning in the *Thompson* case was followed in *Hill v Commissioner of Police for the Metropolis* (1998), where the plaintiff was awarded £45,600 for wrongful arrest, false imprisonment, assault and malicious prosecution. The most contentious award was that of exemplary damages, the bracket having been set by the judge as between £5,000 and £15,000, but the jury awarded the plaintiff £20,000. The Court of Appeal held that the jury had only gone beyond the guidelines to a limited extent and it was clear that they had taken a poor view of the police officers' conduct. In those circumstances, although the total award was high and might be seen to be out of proportion to awards made in personal injury cases, it was not seen as manifestly excessive in relation to Thompson's case.

If the extent of damages has been a particular problem in relation to defamation claims, especially when they are compared to the much smaller awards made in relation to personal injury, it should also be noted that public funding is not normally available in defamation cases, although it is available in relation to malicious falsehood. This effec-tively has made defamation a rich person's claim. As a consequence, people without the necessary wealth to finance legal proceedings find it extremely difficult to gain redress when they have suffered from what subsequently turns out to be false and damaging press coverage of their affairs. But of equal concern is the way some wealthy people were able and allowed to abuse the system. One example was the late and notorious publisher, Robert Maxwell, who often used libel proceedings or the threat of them to silence critics. As it turned out, much of what Mr Maxwell sought to prevent from becoming public knowledge was in fact illegal and harmful business conduct.

The Defamation Act 2013 came into operation in January 2014. For the purposes of this chapter the essential change made is that s 11 of the Act effectively abolishes trial by jury in defamation cases by removing the presumption in favour of jury trial in such actions relating to libel and slander. The Act, however, has made additional significant alterations to the operation of defamation law in England. Thus it:

- includes a requirement for claimants to show that they have suffered *serious reputational harm* before suing for defamation;
- introduces a defence of 'responsible publication on matters of public interest' (effectively replacing the previous *Reynolds* defence);
- implements a single publication rule to prevent repeated claims against a publisher concerning the same material;
- provides increased protection to operators of websites that host user-generated content, providing they comply with the procedure to enable the complainant to resolve disputes directly with the author of the material concerned;
- introduces new statutory defences of truth and honest opinion to replace the common law defences of justification and fair comment;
- extends privilege to cover defamatory statements in peer-reviewed scientific or academic journals;
- removes the courts' jurisdiction to hear actions against a secondary author, editor or publisher if it is reasonably practicable for an action to be brought against the primary author, editor or publisher.

Section 9 of the Act seeks to deal with the problem of 'libel tourism', ensuring that a court cannot hear a case unless it is satisfied that, of all the places publication has taken place, England and Wales is clearly the most appropriate.

Apart from the instances considered previously there is, therefore, a presumption against trial by jury in civil cases. However, under s 69(3) SCA 1981, the judge has the discretion to order a trial by jury. In *Ward v James* (1965), the Court of Appeal decided that a jury should be used in civil cases only in 'exceptional circumstances', although no exhaustive list as to what amounted to exceptional circumstances was provided.

14.6.2 JURIES IN CRIMINAL TRIALS

It has to be borne in mind that the criminal jury trial is essentially the creature of the Crown Court, and that the magistrates' courts deal with at least 95 per cent of criminal cases. In practice, juries determine the outcome of less than 1 per cent of the total of criminal cases for the reason that, of all the cases that are decided in the Crown Court, 71 per cent of defendants plead guilty on all counts and, therefore, have no need of jury trial. Initiatives in the Crown Court and with other agencies, such as offering a discount on sentence for an early plea of guilty and providing early charging advice by the Crown Prosecution Service at police stations, have been put forward as reasons for this significant increase in the guilty plea rate.

It can be seen, therefore, that in absolute and proportional terms, the jury does not play a significant part in the determination of criminal cases.

If trial by jury is not statistically significant, it cannot be denied that it is of major significance in the determination of the most serious cases. Even this role, however, has not gone without scrutiny, as will be seen below.

It should not be forgotten that the right to jury trial has been abolished in Northern Ireland since 1973. In response to the problem of the intimidation of jury members, the *Report of the Commission to Consider Legal Procedures to Deal with Terrorist Activities in Northern Ireland*, headed by Lord Diplock, recommended that cases be decided without juries in particular situations. The so-called Diplock courts operate in relation to certain 'scheduled offences', particularly, but not exclusively, ones associated with terrorism.

With regard to the continuation of no-jury trial in Northern Ireland, the United Nations Human Rights Committee, in its concluding observations on the UK's periodic report under the UN Covenant on Civil and Political Rights, stated its concern. In its words:

> The Committee remains concerned that, despite improvements in the security situation in Northern Ireland, some elements of criminal procedure continue to differ between Northern Ireland and the remainder of the State party's territory. In particular, the Committee is concerned that, under the Justice and Security (Northern Ireland) Act 2007, persons whose cases are certified by the Director of Public Prosecutions for Northern Ireland are tried in the absence of a jury. It is also concerned that there is no right of appeal against the decision made by the Director of Public Prosecutions for Northern Ireland.

In October 2010 *The Guardian* newspaper reported that The Criminal Cases Review Commission (see above, 9.9) had received applications from more than 200 people who claimed that they had suffered injustices under the Diplock trial system. By that time, the Court of Appeal in Belfast had overturned convictions in 24 of 26 cases referred to it by the Commission. The newspaper alleged that a number of men who served as detectives with the Royal Ulster Constabulary (RUC) claimed that senior officers 'encouraged the systematic mistreatment of suspects at Castlereagh interrogation centre in east Belfast' after the establishment of the Diplock courts in 1973. The accusation was that the officers took full advantage of the vague wording of emergency legislation in Northern Ireland, which allowed the courts to admit confessions as evidence, *providing there was no evidence* they had been obtained through the use of torture, or inhuman or degrading treatment. This issue clearly links back to the consideration of the use of torture in Chapter 2. A video report of the allegations may be seen at www.theguardian.com/uk/2010/oct/11/inside-castlereagh-confessions-torture.

Criminal Justice Act 2003: jury tampering

The term 'jury tampering' covers a range of circumstances in which the jury's independence is or may appear to be compromised. Such a situation could come about because of actual harm or threats of harm to jury members. It might equally involve intimidation or bribery of jury members. Alternatively, it could also include similar improper approaches to a juror's family or friends.

Sections 44 and 46 of the CJA 2003 provide for a trial on indictment in the Crown Court to be conducted without a jury where there is a danger of jury tampering, or continued without a jury where the jury has been discharged because of jury tampering. For an application under s 44 to be granted, the court must be satisfied that there is evidence of a real and present danger that jury tampering would take place. In addition, the court must also be satisfied that the danger of jury tampering is so substantial, notwithstanding any steps that could reasonably be taken to prevent it, as to make it necessary in the interests of justice for the trial to be conducted without a jury. Sub-section (6) sets out examples of what might constitute evidence of a real and present danger of jury tampering, which include:

- a case where the trial is a retrial and the jury in the previous trial was discharged because jury tampering had taken place;
- a case where jury tampering has taken place in previous criminal proceedings involving the defendant or any of the defendants;
- a case where there has been intimidation, or attempted intimidation, of any person who is likely to be a witness in the trial.

Section 46 deals with trials already under way, where jury tampering has or appears to have taken place. In these circumstances, if the judge decides to discharge the jury, as he or she has a right to do in common law, and is satisfied that tampering has occurred, he or she may order that the trial should continue without a jury if he or she is satisfied that this would be fair to the defendant. On the other hand, if the judge considers it necessary in the interests of justice to terminate the trial due to tampering, he or she may order that the retrial should take place without a jury.

In March 2010, after the first non-jury criminal trial for more than 350 years, four members of a gang were convicted of a £1.75 million armed raid on a warehouse near Heathrow Airport in February 2004. Following three previous failed trials, the prosecution had applied for a non-jury trial on the grounds that the third trial had had to be halted because of alleged jury tampering. On subsequent appeal to the ECtHR, *Twomey and Cameron v the United Kingdom* (application no. 67318/09), the court stated that the system of trial by jury was just one example among others of the variety of legal systems existing in Europe, and held that the right to a fair trial did not require that the determination of guilt be made by a jury. On a second issue, that the basis of the evidence of jury tampering had not been fully disclosed to the defence, the court held that the procedure afforded the defence sufficient safeguards, taking into account the important public interest grounds against disclosing the evidence.

In July 2010 Lord Judge CJ, in the Court of Appeal, handed down guidance on how the jury tampering provisions of the CJA 2003 were to be operated in two similar but unrelated cases, *R v J, S, M* (2010) and *R v KS* (2010). In overturning orders for non-jury trials Judge LCJ emphasised that the making of such an order:

> remains and must remain the decision of last resort, only to be ordered when the court is sure (not that it entertains doubts, suspicions or reservations) that the statutory conditions are fulfilled. Save in extreme cases, *where the*

necessary protective measures constitute an unreasonable intrusion into the lives of the jurors, for example, a constant police presence in or near their homes, day and night and at the weekends, or police protection, which means that at all times when they are out of their homes, they are accompanied or overseen by police officers, again day and night and at the weekend, with its consequent impact on the availability of police officers to carry out their ordinary duties, the confident expectation must be that the jury will perform its duties with its customary determination to do justice (emphasis added).

However, in relation to s 46 powers he concluded that:

If during the course of this, or indeed any trial, attempts are made to tamper with the jury to the extent that the judge feels it necessary to discharge the entire jury, it should be clearly understood that the judge may continue with the trial and deliver a judgment and verdict on his own. The principle of trial by jury is precious, but in the end any defendant who is responsible for abusing this principle by attempting to subvert the process has no justified complaint that he has been deprived of a right which, by his own actions, he himself has spurned.

Criminal Justice Act 2003: complex Fraud Trials

In 1986, the Roskill Committee on Fraud Trials critically examined the operation of the jury in complex criminal fraud cases. Its report recommended the abolition of trial by jury in such cases. The Roskill Committee did not go as far as to recommend that all fraud cases should be taken away from juries, only the most complex, of which it was estimated that there were about two dozen or so every year. It was suggested that these cases would be better decided by a judge assisted by two laypersons drawn from a panel with specialist expertise. The government declined to implement the recommendations of the Roskill Committee, and instead introduced procedures designed to make it easier to follow the proceedings in complex fraud cases.

After being found not guilty of a £19 million fraud charge, George Walker, the former chief executive of Brent Walker, said: 'Thank God for the jury. It would be madness to lose the jury system.' This enthusiastic endorsement of the jury system is in no little way undercut, however, by the fact that Walker is reported as going on to state that he was sure the jury had not properly understood much of the highly detailed material in the trial, as he admitted: 'I didn't understand a lot of it, so I can't see how they could.'

Mr Walker's enthusiasm perhaps was not shared by his co-accused, Wilfred Aquilina, who was found guilty, on a majority verdict, of false accounting.

The Royal Commission on the Criminal Justice System of 1993 (the Runciman Commission) recognised the particular difficulties faced by jurors in fraud trials but, somewhat surprisingly in the light of its recommendations in relation to offences triable either way, it did not suggest the removal of the jury from such cases. It merely recommended that s 10(3) of the CJA 1988 should be amended to permit judges to put the issues before the jury at the outset of the trial.

In February 1998, the Home Office issued a Green Paper entitled *Juries in Serious Fraud Trials*. The Consultation Paper suggested the need for a new procedure in relation to complex fraud trials, due to the fact that 'the detection, investigation and trial of serious criminal fraud offences have presented certain difficulties not commonly found amongst other types of offences'. A variety of possible alternatives were put forward:

- *Special juries:* these would be made up of qualified people and might be drawn from a special pool of potential jurors. Alternatively, ordinary jurors would have to be assessed as to their competency to sit on the case.
- *Judge-run trials:* specially trained judges, either singly or in a panel, and possibly with the help of lay experts.
- *Fraud tribunals:* following Roskill, these would be made up of a judge and qualified lay members with the power to question witnesses.
- *Verdict-only juries:* in this situation, the judge would hear the evidence and sum up the facts, leaving the jury simply to vote on guilt or innocence.
- A *special juror:* here, 11 of the jury would be selected as normal, but number 12 would be specially qualified in order to be able to assist the others on complex points.

With respect to these alternatives, the government stated that it had no particular preference.

Subsequently, in April 1998, the Home Secretary requested the Law Commission to carry out a review of fraud trials, focusing particularly on whether the existing law was:

- readily comprehensible to juries;
- adequate for effective prosecution;
- fair to defendants; and
- able to cope with changes in technology.

However, in its response in Consultation Paper No 155, *Fraud and Deception* (1999), the Law Commission addressed only the issues of possible criminal offences and did not deal with any procedural issues.

In his extensive *Review of the Criminal Courts* (2001), Sir Robin Auld LJ recommended that in serious and complex frauds, the nominated trial judge should have the power to direct trial by themselves and two lay members drawn from a panel established by the Lord Chancellor for the purpose or, if the defendant requested, by the judge alone.

The White Paper preceding the CJA 2003 claimed that each year 15 to 20 complex fraud trials took place that would be better dealt with by a judge sitting alone and s 43 of the CJA 2003 provided for exactly that possibility. Before granting any application for a non-jury trial, the Court would have to be satisfied that the length or complexity of the trial was likely to make it so burdensome upon the jury that, in the interests of justice, serious consideration should be given to conducting the trial without a jury. The CJA 2003 thus proposed the introduction of measures much more restrictive than any previous body had recommended (the initial Criminal Justice Bill had actually gone further and proposed a similar potential curtailment in all complex or lengthy trials, not just fraud cases). The implementation of s 43 required an affirmative vote in favour by both the House of Commons and the House of Lords, but before any such occurrence it was repealed by s 113 of the Protection of Freedoms Act 2012.

The collapse of the longest ever jury trial, in March 2005, led to calls for the provisions of the CJA to be implemented. The case, relating to alleged bribery in contracts for the £3 billion extension of the London Underground Jubilee Line, lasted for 21 months and cost an estimated £60 million. The trial came to an end only after protests by the jurors, who it was claimed were refusing to continue to participate in the trial. According to one juror, as reported in *The Observer* newspaper, 'It was a nightmare and a total waste of taxpayers' money.' As the newspaper ironically put it, 'Jurors do not usually discuss their experiences; but because this trial collapsed and, since their efforts were in vain, it has been hard to shut them up.'

The protestations of the long-suffering jury members led Lord Falconer to propose the expeditious implementation of the proposals of the CJA 2003. However, in November 2005 the Attorney General, Lord Goldsmith, confirmed that the government would not be pressing ahead with the proposal. In the face of the confirmed resistance, it recognised that it would certainly be unable to get such a vote in the House of Lords, even if it succeeded in the House of Commons, which was not at all certain. No proposed date for implementation has been suggested by the government since.

The Criminal Procedure Rules 2012 reaffirm the original protocol for the conduct of heavy fraud and other complex criminal cases issued by the Lord Chief Justice in 2005 (available at www.justice.gov.uk/courts/procedure-rules/criminal/pd-protocol/pd_protocol).

14.7   FUTURE JURY REFORM

The foregoing has considered the historical decline of the jury trial; it remains to consider its prospects for the future and the related matter of how and whether research can be conducted into the way in which juries operate in practice.

14.7.1   EITHER-WAY OFFENCES: THE ROLE OF THE JURY

In order to understand the full implications of the recommendation, it is necessary to reconsider points that have been discussed previously in Chapter 9.

It is essential to appreciate the distinction between offences to be tried only by summary procedure, offences to be tried only on indictment and offences triable 'either way'. Summary offences are those which are triable only in the magistrates' courts and cases which, as has been noted previously, magistrates decide on their own without the assistance of a jury. There are literally hundreds of summary offences; given the limitations on the sentencing powers of magistrates, they are by necessity the least serious of criminal acts, such as road traffic offences and minor assault. The most serious offences, such as major theft, serious assault, rape, manslaughter and murder, have to be tried on indictment before a jury in the Crown Court. There is, however, a third category, offences triable 'either way' which, as the name suggests, may be tried either summarily or on indictment.

Committal hearings by magistrates to determine whether a particular case should be dealt with in the Crown Court were abolished completely in May 2014, so now serious cases go directly to that court.

The Royal Commission on Criminal Justice

The Runciman Commission's Report stated that defendants should not 'be able to choose their court of trial solely on the basis that they think that they will get a fairer hearing at one level than another' (see para 6.18 of the Report). The conclusion of the Commission seemed to be that, because defendants do not trust the magistrates' court, and there is some justification for this in respect of the rates of acquittal, and do have more faith in the Crown Court than is warranted in terms of sentencing, then they should be forced to use the magistrates' court. As the Report stated: 'Magistrates' courts conduct over 93 per cent of all criminal cases and should be trusted to try cases fairly' (see para 6.18 of the Report). It is at least arguable that, in this conclusion, the Commission missed the point. Put starkly, the evidence supports the conclusion that defendants do not trust magistrates' courts. Indeed, the evidence as to the number of people changing their plea to guilty in the Crown Court would seem to support the conclusion, not so much that defendants trust juries, but more that they do not trust magistrates. This lack of trust in the magistracy is further highlighted by the fact that those who do not plead guilty would rather have their guilt or innocence determined by a jury.

Simply forcing such people to use the magistrates' courts does not address the underlying problem, let alone solve it.

It would have been possible for the Commission to have achieved its end by simply recommending that particular offences that are defined as triable 'either way' at present should be recategorised as offences only open to summary procedure. That it did not do so further indicates the weakness of the underlying logic of its case for removing the right to insist on trial on indictment. The Commission rejected the reclassification of offences partly because of the difficulty and uncertainty inherent in the task. Additionally, and more importantly, however, it rejected this approach because it wished to leave available the possibility of the defendant successfully insisting on trial on indictment in the case of first offenders, where the consequences of loss of reputation would be significant. In the words of the Commission:

> Loss of reputation is a different matter, since jury trial has long been regarded as appropriate for cases involving that issue. But, it should only be one of the factors to be taken into account and will often be relevant only to first offenders (see para 6.18 of the Report).

There are two assumptions in this proposal. First, there is the surely objectionable assumption that the reputation of anyone with a previous conviction is not important. But of even more concern is the fact that it is recognised that in the cases of first offenders, they should be permitted access to the jury. The question has to be asked: why should this be the case if juries do no more than magistrates do? It appears that in the instance of first offenders, it is recognised that juries do offer more protection than magistrates. Again, this demands the question: why should the extra protection not be open to all?

Criminal Justice (Mode of Trial) Bills

The Runciman Commission Report was produced under the auspices of a Conservative government operating under an economic imperative to reduce costs. If those who were opposed to its findings found comfort in the election of a New Labour government in 1997, they were soon to be disabused when the new (now former) Home Secretary, Jack Straw, announced his intention to reduce the rights to jury trials, essentially to the same end as the Runciman proposals. Thus, the first Criminal Justice (Mode of Trial) Bill was introduced in the parliamentary session of 1999–2000. This Bill sought to amend the MCA 1980 by introducing sections that gave the magistrates, rather than the accused, the power to decide whether a case should be tried summarily or on indictment. As Runciman's Report had been, so the new Bill was solicitous of the protection of those accused whose reputation 'would be seriously damaged as a result of conviction'. The Bill was generally criticised as an illiberal measure by civil liberties organisations and the legal professions, but was particularly attacked for the manner in which it sought to protect the rights of individuals with reputations to protect. Such solicitude for those with reputations to protect, apparently as opposed to the common majority of people, was seen as inherently unjust and dangerously class-based. The opposition to the Bill outside Parliament was matched, and more importantly so in relation to its legislative progress, by equal opposition within the House of Lords, which voted against its passage.

Undaunted by the rejection of his Bill, the Home Secretary reintroduced a reformed version of it in the Criminal Justice (Mode of Trial) (No 2) Bill. In acknowledgement of criticisms of the earlier Bill, the (No 2) Bill made it clear that the reputation, or any other personal characteristic, of the accused was not something to be taken into account by the magistrates in deciding on the mode of trial. Nonetheless, the Bill was once again defeated in the House of Lords in 2001.

Although the newly re-elected government insisted that it retained the power to use the Parliament Acts to force a mode of trial Bill through the House of Lords, its approach altered following the publishing of the report on the criminal courts conducted by Sir Robin Auld.

The Auld review

In his extensive *Review of the Criminal Courts* (2001), Sir Robin Auld LJ included recommendations that were aimed specifically at the current operation of the jury within the criminal justice system. In summary, he recommended the following points:

- Jurors should be more widely representative than they are of the national and local communities from which they are drawn.

- No one in future should be ineligible for, or excusable as of right from, jury service. While those with criminal convictions and mental disorder should continue to be disqualified, any claimed inability to serve should be a matter for discretionary deferral or excusal.

- Provision should be made to enable ethnic minority representation on juries where race is likely to be relevant to an important issue in the case.

- The law should not be amended to permit more intrusive research than is already possible into the workings of juries, though in appropriate cases, trial judges and/or the Court of Appeal should be entitled to examine alleged improprieties in the jury room.

- The law should be declared, by statute if need be, that juries have no right to acquit defendants in defiance of the law or in disregard of the evidence.

- If the jury's verdict appears to be perverse, the prosecution should be entitled to appeal on the grounds that the perversity is indicative that the verdict is likely to be unfair or untrue.

- The defendant should no longer have an elective right to trial by judge and jury in 'either-way' cases.

- Trial by judge and jury should remain the main form of trial of the more serious offences triable on indictment, that is, those that would go to the Crown Division, subject to four exceptions:

  (i) defendants should be entitled, with the court's consent, to opt for trial by judge alone;

  (ii) in serious and complex frauds, the nominated trial judge should have the power to direct trial by themselves and two lay members drawn from a panel established by the Lord Chancellor for the purpose (or, if the defendant requests, by the judge alone);

  (iii) a Youth Court, constituted by a judge of an appropriate level and at least two experienced youth panel magistrates, should be given jurisdiction to hear all grave cases against young defendants;

  (iv) legislation should be introduced to require a judge, not a jury, to determine the issue of fitness to plead.

The Criminal Justice Act 2003

As has been seen, the CJA 2003 introduced significant changes in the role and place of juries in the criminal system, but it did so without addressing the contentious issue of either-way offences. Perhaps this course of action was adopted in the belief that the increase in the sentencing power of the magistrates' courts to 12 months would reduce the pressure on the Crown Courts by cutting down the number of cases sent for sentencing. *It is unlikely, however, that the issue will have gone away for ever.*

How true, but not particularly insightful or prescient, was the previous sentence, because within months of the installation of the coalition government in 2010, its 'victims' commissioner', Louise Casey, was calling for jury trial to be removed from petty criminals who were 'clogging up' the courts system and whose cases should be tried by magistrates. In her view, the right to opt for trial by jury in the Crown Court was a 'nicety' of the legal system and was being abused by criminals. As she was quoted as saying:

> In a time of cuts, we need to abandon some of the genteel traditions and niceties of the legal system. How can it be right that a jury can be made to convene to hear arguments about the theft of £20-worth of tea bags, as is the case now, when a magistrate could do the job justly but costing far less?

The simple answer is because it is of *crucial importance* to the person who is charged with the offence, no matter the cost to the state.

14.8 INVESTIGATION OF JURY BEHAVIOUR

The very first recommendation made by the Royal Commission on Criminal Justice was that s 8 of the Contempt of Court Act 1981 should be repealed to enable research to be conducted into juries' reasons for their verdicts. Section 8 makes it an offence to obtain, disclose or solicit any particulars of statements made, opinion expressed, arguments advanced or votes cast by members of a jury in the course of their deliberations in any legal proceedings.

In *Attorney General v Associated Newspapers* (1994), the House of Lords held that it was contempt of court for a newspaper to publish disclosures by jurors of what took place in the jury room while they were considering their verdict, unless the publication amounted to no more than a restatement of facts already known. It was decided that the word 'disclose' in s 8(1) applied not just to jurors, but to any others who published their revelations.

The continued legality of s 8 in the light of Art 6 of the ECHR was considered in *R v Mirza* in January 2004. The appellant Mirza had been convicted on six counts of indecent assault by a majority verdict of 10 to two. He had arrived in the UK from Pakistan in 1988 and, during the trial, he had made use of an interpreter. During the course of the trial, the jury sent a note asking the interpreter whether it was typical of a man with Mirza's background to require an interpreter, despite having lived in the UK for so long. It was explained to the jury that it was usual for people who were not fluent to have an interpreter in complicated and serious cases and, in his summing up, the judge directed the jury not to draw an adverse inference from Mirza's use of an interpreter.

Six days after the case finished, the defence counsel received a letter from one of the jurors claiming that some jurors had, from the beginning of the trial, believed that the use of the interpreter had been a devious ploy. The question of the interpreter was raised early during the jury's deliberations, and the letter writer was 'shouted down' when she objected and sought to remind the other members of the jury of the judge's directions. Members of the jury specifically refused to accept the judge's direction, and some regarded defence counsel's warnings against prejudice in her final speech as 'playing the race card'. The writer concluded that the decision of the jury was that of bigots who considered Mirza guilty because he used an interpreter in court after declining one for his police interviews.

When the case came on appeal to the House of Lords, it was confirmed by a majority of four to one that s 8 of the Contempt of Court Act 1981 prevented any investigation into what had taken place within the confines of the jury room. The majority also relied on a passage in *Gregory v UK* (1998), in which the ECtHR had previously approved the protection of jury secrecy under UK law in deciding that s 8 was not in conflict with Art 6 of the ECHR. In reaching its conclusion, the majority focused on the difficulties involved in assessing and investigating such matters of jury misbehaviour but, as Lord Steyn stated in his minority judgment:

> In my view it would be an astonishing thing for the ECtHR to hold, when the point directly arises before it, that a miscarriage of justice may be ignored in the interest of the general efficiency of the jury system. The terms of Art 6(1) of the ECHR, the rights revolution, and 50 years of development of human rights law and practice, would suggest that such a view would be utterly indefensible.

The issue was further considered by the House of Lords in *R v Smith (Patrick)* in 2005. That case related to a situation where, after a jury had begun its deliberations, the judge received a letter from one of the jurors claiming that some of the other members of the panel were disregarding the judge's directions on the law and were engaging in improper speculation over verdicts. Rather than discharge the jury, the judge, with the approval of the lawyers for both sides, had given further directions to the jury in which he clarified the burden of proof, and told them to decide the case on the evidence and not on speculation. He also stated the need for discussion, but told the jury members to resist being bullied into reaching a verdict they did not agree with. In the event the jury returned majority verdicts of guilty on all counts.

On allowing the appeal against conviction, the House of Lords held that the judge's directions had not been strong enough and that the jury had required much more emphatic and detailed guidance and instruction. The House of Lords held that, without such an emphatic reaffirmation of its role as was required after the allegation made by one of its members, it was difficult to be satisfied that the jury's discussions thereafter were conducted in the proper manner.

In reaching its unanimous decision the House affirmed Lord Carswell's judgment, in which he set out the circumstances that might be taken as undermining the propriety of jury verdicts and the common law principles governing the possibility of inquiring into jury verdicts. In so doing Lord Carswell set out six distinct situations:

(i)   The general rule is that the court will not investigate, or receive evidence about, anything said in the course of the jury's deliberations while they are considering their verdict in the jury room.

(ii)   An exception to the above rule may exist if an allegation is made which tends to show that the jury as a whole decided not to actually reach a decision at all, but decided the case by other means such as tossing a coin. As any such behaviour would be contrary to the function of a jury and the oath they took, any result decided in such a way could not be a proper decision at all (see *R v Young (Stephen)* (1995), the Ouija board case).

(iii)   There is a firm rule that after the verdict has been delivered evidence directed to matters intrinsic to the deliberations of jurors is inadmissible (but see *AG v Scotcher* (2005) below).

(iv)   The common exceptions to the general rule were confined to situations where the jury is alleged to have been affected by what are termed *extraneous* influences, e.g. contact with other persons who may have passed on information which should not have been before the jury. However, those extraneous influences have been extended under the influence of new technology (see below). As an amusing sideline to this very serious issue, a Crown Court judge in 2006 made headline news in the papers by warning a jury that they were not to assume the proactive role that had been assumed by the hero of the popular television series *Judge John Deed*. In the television programme, the eponymous judge, while sitting on a jury, had personally entered into an active investigation of the situation he was supposed to be deciding on. It has to be said that the subsequent attempt by the legal adviser to the programme to justify its ludicrous travesty of the law was much more entertaining than the programme itself.

(v)   When complaints have been made during the course of trials of improper behaviour or bias on the part of jurors, judges have on occasion given further instructions to the jury and/or asked them if they feel able to continue with the case and give verdicts in the proper manner. This course should only be taken with the whole jury present and it is an irregularity to question individual jurors in the absence of the others about their ability to bring in a true verdict according to the evidence.

(vi)   Section 8(1) of the Contempt of Court Act 1981 is not a bar to the court itself carrying out necessary investigations of such matters as bias or irregularity in the jury's consideration of the case. If matters of that nature were raised by credible evidence the judge can investigate them and deal with the allegations as the situation may require.

While point (vi) in Lord Carswell's list was based on a well-established principle, it did not address the issue of a juror who wished to raise a matter of jury impropriety after the trial had been completed and the decision of the court recorded. However, just such a situation arose in *Attorney General v Scotcher* (2005). The defendant had been a member of a jury that reached a guilty verdict against two accused by a majority of 10 to one. On the day after the case, Scotcher wrote an anonymous letter to the mother of one of the convicted men detailing improprieties that he alleged had taken place in the jury room. The letter stated, for example that ([2005] 3 All ER 1 at 6):

Many changed their vote late on simply because they wanted to get out of the courtroom and go home . . . They just decide [*sic*] on prejudice and hearsay (and wanting to get home for tea!). I hope these are grounds in law to show that the verdict was unsafe. Don't know if it can be shown that the Judge misdirected the jury . . . Good luck.

The mother passed the letter on to her son's solicitor, who raised it with the Court of Appeal, which in turn passed it on to the police who had no difficulty in tracing Scotcher, who was ultimately charged with contempt of court under s 8 of the Contempt of Court Act 1981. In rejecting his appeal against an earlier guilty verdict, the House of Lords upheld the principle that the secrecy of the jury room should remain paramount, but it also recognised, for the first time, the need to advise jurors as to what to do if they subsequently feel that they have participated in an unfair trial.

Prior to the judgment in *Scotcher*, jurors were advised by the judge that if they were concerned about the conduct of the jury itself, they could raise the issue with the judge *before* the verdict was passed, but they received no clear direction about what they could do *after* the trial. *Scotcher* set out a variety of options open to a juror in such a situation that did not render them vulnerable to prosecution for contempt of court. Thus jurors can safely alert the judicial authorities by contacting the clerk of the court or the jury bailiff, or even by sending a sealed letter to the court via an outside agency such as the Citizens' Advice Bureau.

In *R v Thompson and others* (2010), the Court of Appeal considered the issue of jury irregularity in a number of conjoined appeals. At the outset of his judgment, Judge LCJ made the following statement before going on to explain how allegations of irregularity can arise and how they should be dealt with:

The common feature of these six cases is alleged jury irregularity. They were heard together. We emphasise at the outset that allegations of this kind rarely trouble the Court of Appeal. The overwhelming majority of jury trials proceed without jury irregularities. Generally speaking, if these problems become apparent during the course of the trial itself, they must be addressed and handled by the trial judge. Depending on the context he may give further directions to the jury, if necessary in severe and unequivocal language (*R v Smith* [2005] 1 WLR 704), which he may or may not combine with discharging an individual juror or indeed, in the ultimate analysis, the entire jury. It is therefore to be expected that any irregularity will have been addressed and cured during and as part of the trial itself.

Much more difficult problems arise when after the verdict has been returned, attention is drawn to alleged irregularities. This may take the form of a complaint from a defendant, or his solicitors, or in a very few cases it may emerge from one or more jurors, or indeed from information revealed by the jury bailiff. It is then beyond the jurisdiction of the trial judge to intervene. Responsibility for investigating any irregularity must be assumed by this court. In performing its responsibilities, it is bound to apply the principle that the deliberations of the jury are confidential. Except with the authority of the trial judge during the trial, or this court after the verdict, inquiries into jury deliberations are 'forbidden territory' (per Gage LJ in *R v Adams* [2007] 1 Cr App R 34). If any complaint about jury deliberations is received by the trial court after verdict it is immediately referred to this court and whether the complaint has been received from the court of trial or by this court directly, the practice is to examine each case to see whether or not, exceptionally, further inquiries ought to be made, and if so, to invite the assistance of the Criminal Cases Review Commission to conduct the necessary inquiry.

In November 2012 the President of the Queen's Bench issued a protocol clarifying the procedure to be followed in regard to allegations of jury irregularities arising both during and after a trial: 'Jury Irregularities in the Crown Court', available on the www.judiciary.gov.uk website.

14.8.1   THE USE OF THE INTERNET AND OTHER ELECTRONIC MEANS OF COMMUNICATION

There has always been a possibility of jurors being influenced by extraneous sources of information, such as press or other media sources, rather than solely relying on the evidence presented in the court. However, the growth of information technology has intensified the problem and generated particular difficulties in relation to juries. In *R v Adem Karakaya* (2005) the Court of Appeal held that material downloaded from the internet and taken into a jury room by one of the members of a jury was contrary to the general rule that jurors were not to rely on privately obtained information or to receive further information after it had retired. However, see also *R v Marshall and Crump* (2007), where the finding of downloaded material relating to sentencing was held not to render guilty verdicts unsafe. The distinction was explained by Lord Judge in *R v Thompson* as follows:

> If, on examination, this material strikes at the fairness of the trial, because the jury has considered material adverse to the defendant with which he has had no or no proper opportunity to deal, the conviction is likely to be unsafe (*R v Karakaya*). If the material does not affect the safety of the conviction, the appeal will fail (*R v Marshall and Crump*).

Subsequently, in *R v Thakrar* (2008), a member of a jury supplied fellow jury members with information, again found on the internet, about the defendant's previous convictions. Unfortunately, the information was incorrect. Just over six weeks into the trial, and at the conclusion of the appellant's examination-in-chief, the jury passed a note to the judge, which revealed that they had received the information from the internet. The judge directed the jury in strong terms that they must disregard the internet information and they went on to find the accused guilty. However, on appeal it was held that there should be a retrial as under the circumstances there was a real possibility that a member, or members, of the jury did not follow the direction given by the judge.

The issue of jurors using the internet and mobile communications to research cases, and in particular details relating to the accused in cases, became a major issue in the course of 2010. In her report on the fairness of juries, released in February 2010, Cheryl Thomas found that in high-profile cases almost three-quarters of jurors will be aware of media coverage of their case. However, the report raised questions about the issue of internet use by jury members in particular. The research revealed that:

- all jurors who looked for information about their case during the trial looked on the internet;
- more jurors said they saw information on the internet than admitted looking for it on the internet;
- in high-profile cases 26 per cent said they saw information on the internet, compared with 12 per cent who said they looked, whereas in standard cases 13 per cent said they saw information, compared with 5 per cent who said they looked.

As Thomas pointed out, as jurors were admitting to doing something they should have been told by the judge not to do, that may explain why more jurors said they 'just saw' reports on the internet than said they 'looked' on the internet.

Interesting and important as these findings were, they did not generate the same degree of heat that subsequent interventions did. In October 2010, a former Director of Public Prosecutions, now Lord Ken McDonald, engaged in a public debate on the matter by expressing the view that:

> This is a serious point and we struggled with it, in criminal justice, for years trying to protect juries from what they might read about a case on the internet, material they weren't supposed to know about while they were trying it . . . In essence, we're finally giving up and just concluding that you have to expect juries to try cases fairly and they're told to do that so I think this is a serious issue around privacy, because policing the inter-net is really, I think, an unmanageable task. I don't think juries should be 'allowed' to do online research, but I do think we need to assume this will occasionally happen and that it should not invalidate a trial. We have to expect them to follow directions to try the case on the evidence. Otherwise, jury trial will go.

Lord McDonald's comments prompted the Lord Chief Justice to intervene with his own views in a lecture delivered to the Judicial Studies Board of Northern Ireland on 16 November 2010, entitled simply 'Jury trials' (available at www.judiciary.gov.uk).

In his speech, Judge LCJ makes his view clear:

> What we seem to do at the moment, is to assume that the occasions when jurors go to the internet for information are rare indeed. It is therefore easy to brush them aside as odd moments of aberration. I wonder whether we will still be thinking that in a year or two from now. Professor Thomas suggests that we should be thinking of it immediately. I respectfully agree.
>
> I should just add that I must record my entire disagreement with the view of the former Director of Public Prosecutions in England and Wales, now Lord MacDonald, that judges are 'giving up trying to stop jurors using Google, Facebook and Twitter to access potentially false and prejudicial' information about defendants. He is reported as suggesting that a trial should not be invalidated if jurors are found to have conducted online research while a case is in progress.

Not only does Lord Judge appear to agree with Professor Thomas that there is a problem, but he also appears to agree with her proposed solution. As she suggested in her report:

> To address both jury impropriety in general and juror use of the internet, the judiciary and HMCS should consider issuing every sworn juror with written guidelines clearly outlining the requirements for serving on a trial.

In the words of Judge LCJ:

> I have to be blunt about this, but in my view, if the jury system is to survive as the system for a fair trial in which we all believe and support, the misuse of the internet by jurors must stop. And I think we must spell this out to them yet more clearly. It must be provided in the information received by every potential juror. It must be reflected in the video which jurors see before they start a trial. Judges must continue to direct juries in unequivocal terms from the very outset of the trial. And I should like the notice in jury rooms which identifies potential contempt of court arising from discussions outside the jury room of their debates, to be extended to any form of reference to the internet.

AG v Fraill & Sewart *(2011)*

The first defendant, Joanne Fraill, had been a juror in a case involving the second defendant as one of the accused in a prolonged drug case trial involving a number of charges against people. Sewart's partner, Gary Knox, was accused of the drugs offences but was also charged with a distinct charge of conspiracy to commit misconduct in a public office together with a serving, although suspended, police officer, Philip Berry.

The judge gave the jury an unequivocal direction that they must not use the internet. He directed them as follows:

> You will make your decision about this case based solely upon the evidence which you hear during this trial, in this courtroom and upon nothing else. Most of us these days have access to the internet, it contains lots of fascinating information, some of it about the criminal justice system and some of it about specific criminal offences. If you do have access to the 'net, members of the jury, please do not go on the 'net during this trial to explore any issues which may arise. That would be wrong. As I have said, you must base your decision in this case solely on what you hear in this courtroom and upon nothing else.

The direction was repeated from time to time throughout the trial.

By 2 August, Sewart had been acquitted of all three charges against her. Knox had been convicted on the conspiracy charge involving Berry, and had been acquitted on one other count. However, verdicts still had to be reached on three other counts. After her acquittal, Sewart continued to attend the ongoing trial of her partner, Knox.

On 4 August, it became apparent to the judge hearing the case that an unknown juror had been in Facebook contact with Sewart, commenting to the effect that she was pleased that Sewart had been acquitted because she was 'with her the whole of the way'. She also suggested that it was a pity that Sewart had not been in court when the verdicts involving Knox were announced because she was not able to see 'the look of delight' on Gary's face when he was acquitted on the remaining charge against him. Sewart had asked her Facebook friend about the conduct of the trial while it was ongoing.

On questioning the jurors individually, the judge established, through her owning up, that the juror in question was Joanne Fraill. Although the judge decided to continue the remainder of the hearings without Fraill's participation, he subsequently decided that the case could not proceed and discharged the rest of the jury.

Both Fraill and Sewart were subsequently found guilty of contempt of court in June 2011. The judgment against Fraill was so stark as to warrant quoting. As Judge LCJ stated (and the structure of what he says is significant):

> 55 . . . it is a feature of this case that when the question of Facebook contact was raised with her in the Crown Court, this woman of good character, immediately and unhesitantly admitted what she had done and apologised for it. During the subsequent investigation she provided evidence against

herself of her misuse of the internet throughout the trial. In effect therefore she acknowledged her guilt at the earliest possible opportunity, and for some months now she has been waiting for the present proceedings to take place, and to know what the consequences of her contempt will be. The effect of all these stresses and strains was virtually palpable here in court.

56 . . . There will be an order for immediate custody for a period of eight months.

Perhaps this is an example of Voltaire's maxim about English justice 'pour encourager les autres'; but it is hardly surprising that this statement was met with overwhelming distress and tears from Fraill. Sewart received a two-month custodial term, suspended for two years.

In November 2011 in *R v Mears*, evidence emerged that a member of the jury had been in mobile phone contact with her fiancé, who had been sitting in the public gallery during a significant part of the trial and had observed proceedings which had taken place in the absence of the jury. A number of texts had been exchanged between them during the trial and the juror admitted receiving texts while in the jury room. One such text sent by the fiancé to the juror during the judge's summing-up read 'guilty'. While the judge at the trial had refused a motion to discharge the jury, the Court of Appeal had no option but to overturn the conviction on the grounds of the risk of prejudice.

Finally, in January 2012, a juror, Dr Theodora Dallas, was gaoled for six months for ignoring instructions to the contrary and conducting internet investigations into the accused person whose trial she was sitting on. When Dallas told the other jurors what she had found – that the accused had been previously accused of rape – they were concerned and informed the presiding judge, who halted the case.

On a related point, following evident breaches of the contempt and libel laws on Twitter, it was announced in December 2013 that the Attorney General would be publishing advisory notes on the gov.uk website and Twitter (@AGO_UK) to help prevent social media users from committing such offences. Advice had previously only been issued to print and broadcast media outlets on a 'not for publication' basis but the new public advice was 'designed to make sure that a fair trial takes place and warn people that comment on a particular case needs to comply with the Contempt of Court Act 1981'.

The change in policy was designed to help inform the public about the legal pitfalls of commenting in a way which could be seen as prejudicial to a court case or those involved. In the words of then Attorney General, Dominic Grieve:

Blogs and social media sites like Twitter and Facebook mean that individuals can now reach thousands of people with a single tweet or post. This is an exciting prospect, but it can pose certain challenges to the criminal justice system. In days gone by, it was only the mainstream media that had the opportunity to bring information relating to a court case to such a large group of people that it could put a court case at risk. That is no longer the case, and is why I have decided to publish the advisories that I have previously only issued to the media. This is not about telling people what they can or cannot talk about on social media; quite the opposite in fact, it's designed to help facilitate commentary in a lawful way. I hope that by making this information available to the public at large, we can help stop people from inadvertently breaking the law, and make sure that cases are tried on the evidence, not what people have found online.

14.8.2   CRIMINAL JUSTICE AND COURTS ACT 2015: JURIES

As has been stated previously at 3.6, the Law Commission report of December 2013, *Contempt of Court: Juror Misconduct and Internet Publications* (Law Com no 340) provided the basis for the sections in Part 3 of the Criminal Justice and Courts Act 2015, which established new criminal offences in relation to jurors' internet activity.

Under s 47 of the CJ&CA 2015, which amends the Juries Act 1974, it is a criminal offence to undertake any research during the trial period. Research, which is defined as intentionally seeking information which a juror ought reasonably to know is or may be relevant to the case, includes:

(a)   asking a question;
(b)   searching an electronic database, including by means of the internet;
(c)   visiting or inspecting a place or object;
(d)   conducting an experiment; and
(e)   asking another person to seek the information.

Information is relevant if it relates to:

(a)   a person involved in events relevant to the case;
(b)   the judge dealing with the issue;
(c)   any other person involved in the trial, whether as a lawyer, a witness or otherwise;
(d)   the law relating to the case;
(e)   the law of evidence; and
(f)   court procedure.

Section 48 creates the related offence of sharing information with a fellow juror, and s 49 criminalises a juror engaging in 'prohibited conduct', defined as 'conduct from which it may reasonably be concluded that the person intends to try the issue otherwise than on the basis of the evidence presented in the proceedings on the issue'.

Section 50 creates the statutory offence of disclosing details of a jury's deliberation and also extends to non-jurors looking to get information relating to those deliberations. However, there is a public interest defence where such disclosures have been made to a police officer, a judge of the court where the proceedings took place, a judge of the Court of Appeal or the Registrar of Criminal Appeals.

14.9   CONCLUSION

It has been repeatedly suggested by those in favour of abolishing, or at least severely curtailing, the role of the jury in the criminal justice system, that the general perception of the jury is romanticised and has little foundation in reality. Runciman did not actually make this point explicitly, but it is implicit in his assessment of the jury system as against the magistrates' courts. Others have been more explicit; thus, the Roskill Committee expressed the view that:

> Society appears to have an attachment to jury trial which is emotional or sentimental rather than logical (para 8.21).

A similar point had been made previously by the Faulks Committee, but that report also recognised the source of the public's opinion and was careful not to dismiss it as unimportant:

> Much of the support for jury trials is emotional and derives from the undoubted value of juries in serious criminal cases where they stand between the prosecuting authority and the citizen (para 496).

The jury system certainly commands considerable public support. A survey published in January 2004, involving interviews with 361 jurors, found that, for the vast majority of respondents, juries were seen as an essential component of providing a fair and just trial process, and the diversity of the jury was seen as the best way of avoiding bias and arriving at a sound verdict. The major conclusions of the survey were as follows:

- The majority of respondents had a more positive view of the jury trial system after completing their service than they did before. Furthermore, despite the considerable personal inconvenience they may have suffered, virtually all jurors interviewed considered jury trials to be an important part of the criminal justice system.
- Confidence in the jury system was closely associated with the process, fairness, respect for the rights of defendants and ability of all the members of the jury to consider evidence from different perspectives. A jury's representation of a broad spectrum of views was a key factor in jurors' confidence in the Crown Court trial.

- Jurors were very impressed with the professionalism and helpfulness of the court personnel. In particular, they praised the judge's performance, commitment and competence.

- The main impediment to understanding proceedings was the use of legal terminology, although jurors also felt that evidence could sometimes be presented more clearly.

- Over half of the respondents said that they would be happy to do jury service again, while 19 per cent said that they 'would not mind' doing it again. The most positive aspects of engaging in jury service were reported to be having a greater understanding of the criminal court trial, a feeling of having performed an important civic duty and finding the experience personally fulfilling.

The ideological power of the jury system should not be underestimated. It represents the ordinary person's input into the legal system and it is at least arguable that in that way it provides the whole legal system with a sense of legitimacy. It is argued by some civil libertarians that the existence of the non-jury Diplock courts in Northern Ireland brings the whole of the legal system in that province into disrepute.

As Lord Devlin noted (*Trial By Jury*, 1966):

> The first object of any tyrant in Whitehall would be to make Parliament utterly subservient to his will; and the next to overthrow or diminish trial by jury, for no tyrant could afford to leave a subject's freedom in the hands of 12 of his countrymen.

Juror satisfaction

It should also be noted that most jurors seem to be reasonably happy with the system despite the stress and inconvenience it can impose on them. The Justice Ministry carries out an annual survey to measure the expectations, attitudes and experiences of jurors (see www.justice.gov.uk/downloads/publications/statistics-and-data/mojstats/crown-court-jurors-survey-2010.pdf). Jurors are asked to rate the service provided during the pre-court, at court and after court stages of their jury service. Among the findings are that:

- over three-quarters of jurors (77 per cent) said they were satisfied with their overall experience of jury service;

- 87 per cent stated that they were satisfied overall with the treatment they received from the Jury Summoning Bureau before they attended court;

- of those who had been on jury service before, 40 per cent felt their experience this time was better than last, while 14 per cent felt their experience was worse;

- 94 per cent were satisfied with both the politeness and helpfulness of staff, and thought that staff treated jurors fairly and sensitively.

However, only 43 per cent of jurors were satisfied with the time spent waiting to be selected for a trial, so this area clearly constitutes the major source of juror dissatisfaction.

Internet use

Although only a minority of 7 per cent of jurors contacted the Jury Central Summoning Bureau by email, this is a significant increase in numbers compared to 2009 (5 per cent). One in 10 (10 per cent) of those aged 18 to 34 used this method of communication. Nearly two-thirds of jurors were very satisfied with the information they received (65 per cent) and the speed of the response (67 per cent).

CHAPTER SUMMARY: THE JURY

THE JURY

The jury has come under close public scrutiny since the Runciman Commission's recommendation to curtail the right to jury trial. It is important to know the standard arguments in favour of the jury and also the arguments showing that it may not be truly random and representative. The detail of the jury's function in a trial and the extent to which its verdict can be appealed against are important. In what ways can the membership of the jury be challenged? Juries lie at the heart of the English criminal justice system but there is debate about whether juries provide any better justice than magistrates' courts or whether the role is purely symbolic.

THE ROLE OF THE JURY

Juries decide matters of fact; judges decide matters of law. Judges can instruct juries to acquit but not to convict. Juries do not have to give reasons for their decision. There is no appeal against an acquittal verdict, although points of law may be clarified by an Attorney General's reference. Civil cases can be overturned if perverse – but not criminal cases. Verdicts can be delivered on the basis of majority decisions. The use of juries has declined in relation to criminal and civil law.

SELECTION OF JURIES

Random in theory – selective in practice. All on the electoral register are liable to serve, but the registers tend to be inaccurate. Service is subject to exemption, excusal and disqualification. Defence and prosecution can challenge for cause. Prosecution can ask jurors to stand by. Jury vetting is checking that jurors are suitable to hear sensitive cases. If Runciman is followed, juries may be required to have a racial mix.

DECLINE IN JURY TRIALS

Under s 69 of the Senior Courts Act 1981, the right to a jury trial is limited to only four specific areas:

- fraud;
- defamation;

- malicious prosecution; and
- false imprisonment.

Even in these areas, the right is not absolute and can be denied by a judge under s 69(1) where the case involves 'any prolonged examination of documents or accounts or any scientific or local investigation which cannot conveniently be made with a jury'.

The Criminal Justice Act 2003 has potentially introduced restriction in jury trials in relation to:

- jury tampering;
- complex fraud cases.

INVESTIGATION OF JURY BEHAVIOUR

Section 8 of the Contempt of Court Act 1981 makes it an offence to obtain, disclose or solicit any particulars of statements made, opinion expressed, arguments advanced or votes cast by members of a jury in the course of their deliberations in any legal proceedings.

FOOD FOR THOUGHT

1   The essential feature of jury selection is randomness, but is that really a value in and of itself? Would an all-male jury be acceptable in a rape trial, even if that were the outcome of a random selection process? If not, why not? Similarly, would an all-black jury be acceptable in a case involving a member of a white supremacist group? However, if these instances are thought to be problematic, why is this the case, and what implications does it have generally for juries' impartiality? Should what goes on in the jury room be sacrosanct, beyond investigation and subject to proceedings for contempt of court, even where the jurors may have engaged in prejudicial behaviour?

2   Some people are concerned that the jury selection process can quite easily result in unsuitable people serving as jurors and, for that reason, suggest that there should be some sort of minimum standard for serving as jurors. Do you agree?

3   In the context of recent development in information technology, should jurors be banned from investigating issues they are deciding about on the internet?

4   In the context of the cost involved, should all jury trials be abolished?

FURTHER READING

Airs, J and Shaw, A, 'Jury Excusal and Deferral' (1999), Home Office Research and Statistics Directorate Research Study No 102, 1999

Arce, R, 'Evidence evaluation in jury decision-making', in Carson, D and Bull, R (eds), *Handbook of Psychology in Legal Contexts*, 2nd edn, 2003, Chichester: John Wiley & Sons

Baldwin, J and McConville, M, *Jury Trials*, 1979, Oxford: Clarendon Press

Barber, JW, 'The jury is still out: the role of jury science in the modern American courtroom' (1994) 31 Am Crim L Rev 1225

Broeder, DW, 'The University of Chicago jury project' (1959) 38 Nebraska LR 744

Carlton, Darbyshire, Harris, Hodgetts and Robbins, in separate articles (1990) 140 NLJ 1264–1276

Chada, R, 'Jury out on justice system' (2009) 106(28) Law Soc Gazette 8

Cornish, WR, *The Jury*, 1970, London: Allen Lane

Corrin, L, '12 heads better than one' (2009) 153(27) SJ 19

Darbyshire, P, 'The lamp that shows that freedom lives: Is it worth the candle?' (1991) Crim LR 740

Devlin, P, *Trial By Jury*, 1956, London: Stevens

Findlay, M and Duff, P, *The Jury Under Attack*, 1988, London: Butterworths

Finkel, NJ, *Common Sense Justice: Jurors' Notions of the Law*, 1995, Cambridge, MA: Harvard UP

Gobert, J, *Justice, Democracy and the Jury*, 1997, Aldershot: Dartmouth

Griffiths, C, 'Jury trial' (1999) Counsel 14

Grove, T, *The Juryman's Tale*, 1998, London: Bloomsbury

Hastie, R, *Inside the Juror: The Psychology of Juror Decision-making*, 1993, Cambridge: CUP

Mathews, R, Hancock, L and Briggs, D, *Jurors' Perceptions: Understanding Confidence and Satisfaction in the Jury System – A Study in Six Courts*, 2004, London: Home Office

Sealy, AP and Cornish, WR, 'Jurors and their verdicts' (1973) 36 MLR 496

Vidmar, N (ed), *World Jury Systems*, 2000, Oxford: OUP

Wolchover, D, 'Twelve good men & true & safe' (2009) Counsel 28

USEFUL WEBSITES

http://4wardeveruk.org/wp-content/uploads/2009/08/p.Diversity-Fairness-in-the-Jury-System.pdf
Diversity and Fairness in the Jury System.

www.justice.gov.uk/downloads/publications/research-and-analysis/moj-research/are-juries-fairre-search.pdf
Are juries fair?

COMPANION WEBSITE

Now visit the companion website to:

- test your understanding of the key terms using our Flashcard Glossary;
- revise and consolidate your knowledge of 'The jury' using our multiple choice question testbank;
- view all of the links to the Useful Websites above.

www.routledge.com/cw/slapper

15.1 INTRODUCTION

In its 1999 Consultation Paper, *Alternative Dispute Resolution*, the Lord Chancellor's Department (LCD) redefined 'access to justice' as meaning:

> [W]here people need help there are effective solutions that are proportionate to the issues at stake. In some circumstances, this will involve going to court, but in others, that will not be necessary. *For most people most of the time, litigation in the civil courts, and often in tribunals too, should be the method of dispute resolution of last resort* (emphasis added).

That extremely useful Consultation Paper also set out the following list of types of alternative dispute resolution (ADR) mechanisms:

- *Arbitration* is a procedure whereby both sides to a dispute agree to let a third party, the arbitrator, decide. In some instances, there may be a panel. The arbitrator may be a lawyer or may be an expert in the field of the dispute. He or she will make a decision according to the law. The arbitrator's decision, known as an award, is legally binding and can be enforced through the courts.
- *Early neutral evaluation* is a process in which a neutral professional, commonly a lawyer, hears a summary of each party's case and gives a non-binding assessment of the merits. This can then be used as a basis for settlement or for further negotiation.
- *Expert determination* is a process where an independent third party who is an expert in the subject matter is appointed to decide the dispute. The expert's decision is binding on the parties.
- *Mediation* is a way of settling disputes in which a third party, known as a mediator, helps both sides to come to an agreement that each considers acceptable. Mediation can be 'evaluative', where the mediator gives an assessment of the legal strength of a case, or 'facilitative', where the mediator concentrates on assisting the parties to define the issues. When mediation is successful and an agreement is reached, it is written down and forms a legally binding contract unless the parties state otherwise.
- *Conciliation* is a procedure like mediation but where the third party, the conciliator, takes a more interventionist role in bringing the two parties together and in suggesting possible solutions to help achieve an agreed settlement. The term 'conciliation' is gradually falling into disuse and the process is regarded as a form of mediation.
- *Med-Arb* is a combination of mediation and arbitration where the parties agree to mediate, but if that fails to achieve a settlement, the dispute is referred to arbitration. The same person may act as mediator and arbitrator in this type of arrangement.
- *Neutral fact finding* is a non-binding procedure used in cases involving complex technical issues. A neutral expert in the subject matter is appointed to investigate the facts of the dispute and make an evaluation of the merits of the case. This can form the basis of a settlement or a starting point for further negotiation.

- *Ombudsmen* are independent office-holders who investigate and rule on complaints from members of the public about maladministration in government and, in particular, services in both the public and private sectors. Some Ombudsmen use mediation as part of their dispute resolution procedures. The powers of Ombudsmen vary. Most Ombudsmen are able to make recommendations; only a few can make decisions which are enforceable through the courts.
- *Utility regulators* are watchdogs appointed to oversee the privatised utilities such as water or gas. They handle complaints from customers who are dissatisfied by the way a complaint has been dealt with by their supplier.

While ADR is usually regarded as referring to arbitration and mediation and the operation of the Ombudsman scheme, this chapter will extend this meaning to allow an examination of the role of the various administrative tribunals that exercise so much power in contemporary society.

ADR in the European Union

The importance of resolving commercial disputes, and the role of ADR in that process, was not lost on the European Union. The fundamental tenet of the EU, the free movement of goods and services within a unified market, runs in to difficulties when consumers are not confident that any problems relating to a particular transaction can be resolved. The single market only works when consumers have confidence that problems can be resolved effectively and relatively cheaply; however, for the moment consumers may be reluctant to enter into cross-border transactions for fear of what happens when things go wrong. An EU-wide system of dealing with such transactions, and particularly online transactions which are most likely to be involved, clearly would greatly facilitate the operation of the market. The EU Commission estimates that if EU consumers could rely on well-functioning and transparent ADR for their disputes, they could save around €22.5 billion a year, corresponding to 0.19 per cent of EU GDP.

In line with this line of reasoning, in June 2013, the European Parliament published a Directive on ADR (Directive 2013/11/EU) for consumer disputes together with Regulation on Online Dispute Resolution for consumer disputes (ODR Regulation (EU) 524/2013). Member states were required implement the Directive by July 2015. The Regulation came into force in January 2016.

The Directive for consumer ADR

The Directive applies to both domestic and cross-border disputes between EU consumers and traders relating to sales or service contracts. It applies to online and other transactions and in all economic sectors, except health and education. It does not apply to trader to business disputes and disputes between traders.

The Directive requires Member states to designate competent authorities to maintain and monitor a list of appropriately qualified ADR providers. All ADR entities will have to meet quality criteria which guarantee that they operate in an effective, fair, independent and transparent way. The use of ADR is not compulsory but those traders who commit to, or are obliged to use, ADR will need to inform consumers about ADR on their websites and in their general terms and conditions. All traders will need to inform consumers about ADR when a dispute cannot be settled directly between the consumer and the trader. The Directive imposes a 90-day time limit for dealing with a dispute and allows consumers to elect to deal with their complaint online or in some other way.

The ODR Regulation

The Regulation requires the establishment by the EU Commission, of an online, interactive portal (the 'ODR platform') for resolving contractual disputes. The Regulation applies to consumer/trader disputes, domestic and cross-border disputes. Member states must propose an ODR contact to assist with disputes submitted through the ODR platform. Once the EU consumer submits their dispute online, they are linked with national ADR providers who will help to resolve the dispute. According to the Commission the procedure will operate as follows:

- Consumers who encounter a problem with an online purchase will be able to submit a complaint online through the ODR platform, in the language of their choice. The ODR platform will notify the trader that a complaint is lodged against him. The consumer and the trader will then agree on which ADR entity to use to solve their dispute. When they agree, the chosen ADR entity will receive the details of the dispute via the ODR platform.
- The ODR platform will be connected to the national ADR entities set up and notified to the Commission, in line with the new rules of the ADR Directive. The platform will help speed up the resolution of the dispute by allowing ADR entities to conduct the proceedings online and through electronic means. A set of common rules will govern the functioning of the ODR platform. These will include the role of national contact points acting as ODR advisers in their respective countries. Their task will be to provide general information on consumer rights and redress in relation to online purchases, assist with the submission of complaints and facilitate communication between the parties and the competent ADR entity through the ODR platform. For this purpose, ODR advisers will also be linked electronically to the platform.

Implementation of the Directive for consumer ADR in the UK

In November 2014, following a consultation exercise, the Department for Business Innovation and Skills published its proposals for bringing the EU rules into effect within the required time period (*Alternative Dispute Resolution for Consumers*). The document set out the intentions as follows:

> To plug existing gaps and ensure ADR is widely available across all sectors, the Government will assist with the set-up of a residual ADR scheme, which will be available to businesses that are not obliged or committed to using another ADR scheme . . .

The current UK ADR landscape can also be complex and confusing for consumers. In order to make the system easier for consumers to navigate, to increase awareness of ADR and the process for accessing it and to ensure as seamless a consumer journey as possible, the Government is intending to work with Citizens Advice to create a consumer complaints helpdesk to provide assistance and advice to consumers attempting to resolve a dispute with a trader . . .

The Government will appoint the Trading Standards Institute (TSI) to act as the UK's competent authority covering ADR schemes in the non-regulated sectors. Operating alongside TSI, the Government will appoint the sector regulators as competent authorities for their sectors where appropriate. In order to help traders meet the statutory information requirements concerning the provision of ADR, government will work with the Trading Standards Institute (TSI) to produce appropriate guidance for business.

In relation to the ODR scheme the Government will establish an ODR contact point to help consumers with cross-border disputes submitted via the Commission's ODR platform but will not extend the ODR requirements beyond that.

In April 2015 the government implemented its proposals to comply with the directive and regulation through the Alternative Dispute Resolution for Consumer Disputes (Competent Authorities and Information) Regulations (SI 2015/542). Amendments to the regulations soon followed (ADR for Consumer Disputes (Amendment) Regulations 2015 (2015/1392), to allow for the extension of the time for businesses to comply until 1 October 2015 and allowing non-UK based ADR providers to apply to operate.

In the simplest terms the regulations:

- *place an information requirement on businesses selling to consumers.* The regulations do not make participation in ADR schemes mandatory for traders but they do require businesses which sell directly to consumers, where they cannot resolve a dispute in-house, to inform the consumer of a certified ADR scheme and state whether or not they intend to use that scheme.

- *establish competent authorities to certify ADR schemes.* The Chartered Trading Standards Institute (CTSI) is the UK Competent Authority and handles applications from bodies, seeking approval, operating in non-regulated consumer sectors. Bodies seeking approval, to operate in regulated sectors, must apply to other Competent Authorities such as:
  - The Financial Conduct Authority (FCA).
  - Legal Services Board.
  - Civil Aviation Authority.
  - Gas and Electricity Markets Authority (Ofgem).

- *set the standards that ADR scheme applicants must meet in order to achieve certification.* The regulations require that any ADR providers wishing to gain certification must meet certain standards with regard to independence, impartiality, and quality of expertise.

Apart from the business information requirement, the regulations came into force in July 2015, the former took effect from October 2015. For the purposes of the regulations,

The CTSA website, www.tradingstandards.uk/advice/AlternativeDispute Resolution.cfm provides a number of extremely useful guides on such aspects of the scheme such as how to apply to become an ADR approved body, what businesses must do to conform with the regulations and a list of approved ADR bodies.

It should also be mentioned that this change accompanied a major alteration in the law relating to consumer transactions, with the passing of the Consumer Rights Act 2015.

15.2   MEDIATION AND CONCILIATION

A number of alternatives to court proceedings have already been listed, but the two most common, or certainly the two that most immediately spring to mind when the topic of ADR is raised, are mediation and conciliation, and as a consequence, although distinct, they are dealt with together.

15.2.1   MEDIATION

Mediation is the process whereby a third party acts as the conduit through which two disputing parties communicate and negotiate, in an attempt to reach a common resolution to a problem. The mediator may move between the parties, communicating their opinions without their having to meet, or alternatively the mediator may operate in the presence of the parties, but in either situation the emphasis is on the parties themselves working out a shared agreement as to how the dispute in question is to be settled.

Before the Woolf reforms introduced the three-track system, the small claims process was referred to as mediation, due to its much less formal procedural rules and practices. Although the small claims track is still relatively informal in comparison with the other tracks (see above, 7.5), the Court Service introduced a distinct and specific mediation process as an alternative to the court-based procedure. This small claims mediation scheme was funded by HMCS and consequently was free to court users who had a defended small claim.

The scheme was assessed positively after a pilot at Manchester County Court, and in 2007 HMCS began to appoint a number of small claims mediators across England and Wales. By June 2008 each of the 23 HMCS Court Areas in England and Wales had an in-house small claims mediator to deal with appropriate cases. The Ministry of Justice also developed a Mediation Helpline to assist individuals to access mediation. However, in October 2011, an online civil mediation directory replaced the National Mediation

Helpline. A spokesperson for the ministry was quoted as saying that 'over recent years calls, mediation referrals and settlements had continued to fall' and 'approximately two-thirds of all calls to the helpline had nothing to do with mediation'. As a result, it was felt not to be worth the £90,000 spent on it annually. Such a statement and action does not fit particularly well with government's supposed commitment to an increased use of ADR.

The new directory has replicated some of the previous functions of the helpline in that it allows individuals to find a mediation provider accredited by the Civil Mediation Council anywhere in England and Wales. The cost of such mediation is based on a fixed fee, depending on the value of the dispute and, although not free, is much cheaper than making use of lawyers and going to court.

The fees for using the National Mediation Scheme are:

Amount claimed	Fees (per party)	Length of session	Extra hours (per party)
£5,000 or less*	£50 + VAT	1 hour	£50 + VAT
	£100 + VAT	Up to 2 hours	
£5,000 – £15,000	£300 + VAT	Up to 3 hours	£85 + VAT
£15,000 – £50,000**	£425 + VAT	Up to 4 hours	£95 + VAT

Mediation is also available for higher value claims and fees are negotiable.

LawWorks (www.lawworks.org.uk), a legal pro bono charity, offers free civil and commercial mediation to those unable to afford to pay for a commercial provider and without other means of paying. This service is available throughout England and Wales and is free to both parties if one party qualifies for pro bono help. Fee remission is an automatic gateway; in other cases, LawWorks will assess whether the applicant can afford to pay.

In the same year as the Helpline was closed, the Legal Services Commission withdrew funding (£12,000) from the ADRnow website, a resource provided by the Advice Services Alliance (http://asauk.org.uk) aimed at steering the public towards mediation and other forms of alternative dispute resolution. As a result, ASA had to cease updating its extremely informative and useful ADR material. The Family Mediation Council provides an online service explaining and promoting the advantages of mediation in separation, divorce and other family law issues. It also operates a compulsory accreditation scheme for all family mediators and helps to locate suitable mediators.

The way in which mediation operates will become clear from the cases considered below. However, the mediator may settle the majority of disputes over the telephone without the need for either party to attend a hearing, consequently reducing time and expense. However, if necessary, face-to-face mediation can be arranged, either on court premises or elsewhere as deemed appropriate. In the event of the parties not being able to reach a settlement at the mediation appointment, the case will be listed for a small claims hearing. As the mediation process is confidential, the judge who deals with the subsequent case in court will not be informed of the content of any discussions at any previous mediation proceedings.

In his final report into the structure of the civil courts: The Civil Courts Structure Review July 2016, Lord Justice Briggs had some critical things to say about the removal of previous ADR facilities:

> . . . [T]he court service used to provide free space after court hours for short mediations, and then funded the National Mediation Helpline. I have tried to ascertain why those two services were discontinued. It appears that the after-hours service was regarded as less satisfactory than a nationally organised service, and that the latter was discontinued because of the expense to the MoJ of funding its administration (but not its performance) on a contracted-out basis. Whatever may have been the justification for the discontinuation of those services, and their replacement by a service which only addresses small claims, (and only a moderate proportion of those), I regard the outcome as less than satisfactory.

Consequently he recommended the re-establishment of a court-based out of hours private mediation service in County Court hearing centres prepared to participate, along the lines of the service which existed prior to the establishment and then termination of the National Mediation Helpline.

15.2.2   MEDIATION IN DIVORCE

Mediation has an important part to play in family matters, where it is felt that the adversarial approach of the traditional legal system has tended to emphasise, if not increase, existing differences of view between individuals and has not been conducive to amicable settlements. Thus, in divorce cases, mediation has traditionally been used to enable the parties themselves to work out an agreed settlement rather than having one imposed upon them by the courts.

This emphasis on mediation was formally strengthened in the Family Law Act 1996. Before receiving legal aid for representation in a divorce case a person was *expected* to have a meeting with a mediator to assess whether mediation was a suitable alternative to court proceedings. The only exception to this requirement was in relation to allegations of domestic abuse. However, excluding those exempted for reasons of domestic abuse, only 20 per cent of people publicly funded in divorce proceedings actually got involved in mediation.

In April 2011 the scheme applying to those making use of legal aid was extended to all parties wishing to go to court to resolve children or property issues following a separation or divorce. Consequently, all applicants to court on family proceedings were *expected* to show that they have already considered mediation and other dispute resolution options by attending a Mediation Information and Assessment Meeting (MIAM). However, the fact was that many applicants did not comply with the expectation.

The expectation that applicants should attend MIAMs became a *requirement* in April 2014 following the enactment of the Children and Families Act 2014 (s 10). The fact that the requirement only applies to applicants and not respondents inevitably reduces the effectiveness of the provision. In November 2014 the Justice Ministry announced that the first mediation session would be funded for both parties, provided at least one of them is already legally aided. Both of these measures may be understood as an attempt to deal with a crisis developing in the recently unified Family Court.

The Legal Aid, Sentencing and Punishment of Offenders Act 2012 introduced reforms, effectively designed to remove legal aid for divorce cases, unless they involve allegations of domestic violence or child abuse. The new Act came into force in April 2013. Among the justifications for cutting legal aid in this particular area was not just the fact that it saved money and reduced pressure on the courts, but that it would also have the additional benefit of reducing antagonism between separating couples as they opted for the, certainly cheaper, but also, unarguably, less confrontational form of mediation. Unfortunately the provisions seem to have had not only an unexpected, but a contrary, outcome. In effect, by removing most access to legal aid in relation to divorce, the government removed the signposts to mediation, which actually led not just to a reduction in the use of mediation, but to a corresponding increase in recourse to the courts and also an increase in self-representation in those courts. In turn, this had the consequence of slowing up of court proceedings as those unused to law and legal procedures attempted to represent themselves.

Following a freedom of information request by family mediator Marc Lopatin, the founder of Lawyer Supported Mediation (now Dialogue First http://dialoguefirst. co.uk/), statistics compiled by the Ministry of Justice revealed a large drop in the number of couples attending family related mediation meetings since the implementation of the legal aid cuts in April 2013. Between April and June 2012, 7,381 couples attended mediation information and assessment meetings in England and Wales, but in the same period in 2013, only 3,854 couples attended such meetings, a drop of 47 per cent.

The irony is that legal aid for mediation was still available; indeed, the government had made an extra £10 million available for such purposes, but no referrals were being made. Couples were avoiding what they saw as the unaffordable expense of funding lawyers through a full divorce hearing, but in so doing they were also avoiding the gatekeepers who could have guided them to a simpler process. Lord McNally, then the Family Justice Minister, was quoted in the press as responding as follows:

> We are aware there has been a recent drop in referrals to mediation and are working closely with the Family Mediation Council and legal profession to address this . . . We are also now changing the law so anyone considering court action over disputes about children or finances will be legally obliged to attend a mediation meeting first.

As stated, making mediation compulsory under the Children and Families Act 2014 would appear to be the response, but whether it is sufficient remains problematic. The underlying tension came to a head in August 2014 when, in a series of linked cases, *Q v Q, Re B* and *Re C* [2014] EWFC 31, president of the Family Court Sir James Munby asked the Justice Ministry to explain how the cases in question could proceed without legal aid. In Munby's words:

> [T]hese are problems which pre-date the implementation in April 2013 of the relevant provisions of the Legal Aid, Sentencing and Punishment of Offenders Act 2012 (LASPO). They are, however, problems which most practitioners and judges with any practical experience of the family justice system would recognise as having been very considerably exacerbated by LASPO . . .

There has been a drastic reduction in the number of represented litigants in private law cases. The number of cases where both parties are represented has fallen very significantly, the number of cases where one party is represented has also fallen significantly and, correspondingly, the number of cases where neither party is represented has risen very significantly.

It is important to realise that there are potential problems with mediation. The assumption that the parties freely negotiate the terms of their final agreement in a less than hostile manner may be deeply flawed, to the extent that it assumes equality of bargaining power and knowledge between the parties to the negotiation. Mediation may well ease pain, but unless the mediation procedure is carefully and critically monitored, it may gloss over and perpetuate a previously exploitative relationship, allowing the more powerful participant to manipulate and dominate the more vulnerable and force an inequitable agreement. Establishing entitlements on the basis of clear legal advice may be preferable to apparently negotiating those entitlements away in the non-confrontational, therapeutic, atmosphere of mediation.

15.2.3   CONCILIATION

Conciliation takes mediation a step further and gives the mediator the power to suggest grounds for compromise and the possible basis for a conclusive agreement. Both mediation and conciliation have been available in relation to industrial disputes under the auspices of the government-funded Advisory, Conciliation and Arbitration Service (ACAS). One of the statutory functions of ACAS is to try to resolve industrial disputes by means of discussion and negotiation or, if the parties agree, the service might take a more active part as arbitrator in relation to a particular dispute.

The essential weakness in the procedures of mediation and conciliation lies in the fact that, although they *may* lead to the resolution of a dispute, they do not *necessarily* achieve that end. Where they operate successfully they are excellent methods of dealing with problems, as the parties to the dispute essentially determine their own solutions and feel committed to the outcome. The problem is that they have no binding power and do not always lead to an outcome. As a result, it is always possible that parties will go through the time and expense of mediation, only to find that, at the end of the procedure, one of them does not agree to a proposed resolution. As a result, the whole process ends up taking longer and being more expensive than it would have been if the dispute had been taken directly to court.

A case study in how not to do it: Burchell v Bullard
[2005] EWCA Civ 358

This unfortunate case, for everyone apart perhaps from the lawyers engaged to pursue it, can be taken as a signal example of the dangers and inappropriateness of pursuing legal action in the courts when ADR is available and a better way of deciding the contended issue.

The appellant in the case was a builder who had contracted to build two large extensions onto the defendants' home. The dispute arose because the Bullards claimed that some of the work carried out by Burchell's subcontractor was substandard. They refused to make a payment, due under the contract, until the allegedly defective work had been rectified. As a result, Burchell left the site. In an attempt to resolve the dispute, Burchell suggested that the dispute be referred to mediation, but on the advice of their chartered surveyor the Bullards refused to mediate, claiming that due to the complexity of the issues the case was not appropriate for mediation.

At first instance the judge, District Judge Tennant, was clear that (para 20):

> There are faults on both sides . . . [o]n balance, however, I am satisfied that quite apart from the net amount actually recovered by the claimant, the defendants are more at fault than the claimant in the sense that they have conducted the litigation more unreasonably.

Nonetheless, he decided that each of the parties should pay the costs of the other in relation to the main claim in the action. Burchell subsequently appealed against those costs orders.

The attitude of the Court of Appeal is scathingly evident in the judgment of Ward LJ. As to the offer of mediation he stated that (para 3):

> [Burchell's] solicitors wrote sensibly suggesting that to avoid litigation the matter be referred for alternate dispute resolution through 'a qualified construction mediator'. *The sorry response* from the respondents' chartered building surveyor was that 'the matters complained of are technically complex and as such mediation is not an appropriate route to settle matters' (emphasis added).

However, as Ward LJ pointed out, 'All the Bullards wanted was for the builder to complete the contract and rectify the defective work.' So what was the underlying 'technically complex' issue that prevented mediation?

As Ward LJ examined the facts of the case he found things, regrettably but not unexpectedly, getting worse (para 23):

> As we had expected, *an horrific picture emerges*. In this comparatively small case where ultimately only about £5,000 will pass from defendants to claimant, the claimant will have spent about £65,000 up to the end of the trial and he will also have to pay the subcontractor's costs of £27,500. We were told that the claimant might recover perhaps only 25 per cent of his trial costs, say £16,000, because most of the contest centred on the counterclaim. The defendants' costs of trial are estimated at about £70,000 and it was estimated the claimant would have to pay about 85 per cent, i.e. £59,500. *Recovery of £5,000 will have cost him about £136,000. On the other hand the defendants who lost in the sense that they have to pay the claimant £5,000 are only a further £26,500 out of pocket in respect of costs.* Then there are the costs of the appeal – £13,500 for the appellant and over £9,000 for the respondents. *A judgment of £5,000 will have been procured at a cost to the parties of about £185,000. Is that not horrific?* (emphasis added)

In examining the situation, Ward LJ emphasised the fact that the appellant's offer to mediate was made long before the action started, and long before the crippling costs had been incurred. The issue to be decided, therefore, was whether the respondents had acted unreasonably in refusing the offer of mediation. While Ward LJ recognised that *Halsey v The Milton Keynes General NHS Trust* had set out the manner in which such a question should be answered, he declined to follow it in the immediate case. His reasoning was as follows (para 42):

> It seems to me, therefore, that the *Halsey* factors are established in this case and that the court should mark its disapproval of the defendants' conduct by imposing some costs sanction. Yet I draw back from doing so. This offer was made in May 2001. The defendants rejected the offer on the advice of their surveyor, not of their solicitor. The law had not become as clear and developed as it now is following the succession of judgments from this court of which *Halsey* and *Dunnett v Railtrack plc (Practice Note)* [2002] 1 WLR 2434 are prime examples. To be fair to the defendants one must judge the reasonableness of their actions against the background of practice a year earlier than *Dunnett*. In the light of the knowledge of the times and in the absence of legal advice, I cannot condemn them as having been so unreasonable that a costs sanction should follow many years later.

However, Ward LJ was as emphatic as he was admonitory in his assessment of the present case and his view as to how future cases should be treated. As he put it (paras 41–43):

> *a small building dispute is par excellence the kind of dispute which, as the recorder found, lends itself to ADR.* Secondly, the merits of the case favoured mediation. The defendants behaved unreasonably in believing, if they did, that their case was so watertight that they need not engage in attempts to settle. They were counterclaiming almost as much to remedy *some* defective work as they had contracted to pay for the whole of the stipulated work. There was clearly room for give and take. *The stated reason for refusing mediation, that the matter was too complex for mediation, is plain nonsense.* Thirdly, the costs of ADR would have been a drop in the ocean *compared with the fortune that has been spent on this litigation.* Finally, the way in which the claimant modestly presented his claim and readily admitted many of the defects, allied with the finding that he was transparently honest and more than ready to admit where he was wrong and to shoulder responsibility for it augured well for mediation. The claimant has satisfied me that mediation would have had a reasonable prospect of success. The defendants cannot rely on their own obstinacy to assert that mediation had no reasonable prospect of success . . . *The profession must, however, take no comfort from this conclusion. Halsey has made plain not only the high rate of a successful outcome being achieved by mediation but also its established importance as a track to a just result running parallel with that of the court system.* Both have a proper part to play in the administration of justice. The court has given its stamp of approval to mediation and *it is now the legal profession which must become fully aware of and acknowledge its value.* The profession can no longer with impunity shrug aside reasonable requests to mediate . . . These defendants have escaped the imposition of a costs sanction in this case *but defendants in a like position in the future can expect little sympathy if they blithely battle on regardless of the alternatives* (emphasis added).

In the final analysis, the Court of Appeal directed the defendants to pay 60 per cent of the claimant's costs of the original claim and counterclaim and related proceedings. However, there was still a sting in the tail, for as Ward LJ stated (para 47):

> We have not heard argument on the costs of this appeal. In order that more costs are not wasted, I say that my preliminary view is that costs of the appeal should follow the event. The appellant has been successful and as at present advised and having regard to the checklist of relevant considerations set out in CPR 44.3, I can see no justification for his not having the costs of the appeal.

FIGURE 15.1 *Alternative Dispute Resolution (ADR): an aide-mémoire.*

So the Bullards faced even more costs for their failure to take advantage of the earlier offer of mediation. (For another case of money being thrown away in pursuit of a 'matter of principle', and perhaps even more scathing comments by Ward LJ, see *Egan v Motor Services (Bath) Ltd* (2007) in which a claim for about £6,000 damages cost £100,000 in fees.)

15.3   THE COURTS AND ADR

15.3.1   THE WOOLF AND JACKSON REFORMS

Alternative Dispute Resolution mechanisms have assumed an increasingly central place in the English legal system in fairly recent times.

Central to Lord Woolf's review of the civil law system was the perception of the lack of control over the antagonistic process of civil litigation allowing, if not necessarily directly leading to, inherent problems of cost, complexity and delay (see 7.2).

And central to Woolf's solution was the avoidance of litigation and the promotion of early, cost-effective settlement.

In his final report, *Access to Justice*, Woolf prefigured a new landscape for civil justice for the 21st century in which ' *litigation will be avoided wherever possible*'. To achieve this end:

- people were to be encouraged to start court proceedings *only as a last resort*, and after using other more appropriate means when these are available;

- information on sources of alternative dispute resolution were to be provided at all civil courts;
- legal aid funding was to be made available for pre-litigation resolution and ADR.

However, although a proponent of ADR, Lord Woolf was very much of the opinion that it could never be forced on individuals if they did not wish to make use of it. However, they should be actively encouraged and indeed might suffer in costs if they did not avail themselves of the opportunities and advantages afforded by such alternative methods of dispute resolution.

In April 1999, new Civil Procedure Rules (CPR) and Practice Directions came into force. As part of the civil justice reforms, the general requirement placed on courts to actively manage cases includes 'encouraging the parties to use an alternative dispute resolution procedure if the court considers that to be appropriate and facilitating the use of such procedure' (CPR 1.4(2)). Rule 26.4 of the CPR enables judges, either on their own account or at the agreement of the parties, to stop court proceedings where they consider the dispute to be better suited to solution by some alternative procedure, such as arbitration or mediation.

CPR 44.2(2) provides that 'if the court decides to make an order about costs:

(a)   the general rule is that the unsuccessful party will be ordered to pay the costs of the successful party; but

(b)   the court may make a different order'.

CPR 44.2(4) provides that in deciding what order (if any) to make about costs, the court must have regard to all the circumstances, including the conduct of the parties, and r 44.2(5) provides that the conduct of the parties includes '(a) conduct before, as well as during, the proceedings and in particular the extent to which the parties followed any relevant pre-action protocol'.

If, subsequently, a court is of the opinion that an action it has been required to decide could have been settled more effectively through ADR, then under r 44.2(1) of the CPR, it may penalise the party who insisted on the court hearing by awarding them reduced, or even, no costs should they win the case.

Some 10 years after Lord Woolf's review of the operation of general civil law system, it fell to Lord Justice Jackson to conduct a review of the specifics of the cost of that system, and his *Review of Civil Litigation Costs* was issued in January 2010. While the report covered some 45 subject areas and ran to 557 pages, with recommendations across the whole spectrum of civil litigation, it did have some specific points to make about ADR. It was Jackson LJ's view that ADR was not fully appreciated by legal practitioners, the public generally and small businesses in particular. Consequently he felt it was under-used, and he strongly supported its increased use, concluding that ADR and, in particular, mediation had a vital role to play in reducing the costs of civil disputes, by facilitating the early settlement of cases. In particular he disagreed with the widespread belief that mediation was not suitable for personal injury cases, as long as such mediations are carried out by mediators with specialist experience of personal injuries litigation. However, he did not consider ADR to be a panacea and recognised that mediation can be expensive and does not always end successfully.

Although not central to the report, in line with the foregoing, Jackson did have two particular recommendations to make with regard to ADR:

(i)   there should be a campaign to ensure that all litigation lawyers and judges are properly informed about the benefits which ADR can bring and to alert the public and small businesses to the benefits of ADR;

(ii)   an authoritative handbook should be prepared, explaining clearly and concisely what ADR is and providing practical and concise guidance on all aspects of ADR. This handbook should be the standard text for use at all Judicial College seminars and CPD training sessions concerning mediation.

Subsequently, such an authoritative handbook, *The Jackson ADR Handbook*, was produced by authors Susan Blake, Julie Browne and Stuart Sime of City University, London. The handbook has been endorsed by Lord Justice Jackson, the Judicial College, the Civil Justice Council and the Civil Mediation Council. It is proposed that it and every judge who hears civil cases will receive a copy as an aide. Its use was recognised and endorsed by the Court of appeal in *PGF II SA v OMFS Company 1 Ltd* (2014) (see, further, below).

The main aim of the Jackson report was to deal with the escalating costs of personal injury cases and, although not strictly within the ambit of this chapter, it cannot go unrecognised that it already has had a significant impact on the substance and process of English law. The legislation introducing these changes was the Legal Aid, Sentencing and Punishment of Offenders Act 2012 and most of the relevant provisions came into force on 1 April 2013.

Amendments to the Civil Procedure Rules

Since April 2013 the Civil Procedure Rules have a revised overriding objective: to enable the court to deal with cases justly *and at proportionate cost*.

Although proportionality is not defined, r 44.3(5) states that costs incurred are proportionate if they bear a reasonable relationship to:

(a)   the sums in issue in the proceedings;

(b)   the value of any non-monetary relief in issue in the proceedings;

(c)   the complexity of the litigation;

(d)   any additional work generated by the conduct of the paying party; or

(e)   any wider factors involved in the proceedings, such as reputation or public importance.

Significantly, and perhaps worryingly, r 44.3 states that costs which are disproportionate in amount may be disallowed or reduced *even if they were reasonably or necessarily incurred*.

The judicial development of ADR

The potential consequences of not abiding by a recommendation to use ADR may be seen in *Dunnett v Railtrack plc* (2002). When Dunnett won a right to appeal against a previous court decision, the court granting the appeal recommended that the dispute should be put to arbitration. Railtrack, however, refused Dunnett's offer of arbitration and insisted on the dispute going back to a full court hearing. In the subsequent hearing in the Court of Appeal, Railtrack proved successful. The Court of Appeal, however, held that if a party rejected ADR out of hand when it had been suggested by the court, they would suffer the consequences when costs came to be decided. In the instant case, Railtrack had refused to even contemplate ADR at a stage prior to the costs of the appeal beginning to flow.

The Court of Appeal subsequently applied *Dunnett* in *Leicester Circuits Ltd v Coates Brothers plc* (2003) where, although it found for Coates, it did not award it full costs on the grounds that it had withdrawn from a mediation process. The Court of Appeal also dismissed Coates' claim that there was no realistic prospect of success in the mediation. As Judge LJ stated (para 27):

> We do not for one moment assume that the mediation process would have succeeded, but certainly there is a prospect that it would have done if it had been allowed to proceed. That therefore bears on the issue of costs.

It is possible to refuse to engage in mediation without subsequently suffering in the awards of costs. The test, however, is an objective rather than a subjective one, and a difficult one to sustain, as was shown in *Hurst v Leeming* (2002). Hurst, a solicitor, started legal proceedings against his former partners and instructed Leeming, a barrister, to represent him. When the claim proved unsuccessful, Hurst sued Leeming in professional negligence. When that claim failed, Hurst argued that Leeming should not be awarded costs, as he, Hurst, had offered to mediate the dispute, but Leeming had rejected the offer. Leeming cited five separate justifications for his refusal to mediate. These were:

- the heavy costs he had already incurred in meeting the allegations;
- the seriousness of the allegation made against him;
- the lack of substance in the claim;
- the fact that he had already provided Hurst with a full refutation of his allegation;
- the fact that, given Hurst's obsessive character, there was no real prospect of a successful outcome to the litigation.

Only the fifth justification was accepted by the court, although even in that case it was emphasised that the conclusion had to be supported by an objective evaluation of the situation. However, in the circumstances, given Hurst's behaviour and character, the conclusion that mediation would not have resolved the complaint could be sustained objectively.

In *Halsey v Milton Keynes General NHS Trust* (2004), the Court of Appeal emphasised that the criterion was the reasonableness of the belief. The only ground of appeal in *Halsey* was that the judge at first instance had been wrong to award the defendant, the Milton Keynes General NHS, its costs, since it had refused a number of invitations by the claimant to mediate. As the court emphasised, in deciding whether to deprive a successful party of some or all of their costs on the grounds that they have refused to agree to ADR, it must be borne in mind that such an order is an exception to the general rule that costs should follow the event. In demonstrating such exceptional circumstances, in the view of the Court of Appeal, the burden is to be placed on the unsuccessful party to the substantive action to show why there should be any departure from that general rule. Lord Justice Dyson said (para 28):

> It seems to us that a fair . . . balance is struck if the burden is placed on the unsuccessful party to show that there was a reasonable prospect that mediation would have been successful. This is not an unduly onerous burden to discharge: he does not have to prove that a mediation would *in fact* have succeeded. It is significantly easier for the unsuccessful party to prove that there was a reasonable prospect that a mediation would have succeeded than for the successful party to prove the contrary.

In taking such a stance, the Court of Appeal was sensitive to the possibility, as it implicitly suggested was the case in relation to the claimants in the *Halsey* case, that (para 18):

> . . . there would be considerable scope for a claimant to use the threat of costs sanctions to extract a settlement from the defendant even where the claim is without merit. Courts should be particularly astute to this danger. Large organisations, especially public bodies, are vulnerable to pressure from claimants who, having weak cases, invite mediation as a tactical ploy. They calculate that such a defendant may at least make a nuisance-value offer to buy off the cost of a mediation and the risk of being penalised in costs for refusing a mediation even if ultimately successful . . .

As regards the power of the courts to order mediation, the Court of Appeal declined to accept such a proposition, finding it to be contrary to both domestic and ECHR law. As Dyson LJ stated in delivering the decision of the Court (para 9):

> We heard argument on the question whether the court has power to order parties to submit their disputes to mediation against their will. It is one thing to encourage the parties to agree to mediation, even to encourage them in the strongest terms. It is another to order them to do so. It seems to us that to oblige truly unwilling parties to refer their disputes to mediation would be to impose an unacceptable obstruction on their right of access to the court. The court in Strasbourg has said in relation to Article 6 of the European Convention on Human Rights that the right of access to a court may be waived, for example by means of an arbitration agreement, but such waiver should be subjected to 'particularly careful review' to ensure that the claimant is not subject to constraint . . . If that is the approach of the ECtHR to an *agreement* to arbitrate, it seems to us likely that *compulsion* of ADR would be regarded as an unacceptable constraint on the right of access to the court and, therefore, a violation of Article 6.

It is clear that a party can refuse to accept an offer to participate in mediation, but any such refusal must be reasonable. Unfortunately, what counts as reasonable cannot be defined with certainty, but its centrality is evident in the two cases below.

In *Rolf v De Guerin* (2011) the claimant succeeded to a degree in her claim but only recovered a small proportion of the amount claimed (£2,500 against a claim of £92,515) and failed on a number of her main allegations. On such grounds the court at first instance decided that the costs should *not* 'follow the event' in this case and awarded costs to the unsuccessful defendant.

On appeal, the Court of Appeal took into account Rolf's repeatedly stated willingness to settle the dispute through mediation. The defendant had refused mediation until it was too late to be effective and the Court of Appeal denied the validity of his reasons for refusal. As the reasons for refusal were unreasonable, the Court of Appeal held that each party should bear their own individual costs.

Subsequently, however, in *Swain Mason v Mills & Reeve* (2012), the Court of Appeal reaffirmed the decision in *Halsey* that under certain circumstances parties could refuse to engage in mediation. On the issue of refusal to mediate, the Court of Appeal took a different view from the trial judge in holding that the defendants had not unreasonably refused to mediate. In reaching its decision the Court of Appeal provided a gloss on *Halsey v Milton Keynes General NHS Trust*, holding that it was authority for the following:

- parties should not be compelled to mediate;
- mediation and other ADR processes do not offer a panacea and can have disadvantages as well as advantages and are not appropriate for every case;

- a party's reasonable belief that it has a strong case is a factor in deciding whether it was unreasonable to refuse mediation;
- where a party reasonably believes that it has a watertight case that may well be a sufficient justification for a refusal to mediate;
- account needs to be taken of whether a meditation would succeed, given the parties' stances;
- the court should be astute to the danger of parties being wrongly put under costs pressure as regards mediation.

As Davis LJ put it:

> The fundamental question remains as to whether it had been shown by the unsuccessful party (the claimants) that the successful party (the defendant) had acted *unreasonably* in refusing to agree to a mediation. In my view, that could not be shown here; and I therefore think that the judge was wrong to bring into account, adversely to the defendant, the defendant's attitude to mediation in deciding what costs overall should be awarded.

The Court of Appeal, taking a broad-brush approach, substituted an order that the defendants recover 60 per cent as opposed to the original court decision to award only 50 per cent of its costs.

PGF II SA v OMFS Company 1 Ltd (2013) is significant in that the Court of Appeal clarified the reasoning in *Halsey* by holding that the defendant's refusal even to respond to the claimant's invitations to mediation amounted to unreasonable conduct. In so doing the court accepted the statement of the law as set out in *The Jackson ADR Handbook*. As Briggs LJ stated:

> In my judgment, the time has now come for this court firmly to endorse the advice given in chapter 11 .56 of the ADR Handbook, that silence in the face of an invitation to participate in ADR is, as a general rule, of itself unreasonable, regardless whether an outright refusal, or a refusal to engage in the type of ADR requested, or to do so at the time requested, might have been justified by the identification of reasonable grounds.

Although the case had been settled with the last-minute acceptance of the defendant's CPR 36 offer, the trial judge nonetheless penalised the defendant's refusal to mediate by depriving it of costs. The Court of Appeal confirmed that decision, although as his words show, Briggs LJ was aware that the decision was on the cusp of what is appropriate:

> The court's task in encouraging the more proportionate conduct of civil litigation is so important in current economic circumstances that it is appropriate to emphasise that message by a sanction which, *even if a little more vigorous than I would have preferred*, nonetheless operates *pour encourager les autres* (emphasis added).

15.4 ARBITRATION

The first and oldest of these alternative procedures to the courts is arbitration. This is the procedure whereby parties in dispute refer the issue to a third party for resolution, rather than taking the case to the ordinary law courts. Studies have shown a reluctance on the part of commercial undertakings to have recourse to the law to resolve their disputes. At first sight, this appears paradoxical. The development of contract law can, to a great extent, be explained as the law's response to the need for regulation in relation to business activity, yet business declines to make use of its procedures. To some degree, questions of speed and cost explain this peculiar phenomenon, but it can be explained more fully by reference to the introduction to this chapter. It was stated there that informal procedures tend to be most effective where there is a high degree of mutuality and interdependency, and that is precisely the case in most business relationships. Businesses seek to establish and maintain long-term relationships with other concerns. The problem with the law is that the court case tends to terminally rupture such relationships. It is not suggested that, in the final analysis, where the stakes are sufficiently high, recourse will not be had to law, but such action does not represent the first or indeed the preferred option. In contemporary business practice, it is common, if not standard, practice for commercial contracts to contain express clauses referring any future disputes to arbitration. This practice is well established and its legal effectiveness has long been recognised by the law.

Thus in *Cable & Wireless Plc v IBM United Kingdom Ltd* (2002) the two parties had entered into a contractual agreement which provided that in the event of any dispute they:

> shall attempt in good faith to resolve the dispute or claim through an alternative dispute resolution procedure as recommended . . . by the Centre for Dispute Resolution ('CEDR'). However an ADR procedure which is being followed shall not prevent any party . . . from issuing proceedings.

However, when an issue arose the claimant declined to refer its claim to ADR, submitting that the above term was unenforceable because it lacked certainty due to its apparent contradictory wording, which suggested the possibility of both ADR and the issuing of court proceedings. It was suggested that the clause amounted to no more than an agreement to negotiate, which was not enforceable in English law. However, Colman J held that the issuing of proceedings was not inconsistent with the simultaneous conduct of an ADR procedure or with a mutual intention to have the issue finally decided by the courts only if the ADR procedure failed. He also concluded that the fact that the parties had identified a particular procedure from an experienced dispute resolution service provider indicated that they intended to be bound by the ADR provision. As regards the uncertainty issue, Colman J made a wider reference to the applicability of ADR agreements after *Dunnett v Railtrack*, holding that the English courts should not go out of their way to find uncertainty, and therefore unenforceability, in the field of ADR references. As he put it, 'For the courts now to decline to enforce contractual references to ADR on the grounds of intrinsic uncertainty would be to fly in the face of public policy.'

15.4.1 PROCEDURE

Section 1 of the Arbitration Act (AA) 1996 states that it is founded on the following principles:

(a)   the object of arbitration is to obtain the fair resolution of disputes by an impartial tribunal without necessary delay or expense;

(b)   the parties should be free to agree how their disputes are resolved, subject only to such safeguards as are necessary in the public interest;

(c)   in matters governed by this part of the Act, the court should not intervene except as provided by this part.

This provision of general principles, which should inform the reading of the later detailed provisions of the Act, is unusual for UK legislation, but may be seen as reflecting the purposes behind the Act, one major purpose of which was the wish to ensure that London did not lose its place as a leading centre for international arbitration. As a consequence of the demand-driven nature of the legislation, it would seem that court interference in the arbitration process has had to be reduced to a minimum and replaced by party autonomy. Under the 1996 Act, the role of the arbitrator has been increased and that of the court has been reduced to the residual level of intervention where the arbitration process either requires legal assistance or else is seen to be failing to provide a just settlement.

The Act, at least to a degree, follows the Model Arbitration Law adopted in 1985 by the United Nations Commission on International Trade Law (UNCITRAL), although it differs from the model code to the extent that it contains mandatory rules as well as provisions the parties can opt into or out of. For example, the power of the court to remove an arbitrator under s 24 cannot be overridden by the parties to the arbitration.

While it is possible for there to be an oral arbitration agreement at common law, s 5 provides that Part I of the 1996 Act only applies to agreements in writing. What this means in practice, however, has been extended by s 5(3) which provides that, where the parties agree to an arbitration procedure which is in writing, that procedure will be operative, even though the agreement between the parties is not itself in writing. An example of such a situation would be where a salvage operation was negotiated between two vessels on the basis of Lloyd's standard salvage terms. It would be unlikely that the actual agreement would be reduced to written form, but nonetheless, the arbitration element in those terms would be effective.

In analysing the AA 1996, it is useful to consider it in three distinct parts: autonomy of the parties; powers of the arbitrator and the court; and appellate rights:

Autonomy

It is significant that most of the provisions set out in the AA 1996 are not compulsory. As is clearly stated in s 1, it is for the parties to an arbitration agreement to agree what procedures to adopt. The main purpose of the Act is to empower the parties to the dispute and to allow them to choose how it is to be decided. In pursuit of this aim, the mandatory parts of the Act only take effect where the parties involved do not agree otherwise. It is actually possible for the parties to agree that the dispute should not be decided in line with the strict legal rules, but rather in line with commercial fairness, which might be a completely different thing altogether.

In *Jivraj v Hashwani* (2011) the Supreme Court, in overruling the Court of Appeal, held that arbitrators were not employees and consequently the requirement to select arbitrators from a particular religious group (in this case the Ismaili community) did not breach the Employment Equality (Religion or Belief) Regulations 2003.

Powers of the arbitrator

Section 30 provides that, unless the parties agree otherwise, the arbitrator can rule on questions relating to jurisdiction, that is, in relation to:

(a)   whether there actually is a valid arbitration agreement;

(b)   whether the arbitration tribunal is properly constituted;

(c)   what matters have been submitted to arbitration in accordance with the agreement.

Section 32 allows any of the parties to raise preliminary objections to the substantive jurisdiction of the arbitration tribunal in court, but provides that they may only do so on limited grounds which require either: the agreement of the parties concerned; the permission of the arbitration tribunal; or the agreement of the court. Leave to appeal will only be granted where the court is satisfied that the question involves a point of law of general importance.

Section 28 expressly provides that the parties to the proceedings are jointly and severally liable to pay the arbitrators such reasonable fees and expenses as appropriate. Previously, this was only an implied term.

Section 29 provides that arbitrators are not liable for anything done or omitted in the discharge of their functions unless the act or omission was done in bad faith.

Section 33 provides that the tribunal has a general duty:

(a)   to act fairly and impartially between the parties, giving each a reasonable opportunity to state their case; and

(b)   to adopt procedures suitable for the circumstance of the case, avoiding unnecessary delay or expense.

Section 35 provides that, subject to the parties agreeing to the contrary, the tribunal shall have the following powers:

(a)   to order parties to provide security for costs (previously a power reserved to the courts);

(b)   to give directions in relation to property subject to the arbitration;

(c)   to direct that a party or witness be examined on oath, and to administer the oath.

The parties may also empower the arbitrator to make provisional orders (s 39).

Powers of the court

Where one party seeks to start a court action, contrary to a valid arbitration agreement, then the other party may request the court to stay the litigation in favour of the arbitration agreement under ss 9–11 of the AA 1996. Where, however, both parties agree to ignore the arbitration agreement and seek recourse to litigation, then, following the party consensual nature of the Act, the agreement may be ignored.

The courts may order a party to comply with an order of the tribunal and may also order parties and witnesses to attend and to give oral evidence before tribunals (s 43).

The court has power to revoke the appointment of an arbitrator on application of any of the parties where there has been a failure in the appointment procedure under s 18, but it also has powers to revoke authority under s 24. This power comes into play on the application of one of the parties in circumstances where the arbitrator:

(a)   has not acted impartially or there are justifiable doubts as to their impartiality (see *Sierra Fishing Co. v Farran* (2015));

(b)   does not possess the required qualifications;

(c)   does not have either the physical or mental capacity to deal with the proceedings;

(d)   has refused or failed to properly conduct the proceedings, or has been dilatory in dealing with the proceedings or in making an award, to the extent that it will cause substantial injustice to the party applying for their removal.

Under s 45, the court may, on application by one of the parties, decide any preliminary question of law arising in the course of the proceedings.

Arbitrators

The arbitration tribunal may consist of a single arbitrator or a panel, as the parties decide (s 15). If one party fails to appoint an arbitrator, then the other party's nominee may act as sole arbitrator (s 17). Under s 20(4), where there is a panel and it fails to reach a majority decision, the decision of the chair shall prevail.

The tribunal is required to adopt procedures fairly and impartially, which are suitable to the circumstances of each case. It is also for the tribunal to decide all procedural and evidential matters. Parties may be represented by a lawyer or any other person and the tribunal may appoint experts or legal advisers to report to it.

Arbitrators will be immune from action being taken against them except in situations where they have acted in bad faith.

Appeal

The AA 1950 allowed for either party to the proceedings to have questions of law authoritatively determined by the High Court through the procedure of '*case stated*'. The High Court could also set aside the decision of the arbitrator on grounds of fact, law or procedure. Whereas the arbitration process was supposed to provide a quick and relatively cheap method of deciding disputes, the availability of the appeals procedures meant that parties could delay the final decision and in so doing increase the costs. In such circumstances, arbitration became the precursor to a court case rather than replacing it. The AA 1979 abolished the 'case stated' procedure and curtailed the right to appeal. The AA 1996 has reduced the grounds for appeal to the court system even further.

Once the decision has been made, there are limited grounds for appeal. The first ground arises under s 67 of the AA 1996 in relation to the substantive jurisdiction of the arbitral panel, although the right to appeal on this ground may be lost if the party attempting to make use of it took part in the arbitration proceedings without objecting to the alleged lack of jurisdiction. The second ground for appeal to the courts is on procedural grounds, under s 68, on the basis that some serious irregularity affected the operation of the tribunal. By serious irregularity is meant:

(a)   failure to comply with the general duty to act fairly set out in s 33;

(b)   failure to conduct the tribunal as agreed by the parties;

(c)   uncertainty or ambiguity as to the effect of the award;

(d)   failure to comply with the requirement as to the form of the award.

The threshold for raising an action under s 68 is very restrictive and will succeed 'only if what had occurred was too far removed from what could reasonably be expected from the arbitral process to be justified' (see *ABB Ag v Hochtief Airport GmbH* [2006] EWHC 388 (Comm)). Thus the court will not intervene on the ground that it would have done things differently (see *Lorand Shipping Limited v Davof Trading (Africa) BV MV 'Ocean Glory'* [2014] EWHC 3521 (Comm) for an example of a successful claim under s 68.

In *Secretary of State for the Home Department v Raytheon Systems Limited* [2015] EWCH 311 (TCC) the judge, on appeal, held that not only should the original finding of the arbitration panel be set aside on the basis of serious irregularity, but also that the issue should be reconsidered and decided by a different arbitrator panel on the grounds that 'there is a *real* risk, *judged objectively*, that even a competent and respectable arbitral tribunal, whose acts or omissions have been held to amount to serious irregularity causing substantial injustice may sub-consciously be tempted to achieve the same result as before'.

Parties may also appeal on a point of law arising from the award under s 69. However, the parties can agree beforehand to preclude such a possibility, and where they agree to the arbitral panel making a decision without providing a reasoned justification for it, they will also lose the right to appeal.

15.4.2 RELATIONSHIP TO ORDINARY COURTS

The attitude of the courts generally to arbitration may be seen in the words of Mrs Justice Gloster in *Soeximex SAS v Agrocorp International PTE Ltd* [2011] EWHC 2743:

> The Commercial Court is very sensitive to the fact that parties have chosen to have their disputes resolved by an industry or trade arbitral tribunal, rather than by the Courts. As a matter of general approach, it tries to uphold arbitration awards and to read them in a sensible and commercial way. It is very mindful that the Court's role on a s 68 application is not to pick holes in an award, or to indulge in an over-nice analysis of what may be understandably brief reasons given by commercial men in areas with which they are far more familiar than the Court.

However, where, as in the case in question, there are clearly legal issues to be addressed that were not dealt with in the arbitration, the court will allow an appeal and may impose its own, contrary, decision.

In general terms, therefore, the courts have no objection to individuals settling their disputes on a voluntary basis, but at the same time, they are careful to maintain their supervisory role in such procedures. Arbitration agreements are no different from other terms of a contract, and in line with the normal rules of contract law, courts will strike out any attempt to oust their ultimate jurisdiction as being contrary to public policy. Thus, as has been stated previously, arbitration proceedings are open to challenge through judicial review on the grounds that they were not conducted in a judicial manner.

In February 2008 the then Archbishop of Canterbury, Rowan Williams, caused a furore when, in a speech, he suggested that the eventual use of Sharia law to deal with disputes was inevitable in the United Kingdom. His comment was taken out of context, but as some commentators pointed out, it was already possible for Sharia Councils to decide disputes on an informal non-compulsory basis using Sharia principles. Similarly,

Jewish people have been able to use their own system of courts, the Beth Din, to decide issues on a voluntary basis. In March 2015, in clear pre-election mode, Home Secretary Theresa May stated that a Conservative government intended to commission an independent figure to complete an investigation into the application of Sharia law in England and Wales on the basis, she claimed, that:

> . . . there is evidence of women being 'divorced' under sharia law and left in penury, wives who are forced to return to abusive relationships because sharia councils say a husband has a right to 'chastise', and sharia councils giving the testimony of a woman only half the weight of the testimony of a man.

Subsequently, in December 2015 the self-styled Commission on Religion and Belief in British Public Life issued a report entitled 'Living with Difference'. The report recognised that many submissions to its inquiry viewed religion-based tribunals negatively, or indeed saw them as having no place in British society. Nonetheless, it did not recommend any immediate action against them; rather, it called for more investigation about the impact that the operation of such tribunals had on women users, and about the impact of state policies on the procedures and substantive rules of these tribunals.

15.4.3 ADVANTAGES

There are numerous advantages to be gained from using arbitration rather than the court system:

Privacy

Arbitration tends to be a private procedure. This has the twofold advantage that outsiders do not get access to any potentially sensitive information and the parties to the arbitration do not run the risk of any damaging publicity arising out of reports of the proceedings.

Informality

The proceedings are less formal than a court case and they can be scheduled more flexibly than court proceedings.

Speed

Arbitration is generally much quicker than taking a case through the courts. Where, however, one of the parties makes use of the available grounds to challenge an arbitration award, the prior costs of the arbitration will have been largely wasted.

Cost

Arbitration is generally a much cheaper procedure than taking a case to the normal courts. Nonetheless, the costs of arbitration and the use of specialist arbitrators should not be underestimated.

Expertise

The use of a specialist arbitrator ensures that the person deciding the case has expert knowledge of the actual practice within the area under consideration, and can form their conclusion in line with accepted practice.

It can be argued that arbitration represents a privatisation of the judicial process. It may be assumed, therefore, that of all its virtues, perhaps the greatest, at least as far as the government is concerned, is the potential reduction in costs for the state in providing the legal framework within which disputes are resolved.

15.5   ADMINISTRATIVE TRIBUNALS

Although attention tends to be focused on the operation of the courts as the forum within which legal decisions are taken, it is no longer the case that the bulk of legal and quasi-legal questions are determined within that court structure. There are, as an alternative to the court system, a large number of tribunals that have been set up under various Acts of Parliament to rule on the operation of the particular schemes established under those Acts.

The generally accepted explanation for the establishment and growth of tribunals in Britain since 1945 was the need to provide a specialist forum to deal with cases involving conflicts between an increasingly interventionist welfare state, its functionaries and the rights of private citizens. It is certainly true that, since 1945, the welfare state has intervened more and more in every aspect of people's lives. The intention may have been to extend various social benefits to a wider constituency, but in so doing, the machinery of the welfare state, and in reality those who operate that machinery, have been granted powers to control access to its benefits, and as a consequence have been given the power to interfere in and control the lives of individual subjects of the state. By its nature, welfare provision tends to be discretionary and dependent upon the particular circumstance of a given case. As a consequence, state functionaries were extended discretionary power over the supply/withdrawal of welfare benefits. As the interventionist state replaced the completely free market as the source of welfare for many people, so access to the provisions made by the state became a matter of fundamental importance, and a focus for potential contention, especially given the discretionary nature of its provision. At the same time as welfare state provisions were being extended, the view was articulated that such provisions and projects should not be under the purview and control of the ordinary courts. It was felt that the judiciary reflected a culture that tended to favour a more market-centred, individualistic approach to the provision of rights and welfare and that their essentially formalistic approach to the resolution of disputes would not fit with the operation of the new projects.

There is some debate as to whether tribunals are merely part of the machinery of *administration* of particular projects or whether their function is the distinct one of *adjudication*. The Franks Committee (Cmnd 218, 1957) favoured the latter view, but others have disagreed and have emphasised the administrative role of such bodies. Parliament initiated various projects and schemes, and included within those projects specialist tribunals to deal with the problems that they inevitably generated. On that basis, it is suggested that tribunals are merely adjuncts to the parent project and that this therefore defines their role as more administrative than adjudicatory. In *Baker v HMRC* (2013) the First-tier Tribunal expressly stated that it could not grant the relief sought as it was not a court and has no jurisdiction to grant such relief.

If the foregoing has suggested the theoretical possibility of distinguishing courts and tribunals in relation to their administrative or adjudicatory role, in practice it is difficult to implement such a distinction for the reason that the members of tribunals may be, and usually are, acting in a quasi-judicial capacity. Thus, in *Pickering v Liverpool Daily Post and Echo Newspapers* (1991), it was held that a mental health review tribunal was a court whose proceedings were subject to the law of contempt. Although a newspaper was entitled to publish the fact that a named person had made an application to the tribunal, together with the date of the hearing and its decision, it was not allowed to publish the reasons for the decision or any conditions applied.

If the precise distinction between tribunals and courts is a matter of uncertainty, what is certain is that tribunals are inferior to the normal courts. One of the main purposes of the tribunal system is to prevent the ordinary courts of law from being overburdened by cases, but a tribunal is still subject to judicial review on the basis of breach of natural justice, or where it acts in an *ultra vires* manner, or indeed where it goes wrong in relation to the application of the law when deciding cases.

The supervisory body, the Administrative Justice and Tribunals Council, which replaced the previous Council on Tribunals, was itself abolished under the Public Bodies Act 2011 (see 3.5.3). The government declared its intention to abolish the AJTC in a strategy document issued in December 2012 entitled 'Administrative Justice and Tribunals: A Strategic Work Programme 2013–16'. As a result there is now only the Administrative Justice Forum, an independent body sponsored by the MoJ whose function is 'to gauge how the administrative justice and tribunals system is working, and identify any areas of concern or good practice and to provide early, informal, testing of policy initiatives'. However, in spite of the House of Commons Justice Committee expressing doubts about the consequences of getting rid of the AJTC, the Ministry of Justice proceeded to do so on the basis that it 'believe[d] that the independence of the tribunals system administered by HMCTS ensures that tribunal members and their administrative support systems are sufficiently removed from decision makers to diminish the case for a standing body to oversee tribunals. We believe that policy development and oversight of the wider administrative justice system should be led from within the MoJ.'

In May 2000, the then Lord Chancellor, Lord Irvine, appointed Sir Andrew Leggatt to review the operation of the tribunal system, and the attendant Consultation Paper stated that:

> There are signs . . . that the complexity of the system (if indeed it amounts to a system at all), its diversity, and the separateness within it of most tribunals, may be creating problems for the user and an overall lack of coherence.

As Sir Andrew found, there were 70 different administrative tribunals in England and Wales, leaving aside regulatory bodies, and between them they dealt with nearly one million cases a year. However, of those 70 tribunals, only 20 heard more than 500 cases a year and many were, in fact, defunct. Three tribunals still account for over 90 per cent of the caseload dealt with in the tribunal system covering the areas of social security and child support, which deals with around half of the total caseload; employment; and immigration and asylum.

Sir Andrew's task was to rationalise and modernise the tribunal structure, and to that end, he made a number of proposals, including the following:

- *Making the 70 tribunals into one tribunals system*

  He suggested that the existing 'system' did not really merit that title and that combining the administration of the different tribunals was necessary to generate a collective standing to match that of the court system.

- *Ensuring that the tribunals were independent of their sponsoring departments by having them administered by one Tribunals Service*

  He thought that, as happened, where a Department of State may provide the administrative support for a tribunal, pay its fees and expenses, appoint some of its members, provide its IT support and possibly promote legislation prescribing the procedure that the tribunal was to follow, the tribunal neither appeared to be independent, nor was it independent in fact.

- *Providing a coherent appeal system*

  He found the current system to be confusing and some tribunals to have too many appeal stages, leading to long delays in reaching finality.

- *Reconsidering the position of lay members*

  He considered that there was no justification for any members to sit, whether expert or lay, unless they have a particular function to fulfil, as they do in the employment tribunal.

Subsequently, in March 2003, the Lord Chancellor's Office, as it then was, announced its intention to follow the Leggatt recommendation in establishing a new unified Tribunal Service. The new organisation formally came into being in April 2005 and was launched operationally in April 2006.

On 1 April 2011 Her Majesty's Courts Service and the Tribunals Service were amalgamated into one integrated agency, Her Majesty's Courts and Tribunals Service (HMCTS), providing support for the administration of justice in courts (up to and including the Court of Appeal) and most tribunals, but importantly not Employment Tribunals. The new Service operates as an agency of the Ministry of Justice.

15.5.3   THE TRIBUNALS, COURT AND ENFORCEMENT ACT (TCEA) 2007

In further pursuance of the Leggatt Review, the stated intention of this legislation (TCEA 2007) was the creation of a new, simplified, statutory framework for tribunals, which was to be achieved not just by the bringing together of existing tribunal jurisdictions but by provision of a new structure of jurisdiction and new appeal rights.

- *Unified structure*

  The Act provides for the establishment of a new unified structure to subsume all tribunals, except for the Employment Tribunals, which will remain independent. This unification is to be achieved through the creation of two new tribunals, the First-tier Tribunal and the Upper Tribunal, and in pursuit of that end the Act gives the Lord Chancellor power to transfer the jurisdiction of existing tribunals to the two new tribunals. The Act also provides for the establishment within each tier of 'chambers', so that existing jurisdictions may be grouped together appropriately. Chambers at the first-tier level will hear cases initially and the role of the upper chambers will be mainly, but not exclusively, to hear appeals from the first tier. Each chamber will be headed by a Chamber President, and the tribunals' judiciary, as the legal members of tribunals will now be entitled, will be headed by a Senior President of Tribunals.

- *Appeals*

  The Act specifically recognises and attempts to deal with the previous unclear and unsatisfactory routes of appeal in relation to tribunals' decisions. Under its provisions, in most cases, a decision of the First-tier Tribunal may be appealed to the Upper Tribunal and a decision of the Upper Tribunal may be appealed to the Court of Appeal. However, an appeal will not be allowed if such procedure is excluded by the specific Act or in any order made by the Lord Chancellor. However, it also provides that any such appeal must relate to a point of law and may only be exercised with permission from the tribunal being appealed from or the tribunal or court being appealed to.

- *Administration*

  The Act restated the role of the Tribunals Service, subsequently replaced by the amalgamated HMCTS, in the successful operation of the new unified system.

- *Supervision*

  The Senior President of Tribunals has responsibility for representing the views of the tribunal judiciary to Ministers and Parliament and for training, guidance and welfare. In addition to the powers under the Act, the Lord Chief Justice has delegated to the Senior President some of his powers under the Constitutional Reform Act, particularly in relation to judicial discipline of most tribunal judges and members.

As has been stated, the Administrative Justice and Tribunals Council (AJTC) was abolished by the MoJ in August 2013, and was effectively replaced by the Administrative Justice Advisory Group. The final report of the AJTC contained the following barbed comment:

> The MoJ has attached much weight to the Administrative Justice Advisory Group (AJAG) which it has established to 'play a dynamic role in helping to address issues for users'. The scepticism of the AJTC towards these arrangements has been echoed in Parliament with such descriptions as a 'poorly planned afterthought' and a 'pawn of the Department'. Despite the reservations, this Response acknowledges that AJAG will be the main forum for future identification and discussion of user concerns. We hope that AJAG, especially with an independent chairman, will be able to work robustly.

In April 2014 Jodi Berg was announced as the chair of the newly named Administrative Justice Forum (AJF).

- *Enforcement*

  In relation to enforcement, at present, tribunals have no enforcement powers of their own. Consequently, if a monetary award is not paid then the claimant must register the claim in the County Court before seeking enforcement. Under the TCEA 2007, claimants will be able to go directly to the County Court or High Court for enforcement.

Composition of the First-tier Tribunal

The following seven chambers operate within the First-tier Tribunal. The scope of the tribunal is so extensive that only limited comment can be made in relation to the chambers, but detailed information on each is available on the HMCTS website.

- **General Regulatory Chamber**

  The GRC was established within the First-tier Tribunal on 1 September 2009. The GRC brings together tribunals that heard appeals relating to various regulatory issues. Included among these are the following specific areas:
  - charities;
  - claims management services;
  - community right to bid;
  - copyright licensing;
  - electronic communications and postal services;

- environment;
- estate agents;
- exam boards;
- food;
- gambling;
- immigration services;
- information rights;
- letting and managing agents;
- microchipping dogs;
- pensions regulation;
- professional regulation;
- transport.

- **Social Entitlement Chamber**

  The SEC deals with the following areas:

  (a) Asylum Support (it does not deal with asylum claims or other immigration matters);

  (b) Criminal Injuries Compensation;

  (c) Social Security and Child Support.

- **Health, Education and Social Care Chamber**

  (a) Care Standards (i.e. appeals from people who have received a decision issued by organisations concerned with children and vulnerable adults, and those which regulate the provision of social, personal and health care);

  (b) Special Education Needs and Disability;

  (c) Mental Health Review;

  (d) Primary Health Lists: this tribunal hears appeals/applications resulting from decisions made by Primary Care Trusts as part of the local management of such lists, which medical practitioners must be on in order to function.

- **Immigration and Asylum Chamber**

  This chamber deals with appeals against decisions made by the Home Office officials in immigration, asylum and nationality matters. These mainly relate to decisions to:

  - refuse asylum in the UK;
  - refuse entry to, or leave to remain in, the UK;
  - deport someone already in the UK.

- **Property Chamber**

  This chamber hears appeals and references relating to disputes over property and land including:

  - residential property disputes;
  - land registration matters;
  - agricultural land and drainage matters.

- **Tax chamber**

  This chamber has two specific areas of competence:

  (a) Tax, where it hears appeals against decisions relating to tax made by Her Majesty's Revenue and Customs (HMRC).

  (b) MPs' expenses, where it hears appeals against certain decisions made by the Compliance Officer. The Compliance Officer is appointed by the Independent Parliamentary Standards Authority (IPSA) and is responsible for determining and paying MPs' expenses. Appeals can be made by MPs under the Parliamentary Standards Act 2009.

- **War Pensions and Armed Forces Compensation Chamber**

  As its title suggests, this chamber hears appeals from ex-servicemen or women who have had their claims for a war pension rejected by the Secretary of State for Defence.

The following is a list of the **Chambers within the Upper Tribunal** already operating:

- **Administrative Appeals Chamber**

  This chamber hears appeals from the present First-tier Tribunals, the General Regulatory Chamber, the Health, Education and Social Care Chamber, Social Entitlement Chamber, and the War Pensions and Armed Forces Compensation Chamber.

- **Tax and Chancery Chamber**

  This chamber hears appeals from the First-tier Tax Chamber Tribunal. This brought together the four existing tax tribunals to hear the full range of direct and indirect tax cases.

- **Lands Chamber (Lands Tribunal)**

  In June 2009 the Lands Tribunal joined the tribunal system established by the TCEA when it became the Lands Chamber of the Upper Tribunal. As its functions have not changed, for the time being the Lands Chamber of the Upper Tribunal is still known as the Lands Tribunal.

- **Immigration and Asylum Chamber**

  In February 2010, immigration and asylum chambers were established in both tiers of the Unified Tribunals framework. The Upper Tribunal is a superior court of record dealing with appeals against decisions made by the First-tier Immigration and Asylum Chamber Tribunal.

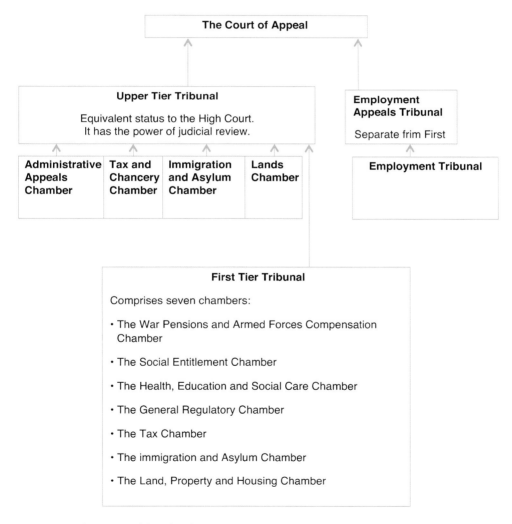

FIGURE 15.2 *The structure of the Tribunals Service.*

The Employment Tribunals

The Employment Tribunal and the Employment Appeal Tribunal continue largely unchanged as a separate 'pillar' of the new system, as do some other specialist tribunals such as Special Immigration Appeals Commission (SIAC) (see 2.5.2). They are subject to the authority of the Senior President for training and welfare purposes and are treated as having the same status as Chambers in the First-tier and Upper Tribunals.

The Employment Tribunals are governed by the Employment Tribunals Act 1996, which sets out their composition, major areas of competence and procedure. They have jurisdiction in relation to a number of statutory provisions relating to employment issues. The majority of issues arise in relation to such matters as disputes over the meaning and operation of particular terms of employment, disputes relating to redundancy payments, disputes involving issues of unfair dismissal and disputes as to the provision of maternity pay.

They also have authority in other areas under different legislation. Thus, they deal with: complaints about racial discrimination in the employment field under the Race Relations Act 1976; complaints about sexual discrimination in employment under the Sex Discrimination Act 1975; complaints about equal pay under the Equal Pay Act 1970, as amended by the Sex Discrimination Act; complaints under the Disability Discrimination Act 1995; complaints about unlawful deductions from wages under the Wages Act 1986; and appeals against the imposition of improvement notices under the Health and Safety at Work Act 1974. There are, in addition, various ancillary matters relating to trade union membership and activities that the Employment Tribunals have to deal with.

The tribunal hearing is relatively informal. As in arbitration hearings, the normal rules of evidence are not applied and parties can represent themselves or be represented by solicitors or barristers. And, as appropriate in an employment context, they may also be represented by trade union officials or representatives, or indeed by any other person they wish to represent them.

Appeal, on a point of law only, is to the Employment Appeal Tribunal.

Although less formal than ordinary courts, the process of taking a case to, or defending a case in, an employment tribunal can be time-consuming and expensive, and employers' representatives have complained about the increased use of tribunals. As an alternative to the formal hearing, the Employment Tribunals offer a Judicial Mediation scheme. This was introduced as a pilot in 2006, and is now available throughout England and Wales. Judicial Mediation involves bringing the parties together for a Mediation Case Management Discussion before an employment judge who remains neutral and tries to assist the parties in resolving their disputes.

In a further attempt to remedy the alleged shortcomings in the Employment Tribunal process, the Advisory, Conciliation and Arbitration Service (ACAS) initiated a voluntary arbitration process for dealing with unfair dismissal claims as an alternative to using the employment tribunals.

However, even before it was introduced, the scheme came under attack from the Industrial Society. In a pamphlet entitled *Courts or Compromise? Routes to Resolving Disputes*, it argued that the new alternative to employment tribunals could well become as rigid, formal and almost as expensive as current tribunal and court processes, and claimed that in any event, the impact on the tribunal system was likely to be slight. While it recognised the advantages in such schemes, that they were faster, cheaper, more informal and flexible than tribunals, it also foresaw inherent risks. The pamphlet argued that ADR does not guarantee fairness or consistency in outcomes. In particular, it highlighted dangers where there is no appeal process, in lack of precedent, and where confidentiality is unjustifiable. It also pointed out the risk that compensation awarded through ADR might be less than in a tribunal or court. In conclusion, it warned that people who opt for ADR need to make sure that they understand the implications, for example, where the decision is binding and leaves no route to appeal.

Employment Tribunal charges

As with the furore over general criminal court charges (see p 490), so there was consternation when the government introduced fees for raising claims in the Employment Tribunal under the Employment Tribunals and the Employment Appeal Tribunal Fees Order 2013 (SI 2013/1893). Under the scheme, claimants were required to pay £160 or £250 to lodge a claim, depending on the type of issue involved, and a further charge of either £230 or £950 if the case was pursued to a hearing. People in receipt of benefits or, on a low income or with only a small amount of savings and investments were eligible to have fees waived or reduced. As detailed in a House of Commons briefing paper, *Employment tribunal fees* (SN07081), following the introduction of fees, the number of single cases *declined by 67 per cent* between October 2013 and June 2015 and the number of cases brought by two or more people *fell by 69 per cent*.

The trade union Unison applied for judicial review of the introduction of tribunal fees on two separate occasions. In February 2014 the first case was rejected by the High Court as insufficient time had passed for the court to assess the impact of the fees order. However, it did allow that, although the fees were not inherently unlawful, they might be deemed so, if they proved discriminatory or rendered it excessively difficult to enforce EU law-derived rights. Consequently, Unison raised a second case in October 2014, and this time included the specific issue that the introduction of fees weighed discriminately more on women, citing statistics that indicated that since the introduction of fees, there had been an 86 per cent drop in sex discrimination claims and an 80 per cent drop in equal pay claims. However, once again the High Court dismissed its action, as did the Court of Appeal, on the basis that the action could not succeed merely on the basis of statistical evidence alone. Unison announced its intention to pursue its case at a later time when specific instances could be used to support the action.

In June 2015 the government announced that it would be conducting a review of the effect of the introduction of fees for the Employment Tribunals. The review will consider how effective fees have been in achieving the objectives of:

- transferring some of the cost from the taxpayer to those who use the employment tribunal service;
- encouraging the use of alternative dispute resolution, such as ACAS;
- improving tribunal efficiency and effectiveness; and
- maintaining access to justice.

The delay in publishing the review and any conclusion to be drawn from it was strongly criticised by the House of Commons Justice Committee in its report 'Courts and tribunals fees' (HC 167). The report stated that: 'We find it unacceptable that the Government has not reported the results of its review one year after it began and six months after the Government said it would be completed'.

In relation to employment tribunals the key findings of the report were that:

●   there has been a significant drop in the number of employment tribunal claims;
●   the government's assertion that the drop is largely attributable to the success of Acas Early Conciliation is '. . . even on the most favourable construction, superficial';
●   fees 'have had a significant adverse impact on access to justice for meritorious claims'.

The Justice Committee recommended that:

●   the 'overall quantum of fees' charged for bringing an employment tribunal claim should be substantially reduced;
●   the type A/type B distinction of tribunal claims should be replaced by a single fee, by a three-tier fee structure, or by a fee set as a proportion of the amount claimed;
●   further special consideration should be given to the position of women alleging maternity or pregnancy discrimination, for whom, at the least, the time limit of three months for bringing a claim should be reviewed; and
●   disposable capital and monthly income thresholds for fee remission should be increased.

15.5.4   COMPOSITION OF TRIBUNALS

Appointment to tribunals is through the Judicial Appointments Commission procedure of application and interview, on the basis of the statutory and non-statutory requirements for the specific post. They are usually made up of three members, only one of whom, the chair, is expected to be legally qualified, although not necessarily a legal practitioner. The other two members are lay representatives. The lack of legal training is not considered a drawback, given the technical and administrative, as opposed to specifically legal, nature of the provisions the members have to consider. Indeed, the fact of there being two lay representatives on tribunals provides them with one of their perceived advantages over courts. The non-legal members may provide specialist knowledge and thus they may enable the tribunal to base its decision on actual practice as opposed to abstract legal theory or mere legal formalism.

Research into the role of lay members in employment tribunals, conducted in 2010–11, by Corby and Latreille, endorsed the role of lay members and considered that they added value to the operation of tribunals. In particular they found support for the

Background to tribunals: Tribunals date back over 200 years and modern, specialist tribunals support the ordinary courts by resolving legal disputes quickly and cheaply within their areas of expertise

The organisation of tribunals: Until recently the organisation of administrative tribunals (i.e. those established by the state) was said to lack coherence. The **Tribunals, Courts and Enforcement Act 2007** (TCEA) was enacted to remedy this, introducing a new system of 'tiers' and 'chambers', each dealing with their own areas of expertise

THE UNIFIED TRIBUNAL STRUCTURE

First Tier: Appeals to First-tier Tribunal against the decisions of government departments and other public bodies. The First-tier Tribunal comprises seven chambers, namely:
- **The General Regulatory Chamber,** covering: Alternative Business Structures, Charity, Claims Management Services, Consumer Credit, Community Right to Bid, Environment, Estate Agents, Examination board, Food, Gambling Appeals, Immigration Services, Information Rights, Local Government Standards in England and Transport
- **The Health, Education and Social Care Chamber,** covering: Care Standards, Mental Health, Special Educational Needs & Disability and Primary Health Lists
- **The Immigration and Asylum Chamber,** covering Immigration and Asylum
- **The Property Chamber,** covering: Land Registration, Agricultural Land & Drainage and Residential Property Tribunal
- **The Social Entitlement Chamber,** covering Asylum Support, Criminal Injuries Compensation, Social Security and Child Support
- **The Tax Chamber,** covering Tax and MP Expenses
- **The War Pensions and Armed Forces Compensation Chamber**, covering War Pensions and Armed Forces Compensation

Upper Tribunal: Hears appeals from the First-tier Tribunal on points of law (i.e. an appeal made over the interpretation of a legal principle or statute). Further appeals may be made, with permission, to the Court of Appeal. The Upper Tribunal comprises four chambers, namely:
- **The Administrative Appeals Chamber**
- **The Immigration and Asylum Chamber**
- **The Lands Chamber**
- **The Tax and Chancery Chamber**

Tribunals which presently remain outside the First/Upper-Tier system: Employment, Employment Appeal, Gangmasters, Licensing Appeals, Gender Recognition Panel, Pathogens Access Appeal Commission, Proscribed Organisations Appeal Commission, Reserve Forces Appeal, Special Immigration Appeals Commission

FIGURE 15.3 *The Unified Tribunal Structure.*

view that unfair dismissal was particularly 'a jurisdiction where lay members added value to decision making, despite a government proposal to enable judges to sit alone in unfair dismissal cases'. Nonetheless, s 4(3) ETA, which details proceedings which may be heard by an Employment Judge sitting alone was extended in 2012 to include actions in relation to unfair dismissal. This is important as, if a judge sitting alone at the Employment Tribunal decides a case, then any appeal hearing at the EAT will normally be decided by a judge sitting alone as well. This may not be as disadvantageous as it seems at first;

the EAT only hears appeals on points of law and in any case further research by Susan Corby has found, perhaps somewhat counter-intuitively, that employee appellants have a significantly better chance of success when a decision is made by a judge sitting alone, rather than a judge with lay members.

The use of multiple panel members in the unified tribunals currently costs the taxpayer around £21m per year in fees alone. In order to reduce such cost the Justice Ministry's paper 'Transforming our justice system: summary of reforms and consultation' ((2016) CM 93321) proposed to amend the First-tier Tribunal and Upper Tribunal (Composition of Tribunal) Order 2008 to give the senior president of tribunals (SPT) greater freedom to adopt a more proportionate and flexible approach to panel composition, by:

- providing that a tribunal panel in the First-tier Tribunal is to consist of a single member unless otherwise determined by the SPT; and
- removing the existing requirement to consider the arrangements that were in place before the tribunal transferred into the unified system.

15.5.5   DOMESTIC TRIBUNALS

The foregoing has focused on public administrative tribunals set up under particular legislative provisions to deal with matters of public relevance. The term 'tribunal', however, is also used in relation to the internal disciplinary procedures of particular institutions. Whether these institutions are created under legislation or not is immaterial; the point is that domestic tribunals relate mainly to matters of private rather than public concern, although at times the two can overlap. Examples of domestic tribunals are the disciplinary committees of professional institutions such as the Bar, The Law Society or the British Medical Association; trade unions; and universities. The power that each of these tribunals has is very great and it is controlled by the ordinary courts through ensuring that the rules of natural justice are complied with and that the tribunal does not act *ultra vires*, that is, beyond its powers. Matters relating to trade union membership and discipline are additionally regulated by the Employment Rights Act 1996.

15.5.6   ADVANTAGES OF TRIBUNALS

Advantages of tribunals over courts relate to such matters as:

- *Speed*
  The ordinary court system is notoriously dilatory in hearing and deciding cases. Tribunals are much quicker to hear cases. A related advantage of the tribunal system is the certainty that it will be heard on a specific date and not subject to the vagaries of the court system. This being said, there have been reports that the tribunal system is coming under increased pressure and is falling behind in relation to its caseload.

- *Cost*

  Tribunals are a much cheaper way of deciding cases than using the ordinary court system. One factor that leads to a reduction in cost is the fact that no specialised court building is required to hear the cases. Also, the fact that those deciding the cases are less expensive to employ than judges, together with the fact that complainants do not have to rely on legal representation, makes the tribunal procedure considerably less expensive than using the traditional court system.

- *Informality*

  Tribunals are supposed to be informal in order to make them less intimidating than full-blown court cases. The strict rules relating to evidence, pleading and procedure that apply in courts are not binding in tribunal proceedings. The lack of formality is strengthened by the fact that proceedings tend not to be inquisitorial or accusatorial, but are intended to try to encourage and help participants to express their views of the situation before the tribunal. Informality should not, however, be mistaken for a lack of order, and the Franks Committee Report itself emphasised the need for clear rules of procedure. The provision of this informal situation and procedure tends to suggest that complainants do not need to be represented by a lawyer in order to present their grievance. They may represent themselves or be represented by a more knowledgeable associate such as a trade union representative or some other friend. This contentious point will be considered further below.

- *Flexibility*

  Tribunals are not bound by the strict rules of precedent, although some pay more regard to previous decisions than others. It should be remembered that, as tribunals are inferior and subject to the courts, they are governed by the precedents made in the courts.

- *Expertise*

  Reference has already been made to the advantages to be gained from the particular expertise that is provided by the lay members of tribunals, as against the more general legal expertise of the chairperson.

- *Accessibility*

  The aim of tribunals is to provide individuals with a readily accessible forum in which to air their grievances, and gaining access to tribunals is certainly not as difficult as getting a case into the ordinary courts.

- *Privacy*

  The final advantage is the fact that proceedings can be taken before a tribunal without necessarily triggering the publicity that might follow from a court case.

15.5.7   DISADVANTAGES OF TRIBUNALS

It is important that the supposed advantages of tribunals are not simply taken at face value. They represent significant improvements over the operation of the ordinary court system, but it is at least arguable that some of them are not as advantageous as they appear at first sight, and that others represent potential, if not actual, weaknesses in the tribunal system.

Tribunals are cheap, quick, flexible and informal, but their operation should not be viewed with complacency. These so-called advantages could be seen as representing an attack on general legal standards, and the tribunal system could be portrayed as providing a second-rate system of justice for those who cannot afford to pay to gain access to 'real law' in the court system. Vigilance is required on the part of the general community to ensure that such does not become an accurate representation of the tribunal system.

In addition to this general point, there are particular weaknesses in the system of tribunal adjudication. Some of these relate to the following:

- *Appeals procedures*

  The previous confusion and complexity relating to means and routes of appeal noted by Sir Andrew Leggatt have been remedied by the TCEA 2007.

- *Publicity*

  It was stated above that lack of publicity in relation to tribunal proceedings was a potential advantage of the system. A lack of publicity, however, may be a distinct disadvantage because it has the effect that cases involving issues of general public importance are not given the publicity and consideration that they might merit.

FIGURE 15.4 *Tribunals: an aide-mémoire.*

● *The provision of public funding*

It was claimed previously that one of the major advantages of the tribunal system is its lack of formality and non-legal atmosphere. Research has shown, however, that individual complainants fare better where they are represented by lawyers. Additionally, as a consequence of the Franks recommendations, the fact that chairpersons have to be legally qualified has led to an increase in the formality of tribunal proceedings. As a result, non-law experts find it increasingly difficult in practice to represent themselves effectively. This difficulty is compounded when the body that is the object of the complaint is itself legally represented; although the parties to hearings do not have to be legally represented, there is nothing to prevent them from being so represented.

15.6   OMBUDSMAN

As with tribunals, so the institution of the Ombudsman reflects the increased activity of the contemporary state. As the state became more engaged in everyday social activity, it increasingly impinged on, and on occasion conflicted with, the individual citizen. Courts and tribunals were available to deal with substantive breaches of particular rules and procedures, but there remained some disquiet as to the possibility of the adverse effect of the implementation of general state policy on individuals. If tribunals may be categorised as an ADR procedure to the ordinary court system in relation to *decisions taken in breach of rules*, the institution of the Ombudsman represents a procedure for the redress of complaints about *the way in which those decisions have been taken*. It has to be admitted, however, that the two categories overlap to a considerable degree. The Ombudsman procedure, however, is not just an alternative to the court and tribunal system; it is based upon a distinctly different approach to dealing with disputes. Indeed, the Parliamentary Commissioner Act 1967, which established the position of the first Ombudsman, provides that complainants with rights to pursue their complaints in either of those forums will be precluded from making use of the Ombudsman procedure. (Such a prohibition is subject to the discretion of the Ombudsman, who tends to interpret it in a generous manner in favour of the complainant.)

The concept of the Ombudsman is Scandinavian in origin, and the function of the office-holder is to investigate complaints of *maladministration*, that is, situations where the performance of a government department has fallen below acceptable standards of administration. The first Ombudsman, appointed under the 1967 legislation, operated, and the present Ombudsman still operates, under the title of the Parliamentary Commissioner for Administration (PCA), and was empowered to consider central government processes only. The PCA also serves as Health Service Ombudsman, in which capacity they investigate complaints that hardship or injustice has been caused by the National Health Service's failure to provide a service, by a failure in service provided or by maladministration. Since that date, a number of other Ombudsmen have been appointed to oversee the administration of local government in England and Wales, under the Local Government Act 1974. Scotland and Northern Ireland have their own local government

Ombudsmen fulfilling the same task. There are also Health Service Commissioners for England, Wales and Scotland, whose duty it is to investigate the administration and provision of services in the health service, and in October 1994 Sir Peter Woodhead was appointed as the first Prisons Ombudsman. This proliferation of Ombudsmen has led to some confusion as to which one any particular complaint should be taken to. This can be especially problematic where the complaint concerns more than one public body. In order to remedy this potential difficulty, a Cabinet Office review recommended in April 2000 that access be made easier through the establishment of one new Commission, bringing together the Ombudsmen for central government, local government and the health service. This initiative moved forward in August 2005 when the Cabinet Office published a *Consultation Paper on the Reform of Public Sector Ombudsmen Services in England*. As yet, the single Commission has not been brought into existence. The Ombudsman system has also spread beyond the realm of government administration and there are Ombudsmen overseeing the operation of, among other things, legal services (see below, 16.6.7, for details), banking and insurance. Some schemes, such as the legal services scheme, have been established by statute, but many others have been established by industry as a means of self-regulation. It is a peculiarity of the system that reference is always made to the Ombuds *man*, irrespective of the gender of the office-holder. The present Parliamentary Ombudsman is in fact Dame Julie Mellor.

The European Parliament appointed an Ombudsman under the powers extended to it by the Treaty Establishing the European Community (EC Treaty) (Art 195, formerly 138(e)). The European Ombudsman has the function of investigating maladministration in all of the Union institutions, including the non-judicial operation of the Court of Justice of the European Union.

Before going on to consider the work of the Parliamentary Commissioner in some detail, mention should also be made of the various regulatory authorities that were established to control the operation of the privatised former state monopolies such as the water, gas, telephone and railway industries. Thus were Ofcom, Ofgem and Ofwat, and so on, set up, with part of their remit being to deal with particular consumer complaints, as well as the general regulation of the various sectors.

15.6.1 PROCEDURE

Although maladministration is not defined in the Parliamentary Commissioner Act 1967, it has been taken to refer to an error in the way a decision was reached rather than an error in the actual decision itself. Indeed, s 12(3) of the Parliamentary Commissioner Act 1967 expressly precludes the PCA from questioning the merits of particular decisions taken without maladministration. Maladministration therefore can be seen to refer to the procedure used to reach a result rather than the result itself. In an illuminating and much-quoted speech introducing the Act, Richard Crossman, the then Leader of the House of Commons, gave an indicative, if non-definitive, list of what might be included within the term maladministration, and included within it bias, neglect, inattention, delay, incompetence, ineptitude, perversity, turpitude and arbitrariness.

In his 1993 Annual Report, the then Parliamentary Ombudsman, Sir William Reid, added the following additional examples to Crossman's list:

- rudeness (though that is a matter of degree);
- unwillingness to treat the complainant as a person with rights;
- refusal to answer reasonable questions;
- neglecting to inform a complainant on request of his or her rights or entitlement;
- knowingly giving advice which is misleading or inadequate;
- ignoring valid advice or overruling considerations which would produce an uncomfortable result for the overruler;
- offering no redress or manifestly disproportionate redress;
- showing bias whether because of colour, sex or any other grounds;
- omission to notify those who thereby lose a right of appeal;
- refusal to inform adequately of the right of appeal;
- faulty procedures;
- failure by management to monitor compliance with adequate procedures;
- cavalier disregard of guidance which is intended to be followed in the interest of equitable treatment of those who use a service;
- partiality; and
- failure to mitigate the effects of rigid adherence to the letter of the law where that produces manifestly inequitable treatment.

Members of the public do not have the right to complain directly to the PCA, but must channel any such complaint through a Member of Parliament. Complainants do not have to provide precise details of any maladministration. They simply have to indicate the difficulties they have experienced as a result of dealing with an agency of central government. It is the function of the PCA to discover whether the problem arose as a result of maladministration. There is a 12-month time limit for raising complaints, but the PCA has discretion to ignore this.

The powers of the PCA to investigate complaints are similar to those of a High Court judge to require the attendance of witnesses and the production of documents; wilful obstruction of the investigation is treated as contempt of court.

On conclusion of an investigation, the PCA submits reports to the Member of Parliament who raised the complaint, and to the principal of the government office that was subject to the investigation. The Ombudsman has no enforcement powers, but if their recommendations are ignored, and existing practices involving maladministration are not altered, they may submit a further report to both Houses of Parliament in order to highlight the continued bad practice. The assumption is that on the submission of such a report, Members of Parliament will exert pressure on the appropriate Minister of State to ensure that any changes needed in procedure are made.

Annual reports are laid before Parliament and a Parliamentary Select Committee exists to oversee the operation of the PCA. The operation of the PCA is subject to judicial review (*R v Parliamentary Commissioner for Administration ex p Balchin* (1997)).

15.6.2 CASE STUDIES

The relationship between the PCA and the government is highlighted by the following case studies:

Channel Tunnel Rail link

As a consequence of the four-year delay on the part of the Department of Transport in deciding on a route for the Channel Tunnel Rail Link, the owners of properties along the various possible routes found the value of their properties blighted, or the property simply unsaleable. The situation was not finalised until the Department announced its final selection in 1994. According to the PCA:

> The effect of the Department of Transport's policy was to put the project in limbo, keeping it alive when it could not be funded.

As a consequence, he held that the Department:

> had a responsibility to consider the position of such persons suffering exceptional or extreme hardship and to provide redress where appropriate. They undertook no such considerations. That merits my criticism.

The unusual thing about this case, however, was the reaction of the Department of Transport, which rejected the findings of the PCA and refused to provide any compensation. The refusal of the Department of Transport led the PCA to lay a special report before Parliament, consequent upon a situation where an 'injustice has been found which has not or will not be remedied' (s 10(3) of the Parliamentary Commissioner Act 1967). Even in the face of the implementation of this extremely rare form of censure, the government maintained its original policy that it was not liable for the consequences of either general or particular blight. The matter was then taken up by the Select Committee on the Parliamentary Commissioner for Administration, which supported the conclusions of the PCA and recommended that:

> the Department of Transport reconsider its response to the Ombudsman's findings, accept his conclusions that maladministration had occurred . . . It

would be most regrettable if the department were to remain obdurate. In such an event, we recommend that as a matter of urgency a debate on this matter be held on the floor of the House on a substantive motion in government time (*Sixth Report of PCA*).

Such a demonstration of solidarity between the PCA and the Committee had the desired effect, leading to the government's climbdown and payments of £5,000 to those property owners who had suffered as a consequence of the housing blight.

Trusting the pensions promise: government bodies and the security of final-salary occupational pensions

On 15 March 2006 the Ombudsman published the above-named report on her investigation into the actions of government bodies in relation to the security of final-salary occupational pensions. She had received more than 200 complaints from MPs relating to the issue, together with 500 direct complaints from members of the public. All of the complaints were against the Department for Work and Pensions, the Treasury, the former Occupational Pensions Regulatory Authority and the National Insurance Contributions Office. However, the claims actually related to some 85,000 people from 400 private pension schemes who had lost part or all of their occupational pensions as a result of their company becoming insolvent between 6 April 1997 and 31 March 2004. Additionally, people whose schemes finished between April 2004 and 31 March 2005 were affected.

The extensive report supported claims that government departments wrongly advised workers that their company pensions were safe and protected by law. In this regard the report focused on leaflets issued by the Department for Work and Pensions advising workers as to the security of their works pensions. Particular weight was placed on one leaflet, issued in January 1996, which proclaimed that the Pensions Act 1995 was introduced specifically because 'the government wanted to remove any worries people had about the safety of their occupational scheme following the "Maxwell affair"'. As a result of such information, many workers who lost out on company pension schemes when their employers went bust felt the government had failed to highlight the risks of occupational pensions.

It was also alleged that on a number of occasions, ministers and officials had ignored relevant evidence when taking policy and other decisions related to the protection of pension rights accrued in such schemes. Thus the government twice reduced the minimum funding requirement (MFR), a formula introduced in 1995 as a result of the Maxwell pensions scandal, designed to make final-salary schemes safer by setting out the level of funding occupational pension schemes were required to have. By reducing the MFR, the government reduced the burden on employers, but in so doing it also decreased the protection offered to members. Although the MFR was never intended to guarantee pensions, the complainants argued that the literature produced by the government agencies implied exactly that. Consequently, many workers thought their pensions were safer than they were.

The investigation uncovered evidence of real suffering, distress and uncertainty about the future among pension scheme members and their families, who had relied on government information when making choices about their future pension provision. Two people had actually committed suicide after learning they would not receive their full pensions.

The report found that official information about the security of final-salary occupational pension schemes provided over many years by the Department for Work and Pensions, the Occupational Pensions Regulatory Authority and other government bodies was '*inaccurate, incomplete, unclear and inconsistent*' and in her conclusion the Ombudsman stated that:

> Government has a unique responsibility in these matters. Government set the pensions policy framework and took upon itself the responsibility of providing information for the public. The maladministration which my investigation has uncovered caused injustice to a large number of people who, as a result, lost the opportunity to make informed choices about their future.

The report made the following five recommendations to the government:

- full restoration of all lost pensions plus any other benefits such as life cover, 'by whichever means is most appropriate, including if necessary by payment from public funds';
- making 'consolatory payments' in recognition of the 'outrage, distress, inconvenience and uncertainty' workers have endured;
- apologising to scheme trustees for the distress they have suffered;
- considering whether to compensate those who are not fully covered by her recommendations;
- reviewing what can be done to reduce the time taken to wind up final-salary schemes.

However, as the report itself revealed that ministers had not accepted the findings of the report and had informed the Ombudsman that they were likely to comply only with the last of her recommendations, she was left to conclude that:

> Therefore, there is no basis on which I can be satisfied that the injustice I have identified will be remedied.

The estimation of costs of compensation was put between £5 billion and £10 billion to be paid over a period of some 40 years, a cost the government refused to meet. While the then pensions minister, Stephen Timms, expressed his sympathy with the workers who lost their pensions, he stated that 'nobody ever said occupational schemes were guaranteed by the taxpayer'. He also claimed that the Ombudsman had made 'an implausible leap' when she suggested literature written by his department backing occupational schemes led to government liability. In his view:

> Responsibility must fall on those companies whose schemes were or are being wound up, and to the trustees who, with the benefit of professional advice, were responsible for protecting members' interests.

Subsequently, the later pensions minister Peter Hain, towards the end of 2007, announced that the government intended to recompense most of the pensioners who had lost out in works schemes.

Equitable life: a decade of regulatory failure

This investigation originally took place into the role of the Financial Services Authority (FSA) and other authorities in regulating the conduct of the Equitable Life Assurance Society. In the 1950s the society started selling pension policies with a guaranteed annuity rate (GAR) that allowed policyholders to opt for minimum pension payouts and a bonus when their policy matured. Such policies were sustainable during the high inflation rates of the 1970s, but with current low inflation and interest rates Equitable found it hard to fund its commitments. Consequently, in an attempt to maintain payments to the majority of its customers who did not hold guarantees, it tried to withdraw the guaranteed payouts. However, in July 2000 the House of Lords ruled (in the *Hyman* litigation) that Equitable was required to make good its promises to the 90,000 holders of guaranteed annuity pension policies. As a consequence of this decision, it was apparent that Equitable was not in a position to maintain its payment to its policyholders; in December 2000 it closed its doors to new business and in July 2001 it announced that it was reducing the value of pension policies for with-profits policyholders by about 16 per cent. Later, in September 2001, Equitable published a compromise proposal for policyholders aimed at salvaging the company's finances and meeting its liabilities. This ensured that the existing GAR policyholders would get a 17.5 per cent increase in the value of their policies, but they would have to sign away their guaranteed pension rights. The other policyholders who were not GAR holders were offered a 2.5 per cent increase on the value of their policies, but they were required to sign away their rights to any legal claims. It has been estimated that some 800,000 policyholders have lost money as a result of the actions of Equitable. In August 2001, the government announced the independent Penrose Inquiry into events at Equitable Life; in October 2001, the then Parliamentary Ombudsman, Michael

Buckley, announced that he would be carrying out a statutory investigation into the FSA's handling of events at Equitable Life beginning in 1999, when it had assumed responsibility for the prudential regulation of the life insurance industry. The investigation by the Ombudsman took 20 months, and when the report was issued by the Ombudsman in July 2003, it was not met with uniform approval. The Ombudsman 'found no evidence to suggest that the FSA . . . had failed their regulatory responsibilities during the period under investigation'. As she pointed out:

> the responsibility for what individual potential investors were actually told when purchasing new policies or annuities was not a matter for the regulator. Given all the publicity surrounding Equitable's high-profile court case and their subsequent decision to put up the company for sale, I would have expected potential investors to have sought independent advice before investing in Equitable.

However, the investigation had highlighted a specific issue that she wished to draw to Parliament's attention. That was the apparent mismatch between public expectations of the role of the prudential regulator and what the regulator could reasonably be expected to deliver. It was never envisaged by those who framed the legislation establishing the regulatory regime that it would provide complete protection for all policyholders. The emphasis was on a 'light touch' approach to regulation and the avoidance of over-interference in a company's affairs. Referring to calls for her to extend her investigation to an earlier period, the Ombudsman stated that:

> I have the very deepest sympathy for those who have suffered financial loss as a result of events at Equitable. However, given my very limited remit and the conclusions I have drawn from the investigation, I do not believe that anything would be gained from my further intervention, nor do I believe I could meet the expectations of policyholders in terms of the remedies they are seeking. It would be offering policyholders false hope were I to suggest otherwise. I have therefore decided not to investigate further complaints about the prudential regulation of Equitable.

The placing of blame on the management of Equitable rather than on the regulator was confirmed when Lord Penrose issued his report in March 2004. The report laid the blame for the affair at the door of Equitable's management in its finding that 'a culture of manipulation and concealment on the part of some of the company's previous senior management allowed a bonus policy to develop that led to the society's financial weakening – a policy left unchecked by its own board'. However, in July 2004, the

Ombudsman reported to Parliament that she would, after all, be conducting a further investigation into the prudential regulation of Equitable Life. As she stated:

> The concerns surrounding the prudential regulation of Equitable Life remain despite the publication of the Penrose Report and the Government's response to it. I took the view that I should consider whether a new investigation by my Office was justified as Lord Penrose did not deal with questions of maladministration – or redress.

In her report, the Ombudsman asked the government to bring the Government Actuary's Department (GAD) into her jurisdiction so that she could assess the GAD's role in the prudential regulation of Equitable. As she stated:

> I consider that there is sufficient initial evidence to suggest that the actions of GAD are key to an assessment of whether maladministration by the prudential regulators caused an injustice to complainants that has not been put right. I believe therefore that GAD's actions must be brought within my jurisdiction.

It was stated that the investigation would cover the actions of the government departments responsible for the prudential regulation of Equitable Life but not concerns around the management of Equitable Life itself, or complaints about the alleged misselling of its policies, neither of which is within the Ombudsman's remit.

When her report, *Equitable Life: a decade of regulatory failure*, came out in July 2008 it set out 10 specific findings of maladministration: one against the former Department of Trade and Industry, four against the Government Actuary's Department, and five against the Financial Services Authority, in relation to their regulation of Equitable in the period before 1 December 2001. Included in those determinations were that:

- during the period before mid-1998, the regulators failed to verify the financial position of Equitable Life, even though they were duty-bound to do so and that such failure 'permitted misleading information . . . to be provided to policyholders and potential policyholders';
- the company's financial position was further obscured by the publication in 1999 of misleading regulatory returns showing a solvency position that was boosted by a 'worthless' reinsurance arrangement;
- after Equitable closed to new business in late 2000, the regulators 'provided misleading information to policyholders and the public, saying that Equitable had always

been solvent for regulatory purposes. The regulators also gave assurances that the company had always met its other regulatory requirements. Neither was the case.'

In addition to the specific findings of maladministration, the Ombudsman also upheld a general complaint about the period before Equitable closed to new business on 8 December 2000, namely that:

> the public bodies responsible for the prudential regulation of insurance companies . . . and the Government Actuary's Department failed for considerably longer than a decade properly to exercise their regulatory functions in respect of Equitable Life.

On the basis of those findings, the Ombudsman recommended, first, that, in recognition of the justifiable sense of outrage felt by those who had complained, the public bodies concerned should apologise for their failures. More importantly, however, her second recommendation was that the government should establish and fund a compensation scheme, with the aim of putting those who had suffered in the position they would have been in had they not invested in Equitable Life policies. Effectively this would mean paying compensation to remedy any financial losses which would not have been suffered had those people invested elsewhere than with Equitable.

As approximately one million people saw the value of their retirement savings affected as a result of the Equitable Life affair, the government's potential payment could amount to £4.5 billion, were it to accept and adopt the Ombudsman's recommendations. Whether it does so remains to be seen, but it is of interest to note that there have already been suggestions in the press that the government will resist making such payment and would rest its case on the Ombudsman's earlier conclusions that perhaps those who suffered should have taken more care and should bear more responsibility for their investments rather than looking to the state to bail them out. The Ombudsman's rejoinder to that approach would surely now be that the losses would not have been suffered had the authorities not been guilty of failure in their supervisory roles such as amounted to maladministration.

In February 2009 the Treasury minister, Yvette Cooper, apologised on behalf of regulators and successive governments for the maladministration found by the Ombudsman. However, she rejected the recommendation that compensation should be provided to all Equitable members and announced that a payment scheme for policyholders would focus on helping those investors who had been 'disproportionately affected' by the maladministration. The retired judge Sir John Chadwick was nominated to determine who was actually to be counted in that category, with of course a consequent further delay in any payment.

In October 2009, in *Equitable Members Action Group (EMAG) v HM Treasury*, in a partial victory for EMAG, Lord Justice Carnwath and Mr Justice Gross, sitting in the Administrative Court, quashed the Treasury's decision to reject a number of findings of injustice and maladministration made by the Parliamentary Ombudsman on the basis of the date when state liability should start. Rather than start after 1995, as the Treasury had argued, the High Court held that the commencement date should be pushed back to 1991, thus greatly increasing the number of potential beneficiaries of compensation. The Court gave the Treasury 21 days to respond to the ruling and say what course of action they proposed to take and refused it permission to appeal.

In a subsequent Parliamentary statement the Chief Secretary to the Treasury, Liam Byrne, did not go out of his way to encourage the hopes of those waiting for payments:

> [Sir John Chadwick's] overall task remains the same, namely to advise the Government on those policyholders who have suffered disproportionate impact as a result of those cases of maladministration leading to injustice which the Government now accepts. The Government remains firmly committed to introducing a fair *ex gratia* payment scheme as soon as possible, taking benefit from Sir John's advice on the apportionment of responsibility and practicality of delivery, *and having taken account of the public finances*. Our goal is to introduce a scheme that is administratively quicker and simpler to deliver than that envisaged by the Ombudsman (emphasis added).

One of the first measures announced by the new coalition government in May 2010 was that a scheme would be established to pay the claims in line with the Ombudsman's recommendations. The Equitable Life (Payments) Bill was introduced in July 2010 and was passed in December of that year. It gives the Treasury statutory authority to incur expenditure in making payments to Equitable Life policyholders. It was initially expected that the total could amount to £5 billion. However, following Chadwick's conclusion that even though people had lost £4.8 billion in the debacle, compensation payments should only range between £400 and £500 million, the coalition government was seen to withdraw from its original promise to the Equitable Life claimants. Thus, in October 2010 the Chancellor, George Osborne, announced that reparation of £1.5 billion would be made. In December 2010, Royal Assent was given to the Equitable Life (Payments) Act 2010, which gave effect to the reparation proposals.

15.6.3 EVALUATION

All in all, the system appears to operate fairly well within its restricted sphere of operation, but there are major areas where it could be improved. The more important of the criticisms levelled at the PCA relate to:

- the retention of Members of Parliament as filters of complaints. It is generally accepted that there is no need for such a filter mechanism. At one level, it represents a sop to the idea of parliamentary representation and control. Yet at the practical level, PCAs have referred complaints made to them directly to the constituent's Member of Parliament, in order to have them referred back to them in the appropriate form. It is suggested that there is no longer any need or justification for this farce;

- the restrictive nature of the definition of maladministration. It is possible to argue that any procedure that leads to an unreasonable decision must involve an element of maladministration and that, therefore, the definition as currently stated is not overly restrictive. However, even if such reverse reasoning is valid, it would still be preferable for the definition of the scope of the PCA's investigations to be clearly stated, and be stated in wider terms than at present;

- the jurisdiction of the PCA. This criticism tends to resolve itself into the view that there are many areas that should be covered by the PCA, but which are not. For example, as presently constituted, the Ombudsman can only investigate the *operation* of general law. It could be claimed, and not without some justification, that the process of *making* law in the form of delegated legislation could equally do with investigation;

- the lack of publicity given to complaints. It is sometimes suggested that sufficient publicity is not given either to the existence of the various Ombudsmen or to the results of their investigations. The argument is that if more people were aware of the procedure and what it could achieve, then more people would make use of it, leading to an overall improvement in the administration of governmental policies;

- the reactive role of the Ombudsman. This criticism refers to the fact that the Ombudsmen are dependent upon receiving complaints before they can initiate investigations. It is suggested that a more *proactive* role, under which the Ombudsmen would be empowered to initiate investigation on their own authority, would lead to an improvement in general administration as well as increase the effectiveness of the activity of the Ombudsmen. This criticism is related to the way in which the role of the Ombudsmen is viewed. If they are simply a problem-solving dispute resolution institution, then a *reactive* role is sufficient; if, however, they are seen as the means of improving general administrative performance, then a more *proactive* role is called for.

Following a review of the current ombudsman provision conducted by Robert Gordon in October 2014, the Cabinet Office issued a consultancy paper in March 2015. It was entitled *A Public Service Ombudsman* and sought views about a proposal to establish a single Public Service Ombudsman taking over the functions of:

- The Parliamentary Ombudsman;
- The Health Service Ombudsman;
- The Local Government Ombudsman;
- The Housing Ombudsman.

As Richard Kirkham and Jane Martin wrote, in support of the proposal, in *The Creation of an English Public Services Ombudsman* (www.democraticaudit.com):

> The basic argument for harmonisation is that the current design of the English ombudsman sector is only explicable as the end product of an unco-ordinated set of historical events. The first ombudsman scheme in the UK was introduced in 1967 with a limited jurisdiction and without proper consideration of the option of a public sector wide ombudsman scheme. This was followed, over time, by the introduction of new ombudsman schemes in response to new pressures in different parts of the public sector. Throughout this process little thought was ever given to the overall structure of the administrative justice system, resulting today in a network of multiple overlapping schemes which do not always map onto the delivery of 21st century public services in a comprehensible, efficient or possibly even effective manner.

CHAPTER SUMMARY: ARBITRATION, TRIBUNAL ADJUDICATION AND ALTERNATIVE DISPUTE RESOLUTION

Alternative dispute resolution (ADR) has many features that make it preferable to the ordinary court system in many areas.

Its main advantage is that it is less antagonistic than the ordinary legal system, and is designed to achieve agreement between the parties involved.

MEDIATION AND CONCILIATION

Mediation: the third party only acts as a go-between. The Family Law Act 1996 proposed a greater role for mediation in relation to divorce. However, following adverse trials, the Lord Chancellor announced in January 2001 that Part II of the Family Law Act would be repealed.

Conciliation: the third party is more active in facilitating a reconciliation or agreement between the parties.

ARBITRATION

This is the procedure whereby parties in dispute refer the issue to a third party for resolution, rather than take the case to the ordinary law courts. Arbitration procedures can be contained in the original contract or agreed after a dispute arises. The procedure is governed by the Arbitration Act 1996. The Act follows the Model Arbitration Law adopted by the United Nations Commission on International Trade Law (UNCITRAL). Arbitration awards are enforceable in the ordinary courts. They must be carried out in a judicial manner and are subject to judicial review.

Advantages over the ordinary court system are: privacy; informality; speed; lower cost; expertise; and it is less antagonistic.

ADMINISTRATIVE TRIBUNALS

These deal with cases involving conflicts between the state, its functionaries and private citizens. Domestic tribunals deal with private internal matters within institutions. Tribunals may be seen as administrative, but they are also adjudicative in that they have to act judicially when deciding particular cases. Tribunals are subject to the supervision of the Council on Tribunals, but are subservient to, and under the control of, the ordinary courts.

Usually, only the chair of a tribunal is legally qualified.

The tribunal structure has been altered by the Tribunals, Courts and Enforcement Act 2007, which introduced a two-tier system of original hearing and appeal.

Examples of tribunals are the: Employment Tribunal; Social Security Appeals Tribunal; Mental Health Review Tribunal; Lands Tribunal; and the Rent Assessment Committee.

Advantages of tribunals over ordinary courts relate to: speed; cost; informality; flexibility; expertise; accessibility; privacy.

Disadvantages relate to: the appeals procedure; lack of publicity; the lack of public funding in most cases.

OMBUDSMEN

The role of Ombudsmen is to investigate complaints of maladministration in various areas of state activity. Members of the public must channel complaints through a Member of Parliament.

The powers of the Parliamentary Commissioner for Administration to investigate complaints are similar to those of a High Court judge. The Ombudsman has no direct enforcement powers as such.

On conclusion of an investigation, the Ombudsman submits reports to the Member of Parliament who raised the complaint and to the principal of the government office that was subject to the investigation. He or she can also report to Parliament.

Shortcomings in the procedure: the Member of Parliament filter; uncertain, if not narrow, jurisdiction; lack of publicity; and the reactive rather than proactive nature of the role.

FOOD FOR THOUGHT

1   One of the most frequently cited advantages of ADR is that it is cheaper than taking cases through the courts, but to what extent does that indicate that it is merely 'justice on the cheap'?

2   Given the much-vaunted advantages of ADR, should it really be made compulsory?

3   One of the most important previous complaints/concerns about administrative tribunals was their lack of independence from the institutions they were

regulating/deciding on. Consider the extent to which the Tribunals Courts and Enforcement Act 2007 and the recently established unified courts and tribunals system has overcome this perception.

FURTHER READING

Abel, R, 'The comparative study of dispute institutions in society' (1973) 8 Law and Society Rev 217

Alle, T, 'Advancing ADR' (2009) 153(15) SJ 18

Baldwin, J, *The Small Claims Procedure and the Consumer*, 1995, London: Office of Fair Trading

Beale, H and Dugdale, T, 'Contracts between businessmen: planning and the use of contractual remedies' (1975) 2 British JLS 45

Betancourt, J and Crook, J (eds), *ADR, Arbitration and Mediation*, 2014, London: Chartered Institute of Arbitrators

Blake, S, Browne, J and Sime, S, *A Practical Approach to Alternative Dispute Resolution*, 3rd edn, 2014, Oxford: OUP

Blake, S, Browne, J and Sime, S, *The Jackson ADR Handbook*,(2nd edn) 2016, Oxford: OUP

Brown, H and Marriott, A, *ADR Principles and Practice*, 3rd edn, 2012, London: Sweet and Maxwell

Corbey, S and Latreille, P, *The role of lay members in employment rights cases – survey evidence*, 2011, gre. ac.uk

Court-based ADR Initiatives for Non-Family Civil Disputes: the Commercial Court and the Court of Appeal, 2002, London: Lord Chancellor's Department

Genn, H and Genn, Y, *The Effectiveness of Representation at Tribunals*, 1989, London: LCD

Hawkins, K, *Law as a Last Resort*, 2002, Oxford: OUP

JUSTICE, *Industrial Tribunals*, 1987, London: Sweet & Maxwell

Justice Mackay (Lord), *The Administration of Justice*, 1994, London: Sweet & Maxwell

Michaelson, J, 'An A – Z of ADR' (2003) 153 NLJ 101, 181 and 232

Payne, R, 'To counsel, not confront: the law on ADR' (1999) Counsel 30

Pedley, FH, 'The small claims process' (1994) 144 NLJ 1217

Qureshi, K, 'Absolute power' (2009) 159 NLJ 1393

Reid, V, 'ADR: an alternative to justice?' (2009) 39 Fam Law 981

USEFUL WEBSITES

www.cedr.co.uk
The official website for the Centre for Effective Dispute Resolution.

www.ciarb.org
The website for the Chartered Institute of Arbitrators.

www.adrnow.org.uk
A useful website on ADR, run by the Advice Services Alliance.

www.justice.gov.uk/about/hmcts
The website for Her Majesty's Courts and Tribunals Service.

www.ombudsman.org.uk
Website of the Parliamentary and Health Service Ombudsman.

www.civilmediation.justice.gov.uk
Online directory of civil mediation providers.

COMPANION WEBSITE

Now visit the companion website to:

- test your understanding of the key terms using our Flashcard Glossary;
- revise and consolidate your knowledge of 'Arbitration, tribunal adjudication and alternative dispute resolution' using our multiple choice question testbank;
- view all of the links to the Useful Websites above.

www.routledge.com/cw/slapper

16.1 INTRODUCTION

The Legal Services Act 2007 (LSA) heralded major changes in the law. The changes prescribed in this new law are comprehensive and radical. The Act was built around Sir David Clementi's proposals and the key components were:

- Creation of the **Office for Legal Complaints** (OLC), which in turn created the Legal Ombudsman (LO) scheme.

- **Alternative Business Structures** (ABSs), which enable consumers to obtain services from one business entity that brings together lawyers and non-lawyers.

- **Legal Disciplinary Practices** (LDPs), which allow firms to have up to 25 per cent non-lawyer or different kinds of lawyers as partners.

- A new **Legal Services Board** (LSB) to act as a single, independent and publicly accountable regulator with the power to enforce high standards in the legal sector, replacing a variety of regulators with overlapping powers.

- A clear set of **regulatory objectives** for the regulation of legal services.

The possible effects of the Legal Services Act 2007

The Legal Services Board (LSB) permitted ABSs from 6 October 2011. This enabled non-law firms to own legal practices and is commonly called 'Tesco Law' by the media. While Tesco may well offer legal services, other large organisations have already registered an ABS. The Co-operative Society became one of the first to obtain a licence and become an ABS. Direct Line, the insurer, has since acquired a licence to become an ABS. Irwin Mitchell, a large legal practice, and Quindell, an AIM listed company, acquired ABS licences. The Solicitors Regulation Authority (SRA) has issued 340 ABS licences to date (SRA website, www.sra.org.uk, March 2015). Slater and Gordon, the Australian quoted law firm, acquired the legal practice of Russell Jones & Walker in April 2012 following the SRA granting an ABS licence. They have been acquiring more law firms. PricewaterhouseCoopers (PWC), a major international accountancy practice, has acquired an ABS for its legal practice, PwC Legal.

Professor Stephen Mayson of the Legal Services Policy Institute of the University of Law wrote in late 2013:

> We are just at the second anniversary of licences being issued for alternative business structures (ABSs). In the first year, about 40 licences were issued, and progress seemed slow. A year later, there are still only two licensing authorities, but there have been roughly another 200 new licences. A year ago, we were told that there were another 200 applications in the pipeline. And we have had another 200 licences issued in the past twelve months. So it appears to have taken a year just to process the pipeline. There are no indications of how many are in the pipeline at the moment (stephenmayson.com, 6 October 2013).

The Law Society has not ignored the ABS threat to its members and, in autumn 2008, it commissioned a report by Lord Hunt, which was published on 5 October 2009 and titled 'The Hunt Review of the Regulation of Legal Services'. This is a lengthy report, which starts by considering the recent background to the legal profession and then considers various matters including professional regulation, education and training and ABS.

In his report (p 102), Lord Hunt, in considering how ABS might work and be regulated, commented: 'How will the inevitable conflict between economic benefits and ethical concerns be resolved?' An example of this conflict might arise where a firm decided to settle a major piece of litigation, believing that it was in the best interest of the client to do so. The practice's shareholders might suffer a consequential loss of potential profit. Under company law the shareholder may be able to sue the directors for making such a decision. The Australian firm Slater and Gordon, the first legal practice in the Western world to be listed on a stock market, worked with its regulator to solve this conundrum. Its constitution states that 'where an inconsistency or conflict arises between the duties of the company, the company's duty to the court will prevail over all duties'. This position has yet to be tested. As Stephen Mayson has pointed out in his excellent discussion paper on ABS and related issues:

> Experience in other jurisdictions (such as New South Wales) suggests that a focus on ethical behaviour and 'education for compliance' with regulation could pay dividends. Work commissioned by the Department for Constitutional Affairs also suggested that it is not the business structure that should be the principal cause for concern but rather the underlying incentives, and that 'traditional' structures and methods of practice involving only lawyers are just as likely to encourage unethical behaviour.

Slater and Gordon specialise as an insurance complainant practice and, compared with the top English law firms, are very small. Their turnover for the 2016 accounting year was AU\$ 908.2 million (£532.1 million) according to their published accounts. The Slater and Gordon business model may well be appropriate for similar practices in the UK, but it is probably less likely to be adopted by the large city corporate law practices.

A new franchise – QualitySolicitors – was founded in 2008 to enable law firms to become members and compete with the changes envisaged by the introduction of ABS. Their objective is to have member law firms across the country in every high street by October 2011. Andrew Holroyd, a former president of The Law Society (and partner in Jackson and Canter, which is now a member of QualitySolicitors), said in the *Law Society Gazette* (7 October 2010): 'The creation of a national legal services brand is essential if we are to compete with the new entrants to the market next year.'

Craig Holt, the chief executive of QualitySolicitors, told the *Law Society Gazette* (7 October 2010) that 'massively increasing our number of fully branded firms will enable us to achieve our goal of becoming the first established household name brand for legal services'. According to their website (www.qualitysolicitors.com, November 2015) they have over 200 branches.

The Institute of Chartered Accountants in England and Wales (ICAEW) was concerned that accountants would not be disadvantaged and in October 2013 applied to the Legal Services Board (LSB) to become an approved regulator and licensing authority for probate under the Legal Services Act 2007. The approval was granted and became effective from 14 August 2014. The ICAEW published a report on 10 November 2015 stating that they had just issued the 100th licence to Tiffin Green Ltd.

In conclusion, the LSA 2007 and its potential effects are beginning to cause both legal and non-legal professions and individual firms to consider how to move forward and compete with the changes that have been taking place since October 2011. It may be that after the initial interest and registration of ABSs by some businesses (e.g. Co-op and Direct Line) there will be comparatively little change. Companies moving into legal services may ultimately find the work less profitable than anticipated, and the risks of professional negligence claims against them may lead to such firms withdrawing from the market. An area of possible major change could be in the insurance claims market and firms seeking stock market listings like the Australian practice Slater and Gordon (see above). There is also the potential for a legal insurer to acquire a legal practice to attempt to reduce costs of defending claims. The emergence of the QualitySolicitors franchise may help to protect the smaller high-street practices against the new 'Tesco Law' type entrants into the marketplace. Further franchises and affiliations may possibly develop. Small- to medium-sized law firms may consider mergers to create larger, more cost-efficient operations.

The introduction of ABSs has not been a total success, with the failure of Parabis Group, formed in 2012 and broken up and sold as part of a pre-pack administration in 2015.

A pilot scheme for trainee solicitors has been started by a company called Acculaw, and approved by the SRA. Acculaw (now known as Accutrainee) will offer training contracts to law graduates and then second them to city law firms and in-house legal departments. Trainees will spend a minimum of three months with any firm and a maximum of three secondments. The trainees will be employed by Accutrainee rather than the law firms. It was announced in *The Times Student Law* on 22 May 2014 that the first two trainees under this scheme had qualified.

16.2   THE LEGAL PROFESSION

The English legal system is one of only three in the world to have a divided legal profession where a lawyer is either a solicitor or a barrister. Each branch has its own separate traditions, training requirements and customs of practice. It is important to remember that it is not only lawyers who regularly perform legal work. As one text noted (Bailey and Gunn, *Smith & Bailey on the Modern English Legal System* (1991), p 105):

> many non-lawyers perform legal tasks, some of them full time. For example, accountants may specialise in revenue law, trade union officials may appear regularly before industrial tribunals on behalf of their members, and solicitors may delegate work to legal executives. Conversely, many of the tasks performed by lawyers are not strictly 'legal'.

16.3 SOLICITORS

The solicitor can be characterised as a general practitioner: a lawyer who deals with clients direct and, when a particular specialism or litigation is required, will engage the services of counsel, that is, a barrister. Looking at the solicitor as a legal GP and the barrister as a specialist, however, can be misleading. Most solicitors, especially those in large practices, are experts in particular areas of law. They may restrict their regular work to litigation or commercial conveyancing or revenue work. Many barristers, on the other hand, might have a quite wide range of work including criminal, family matters and a variety of common law areas like tort and contract cases. The origins of the solicitor go back to the *attornatus*, or later the 'attorney', a medieval officer of the court whose main function was to assist the client in the initial stages of the case. One group of people practising in the Court of Chancery came to be known as 'solicitors'. Originally, they performed a variety of miscellaneous clerical tasks for employers such as landowners and attorneys. Their name was derived from their function of 'soliciting' or prosecuting actions in courts of which they were not officers or attorneys. Eventually, neither of these groups was admitted to the Inns of Court (where barristers worked); they merged and organised themselves as a distinct profession.

It was not, however, until 1831 that 'The Society of Attorneys Solicitors Proctors and Others not being Barristers Practising in the Courts of Law and Equity in the UK' was given its Royal Charter. This body emerged as the governing body of solicitors, the term 'attorney' falling from general use.

One very significant area of development and concern for solicitors at the beginning of the twenty-first century is the extent to which their monopolies of certain sorts of practice have been eroded. They have already lost their monopoly on conveyancing. Then, in 1999, the Access to Justice Act (see Chapter 17) introduced the provision that the Lord Chancellor would in future be able to authorise bodies other than The Law Society to approve of their members carrying out litigation. This, however, should be seen in the wider context of the policy to break down the historical monopolies of both branches of the legal profession. Thus, we can note the growth, since the CLSA 1990, of solicitors' rights of audience in court, and a corresponding anxiety at the Bar when these rights were granted.

The 1990 Act provides that every barrister and every solicitor has a right of audience before every court in relation to all proceedings. The right, however, is not unconditional. In order to exercise it, solicitors and barristers must obey the rules of conduct of the professional bodies and must have met any training requirements that have been prescribed, like the requirement to have completed pupillage in the case of the Bar, or to have obtained a higher courts advocacy qualification in the case of solicitors who wish to appear in the higher courts.

16.3.1 TRAINING

The standard route to qualification is a law degree followed by a one-year Legal Practice Course (LPC) and then a term as a trainee solicitor which, like the barrister's pupillage, is essentially an apprenticeship. The one-year LPC is slowly changing, with Linklaters starting a seven-and-a-half-month course from January 2011 and Clifford Chance a seven-month course one year later. Several of the large city firms favour this course. The Solicitors Regulation Authority (SRA) (see 16.3.3) currently authorises 36 institutions to deliver the LPC. Non-law graduates can complete the Postgraduate Diploma in Law in one year and then proceed as a law graduate. While the Law Society does not require an aptitude test for students wishing to undertake the LPC, the Bar Standards Board requires one. The Bar Course Aptitude Test (BCAT) became compulsory in autumn 2013 and costs £150. After completion of the LPC and trainee-ship, a trainee solicitor may apply to The Law Society to be 'admitted' to the profession. The Master of the Rolls will add the names of the newly qualified to the roll of officers of the Supreme Court. The requirement for a training contract was changed on 1 July 2014 with the introduction of the SRA Training Regulations 2014 to enable qualification provided that 'a period of recognised training' has been completed. This route is currently controversial as to whether the training will be satisfactory and enable the student to become a solicitor. The SRA has recently proposed a final competency examination at the point of qualification for all new solicitors and has commenced a consultation on the proposal.

In October 2013 the SRA published a policy statement, *Training for Tomorrow*, containing three main proposals:

- competency framework to set out the knowledge, skills and attributes that a solicitor requires at the point of qualification;
- continuing professional development (CPD) to focus on effectiveness of post-qualification training;
- removal of layers of regulation which neither assure quality nor enable excellence.

The *Law Society Gazette* (15 April 2015) reported that a paralegal has become the first solicitor to qualify through the alternative method of 'equivalent means'. The SRA accepted evidence that the paralegal had, while working at a law firm, achieved the same standards as someone qualifying through the traditional training period.

The SRA report Regulated Population Statistics for the year to October 2016 states that 6,452 were admitted to the role and the breakdown was:

LPC 5,580, Qualified Lawyer transfer 541, Qualified Lawyer transfer test 27, CILEX 237 and other 67.

Further developments on qualifying as a solicitor can be found in the SRA's second consultation on the Solicitors' Qualifying Examination which commenced on 3 October 2016 and closes on 9 January 2017. The proposals are based on establishing consistency by undergoing 'the same independently-set professional assessment before qualifying' (SRA news release 3 October 2016). The proposals include requiring prospective solicitors to undertake a significant period of training in a legal environment.

In July 2011 the Legal Education and Training Review was commissioned and published in June 2013 (see below, 16.3.2).

To practise, a solicitor will also require a practising certificate issued by the SRA. The fee comprises four parts as listed below. The SRA's fee structure for 2016 is:

Individual practising fee
A flat fee of £290 for every solicitor seeking a practising certificate.

Firm practising fee
A fee payable by every firm seeking or maintaining authorisation to practise. This is a turnover-based fee as shown in the table below.

Individual Compensation Fund contribution
A flat fee of £32 is payable by each individual.

Firm Compensation Fund contribution
A flat fee of £548 is payable by firms which hold client money.

Firm practising fee calculation of turnover for 2016

Turnover range (A)	Pay per cent of turnover within band (B)	Minimum turnover in band (C)	Minimum fee in band (D)
£0 – £19,999	0.76%	£0	£100
£20,000 – £149,999	0.45%	£20,000	£252
£150,000 – £499,999	0.43%	£150,000	£837
£500,000 – £999,999	0.42%	£500,000	£2,342
£1,000,000 – £2,999,999	0.39%	£1,000,000	£4,442
£3,000,000 – £9,999,999	0.27%	£3,000,000	£12,242
£10,000,000 – £29,999,999	0.23%	£10,000,000	£31,142
£30,000,000 – £69,999,999	0.21%	£30,000,000	£77,142
£70,000,000 – £149,999,999	0.19%	£70,000,000	£161,142
£150,000,000 – £9,999,999,999	0.07%	£150,000,000	£313,142

The firm fee is calculated by following the steps below:

* Identify which band the turnover (T) falls in from column A.
* Take T and subtract the figure in the corresponding column C.
* Multiply this figure by the corresponding percentage in column B.

- Finally, add this figure to the corresponding figure in column D.
- Firm fee then needs to be rounded to the nearest pound (i.e. if less than 50p then round down, and if equal to or more than 50p then round up).

Formula: (T – C) × B + D

Example for turnover of £200,000:

(£200,000 – £150,000) × 0.43% + £837 = £1,052

Additionally, solicitors have to pay an annual premium for indemnity insurance.

All solicitors must now undergo regular continuing education, known as continuing professional development (CPD), which means attendance at non-examined legal courses designed to update knowledge and improve expertise. Each year, solicitors are required to complete 16 hours of CPD training in the CPD year that currently runs from 1 November to 31 October each year. One CPD point equates to one hour's training. In November 2016 CPD was replaced by continuing competence and this requires solicitors to assess their own learning and development needs. The SRA's website gives useful guidance on the subject.

The SRA has removed the requirement for all newly admitted solicitors to complete The Law Society's Management Course Stage 1 before the end of the third CPD year of the solicitor being admitted to the role. However, the Law Society has introduced two management courses that satisfy the training requirements under rule 12 of the SRA Practice Framework Rules 2011 ('qualified to supervise') in order to achieve the required 12 hours of management skills training.

16.3.2 LEGAL EDUCATION AND TRAINING REVIEW (LETR)

The Legal Education and Training Review (LETR) was commissioned by the Solicitors Regulation Authority (SRA), the Bar Standards Board (BSB) and ILEX Professional Standards (IPS). In late 2010 the SRA, BSB and IPS awarded the LETR research contract to the UKCLE Research Consortium, led by Professor Julian Webb of the University of Warwick. Research started in June 2011 and the final report was published on 25 June 2013. The aim was to survey the current state and future requirements of legal services education and training (LSET). This has become of significant importance with the advent of the Legal Services Act 2007 and the resultant changes in the legal profession.

The authors carried out detailed research involving 307 academics and an online survey of 1,128 key people. Two expert consultants in legal services, Professors Richard Susskind and Rob Wilson, also provided input to the report. The report is approximately 350 pages long and a brief summary of it can be found in the 15th edition of this book.

This was the profession's governing body, controlled by a council of elected members and an annually elected president. Its powers and duties derived from the Solicitors Act 1974. Complaints against solicitors used to be dealt with by the Solicitors' Complaints Bureau and the Solicitors' Disciplinary Tribunal, the latter having power to strike from the Roll the name of an offending solicitor. It had been sometimes seen as worrying that the Society combined two roles with a possible conflict of interests: maintenance of professional standards for the protection of the public, and as the main professional association to promote the interests of solicitors.

In 2006, The Law Society council began a debate on the future of the society. The question was whether the society should survive, if so in what shape, and what it should do for the solicitors who fund it. Reforms introduced in the Legal Services Bill 2006 have already led to changes, with the society hiving off, in January 2007, its regulation to the Solicitors' Regulation Authority and complaints handling to the Legal Complaints Service, which are new boards managed 'at arm's length' from the central body. The Law Society now deals with the interests of its members and will negotiate with and lobby the profession's regulators and government. The key roles of The Law Society now are to help, protect, promote, train and advise solicitors.

Solicitors Regulation Authority (SRA)

The SRA is the independent regulatory body of The Law Society and was established in January 2007. It was formerly known as The Law Society Regulation Board, but changed its name so that it would be clear that it was independent of The Law Society. The SRA's job is to regulate and discipline all solicitors in England and Wales, who number in excess of 100,000, with its principal aim of giving the public confidence in the profession. The SRA's functions include:

- setting standards for qualifying as a solicitor and the requirements for solicitors' continuing professional development;
- monitoring the performance of organisations that provide legal training;
- monitoring solicitors and their firms to ensure compliance with rules;
- referring solicitors to the Solicitors Disciplinary Tribunal;
- running the compensation fund;
- drafting rules of professional conduct.

In carrying out its functions, the SRA consults with solicitors and other legal professionals, along with the public, consumer groups and the government.

The Compensation Fund was set up in 1941 by The Law Society to protect clients who lost money due to the dishonesty of their solicitor or their solicitor's failure to properly account for clients' money. The fund used to be supervised by the Consumer Complaints Service (CCS). However, the fund is now run by the SRA. Any person, and not just the client of a solicitor, may seek payment from the compensation fund providing the person has suffered financial loss due to a solicitor's dishonesty or financial hardship due to a solicitor's failure to pay over money that he or she has received. The loss must arise during the solicitor's normal work. As a general rule, a person must notify the SRA within six months after they discovered (or should have discovered) the loss. The SRA will require the person making the claim to complete an application form. A caseworker will then investigate the application and if necessary will request more information before an adjudicator or panel determines the application. The SRA will not normally sanction the payment of more than £2 million including interest, costs and any other insurance or other payment the person who has suffered the loss may receive.

The Legal Complaints Service (LCS) may also direct a person to make a claim to the SRA's compensation fund. This may happen following the LCS directing a solicitor to pay compensation for poor service but they are unable to pay it if their firm is insolvent, the SRA having intervened in the firm or their practice is closed.

The Code of Conduct

On 6 October 2011 the Solicitors' Code of Conduct 2011 came into force, which has now codified solicitors' conduct obligations. Rule 1 sets out six core duties which are fundamental rules, and a breach could result in sanctions. Rules 2 to 25 are the rules that arise from the core duties and which basically put flesh on the bare bones of rule 1, breach of which may result in sanctions. After each rule there is guidance which is not mandatory and does not form part of the Code of Conduct.

Outcomes-focused regulation (OFR) is the SRA's new approach to regulation. OFR is a move away from a rules-based approach and instead focuses on high-level outcomes governing practice and the quality of outcomes for clients. Version 18 of the Code of Conduct handbook was published on 1 November 2016. The SRA has announced an 18-months process to reduce the size of the Code of Conduct handbook. The objective is to enable firms to have more flexibility in running their practice.

The Legal Ombudsman

The Legal Ombudsman (see also 16.6.7) is an independent, consumer-focused ombudsman scheme set up to resolve complaints about lawyers in England and Wales. The Legal Ombudsman (LO) was established under the Legal Services Act 2007 and began accepting complaints on 6 October 2010. The LO provides a free complaints resolution service to members of the public, very small businesses, charities and trusts.

The LO deals with complaints about solicitors and the following types of professionals (and generally those working for them): barristers, law costs draftsmen, legal executives, licensed conveyancers, notaries, patent attorneys, probate practitioners, registered European lawyers, solicitors, and trademark attorneys.

The LO runs a remuneration scheme for any person dissatisfied with their solicitor's bill. This service is free, providing that the solicitor's bill does not include work for court proceedings. The LO will check the solicitor's bill to ensure that it is fair and reasonable. If the solicitor's work includes court proceedings, then only the court can assess the bill.

The LO can also instruct a solicitor to pay compensation to their client for distress and inconvenience caused by poor service. If a person is dissatisfied with the service they received from their solicitor, they should first lodge a complaint with their solicitor or the solicitor's complaints handling partner. If the aggrieved party fails to receive a response, or a satisfactory response, they can complain to the LO. The LO can make an award of up to £50,000, including any extra expenses and losses. The LO 2016 report stated that in the year to March 2016 the compensation awarded in 88.6% of cases was less than £1,000. The LO makes awards on the merits of each individual case.

Solicitors' Disciplinary Tribunal (SDT)

The Solicitors' Disciplinary Tribunal is constitutionally independent of The Law Society, although it is funded by them. The SDT's powers arise by virtue of the Solicitors Act 1974. The purpose of the SDT is to consider and determine applications involving allegations of professional misconduct of solicitors or breaches of their professional rules. Such allegations are brought to the attention of the SDT in one of three ways:

* by members of the public;
* on behalf of The Law Society by in-house solicitors/barristers;
* by independent prosecuting solicitors instructed by The Law Society.

In addition, the SRA may refer a case to the SDT if a solicitor's misconduct is likely to lead to a fine, suspension, being struck off or another power given to the SDT.

Whether a referral is made to the SDT depends on two tests being satisfied: the evidential test and the public interest test. The former test requires 'that there is enough evidence to provide a realistic prospect that the solicitor will be found guilty of misconduct' (The Law Society, October 2006). The latter test involves considering the public interest once the evidential test is satisfied. For example, a case may be referred to the SDT if there are grounds for believing the conduct is likely to be continued or repeated, whereas a case may not be referred to the SDT if the misconduct was committed as a genuine mistake or misunderstanding or if the SDT is only likely to impose a small penalty.

The SDT can impose various sanctions which include the following:

* striking off the solicitor from the Roll;
* suspending the solicitor from practice for a fixed or indefinite period;
* ordering the solicitor to pay a penalty (to Her Majesty) for each allegation;
* reprimanding a solicitor.

As mentioned above, the OLC is funded by The Law Society, so there will still be a serious question as to whether this body will be seen as sufficiently independent by the public.

The Chartered Institute of Legal Executives (CILEx) represents over 10,000 legal executives employed in solicitors' offices. They are legally trained (the Institute runs its own examinations) and carry out much of the routine legal work that is a feature of most practices. The Institute was founded in 1892 and incorporated in 1963 with the support of The Law Society. On 30 January 2012 the former ILEX became incorporated by Royal Charter and its members are now known as Chartered Legal Executives. The Managing Clerks' Association, from which CILEx developed, recognised that many non-solicitor staff employed in fee-earning work, and in the management of firms, needed and wanted a training route that would improve standards and award recognition for knowledge and skills. The education and training facilities CILEx offers have developed in number and diversity so that CILEx is able to provide a route to a career in law, which is open to all.

Legal executives are, in the phrase of the CILEx website (www.cilex.org.uk), qualified lawyers specialising in a particular area of law. They will have passed the CILEx Professional Qualification in Law in an area of legal practice to the same level as that required of solicitors. They will have at least five years' experience of working under the supervision of a solicitor in legal practice or the legal department of a private company or local or national government. Fellows are issued with an annual practising certificate, and only Fellows of CILEx may describe themselves as 'Legal Executives'. Specialising in a particular area of law, their day-to-day work is similar to that of a solicitor.

Legal executives might: handle the legal aspects of a property transfer; assist in the formation of a company; be involved in actions in the High Court or County Courts; draft wills; or advise clients accused of serious or petty crime, families with matrimonial problems, and on many other matters affecting people in their domestic and business affairs. Legal executives are fee earners – in private practice their work is charged directly to clients – making a direct contribution to the income of a law firm. This is an important difference between legal executives and other types of legal support staff who tend to handle work of a more routine nature. In March 2000, six legal executives qualified to become the first legal executive advocates under the CLSA 1990. The advocacy certificates were approved by the then ILEX Rights of Audience Committee. The advocates now have extended rights of audience in civil and matrimonial proceedings in the County Courts and magistrates' courts. In some circumstances, Fellows of CILEx can instruct barristers directly. Public Access (the Bar Council's scheme by which barristers can be directly instructed by some professional and voluntary organisations, rather than by solicitors) enables legal executives to access a wide choice of legal advice and representation for their clients and their employers. In December 2010 the first member of ILEX was appointed a deputy district judge (*Law Society Gazette*, 27 January 2011).

16.4   BARRISTERS

The barrister is often thought of as primarily a court advocate, although many spend more time on drafting, pleadings (now called statements of case) and writing advice for solicitors. Professional barristers are technically competent to perform all advocacy for the prosecution or defence in criminal cases, and for a claimant or defendant in a civil claim. More generally, however, established barristers tend to specialise in particular areas of work. Over 60 per cent of practising barristers work in London.

The Bar had been organised as an association of the members of the Inns of Court by the fourteenth century. Today, there are four Inns of Court (Inner and Middle Temples, Lincoln's Inn and Gray's Inn), although there were originally more, including Inns of Chancery and Sergeants' Inns, the latter being an association of the king's most senior lawyers. Until the CLSA 1990, the barrister had a virtual monopoly on advocacy in all the superior courts (in some cases solicitors could act as advocates in the Crown Court). In most situations, they cannot deal direct with clients but must be engaged by solicitors (but see below, 16.6.2).

16.4.1   TRAINING

Entry to the Bar is now restricted to graduates and mature students. An aspirant barrister must register with one of the four Inns of Court in London. Commonly, a barrister will have a law degree and then undertake professional training (the Bar Practice Training Course (BPTC), formerly known as the Bar Vocation Course) for one year leading to the Bar Examinations. Alternatively, a non-law graduate can study for the Common Professional Examination for one year and, if successful in the examinations, proceed to the Bar Examinations. The Bar Standards Board has imposed an aptitude test since autumn 2013, following approval from the LSB, prior to a student undertaking the BPTC (see 16.3.1). The successful student is then called to the Bar by his or her Inn of Court. It is also a requirement of being called that, during study for the vocational course, the student attends his or her Inn to become familiar with the customs of the Bar. The student then undertakes a pupillage, essentially an apprenticeship to a junior counsel. Note that all barristers, however senior in years and experience, are still 'junior counsel' unless they have 'taken silk' and become Queen's Counsel (QCs). Barristers who do not intend to practise do not have to complete the pupillage. See also the section on the LETR at 16.3.2.

16.4.2   THE INNS OF COURT

The Inns of Court are administered by their senior members (QCs and judges) who are called Benchers. The Inns administer the dining system and are responsible for calling the students to the Bar.

16.4.3   THE GENERAL COUNCIL OF THE BAR

The General Council of the Bar of England and Wales and of the Inns of Court (the Bar Council) is the profession's governing body. It is run by elected officials. It is responsible for the Bar's Code of Conduct, disciplinary matters and representing the interests of the

Bar to external bodies like the Lord Chancellor's Department, the government and The Law Society. According to its own literature, this Council:

> fulfils the function of what might be called a 'trade union', pursuing the interests of the Bar and expanding the market for the Bar's services and is also a watchdog regulating its practices and activities.

16.4.4 EDUCATION

The Bar Standards Board (BSB) was established in January 2006 as a result of the Bar Council separating its regulatory and representative functions. That separation was to ensure that there was no conflict of interest between the people whose function was to represent the professional interests of barristers (as trade unions represent the interests of their members) and the people whose function is to regulate standards on behalf of the public and clients. As the independent regulatory board of the Bar Council, the BSB is responsible for regulating barristers called to the Bar in England and Wales. It takes decisions independently and in the public interest, and is not prejudiced by the Bar Council's representative function. The purpose of the BSB is 'to promote and maintain excellence in the quality of legal services provided by barristers to support the rule of law'. It does that by setting standards of entry to the profession and by ensuring that professional practice puts consumers first.

16.4.5 QUEEN'S COUNSEL

Queen's Counsel (QCs) are senior barristers of special merit. In 2015, the Bar had 1,574 QCs in practice. They are given this status (known as 'taking silk' because a part of the robe they are entitled to wear is silk) by the Queen on the advice of the Lord Chancellor. There were, until the suspension of the system in 2003, annual invitations from the Lord Chancellor for barristers to apply for this title. Applicants needed to show at least 10 years of successful practice at the Bar. However, under arrangements announced recently a new independent selection procedure has replaced the widely criticised former system, which relied on secret soundings among senior legal figures. Candidates will be chosen by the Lord Chancellor on the recommendation of an independent panel set up by The Law Society and the Bar Council. If appointed, the barrister will become known as a 'Leader' and he or she will often appear in cases with a junior. The old 'Two Counsel Rule', under which a QC always had to appear with a junior counsel, whether one was really required or not, was abolished in 1977. He or she will be restricted to high-level work (of which there is less available in some types of practice), so appointment can be financially difficult but, in most cases, it has good results for the QC as he or she will be able to considerably increase fee levels.

16.4.6 THE BARRISTER'S CHAMBERS

Barristers were not permitted to form partnerships (except with lawyers from other countries) until April 2010 when the Bar announced new rules following the LSA 2007; they work in sets of offices called chambers. Most chambers are run by barristers' clerks who act as business managers, allocating work to the various barristers and negotiating their fees. Imagine the situation where a solicitor wishes to engage a particular barrister for a case on a certain date and that barrister is already booked to be in another court three days before that date. The clerk cannot be sure whether the first case will have ended in time for the barrister to be free to appear in the second case. The first case might be adjourned after a day or, through unexpected evidential arguments in the early stages in the trial, it might last for four days. If the barrister is detained, then his or her brief for the second case will have to be passed to another barrister in his or her chambers very close to the actual trial. This is known as a late brief. Who will be asked to take the brief and at what point is a matter for the clerk. The role of the barrister's clerk is thus a most influential one. Since 2003, lay clients have been able to enjoy direct access to barristers under the Public Access scheme (previously known as BarDIRECT); see www.barcouncil.org.uk. It is currently possible for barristers to accept instructions from some licensed organisations as opposed to the normal practice of being briefed by solicitors.

16.5 PROFESSIONAL ETIQUETTE

The CLSA 1990 introduced a statutory committee, the Lord Chancellor's Advisory Committee on Legal Education and Conduct (ACLEC), which, until recently, had responsibilities in the regulation of both branches of the profession.

As part of the government's reforms of legal services generally, and publicly funded legal advice specifically, the Access to Justice Act 1999 (s 35) has replaced the ACLEC (considered by some as slow and ponderous) with the Legal Services Consultative Panel, launched at the beginning of 2000. The Consultative Panel has:

(a)   the duty of assisting in the maintenance and development of standards in the education, training and conduct of persons offering legal services and, where appropriate, making recommendations to the Lord Chancellor; and

(b)   the duty of providing to the Lord Chancellor, at their request, advice about particular matters relating to any aspect of the provision of legal services (including the education, training and conduct of persons offering legal services).

The Law Society (through the Solicitors Regulation Authority) and the Bar Council (through the Bar Standards Board) exercise tight control over the professional conduct of their members. Barristers can meet the client only when the solicitor or his or her representative is present. This is supposed to promote the barrister's detachment from the client and his or her case, and thus lend greater objectivity to counsel's judgment. However, since April 2010 the Bar has relaxed the rules on the work a barrister can undertake (see 16.1). Barristers and solicitors must dress formally for court appearances, although solicitors, when appearing in the Crown, County or High Court, are required to wear robes but not wigs. A barrister not wearing a wig and robe cannot be 'seen' or 'heard' by the judge.

Traditionally, lawyers were not permitted to advertise their services, although this area has been subject to some deregulation in the light of recent trends to expose the provision of legal services to ordinary market forces. Solicitors can, subject to some regulations, advertise their services in print and on broadcast media.

16.5.1   IMMUNITY FROM NEGLIGENCE CLAIMS

Until recently barristers could not be sued by their clients for negligent performance in court or for work that was preparatory to court work (*Rondel v Worsley* (1969)); this immunity had also been extended to solicitors who act as advocates (*Saif Ali v Sidney Mitchell* (1980)). The client of the other side, however, may sue for breach of duty (*Kelly v London Transport Executive* (1982)). This was changed in a major case in 2000.

Advocates' liability
Arthur JS Hall and Co v Simons and other appeals (2000)
Background

Lawyers are, for the general public, the most central and prominent part of the English legal system. They are, arguably, to the legal system what doctors are to the health system. For many decades, a debate had grown about why a patient injured by the negligence of a surgeon in the operating theatre could sue for damages, whereas a litigant whose case was lost because of the negligence of his or her advocate could not sue. It all seemed very unfair. Even the most glaringly obvious courtroom negligence was protected against legal action by a special advocates' immunity. The claim that this protection was made by lawyers (and judges who were lawyers) for lawyers was difficult to refute. In this House of Lords decision, the historic immunity was abolished in respect of both barristers and solicitor-advocates for both civil and criminal proceedings.

Facts

In three cases, all conjoined on appeal, a claimant raised a claim of negligence against a firm of solicitors, and in each case, the firms relied on the immunity attaching to barristers and other advocates from claims in negligence. At first instance, all the claims were struck out. Then, on appeal, the Court of Appeal said that the claims could have proceeded. The solicitors appealed to the Lords and two key questions were raised: should the old immunity rule be maintained and, in a criminal case, what was the proper scope of the principle against 'collateral attack'? A 'collateral attack' is when someone convicted in a criminal court tries to invalidate that conviction outside the criminal appeals process by suing his trial defence lawyer in a civil court. The purpose of such a 'collateral attack' is to win in the civil case, proving negligence against the criminal trial lawyer, and thus by implication showing that the conviction in the criminal case was unfair.

Held

The House of Lords held (Lords Hope, Hutton and Hobhouse dissenting in part) that, in the light of modern conditions, it was now clear that it was no longer in the public interest in the administration of justice that advocates should have immunity from suit for negligence for acts concerned with the conduct of either civil or criminal litigation.

Lord Hoffmann (with Lords Steyn, Browne-Wilkinson and Millett delivering concurring opinions) said that over 30 years had passed since the House had last considered the rationale for the immunity of the advocate from suit in *Rondel v Worsley*. Public policy was not immutable and there had been great changes in the law of negligence, the functioning of the legal profession, the administration of justice and public perceptions. It was once again time to re-examine the whole matter. Interestingly, Lord Hoffmann chose to formulate his opinion in a creative mode to reflect public policy, rather than in the tradition of what can be seen as slavish obedience to the details of precedent:

> I hope that I will not be thought ungrateful if I do not encumber this speech with citations. The question of what the public interest now requires depends upon the strength of the arguments rather than the weight of authority.

The point of departure was that, in general, English law provided a remedy in damages for a person who had suffered injury as a result of professional negligence. It followed that any exception that denied such a remedy required a sound justification. The arguments relied on by the court in *Rondel v Worsley* as justifying the immunity had to be considered. One by one, these arguments are evaluated and rejected.

Advocate's divided loyalty

There were two distinct versions of the divided loyalty argument. The first was that the possibility of being sued for negligence would actually inhibit the lawyer, consciously or unconsciously, from giving their duty to the court priority over their duty to their client. The second was that the divided loyalty was a special factor that made the conduct of litigation a very difficult art and could lead to the advocate being exposed to vexatious claims by difficult clients. The argument was pressed most strongly in connection with advocacy in criminal proceedings, where the clients were said to be more than usually likely to be vexatious.

There had been recent developments in the civil justice system designed to reduce the incidence of vexatious litigation. The first was r 24.2 of the Civil Procedure Rules, which provided that a court could give summary judgment in favour of a defendant if it considered that 'the claimant had no real prospect of succeeding on the claim'. The second was the changes to the funding of civil litigation introduced by the Access to Justice Act 1999, which would make it much more difficult than it had been in the past to obtain legal help for negligence claims that had little prospect of success.

There was no doubt that the advocate's duty to the court was extremely important in the English justice system. The question was whether removing the immunity would have a significantly adverse effect. If the possibility of being held liable in negligence was calculated to have an adverse effect on the behaviour of advocates in court, one might have expected that to have followed, at least to some degree, from the introduction of wasted costs orders (where a court disallows a lawyer from being able to claim part of a fee for work that is regarded as unnecessary and wasteful). Although the liability of a negligent advocate to a wasted costs order was not the same as a liability to pay general damages, the experience of the wasted costs jurisdiction was the only empirical evidence available in England to test the proposition that such liability would have an adverse effect upon the way advocates performed their duty to the court, and there was no suggestion that it had changed standards of advocacy for the worse.

The 'cab rank'

The 'cab rank' rule provided that a barrister could not refuse to act for a client on the ground that they disapproved of the client or his or her case. The argument was that a barrister who was obliged to accept any client would be unfairly exposed to vexatious claims by clients for whom any sensible lawyer with freedom of action would have refused to act. Such a claim was, however, in the nature of things intuitive, incapable of empirical verification and did not have any real substance. This rule has been modified by the Bar Standards Board (*Law Society Gazette*, 2 August 2012). A barrister can now refuse to act when work is offered by firms on the List of Defaulting Solicitors.

The witness analogy

The argument started from the well-established rule that a witness was absolutely immune from liability for anything that he or she said in court. So were the judge, counsel and the parties. They could not be sued for libel, malicious falsehood or conspiring to give false evidence. The policy of the rule was to encourage persons who took part in court proceedings to express themselves freely. However, a witness owed no duty of care to anyone in respect of the evidence he or she gave to the court. His or her only duty was to tell the truth. There was no analogy with the position of a lawyer who owed a duty of care to his or her client. The fact that the advocate was the only person involved in the trial process who was liable to be sued for negligence was because he or she was the only person who had undertaken such a duty of care to his or her client.

Collateral attack

The most substantial argument was that it might be contrary to the public interest for a court to retry a case which had been decided by another court. However, claims for negligence against lawyers were not the only cases that gave rise to a possibility of the same issue being tried twice. The law had to deal with the problem in numerous other contexts. So, before examining the strength of the collateral challenge argument as a reason for maintaining the immunity of lawyers, it was necessary to consider how the law dealt with collateral challenge in general.

       The law discouraged re-litigation of the same issues except by means of an appeal. The Latin maxims often quoted were *nemo debet bis vexari pro una et eadem causa* and *interest rei publicae ut finis sit litium*. The first was concerned with the interests of the defendant: a person should not be troubled twice for the same reason. That policy had generated the rules that prevented re-litigation when the parties were the same: *autrefois acquit* (someone acquitted of a crime cannot be tried again for that crime); *res judicata* (a particular dispute decided by a civil court cannot be retried); and issue estoppel (a person cannot deny the fact of a judgment previously decided against him).

The second policy was wider: it was concerned with the interests of the state. There was a general public interest in the same issue not being litigated over again. The second policy could be used to justify the extension of the rules of issue estoppel to cases in which the parties were not the same, but the circumstances were such as to bring the case within the spirit of the rules. Criminal proceedings were in a special category, because although they were technically litigation between the Crown and the defendant, the Crown prosecuted on behalf of society as a whole. So, a conviction had some of the quality of a judgment *in rem*, which should be binding in favour of everyone.

Not all re-litigation of the same issue, however, would be manifestly unfair to a party or bring the administration of justice into disrepute. Sometimes there were valid reasons for rehearing a dispute. It was therefore unnecessary to try to stop any re-litigation by forbidding anyone from suing their lawyer. It was 'burning down the house to roast the pig; using a broad-spectrum remedy without side effects could handle the problem equally well' (Lord Hoffmann (2000).

The scope for re-examination of issues in criminal proceedings was much wider than in civil cases. Fresh evidence was more readily admitted. A conviction could be set aside as unsafe and unsatisfactory when the accused appeared to have been prejudiced by 'flagrantly incompetent advocacy' (see *R v Clinton* (1993). After conviction, the case could be referred to the Court of Appeal if the conviction was on indictment, or to the Crown Court, if the trial was summary, by the Criminal Cases Review Commission.

It followed that it would ordinarily be an abuse of process for a civil court to be asked to decide that a subsisting conviction was wrong. That applied to a conviction on a plea of guilty as well as after a trial. The resulting conflict of judgments was likely to bring the administration of justice into disrepute. The proper procedure was to appeal, or if the right of appeal had been exhausted, to apply to the Criminal Cases Review Commission. It would ordinarily be an abuse, because there were bound to be exceptional cases in which the issue could be tried without a risk that the conflict of judgments would bring the administration of justice into disrepute.

Once the conviction has been set aside, there could be no public policy objection to a claim for negligence against the legal advisers. There could be no conflict of judgments. On the other hand, in civil, including matrimonial, cases, it would seldom be possible to say that a claim for negligence against a legal adviser or representative would bring the administration of justice into dispute. Whether the original decision was right or wrong was usually a matter of concern only to the parties and had no wider implications. There was no public interest objection to a subsequent finding that, but for the negligence of his lawyers, the losing party would have won.

But again, there might be exceptions. The claim for negligence might be an abuse of process on the ground that it was manifestly unfair to someone else. Take, for example, the case of a defendant who published a serious defamation that they attempted unsuccessfully to justify. Should they be able to sue their lawyers and claim that if the case had been conducted differently, the allegation would have been proved to be true? It seemed unfair to the claimant in the defamation claim that any court should be allowed to come to such a conclusion in proceedings to which they were not a party. On the other hand, it was equally unfair that they should have to join as a party and rebut the allegation for a second time. A person's reputation was not only a matter between them and the other party; it represented their relationship with the world. So, it might be that in such circumstances, a claim for negligence would be an abuse of the process of the court.

Having regard to the power of the court to strike out claims that had no real prospect of success, the doctrine was unlikely in that context to be invoked very often. The first step in any application to strike out a claim alleging negligence in the conduct of a previous action had to be to ask whether it had a real prospect of success.

Lords Hope, Hutton and Hobhouse delivered judgments in which they agreed that the immunity from suit was no longer required in relation to civil proceedings, but dissented to the extent of saying that the immunity was still required in the public interest in the administration of justice in relation to criminal proceedings.

Comment

This decision is of major and historic importance in the English legal system for several reasons. It can be seen as a bold attempt by the senior judiciary to drag the legal profession (often a metonymy for the whole legal system) into the twenty-first-century world of accountability and fair business practice. In his judgment, Lord Steyn makes this dramatic observation (*Arthur JS Hall & Co v Simons* [2000] 3 All ER 673 at 684):

> . . . public confidence in the legal system is not enhanced by the existence of the immunity. The appearance is created that the law singles out its own for protection no matter how flagrant the breach of the barrister. The world has changed since 1967. The practice of law has become more commercialised: barristers may now advertise. They may now enter into contracts for legal services with their professional clients. They are now obliged to carry insurance. On the other hand, today we live in a consumerist society in which people have a much greater awareness of their rights. If they have suffered a wrong as the result of the provision of negligent professional services, they expect to have the right to claim redress. It tends to erode confidence in the legal system if advocates, alone among professional men, are immune from liability for negligence.

The case raises and explores many key issues of the legal system, including: the proper relationship between lawyers and the courts; the proper relationship between lawyers and clients; the differences between criminal and civil actions; professional ethics; the nature of dispute resolution; and the circumstances under which the courts should make new law. Above all, however, the case has one simple significance: 'It will', in the words of Jonathan Hirst QC, a former Chairman of the Bar Council, 'mean that a claimant who can prove loss, as the result of an advocate's negligence, will no longer be prevented from making a claim. We cannot really say that is wrong' ((2000) *Bar News*, August, p 3).

16.6 THE COURTS AND LEGAL SERVICES ACT 1990

Both branches of the legal profession have traditionally enjoyed monopolies in the provision of certain legal services (for example, advocacy was reserved almost exclusively to barristers, while conveyancing was reserved to solicitors). In the 1980s, Lord Mackay, the then Lord Chancellor, argued that these monopolies did not best serve the users of legal services as they entailed unnecessarily limited choice and artificially high prices. The CLSA 1990 was introduced to reform the provision of legal services along such lines. Today, many of the old monopolies have been broken. Thus, we have solicitor-advocates and non-solicitor licensed conveyancers.

In 1990 in the CLSA, the government broke the solicitors' conveyancing monopoly by allowing licensed conveyancers to practise. There was initially evidence that this increased competition resulted in benefits to the consumer. From 1985, The Law Society had permitted solicitors to sell property, like estate agents, so as to promote 'one-stop' conveyancing. The Consumers' Association estimated that solicitors' conveyancing prices fell by a margin of 25 to 33 per cent before licensed conveyancers actually began to practise.

Under the CLSA 1990, apart from allowing the Bar Council and The Law Society to grant members rights of audience as before, The Law Society is able to seek to widen the category of those who have such rights. Applications are made to the Lord Chancellor, who refers the matter to their Advisory Committee. If the Committee favours the application, it must also be approved by four senior judges (including the Master of the Rolls and the Lord Chief Justice), each of whom can exercise a veto. The Director General of the Office of Fair Trading must also be consulted by the Lord Chancellor. All those who consider applications for extended rights of audience or the right to conduct litigation must act in accordance with the 'general principle' in s 17.

16.6.1 SECTION 17

The principle in s 17 states that the question of whether a person should be granted a right of audience or to conduct litigation is to be determined only by reference to the following four questions:

- Is the applicant properly qualified in accordance with the educational and training requirements appropriate to the court or proceedings?
- Are applicants members of a professional or other body with proper and enforced rules of conduct?
- Do such rules have the necessary equivalent of the Bar's 'cab rank rule', that is, satisfactory provision requiring its members not to withhold their services: on the ground that the nature of the case is objectionable to them or any section

of the public; on the ground that the conduct, opinions or beliefs of the prospective client are unacceptable to them or to any section of the public; or on any ground relating to the prospective client's source of financial support (for example, public funding)?

- Are the body's rules of conduct 'appropriate in the interests of the proper and efficient administration of justice'?

Subject to the above, those who consider applications must also abide by s 17's 'statutory objective' of 'new and better ways of providing such services and a wider choice of persons providing them, while maintaining the proper and efficient administration of justice'.

Successful applications were made by The Law Society, the Head of the Government Legal Service and the Director of Public Prosecutions (DPP). The Advisory Committee, while rejecting the idea of an automatic extension of solicitors' rights of audience upon qualification (for example, guilty plea cases in Crown Courts), accepted the principle that they should qualify for enlarged rights after a course of advocacy training. Non-lawyers can also apply for rights of audience in the courts: the Chartered Institute of Patent Agents successfully applied for rights to conduct litigation in the High Court. Under s 12 of the CLSA 1990, the Lord Chancellor will use their power to enable lay representatives to be used in cases involving debt and housing matters in small claims procedures. Similarly, under ss 28 and 29 of the CLSA 1990, the right to conduct litigation is thrown open to members of any body that can persuade the Advisory Committee, the Lord Chancellor and the four senior judges that its application should be granted as the criteria set out in s 17 (above) are satisfied.

The historic monopoly of barristers to appear for clients in the higher courts was formally ended in 1994 when the Lord Chancellor approved The Law Society's proposals on how to certify its members in private practice as competent advocates. The innovation is likely to generate significant change in the delivery of legal services, especially in the fields of commercial and criminal cases. The prospective battle between solicitors and barristers for advocacy work can be simply characterised.

16.6.2 SOLICITORS' RIGHTS OF AUDIENCE

There are now 6,680 solicitors qualified as solicitor-advocates with rights to practise advocacy in some or most levels of the court structure (SRA website statistics of solicitor advocates, www.sra.org.uk, November 2016). This development began with changes in the 1990s. In February 1997, the Lord Chancellor, Lord Mackay, and the four designated judges (Lord Bingham, Lord Woolf, Sir Stephen Brown and Sir Richard Scott; see s 17 of the CLSA 1990) approved The Law Society's application for rights of audience in the higher courts for employed solicitors, but subject to certain restrictions.

Lord Phillips, the Lord Chief Justice, put forward proposals that will allow solicitor-advocates to have the same dress code as barristers. The new reforms came into effect in 2008. Solicitor-advocates finally put on wigs in court (*Law Society Gazette*, 10

January 2008). Solicitor-advocates in criminal cases are allowed to wear wigs, wing collars and bands. They can also wear stuff gowns. However, in civil and family proceedings the wigs and other regalia will no longer be worn. The dress code for judges was changed in 2008. The judge's robe, designed by Betty Jackson, received mixed reactions when it was unveiled in May 2008 ('Thumbs down for designer robe', *The Times*, 15 May 2008).

Under The Law Society's 1998 regulations approved by the Lord Chancellor's Department, some solicitors (those who are also barristers or part-time judges) are granted exemption from the new tests of qualification for advocacy. Others need to apply for the grant of higher courts qualifications, either in civil proceedings, criminal proceedings or in both. A holder of the higher courts (criminal proceedings) qualification has rights of audience in the Crown Court in all proceedings (including its civil jurisdiction) and in other courts in all criminal proceedings. A holder of the higher courts (civil proceedings) qualification may appear in the High Court in all proceedings and in other courts in all civil proceedings. On 1 April 2010 new rules came into force for solicitors seeking higher rights of audience. The rules were amended on 1 September 2010. On 17 June 2011, The Higher Rights of Audience Regulations 2011 replaced the 2010 regulations with effect from 6 October 2011. Qualification under the new regulations is solely by advocacy assessment based on the SRA's Higher Rights of Audience competence standard, which is run by organisations authorised by the SRA. A detailed summary can be found in the 15th edition of this book.

All solicitors seeking these rights of audience have to pass an advocacy assessment based on higher rights of audience competency standards.

One benefit for law firms is that those that offer advocacy training are likely to attract the best graduates. This is a worry for the commercial Bar, as some graduates will see a training contract with an advocacy element as a better option than the less secure Bar pupillage. The Bar is determined that it will not lose any significant ground in the face of this new competition. Its representatives claim that solicitors will not be able to compete with barristers because of their much higher overheads.

From 2000, there have been three routes to qualification: the 'development' route leading to the all-proceedings qualification; the 'accreditation' route appropriate for solicitors who have significant experience of the higher civil and/or higher criminal courts; and the 'exemption' route which has existed under both the 1992 and 1998 regulations. The accreditation and exemption routes were phased out in 2005, leaving now only the advocacy assessment route as detailed above. Solicitors who obtained Higher Rights of Audience under previous regulations were transferred under the 2010 regulations and retain their existing rights.

Many barristers are very worried about the threat to their traditional work. A potentially significant development is Public Access (originally known as BarDIRECT), a pilot scheme set up in 1999 that enables certain professions and organisations to have direct access to barristers without referral through a solicitor. While this initiative could be one of the keys to the continuing success of the Bar, it is argued that it makes barristers no different from solicitors and could even encroach on the solicitors' market.

Lawyers' rights of audience before the courts were further addressed in Part III of the Access to Justice Act 1999. It replaces the Lord Chancellor's Advisory Committee on Legal Education and Conduct with a new Legal Services Consultative Panel:

- It provides that, in principle, all lawyers should have full rights of audience before any court, subject only to meeting reasonable training requirements.
- It reforms the procedures for authorising further professional bodies to grant rights of audience or rights to conduct litigation to their members; and for approving changes to professional rules of conduct relating to the exercise of these rights.

The Act also contains sections that:

- simplify procedures for approving changes to rules and the designation of new authorised bodies;
- give the Lord Chancellor power, with the approval of Parliament, to change rules that do not meet the statutory criteria set out in the CLSA 1990 as amended by these sections;
- establish the principle that all barristers and solicitors should enjoy full rights of audience; and
- establish the primacy of an advocate's ethical duties over any other civil law obligations.

The legislation enables employed advocates, including Crown Prosecutors, to appear as advocates in the higher courts if otherwise qualified to do so, regardless of any professional rules designed to prevent their doing so because of their status as employed advocates.

By virtue of s 66 of the CLSA 1990, solicitors are enabled to form partnerships with non-solicitors (multidisciplinary partnerships or MDPs), and the section confirms that barristers are not prevented by the common law from forming such relationships. They are, however, prohibited from doing so (unless with a foreign lawyer) by the Bar. Solicitors are able, under s 89 of the CLSA 1990 (Sched 14), to form multinational partnerships (MNPs). The arrival of MNPs over the coming years will raise particular problems concerning the maintenance of ethical standards by the Solicitors' Regulation Authority over foreign lawyers. MDPs also raise potentially serious problems, as even in arrangements between solicitors and others, it will be likely that certain work (for example, the conduct of litigation) would have to be performed by solicitors.

The business organisation called the limited liability partnership (LLP) was introduced by the Limited Liability Partnership Act 2000. The new business form seeks to amalgamate the advantages of the company's corporate form with the flexibility of the partnership form. Although called a 'partnership', the new form is, in fact, a distinct legal entity that enjoys an existence apart from that of its members. The LLP can enter into agreements in its own name, it can own property, sue and be sued. Traditional partnerships by contrast entail liability for the partners as individuals. Although the LLP enjoys corporate status, it is not taxed as a separate entity from its members. Solicitors do not seem to have been keen to adopt these as their preferred form of firm. The growth in their popularity has been steady. In 2002, fewer than 100 from the then 8,300 law firms had become LPPs. Most were formed because of international constraints in mergers, that is, the foreign firm could not merge with the British one unless the British one became an LLP. In October 2016 1,559 law firms in England and Wales out of 10,415 were practising as LLPs, ((SRA *statistics*).

Law firms

Another feature of change is the evidently widening gap between the work and income of the top few hundred commercial firms and the 2,627 sole practitioners. Compare this number with the very large practices who employ more than 2,627 solicitors.. A series of mergers has created a few relatively huge law firms, and the merger of an English firm with an American one produced the world's first billion-dollar practice. In 1999, partners at Clifford Chance voted to merge with the United States' Rogers & Wells, and Punders in Germany, to form a firm that now employs over 7,000 people in 30 offices worldwide.

The trend of firms merging is continuing. In late 2015, Irwin Mitchell announced that it was taking over Thomas Eggar, which will create a practice with a fee income of approximately £250 million. As firms have merged and also become international the number with a turnover in excess of £1 billion is increasing and comparison with individual firms of the past becomes less relevant. In 2015 the top 100 law firms had a combined fee income of £20 billion and eleven of the top 200 firms had an average PEP (profit per equity partner) in excess of £1 million (Lawyer.com 21 and 27 October 2016).[

16.6.5   EMPLOYED SOLICITORS

This is a fast-growing area of practice with more than one-fifth of those holding a practising certificate working outside private practice. Employed solicitors are professionals who work for salaries as part of a commercial firm, private or public enterprise, charity or organisation, as opposed to solicitors in private practice who take instructions from various clients.

16.6.6   MONOPOLY CONVEYANCING RIGHTS

Historically, barristers, solicitors, certified notaries and licensed conveyancers enjoyed statutory monopolies, making it an offence for any other persons to draw up or prepare documents connected with the transfer of title to property for payment. The CLSA 1990 broke this monopoly by allowing any person or body not currently authorised to provide conveyancing services to make an application to the Authorised Conveyancing Practitioners' Board (established by s 34) for authorisation under s 37. The Board must be satisfied, before granting authorisation, that the applicant's business is, and will be, carried on by fit and proper persons, and must believe that the applicant will establish or participate in the systems for the protection of the client specified in s 37(7) including, for example, adequate professional indemnity cover and regulations made under s 40 concerning competence and conduct. Banks and building societies were in a privileged position (s 37(8)), since they were already regulated by statute. These institutions did not initially appear enthusiastic to compete with solicitors by establishing in-house lawyers. They have preferred instead to use panels of local practitioners.

The solicitors' monopoly on the grant of probate has also been abolished. Under ss 54–55 of the CLSA 1990, probate services were opened up to be available from approved bodies of non-lawyers. Grant of probate is the legal proof that a will is valid, which is needed for a person to put the will into effect. New probate practitioners

1. Solicitors
– Often described as the 'general practitioners' of law, which may be misleading today, as solicitors in larger practices often specialise
– Rights of audience now extend to the senior courts, where a higher court advocacy qualification has been obtained
– In return solicitors have lost their monopoly in areas such as conveyancing
– Training involves a law degree (or GDL/CPE), followed by a Legal Practice Course (LPC) and two years as a trainee
– Supervised by the Solicitors' Regulation Authority, solicitors normally work together in partnerships, while complaints relating to maladministration in the legal profession can be made to the Legal Ombudsman

2. Barristers
– Often thought of as the 'specialists'; the academic stage of training is normally the same as for solicitors, but barristers complete a Bar Vocational Course (BVC), followed by a year's pupillage
– Barristers join one of the Inns of Court, which are responsible for 'calling' members to the Bar
– Supervised by the General Council of the Bar, barristers have rights of audience in all courts
– Senior barristers of merit may 'take silk', becoming Queen's Counsel (QCs)
– Barristers are normally, but not always, self-employed but share offices known as 'Chambers'

3. Legal Executives
The Institute of Legal Executives (ILEX), which was developed from the Managing Clerks Association, represents Legal Executives, who carry out the more routine legal work. Qualified lawyers, such practitioners will be specialists in a particular area of law and now have limited rights of audience in lower courts

THE LEGAL PROFESSION

4. Fusion of the Professions: The ELS is one of only three systems in the world that maintain a divided legal profession. Despite criticism of the present system, the legal professions have argued that fusion would lead to a fall in the quality of advocacy. It has, however, been claimed that there has been 'fusion by the backdoor', as the CLSA 1990 and the AJA 1999 have removed solicitors' monopolies over certain tasks such as conveyancing, as well as barristers' monopoly over advocacy in the senior courts

FIGURE 16.1 *A Breakdown of the Different Legal Professions.*

directly compete with solicitors for probate work. The grant of probate is only a small part of the probate process, but when it was restricted as business that only a solicitor could perform, it effectively prevented others, except some banks, from being involved in probate. The banks seem best placed to take up work in this area as they already have trustee and executor departments.

16.6.7   THE LEGAL OMBUDSMAN

The Legal Ombudsman (LO) scheme, replacing the previous Legal Services Ombudsman (LSO), was established by the Office for Legal Complaints (OLC) under the Legal Services Act 2007. It began accepting complaints in October 2010. The LO claims to be an independent, consumer-focused ombudsman scheme set up to resolve complaints about lawyers in England and Wales. It provides a free service to all members of the public, very small businesses, charities, clubs and trusts.

It deals with complaints about the following types of lawyers (and generally those working for them):

- barristers;
- solicitors;
- law costs draftsmen;
- legal executives;
- licensed conveyancers;
- notaries;
- patent attorneys;
- probate practitioners;
- registered European lawyers;
- trademark attorneys;

and deals with complaints relating to:

- buying and selling a house or property;
- family law such as divorce;
- wills;
- personal injury;
- intellectual property;
- criminal law;
- civil litigation;
- immigration;
- employment issues.

If the LO decides the service received by the complainant was unsatisfactory, it can require the lawyer to put it right. Although most complaints can be resolved informally, it is empowered to carry out a formal investigation.

CHAPTER SUMMARY: LEGAL SERVICES

The main area of debate on this theme is the best approach to supplying the highest number and widest range of people with legal services appropriate to what citizens need. How can the legal profession become more user-friendly? Have the changes made under the CLSA 1990 to increase competition in the provision of legal services been successful? Have the restrictive professional monopolies been properly broken and, if so, will the quality of services offered by non-lawyers (for example, conveyancing, probate, litigation) be reduced? Will the exclusion of millions of people from public funding eligibility have any serious consequences?

The impact of the conditional fee arrangements, the 1995 Green Paper on legal aid, and franchising are of special importance, but to deal with these issues properly you need to be familiar with the details of how legal services are delivered in general.

THE LEGAL PROFESSION

The legal profession, although not fused, comprises solicitors and barristers whose work is becoming increasingly similar in many respects. Additionally, the ending of monopolies on litigation, probate and conveyancing has meant that lawyers' traditional work is increasingly becoming blurred with that of other professionals. The liabilities of lawyers for errors and negligence are key issues. Another is the way in which complaints are handled by the professions.

THE COURTS AND LEGAL SERVICES ACT 1990

The CLSA 1990 was passed 'to see that the public has the best possible access to legal services and that those services are of the right quality for the particular needs of the client'. The detail by which the Act sought to do this is very important, especially s 17 (general principle, litigation and rights of audience); s 11 (lay representatives); ss 28–29 (right to conduct litigation); s 66 (multidisciplinary partnerships); s 89 (multinational partnerships); ss 34–37 (conveyancing); ss 21–26 (the Legal Services Ombudsman); and s 58 (conditional fee arrangements).

THE ACCESS TO JUSTICE ACT 1999

The 1999 Act makes many changes that will have an impact upon the professions. It articulates the principle that all lawyers should have full rights of audience before all courts, provided they have passed the relevant examinations. Also, by reforming the procedures for authorising further professional bodies to grant rights of audience, it signals a widening of those rights in the future.

IMMUNITY FROM NEGLIGENCE CLAIMS

Until recently barristers could not be sued by their clients for negligent performance in court or for work that was preparatory to court work (*Rondel v Worsley* (1969)); this immunity had also been extended to solicitors who act as advocates (*Saif Ali v Sidney Mitchell* (1980)). The client of the other side, however, may sue for breach of duty (*Kelly v London Transport Executive* (1982)). This was changed in a major case in 2000, *Arthur JS Hall and Co v Simons and Other Appeals*.

THE LEGAL OMBUDSMAN

An Ombudsman is a person independent of the government or a given field of activity, who investigates complaints of maladministration. The post of Legal Ombudsman is now operated under the LSA 2007 by the Office for Legal Complaints.

OVERVIEW OF CHANGES TO LEGAL PROFESSION

Historically the legal profession was generally considered a safe, conservative and usually profitable business. However, this is starting to change.

The Legal Services Act 2007 received Royal Assent on 30 October 2007 and became fully operational on 6 October 2011 when it allowed the formation of Alternative Business Structures (ABSs).

The Act came into force during a severe and prolonged economic recession, and the latter may also have contributed to the changes in the legal profession.

There have been significant changes during this period with the creation of the QualitySolicitors franchise, mergers of law firms, the newly created ABS structures and Slater and Gordon acquiring English legal practices. The changes are still in their infancy and the ultimate outcome for the legal profession is still unclear.

The *Law Society Gazette* (5 August 2013) reported that a half-yearly report produced by Law Consultancy Network indicated that 38 per cent of firms of fewer than 10 partners thought that there was a good or definite chance of a merger. This trend towards merging is not limited to small firms, as can be seen by the takeover of Thomas Eggar by Irwin Mitchell ('Irwin Mitchell creates £250m firm with Thomas Eggar merger' (2015) *Law Society Gazette*, 26 November). The *Wall Street Journal* (27 October 2013) reported that a number of US law firms were in merger discussions.

The advent of the ABS has been relatively slow, as stated in Stephen Mayson's report dated 6 October 2013 which indicated that in the first two years, only 240 ABS licences had been issued. However, some major developments have taken place under the umbrella of an ABS.

The Co-op Legal Services, which was formed in 2006, was one of the first firms to acquire an ABS. The financial report for the Co-op group for 2015 reported that the legal business made a profit of £.7 million in the year, compared with a loss of £4 million in 2014 (Co-operative Group Limited, Annual Report 2015).

The AA has obtained an ABS and from 1 December 2013 commenced a joint venture with law firm Lyons Davidson. Direct Line Insurance has also now obtained an ABS licence.

Russell Jones & Walker acquired an ABS licence and were then acquired by Australian law firm Slater and Gordon (a public quoted company), which has subsequently acquired four more English legal practices.

It is unclear at the present time how the legal market will develop with the current changes and new businesses offering legal services. The largest English law firms that tend to specialise in corporate and related work for major companies appear, at the present time, to be relatively unaffected and still producing turnover in excess of £1 billion and PEP of £1 million. What is becoming clear is the need for the legal profession to adapt to the changes in the legal market. We have already seen a number of law firms of varying size collapse including Halliwells, Cobbetts, Follett Stock, Manches and Dewey & LeBoeuf (a large US firm also operating in the UK). In 2015, Parabis Group, an ABS formed in 2012, was sold off as part of a pre-pack administration.

FOOD FOR THOUGHT

1   Why should the legal profession be divided into two discrete sectors? Whose interests does this really serve?

2   Why do barristers make the best judges, if they do?

3   Much is made of the need for greater access to the legal professions. However, given the increase in the number of law graduates and the restrictions in the number of training contracts and pupillages, is progression not a matter of 'who you know rather than what you know'?

4   In legal firms, attention tends to be focused on the partners/solicitors, but what roles do the legal executives play?

5   Does the introduction of 'Tesco Law' (ABSs) necessarily mean a reduction in standards?

6   Consider the extent to which access to online provision reduces the need for legal professionals.

FURTHER READING

Abel, R, *The Legal Profession in England and Wales*, 1988, Oxford: Basil Blackwell

Baksi, C, 'Solicitor-advocates hit bar' (2008) Law Soc Gazette, 28 March

Browne, D, QC, 'A considered response' (2009) Counsel 3

Bryant, J, 'Proactive regulation will hit solicitors where it hurts' (2009) 23(40) Lawyer 6

Cocks, R, *Foundations of the Modern Bar*, 1983, London: Sweet & Maxwell

Farrow, A and Littler, R, 'Raising the bar' (2009) 153(40) SJ 6

Genn, H and Genn, Y, *The Effectiveness of Representation at Tribunals*, 1989, London: LCD

Guise, T, 'Something for everyone' (2009) 153(41) SJ 19

Holroyd, A, 'Moving with the times' (2008) 105(2) Law Soc Gazette 16

Jackson, R, 'Disappointed litigants and doubtful actions' (1995) Counsel 16

Keogh, A, 'Power sharing' (2008) 158 NLJ 717

Lord Hoffmann, *Arthur JS Hall and Co. v. Simons (A.P.)* (2000) UKHL 38

Money-Kyrle, R, 'Advocates' immunity after *Osman*' (1999) 149 NLJ 945 and 981

Susskind, R, *Tomorrow's Lawyers* (2013) Oxford: OUP
Underwood, K, 'Hope continues' (2007) 151(46) SJ 1542
Williamson, P, 'Open and accountable' (2007) 104(48) Law Soc Gazette 11

USEFUL WEBSITES

www.lawsociety.org.uk
The official site of The Law Society.

www.sra.org.uk
The official site of the Solicitors Regulation Authority.

www.barcouncil.org.uk
The official site of the Bar Council of England and Wales.

http://letr.org.uk
The site of the Legal Education and Training Review.

COMPANION WEBSITE

Now visit the companion website to:

- test your understanding of the key terms using our Flashcard Glossary;
- revise and consolidate your knowledge of 'Legal services' using our multiple choice question testbank;
- read the latest news and updates on the Legal Profession in the Student Law Review;
- view all of the links to the Useful Websites above.

www.routledge.com/cw/slapper

17.1 INTRODUCTION

member of the House of Lords, said this ('Wanted – a legal aid fund that meets needs of ordinary citizens', *The Times*, 10 December 2015):

> When Sir Hartley Shawcross, the attorney-general, opened the second reading debate on the Legal Aid and Advice Bill in December 1948, he said it was a 'charter' for the ordinary citizen. It would 'open the doors of the courts freely to all persons who may wish to avail themselves of British justice without regard to the question of their wealth or ability to pay'. He added that no longer would legal rights be 'luxuries' beyond people's reach. The Legal Aid, Sentencing and Punishment of Offenders Act 2012 (Laspo) undermines those objectives.
>
> Before Laspo, civil legal aid was available for most legal disputes, with specified exceptions, for those who satisfy the means-test criteria. Now civil legal aid is available only for specific types of legal dispute with a narrow (in practice, very narrow) 'exceptional funding' provision for excluded areas. So civil legal aid is no longer available for cases concerning, for example, employment, education (apart from special educational needs), immigration (except for detention), family law (apart from domestic violence and child abuse), and most welfare benefit claims. In addition, the means-test criteria have been tightened so that the 'little man' (or woman) referred to by Sir Hartley is most unlikely to qualify.

Lord Pannick QC concluded that the most promising option for reform is for the Ministry of Justice to promote a legal insurance scheme in which funds are provided for claims that have good prospects of success, to be paid for from the costs awarded in successful cases against the other party, plus a percentage of the sums recovered for claimants.

On 10 December 2015, in a debate in the House of Lords, Lord Lester of Herne Hill QC, a Liberal Democrat, reminded fellow peers that the debate coincided with the UN's human rights day. He then said:

> One fundamental human right is effective access to justice. It is a state's duty to provide a system of legal aid that enables everyone, including the poor and not so rich, to have effective access to courts and tribunals.

In the same debate, Lord Howarth of Newport, a Labour peer who defected from the Conservatives in 1995, made an observation about the recent and substantial reductions in legal aid. He said:

> In 1987, the Conservative government commenced a long attrition of public spending on legal aid. The Labour government more or less carried on the policy after 1997. But it was the coalition government that really took the axe to legal aid. The coalition parties had no mandate for this; their manifestos had not hinted at it.

Without access to legal professional advice and representation, a citizen is, in effect, cut adrift from civil society. Whether it would have been possible substantially to reduce public access to basic education or basic health care without an express mandate, as the coalition government did in respect of legal services, is an open question.

In 2015, 70 per cent of respondents to research conducted by Citizens Advice said they would not be able to afford a lawyer to advise on a problem or dispute. Only about 10 per cent were confident they could afford the cost of legal fees. Fewer than 40 per cent of respondents said the English legal system is working well for the entire population ('Responsive justice: how citizens experience the justice system', Citizens Advice, November 2015).

17.2   BACKGROUND TO RECENT CHANGES

In 2006, the government indicated it was determined to curb the spiralling cost of legal aid expenditure, which was £1.5 billion in 1996–97 and rose to almost £2.1 billion in 2003/04, where it peaked before decreasing slightly over the next few years to around £2 billion a year (Lord Hunt, *Hansard*, 19 February 2008, col 134).

The proposals in a report of a review team under Lord Carter of Coles (*Procurement of Criminal Defence Services: Market-based Reform*, 2006) are being gradually implemented and are set to make substantial changes to the system. The system advocated by Carter is one where lawyers have to bid competitively to win contracts for doing criminal legal aid work. Under this new market-based model, all criminal legal aid lawyers are paid fixed fees – rather than being paid by time spent – and compete for contracts for work in police stations and courts.

The reforms prevent the highest-earning barristers being paid £1 million a year from legal aid, as used to be the case. Such a reorganisation could halve the number of the 2,500 legal aid firms and cause wide-scale mergers.

Most criminal trials are now covered by fixed fees, but fees in the long and most complex criminal trials are still the subject of negotiation between the government and the professional bodies.

There are several state-funded schemes to facilitate the provision of aid and advice. Each scheme has different rules relating to its scope, procedures for application and eligibility. Because of the importance of justice and access to the legal machinery, the idea behind legal aid is to give people who could otherwise not afford professional legal help the same services as more wealthy citizens. This raises important social, political and economic questions. Do poorer people deserve the same quality of legal advice as that which can be afforded by wealthy people? If so, how should such schemes be funded? The LSC, in its strategic plan published in April 2009 for the period 2009 to 2012, had a vision of 'fair access to justice to the people who need it but can least afford it'.

17.3   THE LEGAL AID SCHEME

The Access to Justice Act 1999 set up a new legal aid system and made provisions about rights to supply legal services (see Chapter 16), court procedure (see Chapter 9), magistrates and magistrates' courts (see Chapter 12). The provisions in the Act form part of the wide-ranging programme of reforms to legal services and the courts, described in the government's White Paper, *Modernising Justice*, published on 2 December 1998. Except where noted, the Act only affects England and Wales.

Part I of the 1999 Act established a Legal Services Commission (LSC) to maintain and develop the Community Legal Service (CLS) and the Criminal Defence Service (CDS), which replaced the Civil and Criminal Legal Aid schemes, respectively. The Act also enabled the Lord Chancellor to give the Commission orders, directions and guidance about how it should exercise its functions. The Community Legal Service Fund replaced the legal aid fund in civil and family cases.

On 1 April 2013 the Legal Aid, Sentencing and Punishment of Offenders Act 2012 (LASPO) came into force. This Act introduced the Legal Aid Agency (LAA) following the abolition of the LSC.

The LAA publishes (on the website www.gov.uk) full details of all aspects of legal aid for the benefit of both providers and those requiring its services. The information is both detailed and regularly updated, including details of new contracts and application procedures.

Examples are the new 2015 Duty Provider Crime Contract details published on 10 July 2014 and updated on 27 November 2014. The information for applicants extended to 150 pages. Applicants had to apply by 29 January 2015 and the contract was due to commence on 1 October 2015. The LAA announced on 13 November 2015 that because of legal challenges, the existing contract will run from 11 January 2016 to 31 March 2016, with the new contract commencing the following day. However, if because of injunctions, a further extension is required, a backstop date of 10 January 2017 has been set. The LAA withdrew the 2015 contract and replaced it with the Standard Crime Contract 2017. The draft terms extend to 90 pages and specification 149 pages. On 10 June 2015 the *Law Society Gazette* reported that Shailesh Vara, the minister responsible for legal aid, proposed that the number of contracts for providing duty lawyers to advise suspects detained in police stations or defendants at magistrates' courts would be reduced from 1,600 to 527.

17.3.1 CONTROLLED AND LICENSED WORK

As noted at 17.2 above, legal aid funding was granted on a case-by-case basis until the system of franchising was introduced in August 1994, where firms of solicitors meeting certain requirements were able to contract to undertake certain cases without prior approval, and claim funding on a more advantageous basis than previously. This franchise or 'contract' system has formed the basis of the legal aid scheme.

Funded services for all civil contract work fall under the headings of 'controlled work' and 'licensed work'. In non-family cases there are three levels of service for controlled work: legal help, help at court and controlled legal representation, which includes legal representation before a mental health review tribunal or the Asylum and Immigration Tribunal. For controlled work the decision about whether to provide services in a particular case is made by the supplier, who is either a solicitor or a not-for-profit organisation, such as a law centre or Citizens' Advice Bureau (discussed below, 17.9.2).

They bid for a contract to provide legal services funded by the LSC to the Regional Legal Services Committees. Under the contract, the number of cases that may be undertaken by the suppliers is limited.

Licensed work is the equivalent of the case-by-case approval granted for all state-funded legal work prior to 1994 and all non-franchised work prior to the establishment of the LSC. Licensed work is administered through a certification process requiring the Commission's initial approval of the cost, timing and scope of each case. Once the licence is granted, it covers all legal representation before the courts, except for controlled legal representation or services funded by individual case contracts that are managed by the Commission, such as very expensive cases referred to as 'very high cost cases' (VHCCs).

As with all legal aid matters, full details of VHCC contracts are published by the LAA.

17.3.2 CONTRACTING

The work that may be undertaken by a supplier, whether a solicitor or a not-for-profit organisation, covers a wide variety of categories. Civil legal aid work covers family, immigration, social welfare (which covers debt, employment, housing, community care and welfare benefits), mental health, personal injury, clinical disputes, consumer general contract, actions against police, public law and education. Criminal legal aid covers work in police stations, magistrates' courts, Crown Courts, VHCCs and working within the criminal justice system.

The contract for civil work used to be carried out under a General Civil Contract under the CLS. However, this has now been replaced by a new standard contract, which is discussed below, at 17.3.3. Criminal work is now also covered by a new standard contract.

The LAA may terminate the contract for any reason at six months' notice and the providers at three months' notice. Key Performance Indicators (KPIs) are now part of the contract and failure to comply will be a breach of contract.

The coming into force of LASPO introduced new rules from 1 April 2013. An interim contract for Welfare Benefits operated until 31 October 2013. The 2013 Standard Civil Contract (Welfare Benefits) governs the provision of face-to-face Welfare Benefits Services from 1 November 2013.

The 2013 CLA Contract governs the provision of Community Legal Advice from 1 April 2013. CLA services will be provided primarily by telephone and also online and by other 'remote' means.

The 2013 CLA Contract covers remote advice in the categories of Family, Housing and Debt, Education and Discrimination law, as well as face-to-face services in Education and Discrimination law only. Providers may only carry out 'Licensed Work' in the Education and Discrimination categories.

From 1 April 2013, the 2013 Standard Civil Contract governs the provision of face-to-face legal aid services in the categories of Family, Immigration and Asylum, Housing and Debt.

Other categories of law are either not affected by LASPO to the extent that new contracts are required, in which case they will continue to be provided under the 2010 Standard Civil Contract (as amended), or will no longer be within the scope of legal aid provision after 1 April 2013.

The Criminal Legal Aid (Determinations by a Court and Choice of Representative) (Amendment) Regulations 2013 introduced new rules relating to 'Selection of a Queen's Counsel or multiple advocates', which sets out the following conditions:

19. (1) A determination that an individual is entitled to select a Queen's Counsel or more than one advocate under regulation 18 may only be made by the following judges –

   (a) subject to paragraph (2), in the course of a trial or a preliminary hearing, pre-trial review or plea and directions hearing, the judge who has been assigned as the trial judge;

   (b) where a trial judge has not been assigned, by –

      (i) a High Court judge; or

      (ii) subject to paragraph (2), a resident judge of the Crown Court or, in the absence of a resident judge, a judge nominated by a resident judge of the Crown Court for the purpose of making such a determination; or

   (c) where the proceedings are in the Court of Appeal, by the Registrar of Criminal Appeals, a High Court judge or a judge of the Court of Appeal.

(2) A determination made by a judge referred to in paragraph (1)(a) or (b)(ii) does not take effect unless it is approved by a presiding judge of the circuit or by a judge nominated by a presiding judge of the circuit for the purpose of giving such approval.

A contract may be awarded to allow a supplier to undertake work within one or more categories. The contract will state the categories and terms under which the supplier may provide legal advice and representation. The purpose of specifying categories in respect of civil contracts is to ensure an appropriate distribution of legal and advice services to meet demand in each region.

In order to assess demand and ensure that the right kind of services are available to meet the needs of a region, Community Legal Service Partnerships (CLSPs) were set up. The purpose of CLSPs was to provide a forum, in each local authority area, for the local authority and the LSC, and if possible other significant funders, to come together to co-ordinate funding and planning of local legal and advice services, to ensure that delivery of services better matches local needs. The LSC no longer facilitates CLSPs, and the LSC has asked each CLSP to consider whether it has a viable role as a provider forum.

If a law firm is awarded a contract to provide publicly funded legal advice through the LAA, the terms under which it will carry out the work will depend on how it provides the services and the type of legal aid given.

Face-to-face legal aid services for civil cases

Family, immigration and asylum, housing and debt categories of work are governed by the standard civil contract 2013.

Welfare benefits work is governed by the standard civil contract (welfare benefits) contract 2013, except in the north and south-west and Wales, where the welfare benefits contract 2014 applies.

Community care and mental health categories are governed by the standard civil contract 2014.

Amendments to the 2013, 2014 and 2015 Standard Civil Contracts were made on 1 December 2014 and the 2013 CLA Specification was updated 26 May 2016.

Actions against the police, public law, clinical negligence, family mediation, and immigration removal centre categories are governed by the standard civil contract 2010.

Remote legal aid services for civil cases

This includes the provision of legal aid by telephone, online and other remote means. Family, housing and debt, education and discrimination categories of work are governed by the civil legal advice contract 2013.

All legal aid services for criminal cases

All cases that would fall under criminal law are governed by the standard crime contract 2010 or through separate arrangements for Very High Cost Cases (VHCC).

Halted reform

A new set of reforms to criminal legal aid contracts due to be implemented in 2015–16 will now be superseded by the Standard Crime Contract 2017. However, many solicitors firms feared the reforms would entail an unwarranted restriction on who could participate in the duty legal aid rota, and that this would lead to a less diverse and competitive market. Many barristers feared that the commercial model being designed by some solicitors' firms would lead to a diminution in choice and the quality of professional service. In January 2016, faced with 99 separate legal challenges over the prospective procurement process, the Lord Chancellor decided not to introduce the contractual reforms, and to suspend, for a period of 12 months from 1 April 2016 a proposed fee cut for criminal legal aid work (Lord Chancellor and Secretary of State for Justice, Michael Gove MP, Written statement to Parliament Changes to criminal legal aid contracting, 28 January 2016).

The LAA periodically amends the contract terms of legal aid contracts to deal with changes in legislation or court rulings. The Civil Contract was amended on 17 and 31 July 2015 to reflect new legislation, including Care Act 2014 and Modern Slavery Act 2015. Changes to contract terms and details of any new tenders are available on the LAA website.

A new family contract commenced on 1 February 2012, but this ceased on 31 March 2013 and a new contract commenced the following day. The aim of the Unified Contract is to put not-for-profit advisers on the same footing as solicitors who carry out civil legal aid work and to create greater efficiency when working with providers. It is anticipated that one way this will be achieved is by requiring providers to work with the LAA by means of email to reduce administrative time and costs. In addition, providers will be required to meet certain standards that are contained in KPIs.

Another major change to this new system is the move away from issuing separate contracts to each office of a provider and instead issuing a contract to the whole organisation of the provider with each contract containing a schedule detailing the work that an individual office can undertake. The LAA will be able to stipulate a minimum and maximum number of cases that an individual office may start each year.

17.3.4   QUALITY MARK

In order to be a supplier under either the CLS or the CDS, the solicitor or not-for-profit organisation must achieve the minimum standards under the respective Quality Marks. There are four kinds of Quality Mark and all contract holders must hold the SQM or MQM or LEXCEL. Barristers must hold QMB.

There are four Quality Marks applicable as follows.

SQM: Specialist Quality Mark. This will be for complex matters.
MQM: Family Mediation Quality Mark.
QMB: Quality Mark for the Bar.
LEXCEL: Legal Practice Management standard (owned by Law Society).

17.4   THE LEGAL AID AGENCY

As from 1 April 2013, the Legal Aid Agency (LAA) replaced the Legal Services Commission (s 38 of LASPO).

Legal aid has been one of the fastest growing parts of the public sector over the past 25 years, and expenditure has increased at almost 6 per cent per year in real terms, compared to similar increases in health and education expenditure of approximately 4 per cent and 2 per cent, respectively. At approximately £38 per head of the population, the LSC also spent more in England and Wales than is spent by any other jurisdiction for which comparative data are currently available.

The LAA produces highly detailed quarterly and annual statistics of all the legal aid work undertaken and the related costs. Examples of the information for 2015/16 are:

- Crown Court legal aid granted in 104,975 cases out of 105,153 applications.
- Civil representation costs met by LAA £586.9 million.

17.5   THE COMMUNITY LEGAL SERVICE

Since 1 April 2013, Community Legal Service has been known as Civil Legal Aid (CLA), and Community Legal Advice as Civil Legal Advice (CLAD).

The LAA as successor to the LSC provides both civil and criminal legal aid and advice in England and Wales utilising solicitors, barristers and not-for-profit organisations. The LAA's main objectives are to:

- improve casework to reduce cost, enhance control and give better customer service;
- improve organisational capability to meet the challenges ahead, including developing and engaging their people;
- build and maintain strong partnerships to secure quality provision and contribute fully to wider justice and government aims.

17.5.1   CIVIL LEGAL AID CONTRACT

Civil legal aid is currently carried out mainly under the 2013 Standard Civil Contract and 2010 Standard Civil Contracts. There is also provision for some family work that commenced before April 2013 to be carried out under the provisions of the 2012 Standard Civil Contract (Family and Housing).

17.5.2   FINANCIAL ELIGIBILITY TEST

The Community Legal Service (Financial) (Amendment) Regulations 2007 (which amend the Community Legal Service (Financial) Regulations 2000) set out the thresholds for financial eligibility for all applications for funding made on or after 8 April 2008. The test uses the basic concepts of 'disposable income', that is, income available to a person after deducting essential living expenses; and 'disposable capital', that is, the assets owned by a person after essential items like a home. If a person could sell his or her home, pay off the mortgage and still have more than £100,000 left (called 'equity'), then he or she will not qualify for aid.

Certain services are free, regardless of financial resources, such as services consisting exclusively of the provision of general information about the law, legal system and availability of legal services, legal representation in some cases involving the Children Act 1989 and related proceedings, and representation at a mental health review tribunal. Some services are non-contributory and a client is either eligible or not, whereas others are contributory in accordance with a sliding scale, dependent on how much a client's income or capital exceeds a given threshold. There is a cap amount over which a person is ineligible for legal aid. In summary, the financial eligibility amounts for applications are as follows:

- For all levels of service, there is (as of 1 April 2013) a gross income cap of £2,657 per month. This cap may be increased by £222 per month for each child in excess of four. A client who is directly or indirectly in receipt of Income Support or income-based Jobseeker's Allowance automatically satisfies the gross income test for all levels of service.

- For the service of Legal Help, Help at Court and Legal Representation before Immigration Adjudicators and the Immigration Appeal Tribunal, the disposable income must not exceed £733 per month.

- For the service of Family Mediation, Help with Mediation and other Legal Representation (which may be subject to a contribution from income and capital), the disposable income must not exceed £733 per month.

There is a capital limit of £8,000 for all controlled legal representation, except legal representation in respect of immigration matters set out in Regulation 8(3) where it remains £3,000.

When assessing gross income and disposable income, state benefits under the Social Security Contributions and Benefits Act 1992 (Disability Living Allowance, Attendance Allowance, Constant Attendance Allowance, Invalid Care Allowance, Severe Disablement Allowance, Council Tax Benefit, Housing Benefit and any payment out of the social fund), back-to-work bonuses under the Jobseekers Act 1995, war and war widows' pensions and fostering allowances are disregarded. Any person being paid the new Universal Credit will automatically be passported through to legal aid, although capital must be assessed. If a person receives financial support under ss 4 or 95 of the Immigration and Asylum Act 1999 from the National Asylum Support Service (NASS), they are passported through both income and capital tests for controlled work immigration and asylum matters only.

The only level of service assessed by the supplier for which contributions can be sought is Legal Representation in Specified Family Proceedings. However, provided that the client's gross income is below the prescribed limit, clients with a disposable income of £315 or below per month will not need to pay any contributions from income, but may still have to pay a contribution from capital. A client with disposable income in excess of £315 and up to £733 per month will be liable to pay a monthly contribution of a proportion of the excess over £311, assessed in accordance with the following bands:

Band	Monthly disposable income	Monthly contribution
A	£316 – £465	Quarter of income in excess of £311
B	£466 – £616	£38.50 + third of income in excess of £465
C	£617 – £733	£88.85 + half of income in excess of £616

A client whose disposable capital exceeds £3,000 is required to pay a contribution of either the capital exceeding that sum or the likely maximum costs of the funded service, whichever is the lesser.

For example, if disposable income is £480 per month, the contribution will be in Band B, the excess income is £15 (£480 – £465), the monthly contribution would therefore be £43.50 (£38.50 + £5 (a third of the excess income)). The LAA website has an online legal aid eligibility calculator to enable people to check whether they are likely to qualify financially.

Provided it is not disregarded as subject matter of the dispute, a client's main or only dwelling in which he or she resides must be taken into account as capital, subject to the following rules:

(a) The dwelling should be valued at the amount for which it could be sold on the open market.

(b) The amount of any mortgage or charge registered on the property must be deducted, but the maximum amount that can be deducted for such a mortgage or charge is £100,000.

(c) The first £100,000 of the value of the client's interest after making the above mortgage deduction must be disregarded.

17.5.3   THE FUNDING CODE

The basis of funding was governed by s 8 of the Access to Justice Act 1999. This is now governed by LASPO. Under s 4 of the Act the Lord Chancellor can issue guidance and regulations.

The Civil Legal Aid (Merits Criteria) Regulations 2013 replace the previous Funding Code Criteria and the Civil Legal Aid (Procedures) Regulations 2012 replace the previous Funding Code Procedures.

The Lord Chancellor has issued a three-part funding guidance, which replaced the previous Funding Code Guidance. The three parts comprise general guidance, guidance for exceptional funding for inquests and exceptional funding for out-of-scope (non-inquest) cases.

17.5.4   LEGAL SERVICES PROVIDED

Legal services were formerly governed by the Access to Justice Act 1999. This has now been superseded by LASPO. Schedule 1 of LASPO covers civil legal services. These range from the provision of basic information about the law and legal services to providing help towards preventing or resolving disputes and enforcing decisions that have been reached. The scheme encompasses advice, assistance and representation by lawyers (which have long been available under the legal aid scheme), and also the services of non-lawyers. It will extend to other types of service including, for example, mediation in family or civil cases where appropriate.

The Lord Chancellor must designate a civil servant as the Director of Legal Aid Casework. Under s 10 of LASPO the Director can make directions bringing cases that would be excluded within the provisions of the Act in exceptional circumstances.

17.5.5 THE CLA FUND

Unlike the CLS budget, the LAA budget is not established by statute. Instead, the LAA, as a government agency of the Ministry of Justice, submits its budget to the Permanent Secretary (who is the Principal Accounting Officer of the department) and, once it is approved, is required to operate within it. The budget must be approved by a government minister.

17.5.6 EXTENSION OF FINANCIAL CONDITIONS ON AN ASSISTED PARTY

Section 23 of LASPO extends the potential scope of financial conditions imposed on an assisted party in two ways, although there are no immediate plans to use either of these powers:

- It will be possible to make the provision of services in some types of case subject to the assisted person agreeing to repay an amount in excess of the cost of the services provided, in the event that their case is successful (s 23(3)). This might make it possible to fund certain types of case on a self-financing basis, with the additional payments from successful litigants applied to meet the cost of unsuccessful cases. It would also be possible to mix public funding with a private conditional fee arrangement, subject to the same conditions about the uplift to the costs in the event of a successful outcome. The government has suggested that this might be appropriate, for example, where a case could not be taken under a wholly private arrangement, because the solicitors' firm was not large enough to bear the risk of the very high costs likely to be involved.

- It will be possible (s 23(10)) to require the assisted person to repay, over time and with interest, the full cost of the service provided (for example, through continuing contributions from income). This will make it possible to provide services in some categories of case in the form of a loan scheme.

Section 26 of LASPO establishes limits on the liability of the person receiving funded services to pay costs to the unassisted party. The costs he or she must pay cannot go above what is 'reasonable' (s 26(1)), taking into account the financial resources of all parties. It also provides that regulations may specify the principles that are to be applied in determining the amount of any costs awarded against the party receiving funded services, and the circumstances in which a costs order may be enforced against the person receiving funded services.

Today, the regulations that limit the circumstances in which the costs order may be enforced against the person receiving funded services (or the liability of the Agency to meet any costs order on behalf of the person receiving funded services) are made on a more flexible basis. Previously, protection from costs was seen by governments to create too great an advantage in litigation for the person receiving legal aid.

The 2016 annual report of the LAA shows that the 2015/16 spend was £1.638 million.

Following the introduction of new contracting arrangements, there has been a decline in the number of solicitors' firms providing legal aid services from 4,866 in January 2000 to 2,954 by March 2014, of which there were 1,435 (including 13 telephone providers) for civil work and 1,519 (including three telephone providers) for criminal (LAA Annual Report 2014 no later figures are available). Hugh Barrett, executive director for commissioning at the LAA, speaking to the Legal Aid Practitioners Group in October 2015, said the number of firms carrying out criminal legal aid work had fallen from 2,600 to 1,800. The reduction in the supplier base is partly a deliberate move away from reliance on a large number of generalist support firms towards a smaller number of specialist quality-assured providers. However, the reduction also reflects concern among some firms about the level of remuneration offered on civil legal aid work.

17.6   THE CRIMINAL DEFENCE SERVICE

The Criminal Defence Service (CDS), known as Criminal Legal Aid (CRLA) from 1 April 2013, uses criminal legal aid to help people who are under investigation or facing criminal charges. By ensuring that people accused of crimes have access to legal advice and representation, the CRLA also helps the police and courts operate fairly and efficiently.

Criminal legal aid can offer:

- advice and assistance from a solicitor on criminal matters;
- free legal advice from a solicitor at the police station during questioning;
- the cost of a solicitor preparing a case and initial representation for certain proceedings at a magistrates' or Crown Court;
- full legal representation for defence in criminal cases at all court levels;
- a duty solicitor to provide free legal advice and representation at magistrates' court.

The Criminal Defence Service Act 2006 changed the arrangements for the grant of public funding for representation in criminal proceedings in England and Wales. It provides for the power to grant rights to representation to be conferred on the Legal Services Commission (LSC), and now under the direction of the Legal Aid Agency (LAA) instead of that being done by a court. It introduces a test of financial eligibility for the grant of such funding and, in cases where eligibility exists, contributions based on means.

The creation of the Criminal Defence Service (CDS) was part of the government's fundamental reform of the legal aid system, as set out in the Access to Justice Act 1999. The purpose of the CDS is to ensure access for individuals involved in criminal investigations or criminal proceedings to such advice, assistance and representation as the interests of justice require. The CDS was implemented and managed by the LSC, which was also created by the Access to Justice Act 1999. Solicitors are required to work within quality-assured contracts to perform CDS functions.

The LSC was responsible for funding legal representation under the Criminal Defence Service. This is now the responsibility of the LAA. However, under the old structure, it was the courts – and not the LSC – which were responsible for granting the right to have funding. Now the applications for funding are made centrally, not to a court.

The LSC awarded CDS contracts to quality-assured providers. At 31 March 2014, 1,516 solicitors' offices and three telephone providers operated under a CDS contract (LAA Annual Report 2014), a net decrease of 4.78 per cent on 2012/13.

The interests of justice test

The 'interests of justice' test determines whether an applicant is entitled to a Representation Order based on the merits of the case. This is also known as the 'Widgery Criteria' (after the name of the judge in whose 1966 government report on legal aid they were originally formulated).

The applicant must indicate which of the following criteria they believe apply to their case:

- It is likely that I will lose my liberty.
- I have been given a sentence that is suspended or non-custodial. If I break this, the court may be able to deal with me for the original offence.
- It is likely that I will lose my livelihood.
- It is likely that I will suffer serious damage to my reputation.
- A substantial question of law may be involved.
- I may not be able to understand the court proceedings or present my own case.
- I may need witnesses to be traced or interviewed on my behalf.
- The proceedings may involve expert cross-examination of a prosecution witness.
- It is in the interests of another person that I am represented.
- Any other reasons.

If the applicant passes the 'interests of justice' test, he or she must also pass the means test to qualify for legal aid. The aid will be granted to an applicant who does not have the financial means to fund their own representation in a magistrates' court.

The means test in the magistrates' court establishes whether an applicant is financially eligible for legal aid. It only considers income and expenses – capital is not included.

Her Majesty's Courts and Tribunals Service (HMCTS) staff apply the test once they receive a correctly completed application form.

So-called passported applicants are those individuals who automatically pass the means test (for example because of the state benefits they are on). These applicants will still need to pass the interests of justice test to qualify for legal aid. The initial means test assesses the applicant's income and how this is spread between any partners and children.

A full means test is carried out if, through the initial means test, the applicant's adjusted income is calculated (after April 2008) to be more than £12,475 and less than £22,325. It works out an applicant's disposable income after deducting tax, maintenance and other annual costs from the gross annual income. There is also a complex means test for those who have complex financial circumstances. Hardship reviews can be carried out if an applicant can show they are genuinely unable to fund their own representation. A person may qualify for criminal legal aid if their annual disposable income exceeds £3,398 (£283.17 per month), but does not exceed £37,500, subject to making a contribution. This would be refunded if found not guilty. If found guilty and their capital exceeds £30,000, a contribution may be required.

In 2015/16, the public expenditure on the Criminal Defence Service was £889.5 million (LAA Annual Report 2016).

17.7 PUBLIC DEFENDER SERVICE

The Public Defender Service (PDS) was operated by the LSC and since 1 April 2013 has been run by the LAA. The LAA directly employs the PDS staff of solicitors, accredited representatives and administrators. The PDS provides independent advice, assistance and representation on criminal matters.

PDS lawyers are available 24 hours a day, seven days a week to:

- give advice to people in custody;
- represent clients in magistrates', Crown and higher courts where necessary.

All PDS employees must observe the code made under s 29 of LASPO.

The Public Defender Service aims to:

- provide independent, high-quality, value-for-money criminal defence services to the public;
- provide examples of excellence in the provision of criminal defence services nationally and locally;
- provide benchmarking information to be used to improve the performance of the contracting regime for private practice suppliers;
- raise the level of understanding within government and all levels and areas of the Agency of the issues facing criminal defence lawyers in providing high-quality services to the public;
- provide an additional option for ensuring the provision of quality criminal defence services in geographical areas where existing provision is low or of a poor standard;
- recruit, train and develop people to provide high-quality criminal defence services, in accordance with the PDS's own business needs, which will add to the body of such people available to provide criminal defence services generally; and

- share with private practice suppliers best practice in terms of forms, systems and so on, developed within the PDS to assist in the overall improvement of CRLA provision locally.

The Public Defender Service (PDS) is the first salaried criminal provider in England and Wales. There are currently four PDS offices: Cheltenham, Darlington, Pontypridd and Swansea.

17.8 THE MAGEE REVIEW 2009

In October 2009 the Ministry of Justice announced a review of the way the £2 billion legal aid budget was delivered. The resultant conclusions could see separate civil and criminal funds run by different bodies (C Baksi, *Law Society Gazette*, 14 October 2009). The review was established while legal aid lawyers warned that firms providing social welfare legal services were at risk of collapse because of the 'artificial' way work was being distributed by the Legal Services Commission. Lord Bach, the minister for legal aid, appointed Sir Ian Magee, a former permanent secretary at the Department for Constitutional Affairs, to explore ways of optimising value for money in the way legal aid was administered.

Bach told the *Gazette* he was 'ruling nothing out and nothing in'. He said he would be surprised if the LSC ceased to exist, but said it could work alongside another body, with one administering the criminal budget and the other the civil budget. The two budgets could be ring-fenced.

The Law Society had warned that the LSC's policy of capping the number of new social welfare cases or 'matter starts' that a firm can take on could cause some firms to collapse. Nicola Mackintosh of legal aid firm Mackintosh Duncan questioned why the LSC was 'artificially limiting the number of clients who can get access to justice' by allocating firms only a set number of new cases (*Law Society Gazette*, 14 October 2009, p 1).

On 1 April 2013 the LSC was replaced by the LAA.

17.9 THE VOLUNTARY SECTOR

There are over 1,500 not-for-profit advice agencies in England and Wales. They receive their funding – over £150 million a year in total – from many different sources, mainly local authorities, but also charities including the Big Lottery Fund, central government and the LAA. The provision of advice services is not spread consistently across the country. Some areas appear to have relatively high levels of both legal practitioners and voluntary outlets, while others have few or none. For example, the former LSC's South East Area has one Citizens' Advice Bureau per 46,000 people, but, in the East Midlands, 138,000 people share a Citizens' Advice Bureau. The government believes that the fragmented nature of the advice sector obstructs effective planning and prevents local needs for legal advice and help from being met as rationally and fully as possible.

17.9.1 LAW CENTRES

There are currently 45 Law Centres in England and Wales listed on the Law Centres Network's website as at December 2016. These centres are staffed by salaried solicitors, trainee solicitors and non-lawyer experts in other areas like debt management. They are funded by local and central government and charity. They have 'shop-front' access and aim to be user-friendly and unintimidating. They are managed by committees and represented by the Law Centres' Federation (LCF).

Law Centres take on individual cases, providing, for example advice on landlord and tenant matters and representing people at tribunals. Some centres also take on group work since quite often the problems of one client are part of a wider problem. This sort of work is controversial.

Since the introduction of LASPO, the Law Centres' budgets have been cut and sometimes they are now forced to either turn people away or charge for services.

17.9.2 OTHER VOLUNTARY ADVICE

The Citizens Advice Bureaux (CABs) have been assisting people since 1939 and there are now 600 local CAB premises in England and Wales providing free, independent and impartial information and advice from over 2,250 locations (such as community centres, doctors' surgeries and prisons). They deal with a high number of cases (over six million a year) and a very wide range of problems, many of which are legal problems. During 2015/16, bureaux advised 2.7 million clients with 6.2 million issues (CAB annual report 2016). According to the annual report 99.7% of people in England and Wales can access a local Citizens Advice within a 30 minute drive of where they live. There are, however, very few trained lawyers working for the CABs, but over 20,000 volunteer helpers. In keeping with the changing technology of the modern world, the CABs now offers an online help service through its website, providing independent advice on a range of topics such as money, family, consumer matters and civil rights.

In April 2012 the CABs took over Consumer Direct and in its first year dealt with 837,000 matters.

The CLS launched CLS Direct in July 2004, a website providing free advice on a range of matters similar to the CABs. The website offers topics of the month on the home page such as redundancy rights. It also contains an online calculator to assist people to determine whether they qualify for legal aid. Legal information leaflets and factsheets are also available on this site.

The Bar Council supports a Free Representation Unit for clients at a variety of tribunals for which legal aid is not available. Most of the representation is carried out by Bar students supported and advised by full-time caseworkers. A special Bar unit based in London was formed in 1996 through which more senior barristers provide representation. Some colleges and universities also offer advice. For example, the College of Law in London operates a free advice service in which vocational students give advice on such matters as personal injury cases and employment law.

Both barristers and solicitors operate 'pro bono' (from the Latin phrase *pro bono publico*, meaning 'for the public good') schemes under which legal work is done without charge or at reduced cost for members of the public ineligible for legal aid from the LSC but with limited means, or charitable and other non-profit-making organisations. Examples of pro bono activities include: solicitors attending advice sessions at Citizens Advice Bureaux or other free services; free advice to members of organisations, for example, trade union general advice schemes; secondment to Law Centres; and free advice to charitable organisations.

17.10   CONDITIONAL FEE ARRANGEMENTS

These are sometimes known as 'no win, no fee' agreements. They are not used for family or criminal matters, but can be used in many types of civil action. In a 'no win, no fee' agreement, a litigant's solicitor will only be paid if the claim is successful. If so, the solicitor will also be entitled to an extra fee (known as a success fee). Both the basic fee and this extra fee are normally paid in whole or part by the losing party.

There are other incurred costs (such as court fees or the fee for a medical report). These are normally known as disbursements. Again, the losing party should pay all or part of these costs. A litigant is liable to pay his or her solicitor for any costs that the losing party is not ordered to pay.

If, under such an arrangement, a litigant's claim fails, they will not have to pay their own solicitor, but they will still probably have to pay the costs of the successful party – the other side. That is something, however, against which they can take out insurance. They will also have to pay any other incurred costs (such as court fees or the fee for a medical report). These are normally known as disbursements. The insurance in these circumstances is known as 'after the event' insurance. The client may have to pay the insurance premium.

Background

As part of the scheme to expose the provision of legal services to the full rigour of market forces, the then Lord Chancellor chose to devote an entire Green Paper in 1989 to *Contingency Fees*. Following a recommendation from the Civil Justice Review, the Paper had sought opinion on the funding of litigation on a contingent fee basis. This provides that litigation is funded by the claimant only if he or she wins, in which event the lawyer claims fees as a portion of the damages payable to the claimant. The response to this idea was largely hostile.

The traditional opposition to contingency fees in the English legal system was that they were 'maintenance' (the financial support of another's litigation) and 'champerty' (taking a financial interest in another's litigation). Champerty occurs when the person maintaining another takes as his reward a portion of the property in dispute. It taints an agreement with illegality and renders it void (for a discussion of the principle, see *Grovewood Holding plc v James Capel & Co Ltd* (1995)). Section 14 of the Criminal Justice Act 1967 abolished maintenance and champerty as crimes and torts, but kept the rules making such arrangements improper for solicitors.

English litigation uses the Indemnity Rule, by which the loser pays the costs of the winner and thus puts him or her, more or less, in the position he or she enjoyed before the damage was done. Objectors to contingency fee agreements pointed out that such things were incompatible with the Indemnity Rule because, although the winner's costs would be paid for them by the other side, they would still have to pay for their lawyer from their damages (calculated to put them in the position they would have enjoyed if no wrong had been done to them) so they would not really be 'made whole' by their award. The position is different in the United States, where contingency agreements are common in personal injury cases, because there each side bears its own costs.

It was further contended by objectors to the contingency fee that the legal aid system adequately catered for those who were too poor to afford an ordinary private action. Even if there were people who were just above the legal aid financial thresholds but still too poor to pay for an action, this should be dealt with simply by changing the threshold.

Section 58 of the Courts and Legal Services Act (CLSA) 1990 permitted the Lord Chancellor to introduce conditional fee arrangements, although these cannot apply to criminal cases, family cases or those involving children (s 58(10)). However, there are a number of different arrangements for conditional fees, so one issue to be addressed was the type of conditional fee system that should be applied in England and Wales. The Scottish model, for which initially there was reasonable support, is that of the 'speculative fee', whereby the solicitor can agree with their client that they would be paid their ordinary taxed costs only if they won the case. Two other forms of contingency fee were rejected during the consultation period as being unsuitable. The first was a restricted contingency fee system in which the fee payable in the event of a successful action would be a *percentage of the damages*, but where the actual levels of recovery would be governed by rules. The second was an unrestricted contingency arrangement, similarly based on a percentage of damages, but at uncontrolled levels. These plans were rejected because it was thought that to give the lawyer a stake in the claimant's damages would be likely to create unacceptable temptations for the lawyer to behave unprofessionally in order to secure their fee.

The system eventually adopted is that where conditional fees are based on an 'uplift' from the level of fee the lawyer would normally charge for the sort of work in question. Originally, the maximum uplift was to be 20 per cent in order to induce lawyers to take on potentially difficult cases and to help finance lawyers' unsuccessful conditional fee cases. This would have meant they could charge the fee that they would normally charge for a given type of case, plus an additional fifth.

In August 1993, after a long process of negotiation with the profession, Lord Mackay, the then Lord Chancellor, finally announced that he would allow the conditional fee to operate on a 100 per cent uplift. Thus, solicitors receive no fee if they lose a case, but double what they would normally charge if they win the case. The Law Society had campaigned vigorously against the proposed 20 per cent uplift, arguing that such risks as the 'no win, no fee' arrangement entailed would not be regarded as worth taking by many solicitors simply on the incentive that their fee for winning the case would be 20 per cent more than they would normally charge for such a case. The LCD originally decided to restrict the scheme to cases involving personal injury, insolvency and the European Court of Human Rights.

The system came into effect in June 1995. Such agreements are now legal, provided that they comply with any requirements imposed by the Lord Chancellor and are not 'contentious business agreements'. These are defined under s 59 of the Solicitors Act 1974 as agreements between a solicitor and his or her client made in writing by which the solicitor is to be remunerated by a gross sum, or a salary, at agreed hourly rates or otherwise, and whether higher or lower than that at which he or she would normally be remunerated. A valid CFA must comply with the LCD requirements, be in writing, stating the percentage uplift payable if successful (and 'must not exceed the percentage specified in relation to the description of proceedings to which the agreement relates by order made by the Lord Chancellor' – s 58(4)(c) CLSA 1990 as amended by s 27 of the Access to Justice Act 1999). A CFA cannot be used if proceedings do not allow an enforceable CFA.

The right to use 'no win, no fee' agreements to pursue civil law claims was extended by the Conditional Fee Agreements Order 1998. The Order allowed lawyers to offer conditional fee agreements to their clients in all civil cases excluding family cases. Speaking in the House of Lords on 23 July 1988, the then Lord Chancellor, Lord Irvine, said:

> These agreements will result in a huge expansion of access to justice. Today, only the very rich or the very poor can afford to litigate. In future, everyone with a really strong case will be able to secure his rights free of the fear of ruin if he loses. They will bring the majority of our people into access to justice.

Conditional fees have been the means by which at least several hundred thousand personal injury cases have been brought, and many, in all likelihood, would not have been brought but for the existence of conditional fees. The Order retains the old rule that the maximum uplift on the fees lawyers can charge is 100 per cent. Thus, a lawyer may take on a claim against an allegedly negligent employer whose carelessness has resulted in the client being injured. The lawyer, who might normally charge £2,000 for such a case, can say 'I shall do this work for nothing if we lose, but £3,000 if we win'. In fact, as the price uplift can be up to 100 per cent of the normal fee, he or she can stipulate for up to £4,000 in this example. The Law Society has recommended an additional voluntary cap of 25 per cent of damages, and this has been widely accepted in practice.

The real problems continued to be:

(a)   that the new system, designed really to help the millions who have been regulated out of the legal aid system, does not help people whose cases stand only a limited chance of success, as lawyers will not take their cases; and

(b)   the difficulties of a claimant getting insurance to cover the costs that he or she will have to pay, if he or she loses the claim, for the other side's lawyers. Where a personal injury claim arises from a road traffic incident, it is almost always clear to a solicitor where blame and legal liability probably lie. Risks are therefore calculable by insurance companies, so one can presently insure against having to pay the other side's costs in the event of losing an action on a personal injury case for about £100 in a 'no win, no fee' arrangement. There are, however, many areas, and medical negligence cases are good examples, where the chances of success are notoriously difficult to predict. Thus, insurance against having to pay the other side's costs is prohibitively high, running into many thousands of pounds in some cases. It is quite unrealistic to assume that all such cases, arising often from highly distressing circumstances, will be dealt with in future on a 'no win, no fee' basis. Lawyers will generally not want to take on such cases on such a basis, and even where they do, clients will often not be able to afford the necessary insurance. As insurance to cover client costs in medical 'no win, no fee' cases has proven so expensive, legal aid continues to cover clinical negligence cases.

17.10.1 THE ACCESS TO JUSTICE ACT 1999

The Access to Justice Act 1999 (ss 27–31), together with the Conditional Fee Agreements Regulations 2000 and the Collective Conditional Fee Agreements Regulations 2000, reformed the law relating to conditional fees to enable the court to order a losing party to pay, in addition to the other party's normal legal costs, the uplift on the successful party's lawyers' fees and, in any case where a litigant has insured against facing an order for the other side's costs, any premium paid by the successful party for that insurance. The intention was to:

- ensure that the compensation awarded to a successful party is not eroded by any uplift or premium. The party in the wrong will bear the full burden of costs;
- make conditional fees more attractive, in particular to defendants and to claimants seeking non-monetary redress (these litigants can rarely use conditional fees now, because they cannot rely on the prospect of recovering damages to meet the cost of the uplift and premium);
- discourage weak cases and encourage settlements;
- provide a mechanism for regulating the uplifts that solicitors charge. In future, unsuccessful litigants will be able to challenge unreasonably high uplifts when the court comes to assess costs.

In the first version of conditional fee arrangements, only people who expected to win money from their case could benefit from conditional fees. This was the only way that most people could afford to pay the success fee. There were also available insurance policies that could be taken out by someone contemplating litigation to cover the costs of the other party and the client's own costs (including, if not a conditional fee case, a client's solicitor's fees) if the case was lost. However, it meant that a successful litigant would not receive all the money he or she was awarded, so the government made provision in the Access to Justice Act 1999 to make it possible for the winning party to recover the success fee and any insurance premium from the losing party.

The rules, which had become very complex for all using them, were simplified in 2005. The Conditional Fee Agreements Regulations 2000 and the Collective Conditional Fee Agreements Regulations 2000 were revoked by the Conditional Fee Agreement (Revocation) Regulations 2005 (SI 2005/2305). The Access to Justice (Membership Organisation) Regulations 2000 were revoked and replaced by the simpler Access to Justice (Membership Organisation) Regulations 2005 (SI 2005/2306).

The removal of the unnecessary regulation was applied to all CFAs across the range of civil cases, including commercial, insolvency, environmental, intellectual property, human rights, privacy, defamation and injury.

Announcing the simplified arrangements, Parliamentary Under Secretary of State Baroness Ashton of Upholland said (10 August 2005):

> Conditional fee agreements play a valuable role in helping people with valid claims obtain access to justice. For many consumers and businesses this provides the only means of obtaining appropriate redress. A regime that is complex and opaque puts the consumer at a disadvantage. Revoking the existing regulations will help make CFA agreements a simpler product and in particular will help consumers to better understand the agreements they enter into and the risks they could face in contemplating litigation. Consumer safeguards will be improved as responsibility for proper advice falls on the solicitor.

Regulation of solicitors involved in CFA cases is the responsibility of the Solicitors' Regulation Authority. It is required to ensure that clients are fully informed about the strength of their case and prospects of success in clear, simple terms. This is designed to help to ensure that only well-founded claims proceed and benefit both claimants and defendants who will be spared the stress of avoidable court hearings.

Collective conditional fee arrangements

Collective conditional fee agreements are designed specifically for mass providers and purchasers of legal services, such as trade unions, insurers or commercial organisations. A collective conditional fee agreement enables a trade union to enter into a single agreement with solicitors to govern the way in which cases for its members will be run and paid for; by simplifying the standard individual process, it reduces the cost of pursuing separate individual cases. The scheme also benefits commercial organisations which are able to enter collective conditional fee agreements to pursue or defend claims arising in the course of business.

17.10.2   THE ADVANTAGES OF CONDITIONAL FEE ARRANGEMENTS

For claimants, the advantages can be summarised as being:

- that lawyers acting in any case will be confident (they will have had to weigh carefully the chances of success before taking the case as their fee depends on winning) and determined;

- there will be freedom from the anxiety of having to pay huge fees;
- there will be no need to pay fees in advance; and
- there will be no delays or worries with legal aid applications.

For defendants there will be advantages too, as the contingency fee system will probably reduce the number of spurious claims. In a period where legal aid is being cut back so drastically, preventing so many people from going to law, this system can be seen as a way of preserving at least some limited access to the legal process. Losing parties will still be liable to pay the other side's costs, so it will be unlikely that people will take action unless they consider they have a good chance of success.

The taxpayer can also be given the advantage in the form of a significant reduction in the funding of the legal aid system. Furthermore, practitioners who are competent to assess and willing to take the risks of litigation will arguably enjoy a better fee-paying basis, increased fee income and overall business, fewer reasons for delay and more satisfied clients with fewer complaints.

Consider two examples. First, a middle-class couple consult their solicitor about injuries received in a road accident. Their joint income and savings put them outside the legal aid scheme. The proposed litigation is beset with uncertainties as the other driver's insurers have denied liability. The couple have to worry about their own expenses and the possibility under the Indemnity Rule of paying for the defendant's costs. Second, a young man who has been injured at work wants to sue his employer. The case will turn on some difficult health and safety law on which there are currently conflicting decisions. He is eligible for legal aid, but he will have to make substantial contributions because of his level of income, and if his claim fails, he will have to pay the same sum again towards the expenses of his employers. In both cases, the prospective litigants might well drop any plan to litigate. Both cases, however, might proceed expeditiously if they found a lawyer to act on a no win, no fee basis.

17.10.3 THE DISADVANTAGES OF CONDITIONAL FEE ARRANGEMENTS

Critics of the system argue that it encourages the sort of speculative actions that occur frequently in the United States, taken up by so-called ambulance-chasing lawyers. It can be argued that the system of contingency fees creates a conflict of interest between the lay client and the lawyer, with a consequential risk of exploitation of the client. Where a lawyer's fee depends on the outcome of a case, there is a greater temptation for him to act unethically. When the Royal Commission on Legal Services (1979) rejected the idea of contingent fees, it stated that such a scheme might lead to undesirable practices by lawyers including:

the construction of evidence, the improper coaching of witnesses, the use of professionally partisan expert witnesses, especially medical witnesses, improper examination and cross-examination, groundless legal arguments designed to lead the courts into error and competitive touting.

If the case was won, the lawyer claimed a significant part of the damages, but there was also a real danger that lawyers would be pressured to settle too readily to avoid the costs of preparing for a trial that could be lost and therewith the fee. An example would be where an insurance company admits liability but contests the level of damages. The claimant might stand to get substantially higher compensation by contesting the case. Under the new system, however, their solicitor will have a strong interest in advising them to settle. A settlement would guarantee the solicitor's costs and the agreed 'mark-up' (up to 100 per cent more than a normal fee for such work), both of which would be completely lost if the case was fought and lost. This would not occur outside of a conditional fee arrangement. Although the conventional system of payment was not without problems, as Walter Merricks, then of The Law Society, has stated:

> when a lawyer is being paid by the hour, he may have a financial interest in encouraging his client to go on with an open-and-shut case, increasing his own fees.

The Law Society has argued that the system, if not properly regulated, could promote the sort of 'ambulance chasing' practised by American lawyers in the wake of the 1984 Bhopal disaster, in which over 2,500 people were killed by escaping gas from a US company (Union Carbide Corporation) plant in India. American lawyers flew out to act for victims and their relatives and some were reported to be taking fees of 50 per cent of the claimants' damages.

It was argued by some that by allowing lawyers to *double* their normal fee for certain cases, the Lord Chancellor risked eliminating any benefit speculative fees might bring. If the successful client was not to be able to recover the *uplift* from the other side, they would have to fund it themselves out of the damages they had been awarded. In effect, this often resulted in their damages being halved. The uplift can now be recovered, subject to taxation (that is, court official approval), following changes made by the Access to Justice Act 1999.

It is not even clear that the main claim made for the system – that it increases access to the courts – is correct. The Scottish experience is that speculative cases do not exceed 1 per cent of the cases in the caseload of the Faculty of Advocates. One firm opponent of the system is Lord Justice Auld. He has argued that the system will eventually endanger the esteem in which lawyers are held by the public. He has doubted whether the scheme will produce greater commitment by lawyers to their cases: 'There is a distinction to be drawn between the lawyer's commitment to the case and his anxiety to recover his fees. The two do not always correspond.'

Since 1 April 2013, a successful client using a CFA has been obliged to pay any success fee and After-the-Event (ATE) insurance under ss 44 and 46 LASPO.

17.11 RECENT CHALLENGES TO LEGAL AID CUTS

During 2014, the government's schemes and policies to reduce legal aid provision were successfully challenged in the courts on a number of occasions. The latest was in December 2014 when the Court of Appeal ruled that people appealing against deportation had been unlawfully denied legal aid under too-restrictive government guidelines (*R (on the application of) Gudanaviciene and others v The Director of Legal Aid Casework and others* (2014)).

In the ruling, against Chris Grayling, the Lord Chancellor, three appeal judges upheld a High Court decision that the guidance he had issued was 'unlawful and too restrictive'. As Justice Secretary or Lord Chancellor, Mr Grayling had lost seven such challenges in seven months by the end of 2014.

A High Court judge had ruled that the guidance 'sets too high a threshold' and 'produces unfairness' by denying publicly funded legal advice to applicants in 'exceptional cases'. The Court of Appeal decision entailed that six cases in which legal aid had been refused would need to be reconsidered. The High Court had quashed refusals of civil legal aid by the director of legal aid casework, relying on the Lord Chancellor's guidance, to grant legal aid to the six claimants, and the Court of Appeal upheld the decision of the High Court.

All the cases concerned the availability of legal aid in immigration cases under s 10 of the Legal Aid, Sentencing and Punishment of Offenders Act 2012 (LASPO), which deals with exceptional funding applications. Mr Justice Collins said the cases involved EU nationals appealing against decisions that they should be deported following criminal convictions, an alleged victim of trafficking from Nigeria, and other cases involving the right to enter and remain in the UK.

Announcing the court's decision, Lord Dyson said:

> As is well known, the effect of LASPO was to limit the circumstances in which civil legal aid can be granted. Legal aid was withdrawn in a large number of types of case. But provision was made for exceptional case funding by section 10. The Lord Chancellor has issued guidance to which those responsible for deciding whether to grant exceptional case funding must have regard. The aim of section 10 and of the guidance is that legal aid should be provided where it is necessary to ensure that litigants have effective access to justice as required by the Convention on Human Rights and the EU Charter of Fundamental Freedoms
>
> (Frances Gibb, 'Legal aid guidance on deportation cases ruled unlawful by appeal court', *The Times*, 15 December 2014).

Lord Dyson said the court concluded that the guidance 'is unlawful because it mis-states the effect of the relevant jurisprudence'.

While the guidance identified correctly factors to be taken into account in deciding whether to grant exceptional funding, it neutralised their effect by wrongly stating that the threshold for funding was very high and that legal aid is required only in rare and extreme cases.

Lord Dyson stated:

> It is also unlawful because – as is conceded by the Lord Chancellor – it wrongly states that there is nothing in the current case law which says that Article 8 of the convention requires the provision of legal aid in immigration proceedings.

The Court of Appeal ruled (para 45):

> In our judgment, the cumulative effect of [the Lord Chancellor's guidelines] is to misstate the effect of the ECtHR jurisprudence. As we have seen, the Guidance correctly identifies many of the particular factors that should be taken into account in deciding whether to make an exceptional case determination, but their effect is substantially neutralised by the strong steer given in the passages that we have highlighted. These passages send a clear signal to the caseworkers and the Director that the refusal of legal aid will amount to a breach of Article 6(1) only in rare and extreme cases. In our judgment, there are no statements in the case-law which support this signal.

It has been said by some critics of the Court of Appeal's decision (see comments from lawyers under *The Times* article cited above) that the judges, in ruling the Lord Chancellor's guidance unlawful, are acting merely to protect the economic interests of the legal firmament from which they arise. Notably, however, no clear legal reasoning is advanced to refute that of the Court of Appeal.

CHAPTER SUMMARY: THE FUNDING OF LEGAL SERVICES

On 1 April 2013 the Legal Aid, Sentencing and Punishment of Offenders Act 2012 (LASPO) came into force. This introduced the Legal Aid Agency (LAA) and abolished the LSC.

To many people the funding of legal services means legal aid. This effectively relates to two parties, the purchaser (being the person who requires legal assistance) and the seller (being the person who gives the legal advice). Both parties to the transaction have been seriously affected by the government's progressive cutbacks. The person receiving the legal aid is faced with the qualifying earnings limits being frozen since April 2011. In addition, the areas of legal assistance a person can obtain have been reduced since April 2013. The solicitor or other legal professional is affected by reductions in fees payable by the LAA.

On 5 September 2013 the then Justice Secretary, Chris Grayling MP, announced in the House of Commons concessions to the government's legal aid Consultation. This consultation received over 1,600 responses from interested legal parties. The main concessions agreed with The Law Society were the creation of two criminal contracts, one for own client work and one for duty solicitor work, and the scrapping of price competitive tendering. These concessions followed the earlier one announced in July reinstating the ability for a client to choose his own solicitor.

Legal aid fees have been cut by 17.5 per cent across the board in two stages – the first 8.75 per cent in 2014 and the second in July 2015. Barrister and solicitor advocates in the most serious criminal cases – very high costs cases – had their fees cut by 30 per cent. To mitigate the effect of some of the cuts, the ministry will introduce interim payments during long-running cases.

In response to a spokesperson for the Ministry of Justice regarding changes to legal aid, Andrew Langdon QC, writing in *The Guardian* (4 October 2013), challenged the assertion that at approximately £2 billion per annum England has one of the most expensive legal aid systems in the world.

He went on to state that:

> Spending on our Criminal Justice System has *fallen* for a number of years. In the last five years it's fallen from £1.12bn to £975m and the cost of the most expensive category of cases has halved (from £124m to £67m). As for our system being expensive compared to other countries – this line has been peddled before, though the Ministry knows it's wrong. It's wrong because our system is different from other countries – it's 'adversarial'. So our legal aid budget pays for things that in other countries are transferred to other budgets. The true and fair way of making the comparison – don't take it from me, take it from the 2012 EC report on 'Efficiency of Justice' – shows that out of 14 European legal systems, we are *tenth* when you look at legal spend per inhabitant. Behind amongst others, Spain, Norway, Austria and Belgium. Behind Luxembourg and Switzerland – which is twice as expensive. This is not news to the Ministry. They know that. So why the spin? What's wrong with telling it how it is?

This article concluded that it 'was supported by Alistair MacDonald QC, Leader North Eastern Circuit; Gregory Bull QC, Leader Wales and Chester Circuit; Mark Wall QC, Leader Midlands Circuit; Andrew Langdon QC, Leader Western Circuit; Rick Pratt QC, Leader Northern Circuit; Sarah Forshaw QC, Leader South Eastern Circuit'.

FOOD FOR THOUGHT

1   Are legal services really akin to health and social services? In any case, should there be a limit to the funds that are expended on the provision of such services?

2   To what extent can voluntary services fill the gap left by professional legal advisers?

3   Anyone who has a phone has received a call from some ambulance-chasing claim firm. To what extent are such people providing a useful service?

4   Conditional fees were once seen as a way of reducing fees and costs, but are now attacked as having the opposite effect. Which version is true and why?

FURTHER READING

Butler, J, 'The funding drought' (2009) 63 Litigation Funding 16–17

Dutton, T, 'A public – private partnership' (2008) 158 NLJ 1013

Gilg, J-Y, 'Carolyn Regan: legal aid is the fourth plank of the welfare state' (2009) 153(29) SJ 10

Morris, A, 'Spiralling or stabilising? – the compensation culture and our propensity to claim damages for personal injury' (2007) 70(3) MLR 349

Morris, P et al, Social Needs and Legal Action, 1973, Oxford: Martin Robertson

Prior, S, 'Clinical negligence: the cost of claims' (2007) 52 Personal Injury Law Journal 11

Rhode, D, Access to Justice, 2004, Oxford: OUP

Robins, J, 'Are accident victims ill-served by "no win, no fee" agreements?' (2008) 158 NLJ 1125

Rothwell, R, 'Litigation funders face new complaints' (2014) 4(3) Law Soc Gazette, 17 February

Smith, R, 'Time to adjust' (2009) 159 NLJ 1271

Underhill, N et al, 'Law for free' (2003) Counsel 14

USEFUL WEBSITE

www.gov.uk/government/organisations/legal-aid-agency
The Legal Aid Agency.

COMPANION WEBSITE

Now visit the companion website to:

- test your understanding of the key terms using our Flashcard Glossary;
- revise and consolidate your knowledge of 'The funding of legal services' using our multiple choice question testbank;
- view both the links to the Useful Websites above.

www.routledge.com/cw/slapper

GENERAL LEGAL WEBSITES FOR THE ENGLISH LEGAL SYSTEM

It is not unusual for textbooks to provide extremely comprehensive lists of websites for students and other readers to find further information. In reality there are so many such sites that it is simply impossible to do them justice and in any event readers are capable of doing their own internet searches to locate more detailed information on any particular topic. In recognition of that reality what follows is merely a brief indication of the basic sites that have been used as a starting point for our own research.

www.bbc.co.uk
For general stories about the law, legal cases, political issues and current affairs, the BBC site is an excellent source of information.

www.bailii.org
The British and Irish Legal Information Institute (BAILII) offers the most comprehensive set of primary legal materials that are available free and in one place on the internet. It includes 46 databases covering seven jurisdictions.

www.bailii.org/uk/cases/UKHL
This includes all the House of Lords' decisions since 1838.

https://www.supremecourt.uk
The Supreme Court is the final court of appeal in the UK for civil cases. It hears appeals in criminal cases from England, Wales and Northern Ireland. It hears cases of the greatest public or constitutional importance affecting the whole population.

www.parliament.uk
Provides access to Parliament and all parliamentary business. Bills can be followed as they make their way through the legislative procedure.

www.legislation.gov.uk
Provides access to all legislation. This site also houses Explanatory Notes for important legislation, and information about which sections of Acts have been brought into force.

www.gov.uk
All government departments are now accessed through this one site. For example, the Justice Ministry is available at:

www.gov.uk/government/organisations/ministry-of-justice

www.theguardian.com/law/series/guardian-legal-network
The *Guardian* Legal Network brings together the best blogs and sites that cover legal affairs and developments from around the world. The network connects sites that provide high – quality news, comment, analysis, blogs and multimedia.

www.thetimes.co.uk/tto/law (paywall)

The legal site of *The Times*. It is updated continuously every day, and contains a wide range of legal stories, analyses and commentaries. Gary Slapper wrote a weekly column for *Times online*. There are over 600 of his articles in *The Times* online archive.

http://ukhumanrightsblog.com

Barristers from 1 Crown Office Row offer balanced analysis of human rights legal issues.

GENERAL READING

Archbold (Richardson, PJ (ed)), *Criminal Pleading, Evidence and Practice*, 2015, London: Sweet & Maxwell

Ashworth, A, *Sentencing and Criminal Justice*, 2010, Cambridge: CUP

Bailey, SH, Gunn, MJ and Ormerod, D, *Smith & Bailey on The Modern English Legal System*, 5th edn, 2007, London: Sweet & Maxwell

Baldwin, J, 'Police interview techniques: establishing truth or proof?' (1993) 33 British J of Criminology 3

Baldwin, J, 'Power and police interviews' (1993) 143 NLJ 1194

Baldwin, J and Hill, S, *The Operation of the Green Form Scheme in England and Wales*, 1988, London: LCD

Baldwin, J and McConville, M, *Negotiated Justice: A Closer Look at the Implications of Plea Bargaining*, 1993, London: Martin Robertson

Baldwin, J and McConville, M, *Negotiated Justice: Pressures on Defendants to Plead Guilty*, 1977, London: Martin Robertson

Barnard, M, 'All bar none' (1999) 96/26 Law Soc Gazette 20

Barnett, H, *Constitutional and Administrative Law*, 11th edn, 2015, Abingdon: Routledge

Bennett, WL and Feldman, MS, *Reconstructing Reality in the Courtroom: Justice and Judgment in American Culture*, 1984, New Jersey: Rutgers UP

Bennion, F, 'A naked usurpation?' (1999) 149 NLJ 421

Bennion, F, 'Statute law obscurity and drafting parameters' (1978) British JLS 235

Bennion, F, *Statutory Interpretation*, 5th edn, 2008, London: Butterworths

Bindaman, D, 'Crown duals' (1999) Law Soc Gazette, 31 March

Bindman, G, 'Lessons of *Pinochet*' (1999) 149 NLJ 1050

Bingham, T, *The Rule of Law*, 2011, London, Penguin

Black, J, Bridge, J, Bond, T and Gribbin, L, *A Practical Approach to Family Law*, 10th edn 2015, Oxford: OUP

Blackstone's Civil Practice (Sime s and French deds)), 2017, Oxford: OUP

Blake, S, Browne, J and Sime, S, *The Jackson ADR Handbook*, 2nd edn, 2012, Oxford: OUP.

Blom-Cooper, L (ed), *The Law as Literature*, 1961, London: The Bodley Head

Broadbent, G, 'Offensive weapons and the Criminal Justice Act' (1989) Law Soc Gazette, 12 July

Burns, R, 'A view from the ranks' (2000) 150 NLJ 1829–30

Burrow, J, 'Pre – committal custody time limits' (1999) 149 NLJ 330

Cane, P (ed), *Atiyah's Accidents, Compensation and the Law*, 8th edn, 2013, CUP

Cape, E, 'Police interrogation and interruption' (1994) 144 NLJ 120

Card, R and Ward, R, *The Criminal Justice and Public Order Act 1994*, 1994, Bristol: Jordans

Clayton, R and Tomlinson, H, 'Arrest and reasonable grounds for suspicion' (1988) 32 Law Soc Gazette 22

Costigan, R and Stone, R, *Civil Liberties and Human Rights*, 11th edn, 2017, Oxford: OUP

Cragg, S, 'Stop and search powers: research and extension' (1999) Legal Action 3

Craig, P and de Búrca, G, *EU Law: Text, Cases and Materials*, 5th edn, 2011, Oxford: OUP

Crawford, L, 'Race awareness training and the judges' (1994) Counsel 11

Croall, H, *Crime and Society in Britain*, 2008, London: Longman

Darbyshire, P, 'The lamp that shows that freedom lives – is it worth the candle?' [1991] Crim LR 740

De Sousa Santos, B, *Toward a New Common Sense*, 2002, London: Butterworths

Devlin (Lord), *Trial by Jury*, 1966, London: Stevens

Diamond, D, 'Woolf reforms hike costs' (1999) The Lawyer 2

Dicey, AV, *An Introduction to the Study of the Law of the Constitution* (1885), 10th edn, 1959, London: Macmillan

Dixon, D, Coleman, C and Bottomley, K, 'Consent and legal regulation of policing' (1990) 17 JLS 345

Eekelaar, J and Maclean, M, *Family Justice: The Work of Family Judges in Uncertain Times*, 2013, Oxford: OUP

Exall, G, 'Civil litigation brief' (1999) SJ 32

Flemming, J, 'Judge airs concerns over Woolf reforms' (2000) Law Soc Gazette, 10 February

Freeman, M, *Law and Popular Culture*, 2005, Oxford: OUP

Frenkel, J, 'Offers to settle and payments into court' (1999) 149 NLJ 458

Frenkel, J, 'On the road to reform' (1998) Law Soc Gazette, 16 December

Genn, H, *Hard Bargaining: Out of Court Settlement in Personal Injury Claims*, 1987, Oxford: OUP

Genn, H and Genn, Y, *The Effectiveness of Representation at Tribunals*, 1989, London: LCD

Gibb, F, 'Rude judges must mind their language' (1999) *The Times*, 29 June

Gibb, F, 'Thatcher furious at "vindictive" Pinochet decision' (1999) *The Times*, 16 April

Gibb, F, 'Child killer Bell granted anonymity for life' (2003) *The Times*, 22 May

Gibb, F, 'Falconer takes an axe to legal tradition' (2003) *The Times*, 16 September

Gibb, F, 'Fee cuts prompt barristers to reject legal aid work' (2004) *The Times*, 5 April

Gibb, F, 'Commonwealth and common law: our imperial legacies' (2005) *The Times*, 13 September

Gibb, F, 'Some of the EU countries are hypocritical about human rights' (2006) *The Times*, 25 April

Gibb, F, 'Price is important, but quality can't be sacrificed' (2006) *The Times*, 14 February

Gibb, F, 'Legal profession set for historic reforms' (2009) *The Times*, 20 November

Gibb, F, 'Chilcot and legal advice' (2010) *The Times*, 3 February

Gibb, F, 'Gilderdale case prompts fresh calls to clarify the law on assisted dying' (2010) *The Times* 26 January

Gibb, F, 'Divorce courts may be thing of the past under radical overhaul of family justice' (2010) *The Times*, 21 January

Gibb, F, 'No win, no fee' deals cost taxpayers and insurers millions' (2010) *The Times* 15 January

Gibb, F, 'First criminal trial with no jury for 400 years starts' (2010) *The Times*, 13 January

Gibson, B, 'Why Bournemouth?' (1987) 151 JP 520

Glasser, C, 'Legal aid and eligibility' (1988) Law Soc Gazette, 9 March

Glasser, C, 'Legal services and the Green Papers' (1989) Law Soc Gazette, 5 April

Gold, S, 'Woolf watch' (1999) 149 NLJ 718

Goodhart, A, 'The *ratio decidendi* of a case' (1959) 22 MLR 117

Goodrich, P, *Reading the Law*, 1986, Oxford: Basil Blackwell

Grainger, I and Fealy, M, *An Introduction to the New Civil Procedure Rules*, 1999, London: Cavendish Publishing

Griffith, JAG, *The Politics of the Judiciary*, 5th edn, 1997, London: Fontana

Griffiths, C, 'Jury trial' (1999) Counsel 14

Hamer, P, 'Complaints: a new strategy' (1999) 149 NLJ 959

Hanson, S, *Legal Method, Skills and Reasoning*, 3rd edn, 2010, Abingdon: Routledge

Harris, D *et al*, *Compensation and Support for Illness and Injury*, 1984, Oxford: Clarendon

Harrison, R, 'Appealing prospects' (2000) NLJ 1175–76

Harrison, R, 'Cry Woolf' (1999) 149 NLJ 1011

Harrison, R, 'Why have two types of civil court?' (1999) 149 NLJ 65

Hart, H, *The Concept of Law*, 1961, Oxford: OUP

Hayek, FA von, *The Road to Serfdom* (1971), 1994, London: Routledge and Kegan Paul

Hedderman, C and Moxon, C, *Magistrates' Court or Crown Court? Mode of Trial Decisions and Sentencing*, Home Office Study No 125, 1992, London: HMSO

HM Magistrates' Courts Service Inspectorate, *Annual Report 1997–98*, London: HMSO

Holdsworth, W, *A History of English Law*, 1924, London: Methuen

Holland, T, 'Cut price conveyancing' (1994) 144 NLJ 192

Horne, A, Drewry, G and Oliver, D (eds), *Parliament and the Law*, 2013, Oxford: Hart

Hucklesby, A and Wahidin, A, *Criminal Justice*, 2013, Oxford: OUP

Hutchinson, A, *Evolution and the Common Law*, 2005, Cambridge: CUP

Irvine (Lord), 'Community vision under fire' (1999) Law Soc Gazette, 26 May

Jason-Lloyd, L, 'Section 60 of the Criminal Justice and Public Order Act 1994' (1998) 162 JP 836

JUSTICE, *Professional Negligence and the Quality of Legal Services – An Economic Perspective*, 1983, London: JUSTICE

Kadri, S, *The Trial: a history from Socrates to OJ Simpson*, 2005, London: HarperCollins

Kairys, D, *The Politics of Law: A Progressive Critique*, 1982, New York: Pantheon

Keating, D, 'Upholding the Rule of Law' (1999) 149 NLJ 533

Khan, S and Ryder, M, 'Police and the law' (1998) Legal Action 16

Law Society Civil Litigation Committee, 'Unravelling the enigma of *Thai Trading*' (2000) Law Soc Gazette, 9 June

Lee, S, *Judging Judges*, 1988, London: Faber & Faber

Legal Services Ombudsman, *Demanding Progress*, 1999–2000 Annual Report, London: HMSO

Lidstone, K, 'Entry, search and seizure' (1989) 40 NILQ 333

Lidstone, K (ed), *Prosecutions by Private Individuals and Non-Police Agencies*, 1980, London: HMSO

Lidstone, K and Palmer, C, *The Investigation of Crime*, 1996, London: Butterworths

Loughlin, M, *Sword and Scales*, 2000, Oxford: Hart

MacCallum, V, 'Learning lessons' (2001) Law Soc Gazette, 10 January

MacCormick, N, *Legal Rules and Legal Reasoning*, 1978, Oxford: Clarendon

Mackay (Lord), *The Administration of Justice*, 1994, Hamlyn Lectures, London: Sweet & Maxwell

Malleson, K, *The New Judiciary – The Effect of Expansion and Activism*, 1999, Aldershot: Ashgate

Malleson, K and Roberts, S, 'Streamlining and Clarifying the Appellate Process' (2002) Crim LR 272

Mansell, W, Meteyard, B and Thomson, A, *A Critical Introduction to Law*, 3rd edn, 2004, London: Cavendish Publishing

Mayhew, L and Reiss, A, 'The social organisation of legal contacts' (1969) 34 American Sociological Rev 311

McConville, M, Sanders, A and Leng, R, *The Case for the Prosecution*, 1991, London: Routledge

McGrath, P, 'Appeals against small claims track decisions' (1999) 149 NLJ 748

McLaughlin, E and Muncie, J, *Controlling Crime*, 2001, London: Sage and the Open University

Money-Kyrle, R, 'Advocates' immunity after *Osman*' (1999) 149 NLJ 945 and 981

Montesquieu, C, *De l'Esprit des Lois* (1748), 1989, Cambridge: CUP

Morris, P, White, R and Lewis, P, *Social Needs and Legal Action*, 1973, London: Robertson

Motson, S, Stephenson, G and Williamson, T, 'The effects of case characteristics on suspect behaviour during police questioning' (1992) 32 British J of Criminology 23

Murphy, M, 'Civil legal aid eligibility' (1989) Legal Action 4

Napier, M, 'Conditional fees' (1995) 92/16 Law Soc Gazette 1626

News, 'The legal profession and the Community Legal Service' (1999) 149 NLJ 1195

News in Brief, 'Cheap conveyancing' (1998) 148 NLJ 8

Nobles, R, 'The Criminal Case Review Commission' (2005) Crim LR 173

Pannick, D, *Advocates*, 1992, Oxford: OUP

Pannick, D, *Judges*, 1987, Oxford: OUP

Parker, C, 'Judicial decision making' (1999) 149 NLJ 1142

Parpworth, N, 'Breach of the peace: breach of human rights?' (1998) 152 JP 6

Payne, R, 'To counsel, not confront: the law on ADR' (1999) Counsel 30

Popplewell, O, *Benchmark: life, laughter, and the law*, 2003, London: Tauris

Purchas, F (Sir), 'What is happening to judicial independence' (1994) 144 NLJ 1306

Raz, J, 'The Rule of Law and its virtue' (1977) 93 LQR 195

Reid (Lord), 'The judge as law maker' (1972) 12 JSPTL 22

Reiner, R, *Crime, Order and Policing*, 1994, London: Routledge

Reiner, R, 'Responsibilities and reforms' (1993) 143 NLJ 1096

Reiner, R, *The Politics of the Police*, 2nd edn, 2000, Oxford: OUP

Richardson, J (ed), *Archbold on Criminal Pleading, Evidence and Practice*, 2017, London: Sweet & Maxwell

Robertshaw, P, *Rethinking Legal Need: The Case of Criminal Justice*, 1991, Aldershot: Dartmouth

Robertson, G, 'The Downey Report: MPs must realise they are not above the law' (1997) *The Guardian*, 4 July

Rutherford, A, 'Judicial training and autonomy' (1999) 149 NLJ 1120

Rutherford, A, 'Preserving a robust independence' (1999) 149 NLJ 908

Sanders, A, 'Class bias in prosecutions' (1985) 24 Howard J 17

Sanders, A, 'The silent code' (1994) 144 NLJ 946

Sanders, A and Young, R, *Criminal Justice*, 1995, London: Butterworths

Sanders, A and Young, R, 'Plea bargaining and the next Criminal Justice Bill' (1994) 144 NLJ 1200

Sanders, A *et al*, *Advice and Assistance at Police Stations and the 24 Hour Duty Solicitor Scheme*, 1989, London: LCD

Scrivener, A, 'The birth of a new language in the court room: English' (1999) *The Independent*, 26 April

Sedley, S (Sir), 'Human rights: a 21st century agenda' [1995] PL 386

Sidebottom, A, Belur, J, Bowers, K, Tompson, L and Johnson, SD, 'Theft in Price-Volatile Markets: On the Relationship between Copper Price and Copper Theft', (2011) 48(3) Journal of Research in Crime and Delinquency 396–418

Sime, S, *A Practical Approach to Civil Procedure*, 19th edn, 2015, Oxford: OUP

Simpson, A, 'The *ratio decidendi* of a case' (1957) 20 MLR 413

Slapper, G, *Blood in the Bank*, 1999, Aldershot: Ashgate

Slapper, G, 'English legal system' (1999) 26 SLR 31

Slapper, G, *How the Law Works*, 4th edn, 2016, Abingdon: Routledge

Slapper, G, *Organisational Prosecutions*, 2001, Aldershot: Ashgate

Slapper, G and Kelly, D, *English Law*, 3rd edn, 2010, Abingdon: Routledge

Smith, JC, 'Criminal appeals and the Criminal Cases Review Commission' (1995) 145 NLJ 534

Smith, R, 'Judicial statistics: questions and answers' (1994) 144 NLJ 1088

Smith, R, 'Politics and the judiciary' (1993) 143 NLJ 1486

Smith, R (ed), *Achieving Civil Justice*, 1996, London: LAG

Smith, R (ed), *Shaping the Future: New Directions in Legal Services*, 1995, London: LAG

St Luce, S, 'Cutting the lifeline' (1999) 149 NLJ 398

Steyn (Lord), 'The weakest and least dangerous department of government' [1997] PL 84

Susskind, R, *Tomorrow's Lawyers: An Introduction to Your Future*, 2013, Oxford: OUP

Temple Lang, J, 'The duties of national courts under Community constitutional law' [1997] EL Rev 22

Thomas, DA (ed), *Current Sentencing Practice*, 1999, London: Sweet & Maxwell

Thompson, E, *Whigs and Hunters*, 1977, Harmondsworth: Penguin

Thompson, P (ed), *The Civil Court Practice*, 1999, London: Butterworths

Trent, M, 'ADR and the new Civil Procedure Rules' (1999) 149 NLJ 410

Turner, AJ, 'Inferences under s 34 of the Criminal Justice and Public Order Act 1994: Part One' (1999) 163 JP, 27 March

Turner, AJ, 'Inferences under s 34 of the Criminal Justice and Public Order Act 1994: Part Two' (1999) 163 JP, 24 April

Twining, W, *Globalisation and Legal Theory*, 2000, Cambridge: CUP

Twining, W, *Rethinking Evidence: Exploratory Essays*, 2nd edn, 2006, Cambridge: CUP

Twining, W and Meirs, D, *How To Do Things With Rules*, 5th edn, 2010, Cambridge: CUP

Unger, R, *In Law and Modern Society*, 1976, New York: Free Press

Verkaik, R, 'Opinions on counsel' (1998) 95/04 Law Soc Gazette 22

Vignaendra, S, *Social Class and entry into the Solicitors' Profession: Research Study 41*, 2001, London: The Law Society

Wadham, J and Arkinstall, J, 'Human rights and crime' (1999) 149 NLJ 703

Watson, A, 'The right to elect trial by jury: the issue reappears' (1998) 163 JP 636

Weber, M, *Economy and Society* (*Wirtschaft und Gesellschaft*), 1968, Roth, G and Widttich, C (trans), Berkeley: California UP

Wendel Holmes, O, *The Common Law* (1881), 1968, London: Macmillan

Williams, G, 'Letting off the guilty and prosecuting the innocent' [1985] Crim LR 115

Wolchover, D and Heaton-Armstrong, A, 'Jailing psychopaths and prison cell confessions' (1999) 149 NLJ 285

Woolf (Lord), 'Judicial review – the tensions between the executive and the judiciary' (1998) 114 LQR 579

Yarrow, S, *The Price of Success*, 1997, Grantham: Grantham

Yarrow, S and Abrams, P, *Nothing to Lose? Clients' Experiences of Using Conditional Fees*, Summary Report, 1999, London: University of Westminster

Zander, M, *The Law Making Process*, 7th edn, 2015, Oxford: Hart

Zander, M, *Cases and Materials on the English Legal System*, 10th edn, 2007, Cambridge: CUP

Zander, M and Henderson, P, *The Crown Court Study*, Royal Commission on Criminal Justice Study 19, 145, 1993, London: HMSO

INDEX